CHRISTIANITY, PHILOSOPHY, AND ROMAN POWER

This book rethinks the Christianisation of the later Roman Empire as a crisis of knowledge, pointing to competitive cultural reassessment as a major driving force in the making of the Constantinian and post-Constantinian state. Emperor Julian's writings are reassessed as key to accessing the rise and consolidation of a Christian politics of interpretation that relied on exegesis as a self-legitimising device to secure control over Roman history via claims to Christianity's control of *paideia*. This reconstruction infuses Julian's reaction with contextual significance. His literary and political project emerges as a response to contemporary reconfigurations of Christian hermeneutics as controlling the meaning of Rome's culture and history. At the same time, understanding Julian as a participant in a larger debate requalifies all fourth-century political and episcopal discourse as a long knock-on effect reacting to the imperial mobilisation of Christian debates over the link between power and culture.

LEA NICCOLAI is Assistant Professor in Classics (Late Antique and Early Byzantine History) at the University of Cambridge and a Fellow of Trinity College.

GREEK CULTURE IN THE ROMAN WORLD

Series Editors
JAŚ ELSNER, University of Oxford
SIMON GOLDHILL, University of Cambridge
CONSTANZE GÜTHENKE, University of Oxford
MICHAEL SQUIRE, King's College London

Founding Editors
SUSAN E. ALCOCK
JAŚ ELSNER
SIMON GOLDHILL

The Greek culture of the Roman Empire offers a rich field of study. Extraordinary insights can be gained into processes of multicultural contact and exchange, political and ideological conflict, and the creativity of a changing, polyglot empire. During this period, many fundamental elements of Western society were being set in place: from the rise of Christianity, to an influential system of education, to long-lived artistic canons. This series is the first to focus on the response of Greek culture to its Roman imperial setting as a significant phenomenon in its own right. To this end, it will publish original and innovative research in the art, archaeology, epigraphy, history, philosophy, religion, and literature of the empire, with an emphasis on Greek material.

Recent Titles in the Series

Greek Declamation and the Roman Empire William Guast

The Death of Myth on Roman Sarcophagi: Allegory and Visual Narrative in the Late Empire Mont Allen

The Lives of Ancient Villages: Rural Society in Roman Anatolia Peter Thonemann

Roman Ionia: Constructions of Cultural Identity in Western Asia Minor Martin Hallmannsecker

Late Hellenistic Greek Literature in Dialogue Jason König and Nicolas Wiater

Oppian's Halieutica Emily Kneebone

CHRISTIANITY, PHILOSOPHY, AND ROMAN POWER

Constantine, Julian, and the Bishops on Exegesis and Empire

LEA NICCOLAI
University of Cambridge

Shaftesbury Road, Cambridge CB2 8EA, United Kingdom

One Liberty Plaza, 20th Floor, New York, NY 10006, USA

477 Williamstown Road, Port Melbourne, VIC 3207, Australia

314–321, 3rd Floor, Plot 3, Splendor Forum, Jasola District Centre, New Delhi – 110025, India

103 Penang Road, #05–06/07, Visioncrest Commercial, Singapore 238467

Cambridge University Press is part of Cambridge University Press & Assessment, a department of the University of Cambridge.

We share the University's mission to contribute to society through the pursuit of education, learning and research at the highest international levels of excellence.

www.cambridge.org
Information on this title: www.cambridge.org/9781009299275

DOI: 10.1017/9781009299312

© Lea Niccolai 2023

This publication is in copyright. Subject to statutory exception and to the provisions of relevant collective licensing agreements, no reproduction of any part may take place without the written permission of Cambridge University Press & Assessment.

First published 2023
First paperback edition 2025

A catalogue record for this publication is available from the British Library

ISBN   978-1-009-29929-9   Hardback
ISBN0   978-1-009-29927-5   Paperback

Cambridge University Press & Assessment has no responsibility for the persistence or accuracy of URLs for external or third-party internet websites referred to in this publication and does not guarantee that any content on such websites is, or will remain, accurate or appropriate.

To Peter Garnsey
A mia madre

La sesta lettera comparve nel cielo,
era un annuncio, immagino, della Firestone
che torreggiava solo sul Campo Boario
con scritto: in questo segno vincerai,
ma in verde, perché il verde è il mio colore.
E adesso lo rivedo, anche di giorno,
benedico il Testaccio e i suoi dintorni
e soprattutto l'angolo di strada
dove davanti a un semaforo rosso
mi fu concesso di sperare il verde:
la sesta lettera comparve nel cielo
e in quel momento si fusero i secoli,
fuggì il tempo con tutti i suoi cadaveri,
guardai quel segno di trionfo e
mi innamorai di te: questa è la storia
della mia, diciamo, conversione.

The sixth letter appeared in the sky.
It was, I guess, a Firestone announcement
Towering alone over Campo Boario
With the writing 'under this sign, conquer'
(In green though, because green is my colour).
Now I see it again, even in plain daylight,
And I praise Testaccio and its surroundings
And above all that street corner
Where, facing a red traffic light,
I was given hope for green:
The sixth letter appeared in the sky
And suddenly the centuries melt together
Time fled with all its corpses
I saw that sign of triumph and
I fell in love with you: this is the story
Of my, let's say, conversion.

J. Rodolfo Wilcock, 'La sesta lettera comparve nel cielo', Italienisches Liederbuch
J. Rodolfo Wilcock, Poesie, Piccola Biblioteca Adelphi 101: Milan 1980, p. 135

Contents

List of Figures   *page* viii
Preface   xiii
Acknowledgements   xiv
List of Abbreviations, Editions, and Translations   xvii

Introduction   1

PART I AT CONSTANTIUS' COURT: JULIAN CAESAR

1 How Philosophers Should Take Compliments When They Happen to Become Kings   39

2 Climbing the Ladder   73

PART II MAKING AND BREAKING CONSTANTINE: JULIAN AUGUSTUS

3 Holy Hermeneutics   111

4 A Life for a Life   166

PART III AFTER JULIAN: PHILOSOPHY IN THE WORLD

5 Those Who Know If the Emperor Knows   209

6 Wisdom for the Many, and Wisdom for the Few   267

Conclusions   302

Bibliography   308
Subject Index   345
Index Locorum   354

Figures

3.1 Optatian, *Carm.* 19. Reproduction from Squire and Wienand (2017) p. 42, following the layout of the Codex Augustaneus 9 Guelferbytanus (16th c.), folio 4r, (Herzog August Bibliothek, Wolfenbüttel) *page* 136

3.2 Optatian, *Carm.* 8. Reproduction from Squire and Wienand (2017) p. 8, following the layout of the poem as in P. Welser, *Publilii Optatiani Porphyrii panegyricus dictus Constantino Augusto*, Augsburg 1595, p. 33 (Munich, Bayerische Staatsbibliothek, Sign. 2 A.lat.a. 207) 137

4.1 Julian Augustus, bronze, Sirmium 362–363 CE. Obverse: head of Julian, bearded, pearl-diademed, wearing cloak, with the inscription DN FL CL IVLIANVS PF AVG; reverse: standing bull with stars above, with the inscription SECVRITAS REIPVB (wreath). *RIC* VIII Sirmium 106 p. 392. London, British Museum, Department of Coins and Medals, inv. no. B.3808 (© The Trustees of the British Museum) 180

4.2 Julian Augustus, *solidus*, Antioch 362–363 CE. Obverse: head of Julian, bearded, pearl-diademed, wearing cuirass, with the inscription FL CL IVLIANVS P P AVG; reverse: Roman soldier (arguably Julian) holding a trophy and dragging a fettered captive, with the inscription VIRTVS EXERCITVS ROMANORVM. London, British Museum, Department of Coins and Medals, inv. no. 1921,0107.3 (© The Trustees of the British Museum) 180

List of Figures ix

4.3 Julian Augustus, *solidus*, Antioch 362–363 CE. Obverse: head of Julian, with long beard, pearl-diademed, with the inscription FL CL IVLIA-NVS P F AVG; reverse: Julian standing, in full figure, draped with the *toga picta*, bearing *mappa* and sceptre, with the inscription VIRTVS EXERCI-TVS ROMANORVM. London, British Museum, Department of Coins and Medals, inv. no. 1867,0101.928 (© The Trustees of the British Museum) 181

4.4 Diocletian Augustus, *aureus*, Nicomedia 294–305 CE. Obverse: head of Diocletian with a laureate crown and the inscription DIOCLETIA-NVS AVGVSTVS; reverse: Jupiter wearing cloak and holding thunderbolt, with the inscription IOVI CONSE-RVATORI. *RIC* VI Rome 11 p. 554. London, British Museum, Department of Coins and Medals, inv. no. 1864,1128.165 (© The Trustees of the British Museum) 187

4.5 Maximian Augustus, *aureus*, Nicomedia, 294–305 CE. Obverse: head of Maximian with a laureate crown and the inscription MAXIMIA-NVS P F AVG; reverse: Hercules carrying a club and holding four apples, with the inscription HERCVLI VICTORI. *RIC* VI Nicomedia 3, p. 553. London, British Museum, Department of Coins and Medals, inv. no. 1864,1128.176 (© The Trustees of the British Museum) 187

4.6 Constantine, *aureus*, Rome 305–307 CE. Obverse: head of Constantine (Tetrarchic style), with a laureate crown and the inscription CONSTANT-INVS NOB C; reverse: Constantine in military dress holding standard in the right hand and a sceptre in the left, with the inscription PRINCI-PI I-VVENTVT(IS). *RIC* VI Rome 151, p. 369. London, British Museum, Department of Coins and Medals, inv. no. 1868,0331.1 (© The Trustees of the British Museum) 188

4.7 Constantine, *aureus*, Trier 305–307 CE. Obverse: head of Constantine (new type), with a laureate crown and the inscription CONSTAN-TINVS NOB C; reverse: Constantine in military dress, with the right hand raised and holding a sceptre in the left, between ensigns, with the inscription PRINCIPI IV-V-E-NTVTIS. *RIC* VI Trier 627, p. 204. London, British Museum, Department of Coins and Medals, inv. no. 1864,1128.187 (© The Trustees of the British Museum) 188

List of Figures

4.8 Constantius II Augustus, *siliqua*, Antioch 337–347 CE. Obverse: head of Constantius II (Constantinian dynastic style), pearl-diademed, with upward gaze; reverse: inscription VOTIS XV MVLTIS XX within a jewelled wreath. *RIC* VIII Antioch 35 (2). London, British Museum, Department of Coins and Medals, inv. no. 1950, 1006.1588 (© The Trustees of the British Museum)   189

4.9 Constantius II Augustus, *solidus*, Aquileia 337–340 CE. Obverse: head of Constantius II with cloak, wearing diadem with gems, with the inscription CONSTANT-IVS P AVG; reverse: seated Victory and winged genius supporting a shield reading VOT X MVLT XX, with the inscription FELICIT-AS PERPETVA. *RIC* VIII Aquileia 5, p. 315. London, British Museum, Department of Coins and Medals, inv. no. 1974,0904.6 (© The Trustees of the British Museum)   190

4.10 Julian Caesar, *solidus*, Arles 355–359 CE. Obverse: head of Julian (Constantinian dynastic style), no diadem, wearing cuirass, with the inscription FL CL IVLIANVS NOB CAES; reverse: seated Victory and genius supporting a shield reading VOT V, with the inscription VICTORIA AVGVSTORVM CONST. London, British Museum, Department of Coins and Medals, inv. no. 1853,0716.64 (© The Trustees of the British Museum)   190

4.11 Constantine, *solidus*, Ticinum 326 CE. Obverse: head of Constantine with plain diadem and upward gaze, with no inscription; reverse: star above intertwined wreaths, with the inscription CONSTANTINVS AVG. *RIC* VII Ticinum 192, p. 385. London, British Museum, Department of Coins and Medals, inv. no. R1874,0715.137 (© The Trustees of the British Museum)   193

4.12 Silver tetradrachm of Lysimachus, Lampsacus 305–281 BCE. Obverse: head of Alexander the Great with gaze looking upwards, a diadem, and a ram's horn; reverse: Athena Nikephoros (seated), Nike stretching her right hand and resting her left arm on her shield, with the inscription ΒΑΣΙΛΕΩΣ ΛΥΣΙΜΑΧΟΥ (*basileos lysimachou*). London, British Museum, Department of Coins and Medals, inv. no. 1919, 0820.1 (© The Trustees of the British Museum)   194

4.13 Shield portrait of philosopher with upward gaze from Aphrodisias (Caria), Atrium House, late fourth to early fifth century. CE Museum of Aphrodisias, inv. no. 81-112. LSA no. 207   195

Preface

Julian's writings hide something in plain sight. His claim to be restoring philosophy to the imperial throne conceals how his fourth-century predecessors also sought to assert control over metaphysical truths and the Greek intellectual tradition. The writings composed by and around the representatives of the Constantinian household are riddled with references to the wisdom and culture of the emperors. Yet they also ascribe the intellectual proficiency of the rulers to a specific source, one incompatible with Julian's understanding of the origins of knowledge: Constantine's religion of choice, Christianity.

This book rethinks the Christianisation of the later Roman Empire as a crisis of knowledge, pointing to competitive cultural reassessment as a major driving force in the making of the Constantinian and post-Constantinian state. Julian's writings are reassessed here as key to accessing the rise and consolidation of what I label the fourth-century politics of interpretation. This relied on a Christian adaptation of the ideal of the philosopher-ruler, and on the concomitant exploration of exegesis, as self-legitimising devices to secure control over Roman history via claims to Christianity's control of *paideia*. The reconstruction of this politics of interpretation infuses Julian's reaction with contextual significance. His literary and political project emerges as a response to contemporary reconfigurations of Christian hermeneutics as controlling the meaning of Rome's cultural past. At the same time, this recontextualisation of Julian as a participant in a larger debate qualifies all fourth-century political discourse as a long knock-on effect reacting to the imperial mobilisation of Christian debates on the relationship between authority and culture. The application of religiously competitive criteria for the assessment of philosophical leadership established a positive feedback loop between emperors and the Church, bolstering the self-image of bishops vis-à-vis their episcopal rivals, non-Christian philosophers, and the emperors themselves.

Acknowledgements

This book began its life at the Scuola Normale Superiore of Pisa as a *tesi di laurea specialistica* inspired by a book that had taken my sleep away – Gore Vidal's *Julian*. It was then developed as a PhD thesis at King's College, Cambridge, and was duly smashed and rewritten during a research fellowship at Peterhouse. My gratitude goes to all these institutions and to the Wolfson Foundation that generously funded my doctoral studies. I am also deeply thankful to the Cambridge Classics Faculty, which has felt like home for six years and now, to my joy, has become one.

The debts of gratitude I have contracted over these years are too great and too many to do them justice here. The first is to my supervisor, Simon Goldhill: for shattering all my (late antique) certainties and feeding my mind in return with questions of the most exciting kind – and for being an endless source of inspiration and insight. The wisdom and generosity of my PhD examiners, Tim Whitmarsh and Gavin Kelly, has been invaluable and provided me with essential guidance as I began to navigate the process of turning the thesis into a book. Catherine Conybeare and Aaron Johnson offered the most insightful remarks on previous drafts of my work, pointing to fundamental directions for its development. I have also greatly benefitted from the comments of the series editors, Jaś Elsner and Michael Squire, and of the anonymous referees and from conversations with – and the advice of – Gillian Clark, James Corke-Webster, Garth Fowden, Olivier Gengler, Pui Him Ip, Claire Jackson, Aaron Kachuck, Christopher Kelly, Alberto Quiroga, Simone Rendina, and John Weisweiler. Heartfelt thanks must go also to the Cambridge imperial epic reading group (Simon Goldhill, Emma Greensmith, Daniel Hanigan, Anna Lefteratou, Kostantinos Lygouris, Oliver Parkes, Alexander Schwennicke, and Tim Whitmarsh), for creating such a vibrant community of late antique scholars.

I am thankful to all the members of the Cambridge Classics Faculty for being such generous and stimulating colleagues: in particular, Rebecca

Flemming, Renaud Gagné, Philip Hardie, Richard Hunter, John Patterson, Jerry Toner, and Hannah Willey. I must save a line to express my gratitude to Carrie Vout, for her outstanding mentorship, and to Robin Osborne and Franco Basso, for being the infallible point of reference of my years as a PhD first and then as a postdoc. To Tony Brinkman, Stephen Howell, Carmen Preston, Nigel Thompson, and Lina Undicino go my heartfelt thanks for making the Cambridge Classics Faculty and library such a special place to do work and research.

Gianfranco Agosti and Chiara Tommasi provided treasured guidance as I was a graduate student in Pisa; Pier Giorgio Borbone, Giuseppe Cambiano, and Maria Chiara Martinelli inspired me with their teaching.

My years in Cambridge have been brightened by the company of friends whose company honours me: Faraj Alnasser, Clelia Attanasio, Zoë Audra, Hagar Ben Zion, Lorenzo Bondioli, Poppy Farnese Grima, Parwana Fayyaz, Sarah Foster, Stefano Frullini, Isobel Higgins, Talitha Kearey, Christian Keime, Jessica Lawrence, Valeria Pace, Andrea Peripoli, Sarah Sheard, Henry Tang, and Matt Ward. My PhD cohort – Tatiana Bur, Charles Manklow, Chiara Monaco, Tulsi Parikh, Ludovico Pontiggia, Hanneke Reijnierse-Salisbury, Teresa Röger – has been a source of happiness and affection. The company of Maya Feile Tomes and Alessio Santoro made many nights spent in the library seem light and bright. I count the chats over a coffee or beer with Giulia Bertoni, Konstantinos Lygouris, Peter Martin, and Nir Stern among the great joys of these years. Giulia Maltagliati has been a friend and outstanding collaborator, and I look forward to the continuation of our project. To Alex Schulz, my gratitude for her friendship goes mixed with that for her razor-sharp advice, from which the final draft of this book greatly benefitted.

A corner of this page is for my friends from Pisa: Nicola Barbagli, Fabrizio Bianchi, Stefano Bolzonella, Martina Bottacchiari, Marta D'Asaro, Margherita Fantoli, Carlo Ferrari, Domenico Giordani, Edoardo Galfré, Carlo Ferrari, Lorenzo Livorsi, Francesca Modini, Franceso Morosi, Marta Mussi, Emilio Rosamilia, Gennady Uraltsev, and Anna Zago. Arianna Gullo has been a precious friend and a true teacher in all things late antique. To Ilaria Morresi and Marco Senaldi: you know that a part of me is always at the Carducci with you. These acknowledgements would not be complete without a mention of my friends from Ostia, Tübingen, and Hamburg – Livia Campo, Laura Carrara, Katharina Hoyme, and Giorgia Prestigiacomo – and of my inspiring teachers Sandra Baldascino, Angela De Angelis, Nicolina di Palma, Patrizia Miscia, Tamara Nale, and Daniela Pieri.

I am grateful to Salvatore Ponzone for sending me a copy of his splendid Italian translation of Julian's writings. Michael Sharp provided essential editorial help and Douglas Olson impeccable proofreading. Heartfelt thanks go also to my research assistants Oliver Parkes, Harvey Phythian, and Sebastian Tyrrall, with the wish that they might soon be in search of proofreaders for their own books.

The last line is for my mother and father, for their unfailing love and support. This book is dedicated to two people. To my mother, who over the years of my 'abroadedness' never ceased to be a source of strength, wisdom, and inspiration. I owe it to her support if this book ever found its completion. And, finally, *al mio maestro* Peter Garnsey, who back in 2015 put an Erasmus student from Pisa under his wing and guided her ever since: *grazie*, with all my heart, for your insight and advice, your patience, your wisdom, and your kindness.

Abbreviations, Editions, and Translations

Abbreviations

Constantine
OC   *Oration to the Assembly of the Saints* (Oratio Constantiniana)

Constantius II
Dem.   *Address to the Senate* (Demegoria Constantii)

Eunapius
VPS   *Lives of the Philosophers and Sophists*

Eusebius
DE   *Demonstration of the Gospel*
GEI   *General Elementary Introduction*
HE   *Ecclesiastical History*
LC   *Praise of Constantine*
PE   *Preparation for the Gospel*
SC   *Oration on Christ's Sepulchre*
VC   *Life of Constantine*

Gregory of Nazianzus
DVS   *Concerning His Life* (De Vita Sua)

John Chrysostom
Bab.   *On St. Babylas Against Julian and the Gentiles* (CPG 4348, PG 50.533–72)

Catech.	*Baptismal Instructions* (*CPG* 4465–4472, *SC* 50 bis)
In II Cor. hom.	*30 Homilies on 2 Corinthians* (*CPG* 4429, *PG* 61.381–610)
In Jo. hom.	*88 Homilies on John* (*CPG* 4425, *PG* 59.23–482)
Laz.	*On Lazarus Four Days Dead* (*CPG* 4356, *PG* 50.641–644)
In Mt. hom.	*90 Homilies on Matthew* (*CPG* 4424, *PG* 57.13–794)
In Juv. et Max.	*On the Martyrs Juventinus and Maximus* (*CPG* 4349, *PG* 50.571–8)
Regr.	*On His Return* (*CPG* 4394, *PG* 52.421–4)
Sac.	*On Priesthood* (*CPG* 4316, *PG* 48.623–92)
Stat.	*Homilies on the Statues* (or *To the People of Antioch*) (*CPG* 4330, *PG* 40.15–222)

Julian

I Pan.	*First Panegyric in Honour of Constantius II*
II Pan.	*Second Panegyric in Honour of Constantius II*
Ath.	*Letter to the Athenians*
Caes.	*The Caesars*
C. Gal.	*Treatise Against the Galileans*
C. Her.	*To the Cynic Heraclius*
Cons.	*Consolation to Himself upon the Departure of the Excellent Salutius*
Cyn.	*To the Uneducated Cynics*
Ep. Fragm.	*Fragment of a Letter to a Priest* (= ep. 89b Bidez–Cumont)
Eus.	*Panegyric in Honour of Eusebia*
Hel.	*Hymn to Helios*
Mat.	*Hymn to the Mother of the Gods*
Mis.	*Misopogon*
Them.	*Letter to Themistius*

Synesius

Calv. Enc.	*Praise of Baldness*
Dio	*Dio, or on Living by His Example*
Insomn.	*On Dreams*
Prov.	*The Egyptian Tale, or on Providence*
Reg.	*On Kingship*

Note on Texts and Translations

References to Julian's works are given according to the pagination of W. C. Wright (1913–23). For the letters, double reference – to Wright (1923) and to Bidez–Cumont (1922) – is provided.

References to Synesius' works follow the Budé edition (hymns: Lacombrade [1978]; letters: Garzya and Roques [2000]; orations and essays: Lamoureux and Aujoulat [2004, 2008a, 2008b]).

The English translations referred to are the following:

Ambrose: Liebeschuetz (2005); Ammianus: Rolfe (1935–40); Athanasius: Gregg (1980); Clement of Alexandria: Ferguson (1991); Constantine: Edwards (2003); Constantius II: Heather and Moncur (2003); Cyril of Jerusalem: Yarnold (2000); Eunapius: Blockley (1983) (*History*), Wright (1921) (*VPS*); Eusebius: Cameron and Hall (1999) (*VC*), Drake (1976) (*LC*), Ferrar (1920) (*DE*), Gifford (1903) (*PE*); Gregory of Nazianzus: King (1888) (*Or.* 4 and 5), White (1996) (*DVS*); Gregory of Nyssa: Ware (1963); Himerius: Penella (2007); Iamblichus: Clarke (2004); John Chrysostom: Harkin (1963) (*Catech.*), Mayer and Allen (2000) (*Stat.*), Schatkin (1985) (*Bab.*); Julian: Wright (1913–23); Justin Martyr: Falls (2003); *Latin Panegyrics*: Nixon, Rodgers, and Mynors (1994); Libanius: Norman (1969) (*Or.* 18 and 19), Norman (1992) (letters); Palladius: Meyer (1985); Photius: Wilson (1994); Sallustius: Nock (1926); Synesius: Cameron and Long (1993) (*Prov.*); Fitzgerald (1930) (letters and orations); *Theodosian Code*: Pharr (1952); Themistius: Heather and Matthews (1991) (*Or.* 8, 10), Heather and Moncur (2001) (*Or.* 1, 3, 5, 6, 17, 34), Penella (2000) (*Or.* 26, 28, 31).

Introduction

Three centuries after the more-or-less surreptitious beginning of its history as an empire, Rome was administered by provincial elites whose local authority had mostly been subsumed under a centralised bureaucracy. Their identity as a cosmopolitan elite, however, continued to be fostered through a shared commitment to *paideia*, the traditional Greco-Roman education. The word – Greek, as it happens – is a witness to Rome's long history of self-definition in dialogue and rivalry with cultural markers not its own. Already in Augustan times, Horace could play with the idea that the conquered Hellenistic world continued to exercise a different form of dominance – that of culture – over its *ferus victor*.[1] But it is in the way the Roman Empire conceptualised leadership that the great paradox of its interaction with Greek thinking and its pervasive models is found. Over the course of its expansion across the Mediterranean, Republican Rome became the stage for a cultural debate surrounding 'Hellenisation' and its detractors. Over time, this debate mobilised an array of rhetorical poses invested in various degrees in the political utility of claiming anti-Greekness.[2] And yet, when Rome traded Republican institutions for a style of leadership that looked too much like the critical form of government associated with the Greek-speaking world – monarchy – the path to political stability was paved by Greek political theory. The politics of Augustus, the individual single-handedly responsible for this innovation, already illustrates this.

Augustus hoarded old and new individual offices, but until his death he cunningly avoided giving a name to their unprecedented sum. His cultural policy too must be read against the background of his highly strategic management of authority. Suetonius records that he wrote a now lost

---

[1] Hor, *Epist.* 2.1.156.
[2] See, among others, Gruen (1984), (1992); Henrichs (1995); Flaig (1999); Wallace-Hadrill (2008); Smith and Yarrow (2012); Asper (2016).

exhortation to philosophy.³ A sponsor of literature and the arts, and a pupil of the philosopher Arius of Alexandria, Augustus ostensibly exploited the power of patronage to evoke a cultured profile.⁴ The *princeps* was followed by the contrasting fortunes of a Julio-Claudian dynasty caught up in a rivalry with the Roman Senate and by a Flavian succession cut short by the violent death of its despotic final representative, Domitian. Afterwards, the second-century adoptive emperors recovered senatorial support by pursuing the image of lovers of culture, justice, and piety. This image pervades their propaganda but is also, intriguingly, found in the writings of those who sought to challenge official narratives.⁵ Even Trajan (r. 98–117), a ruler mainly associated with military expansion, could still be recorded in the writings of the second-century Greek rhetorician and philosopher Dio of Prusa as available to listen to philosophical advice (which came, incidentally, from Dio himself).⁶ Marcus Aurelius (r. 161–80), who spent almost all his reign fighting Germanic tribes, has come down in history as Rome's philosopher-emperor, the author of Stoic *Meditations to Himself*, which he wrote – eloquently – in Greek.

Augustus, Trajan, Marcus Aurelius, and the Antonines in general were operating within a legacy. Their image was receptive of a process of Hellenistic and post-Hellenistic elaboration of the ideal of the philosopher-ruler: the leader, located at the heart of Greek political theory since Plato's *Republic*, who derives wisdom from a continuous intellectual training.⁷ Between the first and the second centuries CE, the mediation of the representatives of the so-called Second Sophistic – Greek intellectuals liaising with Roman power – helped repurpose this model for a Roman audience.⁸ Prominent rhetoricians and politicians increasingly exploited philosophy as a rhetorical category used in the service of self-projection,

---

³ Suet. *Aug.* 85.
⁴ Suet. *Aug.* 89. On the issue of the identification of Arius of Alexandria with Arius Didymus, see Barbagli (2019) 46 n. 6.
⁵ Nasrallah (2010) 133–35.
⁶ Dio Chrys. *Or.* 57.11–12. On his success in becoming one of Trajan's *amici*, see also *Or.* 45.3, 47.22, and Philostr. *VS* 1.7.
⁷ On the relationship of Augustus' *Res Gestae* to Hellenistic theories of kingship see Bosworth (1999). The question of the influence of philosophy on Roman imperial politics is addressed, among others, by Barnes and Griffin (1989); Clark and Rajak (2002); Trapp (2007) 166–225; Horst (2013).
⁸ On ancient perception of the bond uniting culture and power, see especially Schmitz (1997) and Whitmarsh (2001). Gleason (1995) and Zanker (1995) illustrate the strategies of self-projection and the appearance in art of Greek intellectuals, respectively; Puech (2002) studies their voice and representation in inscriptions. Swain (1996) points to the ties between language and power. Goldhill (2001a) collects studies of how second-century intellectuals drew on cultural authority to navigate socio-political change. Van Hoof (2010a) uses the case of Plutarch to illustrate the social dynamics of philosophy in the Principate.

claiming the status of philosopher (and denying it to their rivals) in the absence of fixed criteria of classification.[9] Emperors too were involved in this process of self-legitimisation. Far from lifting them above criticism, their prominent position in fact made them vulnerable to a critical assessment of their profile. This is implicitly documented by Rome's tradition of pro-senatorial historiography and by the violent fall of emperors like Caligula or Domitian, who exerted a form of power stripped of the language of self-control.[10] Public intellectuals such as Plutarch and Musonius Rufus were keen to assert that rulers would be ill-equipped to rule if not themselves ruled by reason.[11] The above-noted fortune of the Antonines, whom later Roman historiography would consecrate as models of imperial leadership, testifies to how the ruler's stability needed to rest on a carefully crafted consensus. Awareness of 'the intersubjective processes' (thus Lenski) regulating power, and the emperor's capacity to reassuringly appeal to shared values, were central concerns of the Roman government.[12] Suffice it to say that the Antonines' successors, the Severans, continued to present themselves as Antonines.[13] At the same time, the emperor's pursuit of a reputation as an intellectual was key to validating education as a fundamental marker of the upper class. *Paideia* shaped the public face of power and pursuing it required leisure and resources. In other words, it amounted to what is often labelled, in Bourdieu's terms, cultural capital.[14] Proficiency in philosophy was a crucial expression of this.

This book moves from the premises set by the cultural debate of the Principate and asks how this vital dialogue between state institutions and *paideia*-regulated expectations was affected by what may have been the most radical act of transformation performed by the imperial power since its institution: its Christianisation. The emperor who brought about this

---

[9] Stanton (1973) 351–58; Hahn (1989) 46–53; Schmitz (1997) 86–89; Whitmarsh (2001) 158–60; Sidebottom (2009); Eshleman (2012) 1–18; Lauwers (2013).
[10] On the imperial negotiation of consensus during the Principate, see Noreña (2001); Roller (2001) 129–287; Horst (2013); Gangloff (2018). On the evolution of this phenomenon in late antiquity, see Lenski (2016); Burgersdijk and Ross (2018); and (with attention to religious policies) Kahlos (2019) 17–26.
[11] Plut. *Mor.* 779d–82f (*To an Uneducated Ruler*); Muson. *Lect.* 8 (*That Kings Also Should Study Philosophy*).
[12] Lenski (2016) 12.
[13] Marcus' fortune: Bruch and Hermann (2012); Corke-Webster (2019) 264. The Severans' recovery of past models (from Augustus to the Antonines): Cooley (2007); Barnes (2008). The historians Cassius Dio and Herodian, writing in the first half of the third century, both depicted Marcus' reign as a golden age: Hidber (2006); Scott (2015).
[14] Bourdieu (1986). See, e.g., Van Nijf (2008) 223; Van Hoof (2013) 387.

change, Constantine (r. 306–37), inhabited another paradox: he was simultaneously the dynastic successor of the so-called Tetrarchs and someone whose political stability had been secured through open conflict with and violent elimination of his co-rulers. It might appear surprising that a sovereign who arose from civil war and needed to secure consensus would advocate for a cult that disappointed the expectations of the Greco-Roman elites.[15] Christianity was not traditional, and a society whose identity rested on Homer, Virgil, and Plato suspected innovation above all else.[16] Furthermore, despite its history of engagement with Greek philosophy, the religion grounded on the plain language of the Gospels remained in the eyes of its detractors a popular cult offering an uncultivated alternative to canonical literature. The disdain of the young Augustine for the plain speaking of the Bible captures this effectively.[17]

But precisely what might appear a counterintuitive political choice provided Constantine with a key argument to assert the necessity of his success within the same ideological system his new allegiance apparently threatened. This book argues that, taking into consideration (and even exploiting) the fears and expectations of the educated Greco-Roman upper class, Constantine and his supporters consolidated his leadership with an act of translation – or of 'anchoring', if we borrow from a model increasingly used to explore the blend of tradition and innovation characteristic of socio-cultural transformations in antiquity.[18] The most disturbing trait of Constantine's authority, the clean break from tradition, was described by his propaganda as the spontaneous evolution of an authoritative ideal ultimately deriving from and fulfilling classical political theory.

Constantine creatively adapted the cultural gesture the most successful emperors of the Principate had already performed. This translation, I aim to show, was made possible by an argument in two steps. First: responding to commonly held expectations that political leaders be favoured by the divine, Constantine presented his suppression of Rome's recent political instability as tangible evidence that divinity was on his side.[19]

---

[15] On Constantine's relationship with Christianity, and the scholarly debate surrounding his conversion, see Chapter 3, p. 119.

[16] Cf. Themistius' long defence of the concept of innovation at *Or.* 26.315d–20c.

[17] August. *Conf.* 3.5.9.

[18] The metaphor of anchoring, first developed by behavioural economists (Tversky and Kahneman [1974]), has recently been explored to investigate the mix of attachment to the past and profound innovation characterizing socio-cultural transformation in the ancient world. Sluiter (2017) is a programmatic study. On anchoring and late antique art, cf. Elsner (2020) 1–2.

[19] On the diffusion of this belief between Christians and non-Christians alike, see Kahlos (2019) 17–26.

A competitive element, however, was embedded in his exploration of the traditional rhetoric of divine endorsement. Constantine's successes in fact testified to the agency of a different deity from the gods worshipped by the ill-fated emperors who had jeopardised Rome's stability during the critical third century: the Christian divine.[20] Second, and crucially: Constantine's conversion to a superior god was presented as the outcome of an effort of active reflection on history. It was Constantine's critical interrogation of the past that had led him to identify, via a skilful act of interpretation, the true nature of Roman providence.

The consequences of Constantine's self-projection were various and long-lasting. In the first place, his propaganda influenced how Christianity was conceptualised. The motif of the emperor as Christian qua valid interpreter provided official acknowledgement of pre-circulating ideas (which I will consider below) of Christianity as the perfect hermeneutical system – the perfect philosophy, one might say. Furthermore, while Constantine's engagement with doctrine accelerated an ongoing process of identification of Christian belief with exact knowledge, it also put a spin on it by facilitating the encounter of theology with jurisprudence, opening up an avenue for the unprecedented codification of theological knowledge as law.[21] On a socio-political level, Constantine's religious policy marked the beginning of a history of state intervention in metaphysics as articulated through intra-Christian rivalries. Social hierarchies were re-drawn: bishops consolidated their authority by claiming – often in competition with one another – a role as guardians of the system of knowledge the emperor now advertised as directing his political insight. A Christian updating of the Greco-Roman expectation that the good sovereign be receptive to philosophical advice bestowed upon ecclesiastical leaders the power to validate or deny the ruler's intellectual self-image.

But the tightening, through philosophical ideals, of the bond between emperors and bishops also had another fundamental consequence: it affected the authority and social prominence of non-Christian intellectuals. As I argue in Chapters 5 and 6 of this book, at least some representatives of

---

[20] The narrative of a catastrophic third century (on which, cf. Alföldy [1974], MacMullen [1976]) fails to acknowledge the complexity of the socio-cultural and economic developments of the time. See Strobel (1993); Cameron (1998); Watson (1999); Witschel (1999), (2004); Duncan-Jones (2004); Drinkwater (2005); Dossey (2010); Esmonde Cleary (2013). However, while 'crisis' might not describe every reality and location of the time (cf. the relative prosperity of North Africa), the term nevertheless maintains some validity for assessing the status of third-century Roman institutions. External pressure and internal instability showed the inadequacy of the governmental and administrative structures of the Principate: see De Blois (2002) 204–17; Liebeschuetz (2007).
[21] Humfress (2007).

what might be given the practical but twice problematic label 'pagan Neoplatonism'[22] reacted to the official sanctioning of Christianity as superior philosophy. By arguing this, I do not mean to reinstate an artificial representation of the fourth century as organised in blocks of 'pagans' and 'Christians'. Over the last few decades, reflection on lived religion in antiquity has profitably complicated this view. The century of Constantine is now increasingly appreciated as a time not so much of jostling between fixed and neatly defined religious groups, as of active engagement with the process of defining religious identity and its capacity to demarcate all aspects of life.[23] I deliberately linger, however, in my work on precisely those authors who were most invested in this project of demarcation. By doing so, I seek to show that the discourse they animated across the fourth century was grounded on two interlocking efforts: on the one hand, the mobilisation of traditional notions of enlightened leadership in the service of religious competition and, on the other hand, the fostering of religious competition to promote the perception of some forms of power as especially enlightened.

This generated the rise of what I call a politics of interpretation. Interpretation – the fundamental expertise of post-Hellenistic philosophers operating in the legacy of an established canon – has emerged among scholars of late antiquity as a key factor driving the transformation of late antique art and literature.[24] My reconstruction of the Constantinian discourse and its impact throughout the fourth century invites us to bring to centre stage the self-image of the Christian emperor as simultaneously product and cause of this cultural process. The imperial ruler acted as the pivot of the political and theological discourse legitimising his standing as he positioned himself as the supreme interpretive agent who had read Roman history against common beliefs, ultimately achieving comprehension of what truly regulated history's course.

A final but crucial point remains. This book argues that the rise of a Christian politics of interpretation is demonstrated by the (reluctant) testimony of the ruler who is regarded as an anomaly in the history of

---

[22] On 'pagan' as an external denomination originating among Western Christians, see Cameron (2011) 14–32; Kahlos (2019) 3–6. On the origins of the term 'Neoplatonism' in German eighteenth- and nineteenth-century philosophy, see Dillon and Gerson (2004) xiii; Remes and Slaveva-Griffin (2014) 3.

[23] See, among others, Markus (1990); Cameron (1991); Boyarin (2004); Clark (2004); Kahlos (2007), (2009), (2019); Lieu (2004); Sandwell (2007); Schott (2008); Eshlemann (2012); Rebillard (2012); Johnson (2013), (2020).

[24] Elsner and Hernández-Lobato (2017) 6–16.

the Christianisation of the Roman Empire. Most of my arguments are shaped by a slow, insistent engagement with the writings of Constantine's nephew, the Emperor Julian (r. 355–63), also known as the 'Apostate' for his return to and open endorsement of the Greco-Roman pantheon. Julian famously drew on his devotion to Neoplatonism to claim a status as philosopher-ruler that he presented as resurrecting an ideal last embodied by Marcus Aurelius. The next section will illustrate, however, how the intellectual genealogy Julian claimed was constructed in (critical) response to ideas Constantine had already projected for and about himself.

Rethinking Constantine to Rethink Julian: The Case of the *Oration to the Assembly of the Saints*

Perhaps the most productive development in contemporary research on Julian has been the light shone upon the situatedness of his thinking. Julian's clever interaction as a writer and philosopher with the culture of his times has been compellingly explored by – to name only a few modern thinkers – Athanassiadi, Marcone, Baker-Brian, Tougher, and Quiroga.[25] Elm's detection of crucial parallelisms between Julian and his self-confessed nemesis, Bishop Gregory of Nazianzus, has shed light on his intellectual debt to Christianity and illustrated how upper-class imperial culture was pervaded by a debate, transcending religious divides, regarding how philosophy and leadership should interact.[26] Greenwood's analysis of Julian's reaction to Christian doctrine and hierarchies has led to a reassessment of his self-image as a 'recapitulatory overwriting' of Constantine's claims to proximity to the divine.[27] Finally, De Vita has recently produced a compelling illustration of how Julian's attempts to systematise his take on Neoplatonism map out his ambition to organise Greek religion and philosophy as antidotes to 'irrational' Christianity.[28]

All this work underscores that fourth-century developments in Christianity were key factors shaping Julian's theological and sociopolitical thinking, rather than the mere antagonistic target of his final years.[29] But despite this acknowledgement, Julian's militant self-narrative as a philosopher-ruler is perceived as the direct product of his classicising

---

[25] Athanassiadi (1981); Marcone (1984), (2015), (2019); Tougher (1998a), (1998b), (2007), (2020b); Baker-Brian and Tougher (2012); Quiroga (2009), (2017b).
[26] Elm (2012).   [27] Greenwood (2021) 1.   [28] De Vita (2022).
[29] On the relationship between Julian's philosophy and his attitude to Christianity, see further Rothrauff (1965); Athanassiadi (1981); Bouffartigue (1992), (2004); Smith (1995); Tougher (2007), (2020b); Schäfer (2008); De Vita (2011), (2017a), (2022); Long (2012); Hunt (2012);

education. His choice to carve out a profile for himself as a Platonist scholar on the throne is taken as a nostalgic return to an old paradigm, which Julian resumed in support of his argument that contemporary culture and politics were losing interest in philosophy in favour of irrational matters: dogmas and doctrine. But one should ask how Julian's Christian interlocutors would have thematised the relationship between their doctrinal efforts and 'rationality' – or, to put it differently, between Christianity and philosophy. Julian cultivated a dichotomic narrative of his recovery of philosophy in a Christian period, arguing that he was reviving an ideal of imperial commitment to philosophy long dead and buried by the new religion. It therefore seems opportune to test his claims in the light of the self-image of his greatest polemical target, Constantine – the irrational emperor, as Julian had it.[30]

Many features are reminiscent of the rule of Constantine, a figure who almost represents the epitome of the late empire: the unusual length of his reign, which lasted for thirty years; his military successes and brutal family politics; his re-foundation of the city of Byzantium as Constantinople, capital of the eastern half of the empire; and the summoning of the first ecumenical council in Nicaea in 325. Above all, Constantine is remembered as the first Roman emperor to openly endorse Christianity. As interest in the psychological – and somewhat anachronistic – question of the 'genuineness' of his conversion fades away, the focus of scholarship has shifted towards the study of Constantine as a consensus-seeker, strategist, and cultural mediator.[31] Light has been shed on crucial issues concerning his rule, from his legislative and administrative efforts and his awareness of the differences marking the various social groups with which he interacted (including but not limited to the bishops), to his ability to capitalise on the symbolic force of architecture and on Rome's military traditions.[32] The picture seems richer than ever. Yet it does not include an analysis of

---

Nesselrath (2013); Stöcklin-Kaldewey (2014); Marcone (2019); Riedweg (2020); Tougher (2020b); Niccolai (2023).

[30] Cf. Julian. *C. Her.* 227d–28a.

[31] Already Burckhardt (1853) famously argued that Constantine was interested in religion only insofar as it served his political advancement. Earnestness of belief was supported by Seeck (1920); Baynes (1929); Piganiol (1932); Alföldi (1948); Jones (1949); MacMullen (1969); Barnes (1981); Girardet (2007); Odahl (2010). But attempts to distinguish between religious sentiment and political design superimpose modern categories on a world where the sacred was perceived as inherently constitutive of social order; cf. Lenski (2016) 4–6, summarising the debate; Cooper (2019) 243. For an insightful review of scholarship engaging with the issue (and timing) of Constantine's conversion, see Flower (2012).

[32] Drake (2000); Van Dam (2007b); Dillon (J. N.) (2012); Wienand (2012); Barbero (2016); Lenski (2016); Cooper (2019). A discussion of individual contribution in Chapter 3, p. 119.

Constantine as a self-styled philosopher(-ruler), perhaps because we assume that this was not an image he was concerned to project. The recipient of a decent education but still a military leader, Constantine seems to have concerned himself with Christological disputes at most and to have done so pragmatically and with little enthusiasm for theological subtlety. A different story emerges, however, when we consider how he narrated his doctrinal preoccupations to his subjects. A starting point for appreciating this is the Constantinian *Oration to the Assembly of the Saints*, a speech whose authenticity was once questioned but that is now regarded as compatible with Constantinian authorship.[33] A more thorough analysis of the oration will be developed later in this book. Here I mainly wish to draw attention to the way the *Oration* introduces a reflection on the relationship between impermanence and eternity and on the possibility that the human mind might access such matters:

> Let us return once again to the irrefutable argument (τὸν ἀνεξέλεγκτον ... λόγον). Whatever has a beginning has also an end, and a temporal beginning (ἡ ... κατὰ χρόνον ἀρχὴ) is called coming to be (γένεσις). But all things that come to be are corruptible (φθαρτά), and time effaces their form. How then could things that come of corruptible generation be immortal? ... What is visible to the mind and apprehensible to the intellect (τὸ γάρ τοι νῷ θεατὸν καὶ διανοίᾳ περιληπτὸν) neither desires a form by which it may be known (δι' ἧς γνωρισθείη) nor submits to a shape such as an image or representation. (*OC* 3–4)

The topic is metaphysical, the vocabulary fairly technical. As Constantine delves further into his argument, he engages inter alia in criticism of the notion of 'chance' ('the name uttered by persons who ... failing to comprehend the rationale [*logos*], believe through the weakness of their comprehension that those things for which they cannot give an answer are irrationally ordered' [*OC* 7]). He also reflects, among other things, on the relationship between God and time and on the function and corruptibility of the elements and on nature as evidence of a principle of divine ordering.[34] The speech touches more than once upon the legacy – and limits – of Greek philosophy. Socrates and Pythagoras are remembered for the struggles they faced after sharing divine truths with ignorant audiences.[35] Plato is first praised and later criticised for what Constantine

---

[33] See Chapter 3, p. 125–6.
[34] *OC* 3 (on God, time, unicity of the creator, and plurality of the corruptible things); 6 (providential ordering of the cosmos).
[35] *OC* 9.

regards as insurmountable problems in his understanding of divinity.[36] The *Oration*, which presents itself from the outset as a meditation on Christ's crucifixion, clearly postulates no distinction between the religious and the philosophical spheres. Constantine presents Christianity as both the origin and the culmination of the history of thought – a history that, crucially, includes Greco-Roman thought.

This idea of containment and culmination was far from new: as the next section will consider, it had fed early Christian apologetics since the second century CE. But there is innovation in the fact that the argument is now voiced for the first time from the imperial platform, which uses it to redraw the criteria that define a philosopher-ruler and his capacity to interpret the history and politics of Rome. The *Oration* never loses touch with its main concern, the delineation of the ruler's qualities of leadership as demonstrated by his skill as an exegete. In the second half of the *Oration*, Constantine plunges into the interpretation of select passages ranging from the Book of Daniel to the Sibylline oracles and Virgil's fourth *Eclogue*, with the aim of showing how a skilled interpreter can detect their deeper (that is, Christian) significance.[37] A final apparent digression from Constantine's interpretive excursus reveals the stakes. In the last sections of the *Oration*, Constantine re-assesses the life and rule of those of his predecessors who persecuted Christians. He insists that they all met divine retribution: Decius (r. 249–51) died in battle, Valerian (r. 253–60) in captivity.[38] Diocletian (r. 284–305) became mentally enfeebled, and his palace was destroyed by a thunderbolt. 'This outcome', Constantine concludes, 'had indeed been foretold by people of intelligence (ὑπὸ τῶν εὖ φρονούντων, *OC* 25)' – his eloquent definition of the Christians.

The subtlety of the *Oration* lies in bringing to centre stage the troubles faced by past emperors and juxtaposing them with the new course of things, a course made possible by one factor, the Christianity of the ruler. The *Oration* gathers disgraced emperors under the umbrella of their 'folly', which culminated in acts of persecution attempting to propitiate false gods that only attracted punishment from the god who genuinely intervenes in history. Whereas impious rulers met tragic ends, however, Constantine can now write and speak as the victor. The *Oration* finds closure in the gift of a revelation to those who can interpret the evidence provided by the reader-emperor: the God-given intelligence that enabled Constantine to challenge

---

[36] *OC* 9. [37] *OC* 17–21. [38] *OC* 24.

Plato and unlock the Christological meaning of Virgil's *Fourth Eclogue* is the same intelligence that prompted him to understand how to turn the page on the empire's recent history of instability and violence via conversion.

Constantine's *Oration* thus exemplifies how Julian's self-construction as the philosopher-ruler subverting a recent history of unreason took shape after a recent attempt to claim the same thing. Crucially, however, this attempt posited religious allegiance as the fundamental criterion establishing the validity of a philosophical identity, with the intent of rewriting the traditional coordinates of philosophical leadership accordingly. As the next section argues, this power-centred endorsement of a correct identification of the divine as a true marker of the good philosophical life represented the outcome of a long history of reflection on the divine as the source of any philosophical endeavour. The work of the early imperial philosophical circles (including those of the Christians) had competitively mobilised such ideas throughout the Principate. At the same time, one could argue that developments internal to the history of modern thinking were later responsible for obscuring it. Our loss of perception of the competitive component intrinsic in Julian's philosophical self-image, and the concomitant acceptance of a reified dichotomy between 'philosophy' and 'Christianity', are arguably the result of a process much more recent than the fourth century CE. It is to this recent development that I now turn.

The Exclusive Truth: Christian Philosophy and The Post-Hellenistic Schools

The birth of the modern university in the nineteenth century is also the story of a practical but artificial division of knowledge whose influence survives to the present day: the partition into disciplines. In a secular context primarily concerned with the definition of scientific criteria, religious thinking proved especially controversial to allocate, with the study of the Greco-Roman past – the time of the 'classics' but also of the rise of Christianity – as a battleground. Recent scholarship has highlighted the role within this picture of a new discipline, philology, which came to be perceived as simultaneously scientifically rigorous and threatening, with its 'blind' method, to the authority of the sacred texts. The negotiation of philology's status within the study of *Altertumswissenschaft* eventually facilitated the emergence of two separate disciplines, classics and patristics – the study of the early Church – that investigate aspects of the same world.[39]

Contemporary scholars have been breaking down the disciplinary and conceptual boundaries their predecessors erected, challenging the choice to isolate the ancients' religious questions from the world in which they took shape. In the process, we have become aware that the separation of classics and patristics is complementary to and encourages the cultivation in ancient sources of another modern distinction, that between 'philosophy' and 'theology'. Yet the process of formation of the thinking and identity of early Christian communities drew on the same repertoire of technologies of self-definition available to other groups of intellectuals across the empire. Already texts like Paul's letters and the Prologue to John illustrate how Christianity developed from the beginning in dialogue with Greek thinking.[40] But it is with the second century CE that this relationship began to be thematised explicitly. A watershed moment is routinely detected in the apologetic writings of Justin Martyr (d. ca. 165), who defined Christianity as the 'only certain and useful philosophy' and advocated for an understanding of the identity between Christ and the *logos*, the seminal reason present in every individual, the principle of truth, knowledge, and cosmic order.[41]

As the Gospel's message and imagery came to be developed through a series of questions betraying growing metaphysical concerns (e.g., the relationship between soul and matter, or between God and time, and the genesis of the elements), another practice strengthened Christianity's philosophical identity. Through the mediation of Hellenistic Judaism (and especially the Philonic encounter between Plato and the Bible, which inspired Origen and Clement of Alexandria), the practice of allegorical exegesis – the elaboration of the meaning of a text as pointing to another, deeper meaning – became a central mode in the development of Christian doctrine. This phenomenon, it should be noted, unfolded in parallel with

---

[39] Conybeare and Goldhill (2021b); Goldhill (2021).
[40] On Paul's criticism of the wisdom of the world (cf. *1 Cor.* 1–2, 3.18–20) as resonating with the rivalry between types of wisdom characterizing the post-Hellenistic philosophical landscape, see Van Kooten (2010). See Nasrallah (2010) on the nexus between second-century Christian literature and contemporary art and imperial propaganda. See Eshleman (2012) on modes of community formation shared among second-century Christians, philosophers, and rhetoricians. Second-century 'apologists' underscored the idea that 'the task of philosophy' is 'to enquire about the Divine' (Justin, *Dial. Tryph.* 1.3, transl. Falls; cf. also *Dial. Tryph.* 3.5). On the compatibility and comparability of theological concepts between John, Justin, the Orphic hymns, and Aelius Aristides, see Van Kooten (2021).
[41] 'Only sure and useful philosophy' (*Dial. Tryph.* 8.1). On Justin on Greek philosophy and the *logos*, see Boys-Stones (2001) 184–88.

the rise of the genre of the exegetical commentary in the post-Hellenistic schools of philosophy.[42]

This cluster of doctrinal practices is today labelled early Christian 'theology', but the name poses issues of compartmentalisation: 'theologian' is a later definition applied to intellectuals who in the ancient world would have referred to themselves as philosophers. At the same time, the word *theologia* appears for the first time in the writings of Plato, where it denotes knowledge of the divine.[43] Plato was not eccentric in identifying the culmination of his thinking in the contemplation of ultimate realities, for this identification underlay the development of Greek philosophy from its (known) origins. As Thales thought of water as the *arché*, Heraclitus saw the first principle in fire, Democritus reflected on the atom and Aristotle on the Uncaused Cause, their idea of 'philo-sophy' (literally 'love for wisdom') relied on the assumption that any pursuit of knowledge must culminate in an understanding of immutable truth(s).[44] In their thinking, no distinction was drawn between 'natural' and 'supernatural' (or consequently between 'sacred' and 'secular').[45] It should further be stressed that, contrary to contemporary perceptions of philosophy as an intellectual and academic endeavour, Greek philosophy was experienced by its practitioners as a form of care for what, especially under the impulse of Socratic thinking, came to be defined as the soul. Philosophical training coincided with the choice of a way of life in which the purification of the self was pursued, as Hadot famously put it, through 'spiritual exercises'.[46] The Platonic emphasis on reason as the divine element within us had as its corollary the representation of those who spent their life in contemplation as holy individuals.[47] Porphyry's *Life of Plotinus* testifies to the sanctity attached to the re-founder of Platonism: Plotinus is depicted as a daimonic being, a prophet able to predict inter alia future events awaiting the relatives of his disciples.[48] After his death, an oracle of Apollo proclaimed

---

[42] Dillon (2006); Hoffmann (2009); Johnson (2013) 146–55.   [43] Pl. *Resp.* 2.379a.
[44] On reflection on the divine as a springboard for epistemological advancement in early Greek thinking, see Drozdek (2007). Tor (2017) 10–60. On the ancient use of the word 'philosophy' to refer to meditation on god, see Bardy (1949); Malingrey (1961).
[45] Lacoste (2014) 12–13.
[46] Hadot (1981). On religious experience in ancient Greek philosophy, see also Sedley (1989); Frede (2000).
[47] Fowden (1982); Urbano (2013); Johnson (2014). Platonism has often been conceptualised by scholars as a religion: see already Dörrie (1981), Dillon (1986). Boys-Stones (2016) considers the development of the notion of *pronoia* (providence) in second-century Platonism, illustrating how an idea that modern audiences might take as belonging exclusively to the 'religious' sphere was developed within Platonist rationalizing structures.
[48] Porph. *Plot.* 10–11.

Plotinus' achievement of the divinity he pursued during his life, closing with an image of his soul dwelling with the gods and other blessed spirits, including Pythagoras and Plato.[49] The episode, incidentally, also illustrates the role assigned to oracles of the gods in late antique philosophy. The question of the capacity of the philosopher to interpret the voice of god or the gods animated the controversy between adherents of Greco-Roman religion and their opponents: fragments of Porphyry's *Philosophy from Oracles*, a treatise that teaches philosophers how to interpret oracular utterances, survive precisely because a bishop – Eusebius of Caesarea – transcribed some passages in order to attack them.[50]

All this is illustrative of the limits inherent in any attempt to isolate a distinct sphere of activity in antiquity pertaining exclusively to 'religion'. Cultural historians have become increasingly aware of the problems posed by the adaptation of pre-modern manifestations of spirituality to categories shaped by centuries of interaction between power and cult.[51] This contemporary reassessment of ancient spirituality, however, does not aim to deny validity to research on the religions of the Greeks and the Romans (since, as Johnson writes, this would 'occlude as much as it illumines').[52] It seeks instead to question the ways in which a modern and pre-eminently Western understanding of religion might prevent us from capturing crucial aspects of the ancient experience of the sacred. An example is the current appreciation of how the category of 'faith' should be decentralised in early Christianity, as opposed to the modern emphasis placed on the term; in antiquity, belief was conceptualised as originating from reasoning and understanding.[53] Another important contemporary development for this book is the reassessment of the ancient triangulation between philosophy, doctrine, and cult. This has a crucial impact on the way we understand the efforts of post-Hellenistic philosophical schools to bridge the gap between their teachings and traditions born out of ancient literature and folklore. The Stoics in particular drew on allegory to recover myths and elements of cult as primitive sources of truth and to incorporate them into their

---

[49] Porph. *Plot.* 22. See Brisson (1990).
[50] See especially at Euseb. *PE* 4.6–10; 4.23; 5.6–16. Importantly, later in the work Eusebius quotes from the *Detection of Deceivers* of the Cynic Oenomaus of Gadara (*PE* 5.18–36) with the aim of showing that even pagans were critical of oracles. On the relationship between philosophy and divination in late antique Neoplatonism, with special attention to prophecyer and theurgy, see Addey (2014).
[51] Critiques of universalising definitions of religion has been advanced especially by Asad (1993) 27–54 and Nongbri (2013). Both emphasise that such definitions fail to capture the historical determination of specific manifestations of religious experience.
[52] Johnson (2020) 31.   [53] Morgan (2015).

thinking.⁵⁴ Platonism was re-founded on the notion that Plato had fully reconstructed this kernel of divine knowledge, which could therefore be accessed via exegesis of his writings.⁵⁵ Crucially, this post-Hellenistic re-appraisal of philosophy's capacity to access an original truth via interpretation shaped the competition of Christian intellectuals with Greco-Roman philosophers. It provided early Christian thinkers with tools not only to reject the characterisation of their religion as new and derivative but also to reverse it.⁵⁶ In rivalry with Platonist claims of access to divine wisdom, Christianity advocated in various ways for the pre-existence of the Christian message and the reliance of Greek thinking upon it, the so-called dependency theme, as Boys-Stones terms it.⁵⁷ By so doing, early Christianity crafted a story of completion and culmination: the history of Christian thinking was a journey of perfection of a divine knowledge to which a number of societies and cultures, including – but not limited to – the Greco-Roman world, had had restricted access.⁵⁸ The competitive displacement of the belief the Greeks and Romans had of their cultural centrality was accompanied by the contention that the Greek philosophical schools had inspired Christian heresies. In other words, early Christian intellectuals propagated the idea that Greek philosophies were responsible for diversions from exact metaphysical knowledge.⁵⁹

The fostering of a climate of cultural competition had important socio-political underpinnings. The rivalry over issues of primacy and dependency on the matter of knowledge was the other side of early Christian efforts to negotiate an authoritative voice and role in society, and what primarily illustrates this statement is the way such cultural debate took shape simultaneous with the rise of a Christian political discourse.⁶⁰ Doctrine and politics must be envisaged as the two faces of early Christianity's desire to carve out its space in the Greco-Roman world. The work of those

---

⁵⁴ Boys-Stones (2001) 28–59; Schott (2008) 15–51; Van Nuffelen (2011) 29–47.
⁵⁵ Boys-Stones (2001).   ⁵⁶ Lieu (2004) 84; Nasrallah (2010) 5.   ⁵⁷ Boys-Stones (2001).
⁵⁸ See, e.g., Clement of Alexandria's definition of philosophy as 'a kind of preliminary education (προπαιδεία τις) for those who are trying to gather faith through demonstration (τοῖς τὴν πίστιν δι' ἀποδείξεως καρπουμένοις)', *Strom*. 1.5.28.1, transl. Ferguson). A supporter of the idea that the achievements of classical philosophy were either the result of parallel illumination of the Greeks by the Logos or direct influence from the Bible, Clement would refer to Plato as 'the pupil of barbarian (i.e., Christian) philosophy' (ὁ τῆς βαρβάρου μαθητὴς φιλοσοφίας, *Paedagog*. 2.10).
⁵⁹ Displacement of Greeks and Romans to create a new philosophical hierarchy: Johnson (2006). Heresies (now increasingly defined in opposition to orthodoxy) as a product of Greek philosophy: Eshleman (2012) 216–57.
⁶⁰ Cameron (1991); Lieu (2004); Rapp (2005); Johnson (2006), (2014); Sandwell (2007); Schott (2008); Elm (2012); Eshleman (2012).

second-century thinkers conventionally labelled 'apologists'[61] is already indicative of this: Justin's and Athenagoras' imperial pleas for the cause of Christianity relied upon the self-projection, noted above, of second-century emperors as pious and cultured, exploring it to Christianity's benefit. Justin and Athenagoras challenged Antoninus Pius, Marcus Aurelius, and Lucius Verus to prove their love for truth by honouring a Logos that was interpretable either as Christ or reason.[62] But the most ambitious development of early Christianity's competition with *paideia* and the institutions responding to it arguably took place in the early fourth century, and specifically in two texts that prepare the ground for the Constantinian turn. The first is the *Divine Institutes* (ca. 305–10 CE) by the Latin rhetorician Lactantius, who – crucially – worked and thought in proximity to imperial power. Lactantius was professor of rhetoric at Nicomedia in the years Constantine resided there and later served as the tutor of Constantine's eldest son, Crispus. His influence on Constantine's thinking is much debated and ranges from the idea that religion cannot be coerced (cf. Constantine's and Licinius' 'Edict of Milan') and that God punishes persecuting emperors, to the argument, richly exploited by Constantine's *Oration*, that the interpretation of Greco-Roman literature reveals the underlying Christian truth upon which all knowledge rests.[63] This idea of interpretation as an instrument of revelation operates as a guiding principle, with due differences, also in the second work that sets the stage for the fourth-century cultural competition between Greek-speaking Christian and 'pagan' philosophers: the *Preparation for the Gospel* of Eusebius of Caesarea (265–339 CE), which argues for Christianity's intellectual superiority over Greek philosophy through a systematic re-reading of sapiential writings from a variety of cultures.

The writings of Lactantius and Eusebius encapsulate how Christianity's claims to philosophical priority interacted with the socio-political environment of the late empire.[64] But a fundamental difference divided them. Although Lactantius was concerned with issues of divine retribution (see

---

[61] On the label see Nasrallah (2010) 21–28; Van Kooten (2010) 21–22.

[62] See, e.g., Justin, *Apol.* 1, addressing the Antonines as philosophers and lovers of leaning; or Athenagoras pleading that the emperors devote their 'love of learning and truth' (τὸ φιλομαθὲς καὶ φιλάληθες) to the examination of Christian doctrine (*Leg.* 2.6).

[63] For a discussion of Lactantius' political thinking and the areas of intersection with, and possible influence on, Constantine' religious policies, see DePalma Digeser (2000) 134–43; Garnsey (2003) 3 n. 13; Schott (2008) 110–35, Lettieri (2013); Gassman (2020) 19–47.

[64] Cf. especially Schott (2008) for an insightful placement of late third- and early fourth-century Christian apologetics in the Roman imperial discourse negotiating the control, subjugation, and organisation of the *oikoumene*.

his *On the Deaths of the Persecutors*), he aimed above all else to set the reader on a personal path towards the divine. The rise of Constantine did not substantially alter his pre-Constantinian perception of the world, which was based on the assumption that Christians would live and be vexed in Rome until the end of human time.[65] Eusebius, who lived to see the emperor and the bishops meet at Nicaea, had other ambitions and worked to secure an open acknowledgement of the Church as Rome's intellectual compass. Whether he wrote to recast the history of Christianity as the true heart of Rome's history (*Ecclesiastical History*)[66] or to assert Christian thinking as foundational to Greco-Roman philosophy (*Preparation for the Gospel*), he was clear that knowledge and leadership should be the primary, intertwined concerns of fellow ecclesiastics. Perhaps his most incisive translation of the political aspirations of fourth-century normative Christianity unfolds in the document in which he publicly addresses the emperor, simultaneously bestowing and denying praise: his oration *In Praise of Constantine*. Provocatively voicing Eusebius' understanding of the nature of the relationship between church and state, the *Praise* breaks new ground by referring to the emperor as 'the only philosopher-ruler' on account of his adherence to Christianity.[67]

Eusebius' ascription of Constantine's entitlement to a status of philosopher-ruler to his Christianity thus represents an extreme act of public and episcopal sanctioning of the emperor's religious allegiance as proof of his superior understanding. As this book seeks to show, however, this act took place in a larger context or re-elaboration of Constantine's intellectual identity. This ranged from claims to cultural innovation professed at his court (for instance, Optatian's poetic celebration of the emperor as reader and interpreter)[68] to the elaboration of his legacy via the imperial propaganda cultivated shortly after his death by his sons and successors. In Part I, I pick up on the current scholarly re-assessment of the rule of Constantius II – Constantine's longest-surviving son – as driven by cultural concerns and a desire to display an intellectual self-image (Chapter 2). I use this re-assessment to argue that Constantius' public image qualifies as a reception of his father's simultaneously political, cultural, and religious project, and therefore retrospectively validates my reading. Most important, Constantius II and his entourage committed to perpetuating an understanding of the emperor as the guardian of a form of knowledge that encompassed and superseded *paideia*. Ironically, the young

---

[65] Gassman (2020) 23–27. [66] Corke-Webster (2019).
[67] Eus. *LC* 5.4 (μόνος φιλόσοφος βασιλεύς). [68] See Chapter 3, p. 133–7.

Julian was a key participant in Constantius' propaganda effort. Having come to power as Constantius' subordinate Caesar, Julian entered literature with orations I re-assess in Chapter 2 as supporting a representation of him as a philosopher-ruler qua Christian ruler. The same language structuring his entrance into politics provided Julian with the tools he would use later on to articulate his antagonistic response. But before I move on to an introductory reflection on the modalities of this response, a final point should be addressed, having to do with the resonance of the Constantinian message with a larger group of followers, supporters, and detractors. This resonance raises the question that shapes the Part III of my book: which social categories were most influenced by Constantine's propaganda and its competitive intentions, which Julian's reply further mobilised?

Competing for Wisdom: Bishops as Leaders and Advisers in the Post-Constantinian Empire

As is often remarked, what set early Christians apart from other groups of philosophers and rhetors in the Greco-Roman empire was the fact that, although all these communities sought intellectual prestige as a means to secure their social position, only Christianity entrusted central authorities with the task of coordinating its processes of self-definition.[69] Beginning in the second century, the emergence of a hierarchy of presbyters and deacons, presided over by a bishop, made the episcopacy a leading agent in the articulation of Christian doctrine – a role third-century persecutions inadvertently consolidated, as they prompted Christian communities to solidify – as Kahlos puts it – around their spiritual leaders.[70] By the early fourth century, bishops were the uncontested authority figures of the religion to which the ruler was now pleading allegiance. It follows that bishops were also primarily involved in the efforts to define fourth-century leadership, a process that shaped them just as much as they shaped it. In Part III of the book, I show how the Constantinian project of endorsing Christianity as ideal philosophy, and the response it elicited from Julian, trickled down from the imperial to the episcopal platform, transforming the understanding of the relationship between knowledge, culture, and power across Roman society. This process corroborated the role of bishops in society at a time when they were increasingly replacing local elites in matters of urban leadership, structuring their channels of communications with both the central power and the mass of the faithful, strengthening

---

[69] Eshleman (2012) 61.   [70] Kahlos (2019) 40.

their self-image, fuelling their inner rivalries on matters of 'orthodoxy' and 'heresy', and – finally – destabilising the status and political voice of non-Christian philosophers.

Constantine's propaganda generally influenced the social classes he created or advanced and upon which he bestowed legal and financial benefits, such as the order of the *comites* (imperial companions) or the senators. The monuments and official speeches of fourth-century senators appear to have served as spaces for celebration and justification of how these individuals had proved capable of attracting the favour of the celestial emperor.[71] Comparable self-legitimising efforts unfolding under and after Constantine are visible among the bishops, now welcomed into the imperial court and invested with unprecedented privileges, including judicial authority.[72] Constantine's self-image fed their symbolic authority in two complementary ways. First, the bishops, who until this point had been – as the previous section argued – among the primary agents of definition of the philosophical identity of Christianity, now had their self-image protected by a ruler who shared their view and legitimised the open cultivation of the idea. The second way emperors fed the episcopal self-image was via a peculiar blend of cooperation and competition centred on a specific (unexpressed) question. If the prosperity of the empire depended on divine favour, which the emperor was responsible for securing, how was he expected to relate to religious intermediaries who were now for the first time disjointed from state institutions?

This issue, articulated through the question of how fourth-century power should relate to philosophy, became an opportunity for bishops to pursue a strategic distribution of roles. Good sovereignty, as prescribed by Greco-Roman political theory, was under two simultaneous normative demands. It was expected to strive towards an ideal of philosophical leadership but also to receive philosophical advice from qualified advisers. Hellenistic philosophers, and the representatives of Stoicism in particular, had been content to inhabit an advisory role, as their policy of non-engagement with public affairs was nevertheless perceived as compatible with providing advice to political agents.[73] With the consolidation of the

---

[71] Eloquently, Constantine's legislation would even emphasise his desire to protect private individuals at the expense of the *fiscus publicus* (*C.Th.* 10.15.2). On Constantine's bestowal of benefits on various social classes, see Kelly (2012) 192–200; Barbero (2016) 489–512, 667–69; Lenski (2016); Moser (2018) 45–57. On transformations in the senatorial self-image, see Weisweiler (2015), (2016).

[72] Barbero (2016) 596–600.

[73] See Aalders (1975); Garnsey and Winton (1981); Rawson (1989).

imperial institution in Rome, the desire of emperors to project a cultured image interacted with a collective expectation that they should have counsellors at their side.[74] The most successful literary instantiation of this principle, Dio of Prusa's *Orations of Kingship*, helped consolidate the fundamental belief in the right of the philosopher to withdraw approval if an emperor failed to conform to his advice.[75] Intriguingly, this 'conditionality of praise' (thus Moles) already appears operative as a subtext in the critique of the rulers of the Principate formulated by second-century Christian apologists.[76]

We do not know if the speeches of the second-century apologists were actually received at court.[77] We do know, however, that approximately two centuries later episcopal appeals to emperors were. The Constantinian philosopher-ruler, now defined as such by virtue of his religious allegiance, was especially bound to listen to the words of those qualifying by virtue of their grasp of the (exclusive) truth as an upgraded version of traditional philosopher-advisers. A positive feedback loop established itself between the wisdom-loving emperor and his episcopal counsellors. If the wisdom of the emperor was now at one with his religious allegiance, controlling Christianity meant controlling the imperial self-image. Eusebius' *Praise of Constantine* (336 CE), the first panegyric to tell the emperor that praise goes to God first,[78] lays a precocious claim to this idea of symbolic power. Afterwards, various fourth-century preachers indulged in portraying themselves as masters of *parrhesia* – in Greek political theory, the freedom of speech of the philosopher confronting power.[79] Claims to *parrhesia* sanctioned a desire not merely to fulfil the role of the philosopher-adviser in all its traditional attributes but also and most importantly to claim priority in establishing how state authority should accept being addressed and by whom. The principle that Christian philosophy had privileged access to knowledge translated into the assumption that only Christian philosophers were equipped to give blunt advice, which was therefore requalified as the litmus test for ascertaining the speaker's reliance on unshakable truths intended as correct doctrine.

---

[74] Rawson (1989); Roller (2001) 146–93; Van Renswoude (2019) 65–66. Lucian's *On Salaried Posts in Great Houses* (*De Mercede Conductis*) captures satirically how the social ambitions of second-century intellectuals seeking social prominence met the ambition of the powerful to act as patrons. See Goldhill (2002) 63–93; Eshleman (2012) 79.

[75] On Dio as an embodiment of the 'pedagogical paradigm' of the philosophical guide to a Roman emperor, see Whitmarsh (2001) 181–216. Reception of Dio's work in the late empire: Jones (1978) 115; Brancacci (1985); Maisano (1995) 11–12; Heather (1998) 129–30.

[76] Moles (1990) 312.   [77] Nasrallah (2010) 26–27.   [78] See Chapter 5.

[79] Brown (1992); van Renswoude (2019).

Introduction 21

My outline of fourth-century transactions around the theme of (divine) philosophy, however, divides the players too neatly into two groups, 'emperors' and 'bishops'. By so doing, it fails to acknowledge a fundamental consequence of the imperial endorsement of Christianity as exact knowledge and of the consequent state intervention in the management of doctrine. Already prior to Constantine, in a context of multiple 'Churches' (or Christianities), as some prefer to put it,[80] early Christian thinkers were at work defining the differential category 'heresy', measuring their authority through their capacity to advocate for the correctness of their theological statements.[81] This negotiation too was ultimately a product of the question of the priority or dependency of knowledge that, as noted, shaped post-Hellenistic intellectual disputes. At the level of pre-Constantinian Christian communities, debate over heresy soon translated into various attempts to discipline the non-conforming.[82] But only with Nicaea, in 325 CE, did the management of orthodoxy come to be acknowledged as an imperial and governmental responsibility, not least of all because factionalism, as voices critical of Christianity (including Julian) stressed, had severe repercussions for the idea that Christianity relied on exact knowledge.

Crucially, the increasing involvement of the Roman state in theological disputes – and the progressive reliance of bishops on the centre of gravity represented by state power – altered the nature of these disputes.[83] The entrance of the Church into the imperial legal arena prepared for an unprecedented act of state sanctioning of the possibility of policing knowledge (of the divine). The management of theology and, concomitantly, the process of defining theological authority were transformed by the encapsulation of disputes over heresy within a framework provided by Roman law, producing 'a legally enforceable judgment as to the winner and the loser' (thus Humfress).[84] This went hand in hand with the unfolding of a complex conflict between an 'academic' and a 'Catholic' mode of episcopal authority (thus Williams), whose outcome is epitomised by the downfall of Origen and his legacy.[85] The making first of creeds, and later of canon law, could thus be framed within this re-negotiation of the relationship

---

[80] See Hopkins (1998) 90–94; Salzman (2008) 189; Kahlos (2019) 6–7.
[81] There is a vast bibliography on the subject. See, among others, Boys-Stones (2001); Edwards (2009); Eshleman (2012).
[82] Kahlos (2019) 41.
[83] On harmony with the divine as a governmental concern from the Principate into late antiquity, see Kahlos (2019) 20–24.
[84] Humfress (2007) 146.   [85] Williams (2001) 85–87. See further Ip (2022).

between power and philosophy, as stepping stones in a process of delineating formal guidelines for the legal management of metaphysical understanding.

At the heart of this process lay the question of how a self-confessedly perfect system of knowledge should interact with those who had only partial access to divine truth, a definition intriguingly applied both to the faithful relying on preachers for instructions and – most important – to non-Christian philosophers. The impact of the debate on the latter group is epitomised by the way bishops reconceptualised Julian's experience of leadership to their advantage after his death. While he was sole ruler, Julian developed his engagement with the question of the relationship between philosophy and providence in a way analogous but antagonistic to that of Constantine. His death in Persia in 363 CE served on a silver platter to his detractors the refutation of his attempts to re-draw the boundaries between Rome and *paideia*, on the one hand, and Christianity, on the other. His demise was converted into the locus of a providential argument illustrating the historical defeat of Greco-Roman polytheism and the philosophical system connected to it. Beginning with Gregory of Nazianzus, the interpretation of Julian's life was taken to signify the victory of Christian over pagan hermeneutics in accessing the divine design.[86]

The parable of Julian thus came to epitomise the philosophical failure of post-Hellenistic schools, contributing to disqualifying non-Christian philosophers' claims to knowledge and insight into providence. This phenomenon was concomitant with a growing denial of the philosophical utility of a *paideia* seen as representing, at its best, partial and derivative knowledge. Beginning with the great experiment in mass mobilisation that was the Arian controversy,[87] the fourth century saw bishops return in various ways to the question of whether traditional education provided a path to true knowledge. Socio-political empowerment encouraged them to envisage political advantage in the claim that Christianity was not only a privileged source of knowledge but also the only philosophical system that addressed and cared for all social levels.[88] At the same time, the rise of counter-cultural theologians to prominent positions increasingly undermined that elitist, intellectual form of engagement with doctrine that had been essential to asserting Christianity's status among the philosophical

---

[86] See Chapter 5.
[87] Galvão-Sobrinho (2013). On the dispute as exploiting structured conflict to cultivate factions, see Cooper (2019).
[88] On the utility of this argument in processes of episcopal replacement of the local elites, see Brown (1992) 35–70.

schools of Greece and Rome.[89] As highly influential preachers (e.g., John Chrysostom) denied the validity of Plato or Aristotle in the path to (Christian) philosophy, the capacity of non-Christian philosophers to guide the powerful was redefined accordingly. As I suggest through two case studies, some philosophers clinging to a traditional understanding of the relationship between philosophy and *paideia* perceived this shift and objected to it. The first figure exemplifying this reaction is the aristocrat, polymath, and Neoplatonic philosopher Synesius of Cyrene (ca. 373–414). Synesius is usually regarded as an exemplification of flexible, anti-dogmatic religious allegiance. I have argued elsewhere, however, that his writings map out a neat desire to criticise and compete with counter-cultural Christianity, re-asserting the traditional bond between philosophy and *paideia*.[90] This effort sets Synesius on a plane with my second case study, the pro-Julianic historian and biographer Eunapius of Sardis, who I suggest wrote his *Lives of the Philosophers and Sophists* to re-claim the role of non-Christian philosophers in society. An invisible thread links Synesius' and Eunapius' seemingly life-long obsession with philosophical themes – a thread that ultimately leads to Julian. As we observe philosophical claims and identities being weaponised in various ways across a full century by Christian and 'pagan' intellectuals, or by lovers of *paideia* and counter-cultural voices, we can begin to understand that neither Julian nor Synesius and Eunapius lingered on a well-worn, self-representative paradigm inherited from the Second Sophistic, trying to revive an anachronistic image buried in the past. To the contrary, they all reacted forcefully to the Christian exploration of this paradigm after the Constantinian turn had infused it with momentous significance.

From Exegesis to Empire: The Politics of Interpretation

I would like to advance a final point in this introduction, which concerns how this book seeks to propose a new methodological framework for conceptualising the dynamics of socio-political, cultural, and religious transformation during the fourth century. I suggest that the making of the Constantinian (and post-Constantinian) empire was enabled by the development of a politics of interpretation. I define this as an all-encompassing discourse that mobilised literature and history as mutually

---

[89] On the charismatic capital of the ascetic and how, from the late fourth century, the official church absorbed it, see Sterk (1998), (2004); Rapp (2005).
[90] Niccolai (2021).

validating fields and constructed leaders as 'intelligent readers' to signify their capacity to organise cultural and socio-political change.

I will begin to unpack this definition by considering current perspectives on the role of interpretation in late antiquity. It is now uncontroversial to assert that fourth-century intellectuals were deeply invested in the task of making sense of older literature. Writers with different agendas found common ground in their shared receptiveness to the question of how to understand 'classical' authors in a fast-changing world.[91] A blend of reverence and competition towards a crystallising canon drove what Elsner and Hernández-Lobato call an 'era of interpretation' spanning literature and the arts.[92] But the investment of intellectuals in interpretation was not limited to these two fields. The rubrics of 'exegesis' and 'allegory' open a wide, dynamic scenario in which, as noted above, all post-Hellenistic schools of philosophy participated, from Stoic philosophers to the Jewish Platonists of Alexandria and early Christian thinkers. Interpretation provided a key heuristic practice for philosophers working around an increasingly authoritative canon and seeking to link old texts and new ideas through increasingly ambitious theories of signification.[93] It should also be stressed that this engagement with literary and philosophical exegesis was accompanied and arguably incentivised by technological advances, which set in motion a range of transformations in the way late antique readers approached textuality.[94] The increasing dominance of the codex in late antiquity had an impact on exegetical practices: compared to the scroll, it offered new possibilities for collecting texts and engaging with their contents. For example, the codex enabled the inclusion of entire corpora in a single binding, facilitating cross-referencing. The flourishing of the genre of the commentary (with Servius, Donatus, and Macrobius as famous representatives) testifies to how fourth- and fifth-century scholars took full advantage of this possibility. At the same time, it does not seem coincidental that one of the figures most invested in reinterpreting *paideia* in the light of Christian thinking, Eusebius of Caesarea, also had an impact on codex technology and the way this was put to the service of biblical exegesis. A key innovation ascribed to Eusebius is the invention of the

---

[91] On textual exegesis and rhetorical practice in late antique poetry, see Pelttari (2014) 12–44; Elsner and Hernández Lobato (2017); Hadijttofi and Lefteratou (2020).

[92] Elsner and Hernández-Lobato (2017) 6. On the reflection of typological exegesis in Christian art, see Elsner (1995) 271–87, (2000); Schrenk (1995).

[93] Turner (2010). On incarnational theology as a motor of Christian allegory, see Boyarin (2010).

[94] On the transformation of textuality in late antiquity, see Grafton and Hale Williams (2006); Chin (2008); Riggsby (2019) 216–22; Coogan (2021).

canon tables, the influential cross-referencing system employed in codices that collected the four canonical gospels.[95]

Within this scenario of widespread mobilisation of exegesis, however, we should also incorporate another recent characterisation of the fourth century: the 'century of miracles', as Drake terms it.[96] This view originates in the observation that fourth-century sources variously connected to imperial or episcopal power were all highly invested in the propagation of miracle narratives. As Drake observes, the century is framed in authoritative sources by two supernatural events: Constantine's vision of the celestial cross in 312 and the miraculous windstorm that saved the army of Theodosius, the emperor who (re)asserted Nicene Christianity as orthodoxy, in 394. The timeline between these two events is punctuated in homilies, biographies, panegyrics, and historical writings generally by several other allegedly God-sent events. The 'era of interpretation' in literature and philosophy and the 'century of miracles' might at first seem to be unrelated concepts. In fact, each explains the other. They are two faces of the same coin, capturing from different angles the unfolding of a politics of interpretation – of the signs of the divine interspersed in texts and the world – intended as a laboratory of political and ideological transition towards and beyond the Constantinian state.

The writings examined in this book converge in showing that fourth-century politicians and intellectuals engaged with two interconnected strategies to legitimise change (or anchor innovation, if we wish to continue to draw on this concept). First, agents of historical change (Constantine, Constantius II, Eusebius, Julian, Gregory of Nazianzus, and others) appear particularly keen in their writings to engage in exegetical performances. Their aims, as this book will note, range from efforts to demonstrate their intellectual capacity to attempts to demonstrate their assimilation to ideals of philosophical leadership and suggest their superior grasp of a history shaped by a divinity coinciding with reason (Logos). Second, the writings I examine converge in reflecting on how to produce evidence in support of their statements, backing up a display of interpretive methodology with attempts to guide audiences to recognise points of validity in the arguments advanced. Miracle narratives circulated by official sources appear in this light as a strategy for a Christian politics of interpretation to operate by cutting across social levels. Narratives of divine intervention in fact provide tokens for guided exegesis: they seek to reveal the world as Christian by pointing to events that, if read correctly,

---

[95] Canon tables: Crawford (2019); Bausi, Reudenback, and Wimmer (2020).   [96] Drake (2020).

demonstrate the agency of the divine in the cosmos. But what is essential is that, in doing so, they are able to address simple audiences: the story of a miracle indicating the agency of Christ in history is not on the same intellectual level as exegetical projects addressing scriptures. Like them, however, it establishes a channel of communication between divine and human and resolves accordingly the tension between the meaning of the past – of history, turned into a series of miraculous manifestations of God – and of the present. The latter, for Christian authors, must coincide with that which separates the Bible from Roman actuality. This resolution, I suggest, was obtained through what could be described as a 'master argument' legitimising all others: the production of the life of the emperor, in its specifics, as evidence supporting theological demonstration. What is more, the emperor himself, in an intriguing twist, was invested in the use of his own life to the same argumentative end.

The text introduced above, Constantine's *Oration to the Saints*, can provide a matrix for illustrating the claims just advanced. By presenting Constantine as the intelligent reader of Rome's history, the *Oration* relies, as argued, on a Christian adaptation of the ideal of philosophical leadership. It does so, however, in order to engage with a long, authoritative tradition of what could be defined as future-oriented knowledge: the ambition, marking all sorts of rhetorical and historiographical works from Greco-Roman antiquity, to suggest that an author's intellectual grasp on past and present is the condition for a general understanding of history as it might unfold in the future.[97] Constantine's *Oration*, with its engagement with Rome's past, relies on this idea. Crucially, however, the piece also presents Constantine's reading of recent history not merely as proof of his understanding of history's rules but as a demonstration of his comprehension of history intended as divine design.[98] This claim is validated by producing what Greek oratory labels a *tekmerion*, necessary evidence: Constantine's decades of success give visible support to the claim that he has found endorsement in the god who truly operates in history.[99] The Christian emperor sews himself into his own interpretive framework.[100]

---

[97] On future-oriented knowledge in historiography, see Grethlein (2013); Lianeri (2016). On the Attic orators' use of past exempla in deliberative contexts, see Maltagliati (2020).
[98] On the interdependency between prophecy and Roman power, see Potter (1994).
[99] On Aristotle's definition of *tekmerion* in relationship to *semeion* and *eikos*, see Grimaldi (1980).
[100] This principle also regulates the way Optatian's picture poems capture, through the encounter between the verbal and the visual, the 'interpretability' of Constantine's rule. See Chapter 3, p. 133–7.

The outcome of his life – visible to everyone – provides through this visibility itself the opportunity to ascertain Constantine's claims against the background of decades of turmoil.

But Constantine's advertisement of his ability to interpret providential history does not put itself to the test only in the study of the past. As noted above, a large part of the *Oration* – perhaps the majority of it – builds a case for Constantine as an intelligent reader of literature, which he treats as an alternative source of evidence demonstrating the presence of Christ in the world. His readings of literature and history validate each other. Divine presence must be discernible everywhere, both in providence-led history and in the divinely inspired writings of God's creatures. This interplay – or collapse – between political and literary modes of exegesis, I suggest, is a (the) fundamental feature of the dynamics of Constantinian and post-Constantinian socio-cultural discourse. The fourth-century politics of interpretation is a space of exploration (for the ancient) and of observation (for us) of a readable cosmos. It invites approaches that blur the boundaries between the written page and the world or, one might say, between allegory and divination.

The challenge to such boundaries was prepared by intellectual developments long predating the era I am considering; in ancient Greece and Rome, literary hermeneutics and the interpretation of divine signs were always marked by a semantic overlap.[101] 'Symbol' (σύμβολον), one of the terms most often used in ancient allegory, also designated divine omens.[102] 'Enigma' (αἴνιγμα), another key word for allegorical elaboration, was fundamental to divination. The arts of exegesis and of the interpretation of divine signs thus had common roots, and it is no accident that Stoicism, the Hellenistic school most invested in allegory, also believed that divine reason (*logos*) manifested itself in every part of the cosmos, including in myths and rites.[103] Belief in cosmic sympathy (*symphateia*), an ideal of universal interconnection, emanates from Greek and Roman reflections on divination. Cicero's brother Quintus in *On Divination*, for example, draws an analogy between interpreters of divine signs and those who

---

[101] Ford (2002) 80–85; Struck (2010) 164–65.
[102] In Classical Greek, *symbolon* was the word authenticating a contract, but came to serve also as an 'ontological signifier'. See Struck (2004) 77–90, 162–203.
[103] Most (2010) 28. The absurdity of stories or practices could be perceived as an indication that they carried a deeper, hidden meaning, an idea cultivated also in early Christianity (Turner [2010] 76). For discussion, see Chapter 3, p. 155–61.

comment on poetry.[104] Neoplatonism preserved Stoic ideas of cosmic sympathy.[105]

Constantine's *Oration* thus exemplifies how the imperial leader was both at the receiving end of a contemporary culture of signification and interpretation and contributed to steering it onto a new course. It is equally meaningful that the Neoplatonic philosopher who responded most vocally to Constantine – Julian himself – also articulated his reaction at the intersection between literature and history. As I show in Chapters 3 and 4, the writings dating to Julian's time as sole emperor (*Against Heraclius*, *Caesars*, *Misopogon*) capitalise on the hermeneutical possibilities raised by the historical fact that he had survived the whole house of Constantine; even Julian's public image must be conceptualised in this respect as targeting the way Constantine explored his own iconography as the space of (re)production of his idea of the imperial life as primary evidence for theology.[106] At the same time, Julian's writings map out his ambition to present himself as the true interpreter of myths and philosophy (*Against Heraclius*, *Against the Galileans*, *To the Mother of the Gods*, *To King Helios*) in a direct challenge to the Christian emperor's approach to *paideia*. Hermeneutical concerns pervade Julian's orations, to the point that his main adversaries (Themistius and Constantius II) are repeatedly warned or threatened outright via challenges to their skills as exegetes.[107]

Finally, it should be stressed that the meaning of Julian's exegetical reply, and how it highlights the unfolding of a pervasive culture of signification, is both evident in and demonstrated by the way Christian responses to Julian were organised as an interpretive backlash addressing his claims to superior interpretative abilities. Part III of this book – Chapters 5 and 6 – focuses on the polemical response to Julian's turning of the tables: episcopal attacks on Julian pointed to the ill-fated trajectory of his own life as proof of a poor exegesis of providential history and, consequently, as evidence of the need to reassert a Christian and Constantinian reading of the world.[108] This wide mobilisation of imperial and episcopal exegesis through various literary and

---

[104] On cosmic sympathy, see Struck (2004) 188–92. Quintus' analogy between diviners and commentators: Cicero, *Div.* 1.18(34). On Cicero's (seemingly open-ended) relationship with Stoic opinions in this work, see Beard (1986).

[105] See, e.g., Iamblichus' belief that the divine sprinkles seeds of itself as *symbola* throughout the cosmos; the theurgist can recognize them in various objects (Iambl. *Myst.* 1.11 (37); 1.21 (65); 2.11 (97), 4.2 (184); 4.12 (195–97) Clarke. On Iamblichus' idea of an interconnected cosmos, see further *Myst.* 3.15–16 (135–40) Clarke. See Struck (2004) 218–24; Tanaseanu-Döbler (2013) 104–6; Addey (2014) 28–32, 215–90; De Vita (2022) lviii–lix.

[106] See Chapter 5. [107] See Chapters 1 (Themistius) and 2 (Constantius II), respectively.

[108] See Chapter 5.

artistic forms points to a final point that must be addressed: how the fourth-century politics of interpretation was voiced through what could also be designated a 'rhetoric of interpretation' structuring all the key writings I examine, from Eusebius' *Praise of Constantine*, to Constantine's *Oration to the Saints*, to Julian's panegyrics and satires, to Themistius' encomia, Synesius of Cyrene's *On Kingship*, and Eunapius' *Lives of the Philosophers and Sophists*. By 'rhetoric of interpretation', I mean a technique for constructing texts that both inclines to advertise the exegetical skills of the author and advertises the presence in the text of layers of meaning that, by demanding scrutiny, seal the complicity between author and audience. Goldhill's re-opening of the discussion on the agency of the literary form in late antiquity has emphasised that the manifestation of the unexpected in traditional genres facilitated cultural transition by inviting recognition (and thus demanding approval) of the ideological processes underlying modifications.[109] Here I follow on from this reflection to consider how the fourth-century rhetoric of interpretation infused traditional genres with new meaning, exploring an array of possibilities through which old literary forms, once revised, could activate socio-political change.

A key case study will be biography. As I show, fourth-century biographical writings are invested with the task of communicating the philosophical perfection of (Christian) leaders by reconciling the two guidelines that shaped the history of the genre: an interest in rulers (from Suetonius and Plutarch to Aurelius Victor and the *Historia Augusta*) and in philosophers – or saints, as Christians put it. In other words, fourth-century biographers or para-biographers systematically constructed lives of bishops as lives of leaders (as already in Eusebius' *Ecclesiastical History*) and presented rulers as philosophers (cf. Eusebius' *Life of Constantine*) to suggest that the perfect leader and the perfect sage must coincide.[110] The counterpart of this fourth-century use of biography is a reflexive exploration of autobiographical forms within literary spaces seemingly less suitable for the negotiation of power. I see as an overall intent here a desire to

---

[109] Goldhill (2020).
[110] Chapters 1 (Lives of Pythagoras), 4 (on Eusebius' *Life of Constantine* and Julian's autobiographical experiments), 5 ('mirrors of bishops' as prescriptive hagiography), 6 (Eunapius' *Lives of the Philosophers and Sophists*). On hagiography as one of the main spaces of negotiation of Christian identity at all levels, see Momigliano (1971), (1987); Cox (1983); Hägg and Rousseau (2000); Williams (2008). Urbano (2013)163–204 is key to appreciate how fourth-century cultural and philosophical competition were channelled into the imperial biographies of Constantine and Julian. On the Talmud's avoidance of the biographical form as a possible rabbinical reaction to the hegemony of hagiography in Greco-Roman Christianised literature, see Goldhill (2020) 194–235.

suggest introspection and authors' intellectual capacity to infuse their experience of leadership with meaning. Letter writing, for example, activated pretensions of intimacy to disguise competitiveness and claim spontaneity of expression, as is evident, for example, in Julian's *Letter to Themistius* or Synesius' *ep.* 105, both of which foster the illusion of a conversation *à deux* to public and political ends.[111]

The other main genre I will address to examine the fourth-century exploration of interpretive power is epideictic rhetoric. The interaction between praise and politics in late antiquity has been a subject of discussion since scholarship began to move away from the assumption that encomia were empty performances with little or no impact on political actuality. MacCormack's *Art and Ceremony in Late Antiquity* was pioneering in showing the role of panegyrics in defining the sublime status of the Tetrarchic sovereign, to whom they provide a new vocabulary of light, epiphany, and salvation.[112] Recent studies have further emphasised that late antique praise served a crucial communicative junction. As Sabbah suggests, panegyrics facilitated dialogue in two directions, downwards and upwards.[113] They conveyed imperial messages to larger audiences, influencing historical understanding, but at the same time their prescriptive descriptiveness informed the emperor as to what was expected from his rule.[114] The presence in Tetrarchic and Constantinian panegyrics, for example, of Neoplatonic themes associated with the sovereign (e.g., the emperor's capacity to achieve a resemblance to the divine, the purificatory value of virtue, the divinity of the reason dwelling in his mind) simultaneously sanctioned his proximity to the divine and reminded him of the elite ambition to frame imperial power in cultured language.[115]

The orations analysed in this book converge in displaying an authorial desire to signal self-reflection, a shortcut to intellectual self-projection. To this end, they repeatedly present as a common trait the signposting of the

---

[111] See Chapters 1 (Julian's *Letter to Themistius*) and 6, p. 288–91 (Synesius' *ep.* 105).
[112] MacCormack (1981).
[113] On his model of *communication descendante* and *communication ascendante*, see Sabbah (1984).
[114] Pioneering in the field: MacCormack (1981); Nixon (1983); Pernot (1993); Whitby (1998). See more recently Hägg and Rousseau (2000); Quiroga Puertas (2013), (2017a), (2018); Burgersdijk and Ross (2018); Omissi and Ross (2020). On the panegyrics' influence on politics and historiography, based on the case study of Roman imperial usurpations: Omissi (2018) 41–68. On rhetoric as shaping social and religious identity, see most recently Pernot (2000), (2015); Cribiore (2013); Quiroga Puertas (2013), (2017a), (2018); Van Hoof and Van Nuffelen (2015); Flower and Ludlow (2020).
[115] Neoplatonic imagery in panegyrics: Burgersdijk (2020), with particular attention to *Pan. Lat.* VIII (4); VI (7); XII (9); and IV (10). An exploration of its permanence in Constantinian propaganda in Bardill (2012) 126–50.

speaker's awareness of the addressee's expectations. Eusebius' *Praise of Constantine* is in this regard an exemplary case study. The piece presents itself as a rhetorical challenge set by the bishop for the emperor, one programmed to secure the victory of the ecclesiastical contestant. Nevertheless, I suggest, Eusebius framed his challenge in such a way that he could rightfully assume that Constantine would be interested in joining his game. And Constantine, this book contends, did indeed play along.[116]

The author's ability to allude to his prediction of the possible reactions of his listener(s) was thus highly self-legitimising, since it communicated method and intellectual authority to interlocutors who were well aware of the political utility of such qualities. The result is an *agon*-like quality of the texts under analysis, whereby literary communication presents itself as a contest regulated by a set of double-binding rules. These might be implicit or obliquely hinted at, but understanding them is essential for victory: Van Hoof describes it as *Fingerspitzengefühl*, a 'feel for the game'.[117] It might be said on this basis that late antique intellectuals experienced rhetoric as a kind of fugitive art. The element of crisis perpetually embedded in public oratory – the threat of predictability – was also primarily responsible for continuous self-reinvention.[118]

Outline of the Chapters

Part I ('At Constantius' Court: Julian Caesar') focuses on the early years of Julian's reign (355–60 CE), the period when he ruled as the imperial associate, or Caesar, of the senior emperor Constantius II, Constantine's last surviving son. In this part, I show how Julian's rhetoric simultaneously casts light on the political discourse developed at Constantius' court and maps Julian's desire to define his imperial profile against Constantius' propaganda and its religious implications. I suggest that Constantius' propaganda, invested as it was in a project of Christian translation of the traditional ideal of philosophical leadership, wrote the script for Julian's entrance into politics but over time unintentionally provided him with

---

[116] See Chapters 3 and 5.   [117] Van Hoof (2013) 402.
[118] On the 'crisis of posterity' as already a defining trait of the Second Sophistic, see Whitmarsh (2001) 41–89. Fourth-century rhetoric found itself in an especially complex position: it perceived itself as in direct continuity with the Second Sophistic, with which it shared methodology and a strong sense of cultural identity but from which it was also separated by socio-cultural change. On the debate concerning whether to label fourth-century rhetoricians 'Third Sophistic', to differentiate them from their predecessors, see Quiroga Puertas (2007); Van Hoof (2010b); Cribiore (2013) 21; Fowler and Quiroga Puertas (2014) 5–6; Pernot (2021).

tools enabling his philosophical self-assertion at the expense of the senior emperor.

Chapter 1 ('How Philosophers Should Take Compliments When They Happen to Become Kings') is constructed around a case study, exploring what is arguably Julian's earliest known piece of writing, the *Letter to Themistius*. The *Letter* is a response to a celebratory address composed by the famous philosopher-cum-politician Themistius. It is usually read as Julian's attempt to revive an early ideal of subordination of the emperor to the law against the late antique (and Themistian) celebration of the emperor as 'living law', an entity closer to the divine than to the human sphere. I challenge this reading and argue that the *Letter* is a competitive assertion of Julian's competence as a philosopher and interpreter of Plato. The text strives to signal this competence by engaging in a discussion about the relationship between power and (divine) reason. Through a survey of select works of third- and fourth-century philosophers engaging with political theory, I consider first how the *Letter* must be read against the background of a general reflection on the relationship between leadership and culture. Second, I argue that, for a full appreciation of how such matter was infused with significance in the context in which Julian operated, we must consider the contribution of Christian philosophers to the debate. Lactantius' *Divine Institutes* and Eusebius of Caesarea' *Preparation for the Gospel* are revealing for the sense of urgency they communicate in regard to this topic. They exemplify how Christian intellectuals at the dawn of the Constantinian regime committed to negotiating the relationship between Christianity and Rome by thematising, with increasing assertiveness, Christianity's interpretive control over classical philosophical resources.

Chapter 2 ('Climbing the Ladder') expands on the question of the political and intellectual context in which Julian operated. Here I reflect on the interaction between his early rhetoric and the culture fostered at Constantius' court, where Julian first began to compose what he presents as public speeches. Julian's early writing provides us with a commentary on the propaganda of Constantius, who has been re-assessed by contemporary scholarship as pursuing a reputation as an intellectual and a patron of culture. Crucially, Constantius saw this profile as dependent on his allegiance to Christianity. As I show, Julian's early orations supported Constantius' imperial image by presenting him as Julian's enlightened patron and by advertising their intellectual synergy. Yet Julian's narrative began to change with the success of his Gallic campaign and his growing authority, and he repurposed his previous engagement with Constantius' propaganda to his own advantage. Philosophical themes remained the focus of Julian's texts but were now used to diminish rather than affirm Constantius' reputation. Julian also began to challenge the nexus between philosophical leadership and Christianity. The apparently intimate piece *A Consolation to Himself upon the Departure of the Excellent Sallust* is read in the final section of the chapter as a document subtly but decisively voicing Julian' definitive break with the senior ruler.

Part II ('Making and Breaking Constantine: Julian Augustus') considers Julian's political rhetoric during the twenty months of his sole rule (361–63) following Constantius' sudden death. I suggest that the shift of Julian's literary target from Constantius to Constantius' father, Constantine, reveals his ambition to challenge the association between Christian sovereignty and philosophical leadership by disavowing the emperor who first promoted this nexus. Chapter 3 ('Holy Hermeneutics') shows that Julian's mature output was grounded in the intuition that political Christianity had to be challenged by attacking its identity as a superior interpretive system. In the first section of the chapter, an analysis of key texts by Constantine and his supporters demonstrates that Constantine's propaganda presented him as a sublime exegete whose engagement with Christian philosophy had led him to understand providence and secure divine protection. This argument was further used to encourage a general narrative of Christianity as an intellectual achievement, which had an impact on the way doctrine was spoken of at court. The second section of the chapter details the strategies devised by Julian to deny validity to Christianity's hermeneutical claims, which he argued were built with philosophical tools that, being Greek, were external to Christianity. This critique was articulated through a twofold attack on Christian scriptural exegesis and what Julian perceived as Christianity's exploitative relationship with *paideia* (*Against the Galileans*). The chapter also considers Julian's attempt to rethink Greek allegory in competition with Christian exegesis and his composition of hymns and philosophical writings that aimed at characterising Greek religion as a 'cult of culture'.

In Chapter 4 ('A Life for a Life'), I examine how Constantine's supporters committed to a projection of his life as evidence of the validity of the Christian interpretation of Roman history. Julian's autobiographical experiments, which dominate the final stage of his literary production, are consequently open to being read as the culmination of his attack on the Christian hermeneutics of history. Julian was especially concerned with how the construction of the Christian sovereign as a model of philosophical leadership devalued the non-Christian and pre-Constantinian history of the empire. He responded by projecting his own life as the token of his superior understanding of history as providential (*Against Heraclius*) and by putting Constantine back in a Roman history now presented as a source of counter-exempla disproving Christian interpretations (*Caesars*). In the process, Julian also mobilised a crucial element of Constantine's propaganda, imperial iconography, repurposing it as definitive proof of his own superiority as an authentic philosopher-ruler (*Misopogon*) vis-à-vis Christianity's exegetical weaknesses.

Part III ('After Julian. Philosophy in the World') deals with the impact of Constantinian propaganda – and Julian's reaction to it – on the new type of leaders rising to prominence in the Christianised empire: the bishops. Julian's death in Persia in 363 marked the beginning of a new period of Christian elaboration on the themes of divine providence and the philosopher's capacity to access its design. I argue that the Christian preachers who capitalised on the failure of Julian's response to Constantine also had to confront two crucial issues he had raised: first, his re-assessment of the power dynamics emerging between ruler and priests in the Constantinian empire; and second, the question of the value of *paideia* to philosophy, and of how (restricted) access to the former had an impact of the possibilities of dissemination of the latter. Chapter 5 ('Those Who Know If the Emperor Knows') explores how the identification of religious allegiance as the criterion establishing whether an emperor was a philosopher-ruler affected the power dynamics between the emperor, now decentred from his religious structures of choice, and ecclesiastical leaders. I argue that Julian was especially wary of episcopal power and pursued his religious reform with the aim of re-centring imperial authority in religious matters. A survey of the writings of key fourth-century bishops (John Chrysostom, Gregory of Nazianzus, Athanasius of Alexandria, and Ambrose of Milan) illustrates that engagement with philosophical imagery and expectations both shaped the relationship between emperors and bishops and provided a tool for responding to Julian's reaction. This episcopal response, crucially, resulted in a stricter assertion of spiritual control over imperial authority via the exploitation of Julian as a negative example of the relationship between power and philosophy. The chapter further shows that engagement with philosophical concerns did not merely structure the communication between emperors and bishops but also regulated rivalries over the matter of heresy among the bishops themselves, who capitalised on the state's support of their philosophical self-image to gain the upper hand in doctrinal debates. Finally, episcopal appeals to an exclusive philosophical identity, and the state's endorsement of such appeals, also affected the public role of non-conforming philosophers. The writings of Synesius of Cyrene reveal in this regard the development of competitive feelings around the question of who should be deemed qualified to advise imperial power and which criteria are significant for this assessment.

In Chapter 6 ('Wisdom for the Many, Wisdom for the Few'), I investigate the debate surrounding Julian's final – and, at least in the eyes of late antique Platonists, fundamental – objection to Christianity: his critique of its exploration and exploitation of universalising rhetoric. Third- and fourth-century bishops legitimised their increasing political presence and urban leadership through competitive arguments pointing to Christianity as the only philosophy also accessible to the uneducated and therefore best suited to taking care of all imperial subjects. To this argument, Julian opposed the Platonist belief that a philosophy that appeals to the many is not a valid system of knowledge but a deceptive, crowd-pleasing imitation of one. The reaction of contemporary theologians – especially Gregory of Nazianzus – to Julian's response reveals that discussion of the place of the ill-educated in Christianity was a neuralgic point for Christian intellectuals seeking to expand their political voice. Most theologians appealing to Christianity's universalism were themselves educated members of the upper class and consequently shared Julian's elitist understanding of philosophy. This generated tension between the two, to some extent irreconcilable, episcopal ambitions of wishing and not wishing to be perceived as interlocutors of the crowds. Skilful intellectuals (read: Synesius of Cyrene) capitalised on this tension to negotiate their place in ecclesiastical hierarchies, whereas the increasing social prominence of bishops projecting themselves as 'lovers of the crowds' brought this debate to unexpected ends. First, Neoplatonic objections to the Christian rhetoric of universalism ironically ended up facilitating the displacement of non-Christian philosophers from the political scene, as illustrated by Eunapius' *Lives of the Philosophers and Sophists* and its prescriptive politics of seclusion. Second, the rising popularity of ascetic Christian leaders, combined with use of Julian's life as evidence of the limits of Greek philosophy, encouraged authoritative ecclesiastical voices to question the validity of Greco-Roman *paideia*. This resulted in a second irony: a power-driven challenge to the validity of the cultural system whose competitive adaptation had been indispensable to anchoring Christian leadership to Roman power.

PART I

At Constantius' Court: Julian Caesar

CHAPTER I

How Philosophers Should Take Compliments When They Happen to Become Kings

> I read yesterday almost all your speech before breakfast, and after breakfast, before resting, I gave myself up to reading the remainder. Happy man to be able to speak so well, or rather to have such ideas! O what a discourse! What wit! What wisdom! What analysis! What arguments! What arrangement! What openings! What diction! What symmetry! What structure! (ὢ λόγος, ὢ φρένες, ὢ σύνεσις, ὢ διαίρεσις, ὢ ἐπιχειρήματα, ὢ τάξις, ὢ ἀφορμαί, ὢ λέξις, ὢ ἁρμονία, ὢ συνθήκη).[1]

Antioch, 362.[2] Julian is writing to Libanius, expressing a pupil's admiration for the writing skills of the great rhetorician. (Irony is a matter that will not concern us for now.)[3] The accumulation of compliments might read like an outburst of enthusiasm. Yet comparison with another document sent almost two hundred years before points to the possibility of reading the words somewhat differently. In this case, Rome's most famous philosopher-ruler – Marcus Aurelius – addressed his teacher, adviser, and confidant Fronto with the following words:

> Oh, happy you to be gifted with such eloquence! Oh, happy me to be in the hands of such a master! What arguments! What arrangement! What elegance! What wit! What beauty! What diction! What brilliance! What subtlety! What charm! What practised skill! What everything! (O ἐπιχειρήματα! O τάξις! O elegantia! O lepos! O venustas! O verba! O nitor! O argutiae! O kharites! O ἄσκησις! O omnia!)[4]

By evoking Marcus' phrasing, Julian summons also the intellectual and political legacy of the Antonine emperor. His seemingly spontaneous outburst appears as the calculated gesture of a man of letters who knows

---

[1] *Ep.* 53 Wright (= 97 Bidez–Cumont), transl. Wright.
[2] Wright (1923) xxxiii–xxxv; Caltabiano (1991) 200.
[3] For Julian's praise of Libanius' style, cf. *Mis.* 354c.
[4] *Ad M. Caesar.* 2.3.1 (Naber [1867] 28; transl. from Haines, adapted). See further Pack (1953) 173; Caltabiano (1991) 269 n. 9; Bouffartigue (1992) 515.

how to use a few words to write himself and his addressee into a story that stretches back to the golden – and most philosophical – days of the Antonines. But if Julian's words were calculated, Marcus' were no less so. In the context of the early imperial negotiation of the relationship between power and culture, epistolography, this most intimate genre, was cleverly explored as a space of delineation of the cultivated self.[5] Letters facilitated the cultivation of the self-image of emperors who, since Augustus and Claudius, had used them to experiment with their literary voice.[6] At the same time, letters provided a platform for self-projection for those who enjoyed the privilege of being imperial correspondents. In Pliny's book 10, which collects his correspondence with Trajan, the governor's ability to edit his own writings has often been appreciated. What is less frequently noted is that Trajan's own texts reveal his commitment to projecting himself as a benevolent ruler.[7] In writing letters full of pedagogical themes, Platonic models, and glimpses of eros, Marcus Aurelius and Fronto were similarly engaged in an effort to delineate their portraits within the most sophisticated framework *paideia* offered.[8]

This story did not end with the Principate, for the significance of imperial epistolography came crucially into focus when imperial power emerged from the third-century crisis. The Tetrarchs' ambition to seek a pervasive presence in the state translated into an unprecedented dissemination of imperial correspondence. The distinction between *epistula* and edict was blurred.[9] Constantine took over from his predecessors both the cultivation of the art of the rescript and the desire to use letters to communicate his cultural concerns, religious beliefs, and views on history and Rome.[10] It is against this background that Julian's borrowing of Marcus' vocabulary finds place and meaning. His letter displays an awareness not only of the tradition of the imperial epistolography preceding him

---

[5] On letter-writing and rhetorical self-styling in Rome, see among others Hutchinson (1998); Henderson (2002); Marchesi (2008); Lowrie (2009) 215–75; Goldhill (2009); Zeiner-Charmichael (2013) 23–42; Whitton (2015).
[6] Augustus' *Res Gestae*: Elsner (1996); Bosworth (1999); Cooley (2009) 22–43; Lowrie (2009) 279–308; Levick (2010) 202–50. On Claudius as author, see Sordi (1993); Schmidt (1994); Briquel (1995); Perl (1996).
[7] Lavan (2018).   [8] Freisenbruch (2007); Taoka (2013).
[9] Corcoran (1997) 2–5, 198–203; Rees (2004) 30–33.
[10] On Constantine's clever use of the form of petition and response to advance his political and religious agenda, see Lenski (2016), esp. 87–113 (on the dossier of petitions from Orcistus) and 114–49 (the Hispellum rescript).

but also of the power letters had to define both senders and receivers. Through Julian's intercession, Libanius received permission to take on the role of a fourth-century Fronto.

In this chapter, I aim to show that Julian's engagement with literature was initially negotiated through the rules of letter-writing, which he exploited to secure an image as a leader and a man of culture. His arguably earliest piece,[11] the *Letter to Themistius*, addresses one of the most prominent intellectuals at Constantius' court. The text presents itself as a reflection on ideal leadership pivoting on selected readings from works of classical Greek philosophers, with a special focus on Plato and Aristotle. What the text offers, however, is not what it claims to offer. The *Letter* is not a confession of uncertainty at taking up the imperial role. It does not seek to celebrate, as interpreters assume, an ideal of law-abiding leadership conceived as an alternative to the quasi-divine status of the Diocletianic and post-Diocletianic ruler. My investigation into the fourth-century language of power begins with this apparently marginal piece, and deliberately lingers on it, as I attempt to show that Julian's *Letter* is a declaration of awareness of the dynamics, expectations, and assumptions regulating the political environment he had just entered. The text's efforts to locate itself within a centuries-old reflection on how power relates to wisdom, and its display of the ability to read the classics against someone (the addressee), announce the birth of a sophisticated imperial voice concerned both with establishing a hierarchy of interpreters and with claiming a place on top of it.

The Content of the *Letter to Themistius* – and What It Is Not About

The *Letter to Themistius* is a response. Julian composed it in reply to a message from Themistius, the renowned professor of philosophy who in the 340s had risen to fame in Constantinople, where he held his chair. When Themistius wrote to Julian, however, his days as a teacher had been left behind. After becoming a protégé of Constantine's son Constantius II, Themistius was appointed a senator of Constantinople in 355 – the same year Julian was elevated to the throne.[12] Themistius' now lost message to Julian conveyed his congratulations on the latter's enthronement (and was

---

[11] I follow Bradbury (1987). See discussion at n. 13 below.
[12] On Themistius' political career, see Vanderspoel (1995); Errington (2000); Heather-Moncur (2001).

not, as some scholarship has assumed, a celebration of Julian's emergence as sole ruler in Constantinople in 361).[13]

Julian locates his motive for writing the *Letter* in a desire to elaborate on the reasons that led him to disagree with his addressee. The text opens with a confession of the unease he felt at receiving Themistius' praise (*Them.* 253a). Two things troubled him. In the first place, Themistius had claimed – presumably in consideration of Julian's reputation as a scholar of philosophy – that God expected the young emperor to emulate Heracles and Dionysus, 'at once philosophers and kings' (φιλοσοφοῦντες ὁμοῦ καὶ βασιλεύοντες, 253c), as well as a series of lawgivers of the stature of Solon, Pittacus, and Lycurgus.[14] Second, Themistius had exhorted him to 'shake off all thought of leisure and inactivity' (254a), inviting him to trade the contemplative life for action.

Julian offers in response a profession of inadequacy. He argues that past events – no doubt being appointed emperor while still a student – had prevented him from attaining proficiency in philosophical matters and criticises the Stoic misrepresentation of human agency, which ignores the role of chance (255d–56c). With his exhortation, Themistius has forgotten that politics is ultimately in the hands of God. To support this thesis, Julian produces a long quotation from Plato's *Laws* (257d–59a) with

[13] The dating of the exchange between Themistius and Julian to 355 was already supported by early twentieth-century scholars (e.g. Seeck [1906] 470; Asmus [1914] 522; Rostagni [1920] 371–85). Nevertheless, the 361 dating of Julian's *Letter* later prevailed due to a reading of the *Vossianus Graecus* 77, the best manuscript of his orations, which calls the piece a work of Julian Augustus (Bidez [1929] 137; Athanassiadi [1981] 94; Fontaine [1987] xxxv; Pagliara [2012] 27–28; De Vita [2013] 50, [2022] clvii–cviii n. 304; García-Ruiz [2018] 217). But Bradbury (1987) convincingly illustrated the problems posed by this dating: it would have made no sense for Julian to present himself as apprehensive about leadership in 361, after years of successful military campaigns; and it would have been equally bizarre for Themistius to exhort Julian to action following the latter's re-conquest of Gaul. Julian's *Letter* alludes to no events after 355/6, but lists a series of commitments Julian clearly undertook prior to his Gallic campaign (see *Them.* 259b–60b). Julian's reference to Themistius as a philosopher uninvolved in active life (*Them.* 266a) would hardly have made sense in 361, when Themistius had been a senator for almost six years (and perhaps also Constantinople' proconsul in 358/9, although this is challenged by Vanderspoel (1995) 106–8; Heather and Moncur (2001) 44–47). Finally, Julian's cautious religious language matches the vocabulary of his early works. Barnes and Vanderspoel (1981) suggest that Julian composed the bulk of his *Letter* in 356 but edited and dispatched it sometime between February 360 and November 361. The hypothesis is followed by Smith (1995) 28; Tanaseanu-Döbler (2008) 111; and Elm (2012) 82–83 nn. 86, 106. Elm reads the *Letter* as Julian's act of public self-distancing from Constantius following the latter's death. But it is unclear why Julian would use an old text, which had long ceased to represent his public image, to negotiate his role as sole ruler. It seems more plausible that, in this specific case, the *Vossianus* might be wrong. In support of the 355 date, see also Bouffartigue (2005) 121–27; Swain (2013) 53–57; Chiaradonna (2015) 149; Nesselrath (2020) 41–42, Greenwood (2021) 21.

[14] On associations with Heracles and Dionysius in the cult of Alexander the Great, see Bosworth (1999) 2.

which he expects Themistius to be familiar (257d).[15] Plato describes how, during the Golden Age, Cronos enthroned superior beings, the 'race of daimons' (258b) to ward off the injustice intrinsic to human nature. In Plato's view, this points to a historical necessity, that every polity must imitate the time of Cronos by entrusting its management to 'the principle of immortality in us' (ὅσον ἐν ἡμῖν ἀθανασίας ἔνεστι): *nomos*, the law. Plato etymologises *nomos* by connecting it to (δια)νέμω ('to distribute, assign') and νοῦς ('intellect') and interpreting it as 'the regulation by reason' (τὴν τοῦ νοῦ διανομήν): the rule, in other words, which reason establishes.[16]

The *Letter*'s commentary on this passage emphasises that Plato's ideal sovereign is 'divine and daimonic in his disposition (τῇ προαιρέσει)', having eradicated everything mortal or bestial from his soul. Aristotle too, Julian argues, maintains that ruling is a task beyond human powers, since he proclaimed Law the only entitled ruler, being 'reason without appetite' (ἄνευ ὀρέξεως ὁ νοῦς).[17] Even when human intentions are good, they are still tainted by passions and desire.

Julian's climactic harmonisation of Plato and Aristotle prepares the ground for his reply to Themistius' argument that the active life is preferable to the contemplative one (263c). He criticises Themistius' commentary on a passage from Aristotle's *Politics* defining happiness as virtuous action (τὴν εὐδαιμονίαν ἐν τῷ πράττειν εὖ τιθέμενον, 263c), celebrating the 'architects' of noble deeds.[18] Themistius' position, according to Julian, relies on a faulty interpretation of Aristotle, who clearly identified the architects of noble deeds (τοὺς τῶν καλῶν πράξεων ἀρχιτέκτονας, 263d) with people who aspire to do good. This, Julian states, includes 'lawgivers and political philosophers and, to put it simply, all those operating with intelligence and reason (πάντας . . . τοὺς νῷ τε καὶ λόγῳ πράττοντας, 263d)'. The example of Socrates, who never ruled but had a larger impact on history than Alexander the Great, is brought up to illustrate the limits of Themistius' interpretation (264b–65a).

It follows that Themistius' theory not only originated in a misunderstanding of Aristotle but also undermined his public profile: he more than anyone should know the social value of his activity as teacher (266a). Julian concludes the *Letter* by invoking God and expressing his hope that, despite the present difficulties, good things might now be realised through himself, through the operation of the divine will.

---

[15] Pl. *Leg.* 4.709b.   [16] Pl. *Leg.* 4.713c–14a, in *Them.* 258d.
[17] Arist. *Pol.* 3.1287a, in *Them.* 261c.   [18] Arist. *Pol.* 7.3.1325b.

We have no means of assessing the fairness of Julian's response to Themistius' original message.[19] But Themistius' ideas on kingship can be recovered, at least in the form he chose to make public, from what survives of the imperial addresses he composed over three decades. A theory of sovereignty emerges from his orations that is generally interpreted as conflicting with the idea of leadership expressed in the *Letter*. Themistius was a committed advocate of the post-Hellenistic belief in the ruler as 'ensouled Law' (*empsychos nomos*) – in his own words, as 'he himself the Law and above the laws'.[20] The idea, which recurs in his orations to Constantius II in the 350s, is still present in his pieces for Theodosius in the 380s, an implicit demonstration of the continuing importance of this ideal throughout the fourth century.[21]

Passages from Julian's *Letter* have been singled out to suggest that it criticises Themistius' belief in the superiority of the ruler over the laws and supports against it an ideal of a sovereign who willingly subordinates himself to the power of legislation.[22] For instance, it has been noted that Julian's long quotation from Plato's *Laws* concludes with the statement that no good government is possible if 'one rules ... having first trampled on the laws' (*Them.* 258d). Elsewhere in the text, Julian stresses that Plato and Aristotle agree that governors should do everything they can to observe the laws (262a), here defined – a point to which I return below – as rules formulated by a lawgiver who has 'purified his mind and soul' and legislates 'with regard to the whole of humankind' and 'an eye to posterity' (262b–c). Finally, the declarations of political unworthiness and intellectual modesty running through the *Letter* are usually read as further expressions of Julian's awareness of his inferiority, as a human being, to a higher principle of government. Additional support for this reading is found in a piece Julian wrote at the beginning of his reign, the *First Panegyric to Constantius II*; here Constantius II is praised for behaving

---

[19] Swain (2013) 41, 87–91 suggests that the *Letter to Julian* ascribed to Themistius, which survives only in an Arabic version, might be the translation of a response which Themistius composed to address Julian's remarks.

[20] Them. *Or.* 1.15b, transl. Heather and Moncur.

[21] αὐτὸς νόμος ὢν καὶ ὑπεράνω τῶν νόμων, Them. *Or.* 1.15b–c (to Constantius II). See also 5.64b (to Jovian); 9.127b (to Valentinian II); 16.212d, 19.228a, 34.10 (to Theodosius). Cf. Vanderspoel (1995) 151; Heather and Moncur (2001) 93 n. 138.

[22] Thus Dvornik (1955), (1966) 659–66; Browning (1975) 130; Athanassiadi (1981) 175; Mazza (1986) 121; Curta (1995) 206; Maisano (1995) 21, 144 n. 47; Smith (1995) 27; Vanderspoel (1995) 124–26; O'Meara (2005) 93–94; De Vita (2011) 46; Elm (2012) 105, 355–56; Urbano (2013) 186; Schramm (2014) 137; Chiaradonna (2015) 151–53; O'Meara (2017) 409; Rebenich and Wiemer (2020) 28; Nesselrath (2020) 40; Schmidt-Hofner (2020) 168; De Vita (2022) cxxxviii, clxi–iv.

'like a citizen who obeys the laws, not like a sovereign who is above the laws'.[23]

This reading of Julian's *Letter* has important political implications. If this text truly rejects the ideal of the ruler as ensouled law, its political vision represents a unique response to the transformation of the imperial image following the third-century crisis of succession. A general understanding of Julian as a ruler nostalgically looking back at a pre-Christian past certainly contributed to the theory that he still believed in an ideal of ruler as *primus inter pares* that was lost with the Principate. Already in 1955, Dvornik argued that the *Letter* showed Julian 'as reactionary in politics as he was in religion', going so far as to claim that Julian's model was not even located in the early empire but in the Roman republic.[24]

But an interpretation of Julian's *Letter* as postulating the subordination of the ruler to the laws poses significant problems. First, it forces us to confront Julian's later expressions of his theocratic understanding of imperial power. In the writings issued when he was sole Augustus (361–363 CE), Julian presents himself as a descendent and associate of the gods, the prophet of Apollo, and the leader of his priests, whose training he personally designed.[25] It might be objected that Julian's thoughts on the matter evolved over time or were adapted contextually.[26] It might also be noted that the ideals of *civilis princeps* and (quasi)divine ruler actually coexisted in the late Roman political discourse. This shows that representation of these ideals as a binary does not capture the complexity of the late antique construction of authority. (Consider, for instance, how the *Jovius* Diocletian and the *Herculius* Maximinian could be celebrated through forms of association with Augustus and the Antonines.)[27] Crucially, and in continuity with this point, the idea that Julian's self-positioning opposed the Themistian ideal of the ruler as 'ensouled law' relies on another false dichotomy, one that misrepresents the function of this ideal of sovereignty in Greco-Roman political theory.

---

[23] *I Pan.* 45d (καθάπερ πολίτου τοῖς νόμοις ὑπακούοντος, ἀλλ' οὐ βασιλέως τῶν νόμων ἄρχοντος). Cf. *I Pan.* 14a, 16a.
[24] Dvornik (1955) 659–60.
[25] Cf., e.g., Julian's allegory of his divine task as ruler in *Her.* 227c–34c, where Julian presents Helios as his father (*Her.* 229c). Prophet of Apollo: *ep.* 18 Wright (= 88 Bidez–Cumont). Training of the priests: see *Ep. Fragm.* (= *ep.* 89b Bidez–Cumont).
[26] See, e.g., Criscuolo (1983); De Vita (2022) cclxx–cclxxiv.
[27] In architecture: cf. Marlowe (2016), on the Vicennalia Monument in the Roman Forum. In rhetoric: see Ware (2018), also illustrating the use of Augustus in managing Constantine's image as he parted ways from the older Tetrarchs. On the complex self-positioning of the late Roman emperor in regard to the divine, see Elm (2021).

Classical political philosophy promoted an interest in what could be defined with Agamben as the 'relation of exception' of the ruler to state institutions.[28] This expression indicates the paradox of the sovereign's position simultaneously within the laws, which sanctioned his existence, and beyond the laws, which he could create and abrogate and that he therefore transcended. Given this premise, the Hellenistic and post-Hellenistic ideal of *empsychos nomos* did not amount to a theorisation of the sovereign's entitlement to dismiss or subvert legislation. This behaviour was also perceived as a mark of tyranny in the time of the Principate, which continued to cultivate Republican ideals. In other words, reflection on the freedom of agency of the ruler as opposed to the fixity of written laws was never oblivious to the despotic quality conveyed by an idea of a sovereign who is above all regulation. In this regard, the celebration of the sovereign as ensouled law posed, as Van Nuffelen argues, a normative demand, which reminded rulers of the need for their government to be regulated by the higher principle of the divine law residing in their intellect.[29] This principle, however, ultimately appealed to the Platonic and Aristotelian assumption that reason is the divine in us. Already formulated by Xenophon in reference to King Cyrus, and by Philo of Alexandria for the Patriarchs and Moses, the theory of the *empsychos nomos* first gained momentum in the Hellenistic cultural environment.[30] From there, it flowed into the legal debate early imperial Rome was developing regarding the emperor's unprecedented powers.[31] The theory was mediated for a Roman audience by intellectuals such as Musonius Rufus, Plutarch, and Dio of Prusa.[32] But Roman imperial

---

[28] Agamben (1995) 18–35.
[29] Van Nuffelen (2011) 115–18. On the notion of *nomos empsychos* in ancient political theory, see also Aalders (1969); Martens (1994); Ramelli (2006); Alvino (2019) 69–110.
[30] Xen. *Cyr.*, 8.1.22; Philo, *Abr.* 5 (on the Patriarchs), *Mos.* 1.162 (on Moses).
[31] The first known legal regulation of the relationship between sovereign and laws is the *Lex de imperio Vespasiani* (*CIL* VI 930, 31207 = *ILS* 244) issued in 70 CE, which may have aimed to give Vespasian's authority a legal basis following the fall of the Julio-Claudian dynasty (thus Lucrezi [1995] 166–67. Discussion in Brunt [1977] 97–102; Mantovani [2009]; Tuori [2016] 19–20, 174–7). See Ullmann (1975) 56–57 on Roman jurists (especially Ulpian) on the transferal of the powers from the Roman people to the ruler.
[32] In his *That Kings Also Should Study Philosophy*, Musonius Rufus argues that 'it is of the greatest importance for the good king to be faultless and perfect in word and action if, indeed, he is to be a living law' (Muson. *Lect.* 8.8, transl. Lutz). According to Plutarch, the good king is similar to animate law due to 'reason endowed with life within him' (*Mor.* 780c). Cf. also Dio Chrys. *Or.* 3.10; 76.4. The king as ensouled law is prominently theorised in the writings of the Neo-Pythagoreans (of uncertain chronology but presumably post-Hellenistic: Centrone (2000) 570–75; Garnsey (2000)). See especially Diotogenes, *On Kingship* 72.19–23 ed. Thesleff (= Stobaeus, *Anth.* 4.7.61).

rhetoric primarily conceived of this reflection as a tool to legitimise the ruler by differentiating him from negative models such as Caligula, Nero, and Domitian, who had not sought to conceal their perception of their role as beyond regulation.[33] An example of this diplomatic employment of the issue of the relationship between the emperor and the law is provided by Pliny the Younger's famous remark, in his *Panegyric* to Trajan (100 CE), that 'it is not the emperor who is above the laws, but the laws that are above the emperor'.[34] The meaning of this statement can be fully grasped only if the historical context is taken into consideration. Pliny's *Panegyric* is pervaded by the spectre of the tyrant Domitian and negotiates Trajan's imperial identity as antithetical to that of his despised predecessor. But the same Trajan could be unproblematically celebrated as 'greater than the laws' (so Dio of Prusa) when a rhetorician wanted to emphasise the ruler's capacity to mitigate legislation with enlightened regulations.[35]

This flexibility of representation survives in the rhetoric of the post-Diocletianic empire, where speakers might decide, depending on the circumstances, either to emphasise the ruler's capacity for self-restraint or to celebrate the might of his will. Themistius, as noted, could praise the Emperor Constantius II as greater than the laws; thus his *Or.* 1. It should be noted, however, that the same text simultaneously celebrates Constantius' capacity to exercise perfect self-control in his interactions with institutions: the laws that are 'inferior' to Constantius are the rigid human regulations he improves via his intellectual access to divine law.[36]

The celebration of Constantius as abiding by the laws seems also to have had a place in the emperor's own propaganda. Testimony to this comes in the aforementioned passage from Julian's *First Panegyric* in which Constantius is praised for behaving 'like a citizen who obeys the laws, not like a sovereign who is above the laws'.[37] The argument that Julian's

---

[33] See, e.g., the famous declaration, ascribed to Severus and Caracalla and preserved in Justinian's *Institutes*, that although free from the laws, the emperor lives by them (*Instit.* 2.17.8, cf. Ulp. 1.3.31). The statement seems to have been made originally in regard to Augustan marriage laws (Metzger [1998] 125, n. 20).
[34] Plin. *Pan.* 65.1–2 (Non est princeps super leges, sed leges super principem).
[35] Dio Chrys., *Or.* 3.10.
[36] See Chapter 2. Julian's *Second Panegyric* similarly describes the emperor as a 'good guardian of the laws' but in a context that simultaneously emphasises Constantius' active role as a legislator (*II Pan.* 88d–91d).
[37] *I Pan.* 45d (καθάπερ πολίτου τοῖς νόμοις ὑπακούοντος, ἀλλ' οὐ βασιλέως τῶν νόμων ἄρχοντος). Cf. also *I Pan.* 14a, 16a.

claim points to his fascination with a conservative political ideology obscures the fact that the panegyric was written in concert with Constantius' efforts to adjust his public image after his defeat of the usurper Magnentius in 354.[38] Magnentius' rule has not left many traces in the sources, but it is clear that he sought to construct himself in opposition to Constantine and his sons. Following the customary pattern of delegitimising imperial rivals, he presented them as despots.[39] Magnentius' defeat of Constans was narrated as a tyrannicide, with coinage and inscriptions celebrating his liberation of the state and restoration of freedom to the Romans.[40] Constantius' propaganda repaid Magnentius in kind,[41] casting him as a wild barbarian (courtesy of his Gallic origins)[42] and as a tyrant lacking self-restraint, to the extent that he tortured citizens for amusement.[43] Constantius' image was recovered within this context as a symbol of *civilitas*, moderation, and forgiveness.[44] Julian's depiction of the Augustus' deliberate self-subordination to the authority of the laws thus appears above all else as a celebration of Constantius as the nemesis of tyrants. This portrayal does not clash with the theory of the *empsychos nomos* but simply emphasises that the enlightened emperor was animated by a sense of deep respect for Roman institutions. In Julian's words, Constantius was willing to endure anything 'rather than see a barbarian ... make himself master of the laws and constitution (νόμων κύριον καὶ πολιτείας)'.[45]

An external witness to Julian's early politics – the historian Ammianus, reporting on his military campaign in Gaul – further attests that Julian did not disavow the political ideal of his times. He reports an episode in which the young emperor, while presiding over trials, voiced his belief in the 'right of an emperor of highly merciful disposition to rise above all

---

[38] See Chapter 2, p. 77.   [39] Tantillo (1997) 41.
[40] Inscriptions dedicated to Magnentius celebrated him as *restitutor libertatis et reipublicae, conservator militum et provincialium, liberator orbis Romani* (e.g., *CIL* V 8061, 8066, IX 5937, 5940, 5951, XI 6640). Coins document Magnentius' preference for the title of *imperator* over that of *dominus* and his rejection of the imperial symbol adopted by Constantine towards the end of his rule, the diadem (featured only in his earliest coins, which were presumably issued before the mints were notified of Magnentius' abandonment of the symbol). See Tantillo (1997) 331–32 (n. 202); Omissi (2018) 165.
[41] On the consistency in Magnentius' portrait between Julian's *First* and *Second Panegyric* and Themistius' *Or.* 2, 3, and 4, and the hypothesis of official guidelines, see Omissi (2018) 163–79.'
[42] Zos. 2.54.1. On Magnentius' lineage, see Maraval (2013) 85–86.
[43] Omissi (2018) 53, 169–79; (2020) 225. Cf. Jul. *I Pan.* 31b, 33c–5d, 39d–40a (torture for amusement), 42a; *II Pan.* 56c–7a, 97c–d. Them. *or.* 2.33d–4a; 3.43a–c; 4.56c–d. Similar considerations in Tantillo (1997) 27–28, 41–50.
[44] See, e.g., Julian. *I Pan.* 9b, 33b–d, 38b.   [45] *I Pan.* 42b.

other laws'.⁴⁶ Julian's ideal of kingship thus seems to align with Themistius'.⁴⁷ The *Letter* is an unquestionably agonistic (and antagonistic) text, but the reasons for this lie elsewhere.

What the *Letter* Is About: Providing a Philosophical Definition of the Principle of Authority

Analysis of Julian's use of a dense passage from Aristotle's *Politics* indicates both the limits of reading the *Letter* as a celebration of constrained sovereignty and the actual aim of its argument:

> Regarding the so-called according-to-law king (περὶ τοῦ κατὰ νόμον λεγομένου βασιλέως), who (ὅς)⁴⁸ is both a servant and a guardian of the laws (ὑπηρέτης καὶ φύλαξ τῶν νόμων), he (i.e., Aristotle) does not call him a king at all, nor does he consider such a king a distinct form of government; and he goes on to say 'Now as for what is called unconstrained monarchy (περὶ δὲ τῆς παμβασιλείας καλουμένης), that is to say, when a king governs all other men according to his own will, some people think that it is not in accordance with the nature of things for one man to have absolute authority over all citizens; since those who are by nature equal must necessarily have the same rights'. Again, a little later he says (εἶτα μετ' ὀλίγον φησίν) 'it seems, therefore, that he who bids Reason rule is really preferring the rule of God and the laws, but he who bids man rule adds an element of the beast. For desire is a wild beast, and passion perverts the mind of rulers, even when they are the best of men. It follows, therefore, that law is Reason exempt from desire'. You see that the philosopher seems here clearly to distrust and condemn human nature.⁴⁹

At the beginning of the quotation, Julian introduces the expression 'a servant and guardian of the laws' (ὑπηρέτης καὶ φύλαξ τῶν νόμων) to

---

⁴⁶ Amm. Marc. 16.5.12 (*imperatorem mitissimi animi legibus praestare ceteris decet*). Schmidt-Hofner (2020) shows how Julian's strategic use of his activity as legislator and judge conveyed a message of enlightened control over legislation. Julian's commitment to service as a judge was praised by his supporters (e.g., Amm. Marc. 16.5; Lib. *Or.* 18.182–90) and criticised by his detractors (Greg. Naz. *Or.* 5.20–21).

⁴⁷ See on this already Schofield's remark that the *Letter* offers a 'rationalistic version' of Themistius' ideal, which Julian substantiates through an engagement with classical philosophical texts (Schofield (2000) 664–65).

⁴⁸ I read the MSS's text with Rochefort (1963), rather than adopting Klimek's ὡς (as Wright [1913] does). The definition of the 'according-to-law king' as 'servant and guardian of the laws' is Julian's explanation. Furthermore, Aristotle's 'according-to-law king' does not describe a monarch who subordinates himself to legislation; Aristotle uses the label to describe sovereigns who exercise unconstrained power but have a legally inherited kingship and thus did not create or usurp the throne (Atack [2015] 307–8).

⁴⁹ *Them.* 261a–c, summarising Arist. *Pol.* 3.16.1287a1–32.

explain Aristotle's notion of 'according-to-law king' (ὁ κατὰ νόμον ... βασιλεύς). But his attempt to clarify this notion does not aim to support its validity, just as Julian does not express any preference for Aristotle's opposite notion of 'unconstrained monarchy' (*pambasileia*), which the text brings up immediately afterwards. Julian is merely summarising Aristotle's definitions of constrained and unconstrained monarchy before moving on to quote another Aristotelian statement from the same passage in the *Politics*. This statement argues that 'he who bids Reason rule is really preferring the rule of God and the laws'. Julian, as he himself acknowledges, has skipped a section from the text, which claims that 'the rule of the law is preferable to that of any citizen'.[50]

The *Letter*'s treatment of the myth of the Golden Age, from Plato's *Laws*, lends itself to similar remarks.[51] Julian's quotation ends just before Plato's development of the idea that the rulers of the ideal city are to be understood as 'servants of the laws'. This statement is left out of the *Letter*.[52] If we move from the assumption that Julian cited the *Politics* and the *Laws* to legitimise an ideal of the superiority of legislative over imperial authority, we could only be surprised at this repeated avoidance of sentences that support such an argument. But when one considers how comparable Julian's quotations from Plato and from Aristotle are, it becomes evident that his focus is elsewhere. Both quotations culminate with a definition of 'law', which Plato explains as 'regulation by reason' (*Them.* 258d), and Aristotle as 'reason without passion' (*Them.* 261d). Julian thus appears invested in showing that Plato and Aristotle agreed that the authority of the law resides in its rationality. Julian's *Letter* seeks not a comparison between living ruler and written law but, on a more fundamental level, a reflection on what legitimises power.

Having considered this, we can re-read on this basis all the passages of the *Letter* that have been taken to support the idea of an absolute authority of legislation over sovereignty. Julian's quotation of Aristotle's argument that 'it is not just that one man should rule over many who are his equals (*Them.* 261d)' is accompanied by the remark that a king must overcome his humanity by eliminating all irrational and bestial impulses (260c; 262a). Aristotle is thus quoted to argue against the rule of individuals insofar as Julian expects good rulers to transcend humanity through the cultivation of (divine) reason. Analogously, his allusion to Plato's criticism of governors who 'trample on the laws' (259a), and his insistence that

---

[50] Arist. *Pol.* 3.16.1287a18 (τὸν ἄρα νόμον ἄρχειν αἱρετώτερον μᾶλλον ἢ τῶν πολιτῶν ἕνα τινά).
[51] *Them.* 258a–9a.   [52] Pl. *Leg.* 715c–d.

Aristotle agrees with such criticisms (262a), are accompanied by a crucial sidenote: the laws that should be respected are those formulated by a lawgiver who has purified his mind and soul and legislates with an eye to posterity and the entirety of humankind (262a–c). This definition clearly does not apply to ordinary laws; it defines an ideal type of legislation, which is the product of – and synonymous with – reason. Julian attacks despots who disregard legislative reason, but this is in no way tantamount to a celebration of the sovereign as *primus inter pares*. In fact, the contrary is true: Julian's ideal sovereign, who is expected to remove every 'irrational' element from himself, must eventually be closer to the divinity than to humankind. Julian's denial of having (at the moment) attained this ideal does not mean that he is challenging it. Instead, it confirms that the *empsychos nomos* model is for him the highest ideal and the pursuit of a lifetime.

It remains to be explained why Julian articulates his position as in opposition to Themistius, given that the *Letter*'s understanding of the role of the enlightened sovereign seems in fact to align with that of his addressee. We might begin to sketch an answer by considering the text's engagement with classical sources. Throughout this piece, Julian strives to put on display his ability to read critically and derive meaning from authoritative texts. The quotation from Aristotle's *Politics* mentioned above makes this especially evident: Julian touches upon both types of Aristotelian leadership (law-abiding and 'absolute' kingship), while being ultimately unconcerned with them. But I suggest that their significance lies precisely in their marginality. Julian wants to signal his thorough knowledge of the entire passage excerpted from the *Politics*: the focus of his interest, the Aristotelian equation between law and rationality, is given enough textual context to prove his expertise with the text and his ability to summarise its contents methodically and with full understanding.

Analogous considerations can be advanced in regard to Julian's treatment of Plato's myth of the Golden Age. Julian explicitly remarks that he is reporting the passage in its entirety to reassure his interlocutor of the textual basis that supports his statements. By doing so, he implicitly indicates that a copy of the *Laws*, either entire or partial, is with him as he writes.[53] Crucially, both the *Politics* and the *Laws* were scarcely read in

---

[53] *Them.* 257d, 259a. The verb Julian adopts to describe his operation is παραγράφειν, which has legal implications (indicating the attachment of clauses to contracts).

late antiquity. It has been suggested that the disappearance of the *Politics* from political and philosophical discussion was a consequence of its focus on the life of the *polis*, which had ceased to exist as a political reality.[54] In the case of the *Laws*, the picture is more complex. The name continued to evoke political authority: both Themistius and Julian summon it here and there in their panegyrics. But its employment in court oratory remained nominal and symbolic.[55] Perhaps precisely by virtue of its reputation as a difficult text, the *Laws* was also absent from the Iamblichean school curriculum.[56] Although late antique traces of Neoplatonic interest in Plato's posthumous work exist, they are thin on the ground and seem either to converge on Book 10 (the metaphysical core) or to be generalities.[57]

When seen in the context of his times, therefore, Julian's use of the *Politics* and the *Laws* in the *Letter* appears to be in tension with the claims of intellectual inadequacy scattered throughout the text. Julian declares that he did not have the time or opportunity to finalise his love for philosophy, but his readings reveal his piece as the work of a man with a solid training. By allowing his arguments to arise from comparison between texts, Julian simultaneously professes a scholarly devotion to Plato and Aristotle and suggests that he can find in the classics everything he needs to ground his case. His harmonisation of the *Laws* and the *Politics* (262a) can be interpreted in this light. Late antique Platonists believed in the ultimate unity of Platonic and Aristotelian thinking; Julian's synthesis, which follows this assumption, resonates fully with the philosophical expectations of his times.

[54] Pellegrin (2012) 582.
[55] Themistius explicitly summons the *Laws*, which he calls 'divine' (θεσπέσιοι), at *Or.* 2.32c. In other orations he quotes from the work, but whether he expected his audience to know the source of his quotations is an open question. They are used as aphorisms and might have been circulating as such within anthologies (Maisano [2006]). Julian's orations draw on analogously short excerpts that sound like maxims (see Bouffartigue [1992] 191–93). He refers twice to the *Laws* as 'wonderful' (θαύμασιοι νόμοι, *Them.* 257d and *II Pan.* 70a) and brings up the figure of the Athenian Stranger at *Mis.* 353d.
[56] Iamblichus' *curriculum studiorum* consisted of a group of ten writings followed by the two 'perfect' dialogues, *Timaeus* and *Parmenides*. The curriculum had a great influence on later Neoplatonic thought, as most schools used it. It remained substantially unchanged for generations (Tarrant [2014]).
[57] The *Anonymous Prolegomena to Platonic Philosophy* exemplifies the limited interest of the Neoplatonists in the *Laws*. The text only considers the *Laws* and the *Republic* because they typify a form of constitution ἐξ ὑποθέσεως (i.e., depending on a given situation) and ἄνευ τῆς ὑποθέσεως (free of presupposition), respectively (*Anon. Prol.* 26, l. 37–45 Westerink). The *Anonymous* is presumably describing the *Laws* as contemplating the preservation of social conventions, such as family and property, which the *Republic* does not accept. Other features of the works are ignored. On the Neoplatonic reception of Plato's *Laws*, see Dillon (2001).

It thus seems that the strategies developed by Julian's *Letter* to articulate his reflection on what legitimises power converge in prioritising interpretive concerns. Julian offers a demonstration of the soundness of his exegesis: he has looked back at foundational texts of Greek philosophy, read them thoroughly, sought definitions of the normative principle (Plato's 'regulation by reason', Aristotle's 'reason without desire'), and eventually showed that these definitions express the same truth. The *Letter* subtly exploits the tension between Julian's self-effacing statements and his active performance of philosophical exegesis. Its quotations expose the performative quality of Julian's lament over the premature end of his education. Performance, as the next section argues, is the fundamental trait of the *Letter*: its constant efforts to subvert – or exploit – Julian's claims of unworthiness ultimately amount to a search for intellectual recognition.

Challenging Themistius, Constructing (Interpretive) Authority

The *Letter* also laments Julian's political incompetence. Julian's insistence on his need for hard work and improvement has often been taken in the past as a witness to his early insecurity and has been read alongside other texts voicing his dismay at being appointed emperor. In his *Speech of Praise* in honour of the empress Eusebia, composed about a year after the *Letter*,[58] Julian reminisces about the anxiety he felt at taking up power and compares himself to someone unskilled in driving a chariot who was nevertheless 'compelled to manage a car belonging to a talented, noble charioteer'.[59] His later *Letter to the Athenians* (361 CE) also returns to his imperial appointment and argues that it drove him to the brink of suicide; he only held back after considering that his enthronement was the will of the gods.[60] The *Letter to the Athenians*, which also focuses on Julian's subsequent appointment as Augustus (that is, senior emperor) in February 360, remarks that on that occasion too he accepted his elevation only after receiving an approving sign from Zeus.[61]

A passage from Ammianus' *Res Gestae* is nevertheless revealing of how Julian's expressions of inadequacy and fear of power responded to ancient expectations concerning the self-presentation of newly appointed leaders. Having recorded the celebrations for Julian's enthronement as Caesar, an event presided over by Constantius II and attended by the populace of

---

[58] See Chapter 2, p. 78–81.   [59] *Eus.* 122a. Cf. also *ep.* 8 Wright (= 26 Bidez–Cumont).
[60] *Ath.* 275a–7a.   [61] *Ath.* 284b–d.

Milan, Ammianus gives a brief description of Julian's behaviour during the parade that followed:

> Finally, taken up to sit with the emperor in his carriage and conducted to the palace, he (i.e., Julian) whispered (*sussurabat*) this verse from the Homeric song: 'by purple death I am seized and fate supreme'.[62]

Julian's gesture pretends to be private – he whispers to himself – but is in fact extraordinarily performative. (Did he say these words over and over?) The sentence is also effective in conveying at once a set of traits Julian wanted to be perceived as crucial features of his rule: his use of a Homeric line to compare imperial purple and death signals not only his lack of ambition but also profound culture and wit. Ammianus reports the anecdote with admiration. Regardless of whether he learned it directly from Julian or from someone who was equally struck by Julian's words, his awareness of the episode further confirms the volume of Julian's whisper. As recent scholarship has stressed, we should approach the *Letter*'s proclamations of inadequacy as actually engaging with the self-legitimising rite of the *recusatio imperii*, the hesitation displayed when taking up a prestigious role. In the ancient world, flight from a high position was interpreted as meritorious: those who rejected power proved they truly deserved it. This practice formed a vital line of self-legitimisation for newly appointed authorities throughout Roman history and, as I consider in Chapter 5, became especially productive in the late empire in respect not just to emperors but to bishops as well.[63]

But *recusatio* was also a gesture derived from the philosophical tradition: Plato had theorised it in the *Republic*, arguing that the real philosopher-ruler must be taken away from the contemplative life and compelled to rule for the good of the state.[64] Engagement with the practice of *recusatio* thus likewise signified the intellectual nature of the leader. When one considers Julian's oblique self-advertisement as philosopher in the *Letter*, the irony

---

[62] Amm. Marc. 15.8.17. Julian quotes *Iliad* 5.83 = 16.334 = 20.477 (ἔλλαβε πορφύρεος θάνατος καὶ μοῖρα κραταιή). Cf. Libanius' account of Julian's lack of desire to become emperor (Lib. *Or.* 12.38; 18.22–23, 31–32) and his reluctant yielding to the acclamation of the soldiers in Paris (Lib. *or.* 12. 59–61).

[63] Tool of imperial self-legitimisation: Béranger (1948); Hahn (1989) 161–63, 192–208; Huttner (2004); Freudenburg (2014); Omissi (2018) 25–26. Constantine's flight from power: *Pan. Lat.* VI (7), 8.4 (see Potter [2013] 112). On *recusatio* in Julian, see Elm (2012) 73–75, 79; (2021) 136; Chiaradonna (2015); De Vita (2022) clv–vi, clix–x. Themistius celebrates Jovian's lack of desire for power at *Or.* 5.66d. For the *recusatio* of high officials, see Mamertinus' *Speech of Thanks* to Julian upon his appointment as consul (*Pan. Lat.* III (11) 17.1). On episcopal *recusatio*, see Chapter 5, p. 222–5, 238–40.

[64] Pl. *Resp.* 1.346e–7d, 6.489b–c.

shaping the text becomes even more evident. By making haste to distance himself from Themistius' excessive praise comparing the new Caesar to legendary lawgivers and mythical philosopher-kings, Julian is implicitly confirming that he has, at least potentially, the qualities of a philosopher-ruler. His *Letter* proves him an enlightened ruler in the making.

At the same time, Julian's oblique confirmation of Themistius' praise is pursued in a way that denies Themistius any authority over the establishment of Julian's imperial profile. Julian's self-assertion as a (potential) philosopher-ruler unfolds by deflecting Themistius' compliments: he denies Themistius' prescriptive authority by questioning his models of ideal sovereignty and criticising his philosophical reading. This brings us back to the issue that opened this chapter, that is, Julian's understanding of how correspondence defined not only the sender's profile but also that of his addressees – especially imperial addressees who sought to project themselves as holding a confidential relationship with rulers. It could be argued in this regard that Themistius was interested in claiming a Fronto-like role, of the kind Julian would later offer to Libanius, or at least that Julian assumed that Themistius was interested in claiming such a role.

The year 355, as anticipated above, did not see the rise of Julian alone on the political scene. Themistius too was appointed a member of the Constantinopolitan senate. His *Speech of Thanks* (*Or.* 2) to Constantius II for the *adlectio* eloquently closes with a celebration of Constantius' elevation to the throne of a younger ruler versed in philosophy: Julian himself.[65] Two implications are evident. The first is that Themistius' *Speech* seeks an implicit juxtaposition between the two appointees in order to project Constantius as an enlightened patron of intellectuals – a point to which I return in Chapter 2.[66] At the same time, however, Themistius' public celebration of Constantius' appointment of Julian seeks to establish an intellectual – and political – hierarchy: the sanctioning of Constantius' patronage of Julian seals Themistius' primacy as interpreter (of the policy) of the ruler. Implicit in this is a further assertion of Themistius' philosophical seniority, in that he holds the authority to confirm that the young ruler who has just appeared on the political scene deserves to be celebrated as an intellectual. Themistius' lost message of congratulations to Julian, which Julian's summary allows us to reconstruct as distributing philosophical and political advice, arguably sought to consolidate his reputation. By claiming a role as the correspondent of the emperor, Themistius presented

---

[65] Themistius, *Or.* 2.40a. See also *Or.* 4.58d–9b.   [66] See Chapter 2, p. 81–9.

himself as the philosophical adviser of a ruler who had already come to the throne with a reputation for being a philosopher.

The question of how public Themistius' pursuit was, given that we know nothing about the early distribution of Julian's *Letter*, let alone of the message to which it replied, remains open. But there is a clue from Themistius himself that suggests that the *Letter* might have enjoyed significant circulation. In his *Or.* 31, a speech given approximately thirty years later (Lent 384), an aged Themistius defends his activity as the prefect of Constantinople, which had been criticised as an unphilosophical commitment. He argues that the appointment, offered to him by the Emperor Theodosius in person, represented the culmination of a history of imperial appreciation of his philosophy: already in the 350s, Constantius had regarded it as an 'adornment of his power', and Julian himself had 'acknowledged in writing' (ἐν γράμμασιν ὁμολογήσας) that he had learned the very 'foundations of philosophy' (τὰ πρῶτα ... φιλοσοφίας) from Themistius.[67] No surviving text of Julian makes such a statement. One might conclude that either Themistius invented the homage (but also expected the senators to believe him) or Julian's compliment was contained in a lost text. There is a third option. In the *Letter*, Julian does in a way acknowledge in writing his debt to Themistius' teaching, although in a spirit that could hardly be called deferential. These are the words with which he introduces the Golden Age quotation from Plato's *Laws*:

> And to show that I am not the only one who thinks that Fortune has the upper hand in practical affairs, I would quote to you now the passage of Plato, from his marvellous *Laws*, which you know well and taught to me (λέγοιμ' ἂν ἤδη σοι τὰ τοῦ Πλάτωνος ἐκ τῶν θαυμασίων Νόμων, εἰδότι μὲν καὶ διδάξαντί με). (*Them.* 257d)

This recognition prepares the ground for Julian's polemical self-assertion at Themistius' expense. It is nevertheless a recognition that Julian had in a sense learned the 'foundations of philosophy', that is, (a passage from) Plato, from Themistius. We might hypothesise that, thirty years later, Themistius was still making selective use of these words, capitalising on the literal meaning of Julian's statement. If so, the fact that Themistius could still allude to the *Letter* in the 380s and expect his audience of senators to know what he was referring to indicates that Julian's text had lasting resonance.

---

[67] Them. *Or.* 31.354d.

This is of course a hypothesis. But a reading of Julian's *Letter* as a public response infuses its subtle assertiveness with significance. The text betrays an ambition not only to draw on diplomatic language but also to suggest control of oblique speech. An eloquent example is provided by the opening section, which hastens to dismiss suspicions that Themistius' excessive compliments might be an attempt to 'flatter or deceive' (κολακεύειν ἢ ψεύδεσθαι, 254b–c) Julian. Flattery was a critical category in Greek literature, from Attic rhetoric to the Second Sophistic, and would be routinely activated to disqualify adversaries.[68] Julian quickly declares that what is false in Themistius' statements does not aim to deceive but rather seeks to provide encouragement. But this reads as an *excusatio non petita*, an unrequested apology: if Julian truly did not want to raise the suspicion that Themistius was flattering him, why mention the possibility in the first place? The reader is obliquely invited to suspect that Themistius might fall in some way into the category of sophist, as a social climber seeking to secure his position through Julian's endorsement.

Julian may have sensed an element of challenge in Themistius' text. Many inferences could in fact be drawn from his reply to the comparison of his rule with the legacy of Dionysus, Heracles, Solon, Pittacus, and Lycurgus. The *Letter* cuts such speculation short. By doing so, however, it transforms Themistius' attempt to cast himself as Julian's adviser into an opportunity for the latter to assert himself at the expense of a famous professor of philosophy. Julian implies that Themistius' message betrays a lack of understanding of the role of fate and God in politics, pointing out that Themistius' faulty arguments inadvertently challenged his own role in society. If one considers that Themistius' fame as a philosopher and teacher of philosophy rested primarily on his paraphrases of Aristotle,[69] the accusation that he failed to understand a passage by that author appears especially severe:

> But I should like to make clear to you the points in your letter by which I am puzzled (ὑπὲρ δὲ ὧν ἀπορῆσαί μοι πρὸς τὴν ἐπιστολὴν τὴν σήν), my dearest friend to whom I am especially bound to pay every honour; for I am eager to be more precisely informed about them. You said (ἔφησθα) that you approve a life of action rather than the philosophic life, and you called to witness (μάρτυρα) the wise Aristotle, who defines happiness as virtuous activity ... in this place, you say he approves the architects of noble actions.

---

[68] See, among others, Konstan (1996); Whitmarsh (2001) 194–97; Pownell (2020) 260. Themistius himself celebrated in writing the free speech and bold advice coming from friends, see Vanderspoel (1995) 13, 22.
[69] Heather (1998) 127.

But it is you who assert that these are kings, whereas Aristotle does not speak in the sense of the words that you have introduced (Ἀριστοτέλης δὲ εἴρηκεν οὐδαμοῦ κατὰ τὴν ὑπὸ σοῦ προστεθεῖσαν λέξιν): and from what you have quoted, one would rather infer the contrary.[70]

The gap Julian's *Letter* seeks to open between his position and Themistius' correlates to Julian's (oblique) celebration of his own lucid political analysis. His ideal sovereign might be as much 'ensouled Law' as Themistius' model ruler, but the crucial difference between their political visions is that Themistius' is not grounded in a solid understanding of the classics and thus falls prey to political misconceptions. This line of argument emerges in the second part of the *Letter*, where Julian attacks Themistius' claim that a life of action is superior to a life of contemplation.[71] Here, contrary to what we tend to assume,[72] Julian is supremely uninterested in taking sides. His response to Themistius has the much subtler aim of underscoring that, by stating that a sovereign should rank the active life over contemplation, Themistius misses the fact that, without constant philosophical self-perfectioning, no ruler can achieve the level of rationality that is a condition for enlightened action. Only those who fail to understand this fundamental connection can claim that one of the two activities should be prioritised over the other. Themistius has proven himself an interpreter without a method.

Julian is arguably trying to claim for himself what imperial rhetoric mobilised as a somewhat differential label, that of 'philosopher', by challenging his interlocutor's security in the same status.[73] The political repercussions are undeniable: if the fundamental quality of good leadership, as it emerges from the *Letter*, is a well-trained reason, the emperor who proves himself a better interpreter than a famous philosopher is on his way to ideal sovereignty. Julian reminds his addressee (through what is presented as a compliment but clearly a double-edged one) that Themistius advocated for the superiority of action over contemplation without ever having engaged with the former: his activity is teaching philosophy.[74] The force of this remark becomes apparent when one considers that its author, having been appointed emperor, had just become the second most powerful man in the empire. Themistius celebrates power

---

[70] *Them.* 263c–d, referring to Arist. *Pol.* 7.3.1325b.   [71] *Them.* 263c–6b.
[72] See, e.g., Tanaseanu-Döbler (2008) 112; Stenger (2009) 136–37; Elm (2012) 84–86. For a discussion of Julian's position in the light of Iamblichean political theory, see De Vita (2022) clxii–clxviii.
[73] On the competitive mobilisation of the label 'philosopher', see the Introduction, p. 2–3, 12–15.
[74] *Them.* 266a.

without having had it; Julian celebrates contemplation, which he has practised, from a position of (quasi)absolute agency. Themistius' own weapon, the rhetoric of the self-conscious engagement of the professional philosopher with political rhetoric, ultimately becomes the instrument with which Julian seals his victory in his first rhetorical *agon*.

Handling the *Laws*: Authoritative Knowledge, and Knowledge as a Source of Authority

My analysis of the *Letter* has so far focused on the value of its performative display of philosophical competence and on how Julian perceived this as key to undermining the authority of his interlocutor in what was ultimately a political debate. The remainder of this chapter will attempt to put Julian's operation in context, by asking whether the *Letter*'s method of enquiry and interest in classical philosophical sources can point to meaningful trends in the cultural and political debate of his times. Let us approach this issue by considering first Julian's engagement with his main author of reference, Plato, and in particular the *Laws*. The *Letter* is not the only text by Julian that displays an interest in Plato's posthumous treatise. The extant writings refer to it about a dozen times; on occasion, the work is called 'wonderful' (οἱ θαυμάσιοι Νόμοι).[75] The *Misopogon*, Julian's final piece and a work much concerned with issues of philosophical self-projection, evokes the *Laws* twice. In one case, the quotation is so long and precise that it appears that Julian had either an entire or a partial copy of the text before him as he wrote.[76] In the *Letter to Themistius* as well, as noted, Julian transcribes a long passage from the *Laws*. It thus seems that Julian, who in one letter declares his habit of carrying Plato's works with him, regardless of whether he had the time to read them,[77] considered the *Laws* essential travel equipment: excerpts from it literally feature from his first composition (the *Letter*) to his last (*Misopogon*).

Julian's commitment as a ruler to advertising his acquaintance with the *Laws* is meaningful insofar as Plato's final treatise engaged in great depth with legislative and governmental issues. Regardless of whether specific aspects of this work, such as its emphasis on piety as the fundamental civic virtue, later influenced Julian's religious reforms,[78] the display of engagement with it projected competence in political philosophy. An oblique

---

[75] See n. 55 above. [76] *Mis.* 353d–4a, cf. Bouffartigue (1992) 192.
[77] *Ep.* 29 Wright (= 80 Bidez–Cumont). [78] O'Meara (2005) 120–23.

confirmation of how Julian thought audiences would read his references accordingly comes from the way that Themistius as well, in his speeches to the emperor and senators, occasionally refers to the *Laws*.[79]

A closer look at Themistius' orations shows differences between his appeals to the *Laws*, and to Platonic works in general, and those of Julian. Quotations from Plato in Themistius' orations do not develop into exegetical commentaries on the texts employed. His references to classical authors of philosophy in his panegyrics and other speeches tend to be functional and nominal.[80] An example is the way five of his orations invoke as a Platonic pronouncement the – extremely simple – statement that 'life will achieve its best and happiest condition when the king is young, self-controlled, mindful, brave, majestic, and a ready learner' (a quote, incidentally, from the *Laws*).[81] The sentence is little more than an aphorism, and one might understand Julian' presentation of Themistius in the *Letter* as a superficial reader as targeting this feature of his public work, conveying an implicit accusation as to how it tainted his philosophical integrity.

There might seem to be some irony in Themistius' oratorical handling of his sources. As a professor of philosophy, he had become famous precisely thanks to his paraphrases, a type of work that relied on close engagement with original texts.[82] His reputation as an exegete, which Julian's *Letter* tries to challenge, was foundational to his public profile. Themistius' shift in textual approaches is therefore revealing of his sense of the audience. When operating in a political context, Themistius appears aware that what truly matters to his addressees is to be given clues confirming his identity as a philosopher. His orations engage in a performative display of intellectual authority. This also means that they alert us to something essential: philosophical language had political currency at court. Although Themistius' audience of senators might not have been inclined to dive into philological minutiae – or so Themistius seems to have assumed – they could still be expected to be alive to references to their own cultural capital.

In Chapter 2, I return to Themistius' symbolic role as mouthpiece of *paideia* at Constantius' court. Here, I want to consider instead how his display of engagement with Plato's oeuvre, and Julian's challenge

---

[79] See Maisano (1994).
[80] Cf. Maisano (1994), (2006); Vanderspoel (1995) 22; De Vita (2006); Penella (2014); Vossing (2020) 176.
[81] Them. *Or.* 3.46a; 4.62a; 8.119d; 17.215c; 34.16 (cf. Pl. *Leg.* 4.709e). [82] See above, p. 57.

targeting Themistius' interpretive control of it, point to the importance of claiming intellectual primacy in negotiating public and political authority. It is generally assumed that Themistius introduced Julian to the *Laws* – perhaps in the context of the classroom, perhaps elsewhere – at the time when the latter briefly lived and studied in Constantinople, around 348–349.[83] This might be the case. It should be stressed, however, that the assumption relies exclusively on the passage from the *Letter* where Julian states that Themistius taught him Plato's account of the Golden Age. Although Julian maintains that Themistius taught him this passage, the statement is more ambiguous than is usually acknowledged. Julian does not say whether Themistius introduced him only to this specific passage or to the entire work. Nor does he say to what extent his understanding of the work relied on Themistius' teaching and – most important – whether he regarded Themistius as having any authority in interpreting it. In fact, the entire *Letter* seems constructed to deny this final point.

In the previous section, I argued that Julian's disavowal of Themistius as an interpreter is part of an attempt to prevent Themistius from asserting himself as his adviser. At the same time, we should consider that Julian's and Themistius' allegiance to different schools of thought might have triggered intellectual disagreement between them: Julian admired the Neoplatonic mysticism of Iamblichus, whereas Themistius could be better classified as an eclectic Aristotelian.[84] But Julian's disagreement with Themistius also appears driven by another factor, and one that in my view should not be ascribed to philosophical factionalism: Julian's *Letter* voices a straightforward desire to come across as an independent reader of Plato. The connection made between the Golden Age passage and Aristotle's *Politics* is presented as something Themistius neglected and to which Julian is now drawing attention. In challenging a famous interpreter, Julian is equally concerned to signpost the proficiency with which he handles authoritative sources.

---

[83] Prato and Fornaro (1984) 47–49; Vanderspoel (1995) 118; Dillon (2001) 245 n. 6; Henck (2001) 175; Elm (2012) 83. Bouffartigue's remark that, although Julian read Themistius, they likely belonged to different philosophical circles (cf. note below), seems to imply an objection against the hypothesis that Themistius exercised a substantial influence on Julian's thinking and education (Bouffartigue (1992) 296–97).

[84] Julian on Iamblichus: *Hel.* 146a, 150d; *Cyn.* 188b; *C. Her.* 222b, 235a–b. The traditional view of Themistius' Aristotelianism as free from Platonism has been profitably challenged; see Ballériaux (1994); O'Meara (2005) 206–8; Quiroga (2013b) 612. He was distant, however, from the theurgical and mystical developments of Iamblichean Neoplatonism (Penella [2000] 13; Chiaradonna [2015] 157 n. 31; Zucker [2016] 360).

For a philosopher to lay claims to control over the meaning of a text in competition with another intellectual is not unique to Julian's *Letter*. As seen in the Introduction, the growing investment in exegesis shaping the intellectual developments of the post-Hellenistic schools of philosophy had mobilised an array of competitive dynamics. What seems meaningful, however, is that Julian's letter betrays an interest – an anxiety, even – to ground his political legitimacy on an act of competitive exegesis.

Recent scholarship has challenged the assumption that the strong metaphysical drive of Neoplatonism implied its practitioners' indifference towards society and its institutions. How its representatives positioned themselves regarding the outspokenness and open participation of the philosopher in politics is another complex matter, to which I return in a later chapter.[85] What is relevant here is that third- and fourth-century Platonism cultivated an interest in reflection on the relationship between philosophy and power. O'Meara's *Platonopolis* was pioneering in drawing attention to the Neoplatonic concern for fostering the virtues that facilitate the good civic life. As he shows, this belief was not in contradiction with but in fact depended on the Neoplatonists' self-understanding as mediators between divinity and humankind.[86] This argument is complemented by another point considered in the Introduction, the political currency of Neoplatonic vocabulary in the late Roman Empire.[87] A rhetorical adaptation of Neoplatonic ideas provided ideological scaffolding for the Tetrarchic propaganda.[88] This too points to the activation of a positive feedback loop between cultural expectations and (diluted) philosophical imagery. The very notion of 'ensouled law' resonated with the Platonist belief in the connection through reason between human and divine minds.

It would thus seem both that Neoplatonic philosophers were committed to political ideals and that their language resonated with the upper class. The resulting question is how their literature engaged with the themes of the relationship between power and wisdom and with the agency of philosophical literature in constructing authority. Interestingly, no surviving third- or fourth-century Neoplatonic writing provides a template that precisely matches the *Letter*'s mobilisation of a close reading of classical texts with an attempt to navigate contemporary political dynamics. One could certainly argue that the uniqueness of Julian's social position at the moment must speak to the uniqueness of his strategies of self-negotiation.

---

[85] See Chapter 6.   [86] O'Meara (2005). See also O'Meara (2014).   [87] See Introduction, p. 30.
[88] Burgersdijk (2020).

But comparison of his *Letter* with select contemporary works leads to further insights. Some scholars have singled out Iamblichus' fragmentary *Letter to Agrippa* as anticipating the ideas advanced in Julian's *Letter*, since it lays special emphasis on the centrality of the Law and argues that 'the ruler ... must have a completely pure (εἰλικρινῶς ἀποκεκαθαρμένον) insight into the absolute correctness from the laws' and 'must be immune from corruption (ἀδιάφθορον) as is humanly possible'.[89] Julian's admiration for Iamblichus makes it possible, even plausible, that he was acquainted with the text. It should nevertheless be noted that neither the theme of the authority of the Law nor the understanding of rationality as the political *summum bonum* are exclusive to Iamblichus. In fact, both are essential components of the theory of the ruler as *empsychos nomos*, which, as noted earlier, thrived in Platonising environments. At the same time, Iamblichus is unconcerned with textual definitions and does not look back to earlier philosophical authorities to ground the principle of legislation on their statements.

While theories of direct inspiration thus do not seem to bring us far, the *Letter to Agrippa* nevertheless confirms a Neoplatonic interest in the question of the origins of authority, here found in the intellect and in rational law. A similar interest seems to drive another genre visited by the two canonical figures of post-Plotinian Platonism, Porphyry and Iamblichus: (philosophical) biography. This genre might at first seem at the margins of my discussion. It is in fact profoundly connected to it, especially when one considers that both Porphyry and Iamblichus devoted attention to the archetypical philosopher-leader Pythagoras of Samos.[90] They looked at Pythagoras from different angles and with significant differences in their perspectives and approaches.[91] But their interest in Pythagoras intersects in two respects. First, both Porphyry and Iamblichus record Pythagoras' activity as a unity of intellectual and social engagement. The community-shaping role of the great philosopher is twofold: he is the founder of a close group of disciples who regulate their life according to his

---

[89] Iambl. *ep. fr.* 2 (= Stob. *Ecl.* 4.5.77), transl. Dillon and Polleichtner. Hypothesis of Iamblichean influence on Julian: Schramm (2014) 137; De Vita (2022) clxiv–v. Swain (2013) 37–38 notes the affinity but does not postulate any dependence.

[90] Porphyry's life of his teacher Plotinus will not be discussed here, as this chapter is primarily concerned with what could be defined as a late antique 'archaeology' of philosophy. But see Clark (2000a) for an analysis of Porphyry's and Iamblichus' biographies that also includes the *Life of Plotinus*.

[91] Porphyry's life is the first of four books of a (now lost) *Philosophical History*. It mostly presents itself as an erudite compilation of anecdotes. Iamblichus' *On the Pythagorean Life*, which explicitly presents (the 'divine', *Pyth.* 1 [1]) Pythagoras as an example of the perfect philosophical life, shares material with Porphyry's work and may be directed against it: Clark (2000a) 31–37; Urbano (2013) 91–95.

precepts[92] but also the legislator and teacher of virtue to Samian society at large and to the cities of Southern Italy. (Iamblichus calls him the 'inventor of the whole system of political erudition'.)[93] His listeners get ordinances from him as if they were 'divine commands' (θεῖαι ὑποθῆκαι).[94] He teaches his closest pupils how to become guardians of the laws, as well as excellent legislators.[95] Pythagoras thus provides a historical exemplification of the idea that the enlightened legislator must coincide with the perfect philosopher, implying that the political life must find fulfilment under the guidance of an individual with access to divine reason.

Second, both Porphyry and Iamblichus are invested in reflecting on intellectual authority through the questions of origins and of exemplarity. But the points raised by their biographies do not overlap precisely with Julian's questions. Julian's *Letter* approaches philosophical origins in terms of classical philosophical sources, which he interrogates through exegesis to the twofold end of political theorisation and hierarchical self-positioning. Porphyry and Iamblichus, by contrast, are driven by a desire to root their intellectual lineage in ancient history. Despite their differences, both utilise Pythagoras to pursue what might be called a philosophical archaeology of political theory. In the market of the post-Hellenistic philosophical schools, access to original truth through myth and history was perceived as essential to bestowing authority on a philosophical system.[96] The passage in which Porphyry quotes from Pythagoras' prescription 'not to pluck [the leaves] from a crown' (στέφανόν τε μὴ τίλλειν) is meaningful in this regard.[97] Porphyry explains this as an esoteric exhortation to respect the laws (τοῦτ' ἔστι τοὺς νόμους μὴ λυμαίνεσθαι), 'for they are crowns of cities (στέφανοι γὰρ πόλεων οὗτοι)'. Political and legal theory are here

---

[92] Iamblichus is especially interested in the process of selection and training of Pythagoras' philosophical community: see Iambl. *Pyth.* 17 (70–74), on the examination of followers; 18 (80); on the organisation of the disciples; and 20–22 (94–102), on examining the nature of his pupils, establishing a daily regime, and passing down precepts.

[93] Iambl. *Pyth.* 27 (129). See Clark (2000a); Schott (2003) 503–10; Urbano (2013) 83; Key Fowden (2008) 22–25. According to Iamblichus, the Samians expected Pythagoras to participate in every embassy and civic obligation, see *Pyth.* 6 (28). After his arrival in Kroton, he first advised the population on matters such as piety, self-control, the importance of education, religion, and justice (Porph. *Pyth.* 18; Iambl. *Pyth.* 8 [37]–11 [57]).

[94] Porph. *Pyth.* 20; Iambl. *Pyth.* 6 (30).

[95] Guardians of the laws: Iambl. *Pyth.* 27 (129); legislators: Iambl. *Pyth.*, 27 (130); 39 (172). Porphyry adds that the legislation of Pythagoras' pupils Carondas of Catania and Zaleucos of Locris attracted the envy of neighbouring cities (Porph. *Pyth.* 21). On Porphyry and the *empsychos nomos*, see *Phil. Orac.* fr. 344 Smith. It reports an oracle delivered in response to the question of whether reason or law is better. The mention of the oracle might have served to introduce a (lost) discussion on the rational basis of law.

[96] See the Introduction, p. 14–17.   [97] Porph. *Pyth.* 42; cf. also *Pyth.* 38.

grounded on the interpretation of an obscure archaic maxim, which communicates a superior truth to intelligent readers. Iamblichus identifies in 'symbols (σύμβολα) . . . handed down as education only to those who know' the crucial feature of Pythagoras' teaching.[98]

There are important resonances in the ways Porphyry, Iamblichus, Themistius, and Julian think of the relationship between knowledge and power. They share an interest in postulating philosophy as a source of legitimate authority and in considering sources and origins as fundamental to political thinking. But it is essential to note that, by expanding the picture, we can see that their engagement with the motifs of authority and interpretation was simultaneously cultivated by another category of intellectuals; and that it was this category that approached the issues of exegesis and intellectual lineage with a competitiveness comparable only, of all the sources considered so far, to Julian's *Letter*. But its competitiveness was driven by different factors.

Textual Interpretation and Political Self-legitimation in Lactantius' *Divine Institutes* and Eusebius' *Preparation for the Gospel*

My enquiry so far has been restricted to members of the philosophical schools acknowledged by the system of *paideia*, be they of Aristotelian leanings (Themistius) or operating in the legacy of Plotinus (Porphyry and Iamblichus). Christian theologians would have been surprised to find themselves excluded from this survey. They too thought of themselves as philosophers (or, when they rejected the label, still conceived of their wisdom as competing with the teachings of the traditional philosophical schools).[99] Most important, they were increasingly committed to asserting their philosophical identity in the eyes of contemporary society.

The remainder of my analysis considers how two critical figures operating in the early fourth century, the Latin rhetorician Lactantius and the slightly – but crucially – younger Eusebius Pamphili (ca. 260–340 CE), bishop of Caesarea, thematised the relationship between (Christian) knowledge and Roman society.[100] Lactantius' *Divine Institutes*, composed between 305 and 310, represents an unprecedented turn in Latin apologetics.[101] Dating in its first redaction to a time when Christians were still

---

[98] Iambl. *Pyth.* 23 (102–5), transl. Clark (1989).
[99] On Lactantius' self-definition as a rhetorician, rather than a philosopher, see Chapter 3, p. 141–2.
[100] See the Introduction, p. 16–17.
[101] Discussion of the date and place of authorship in Barnes (1981) 291; Garnsey (2003) 1–3; Heck (2009); Gassmann (2020) 19–20.

experiencing persecution, the work takes a deliberately original route to reply to the detractors of Christianity (including a Greek philosopher of uncertain identity, who is identified by part of scholarship with Porphyry himself).[102] Lactantius is concerned with what he perceives to be the inability of Christians to advocate eloquently for their religion in a way that would make it acceptable to the educated Roman upper class with its set of cultural expectations. He therefore sets out to produce an exposition of Christianity that relies on a targeted use of what his non-Christian interlocutors would perceive as authoritative sources. In other words, Lactantius argues that the sources upon which he grounds his apologetic claims must be different from the Bible; otherwise, the scepticism of the adherents of Greco-Roman religion towards a text they perceive as 'fiction and lies' would continue to invalidate any Christian argument a priori.[103] In doing so, Lactantius gives pride of place to Cicero, with whom he has an ambivalent relationship. For Lactantius, Cicero stands as the culmination of Rome's aspiration to ethical thinking but also simultaneously as proof of the limits of any search of knowledge that excludes Christianity.[104] Two points are remarkable. First, Lactantius' assessment of Cicero is substantiated by a close engagement with the texts he produced, as he negotiates his interpretive authority by putting his knowledge of Ciceronian writings on display.[105] Second, Lactantius' interest falls remarkably on Cicero's ethical and political works, *On the Commonwealth* (*De re publica*) and *On the Laws* (*De legibus*).[106]

Lactantius' thorough engagement with this portion of the production of his author of reference stands in stark contrast to the way Eusebius of Caesarea handles his own reference author in *paideia*, Plato. Eusebius' work matches Lactantius' ambition to advocate for Christianity by demonstrating its control of sources its detractors regard as authoritative. Since he comes from the Greek side of the debate, however, he is especially concerned with Christianity's relationship with Platonic thinking. This must be one of primacy and simultaneously dominance. Eusebius' attempts to mobilise exegesis in the construction of the so-called

---

[102] Porphyry: DePalma Digeser (2000) 93–107; Schott (2008) 179–85; Simmons (2015) 42–43, 64. See, however, Gassman (2020) 19 n. 3.
[103] Lactant. *Div. inst.* 5.4.4 (*uanam fictam commenticiam*). See DePalma Digeser (2000) 7–12; Garnsey (2003) 14–21.
[104] Cf. Lactant. *Div. inst.* 3.15.1. DePalma Digeser (2000) 56–63; Garnsey (2003) 14–15, 20–22, 26–36; Lettieri (2013); Gassman (2020) 26.
[105] Garnsey (2004) 13–16, 20–23.   [106] Garnsey (2004) 26, 31–35.

dependency theme (i.e., the dependence of Greek philosophy on Christianity) are illustrated by his *Preparation for the Gospel*.[107] This treatise in fifteen Books makes the argument that Greek philosophy was derived from an original wisdom also documented in the writings of other peoples (especially the 'Hebrews', intended in the Eusebian sense of proto-Christians).[108] The *Preparation* is strikingly constructed on the assertions of others: more than two-thirds of the work consists of direct quotations.[109] This impressive display of mastery of the philosophical tradition from various cultures, be they Phoenician, Egyptian, Chaldean, Jewish, or above all Greek, seeks to demonstrate Christianity's complete hermeneutical control over the intellectual history of the world and consequently the limited authority of Greek philosophy.

As anticipated, Plato plays a crucial role in the picture. Eusebius acknowledges him as the best classical philosopher, who overcame Greek superstition through access to the same truth that inspired Moses.[110] The model is less conciliatory, however, than it is competitive. As Johnson shows, Eusebius gradually transitions from a thesis of shared inspiration to one of Platonic appropriation of Moses' doctrine.[111] The approach culminates in Book 13, where Plato's discrepancies with Christian metaphysics and ethics are presented as demonstrating the failure of Greek philosophy even in its highest form.[112] And, crucially, Plato's political thinking is at the heart of the process. Eusebius' final dismissal of Plato is preceded by a long examination of the latter's political theory, which stands as the protagonist of *Preparation* Book 12. The book opens with a quotation from the *Laws* in which Plato argues that the best law is one whose divine exactitude is self-evident to everyone.[113] In a programmatic gesture, Eusebius seizes the opportunity to show that the passage in Plato is in harmony with lines from Isaiah and the Psalms.[114] This simultaneously signals Eusebius' interpretive control of Plato's most political works and his ability to find meaning in it via his control of the Bible. Throughout Book 12, Eusebius returns over and over to the *Republic* and the *Laws* – although the number of quotations reveals the latter as Eusebius' real

---

[107] Discussion in Boys-Stones (2001) 176–202.
[108] See, e.g., Euseb. *PE* 10.4.1; 14.3.1. Kofsky (2000) 103–6; Johnson (2006) 20–23, 100–24; Urbano (2013) 107–9.
[109] 71 per cent of the *PE* (Johnson [2014] 26).   [110] See already *PE* 2.6.23–4; 2.7.
[111] Johnson (2006) 21, 137–40; Johnson (2014) 34. On how Plato appropriated Mosaic doctrine, see, e.g., *PE* 11.9.4; 12.11.1; 12.13.1.
[112] See Euseb. *PE* 13.14–21.   [113] Pl. *Leg.* 1.634d–e in Euseb. *PE* 12.1. See Schott (2003) 517–18.
[114] *Is.* 7.9, *Ps.* 116.10 in Euseb. *PE* 12.1.

focus.[115] The book itself, as Schott observes, seems to be structured according to the agenda outlined in Plato's work.[116] Eusebius progresses from a reflection on the appointment of political chiefs and the management of education to elaborating communal regulations (with attention to cultural and religious practices) and concludes with the question of how to structure the ideal city, which according to the *Preparation* must be inspired by Jerusalem and provide to its citizens a training that leads to the knowledge of God.[117] Eusebius evidently shares with Plato (and the Platonists) a belief that the practice of politics, if inspired by philosophy, prepares for the contemplation of the divine. Eusebius and the Platonists also both believe that access to the truth is the precondition for creating a polity where citizenship can foster virtue.

A *fil rouge* links Lactantius' and Eusebius' works. Both rely on the 'classics' to advocate for the superiority of their religion, which they argue is precisely demonstrated by texts that are – apparently – external to it. Both are competing with *paideia* while simultaneously seeking to derive authority and legitimacy from their control over it. Furthermore – and most important – both betray a special interest in the political output of the authors they envisage as their *maîtres à penser* within the classical tradition (Cicero for Lactantius, Plato for Eusebius). This too points to a shared concern: how to draw on traditional culture to demonstrate, in the eyes of a ruling class invested in the cultural capital of *paideia*, that Christianity is a valid – indeed, the most valid – tool for government.

After this, considerations begin to diverge. As recent scholarship has stressed, Lactantius' primary ambition was to lead his readers to an understanding of God, and his concern with Roman politics mostly originated with the fact that he saw it as an expression of what he envisaged as the moral and social limits of polytheism.[118] Throughout his work, Lactantius seeks to show that the Christian life overcomes such sociopolitical systems – including its highest expression, which he found in

---

[115] The *Laws* already feature in book 11 (*Leg.* 4.715e–16b at *PE* 11.13.5; *Leg.* 10.896d–e and 10.906a at *PE* 11.26). In Book 12 alone, Eusebius quotes from the following passages (which I list according to their order of appearance in the text of the *PE*): *Leg.* 1.634d–e, 629e–30c; 11.926e–78a; 3.689b–e, 677a–c, 677e; 1.631a–2a, 632c–d, 643b–d, 643d–4b; 2.653b–c, 659c–60a, 660e–61d, 657a, 658e–9b, 671a–d, 673e–4c; 1.626d–e, 644c–d, 644e–5c; 10.896c–d; 2.663d–e, 665b–c; 1.639a; 7.801e–2a; 11.931e; 8.842e–43a, 843c–d; 9.856c–d, 857a, 874b–c, 873d; 6.760b, 755d–e; 4.704b–5b; 10.888e–90b, 891b–d, 892a–c, 893b–c; 895a–99a. The passages taken from the *Republic* are (in their order of appearance): 2.376e–77a, 377a–c; 1.346e–47a; 2.361b–d, 361d–62a; 6.500c–501c, 499c–d; 5.455c–56b; 4.421e–22a; 5.469c; 3.415a–c; 1.345b–e; 9.588b–89b; 10.595b–c.

[116] Schott (2003) 523.   [117] Euseb. *PE* 12.48 (Jerusalem); 12.49–51 (Plato's educational project).

[118] See Gassman (2020) 23–27.

Ciceronian ethics.[119] But Eusebius had a different agenda, rooted in an understanding of something Lactantius does not seem to have brought entirely into focus: the intuition that the course of history might now be on his party's side. The *Preparation* was composed a few years after the first edition of Lactantius' *Institutes*, between 313 and 324, at the time when Constantine was sharing power with his co-Augustus in the East, Licinius. The 'Edict of Milan' and the well-timed association of the Church with the ruler implied that the moment for pervasive political action had come.[120] Eusebius' close engagement with and actualisation of the *Laws* points, I believe, to his general sense that Christian political thought had acquired a context of application. What Plotinus had once envisaged as Platonopolis could now find concrete realisation in its final form, Christopolis. 'The polity of the Church of Christ', Eusebius writes, 'has replaced (ἐπανίστατο) the polities of the heathen nations (τοῖς τῶν ἀπίστων ἐθνῶν)'.[121]

But such a city and polity needed to be administered. Eusebius' entire literary activity is a testament to that. His invention of a new historiographical genre with his *Ecclesiastical History* (of uncertain date but largely complete by 315/316)[122] aimed to re-cast the relationship between State and Church in a way that would support the presence and voice of Christianity in the public sphere. Christians, Eusebius argues, had always been committed citizens, embodying Roman virtues. As Corke-Webster shows, the *Ecclesiastical History* in this regard turns the traditional narrative on its head, by arguing that the Roman rulers opposing or persecuting Christians had proven, by so doing, their tyrannical and thus anti-Roman nature.[123] At the same time, Eusebius casts his fellow Christians not only as good citizens but – crucially – as members of what he saw as the best philosophical school.[124] From this, he deduced that they were those best equipped to wield spiritual and political authority. It is against this

---

[119] Garnsey (2003) 25–36.
[120] Licinius' relationship with Christianity remains an open historiographical issue, as his image as an enemy and persecutor of the new religion may have been created and was certainly exploited by Constantinian propaganda (Barbero (2016) 88–92).
[121] Euseb. *DE* 6.20.16. Cf. Schott (2003) 528.
[122] Discussion in Corke-Webster (2019) 42, 57–65.
[123] Corke-Webster (2019) 249–79. See also Johnson (2006) 156, 186–87 and Schott (2008) 157 on Eusebius' perception of the joint end of polytheism and polyarchy.
[124] Cf. Euseb. *PE* 14.3.1. See also *GEI* (= *Eclog. Prophet.*) p. 141 Gaisford ('among us there is a crowd of those who entirely lack a formal education, exhibiting a virtuous, philosophic way of life (ἐμφιλόσοφον πολιτείαν) such as one cannot easily find even among those trained in philology and boasting in their care of books', transl. Johnson [2014] 58). Momigliano (1963) already suggested that Eusebius' *Ecclesiastical History* reflects the histories of the philosophical schools. On

background that his treatment of Plato's *Republic* and *Laws* is significant. The *Preparation* might conclude that Plato the philosopher is passé, since he does not entirely share in the truth of God's message. But Eusebius the political theorist must still reckon with his legacy if he wants to carve out a space for his political design in imperial discourse, demonstrating that Roman history is Christian history. Control of the sources is his tool for competition and draws on mastery of the philosophical literature to substantiate a project of Christian re-negotiation of socio-political hierarchies.

We are back to Julian, the freshly appointed emperor testing his political voice through a philosophical *agon*. We have seen that the intellectual agenda driving the *Letter to Themistius* finds its place in a larger context, visited both by pagan and Christian thinkers, involving how knowledge legitimises authority and how sources and origins, when authoritatively handled, substantiate claims to political and intellectual primacy. Julian's competitiveness, I noted above, is greater than that of the other 'pagan' Neoplatonists considered in this chapter. In fact, we might even want to – provocatively – compare Julian's voice to Lactantius' and Eusebius' aggressive self-positioning with regard to ancient sources. It could be objected that very different agendas drove their efforts. At the same time, one might respond to this that both Julian, on the one hand, and Lactantius and Eusebius, on the other, envisaged the outlining of interpretive credentials as essential to their entrance into the political field, be it qua having recently been appointed emperor or because they represented a new political voice. Like Eusebius, Julian does not merely resort to name-dropping Plato or to a brief use of quotations from anthologised maxims drawn from the most famous dialogues – as Themistius, relying safely on his public reputation, would do. Julian's need to assert himself finds expression, as noted, through engagement with long excerpts, which invite the audience to see that his control of literature is metonymic with his control of politics.

Julian, who is unlikely to have ever read Lactantius, knew Eusebius. In the polemical treatise *Against the Galileans* (his name for the Christians),[125] written towards the end of his rule, the 'knavish' (μοχθηρός) Eusebius is the only theologian named and targeted explicitly, at least from what we can reconstruct from the fragments. The way Julian attacks him is

---

Eusebius' patterning of the relationship between Church and empire as that between traditional philosophers and the Roman elites, see Corke-Webster (2019) 89–120.
[125] An analysis of the treatise in Chapter 3, p. 148–52.

significant: the text addresses Eusebius' argument for the priority of the Hebrews over the Greeks in various disciplines, including logic ('something whose name he learnt among the Greeks', Julian comments).[126] *Against the Galileans* displays a concern for Eusebius' celebration of Christianity's intellectual priority and for the way this came at the expense of Greek thinking.

Almost seven years – if one accepts, as I do, the dating of the *Letter to Themistius* to 355 – separate Julian's response from *Against the Galileans*. By stressing an affinity in the method and agenda of the *Letter* with Eusebius' *Preparation*, I do not seek to argue that Julian's earliest piece interacts with Eusebius' use of Platonic philosophy or that it voices an anti-Christian position; for Julian's allegiance to the traditional gods to find expression in his writings, a few more years were needed. But the identification of a largely comparable agenda shaping Julian's and Eusebius' use of philosophical sources, and the way they both drew on such sources to gain access to imperial politics, points to something important. It outlines the contours of a political environment still invested in the 'classical' question of what philosophy is and what it does to power. This relatively generic remark can serve as a springboard for further reflection. Having dismissed the hypothesis of Julian's engagement with Eusebius in the *Letter*, I will argue in Chapter 2 that the vocabulary Julian deployed upon his entrance into politics nevertheless interacted with the discourse cultivated by a *Christian* court that had internalised Eusebius' (or a Eusebius-like) cultural vision. Within this picture, Julian's precociously aggressive self-image as exegete appears as the product of expectations fostered by Constantius II – the last living son of Constantine.

Conclusions

This chapter has shown that the primary aim of Julian's *Letter to Themistius* is not, as usually assumed, a critique of the late antique theory of the ruler as 'ensouled law' but an advertisement of Julian's philosophical expertise via a discussion of the relationship between state authority and (divine) reason. At the heart of the text is a challenge to its addressee, the famous philosopher and senator Themistius, to whom Julian's *Letter* denies the possibility of portraying himself as the correspondent and

---

[126] *C. Gal.* fr. 53 Masaracchia (222a). Bouffartigue (1992) 386, suggests that other arguments in the treatise might also be constructed in reply to Eusebius' commentary on the *Timaeus* (*PE* 11.29). The hypothesis is intriguing but unprovable.

adviser of the young philosopher-ruler. Julian downgrades Themistius to a superficial interpreter and thus implicitly sanctions his own status as philosopher-ruler in the making.

Interpretation is the great protagonist of Julian's *Letter*. His quarrel with Themistius involves exegetical control over the great philosophical authorities preserved as reference points in the contemporary political scene. The third- and fourth-century engagement with philosophical sources and origins displays a shared interest in prescribing a virtuous symbiosis between knowledge and power and in ascribing such prescriptions to an authoritative past (Porphyry, Iamblichus). It is the early fourth-century apologists, however, who appear most invested in the exercise of performing, in literature, their dominance of classical texts. Their intent was to argue that Christianity was key to the interpretive control of *paideia* and consequently of Roman politics. Eusebius in particular shows that domination of classical political philosophy marks Christianity as equipped for the task of ruling – in fact, as better equipped for it than its non-Christian counterpart. Eusebius' and Julian's competitive efforts to legitimise their political voice were driven by different exigencies. The sense of urgency both displayed in entering politics through interpretation, however, serves as an initial indication of the importance of philosophical exegesis in the fourth-century debate about political leadership.

CHAPTER 2

Climbing the Ladder

In this chapter, I show that the self-assertive strategy Julian pursued in the *Letter to Themistius* was not a one off but the first in a series of attempts to define his authorial voice. His early writings, especially the crucial but sidelined *Consolation to Himself upon the Departure of the Excellent Salutius*, illustrate how Julian's literary output from his years as a Caesar (355–60) sought to mirror the growth in authority that resulted from his military campaign in Gaul and to use rhetoric to rewrite the dynamics of his interaction with the senior emperor, Constantius II. What is most relevant about Julian's literary evolution, however, is that it implicitly provides us with a commentary on Constantius' propaganda. As I will show, it is precisely from this that Julian's voice as philosopher-emperor derived meaning and legitimacy. When placed in the culture of the court of the last surviving son of Constantine, Julian's early panegyrics and orations are revealed as first catering to and later antagonising Constantius' intellectualising self-image and the role this played in delineating a project of Christian philosophical leadership.

Praising the Augustus: Julian's *First Panegyric to Constantius II*

Julian the panegyrist has always intrigued scholars. His two surviving encomia of Constantius II and his *Speech of Thanks* addressing Constantius' wife, the empress Eusebia,[1] are the only examples in Roman history of one emperor writing speeches in praise of another, a gesture that points in equal measure to Julian's awareness of his subordinate position and to his ambition to present himself as highly cultivated.

Julian needed to consolidate his image after his appointment as Caesar. He had been placed on the throne as the successor of his half-brother, Gallus, whom Constantius II appointed Caesar in 351 and executed on

---

[1] On the relationship between χαριστήριος λόγος and *encomium*, see Pernot (1993) 284–86.

account of his unstable imperial profile in 354, only one year before Julian's elevation to the throne. Julian too, accused of having met with his brother in Constantinople to conspire against the Augustus, fell temporarily into disgrace and was rescued only due to the intercession of the Empress Eusebia (or so, at least, Julian tells us).[2]

It is therefore inevitable that we look at Julian's panegyrics as the product of difficult circumstances but also in the light of his retrospective reassessment of Constantius, following their fallout in 360, as a life-long enemy. In the *Letter to the Athenians*, a pamphlet composed in 361 as their armies marched against each other, Julian not only accuses the senior Augustus of murdering his half-brother but also singles him out for commissioning the dynastic purge of Constantine's relatives that in the summer of 337 cost Julian's father and elder brother their lives.[3] The piece also highlights how Constantius deprived the young Julian and Gallus of their inherited wealth and forced them to live as exiles.[4] And yet Constantius, presented here as a perpetual source of fear, threat, and hatred, had only a few years before been the subject of Julian's praise. Recent scholarship has explored the question – which often looms large over studies on epideictic rhetoric – of whether and to what extent Julian's panegyrics should be understood as voicing oblique criticism. As Chapter 1 noted, Julian was skilful with figured speech intended to say one thing while implying something far more critical.[5]

This chapter addresses ambiguity in Julian's epideictic rhetoric and its evolution over time. But it also argues that a primary focus on oblique speech and the search for resentment in Julian's early writings may have diverted attention from the efforts these pieces put into communicating cooperative intent. An initial text to illustrate this point is Julian's earliest encomium, the *First Panegyric to Constantius II*, which he arguably composed in 356 or, at the latest, in the summer of 357.[6] Although the text is

---

[2] *Eus.* 118b–c. Cf. also *Eus.* 120c–21b.
[3] *Ath.* 270c–71a. Discussion on Constantius' responsibility in the purge in Burgess (2008).
[4] *Ath.* 270d–71b; cf. also 273b (seizure of property).
[5] Ahl (1984); Pernot (2015). On Julian's rhetorical formation, see now De Vita (2022) xli–xlviii.
[6] Bowersock (1978) 37 and Marcone (2019) 83 believe it possible that Julian started writing it in December 355 as he was wintering in Vienna and then completed it during the following year. A date in 356 is also favoured by Rosen (2006) and Tougher (2012) 21. Tantillo (1997) 39 suggests that the *First Panegyric* and Julian's *Speech of Thanks* to Eusebia were written in preparation for the celebrations of Constantius' *Vicennalia*, which were held in Rome in spring 357. See also Pagliara (2012) 47; (2015) 90; De Vita (2022) cxiii n. 96. Julian did not attend the celebrations and is unlikely to have ever delivered the piece in Constantius' presence, but he might have sent the orations through someone else.

apparently a simple, straightforward encomium, Athanassiadi has pointed to its frequent display of adhesion to the parameters of imperial praise — Julian repeatedly stresses his compliance with the prescribed structure of the encomium — as a performance of critical detachment.[7] Her interpretation postulates that the *First Panegyric* envisages the celebration of the Augustus as a duty with which Julian was forced to comply.[8]

Later scholarship has complicated Athanassiadi's reading by highlighting how Julian's box-ticking show seeks to make his audience appreciate his attempt at writing praise despite being not a rhetorician but someone committed to 'another form of learning' (ἕτερον παιδείας εἶδος) – an allusion to what the audience would recognise as his philosophical training.[9] Chapter 1 considered how the competitive distinction between philosophers and rhetoricians was a self-legitimising strategy frequently employed by fourth-century intellectuals.[10] In the case of Julian, use of it could also arguably rely on the audience's awareness that until recently he had been a proper student of philosophy in Athens. Thus, although Julian's studied display of engagement with the rules of praising can be read as performance, this does not straightforwardly equate with a denial of praise. Julian's pose as a philosopher who has just ventured into rhetorical territory in fact emphasises how the praise of Constantius comes from someone with a reputation for knowledge and wisdom.

At the same time, Julian the philosopher presents himself as especially enticed by the prospect of celebrating the culture of the Augustus. The opening praise of the virtues of Constantius' ancestors prepares for the mention of Constantius' learning (4d; cf. further 10d, 11d). Constantius' wisdom (*phronesis*) is described as the result of a powerful blend of natural talent, the teaching about statecraft he received from the wisest citizens (12c) – a reference to Themistius? – and, above all, God's guidance (13d–14a). His father, Constantine, is celebrated as instrumental in facilitating Constantius' acquisition of wisdom; Julian claims that Constantine's greatest achievement was that he 'begat, reared, and educated' his son.[11] He also presents Constantine's training of Constantius as abiding by Plato's precepts (11d–12b).[12]

---

[7] See, e.g., at *I Pan.* 4c–d, 5b, 6c.   [8] Athanassiadi (1981) 61. See also Browning (1975) 74.
[9] Cf. *I Pan.* 2a–c. See Tougher (1998a) 108; (2012) 24–28; Ross (2018) 191; Marcone (2019) 83; De Vita (2022) cxiv–viii.
[10] Cf., e.g., Them. *Or.* 1.1a–2b.
[11] *I Pan.* 9a (πολλῶν δὲ καὶ καλῶν ἔργων τῷ πατρὶ τῷ σῷ πραχθέντων ... πάντων ἄριστον ... τὴν σὴν γένεσιν καὶ τροφὴν καὶ παιδείαν).
[12] *I Pan.* 11d–12b (καθάπερ ὁ γενναῖος ἠξίωσε Πλάτων). A reference to Pl. *Resp.* 5.467e.

Some of the statements advanced in this text read, and have been read, as problematic.¹³ For instance, Julian's allusion to 'he who first showed philosophy to humankind' (τοῦ πρώτου φιλοσοφίαν ἀνθρώποις φήναντος, 3c) who is unquestionably Apollo – how appropriate a reference is this for Constantius? Julian also explicitly refuses to mention portents that might aggrandise the *laudandus* (10b), despite this being an encouraged rhetorical practice.¹⁴ His reference to the battle of Singara, which the audience knew – by Julian's admission – had ended in defeat (23b), appears similarly critical. The same could be argued of the allusion to Constantius' mother Fausta, who had fallen into disgrace after her death (7c–d, 9b–c).¹⁵

These remarks are all ambiguous and were arguably meant to be. Ambiguity, while potentially serving as a vehicle for conveying hidden content, is also defensive, in that it simultaneously deflects readings that try to signpost it as outright criticism. One example: Julian's refusal to report portents (10b) is accompanied by a statement that stories of omens and signs belong to the realm of poetry – which in ancient literary theory was closely associated to rhetoric.¹⁶ If Julian's self-projection in the *First Panegyric* relies on his denial that he is a rhetorician, his apparent violation of rhetorical norms is potentially available to a positive reading: by refusing to introduce poetic (and hence rhetorical) material into his work, Julian signals his distance from fiction and sophistry, inviting his audience to consider that everything in his piece must be a true event deserving real praise.¹⁷ Similarly, Julian's mention of the lost battle of Singara can

---

¹³ Tougher (2012), followed by García Ruiz (2015); Greenwood (2021); De Vita (2022) cxiv–xxi (the last reading the piece as Julian's first and covert expression of what he was in the process of elaborating as key points in his political and religious agenda). Ross (2018) acknowledges the problems posed by the text but also shows how it constructs Constantius as a triumphant military leader, presumably to the benefit of a Western, Italian audience.

¹⁴ Cf. Men. Rhet. 2.371.2–14 Russell–Wilson.

¹⁵ Cf. also the mention at *I Pan.* 19b–20a of Constantius' benevolent treatment of his brothers (and, therefore, of Constantine II, who had fallen into disgrace after his death). At *I. Pan* 16d, the celebration of Constantius' justice and moderation is followed by a remark on the few exceptional cases in which, 'forced by the critical state of affairs', Constantius could not – despite his wishes – 'prevent others from going astray' (ἑτέρους ἐξαμαρτεῖν οὐ διεκώλυσας, 17a). Tougher (2012) 26–28 reads this as an allusion to Gallus.

¹⁶ Walker (2000).

¹⁷ Forms of philosophical rejection of poetry and rhetoric date back to the Presocratics (Bryan [2012]). The topic was highly debated by Plato (a survey of the discussion in Ferrari (1990)). A reading of Julian's refusal to mention portents as an expression of the piece's philosophical agenda in Tantillo (1997) 200–201 n. 76; cf. also Tougher (2012), 33 n. 61.

(and has been) read as an attempt to make Constantius' enterprises in the West stand out in comparison.[18]

The question of how to read these remarks is complicated by the fact that we know almost nothing of the contemporary dissemination of the *First Panegyric*.[19] It is likely, however, that the text circulated at least somewhat. This is suggested in part by the implausibility of a public figure such as Julian, at the beginning of his imperial career and surrounded by Constantius' subordinates, deciding to write a speech centred on the Augustus in the hope that it would not be leaked. But we also know that the text was sent around in some form, since the rhetorician Libanius, living in Antioch – that is, on the other side of the empire – received a copy of it. The letter in which he comments on Julian's piece intriguingly juxtaposes praise for Julian's oratory with the statement that the Caesar has given to his 'colleague in the empire' (Constantius) 'no cause to repent for his gift of it (i.e., power)'.[20] Is this to be read as a comment not merely on Julian's deeds – which are listed afterwards – but also on his literary production? Did Libanius have an interest in pressing a positive reading of the synergy between the Augustus and the Caesar? Or could it be that his juxtaposition of topics amounts to an oblique remark – the allusive comment of a seasoned rhetorician – concerning Julian's equally oblique rhetoric?

These questions might have to remain open. It is relevant, however, that the contemporary scholarly reassessment of Constantius' attitude towards his Caesar shows that, despite Julian's later retrospective narratives, the Augustus was favourable to his second-in-command and displayed trust in him, especially in religious matters.[21] Constantius' early approval of Julian might have relied on a series of factors, such as reports from collaborators, and did not necessary involve an assessment of Julian's writings. I believe, however, that a text such as the *First Panegyric* nevertheless illustrates a key aspect of the relationship between Julian and Constantius, one that can perhaps also help us to interpret Libanius' comment. Julian's text voices a declaration of commitment to the rules of what might be defined as Constantius' imperial contract. Regardless of whether the text contains

---

[18] Ross (2018).
[19] Tantillo (1997) 36–40; Tougher (2012); Ross (2018) 187; Greenwood (2021) 26–27. For a hypothesis of later re-editing, see García Ruiz (2015).
[20] Lib. *Ep.* 369 Foerster (= 30.6 Norman). On the relationship between Julian's panegyric and Libanius' letter, see Whitby (1999) 74–75; Ross (2018) 187.
[21] Greenwood (2021) 10. On Julian's involvement in the synod of Beziers in 356, see further Beckwith (2005) 34–35.

elements of allusive defiance, as it may, it simultaneously issues a statement of alignment with priorities that, as Libanius too arguably saw, were Constantius'.

To argue this, I will consider how the text channels intellectual themes through Julian's persona, developing this motif as a celebration of the connection between political legitimacy and intellectual authority. The *Panegyric* opens with an allusive mention of Constantius' suppression of a tyranny – that of the usurper Vetranio, in 350 – 'by means of speech and persuasion' (λόγῳ καὶ πειθοῖ, 1d). The account of Vetranio's defeat is recovered later in the text, in a passage in which Julian describes how Constantius persuaded the entire army, with 'the force of his arguments' (ἡ ῥώμη . . . τῶν λόγων, 33a) to recognise him as sole ruler (32d–33d).[22] Constantius' success was therefore achieved 'through intelligence (συνέσεως) rather than force (ῥώμης, 47d)'. Julian further implies that appreciation of Constantius' profile as ruler can truly be voiced only by an intellectual such as himself: his focus on his philosophical identity appears instrumental to the validation of Constantius' intellectual identity. The *First Panegyric* could almost be framed in this light as an act of recognition among (intellectual) equals, its explicit message being a display of concern to celebrate Constantius as a lover of wisdom and an emphasis on the fact that the praise of such wisdom comes from a man who is equally fond of culture. How does this amount to Julian's expression of adherence to what I defined as Constantius' imperial contract? Julian's *Speech of Thanks* to Constantius' wife Eusebia, a text that arguably formed a diptych with the *First Panegyric*, can help us see this.[23]

Praising Eusebia: Julian's *Speech of Thanks*

The *Speech of Thanks* is the only extant example of a prose encomium from the Roman imperial period addressed to a woman.[24] The first part of the text acknowledges its exceptional character.[25] But Julian also argues that his gratitude could not remain unvoiced.[26] Eusebia had been responsible

---

[22] This story of a quiet demise obscures the direct involvement of the imperial family in the elevation of Vetranio, who was presumably proclaimed emperor to slow down Magnentius' expansion (Bleckmann [1994]; Hunt [1997] 15–17).

[23] On *I Pan.* and *Eus.* as a possible diptych, see Tantillo (1997) 39; García Ruiz (2015) 162–65; Washington (2020) 95.

[24] Although see Washington (2020) 99 on the possibility that more women were mentioned in lost panegyrics.

[25] *Eus.* 104b–5d.   [26] *Eus.* 102b–3c.

for rescuing him from disgrace after Gallus' execution, helping him to reassert his loyalty to Constantius II. And yet, despite the compliments paid to the empress, and Julian's effort to adapt elements of the preexisting literary tradition of female praise to the grid of the male encomium,[27] the *Speech* is hardly praise of Eusebia. Instead, it is a play of mirrors, and not only because its praise of Eusebia as a faithful wife enables Julian, as Washington observes, to reassert his own loyalty to the Augustus.[28] As I aim to show, Julian creates a complex structure that apparently pays homage to the wife but in fact addresses the husband. But this displacement of the female subject is not (or better, not only) an accident of patriarchy or the result of Julian's desire to display his literary creativity. It is in fact instrumental to the main aim of the piece, which is to celebrate Constantius' capacity as a patron of intellectuals.

The *Speech* presents itself from the outset as composed under the sign of philosophy. Eusebia bears the imprint of her land, Macedonia, where Alexander the Great was educated by 'the wise Stagyrite' (107b), Aristotle. Her origins are thus located in a place that epitomises the encounter between power and philosophy. This encounter structures the rest of the *Speech* and especially a seeming digression that in fact holds the key to decoding it: Julian's description of how Constantius chose his wife – or, in Julian's words, recognised her as 'worthy of *koinonia*' (109b) – a word whose range of meaning can encompass sexual union as well as partnership and alliance. Julian presents us with an account of a rigorous selection process: Constantius sought what Julian labels 'evidence' (μαρτυρίαν, 109b) of Eusebia's endowment with all desired qualities, including, above all, culture and intelligence (109c). The emperor thus embarked in a long deliberation process (πολλάκις βουλευσάμενον, 110a), 'partly making enquiries about all that was needful to learn about her by hearsay (δι' ἀκοῆς), and judging (τεκμαιρόμενον) also from her mother of the daughter's noble disposition' (110a).

Julian the philosopher offers his reading of Constantius' process of selection, giving his audience a sample of his own interpretive skills, here applied to Constantius' thinking. But also, and most important: Julian the interpreter publicly sanctions the validity of what he has just interpreted, that is, Constantius' method. The implications of this extend beyond the

---

[27] James (2012); García Ruiz (2015); Washington (2020) 94, 99.
[28] Assertion of loyalty through praise of Eusebia's fidelity: Washington (2020) 103–12. De Vita reads the piece as an ideal portrayal of Julian (De Vita [2022] cxxviii–cxxxi). On the classical use of female figures as the 'enhancing mirror of a self-loving representation' of men for men, see Sissa (2009) 114. See also Cooper (1992), (1996).

specific matter of Constantius' marriage. The motif of how a good emperor should choose friends and allies (as opposed to the tyrant, who picks only flatterers) had a special place in the political theory of the Principate. This theme runs through Plutarch's treatises; it is also in Dio's *Kingship Orations*, where the emperor Trajan is repeatedly invited to reflect on his need to have a sincere adviser by his side.[29] Eusebia, whom Constantius had deemed worthy to become the 'partner of his counsels' (κοινωνόν ... τῶν βουλευμάτων, 114a–b), is here clearly turned into the female equivalent of such a figure.

The true importance of the celebration of Constantius' relationship to Eusebia as an act of patronage, however, is in the way it reflects on Julian and his role at court. If Constantius led his investigation of Eusebia and chose to marry her, so too Eusebia, the reader is told, led her own personal investigation (διελέγχειν, 118b) concerning Julian's reputation, refusing to listen to false accusations (118b) and using Julian's life as 'plain proof' (ἐναργεῖ τεκμηρίῳ, 121a) against slander. On the one hand, Eusebia's actions offer the final demonstration of her wisdom and prudence: she rescued an innocent man, supporting him out of respect for philosophy (120b), for which Julian had a – unjustified, he claims – reputation (120b–c).[30] On the other hand, Constantius' exemplary assessment of Eusebia certifies that Julian is a valid associate: he was deemed worthy by someone who had been carefully selected by Constantius himself. Finally, Julian's validation of Constantius' process of selecting his wife appears in this light to round off the virtuous circle. Julian was properly chosen because Eusebia was properly chosen; now the wisdom of Constantius is further confirmed by Julian's display of appreciation of the criteria regulating Constantius' choice.

There is a fair amount of abstraction in all of this. As Tougher argues, it is very possible – and plausible – that the idea of redeeming Julian after Gallus' disgrace had first come to Constantius at a moment when the pressure of the Germanic tribes against Gaul and of the Persians on the eastern border prompted him to confront the need to find a new co-ruler.

---

[29] Cf., e.g., Plut. *Mor.* 49f–74e (*On How to Tell a Flatterer from a Friend*) or Dio's long digression on friendship as the best external possession of the sovereign at Dio Chrys. *Or.* 3.12–28 (on which see Desideri [1978] 302–3; Whitmarsh [2001] 183–215; Vagnone [2012]). On flattery, see further Konstan (1996); Pownell (2020) 260.

[30] Julian also presents Eusebia as primarily responsible for the continuation of his philosophical training through her decision to send him to study in Athens (*Eus.* 118c) and records that, following his elevation to the throne, she gave him books 'on philosophy and history, and of many of the orators and poets' (*Eus.* 123d–24a).

Constantius would have employed Eusebia as a mediator and peacemaker, roles traditionally assigned to the female members of the imperial household, to protect his reputation while family policy was being redrawn.[31] If this is the case, the hypothesis of Julian's instrumental use of the character of Eusebia in the *Speech* is even more poignant. Just as Constantius communicated with Julian through Eusebia, so too Julian's *Speech* addresses Eusebia to talk to Constantius. Through literature, the empress is sealed in her role as mediator. In the process, Julian also seizes the opportunity to portray the three of them as a unity of wisdom, an intellectual family thriving under the protection of the Augustus.

The Philosopher Themistius for Constantius, Philosopher

A question has been lingering: why is Julian's encomiastic production so concerned with presenting his philosophy as the mirror of Constantius' wisdom? Two mutually exclusive answers are available. Julian's panegyrics might be giving voice to a solipsistic fixation: philosophy was the only topic the philosopher-turned-Caesar felt confident to address. Alternatively, Julian knew that Constantius would have appreciated the celebration of his own wisdom. On this line of argument, Julian the panegyrist was engaging dialectically with the Augustus' expectations. The validity of the second hypothesis is shown by the place of Julian's pieces in the larger context of Constantius' propaganda.

Julian's reputation as a scholar preceded him, as Themistius proves. In his *Speech of Thanks* to Constantius (*Or.* 2), delivered in the senate of Constantinople at the end of 355 – the year of Julian's appointment as Caesar – Themistius praises the Augustus for enthroning a philosopher.[32] Chapter 1 considered this remark as part of Themistius' strategy to assert his intellectual authority in the eyes of the senior emperor but also as a way of showing respect to Julian, to whom, around the same time, he sent the missive of congratulations that would prompt Julian's response in the *Letter to Themistius*. Themistius' *Speech of Thanks* epitomises a cultural process at work throughout the history of imperial Rome: the elites' use of patronage as a means to cultural authority, achieved by capitalising on the intellectual prestige of their protégées.[33] Themistius argues eloquently that, through the joint appointment of Themistius as senator and Julian as emperor, Constantius had proven himself a true lover of wisdom. But

---

[31] Tougher (1998b).   [32] Them. *Or.* 2.40a.
[33] Cf. Goldhill (2002) 63–93; Eshleman (2012) 79; Hafner (2017).

the *Speech* does not restrict itself to claiming that the Augustus is a friend of philosophers; it also constructs Constantius as philosopher. Drawing on the argument of the superiority of action over contemplation that Julian would challenge in the *Letter to Themistius*,[34] Themistius writes:

> The supremely wise Plato argues almost everywhere that the true king and the philosopher advance together (ξύνδρομα πορεύεσθαι) because both strive towards the same model (τὸ αὐτὸ παράδειγμα). But one limits himself to reasoning and knowledge (τῷ μὲν ἄχρι λόγου καὶ ἐπιστήμης), whereas the other resorts to concrete action (τῷ δὲ ἄχρι τοῦ πράγματος καὶ τοῦ ἔργου). The former must limit himself to knowing the king of the universe, whereas the latter imitates him (τὸν μὲν γὰρ τοῦδε τοῦ ξύμπαντος βασιλέα ὁ μὲν ἐπίσταται μόνον, ὁ δὲ καὶ μιμεῖται); and action always generates more resemblance than knowledge (ὁμοιότερον δὲ ἀεὶ τοῦ γιγνώσκοντος τὸ ἐργαζόμενον).[35]

If the goal of philosophers is to assimilate themselves to the divine, it follows that the man endowed with the greatest agency can actively imitate (μιμεῖται) God in a way precluded to the contemplative man.[36] He is therefore a better philosopher than philosophers are.

Themistius' *Speech of Thanks* is a response that addresses a text Constantius had previously composed for Themistius' appointment to the Constantinopolitan senate. In his *Address to the Senate*, Constantius places great emphasis on the importance of philosophy in politics, arguing that, through the *adlectio* of Themistius, philosophy was being honoured in its social and civic function.[37] Intriguingly, the argument of Themistius' *Speech of Thanks* draws precisely on Constantius' words in the *Address* to round off his celebration of the emperor as a philosopher. Themistius argues that, in order to represent the unworthy Themistius as worthy of praise, Constantius resorted to a generous stratagem: he modelled his portrait of Themistius upon himself, finding in his philosophical nature the qualities he celebrates in the newly appointed senator (*Or.* 2.29c–30a). But Constantius' enlightened, philanthropic rule, Themistius argues, proves that the sovereign was truly praising himself rather than his senator (2.31a–32d). In particular, Constantius has also shown his capacity to entrust his actions 'to the government of reason'

---

[34] Them. 263c–66b. [35] Them. *Or.* 2.34b–c.
[36] See also Them. *Or.* 2.31b–c, where Aristotle is summoned to argue that philosophy coincides with the practice of virtue.
[37] Constantius, *Dem.* 20a–23d. On his authorship, see Van Hoof (2013). Themistius references Constantius' piece at *Or.* 2.26bc, 28c–30a.

(τῇ τοῦ λόγου ἡγεμονίᾳ, 2.36a) by appointing as second-in-command a 'next-in-virtue', Julian (2.40a).

Intriguingly, Themistius further corroborates his portrait of Constantius by arguing that Constantius' philosophical nature is proven by his success. 'It is a sign of the philosopher', he writes, 'that he is loved by God and his deeds are guided from above'.[38] This formulation should not be dismissed as hyperbolic or eccentric. Its conciseness partly obscures the reasoning behind it, but the statement is of fundamental importance. Themistius is hinting at an ideal that, Chapter 3 argues, had been mobilised by Constantinian propaganda to promote the recognition of Constantine as a (Christian) philosopher-ruler: victory and longevity mark the ruler as a philosopher because they prove that he acts according to the divine will. This means that his mind has gained insight into God's intellect.

The joint claims that the ruler is shown a true philosopher by his victories, and that his agency, being a *mimesis* of the divine, is the highest expression of philosophy, explain how Themistius' *Speech of Thanks* can venture to juxtapose Constantius with Plato and claim the superiority of the former over the latter. History is summoned as the arbiter of this comparison: Plato was unable to convince the tyrant Dionysius of Syracuse to become a philosopher, but Constantius' words had been enough for Vetranio to renounce power (*Or.* 2.37d–38a). According to Themistius, Vetranio had personally 'experienced what it means to be conquered by the speech of a true philosopher'.[39]

Themistius' hyperbolic characterisation of Constantius as philosopher in the *Speech of Thanks* certainly served a contextual function: his over-the-top reciprocation of Constantius' own praise of Themistius sent the emperor's words, aggrandised, back to the sender. It should be noted, however, that Themistius' first address to Constantius – *Or.* 1, delivered in either 347 or 350[40] – already celebrated the emperor as an intellectual. Following an opening that asserts Themistius' distance, as a philosopher, from rhetoricians and flatterers (*Or.* 1.1a–2b), the oration takes a hybrid shape between an encomium and an offer of philosophical advice on sovereignty. Dio of Prusa's orations *On Kingship* are its model.[41] The oration is unconcerned with the Augustus' deeds (except those that manifest his benevolence, such as his abolition of the death penalty).[42] Instead,

---

[38] Them. *Or.* 2.38b–c (ἐστὶ φιλοσόφου ἀνδρὸς σημεῖον, εἰ θεοφιλής τε εἴη καὶ τὰ πράγματα ἄνωθεν αὐτῷ κυβερνῷτο).
[39] Them. *Or.* 2.38a (ὁπόσον δέ ἐστιν ὑπ' ἀληθινοῦ φιλοσόφου λόγῳ ἁλῶναι ᾔσθετο).
[40] For the date, see Heather and Moncur (2001) 69–70, preferring 347; Van Hoof (2013) 389 n. 11.
[41] Ross (2018) 191; Alvino (2019) 6.   [42] Them. *Or.* 1.14b–16a.

it seeks to bring into focus (through a strategy that Julian's *First Panegyric* perhaps seeks to emulate) Themistius' own philosophical identity, which explains and legitimises his focus on Constantius' spiritual qualities.[43] Intriguingly, Themistius counts philanthropy among these qualities. Not one of the traditional philosophical virtues, philanthropy is nevertheless presented here as a philosophical trait because it enables the emperor's soul to become an image of God through his love for his subjects:

> I laugh when I call to mind one of the rulers of the past[44] because he … compelled men to dedicate temples and statues to him as to a god, but in no way whatsoever chose to love (φιλεῖν) men as God does…. Whoever seeks not His honours but His virtue is he who truly imitates God…. Hence it is natural that a king who is dear to God (θεοφιλὴς βασιλεὺς) is one who loves mankind (φιλάνθρωπος): mutual friends are those who take delight in the same things (φίλοι γὰρ ἀλλήλων οἱ τὰ αὐτὰ ἀγαπῶντες) …. This is what it is to admire Him, this the great hymn, this the true reward, this a fitting dedication for a king: to fashion not bronze, silver or gold, but his own soul into an image of God (τὴν αὑτοῦ ψυχὴν εἰκόνα θεοῦ κατασκευάσθαι).[45]

Here as well, the philanthropic emperor is favourably contrasted with the philosopher, who has the same desire to imitate God but 'is defective (χωλεύειν) because he lacks power' (9b). It would seem that Themistius' *Or.* 1 was already trying to pitch the active against the contemplative life to the emperor's advantage: through his leadership, Constantius is more philosophical than any philosopher could ever be.

The other two surviving Themistian orations addressing Constantius, *Or.* 4 and 3, delivered in Constantinople in January 357, and in Rome in the May of the same year, respectively, continue to build on the theme of philosophical kingship. Both speeches have a primarily urban focus: *Or.* 4 celebrates Constantius' love for Constantinople, whereas *Or.* 3 is especially concerned with the relationship between Constantinople and Rome. Yet both texts unquestionably strive to convey the interrelated points that Constantius is a philosopher-ruler and that it takes a philosopher – Themistius – to acknowledge him as such.[46]

---

[43] On the centrality of Themistius' ethos in the piece, see Van Hoof (2013) 392. See also Vanderspoel (1995) 73–83.
[44] Caligula according to Maisano (1995) 130; Domitian according to Heather and Moncur (2001) 86 n. 116.
[45] Them. *Or.* 1.8d–9b.
[46] At *Or.* 3.44c, Themistius explicitly states that Constantinople chose a philosopher (Themistius himself) to honour the philosopher-ruler.

The theme of the emperor's care for the city sets the agenda for both texts. *Or.* 4 opens with a celebration of the extraordinary inner beauty of Constantius (51c–d), accessible only to those who have 'purified their gaze with the cure of philosophy' (52a). This beauty is reflected in the eastern capital, mirror (κάτοπτρον, 52a) of the emperor's soul. The emperor honours philosophy through the joint effort of valorising Constantinople and obtaining bloodless victories. Vetranio is mentioned again as having been 'subjugated by reason' (ὑπὸ λόγου ἠνδραποδίσθη, 56b). Among Constantius' actions on behalf of the city, the 'best and most beloved by God' (59c), is the construction of a library with a *scriptorium* for the transcription of ancient manuscripts, an act that will revive the great authors from the past, in particular Plato and Aristotle (60a). The speech closes with the argument that Constantius fulfils Plato's ideal of the perfect ruler (62d). The shorter *Or.* 3 likewise relies on the themes of Constantius' promotion of culture (45b) and pursuit of philosophy (φιλοσοφίαν μεταδιώκεις, 45b) and alludes to Vetranio's demise as achieved through philosophy (45b). Plato's description of the ideal ruler is again presented as 'sketching a portrait of Constantius' and his 'divine mind' (θεία κεφαλή, 46b).

The consistency between the pieces is striking. Themistius must have pressed lines approved by Constantius: we learn from Themistius himself that Constantius liked his words. *Or.* 4 describes Constantius' joy at receiving what can be identified as Themistius' *Speech of Thanks*, 'the crown woven with flowers plucked from the meadows of Plato and Aristotle' (54b). The piece also tells us that Constantius rewarded Themistius' *Speech* with the dedication of a bronze statue (54b–c).[47] Themistius' prestige grew quickly and steadily under Constantius' rule: he was appointed leader of the embassy on behalf of the Constantinopolitan senate for the celebration of Constantius' *Vicennalia* in Rome (which provided the occasion for the delivery of *Or.* 3).[48] He rose to become the equivalent of a *princeps senatus* and was tasked with travelling across the *pars Orientis* to appoint senators in 358/359.[49] A law of 3 May 361 declares that ten senators must be present during the election of praetors by senatorial decree, including Themistius, 'whose

---

[47] On the statue, see Vanderspoel (1995) 96; Heather and Moncour (2001) 44.
[48] On Themistius' testimony regarding his embassies for Constantinople, see also *Or.* 17.214b; 31.352c–d; 34.29.
[49] Henck (2001) 176; Elm (2012) 82; Moser (2018) 265. Cf. Themistius' retrospective description of his activities for the Senate in *Or.* 34.13.

learning enhances his rank' (*cuius auget scientia dignitatem*).⁵⁰ We also know from Libanius that Constantius honoured Themistius by allowing him to dine with him.⁵¹

Constantius the Wise: Urbanistic Efforts and the Concern with Doctrine

Constantius' reputation among his contemporaries seemingly stands in the way of assessing him as an aspiring philosopher-ruler. Not all those writing about Constantius emphasised his intellectual profile; in fact, several fourth-century sources offer a bleak portrayal of Constantine's son as an obtuse ruler and an enemy of culture. Following Constantius' death, Libanius criticised the deficiency of his education, blaming Constantius for excluding philosophers and orators from the court and replacing them with eunuchs, who would have then 'introduced those pale men (ὠχρούς), the enemies of the gods, who frequent the tombs (τοὺς περὶ τοὺς τάφους)' – that is, the monks.⁵² In sketching an assessment of Constantius' rule in his obituary notice, Ammianus mentions the emperor's 'dullness of mind' (*ingenium obtunsum*).⁵³ The consul Claudius Mamertinus in 362 describes Constantius' court as a corrupt place where ignorance and sycophancy thrived and wealth alone mattered; in his words, it was Julian who first restored the value of education.⁵⁴ Constantius is portrayed as a tyrant in the invectives of bishops Hilary of Poitiers, Athanasius of Alexandria, and Lucifer of Cagliari, whose writings blend biblical and historical paradigms to capture Constantius' immorality and – what was for them the greatest cause of concern – his Arian sympathies.⁵⁵

But all these authors had one thing in common: a motive to attack Constantius and his memory. Athanasius, Hilary, and Lucifer were Nicene bishops who opposed Constantius' religious policy; Libanius, Ammianus, and Mamertinus were supporters of Julian writing after Julian's fallout with Constantius. As a consequence, scholars have recently been

---

⁵⁰ *C.Th.* 6.4.12 (transl. Pharr).
⁵¹ Libanius *ep.* 66.2 Foerster (= 52.2 Norman). See also Themistius, *Or.* 31.353a. Cf. Henck (2001) 176.
⁵² Lib. *Or.* 62.10.   ⁵³ Amm. Marc. 21.16.4.
⁵⁴ *Pan. Lat.* III (11) 19.3–20.4; vf. also 23.4–5. On Julian as the restorer of culture and religion, cf. Lib. *Or.* 18.157–58. Julian's apologetic *Letter to the Athenians* produces a portrait of Constantius as a ruthless, greedy tyrant (*Ath.* 270c–71b, 272d–73b).
⁵⁵ Flower (2013).

reassessing his imperial profile, illustrating how hostile sources obscured crucial traits of his rule and self-image.[56]

Constantius' urban commitment, considered above, for example, which arguably led to a transformation of Constantinople, betrays a cultural agenda.[57] In addition to the foundation of the library with a *scriptorium*, which Themistius celebrates,[58] it appears that special imperial arrangements were put in place to regulate the appointment of public teachers in the eastern capital, whose salary seems to have come from imperial rather than municipal funds.[59] Bishop Gregory of Nazianzus argues that in a few years the city managed to establish itself as a centre of philosophy.[60] Writing in 359, the rhetorician Himerius claims that Constantinople brims with cultural activities and succeeds in attracting intellectuals from everywhere – he himself included.[61]

Addressing Libanius' and Mamertinus' criticism of Constantius' policy of excluding intellectuals from the court, modern scholarship has observed that prosopographical studies show that cultural credentials were an important prerequisite for social and political advancement in Constantius' court.[62] A law jointly issued by Constantius and Julian concerning the appointment of decurials – the clerical officers working for the imperial administration – takes care of underscoring that 'no person shall obtain a

---

[56] Klein (1977); Seiler (1998); Whitby (1999); Henck (2001), (2002); Barceló (2004); Elm (2012); Van Hoof (2013); Moser (2018); Baker-Brian and Tougher (2020); Tougher (2020a); Greenwood (2021) 3.

[57] Henck (2002); Bassett (2004); Isele (2010) 15–79; Moser (2018) 259–76. The reconstruction of Constantius' urban commitment is however complicated by the lack of archaeological evidence and our exclusive reliance on literary sources. Them. *Or.* 4 reports the construction of a colonnade and the rich decorations embellishing the imperial agora (58c), and mentions a theatre with arcade, the hippodrome (60d), and improvements in the harbour facilities (60d; cf. Himer. *Or.* 62.3). Constantius was also responsible for initiating construction of the so-called Senate House and for importing antiquities in the cities, including ancient books (cf. Them. *Or.* 4.59d–61b). He also promoted Christian architecture, from the modification of Constantine's mausoleum to the transformation of a Constantinian audience hall into the church that would later be known as *Hagia Sophia*. (For a revised chronology of the church as begun in 350 or 351 and dedicated in 360, see Bardill [2004] 54–55.) It would be intriguing to explain the dedication of the church to the Holy Wisdom of God in the light of Constantius' intellectual concerns, but there is no evidence to support the claim (Downey [1959] 40–41, Cameron [1965]). According to Socrates, *HE* II 16.16, in Constantius' times the building was simply known as the Great Church (ἡ μεγάλη ἐκκλεσία). Bardill links the name *Hagia Sophia* to Aelia Pulcheria's vow of virginity in 414, following the rebuilding of the church.

[58] Them. *Or.* 4.59d–60c.

[59] Kaster (1983) 39–44; Schlange-Schöningen (1995) 93–96; Moser (2018) 135–36.

[60] Greg. Naz. *Or.* 43.14.1.

[61] Himer. *Or.* 62.7 Penella (2007). On the dating of the piece, see Penella (2007) 38–39.

[62] Brown (1992) 38. Henck (2001) 180–81 lists figures in Constantius' entourage who were accomplished in literary studies. On the presence of rhetoricians in Constantinople during his rule, see further Barceló (2004) 29; Van Hoof (2013) 397; Moser (2018) 265.

post of the first rank unless it shall be proved that he excels in long practice of liberal studies and that he is so polished in literary matters that words flow faultlessly from his pen'.[63] It might be objected that education would be especially important for this type of appointment; at the same time, it should be underscored how the imperial formulation, with its emphasis, seemingly parades the fact that it is setting a high cultural demand. Themistius' career alone disproves Libanius' accusation that monks replaced philosophers in the court. Finally, an argument against the emperor's hostility towards culture comes from the way Constantius himself spoke of his commitment to philosophy.

I considered above how Constantius' *Address to the Senate* explains to the senators that the *adlectio* of the great Themistius honoured philosophy and its synergy with politics. Van Hoof has shown the self-reflective implications of Constantius' argument.[64] The *Address* is pervaded by the emperor's effort to present himself as dominating two worlds intellectually: he lectures about philosophy and its ethical and social function to senators, but he also projects himself as the supreme political agent who can teach philosophers how to participate in civic life. His *Address* – and the implicit self-portrayal that emerges from it – ends in an eloquent transition from praise of Themistius to praise of culture *tout court*. Constantius encourages the honouring of rhetoric (οἱ λόγοι), wisdom, and education, and he lays particular emphasis on philosophy as 'the noblest of sciences (ἡ ἀρίστη τῶν ἐπιστημῶν)', wishing to see it 'shine forth from everywhere and among all men (πανταχόθεν καὶ ἐν πᾶσιν ἐκλαμπάνειν, *Dem.* 23c)'.

Constantius' self-advertisement as a teacher of philosophy certainly operated on the same propagandistic level that moved, to opposite ends, the emperor's detractors.[65] This is obliquely confirmed by the ability of some ex-supporters of Constantius – Julian the panegyrist, Libanius, and Athanasius – to completely reverse their assessment of the emperor after falling out with him or in the wake of his death. Their writings point to a switch from celebrating Constantius as a philosopher and patron of philosophers to characterising him as an ignorant and irrational tyrant.[66] At the same time, we should ask if stopping at an assessment of

---

[63] *C.Th.* 14.1.1, transl. Pharr (1953). See Henck (2001) 178; Van Hoof (2013) 388. The dating of the law was emended from 357 to 360 due to Constantius' location at the time (Long [1996] 189).

[64] Van Hoof (2013).

[65] Cf. Van Hoof (2013) 389, underscoring that both sides were pressing a rhetorical agenda.

[66] See, e.g., Libanius' praise of Constantius (and his brother Constans) for the clever use of words and a good education (Lib. *Or.* 59.33–34). Libanius had presumably been instructed about how to praise the sovereign (Whitby [1999] 74; Karla [2020] 69).

Constantius' self-image as rhetorical and performative prevents us from appreciating two things. The first is Constantius' acute awareness of the political utility of displays of intellectual authority. His efforts to control his public image further suggest that he was actively concerned with this issue: his patronage of Themistius arguably represents the concluding act in a prolonged quest for a permanent imperial panegyrist that saw him try – unsuccessfully – to secure Libanius' services.[67] Second, and crucially, Constantius' philosophical self-projection seems especially performative if we focus on isolated efforts and episodes, such as his patronage of Themistius (and Julian), occasional rhetorical statements, urban planning, and an interest in libraries. But these are all parts of a more complex and cohesive picture, which has at its heart Constantius' life-long commitment to the Christianisation of the Roman state and neighbouring regions.

Divisive Wisdom: Supporters and Detractors of Constantius' (Christian) Philosophy

The rules for intellectual competition that shaped Rome's political scene demanded that efforts to damage someone's reputation be accompanied by a depiction of him as ignorant, obtuse, and an enemy of learning.[68] I am convinced, however, that the reduction of these accusations to a rhetorical trope obscures the fundamental reason that led Julian's supporters to dismiss Constantius' cultural ambitions. Libanius' above-mentioned accusation that monks ('those pale men'... 'who frequent the tombs') had replaced philosophers at Constantius' court is a powerful indication of how the rhetorician from Antioch perceived – and wanted his readers to perceive – the central position Christianity occupied in Constantius' understanding of culture.[69] Ammianus' obituary notice obliquely confirms this. The historian juxtaposes his criticism of Constantius' 'dullness of mind' with a description of how he strove to engage with an ascetic lifestyle: he exercised moderation in eating and drinking (even abstaining from eating fruit, arguably because of its sweetness),[70] slept only when

---

[67] Control of public image: Whitby (1999) 73. Attempt at patronise Libanius: Henck (2001) 177. Libanius reports that in 349, shortly after delivering his panegyric for Constans and Constantius (*Or.* 59), he was compelled by an imperial letter to move to Constantinople (Lib. *Or.* 1.74; cf. also 2.17). In order to be able to return to his city, Antioch, he had to repeatedly petition the Caesar Gallus until this was finally authorized in 354. On the imperial attempts to have him back in Constantinople, see Wintjes (2005) 99–115; Van Hoof (2013) 398 n. 53.
[68] See Introduction, p. 2–3.   [69] Lib. *Or.* 62.10.
[70] Rohrbacher (2005) reads abstinence from fruit as a Manichaean gesture, but Jerome describes Hilarion's same habit in a way that clearly qualifies it as an ascetic practice ('until the sixth-third year

time and circumstance allowed, and led an extraordinarily chaste life.⁷¹ These behaviours suggest that Constantius patterned his life to signal a concern for spiritual matters; Julian himself would later engage in the same practices.⁷² In the same obituary notice, Ammianus documents Constantius' intellectual concerns. He first diagnoses obtusity from the fact that Constantius, in his own words, 'made great pretension to learning' (*doctrinarum diligens affectator*) but failed to achieve anything remarkable in rhetoric and poetry.⁷³ Then he presents as another expression of Constantius' sterile engagement with theoretical matters his approach to the creed. The emperor is described as 'obscuring by a dotard's superstition (*anili superstitione confundens*) the plain and simple religion of the Christians (*Christianam religionem absolutam et simplicem*)'; Ammianus further argues that Constantius, 'by subtle and involved discussions, rather than by seeking agreement, aroused many controversies (*excitavit discidia plurima*)'.⁷⁴ The historian seems therefore to misunderstand – or misrepresent – the emperor's ambition to project his piety as an intellectual concern.

The management of doctrine appears to have been a constant component of Constantius' rule. Beginning with the defeat of the usurper Magnentius and the reconquest of the West, he summoned various councils in an effort to seal his control over the re-unified empire through the establishment of a centralised orthodoxy.⁷⁵ In a pivotal year, 359, he set out to enforce the Homoean creed of Sirmium upon western and eastern bishops gathered at Ariminum and Seleucia, respectively. This extraordinary imperial intervention had no precedents and was met with anxiety by religious authorities, who saw it as an unacceptable show of force.⁷⁶ Constantius banished Christians whose views he considered heretical and over time antagonised the pro-Nicene bishops who would later count among his harshest critics – Hilary of Poitiers, Athanasius of Alexandria, and Lucifer of Cagliari. In the 350s, these bishops targeted

---

of his life he continued at this level of abstinence, tasting neither fruit nor beans nor anything else', Jer. *Vit. S. Hilar.* 11, transl. White).

⁷¹ Amm. Marc. 21.16.5–7 (see also 16.10.10–11).
⁷² On Julian's rigorous lifestyle, see, e.g., *Pan. Lat.* (Mamertinus) III (11) 14.3; Amm. Marc. 16.5.1–5.
⁷³ Amm. Marc. 21.16.4, transl. Rolfe.   ⁷⁴ Amm. Marc. 21.16.18.
⁷⁵ Antioch (341); Serdica (343); Sirmium (351); Milan (355); Seleucia and Ariminum (359); Constantinople (360).
⁷⁶ See Chapter 5, p. 231–2.

Constantius with invective linking him to biblical and historical accounts of tyrants and religious persecutors, including the Tetrarchs.[77]

At the same time – and this is a key paradox in the interaction between emperors and bishops in late antiquity, to which I return in a later chapter[78] – bishops who did not want to be controlled by Constantius nevertheless continued to reinforce his authority on ecclesiastical matters. They engaged in correspondence with him, sanctioning his agency and responsibility in the management of the life of the church. Like his father before him, Constantius exploited epistolography to control the episcopal network, asserting his authority over the rise and fall of bishops, as when he levelled open attacks on Athanasius of Alexandria and Liberius, the bishop of Rome.[79] Letters also served him as a platform to advertise his expertise in religious matters. This is effectively captured by a text composed in 351 by Cyril, the new bishop of Jerusalem.[80] His *Letter to Constantius* ostensibly seeks to please the emperor: Cyril was in a difficult situation following the doctrinal controversies that had surrounded his appointment to the bishopric and was trying to gain the emperor's favour.[81] Intriguingly, he does so by reporting on the vision of a shining cross in the sky above Jerusalem and connecting this description to scriptural interpretation: Cyril explains the vision in the light of the apocalyptic prophecy of the 'sign of the Son of Man' in the Gospel of Matthew.[82] This hermeneutical digression was once read by scholars as pointing to Cyril's engagement with diverse audiences: the ruler who receives the announcement of the vision and the theologians who are interested in exegesis. As Gassman shows, however, it is precisely Constantius who is being here addressed as interpreter.[83] Cyril expects him to engage with and appreciate his reading of the omen as a joint demonstration of the historical necessity of Christianity and of God's love for Constantius' rule. Constantius is further presented as someone who possesses full interpretive control of the holy writings. His textual

---

[77] Flower (2013) 78–126. On the relationship between Constantius and Athanasius, see also Barnes (1993).
[78] See Chapter 5.   [79] Baker-Brian (2020).
[80] Chantraine (1993–94) dated the vision to May 351. On other late antique sources reporting it, see Gassman (2016) 120 nn. 2–4. It has been suggested that what Cyril saw might have been a solar halo (similar to what Weiss (2003) argues in relationship to Constantine's more famous vision of the celestial cross near Rome). I remain sceptical that natural phenomena can be used to support ancient reports of visions and omens (cf. Barbero (2016) 41–43, 142–43): the Roman and late-Roman world expected pivotal historical moments to be accompanied by divine signs (cf. Potter [1994]), as obliquely confirmed also by the accumulation of anecdotes concerning divine visions that accompanies Constantine's rise to power.
[81] Yarnold (2000) 4–6, 68; Gassman (2016) 122.   [82] Mt. 24.30.   [83] Gassman (2016).

knowledge is celebrated in the introductory section of the letter, where Cyril declares:

> Our purpose is to bring with all speed to your Piety's (εὐσεβείας) attention the display of divine energy that took place in the sky over Jerusalem during your reign so favoured by God. I do not presume to imagine that I am leading you from ignorance (ἄγνοιαν) to divine knowledge (θεογνωσίαν): your piety already equips you to instruct others (φθάνεις γὰρ καὶ ἑτέρους διδάσκων δι' ὧν εὐσεβεῖς). My hope is rather that you may be confirmed (βεβαιωθῇς) in the knowledge you already possess (ἅπερ ᾔδεις).[84]

Cyril congratulates Constantius on his proficiency in doctrine, which puts him in the position of instructing others, and states that the announcement of the vision of the cross will only add knowledge to the 'excellent foundation of the pre-existing faith' of the sovereign.[85] Later in the text, Cyril stresses that he is inviting the emperor to consider texts (the Gospels, and specifically Matthew) he already reads 'habitually' (συνήθως).[86] His words betray an awareness that Constantius appreciated not only a scriptural and eschatological framing of his rule but also being invited to assess the validity of such framing as a reader and teacher of doctrine. It's intriguing to consider further that, when trying to regain Constantius' favour, Bishop Athanasius of Alexandria would choose to praise him specifically as a 'lover of learning' (*philologos*) – just as Themistius had done in his *Or.* 4.[87]

Constantius' theological commitment did not obliterate *paideia*-related commitments. The two aspects coexisted, and this is an essential point, since it helps us identify a consistent cultural project: Constantius' intellectual image was informed in equal measure by his acts of patronage of traditional intellectuals and by his active participation in making Christian doctrine.[88] It was arguably this synergy that troubled critics like Julian, Ammianus, Libanius, and Mamertinus. Constantius' twofold commitment appears to instantiate the principle that Christianity can ultimately

---

[84] Cyril, *Ep. Const.* 2, transl. Yarnold.
[85] Cyril, *ep. Const.* 5 (ἀγαθῷ θεμελίῳ τῆς παρὰ σοὶ προϋπαρχούσης πίστεως).
[86] Cyril, *ep. Const.* 6.
[87] Athanasius, *Apol. Ad Const.* 18; Them. *Or.* 4.54a. See Henck (2001) 173.
[88] It should be further noted that, throughout his rule, Constantius presented himself as a devout Christian who nevertheless remained committed to preserving Roman traditions. He continued to support the traditional cults financially, although ruling against sacrifice and divination, and sought to avoid religious conflict (for instance, when, during his visit to Rome for the *Vicennalia*, he performed his duties as *pontifex maximus*: Symmachus, *Rel.* 3.8). As Elm (2012) 121–22, argues, Constantius' policy betrays a concern with how to combine 'the old and the new' in a conservative society.

coexist with Greco-Roman culture because it contains and dominates it, having the power to establish what is valuable and what is not in the space of *paideia*. As Chapter 1 argued, this claim drove the agenda of the encyclopaedic efforts of Lactantius in the West and Eusebius in the West, both of whom strove to assert Christianity's (interpretive) control of the classical past through a display of mastery of its literature and traditions.[89]

Themistius' acquisition of extraordinary prominence at court, his mobilisation as a 'talismanic' figure (thus Heather)[90] for Constantius' power, is invested in this light with additional significance. Themistius, who never disguised his allegiance to the Greco-Roman gods, is interpreted by scholars as a figure who served as a catalyst for eastern landowning elites who had not yet converted but were reassured by his presence in the imperial court.[91] It should also be considered, however, how Themistius fulfilled, somewhat obliquely, a project of cultural Christianisation. He was distant from the normative agenda of contemporary intellectuals on both sides of the religious spectrum, who demanded that one's religious allegiance be put on display in every part of life.[92] Already under Constantius, Themistius used a non-specific notion of *eusebeia*, piety (even paying homage to Eusebius' theology of power),[93] to emphasise that he could align with the Christian emperor on fundamental ethical, political, and social issues. After Julian's demise, he made a speech approving of the policy of religious tolerance of the new emperor, Jovian, in which he also attacked Julian's policy on the same matter.[94] Themistius thus was not – and did not wish to be – a spokesperson for the Eusebian claim that Christianity controlled *paideia*. At the same time, it was inevitable that such religious adaptability, once subsumed under Constantius' patronage, would translate in practical terms into a real-life *exemplum* of how Christianity could contain all obliging wisdom. It might be worth observing that Christians greatly enjoyed Themistius' prose: Gregory of

---

[89] P. 65–70.   [90] Heather (1998) 137–38; Heather and Moncur (2001) 23–24.
[91] Heather (1998); Heather and Moncur (2001).
[92] On the confrontation between normativism and pragmatism in fourth-century theology, see especially Sandwell (2007) 3–33.
[93] Cameron (1991) 131–33. Themistius' celebration of Constantius' philanthropy (see, e.g., Them. *Or.* 1.8b–c) can be seen in this light as one of his strategies to seek alignment: the love for his subjects the renders the emperor similar to God voiced the Neoplatonic desire to assimilate oneself to divinity but could also be appreciated by Christians (cf. Van Hoof [2013] 389). Themistius' use of the verb ἀγαπάω in this context (*Or.* 1.9a; 10a–c) also seems to be seeking a connection with Christian vocabulary. See also Eusebius' celebration of Constantine's philanthropy at *VC* 1.43.1–2 (cf. Alvino [2019] 113).
[94] Chapter 5, p. 249–50.

Nazianzus calls him a 'king of words'.⁹⁵ Julian seems not to have liked him as much.⁹⁶

In Chapter 3, I return to Constantius' cultural project and consider its interaction with the later stage of the propaganda of his father Constantine – of which Constantius' policy qualifies, I suggest, as reception. But before addressing the issue of whether and to what extent Constantius' self-image finds a place in a larger dynastic effort, I want to consider another type of evidence that corroborates my reading of Constantius' ambition to project himself as an intellectual ruler, especially by virtue of his religious allegiance. This lies in the evolution of Julian's early rhetoric. As Julian progressed in his role as Caesar, gaining seniority and confidence, he began to find ways to challenge Constantius' cultural policy by relying on its vocabulary and expectations. The result was a new exploration of Constantius' self-image but this time to Julian's advantage and at Constantius' expense.

Julian the Panegyrist, Again: The Second Panegyric to Constantius II

Julian's early panegyrics, as argued above, derive their meaning from Constantius' propaganda. Between the *First Panegyric* and the *Speech of Thanks* for Eusebia, Julian offers himself as a mirror of Constantius in celebration of the philosopher-ruler who protects and promotes philosophers. But we observe a marked shift in rhetoric between these two pieces and the texts, dating later in Julian's Caesarship, which turn his image as a court philosopher from an instrument of support into a threat. I aim to show that this shift had two aims. On the one hand, it constructed Julian's authority through literature, by subverting his own previous self-narrative as Constantius' subordinate. On the other hand, this subversion was accompanied by Julian's first attempt to destabilise the Constantinian assumption that Greek philosophy and culture were contained in Christian doctrine.

Julian's *Second Panegyric to Constantius II* illustrates both points. The piece is of uncertain date; most hypotheses put it between 358 and 359.⁹⁷

---

⁹⁵ Greg. Naz. *Ep.* 24 (βασιλεύς ... τῶν λόγων). See Elm (2012) 225–28. ⁹⁶ See Chapter 1.
⁹⁷ The hypothesis of composition around summer 358 is favoured by Bidez (1932) 172; De Vita (2011) 26; (2022) cxxxi; Drake (2012b) 39; Pagliara (2015) 98–101; Bleckmann (2020) 110; and Greenwood (2021) 25. The mention of the peace with the Persians at *II Pan.* 66d–67a has been read as indicating composition before spring 359, when hostilities resumed. Curta (1995) 196, who believes that the confrontational nature of the text demands a later date, dates it to summer 359,

What is essential is that it was written after the summer of 357, when Julian's army defeated the Alamanni in a celebrated victory at Argentoratum (modern day Strasbourg). From this moment onwards, Julian's military ascent was relentless. His heightened status is perceptible in the *Second Panegyric*, a text that seeks to translate into literature the authority the Caesar has acquired on the battlefield. The piece, incidentally, seems to open precisely with a polemical allusion to Argentoratum – a reference to Achilles' anger (49c), explained as the outcome of Agamemnon's appropriation of Achilles' γέρας – his prize of valour (50a) – in *Iliad* 1.[98] We know from both Ammianus and Julian that Constantius celebrated the victory as his own success. That the Augustus did so at the expense of the Caesar seems to have been standard procedure,[99] but both Ammianus and Julian resented it.[100] The *Second Panegyric* describes as Achilles as refraining from retaliating against Agamemnon. Julian's Achilles rather chooses to sit down and sings:

> Achilles, as the poet tells us, when his wrath was kindled (ἐμήνισε) and he quarrelled with the king, let fall from his hands spear and shield; then he strung his harp and lyre and sang and chanted the deeds of the demi-gods, making this the pastime of his idle hours, and in this he chose wisely (εὖ μάλα ἐμφρόνως τοῦτο διανοηθέντα). For to fall out with the king and affront him was excessively rash and violent (λίαν αὔθαδες καὶ ἄγριον). (*II Pan.* 49c–d)

No explicit parallel is drawn here between Julian and Achilles (or between Constantius and Agamemnon). Julian's next remark, however, that the image of the quarrelling Agamemnon enables him to exalt by contrast the magnanimity of the senior emperor, inevitably directs attention to the oblique significance of his words. Praise by contrast is certainly not the most appropriate way to open a panegyric, especially if it creates an interplay with arguably well-known critical events.[101] Julian lures his

---

arguing that Julian might have been unaware that the war with the Persians had resumed (cf. similarly Omissi [2018] 170 n. 91).

[98] On Briseis as Achilles' *geras*, see *Il.* 1.13 56, 138, 185, 507.
[99] Browning (1975) 88; Tougher (2007) 40.
[100] Cf. Amm. Marc. 16.12.70 (arguing that, in his public records, Constantius 'falsely' claimed all the merit and 'would have buried in oblivion' Julian's deeds 'had not fame been unable to suppress his splendid exploits'); Julian, *Ath.* 279c–d (his statement *ad loc.* that he 'did not begrudge' – οὐκ ἐφθόνησα – the emperor must be read as self-aggrandising, and an oblique accusation). Julian may have set out to write a (now lost) account of the battle to reclaim his victory (Tougher [2007] 39).
[101] On the identification of Julian with Achilles and of Constantius with Agamemnon, see Athanassiadi (1981) 62; Kennedy (1983) 30; Curta (1995) 184; Elm (2012) 63; Drake (2012b) 38; Pagliara (2015) 99; Omissi (2018) 202; Greenwood (2019). Curta (1995) 177 rejects (unconvincingly, in my view) the polemical implications of the parallelism, arguing that the Iliadic quarrel was too popular a motive in late antiquity to convey criticism.

audience up to the threshold of criticism before abruptly changing direction and turning blame into praise. But the troubling image cannot be erased. It alerts the readers, preparing them for the mode of communication they should expect from the text: hermeneutical challenge.

The peculiar (read: excessive) length of the *Second Panegyric* makes it impossible that the text was composed for oral delivery, unless one resorts to the unverifiable hypothesis that it was re-edited. This inevitably raises the question of its circulation, which is undocumented.[102] It has been argued that such a piece could not have been presented to the emperor, since its ambiguous beginning alone serves to illustrate its controversial nature. Yet in the uncertainty about whether the text reached Constantius, the ways it advertises its use of core themes of his propaganda in the service of new aims are remarkable. These are admonishment (which might suggest that Julian hoped the text would reach Constantius' supporters in some form) and the consequent re-representation of Julian's public role.

Following its Iliadic opening, the panegyric continues by comparing Constantius to a plethora of Homeric heroes, showing how superior the Augustus is to each of them.[103] Late antique panegyrics are at ease with excess; consider, for example, Nazarius' account of how an army of celestial beings commanded by Constantius I led Constantine to victory at the Milvian Bridge.[104] But Julian's celebratory motif, following an allusive, bitter proemium, strikes one as so hyperbolic as to be almost derisive.[105] I suggest, however, that what is essential here is not assessing whether derision is at play. More important than Julian's extravagant comparisons is his decision to intersperse them with theoretical digressions, including an especially long, structured meditation pivoting around the theme of ideal sovereignty (79a–92d). As is often remarked, in this digression Constantius – the addressee of the panegyric – is oddly absent from the picture.

Like Julian's previous panegyrics, the *Second Panegyric* relies on his self-projection as a philosopher who temporarily lends himself to rhetoric to

---

[102] See Kennedy (1983) 30; Curta (1995) 197; Greenwood (2021) 26–27.
[103] See *II Pan.* 49c–51d, 54a–55c, 67b–68c, 71a–b, 73c–74d (Constantius as braver than Achilles, Ajax, and Sarpedon; more noble and generous than Agamemnon; more pious than Hector, and wiser than Nestor and Odysseus). Cf. Drake (2012) 44.
[104] *Pan. Lat.* IV (10) 14.
[105] See, e.g., the celebration of Constantius as able to speak to the simple-minded (*II Pan.* 77a–b): an homage to his communicative skills, or a hint that he was on the same level as his audience? Drake suggests that Julian's Homeric pastiche should be regarded as harmless play (Drake [2012b] 41). But whether an emperor writing parody of another emperor could ever conceive of his activity as entirely playful and apolitical is open to question.

praise Constantius. Julian insists that the genre of the panegyric and its laws are extraneous to him (69c) and that his training inevitably leads him to mix praise with philosophical theories (ἐπαίνους ἅμα καὶ δόγματα ᾄδειν, 69c). He repeatedly appeals to Platonic works, among which, perhaps unsurprisingly, pride of place is reserved for Plato's ('wonderful', 70a) *Laws*.[106] Not only does the *Second Panegyric* cite Plato, however, but it explains him. Quoting from the *Menexenus*, Julian writes that 'the man, and especially the king, best equipped for this life is he who depends on God (ἐς τὸν θεὸν ἀνήρτηται, 68c) for all that relates to happiness'. Julian reveals that he has replaced a word in Plato's text with one of his own, since the *Menexenus* actually says 'he who depends on himself' (εἰς ἑαυτὸν).[107] This intervention, Julian claims, is not arbitrary. In fact, it captures and clarifies Plato's true message: his reference to the self should not be interpreted as having to do with a man's body but is a description of 'his mind (νοῦς), his intelligence', which Julian explains as 'that god that is in us' (68d–69a).

The *Second Panegyric*, however, does not only build a case for Julian as a Platonic exegete. It also strives to present him as a wise interpreter of poetry. Julian adapts the customary self-validating attack on fellow panegyrists as sophists by presenting his 'adversaries' as poor interpreters. Flatterers, Julian explains, produce incorrect readings of poetry as they seek to make Homer say what he never intended:

> I have given this brief account of the Emperor's achievements, not adding in flattery and trying to exaggerate things that are perhaps of no special importance, nor dragging in what is farfetched and unduly pressing points of resemblance with those achievements, like those who interpret the myths of the poets (οἱ τοὺς μύθους ἐξηγούμενοι τῶν ποιητῶν) and analyse them into plausible versions (λόγους πιθανοὺς) which allow them to introduce fiction (πλάσματα), though they start out from a very slight analogy (μικρᾶς ... ὑπονοίας) and, having recourse to a very shadowy basis, try to convince (πειρῶνται ξυμπείθειν) us that this is the very thing the poets intended to say. (74d–75a)

This passage has been interpreted as a rejection of allegory.[108] However – and I return to this point in Chapter 3 – it merely sets the rules for its

---

[106] Passages (or expressions) from Plato's *Laws* feature also at *II Pan.* 81a (*Leg.* 5.728a), 82b (*Leg.* 1.642c), 85b (*Leg.* 8.832a), 87c (*Leg.* 7.808b), 91b (*Leg.* 11.937d).
[107] *II Pan.* 68d, quoting Plato, *Menex.* 247e–48a.
[108] Lamberton (1986) 134–39. On Julian as an anti-allegorist, see further Masaracchia (1990) 38; Riedweg (2008).

correct employment.[109] Julian criticises a manipulative approach that prioritises the message of the self-styled interpreter over the true significance of the text. This critique facilitates his self-advertisement as an excellent exegete who is equally aware of the potential and limits of Homeric poetry. Homer invented the 'strange and unnatural' (καινὸν καὶ ἄτοπον, 60d) duel between Achilles and Scamander and the battles of the gods (61a) to the end of 'embellishing his poems with such tales (ἐπικοσμῶν μύθοις τὴν ποίησιν, 61b).

This criticism of Homer's representation of the divine reveals a critical feature of the *Second Panegyric*. Julian's claim that the Homeric battles of the gods are an invention might lend itself to two alternative interpretations: he might be arguing that Homeric deities are fiction, or he might be saying that the poet represents the gods in a way that does not befit their divinity. Julian's subsequent criticism of Zeus' order to Hector to stay away from battle in *Iliad* 11.202–4, on the ground that Zeus would not 'give such base and cowardly advice' (68a), supports the second hypothesis. The advertisement of Julian's interpretive control of Homer is progressively revealed as related to another expertise of his, that concerning divine matters.

It has been observed that the *Second Panegyric* is an early witness to Julian's adherence to traditional religion, which, according to contemporary accounts (including his own), he would have kept hidden until the appointment as Augustus.[110] The *Second Panegyric*'s critique of Homer, however, invites a challenge to such stories. Elsewhere in the panegyric, Julian attacks the despoliation of the temples of the Sun (80c) and calls the ancients 'natural philosophers' (αὐτοφυῶς φιλοσοφοῦντες) due to the fact that they labelled those endowed with excellent souls 'children of the gods' (82b). He also distinguishes between intelligible and visible gods (82d) and recalls when the Pythian oracle proclaimed Socrates' wisdom (79a). Even more explicitly, Julian calls for observation of the 'lawful form of worship' (τῆς ἐννόμου θεραπείας, 70d), writes that a good sovereign 'does not neglect the worship of the gods (θεραπείας θεῶν, 86a)', and argues that violence to a country's laws is 'a greater impiety than sacrilegious theft of the money that belongs to the gods (τὰ χρήματα τῶν θεῶν, 89a)'. Finally, in commenting on ideal kingship, Julian argues that the gods respond

---

[109] P. 155–61.
[110] Athanassiadi (1981) 65; Tougher (1998a) 109; Drake (2012b) 42; De Vita (2022) cxxxvii–ix. Cf. also Julian's *Ep.* 8 Wright (= 26 Bidez–Cumont), dated to November 361, in which Julian declares he now worships the gods in public (ἀναφανδόν); and Lib. *Or.* 18.114.

reciprocally to the pious ruler, giving him celestial rewards and 'making him their follower and associate' in case of misfortune (92b).

There is a clear and problematic disconnect between this type of ideal sovereign and Constantius' projection of his sovereignty as ideal: his Christianity is the unexpressed foil against which Julian projects his own good ruler. Scholarship has often concluded that the *Second Panegyric*'s excursus on ideal sovereignty should be read as Julian's implicit celebration of himself.[111] This argument, however, conflates the layers of Julian's argument. The *Second Panegyric* does seek to accomplish an ironic displacement of Constantius' centrality from within the literary piece that is presented as composed for him. Yet if we argue that the ideal sovereign Julian is describing is his own mirror image, we lose sight of how he is producing an extremely generic figure built on post-Hellenistic kingship theory. Once he was sole ruler, Julian certainly sought to present himself as endowed with such virtues. But this is a different matter: the *Second Panegyric* predates Julian's time as Augustus. What is remarkable about this theoretical excursus is not that Julian compliments himself upon something he has yet to achieve but that he formulates a theory of kingship in the first place. His digression indicates his philosophical expertise, rendered manifest by his ability to produce advice. Julian writes reflections on political theory of the kind Dio of Prusa could have issued. Conversely, Constantius emerges from the picture as a man who can only receive advice – to which, incidentally, he does not conform.

The unusual length of the *Second Panegyric*, noted above, is itself instrumental to Julian's project of displacing the Augustus. The piece deliberately blurs the lines that separate the oration from the treatise. How long is it before an argument becomes too long and too conceptual for what presents itself, even if only on the level of fiction, as encomiastic rhetoric? Julian quotes from Plato and Homer just as Constantius – the intellectual and patron of intellectuals – would have wanted him to. Yet he also pauses to interpret Plato and corrects those who misread Homer. Julian's insistence on Plato's texts, and the *Laws* in particular, invites comparison with the *Letter to Themistius*. This comparison, however, simultaneously points to a crucial difference: the *Letter* styles itself as a (private) conversation with a famous philosopher, while the *Panegyric* presents itself as a (public) performance of praise. It is very different to correct Plato's *Menexenus* in a philosophical discussion and to do so in an

---

[111] Cf., e.g., Athanassiadi (1981) 66; Drake (2012a) 41–42; Greenwood (2021) 25. De Vita (2022) cxl–li rather sees the text as Julian's outlining of future plans.

encomium. The implicit message is that Julian's urge to philosophise is too great to be contained by traditional rhetorical forms, which are therefore transformed by his philosophy.

The *Second Panegyric* therefore relies on an aggressively revisited version of the public role Julian had agreed to perform after his appointment as Caesar. It has been argued that the speech is a token of his duplicity, putting up a submissive façade towards Constantius at a time when their relationship was beginning to deteriorate.[112] I believe the contrary is true: the piece never seeks to hide conflict.[113] Displacement – destabilisation, even – of the Augustus is presented as illustrative of Julian's intent to recalibrate the power dynamics between him and Constantius based on the Caesar's new understanding of his authority.

Analysis of Julian's self-projection in the *Second Panegyric* as a philosopher and scholar of Homer has thus begun to show that his attempt to renegotiate his status vis-à-vis Constantius pivots on notions of philosophical leadership. This time, however, such notions are evoked competitively. Julian's philosophical identity is brought up not to illuminate Constantius but to obscure him. The reassuring, tamed image of the court philosopher that pleased the Augustus has disappeared. Julian responds to Constantius' self-promotion as an intellectual by implicitly suggesting who, of the two of them, is the actual philosopher. By doing so, he also begins to erode the idea, cultivated by Constantius and his supporters, that Christianity contains classical culture. Worship of the gods is presented as a mark of the wisdom of a sovereign. An ideal link ties true philosophical competence – of the kind, incidentally, that Julian possesses – to Greco-Roman religion.

Julian's *Consolation to Himself*: What Doesn't Kill You, Makes You Wiser

The gap separating Constantius' intellectual pretensions from Julian's philosophy is the subject of another text from the later phase of Julian's Gallic campaign, the *Consolation to Himself upon the Departure of the Excellent Salutius*. The *Consolation* is addressed to a man named Saloustios in the heading. Scholars tend to identify him with Saturninus Secundus Salutius, *quaestor sacri palatii*, who was assigned to Julian as an

---

[112] Bowersock (1978) 43.
[113] Cf. Curta's analysis of the alternation in the text between an 'explicit oration' (the Homeric praise of Constantius) and an 'anti-oration' that 'permanently undermines' its counterpart (Curta [1995] 196–97).

adviser following his appointment as Caesar. Salutius, who was well versed in Neoplatonic philosophy (he may be identical with the author of the Neoplatonic pamphlet *On the Gods and the World*) ended up becoming Julian's closest friend during the campaign in Gaul and would later feature in the opening of Julian's *Caesars* and as the dedicatee of his *Hymn to King Helios*.[114]

A letter by Julian to his physician Oribasius, his *Letter to the Athenians*, and a passage from Ammianus, provide together (slightly contradictory) evidence on the historical background to the *Consolation*.[115] Following Julian's rejection of the tax plans of the praetorian prefect Florentius for the province as extortionate, Florentius accused Salutius of arousing Julian against Constantius; Constantius recalled Salutius from Gaul in 358.[116] The *Consolation* therefore presents itself as the literary space in which Julian elaborates on the loss of his friend and tries to comfort them both. 'Unless I tell you all I said to myself when I learned you were compelled to journey far from my side, my dear friend', reads the beginning, 'I shall think that I am deprived of some comfort' (240a). Scholars express no doubt that this was the genuine motivation for writing the *Consolation*.[117]

The piece has a completely different aim, however, than offering private comfort. The act of consolation serves as a springboard for pressing a simultaneously political and philosophical argument, which is as follows: Constantius is unaware of the consequences of his actions, which means that his decisions are not the outcome of orderly and rational planning (as would be expected from a philosopher-ruler). Conversely, Julian's intellect is so trained and self-sufficient that it has the power to transform every

---

[114] *PLRE* I 797–98 *s.v.* Saturninius Secundus Salutius. An alternative identification would be Flavius Sallustius, praetorian prefect of Gaul (cf. *PLRE* I 797–98 s.v. Flavius Sallustius 5). Both Salutius and Flavius Sallust and are called 'Saloustios' in the Greek sources. Ammianus distinguishes between Sallustius and Salutius, but the naming is irregular (Barnes [1998] 62). Discussion in Bowersock (1978) 125; Athanassiadi (1981) 68 n. 74; Smith (1995) 33; Rosen (2006) 269; Stenger (2009) 320; Liebeschuetz (2012) 226 n. 48; Lössl (2012) 62; De Vita (2022), lxxvii–viii n. 220.

[115] Jul. *Ep.* 4 Wright (= 14 Bidez–Cumont); *Ath.* 282c; Amm. Marc. 17.3.2–5.

[116] In *Ep.* 4 Wright the misbehaviour of an official (arguably Florentius) towards the provincials is mentioned, and the possibility is mentioned that Saloustios might be sent away as a result of Julian's reaction; in *Ath.* 282c Florentius only becomes Julian's enemy after Saloustios has been removed; Amm. Marc. 17.3.2–5 mentions the tax-related quarrel with Florentius but not Salutius' removal. Reconstructions of the episode in Ugenti (2014) 16; Greenwood (2021) 23–25.

[117] Cf., e.g., Browning (1975) 96; Bowersock (1978) 45; Athanassiadi (1981) 20, 68–70; Smith (1995) 33; Lössl (2012); Greenwood (2021) 23–25. A reading of the text as consolatory also in Libanius, *Or.* 18.86. See, however, De Vita (2022) cxlv–vi for an analysis of the *Consolation* as a vehicle for Julian's statement of adhesion to traditional *paideia*.

experience, including the most challenging, into an opportunity for self-improvement: hardship only makes him wiser.

The choice of literary form is, in this regard, highly significant. Julian inscribes his piece in a codified genre – the consolatory speech (παραμυθητικὸς λόγος) – something that naturally prepares the expectations of the audience: the choice suggests resignation. Julian is not rebelling (for now). He has accepted the Augustus' decision and does not plan to overturn it or prevent Salutius' exile. At the same time, the genre draws attention to his intellectual credentials: the literary tradition of consolation for bereavement and exile is a preserve of the philosophers, having been practiced by Cicero, Seneca the Younger, Musonius Rufus, and Plutarch, among others.[118] Philosophers know the value of endurance and how to teach it to others.

Julian also makes it clear that he knows exactly what he is enduring and why. The theme of his finesse as exegete is developed in the text through a display of his capacity to interpret the events that led to Salutius' departure. Julian identifies himself as the true target of his friend's exile and depicts the punishment as a form of political retaliation ('sycophants ... desired to wound me through you').[119] Crucially, his acknowledgement of the nature of Salutius' punishment is preceded by his own explicit identification with Odysseus: 'Then too there came into my mind the words "Then was Odysseus left alone" (οἰώθη δ᾽Ὀδυσεύς)', he writes, 'for now I am, indeed, like him' (ἐκείνῳ παραπλήσιος, 241d).

The line is borrowed from *Iliad* 11.401. Julian expects the reader to know that its implications go beyond the literal meaning of the words: Odysseus, in the Iliadic context, remains alone on the battlefield because he selflessly sheltered the wounded Diomedes, allowing him to escape on his chariot. The Odysseus to whom Julian is pointing as his model is a man free of shadows: he is not the trickster but the high-minded hero. He is described elsewhere in the *Consolation* as 'god-beloved' (θεοφιλής), precisely due to his being 'wary', 'ready of wit', 'prudent' (ἐπητής, ἀγχίνοος, ἐχέφρων).[120] He is a philosopher-ruler, whom the gods love. Julian's readers must also know that, in the Iliadic scene of Odysseus' abandonment, Athena protects him from his attacker, Sokos, whom Odysseus eventually kills (*Il.* 11.437–55).

---

[118] Cicero, *Consolatio*; Seneca, *Consolatio ad Marciam, Consolatio ad Polybium, Consolatio ad Helviam Matrem*; Muson. *Diss.* 9; Plut, *Mor.* 608a–12b.

[119] *Cons.* 241d–42a (ἐμὲ διὰ σοῦ τρῶσαι βουλόμενοι). Greenwood (2021) 24–25 detects oblique criticism of Constantius and Constantine in the passage.

[120] *Cons.* 250c, quoting *Od.* 13.332.

In addition to suggesting that he is fully aware of the reasons that led to the exile of his friend, Julian also signals that he is not allowing himself to become despondent. The consolatory genre is especially conducive to reflection on what might be labelled resilience, as it helps frame Julian's intellectual control of events. Within a context of reflection on what defines a philosopher-ruler, however, this assertion of intellectual dominance in the face of adversity introduces an unexpected, paradoxical consequence: it permits Julian to present an event designed to weaken him as what will in fact help his intellect become stronger, enabling him to progress in his status as philosopher-leader.

This idea is introduced from early in the text, where Julian states that, according to the wise (οἱ σοφοί), 'he who is endowed with reason (τῷ νοῦν ἔχοντι) derives from the greatest trials as much felicity (τὴν εὐπάθειαν) as vexation' (241a). Following a description of healthy bodies that can be nourished by any kind of food (to the extent that 'food that often seems unwholesome for others, far from injuring them, makes them strong', 241b), Julian develops an analogy with the human mind, arguing that 'those who have trained it ... will probably be able to remain cheerful (εὐφραίνοντο) in more trying conditions' (241b–c). Readers may observe that the way Julian deactivates the threatening element embedded in his comparison between bodies and mind deploys a strategy very similar to that of the proemium of the *Second Panegyric*. There, as noted, Julian (unconvincingly) reassured his readers that his account of the quarrel between Achilles and Agamemnon was a veiled attempt to praise Constantius by contrast. In the *Consolation*, the comparison between healthy bodies and healthy minds makes it evident that Julian's goal is not simply 'to remain cheerful in trying conditions'. Bodies that react to challenges, he tells us, do something more: they become stronger. Later in the piece, someone else is summoned to explicitly formulate a theory of the strengthening of souls through difficulties that brings Julian's argument full circle. This is the fifth-century statesman Pericles of Athens, whose long speech (246a–48b), riddled with philosophical content, holds the key to understanding the self-assertive purposes of the *Consolation*.

After listing a series of great philosophers from the past (Pythagoras, Plato, and Democritus, 245c–d), all of whom were compelled to leave friends at home when embarking on their endeavours, Julian introduces Pericles into the text. As his intellectually ambitious (and highly Neoplatonic) speech makes evident, the statesman is summoned in the capacity of philosopher-ruler. Julian's readers are first informed that Pericles set out on his campaign against the island of Samos without taking his friend, the philosopher Anaxagoras, with him. He nevertheless conquered Euboea by relying on Anaxagoras' advice. (He is thus incidentally a conqueror, just as Julian has proven to be.) Having previously been advised by Anaxagoras, he had learned from his suggestions and had now acquired the capacity to control them autonomously (245d–46a). Through his account of Pericles' friendship with Anaxagoras, Julian introduces the theme that enlightened rulers are able to find wise friends and accept their teachings. This time the theme is not developed to the benefit of Constantius, as it was in the *Speech of Thanks*, but reflects on Julian's friendship with Salutius. From its very beginning, the *Consolation* insists on the true intellectual quality of their company. Julian praises their 'unfeigned and candid conversation, innocent and upright company, and co-operation in all that was good' (241c–d).[121]

The reason Pericles could not take Anaxagoras with him to Samos, we are told, was because the Athenians prevented him from doing so. 'Wise man (ἔμφρων) that he was', Julian comments, 'he bore the folly (ἄνοιαν) of his fellow-citizens with fortitude and mildness' (246a). Once again, as with the quarrel of Achilles and Agamemnon, Julian lets the myth (or history, in this case) speak on his behalf. To separate a talented statesman from a valuable adviser was nothing but an act of folly. To this, Pericles responded with fortitude and mildness.

Following this introduction, Julian lets Pericles speak. The opening of his oration is invested with philosophical grandeur: 'The whole world is my city and fatherland', Pericles says, 'and my friends are the gods and lesser divinities and all good men, whoever and wherever they may be. Yet it is right to respect also the country where I was born, since this is the divine law (θεῖος ... νόμος), and to obey all her commands and not oppose them' (246a–b). Julian is showing his credentials. He has Pericles invoke divine law, which, the *Letter to Themistius* argued, is for Julian identical with rationality. That this speech is especially concerned with rationality and its achievement is highlighted by Pericles' deliberate self-distancing from the animals. 'Pericles', the statesman asks himself, 'if Nature had given you eyes only, as she has to birds,[122] it would be natural for you to feel excessive grief' (246c). But human eyes are meant to provide reason through the faculty of imagination (ἡ φαντασία, 246d), which creates images that perfectly resemble the physical object from which they derive

---

[121] See also *Cons.* 243c.
[122] I follow Bidez in accepting the reading of the manuscripts (ὄρνισι) rather than Cobet's normalising θηρίοις (printed by Wright [1913]).

but without being tarnished by matter (247c–d).[123] This process of generation of pure images is precisely what allows the mind to grow stronger. In the words of Pericles, the wise man who is deprived of a good friend will actually gain strength from separation because their conversations will move to the noetic level. The faculty of imagination enables beautiful souls to interact in the absence of bodies, continuing in solitude the process of self-perfectioning first undertaken with a now distant friend. Pericles' conclusions break the historical fiction, bringing out the contemporary implications of his reflection. 'If you employ your mind (*nous*)', he says, 'you will easily see from Athens one who is in Ionia, and from the country of the Celts one who is in Illyria or Thrace' (247b). The reference is to Julian's and Salutius' present situation.

Connection with the divine is central to Julian's analysis of Pericles' argument. He celebrates the inward turn of the mind as preparing us to commune (ξυγγένηται) with god (249b–c). When seen in light of Julian's ideas of kingship theory (as illustrated, for instance, in the *Letter to Themistius*), this idea appears in its full potential. The training of the mind through a purely intellectual friendship will enable Pericles – and therefore Julian – to achieve a level of reason close to the divine, something that in turn will sanction their achievement of perfect (qua perfectly philosophical) leadership. We have already seen that Odysseus, Julian's other alter ego in the piece, is described as 'god-beloved' (θεοφιλής, 250c). The *Consolation* creates a literary network of rulers and philosophers (including Socrates and Achilles, 249b) enjoying a privileged relationship with the divine, to illustrate the models that shape Julian's understanding of his philosophy and rule.

Citations are used as a vehicle of theological content. At the beginning of his speech, Pericles declares that his friends are, next to serious men, 'the gods and lesser divinities' (246a). When one considers Pericles in his historical context, this comes as no surprise. But readers know that the Pericles of the *Consolation* stands for Julian. In a similar fashion, at the conclusion of the piece Julian summons Zeus as *xenios* and *philios* (that is, in his capacity as patron of hospitality) and asks him to receive Salutius benevolently (252b–c). He then writes: 'In these prayers for you (i.e., Salutius) I am echoed by all good and honourable men; and let me add one

---

[123] The reflection on the role of *phantasia* in the mediation between sense-apprehension and knowledge was a Neoplatonic concern; see Porphyry's elaboration on the theme in his *Commentary on Ptolemy's Harmonics*, 13d.21–15d.9 (for which, see Sheppard [2007]; Barker [2015] 19–20).

prayer more, "Health and great joy be with you, and may the gods give you all things good, even to come home again to thy dear fatherland!"' (243d–44a).[124] The Homeric prayer gives Julian licence to mention the gods in the plural. Conversely, Constantius' relationship with the divinity is thematised ironically:

> And now that I have been deprived of all these things at once, with what arguments shall I supply myself (τίνων ἂν εὐπορήσαιμι λόγων), so that . . . they may persuade me to be calm and to bear nobly whatever God has sent? For in accordance with His will (αὐτῷ νοῶν) our mighty Emperor has surely planned this as all else.' (*Cons.* 243d–54a)

Since the *Consolation* presents Salutius' exile as ultimately strengthening Julian, this description of Constantius' enactment of it might be read as emphasising that the ruler in a sense operated in accord with divine design – but as Julian conceived it. He facilitated the process of approximating his second-in-command to the divinity. Furthermore, he did so without being aware of the consequences of his actions and, most importantly, of how his decision would turn against him. Constantius' (faint) understanding of providence is further attacked through a teasing reference to the rhetorical opposition between barbarity and Hellenism. Julian contrasts the Greeks 'seeking after truth by the aid of reason' with the barbarians, who pay heed to 'incredible fables or impossible miracles' (ἀπίστοις μύθοις . . . παραδόξῳ τερατείᾳ, 252b). It is difficult not to read this allusion to impossible miracles as a reference to Christianity, which had often been defined – even by its own representatives, and defiantly – as a barbarian wisdom.[125] This explicit antagonisation of Greek truth and 'barbarian' fables, which seems to interact polemically with theories of Christianity as foundational to Greco-Roman wisdom, crops up here for the first time in Julian's writings. It soon becomes a leitmotiv.[126]

It seems thus clear that Julian's *Consolation* serves above all else as a celebration of Julian as a sovereign endowed with special intellectual might. He can simultaneously advise and be the first recipient of his own wisdom – a wisdom that incidentally communicates with a divinity different from Constantius' god. While the question of the audience of this piece necessarily remains open, its subtlety and politically charged tones are in tune with the other writings from Julian's Caesarship, from the

---

[124] *Cons.* 252d (first line quotes *Odyssey* 24.402; the second adapts Sarpedon at *Il.* 6.587).
[125] Reference to Christian miracles: Stenger (2009) 29; Lössl (2012) 70; De Vita (2022) cxlvi. Ancient representations of Christianity as barbarian wisdom: Antonova (2018).
[126] See Chapter 3, p. 146–64.

Letter to Themistius to the *Second Panegyric*. They dispel the image of an author writing private pieces, riddled with allusion, whose circulation he feared. In turn, they draw the profile of a skilful rhetorician constantly challenging the boundary between what could and could not be said. The intimate tone of the *Consolation* appears just as fictional as that displayed in the complex artefact of literary self-fashioning that is the *Letter to Themistius*.[127] A pretence of formality towards Constantius is maintained – Julian writes 'may God make the emperor gracious to you!' in the closing lines (252c) – although this pretence has evidently become something to play with. Christianity can be mocked, at least allusively. Constantius can be criticised – again allusively. Julian's celebration of his own ability to deal with good advisers can be separated only with difficulty from the fact that Constantius has conversely proven himself a ruler prone to listening to individuals like the praetorian prefect Florentius.[128]

The praise the intellectual benefits of long-distance friendship culminates in an explicit note of defiance. 'Since no one can deprive us of our thoughts, we shall surely commune with ourselves in some fashion, and perhaps God will suggest an alleviation' (249a), he writes. Some decades later, the Neoplatonist Synesius would similarly claim that the state cannot forbid dreaming (intended as the practice of dream divination).[129] In the case of both Julian and Synesius, authority is challenged by pointing at something (interiority) that only divinity can reach. The idea that no one is allowed to interrupt the dialogue between interiority and divine rationality suggests that they are connected by a special bond. Constantius ironically enabled his subordinate Caesar to progress in his status of philosopher-ruler to a level where the senior emperor can now only make empty claims.

Conclusions

Julian's earliest speeches insist on his philosophical identity and its virtuous synergy with the enlightened Augustus, Constantius II. This chapter has argued that this line of argument was encouraged and indeed expected at Constantius' court. Julian's *First Panegyric* and *Speech of Thanks* to Eusebia have their place in the context of the Augustus' propaganda, which Julian interprets cleverly (and not without ambiguity). A survey of the rhetorical environment of Constantius' court confirms that the Augustus was especially concerned with intellectual self-projection and sought to be

---

[127] See Chapter 1. [128] On the friendship *topoi* in the *Consolation*, see Lössl (2012) 66.
[129] Syn. *Insomn*. 12.6. See Chapter 5, p. 254.

represented as a scholar, interpreter, and patron of philosophers, among whom Julian was to be counted. Even the criticism directed at Constantius by his detractors (Ammianus, Libanius, and Mamertinus) obliquely confirms his desire to broadcast his image as a cultured sovereign, as well as the fact that religious allegiance constituted a fundamental component of his intellectual self-image.

Julian's writings composed after his successes in the Gallic campaign appear to be shaped by an ambition to repurpose his previous engagement with Constantius' propaganda to his own advantage. Julian's depiction of his philosophical identity becomes defiant, as he seeks strategies to express in literature his change in status and play with the nexus Constantius postulated between enlightened leadership and Christian piety. The section of philosophical advice delivered in Julian's *Second Panegyric* (ca. 359) reverses the intellectual hierarchy he previously posited between himself and Constantius, sending the message that it is actually Julian who exercises interpretive control over the philosophical and literary tradition. Julian's *Consolation to Himself* also outlines a declaration of intellectual superiority. Following Constantius' recall of Julian's closest adviser from Gaul, the piece implies that the Augustus is unaware of the consequences of his own decisions: he failed to see that Julian, as an authentic philosopher, would grow in wisdom when made to face adversity. The more Constantius punishes, the more Julian lifts himself above the Augustus as an intellectual – implying that in the process he will become a better ruler.

PART II

*Making and Breaking Constantine:
Julian Augustus*

CHAPTER 3

Holy Hermeneutics

The death of Constantius II marks the beginning of Julian's short-lived rule as sole emperor. In Part II, I argue that the two main concerns emerging from his writings of the time – his open challenge to Christianity and his enhanced self-portrayal as a philosopher-ruler – are two faces of the same coin and both illuminate the cultural discourse pursued by his predecessors. The orations and treatises written by Julian as Augustus indicate that he located Constantine's and Constantius' strategy of self-legitimisation in their assertion of Christian leadership as the ideal embodiment of the philosopher-ruler. These writings also clarify that Julian's dissent originated in his assessment of Christianity as a system capitalising on philosophical tools that were not its own. The present chapter brings to light the core idea organising Julian's cultural and political response. I show that the entirety of Julian's final output relied on the intuition that any challenge to Christianity's political rise had to be grounded in a process of destabilisation of its identity as an interpretive system. The first section of the chapter provides an analysis of the writings of Constantine and his supporters, showing that they consistently endorsed an idea of a Christian ruler as the perfect interpreter of Greco-Roman culture and history. In the second section, I consider Julian's ambition to provide a commentary on *paideia* that might rewrite the intellectual hierarchy between Christian and Greek thinking as the Constantinian discourse had (re)defined them.

The Sign of Zeus

Julian's reckoning with Constantius II reached a turning point with Julian's impromptu proclamation as Augustus. Following unsuccessful attempts to negotiate with the senior emperor, who had ordered more than half of Julian's troops to travel to the Persian border to join his campaign against Shapur II, the soldiers revolted. This took place in

February 360, in the Parisian winter quarters. Julian describes how the legions stationed themselves for an entire day in front of the palace of Constantius I, Julian's seat for the winter. At about sunset, they began to shout vociferously. 'Until that time', he protests, 'I knew nothing of what they had determined'.[1]

The veracity of this statement has been challenged.[2] Julian places his story at the climax of his *Letter to the Senate and People of Athens*, a message dispatched in late summer 361, when all attempts at reconciliation with Constantius II had failed, civil war was imminent, and Julian sought to rally his supporters. What he needed at this stage was to dispel the accusation of having usurped the throne. Julian wrote to deny that he had ever plotted against his cousin, supporting his claims with a parallel narrative positioning Constantius as the truly illegitimate sovereign.[3] No divinity had endorsed his tyrannical power; Julian was his god-sent adversary. The *Letter to the Athenians* seeks to illustrate that the gods had been on Julian's side throughout his life, saving him from Constantius' abuse. Intriguingly, philosophy is presented here as the weapon the gods gave Julian to resist his cousin.[4] When he first wrote his appeal to the Athenians, Julian could not know that Constantius would die of illness in November of the same year. But as Mamertinus' panegyric shows, the end of the threat of civil war at a stroke could only bolster his narrative of divine assistance.[5]

The *Letter to the Athenians* constructs Julian's rise to power as part of a providential design. One passage of the *Letter* explicitly declares that the god who summoned him to power was Zeus himself:

> It was already late ... and suddenly the palace was surrounded, and everyone shouted aloud .... I prayed to Zeus. And when the shouting grew

---

[1] *Ath.* 284b.
[2] Amm. Marc. 20.4–5 and Lib. *Or.* 12.59–61, 13.33–35 also support the thesis that Julian was unaware of the proclamation. Bowersock (1978) doubts Julian's reconstruction. Drinkwater (1983) argued that Julian's supporters engineered the proclamation but without his complicity. Discussion also in Szidat (1981) 129–34; Matthews (1989) 93–100; Bleckmann (2020); Heather (2020).
[3] See Humphries (2012).
[4] *Ath.* 272a ('the gods by means of philosophy caused me to remain untouched by it [i.e., Constantius' cruelty] and unharmed').
[5] *Pan. Lat.* III (11) 27.2. The idea that Constantius' death was proof of divine assistance would arguably have been relevant also for the re-editing of the *Letter*. Labriola argues that the text we have today is an expanded version for publication, which came out in Antioch between January and March 363 (Labriola [1972] 18; [1975]; see also Elm [2012] 61; De Vita [2022] cxlviii–ix). Gregory of Nazianzus argues that Julian plotted Constantius' assassination (Greg. Naz. *Or.* 4.47): the claim is indicative of Gregory's sense that Constantius' spontaneous death was a known event to which an invective targeting Julian's theological statements urgently need to respond.

still louder, and all was in tumult in the quarters, I entreated the god to give me a sign (τέρας). And thereupon he showed me a sign and bade me yield (αὐτὰρ ὅ γ'ἡμῖν δεῖξε καὶ ἠνώγει πεισθῆναι).[6]

Julian's story of a god manifesting his will through a sign at a moment of dramatic upheaval evokes comparison with a far more famous episode of divine endorsement in a military setting: the apparition of a cross and the words 'By this conquer' (τούτῳ νίκα), with which the Christian god is said to have saluted the young Constantine fighting his rival Maxentius in 312. The question of whether Julian was acquainted – as I believe he was – with Eusebius' *Life of Constantine*, which reports Constantine's vision, will be addressed in Chapter 4.[7] Here it suffices to note that the coinage series minted by the usurper Vetranio in 350 and by Constantius II in 351 carried the legend *hoc signo victor eris*, which suggests that the episode was known to the public.[8] Julian's story of his rise to power thus seems structured to displace the theology of his predecessor(s), although not its modes of signification.[9] In the *Letter to the Athenians*, divinity still addresses humankind through signs. Constantine was offered the Christian cross; Julian, Zeus' *teras*. Julian's story is infused with a polemical declaration of intellectual priority.

In this chapter, I suggest that Julian organised his response to Christian leadership through narratives shaped around his capacity to interpret divine signification because he recognised that the claim to a correct decoding of divine signs was central to his Christian predecessors' efforts to negotiate authority. Constantine had tied the assertion of his power to the idea that Christianity offered the only interpretive framework able to access the divine will underlying Rome's providential history. The motif of exegesis therefore linked the two great ambitions of the mature Constantine: the delineation of a self-image that fulfilled the expectations of the Roman elites, who cherished the ideal of a high-minded ruler, and

---

[6] *Ath.* 284b–c.
[7] The reconstruction of the early circulation of the story of Constantine's vision is complicated by discrepancies among contemporary authors who claim the emperor saw a divine omen. *Pan. Lat.* VI (7) 21.4–5 speaks of a vision of Apollo; Lactantius reports that Constantine dreamed of Christ (*Mort. Pers.* 44.3–6); Eusebius offers the account of the celestial cross but also includes the story of Christ's dream (*VC* 1.32). Weiss (2003) famously attempted a *reductio ad unum* of these three sources, arguing that they are independent witnesses to the same phenomenon, a solar halo witnessed by Constantine in 310. See *contra* Van Dam (2011) 12 n. 18; Barbero (2016) 41–44, 142–43. A discussion on how different scholarly positions intersects with wider themes of Constantinian historiography in Flower (2012).
[8] Chantraine (1993–94); Dearn (2003); Barbero (2016) 140–41; Omissi (2018) 176.
[9] For the argument that Julian mirrored the Christian theological framework that he opposed, see especially Elm (2012); Cribiore (2013) 180–81; Greenwood (2014), (2017a), (2017b), (2021).

the wish to project a subversive side of his rule – the endorsement of a new religion – as being in fact an act of restoration. Julian, who was only a child at the time of Constantine's death, had not been exposed personally to his uncle's propaganda. I argued in Part I, however, that Julian began to cultivate his political voice at the court of Constantine's son Constantius, who was also concerned to project an intellectual self-image. Furthermore, Constantine's son made no secret of the continuity between his own public profile and that of his father. If anything, as the next section will show, he capitalised on it.

Constantius II, True Son of Constantine.

Appointed consul in 362, Claudius Mamertinus thanked his benefactor – Julian Augustus – with the composition of an encomium (*Pan. Lat.* III [11]) that reads as a compendium of Julianic propaganda.[10] The piece, written after Constantius' death, disqualifies his cultured profile to Julian's advantage. Although never mentioned by name, Constantius is discernible in the text as an enemy of culture who surrounded himself exclusively with worthless men.[11] The oration contrasts this bleak figure with its portrait of Julian, who promoted figures of merit (including, *ça va sans dire*, Mamertinus himself) and was committed to restoring culture at court and liberating philosophy (23.4).

Within his comparative project, Mamertinus implicitly but unmistakably juxtaposes Julian's understanding of the divine will with that of Constantius. Julian is celebrated as able to anticipate a future of happiness for the Roman state through his access to divine knowledge (14.6); his successes – in particular, the fact that he did not even have to fight in the civil war with Constantius – are summoned as testifying to his connection with the gods (27.2). Conversely – and intriguingly – Mamertinus advanced the claim that under Constantius the interpretation of celestial signs was prohibited to the point that farmers could not plan their work, and sailors their routes, based on observation of the skies (23.5). This criticism is certainly instrumental to Mamertinus' exaggerated elaboration on Constantius' rule as a time of subversion ('people lived on land and at sea not in accordance with heavenly science [*ratione caelesti*] but

---

[10] On the proximity between Mamertinus and Julian, see Tougher (2020).
[11] The attack is generalising (*Pan. Lat.* III [11] 19.4–20.4) but Mamertinus argues that this course of things was only changed by Julian (*Pan. Lat.* III [11] 21) – hence, Constantius was fully implicated in it.

haphazardly and at random [*casu ac temere*]', 23.5). It remains the case, however, that the oration presents Constantine's son as tampering with the channels of communication with the divine. Is Mamertinus implying that Constantius deliberately tried to prevent his subjects from engaging with omens? And, if so, does this hint to Constantius' fears that divine signs might cast a shadow on his rule?

Constantius' cultural self-image, as Chapter 2 noted, was in dialogue with contemporary debates theorising Christianity's dominance over the classical tradition.[12] Crucially, Constantius never claimed that his self-image was his invention. On the contrary, he always located his policies in the legacy of those of his great father. Constantius' propaganda, as well as that of his brothers Constantine II (d. 340) and Constans (d. 350), put special emphasis on continuity with Constantine.[13] Culture was key to the picture. From iconography to religion, Constantius' *imitatio* of Constantine posited cultural commitment as something that fulfilled and overcame his father's legacy.[14] His doctrinal commitment, active involvement in councils, and epistolary correspondence with bishops were all pursued in the awareness that Constantine had done the same.[15] His urban efforts too, with their focus on Constantinople – the city Constantine had (re)founded – look like an assertion of filial piety. This assertion was arguably cultivated with a twofold aim: to secure stability of succession (Eusebius' *Life of Constantine* already advises Constantine's sons to continue his legacy of enlightened leadership)[16] but also to claim (filial) primacy over Constantine II and Constans in a context of increasing rivalry. Constantine-themed coinage was issued by Eastern mints throughout the 340s.[17] Statues of Constantine and Constantius decorated the

---

[12] See Chapter 2, p. 86–94.
[13] Humphries (1997); Moser (2018) 156–66, 272–75, 303–11. On Themistius' panegyrics as reflecting the concerted self-image of Constantine's sons see Greenlee (2020).
[14] On iconographic continuity in the house of Constantine, see Chapter 4, p. 186–9. Whether their religious policy truly followed their father's agenda (as they claimed, cf. *C.Th.* 16.10.2) or re-thought it remains a subject of debate: see Drake (1976) 150 n. 17; Corcoran (1996) 315–16 n. 17; Edwards (2006) 153; Lee (2012) 173–74; Barnes (2011); Bardill (2012) 286, 305.
[15] On continuity in epistolary practices between Constantine and Constantius II, see Baker-Brian (2020).
[16] Euseb. *VC* 1.9.2; 4.72.
[17] Pietri (1989) 125; Moser (2018) 148–50, 157–63. Already in late 337, only a few months after Constantine's death, the mints at Constantinople produced a *solidus* depicting a veiled Constantine on the obverse and a toga-clad figure (Constantine himself) on a chariot driving towards the sky on the reverse (*RIC* VIII Constantinople I). Around 342, Constantius issued a series of small bronze coins depicting a veiled Constantine (*RIC* VIII Heraclea 41, *RIC* VIII Constantinople 62, *RIC* Nicomedia 45, *RIC* VIII Cyzicus 35; *RIC* VIII Antioch 64. For the dating, see Pietri (1989) 128; Maraval (2013) 65; Moser (2018) 157).

Senate House of Constantinople.[18] Even Constantius' realisation of a scriptorium in the Eastern capital bears comparison with Constantine's request to Bishop Eusebius of Caesarea for fifty Bibles from the scriptorium of Caesarea.[19]

Constantius' supporters understood that his politics of filial piety wrote the script for his style of government. They shaped their praise accordingly, picking up the theme of Constantius as imitating – and surpassing – his father.[20] The motif is apparent in Libanius,[21] and Themistius rarely calls Constantius by his name, preferring to address him as 'son of Constantine'.[22] In his panegyrics, Julian eloquently connects his philosophical leitmotiv – Constantius' education – to the theme of Constantius' lineage. Among other things, he argues that Constantine's most notable achievement had been to 'beget, rear, and educate' Constantius.[23] In his *Letter to Constantius*, Cyril of Jerusalem claims that Constantius 'surpassed his father's piety'.[24] He openly invites Constantius II to engage in an act of interpretation of the vision of the cross in the sky the bishop (allegedly) had in Jerusalem, claiming that this would cast light on the divine significance of his rule. According to Cyril, the omen signified Constantius' closer proximity than Constantine to the divine: his rule had been blessed with a heavenly token – a celestial cross – whereas his father had only received a terrestrial sign (Helena's discovery of the cross?).[25] What is essential, however, is that Cyril's *Letter* invites Constantius to assess the validity of his interpretation by summoning the emperor as a reader of the Bible. Constantius' ability to dominate the Scriptures with his understanding equips him to operate as the interpreter of divine signification as it manifests itself in the world.

In another text – one of his panegyrics for Constantius – Themistius raises an intriguing question, asking the emperor if he thought that Plato

---

[18] Cf. Them. *Or.* 4.52d–53a.
[19] Euseb. *VC* 4.36. Cf. Constans' comparable commission of Bibles as reported by Athanasius, *Apol. ad Const.* 4.2.
[20] Bleckmann (1999) 63–64; Barbero (2016) 338–40 (with attention to Roman epigraphs); Moser (2018) 273–74. See, e.g., Julian, *I Pan.* 8a–b, 37b, *II Pan.* 52a–b, Them. *Or.* 3.44a–b, 4.53a–b, 55b–c, 58b–c.
[21] Lib. *Or.* 59.16–19, 34, 36, see Greenlee (2020) 146. A reversed paradigm applies also to invectives, with Hilary of Poitiers and Athanasius insisting that he failed to live up to Constantine's expectations (Flower (2013) 90).
[22] Marcone (2019) 148. [23] Julian, *I Pan.* 8d–9a. [24] Cyril, *Ep. Const.* 3.
[25] If this is a reference to Helena's discovery of the Cross, it suggests that Cyril, writing from Jerusalem, was unaware of the story of Constantine's vision: Barbero (2016) 140–41; *pace* Drijvers (2004) 162; Van Dam (2011) 50.

was 'inferior to the Erythraean Sibyl as a prophet'.[26] The Sibyl was evoked by fourth-century Christians as bearing prophetic witness to the coming of Christ; Constantine too, as I show below, shared his thoughts about her position in respect to pagan (and Platonic) wisdom. The summoning of this comparison is therefore not only a signal of Themistius' willingness to engage with issues raised by Christian theologians but also an indication that Constantius was (expected to be) involved in the debate. A final piece of evidence should be added to the interpretive network Constantius' supporters were weaving around him. This time, though, it comes from one emerging critical voice: in his *Res Gestae*, Ammianus describes how Constantius responded to the accidental death of an enemy by suggesting that he had predicted it.[27] When all these passages are considered, two observations can be advanced. First, an important component of Constantius' cultural and political agenda seems to be represented by the motif of his capacity to interpret texts and omens – the two abilities his opponent Mamertinus, as noted, denied to him. Second, the theme of prognostication as well points to Constantius' father. It resonates, for instance, with Eusebius' telling of the story of Constantine's planning of the Church in the Holy Sepulchre. Here, the bishop claims that Constantine's provisions suggested he had been planning the construction for a long time, as if he had 'looked into the future with superior foreknowledge' (concerning the finding of the Sepulchre's site).[28] More generally, analysis of the writings of Constantine's mature period and of those of his supporters shows that the motif of the emperor as an interpreter was central to the first Christian emperor's project of self-legitimisation.

Constantine the Interpreter

Although the chronology of Constantine's conversion to Christianity remains one of the most debated issues connected to his life, it is uncontroversial to assert that, from an early date onwards, Constantine claimed ties to the divine. The Latin panegyric pronounced in Autun that addresses him after the disgrace in 310 of his former protector, the Tetrarch Maximian, reports Constantine's vision of what the author eloquently

---

[26] Them. *Or.* 3.46a.   [27] Amm. Marc. 21.6.2–3. See Potter (1994) 165
[28] Euseb. *VC* 3.29.2. See Drake (2020) 104.

calls 'your Apollo'.²⁹ In the same year, *Sol Invictus* begins to appear on Constantine's coinage as the emperor's divine companion, in an effort to differentiate Constantine's profile from that of the Tetrarchs, who sought association with Jupiter and Hercules.³⁰

The appeal to divine protectors was not an innovation. Roman political theory revolved around the assumption that providence underlay the history of the empire, supporting or impeding the historical agency of individual rulers. The idea that the state should be governed to maintain a good relationship with the gods, and that this regulation was a responsibility of the emperor, was widespread.³¹ Augustus famously attempted to involve his subjects in a collective project of commemoration of his rise to power that included the construction of an *horologium* with an obelisk that indicated the position of the stars at his conception and birth.³² All emperors of the Principate sought to advertise in one form or another that they benefitted from divine favour.³³ The art of divination was generally cultivated (although critical voices did exist) to gather confirmatory evidence that the gods were on the rulers' side.³⁴ Even the so-called oppositional historians – intellectuals who committed to writing history from an anti-Roman perspective – obliquely document the importance of this theme. Oppositional historians sought to challenge interpretations of Roman power as a historical necessity by positioning the empire's success as the outcome of random chance unrelated to piety or virtue.³⁵ The little evidence we can harvest from the third century suggests that rulers attempting to strengthen their imperial profile might seek to emphasise their bond with the divine (thus Aurelian with the cult of the Sol Invictus, on which see Probus' coinage).³⁶ After the difficult third century, the Tetrarchy stabilized the imperial image especially by cultivating Rome's

---

[29] *Lat. Pan.* VI (7) 21.4–5. The same text claimed that temples sprang up in Constantine's footsteps like flowers (22.6).
[30] On Constantine's solar coinage, see Chapter 4, p. 174–5. [31] Kahlos (2019) 17–24.
[32] Potter (1994) 146–47.
[33] Cf. Pliny's gift to Trajan of an oracle predicting greatness (*Pan.* 5.3–4). See Swain (1989) on Plutarch's concern with Roman providence.
[34] Potter (1994). On the perplexities advanced by some adherents of the philosophical schools in regard to Roman practices of prognostication, see already the second book of Cicero's *On Divination*. Cicero is a witness to a late Republican debate about the validity and limits of traditional divination. It is significant that, while raising the issue, he ultimately leaves the matter open (Beard (1986)).
[35] Whitmarsh (2018).
[36] Critical discussion of Aurelian and *Sol* in Ando (2012) 217. Note also that prior to the crisis Caracalla's grant of universal citizenship in the empire (212 CE) might have (also?) aimed at propitiating the gods by enlarging the community of worshippers. Decius' order for universal sacrifice to the gods for the eternity of the empire was a response to the approach of the Roman

penchant for providentialism. Tetrarchic propaganda and the Neoplatonising discourse that flourished around it dramatically heightened the rhetoric of the rulers' proximity to the divine.[37] It was in this context – and, as I set out to show, with full understanding of its mechanisms – that Constantine came to power.

Contemporary scholarship has become progressively detached from the question of the genuineness of Constantine's conversion.[38] The construction of a monolithic Constantine, the man of one decision, has been replaced by appreciation of his understanding of the 'intersubjective processes', as Lenski put it, that shaped his power.[39] Recent studies have engaged with Constantine's seemingly life-long exploration of his imperial voice as a tool to secure authority, considering *inter alia* how religious controversies sharpened his ability to negotiate his leadership vis-à-vis factional leaders.[40] Bardill, for instance, explores the interaction between Constantinian iconography and the traditional imagery of power, reflecting on Constantine's use of his public image as a means to anchor the novelty of his rule and communicate divine favour.[41] By bringing Constantine the warrior to centre stage, Wienand has demonstrated that the emperor's use of the language of military victory responded to elite concerns, neutralising the danger that he could be portrayed as the initiator of fratricidal civil wars.[42] Barbero's painstaking re-examination of Constantinian legislation has shown it to be a laboratory of construction of social consensus, catering to the interests of landowners, senators, clergymen, provincial elites, and others.[43] Lenski's investigation of Constantine's creative exploitation of the system of petition and response has cast light on his capacity to tailor persuasion based on the profile of the targeted communities.[44]

I am convinced, however, that Constantine's most daring strategy of self-legitimisation was the way he catered to public expectations that the ruler be both wise and favoured by the divine in a way that allowed him to assert his primacy over the emperors who preceded him. Constantine's writings allow us to access his strategy. A methodological caveat is

---

Millennium. On the religious underpinnings of Caracalla's and Decius' enactments, see Ando (2012) 52–55, 134–39.

[37] See the Introduction, p. 30.

[38] Discussions on the history of scholarly engagement with the theme of Constantine's conversion in – among others – Van Dam (2011); Flower (2012); Lenski (2016) 4–6; Cooper (2019) 243.

[39] Lenski (2016) 12.   [40] Drake (2000); Veyne (2010); Dillon (2012); Cooper (2019).

[41] Bardill (2012).

[42] Wienand (2012). On the late antique interest in victorious emperors, see also McCormick (1986).

[43] Barbero (2016) 473–669.   [44] Lenski (2016).

nevertheless necessary: the use of Constantinian texts always raises the question of forgery. Despite current scholarly agreement on the authenticity of several key Constantinian documents, the suspicious nature of some letters invites caution.[45] Already in the mid-fourth century, Athanasius of Alexandria attested that forgeries circulated.[46] Two considerations have therefore influenced my reading of the sources. First, I have attempted to ensure that the general argument would remain meaningful if one or more letters I analyse were later to have their authenticity questioned. It is extremely unlikely that all the texts I am considering were forged. Most of the letters presented here were transmitted by Eusebius of Caesarea, whose reliability in transcribing imperial sources is regarded as higher than that of his contemporaries.[47] Second, the possibility that some of these letters might be forgeries raises the question of their immediate reception, supporting the idea that key points of Constantine's propaganda were received and circulated in his lifetime. Eusebius gathered the imperial documents in a text, the *Life of Constantine*, whose final version is dated to around 339, that is, two years after the emperor's death.

The letters I will consider were written after Constantine's defeat of his former co-emperor Licinius in 324. This victory marked the beginning of Constantine's sole rule over a unified empire. Constantine's championing of Christianity had become explicit. But the most striking feature of his post-324 letters is that the emperor's efforts to embed his victory in a providential narrative are supported by an insistent engagement with terms that relate to reason and method. The long letter *To the Provincials of Palestine* (transmitted by Eusebius at *VC* 2.24–42) opens with the remark

---

[45] Constantine's letters were transmitted in non-neutral contexts (Eusebius, Optatus of Milevi, Augustine, Athanasius of Alexandria). On the opportunity to re-open the question of their authenticity in respect to items such as the so-called Optatus dossier or the appendix to Athanasius' *de decretis*, see Barbero (2016) 371–98, 427–44. There were clear advantages in forging or modifying early Constantinian letters like those to the Donatists: documents proving his sternness towards heretics would have dispelled suspicions that Constantine might have been accommodating with the Donatists.

[46] Athanasius, *Apol. ad Const.* 11.

[47] An important role was played in the debate by the discovery of *P. Lond.* 878. The papyrus, dated to 324, contains an independent version of Constantine's letter *To the provincials of Palestine*, which Eusebius reports in the *Life of Constantine* (*VC* 2.24–42). Eusebius' transcription of the document appears exact, with minimal variants. *P. Lond.* 878 has consequently been used to claim that the letters contained in the *Life* must be authentic; see Jones (1954) and Dörries (1954) 12–13, 46–50; Silli (1987) xvii; Cameron and Hall (1999) 16–21; Bleckmann (2012) 22. Barbero (2016) 165–67 calls for caution, pointing out that the papyrus validates Eusebius' accuracy but leaves open the possibility that the bishop inadvertently copied forgeries. I take the methodological point but believe that Eusebius' proximity to Constantine in the years he was composing the *Life of Constantine* gave him general access to high-quality materials.

that God's power 'has been demonstrated' (ἀποδέδεκται) by Constantine's 'manifest deeds and brilliant achievements' to those 'holding right and sound views about the supreme divinity' (τοῖς ὀρθῶς καὶ σωφρόνως περὶ τοῦ κρείττονος δοξάζουσιν, 2.24.1). Facts are invoked as tokens of the divine will (2.24.3). Constantine's letter invites his addressees to reconsider the course of history, finding in past events proof that a system of retribution exists and that the impiety of political leaders destabilises the state (2.27). Constantine appeals to the principles of intellect and reasoning (νοῦς and λογισμός, 2.25) and claims that divine things (and the 'true being', ὄντως ὄν) are to be investigated using 'the hidden eye of reason' (ἀπορρήτῳ τῆς διανοίας ὀφθαλμῷ, 2.65.2).[48]

As noted, claims to divine support were widespread in Roman political history. But it is intriguing to see, for the first time in imperial literature, this belief articulated competitively in opposition to the traditional Roman deities. The divine favouring of Constantine does not belong to the Tetrarchic religious system. Constantine re-asserts his point in his letter *To the Provincials of the East* (also known as *Against Polytheistic Worship*, transmitted by Eusebius in *VC* 2.48–60). Here the philosophical vocabulary is even more pronounced. The letter opens with a preamble describing Christianity as the correct method to train the mind and intellect to apprehend the cosmos. The divine is said to manifest itself through the sovereign laws of nature (κυριωτάτοις τῆς φύσεως νόμοις), providing sufficient evidence (ἱκανὴν αἴσθησιν) of its existence. The letter further states that the capacity to achieve accurate apprehension (ἡ ἀκριβὴς κατάληψις) of divine matters by a correct method (κατ' εὐθεῖαν γνώσεως ὁδόν) is a faculty of the intellect (ἡ διάνοια) and a healthy mind (τοῦ ὑγιοῦς λογισμοῦ).[49]

The text also places great emphasis on the idea that impiety (that is, the worship of the Greco-Roman gods) is 'perverse unreason' (2.48.2). In an act of self-distancing from his predecessors, Constantine writes that he regards 'the previous emperors as exceedingly harsh because of their savage ways ... all the rest were mentally sick' (οὐκ ὑγιαίνοντες τὰς φρένας, 2.49). His father is singled out as the only exception – a mark of dynastic

---

[48] Cf. also *VC* 2.56.2 (the faithful described as 'those of good understanding' [εὖ φρονοῦντες]); 2.59 ('the doctrines of the divine word' [τὰ τοῦ θείου λόγου μαθήματα] are understood by 'those who think right' [τοῖς ὀρθότερον φρονοῦσι]); 3.19.1 (the issue of the dating of Easter solved by 'correct computation'); 3.64.2 (the heretics 'argue falsehoods'); 4.10.2 (God requires men with 'a pure mind').

[49] *VC* 2.48. The idea that cosmic order demonstrates the existence of providence is taken up again at *VC* 2.57–58.

concerns, and a point to which I return below. Intriguingly, the letter includes an anecdote depicting Diocletian, the persecuting emperor, as incapable of interpreting divine messages, a gullible pawn of Apollo's deceitful oracles.[50] Divine retribution, through the mention of the 'shameful death' of the persecuting emperors (2.54), closes Constantine's account. This thus offers itself as a demonstration for 'people of good sense' (τοὺς δ' εὖ φρονοῦντας) of the need to live according to God's laws.

Similar themes surface in other Constantinian documents from the same years. A circular letter received by Eusebius reflects on how the restoration of liberty that followed the end of the persecutions was evidence of God's agency (*VC* 2.46). The claim that wonders provided 'evidence for the truth' (ἡ τῆς ἀληθείας πίστις) also features in a letter in which Constantine gives instructions concerning the construction of the Church of the Holy Sepulchre in Jerusalem (*VC* 3.30.3). In addressing the quarrelling bishops Alexander and Arius, Constantine returns to the theme of the hidden eye of reason (ἀπορρήτῳ τῆς διανοίας ὀφθαλμῷ) that captures divine truth, arguing that impiety is madness (*VC* 2.65).[51] Constantine's letter to the Persian king Shapur II, a text of uncertain authenticity, further presents the emperor as declaring his intent to serve as 'the teacher of the knowledge of the most holy God'.[52]

The key to accessing Constantine's language is in the way the question of the relationship between the ruler and the divine had been influenced by the circulation of philosophical ideas at the Tetrarchic court. As the link between the ruler and the divine was tightened by rulers refusing to equate their subdivision of imperial leadership with diminishing their imperial status,[53] a philosophical vocabulary gradually suffused the rhetoric of the

---

[50] *VC* 2.51. In conformity with early Christian views, Constantine does not deny the existence of Apollo but disqualifies him as a mischievous daemon.

[51] The letter (*VC* 2.65–72) was perhaps addressed not simply to Alexander and Arius but to a synod of bishops that gathered in Antioch at the beginning of 325 (Hall [1998]; Cameron and Hall [1999]; Barbero [2016] 176).

[52] *VC* 4.9. On the question of the text's authenticity, see Lee (1993) 37; Cameron and Hall (1999) 313–14; Poggi (2003); Barbero (2016) 204–5.

[53] On the evolution of court ceremonial, the assumption of the diadem, and the practice of the *adoratio*, see DePalma Digeser (2000) 28; Kolb (2004); Rees (2004) 46–56; Bowman (2005) 70–71; Van Dam (2007b) 229–33; Potter (2013) 53. Aurelius Victor (39.2–4), Eutropius (9.26), Ammianus (15.5.18), and Jerome (*Chron.* 292–93) attribute to Diocletian the use of expensive purple dyes, jewels, and silks, as Victor reports that Diocletian demanded, rather than merely allowing, worship and appellatives like *dominus*, 'Lord' (*Caes.* 39). The request was previously seen as a mark of tyrannical behaviour (cf. Suetonius on Domitian's desire to be called *dominus et deus*, in *Dom.* 13.1–2) and mostly used as a flattering address in private contexts (Roller (2001) 257–58). See however Carlà-Uhink (2019) for a problematisation of the sources. For a reassessment of the

panegyrists.⁵⁴ The speeches addressing sovereigns locate the ideal character of the emperors in the capacity of their mind to access divine will. Divine favour was thematised as originating from the synergy between the sublime mind of the sovereign and the divine intellect enlivening the cosmos; this conviction to some extent explains the late antique fortune of the ideal of the ruler as 'ensouled law', whose mind is a source of perfect justice.⁵⁵

The young Constantine – the son of a Tetrarch, raised in Tetrarchic courts – grew up immersed in this rhetoric. A fleeting reference to the 'divine mind' of the Tetrarch Maximian, who favoured Constantine's ascent to the throne, features in a Latin panegyric dated to March 307.⁵⁶ This is one of the first documents attesting to the rise of Constantine as an associate of the emperors. Comparison of Constantine's mind with the 'divine mind, which governs the whole of this world', also appears in the Latin panegyric of 311, composed after Maximian's fall into disgrace.⁵⁷ In addition, praise of Constantine's *ratio* surfaces in the panegyric from 313 that celebrates Constantine's victory over Maximian's son, Maxentius.⁵⁸ In this text, the divinity is nameless⁵⁹ – its indeterminacy being a marker of universality – but it is undisputed that the emperor's intellect communicates with it. Constantine is described as 'sharing some secret with the divine mind' (*illa mens divina*) and being guided by divine inspiration.⁶⁰ The same rhetoric of the 'prompting of the divinity' behind Constantine's victory and the magnitude of his mind (*mentis magnitudo*) characterises the inscription on the Triumphal Arch the Senate of Rome dedicated to Constantine in 315, which sanctioned his civil war as a *bellum iustum*.⁶¹

Although Constantine's progressive personalisation of his imperial image eventually culminated in the endorsement of a new religion, Neoplatonic expectations continued to underlie his communications. But they did so with a subtle but key change, which I see as a crucial instrument of legitimisation of what was in essence a paradigm shift. As the letters from the mid-320s show, Constantine's description of his

---

monumental Tetrarchic images in the temple of Luxor, ancient Thebes, as marking a site for imperial worship while the emperors were still alive, see Barbagli (2020).
⁵⁴ Burgersdijk (2020). ⁵⁵ See Chapter 1, p. 44–9. ⁵⁶ *Pan. Lat.* VII (6), 7.1.
⁵⁷ *Pan. Lat.* V (8), 10.2. ⁵⁸ *Pan. Lat.* XII (9), 4.2.
⁵⁹ It is referred to as *deus* (XII (9) 2.4, 13.2), *maiestas* (2.4), *mens divina* (2.5, 16.2), *divinum numen* (4.1), *numen* (5.5), *divinum consilium* (4.5), *divinus instinctus* (11.4), *creator* (13.2) and *divinitas* (22.1, 25.4). See Nixon and Mynors (1994) 292; Wienand (2012) 247.
⁶⁰ *Pan. Lat.* XII (9), 2.5; 11.4. ⁶¹ *ILS* 694.

understanding of divine providence does not rely on claims of an intuitive connection with the divine. The Christian emperor instead seems interested in exploring, as noted, a vocabulary that addresses questions of rational method and intellectual training via the observation of nature and history. The change is less drastic than it might seem. Neoplatonism owed to Plato an understanding of reason as the godly element residing in us and thus conceived of philosophy as the path to self-divinisation.[62] The emperor describing how he cultivated his reason could thus be interpreted as celebrating his mind's achievement of a perfect (and consequently divine) harmony with God. But Constantine's emphasis on training remains striking. Tetrarchic panegyrists simply assumed that the emperors knew; Constantine underscores that his knowledge is acquired. The gesture is eloquent. It marks what I see as the ambition of neutralising change as an act of restoration. Constantine's rhetorical shift signifies his intention to recover the old, authoritative paradigm of the philosopher-ruler, which, as the Introduction considered, the rulers of the Principate had revisited and third-century emperors too might have attempted to resurrect.[63] The emperor endorsing a religion regarded as both subversive and appealing to the uncultured assuaged elite concerns that the emperor must be both wise and favoured by the divine by reviving a traditional political model.

This apparently reassuring gesture had two transformative implications. First, Constantine injected a contemporary representation of Christianity as the highest (or exclusive) source of wisdom into the imperial political debate. As noted, Christian apologists had been negotiating the place and status of Christianity among the philosophical schools of Greece and Rome since the second century.[64] Constantine's proximity to Lactantius, one of the key advocates of Christianity as the foundation and goal of all knowledge, may have facilitated his assimilation of this ideal.[65] The second edition of Lactantius' *Divine Institutes*, dated to around winter 312/313,

---

[62] Discussion in Chapter 1.
[63] Gallienus (r. 253–68) acted *inter alia* as the patron of the philosopher Plotinus (cf. Porph. *Vit. Plot.* 12). On Gallienus' penchant for Greek literature and art, see also *H.A.* (*Gallieni*), 6. Cf. Mathew (1943); De Blois (1976); Key Fowden (2008) 97; Ando (2012) 173. See also the case of emperor Macrinus (r. 217–18), who prior to the crisis briefly tried to take up the persona of a philosopher-ruler (Herodian 5.2.3, cf. Brown [1992] 58).
[64] See the Introduction, p. 1–4.
[65] For Constantine's knowledge of Lactantius' work and the hypothesis of influence, see DePalma Digeser (2000) 91–143; Garnsey (2003) 3 n. 13; Schott (2008) 110–35; Lettieri (2013); Potter (2013) 63–64; Gassman (2020) 19–47. Constantine knew Lactantius personally. The Numidian rhetorician operated in Nicomedia in the years Constantine resided there, at Diocletian's court, and later joined Constantine's court in Trier, where he also served as teacher of Constantine's eldest son Crispus (Jer. *Vir. Ill.* 80). Constantine's (and Licinius') decision to grant freedom of religion to the

includes two dedications to Constantine, whom Lactantius describes as 'the first emperor of the Romans who repudiated errors (*repudiatis erroribus*) and recognized (*cognovisti*) and honoured the majesty of the one true god'.[66]

Second, Constantine's endorsement of an idea of Christianity as a perfect theory of the cosmos turned the self-projection of the ruler into a competitive exercise. The argument that a Christian emperor was a philosopher-ruler by virtue of his religious allegiance inevitably entailed a disqualification of the religious and intellectual system that preceded him and that claimed ties with a different divine. This point is captured with unique effectiveness in a text written at some point during the rule of the mature Constantine: the *Oration to the Assembly of the Saints*.[67] As the next section will show, the *Oration* is shaped around two ambitions: it validates Constantine's self-projection as a philosopher-ruler by illustrating his methodology as an exegete, and it produces (antagonistic) evidence supporting the theological and historical necessity of his rule.

Exegesis and Empire in Constantine's *Oration to the Assembly of the Saints*

Earlier scholarship debated the authenticity of this text, which is transmitted as an attachment to Eusebius' *Life of Constantine*.[68] Scepticism mostly

---

Roman oecumene through the so-called Edict of Milan of 313 has also been suspected of bearing the imprint of Lactantius (cf. *Div. inst.* 5.19.23, arguing that persecutions harm any cult they seek to protect; DePalma Digeser (2000) 92; Garnsey (2003) 46; Lettieri [2012]). Constantine's letter *To the Provincials of the East* (Euseb. *VC* 2.56.1) has been called an 'epitome' of Lactantius' *Divine Institutes* (Lettieri [2013] 51).

[66] Lactant. *Div. inst.* 1.1.13. See DePalma Digeser (2000) 134; Schott (2008) 106; Lettieri (2013) 49; Lenski (2016) 37.

[67] An early date is supported by Girardet (2013) 28–49; and Edwards (2003) xxiii–xxix, favouring Rome 315. This presupposes that the *Oration* was composed when Constantine was still based in Rome and had a Western audience in view. However, the piece's hybrid cultural references, its resonance with the Constantinian writings from the 320s, and the allusive political geography mapped out in *OC* 22–25, have led most scholars to favour the hypothesis of a later composition. Piganiol suggested delivery in Thessalonica in 323 (Piganiol [1932]); Lane Fox (1986) Antioch 325; Bleckmann (1997) Nicomedia 328; Barnes (2001) Nicomedia 325; Cristofoli (2005) 12–28 argues for the *Oratio* as a draft delivered before the summer of 325 somewhere in the East; Schott (2008) 111 and Lenski (2016) 35 favour Spring 325. Cf. also Drake's hypothesis that the *Oration* was not destined for a specific date and place of delivery but was a draft meant to be adapted for various occasions (Drake (2000) 292–305).

[68] Discussions of its authenticity in Piganiol (1932); Dörries (1954) 147–61; Barnes (1976), (2001); Lane Fox (1986) 627–53; Silli (1987) xiii; Bleckmann (1997); Cameron and Hall (1999) 51; Drake (2000) 292–305; Edwards (2003) xviii–xxii; Cristofoli (2005); Girardet (2013); Barbero (2016) 226–33; Lenski (2016) 35 n. 56.

originated with the question of whether Constantine would have been able to author what looks and reads like a short theological treatise.[69] But recent scholarship has emphasised that authorial intention does not exclude collaboration. The text of the Constantinian oration might be, in smaller or greater part, the product of the assistance and intervention of the Christian theologians who gravitated around Constantine's court.[70] What is more relevant here is the question of whether the *Oration* conveys a Constantinian message, and the answer, I aim to show, is that it does. The *Oration* is concerned with establishing Christianity as the source of Constantine's superior understanding of the divine providence ordaining the history of Rome and with demonstrating on this basis the necessity of his rule. Engagement with exegesis simultaneously showcases Constantine's interpretive methodology and solidifies his bond with the subjects invited to assess his claims based on the evidence he himself provides.

The *Oration*, a Good Friday sermon, revolves around Christology. Following a preface that celebrates the Passion of Christ for redeeming humankind, a long section outlines elements of theology and debates cosmic principles, discussing the genesis of the elements, the eternal substance of God, and the failure of pagan gods to maintain concord in the universe (*OC* 2–10). A celebration of Christ's message against the background of Greek philosophers (Constantine challenges Socrates, Pythagoras, and Plato)[71] leads to what might seem a long, redundant digression: a commentary on a set of Christological texts. After some scenes from Matthew's gospel (*OC* 15), Constantine lingers on the book of Daniel, reading famous episodes (the fiery furnace and the lion's den) as stories of faith and prayer 'rewarded by Christ's providence' (*OC* 17).[72]

---

[69] Other issues have been raised to question Constantine's authorship, but they all appear minor. Socrates and Photius, speaking of the writings of Eusebius, seem unaware that something (the *Oration*) was attached to Eusebius' *Life* (but see Cristofoli [2015] 11–12, envisaging various solutions). Secondly, Constantine quotes a Sibylline oracle in a version that seems to differ from the text known by his contemporaries Lactantius and Augustine (see n. 73 below); but Constantine's quotation might have been modified by his Greek translators or a later interpolator. Finally, the structure of the *Oration* seems to differ from the standard outline of the Constantinian orations that Eusebius provides at *VC* 4.29.3–4. The *Oration*, however, is a text with a very precise agenda, something that might have encouraged its eccentric structure (while, conversely, a forger might easily have tried to reproduce Constantine's standard rhetoric).

[70] Barnes (2001); Cristofoli (2005) 8; Lenski (2016) 65. Eusebius claims that Constantine wrote his orations alone (*VC* 4.39). This is certainly a propagandistic statement, although it should be noted that Constantine was properly educated (although Eusebius' reference to the 'excellence of his rhetorical education' at *VC* 1.19.2 is probably another exaggeration. See Barnes [1981] 73–75; Edwards [2003] xii; Lenski [2012] 60).

[71] See *OC* 9, 16.   [72] All translations of the *Oration* from Edwards (2003).

After the disquisition on Daniel, Constantine's statement that he will be 'commemorating foreign witnesses (ἀλλοδαπῶν μαρτυριῶν) to the divinity of Christ' (*OC* 18) brings him out of the realm of Scripture. He first introduces the Erythraean Sibyl, a priestess of Apollo who, having become 'full of truly divine inspiration', foresaw the coming of Christ. At this point, breaking the flow of his argument, Constantine transcribes a long section of a poem ascribed to the Sibyl, which forms the acrostic *Iesous Christos theou huios soter* ('Jesus Christ, son of God, Saviour').[73] Next, he introduces Virgil's *Eclogue*, celebrating the birth of a *puer* who ushers in the Golden Age, which is read by Constantine as another announcement of the coming of Christ. A long section of the *Oration* (almost two full chapters, 19 and 20 in current editions) is dedicated to quoting from the *Eclogue* and explaining how it should be interpreted. In contrast to Lactantius, who argued that Virgil unwittingly became the intermediary of the Logos,[74] Constantine makes Virgil a conscious prophet. The poet deliberately hid his announcement of the coming of Christ under the veil of allegory out of fear of persecution (*OC* 20).

The end of the commentary rebukes 'those who lack intelligence' (τῶν οὐκ εὖ φρονούντων) and might therefore reject Constantine's analysis. Then the *Oration* resumes its general argument and offers a critique of contemporary history, attacking Constantine's third-century predecessors who had persecuted Christianity (or were considered to have done so). This provides readers with a concise version of an argument with a Lactantian resonance: the view, famously expounded in *On the Deaths of the Persecutors*, that God punishes those who persecuted Christianity 'by great and marvellous examples'.[75] Constantine illustrates the miserable end of his predecessors Decius, Valerian, and Diocletian. Decius, 'who trampled upon the toils of the just, in hatred', died on the battlefield as he 'led the renowned power of Rome to contempt against the Getae' (*OC* 24). Valerian is said to have 'made the holy judgment manifest' (τὴν ὁσίαν κρίσιν ἐξέφηνας) by dying in captivity as a prisoner of the Persians. Diocletian descended into madness:

> What good did it bring to this man to have kindled war against our God? I suppose that of passing the rest of his life in fear of the thunderbolt . . . .

---

[73] Constantine's quotation of the text includes the acrostic of an extra word, *stauros* (cross), which is missing in Lactantius' and Augustine's citations of the poem (*Div. inst.* 7.16, 19, 24; *Civ. D.* 18.23). On the relationship between these testimonies, see Kurfess (1918); Cristofoli (2005) 14-15; and Girardet (2013) 101-6.
[74] Lactant. *Div. inst.* 7.23.9–15. Garnsey (2003) 18; Cristofoli (2005) 123.
[75] Lactant. *Mort. Pers.* 1.5–7.

For I saw him cry out, when he was mentally enfeebled (εὐτελὴς τὸ φρόνημα) and in fear of every sight and sound, that the cause of the evils surrounding him had been his own folly (τὴν ἀφροσύνην ἑαυτοῦ) when he invoked against himself God's protection of the just. Nevertheless, the palace and his house were destroyed, after the dispensation of the thunderbolt and the fire from heaven. The outcome of these actions had been foretold, in fact, by intelligent people (προείρητό γε ἡ τούτων ἔκβασις ὑπὸ τῶν εὖ φρονούντων). (*OC* 25)

The final sentence of the account, focusing on the capacity of 'intelligent people' to predict the tragic outcome of Diocletian's folly, is essential. The *Oration* is thoroughly concerned with establishing a connection between Christianity and intelligence: those who make nature rather than providence the cause of the ordering of the cosmos are guilty of 'stupidity' because they fail to read the 'proofs' that are 'clear and before our eyes' (*OC* 8–10).[76] Belief in chance is detected as originating in 'haphazard and irrational thoughts' (*OC* 11). 'Reason and providence', Constantine claims, 'are God' (*OC* 12), who made the human being 'a rational creature' (*OC* 30) and guides our intellect (*OC* 36).

Most important, the appeal to 'intelligent people' evokes comparison with Constantine's attribution of stupidity to those who dissent from his interpretation of Virgil as a conscious prophet – a comparison that reveals the meaning of the *Oration*'s exegetical digression. This seemingly redundant excursus is the heart of Constantine's piece: it provides a world desiring a providential ruler with a demonstration of the ruler's capacity to recognise the presence of the divine in the world. It should be remembered, incidentally, that this claim ties into the long-standing practice of Roman politicians of engaging with inductive prognostication, which Cicero's brother Quintus describes, in *On Divination*, as the practice of those who 'having learned the known by observation, seek the unknown by conjecture'.[77] Constantine's insight into God's plans is first illustrated through his interpretations of actual texts: for post-Hellenistic philosophical schools, allegory and divination were the complementary means by which the wise decoded the presence of God in its creatures, be these natural entities or literary artefacts.[78] The first half of the *Oration*, with its enunciation of the metaphysical principles of Christianity, thus appears as

---

[76] Cf. also Schott (2008) 117–22, who sees in the *Oration* a demonstration, developed with a pedagogical intent, of how Christianity overcomes the errors of polytheistic traditions in which Greek philosophers too are caught up despite their claims to universal knowledge.

[77] Cic. *Div.* 1.18.34. On inductive prognostication, see Potter (1994) 15. On the connection of this practice with future-oriented historiography, see Introduction, p. 26.

[78] On the semantic overlap between literary hermeneutics and the interpretation of divine signs in antiquity, see Ford (2002) 80–55; Struck (2010) 164–65.

the exegete's display of his interpretive toolbox, which enables him to crack open the Christological meaning of divinely inspired texts.

Two points are crucial. First, the truth of Constantine's reading is confirmed by the outcome of his greatest act of interpretation, the reading of Roman history. Second, the validity of this interpretation is sanctioned by the evidence provided by Constantine's own life. Constantine was addressing audiences aware that the stability of his power followed decades of political struggle, of which the collapse of the Tetrarchy represented a final act. It is in the handling of the Tetrarchy's downfall and Constantine's role in facilitating it that the cleverness of the *Oration*'s structure becomes evident. Rome's past crises are not hidden but brought into focus. When the reader-emperor argues that the wise could have predicted the destiny of his persecuting predecessors, he is conflating Rome's problems with those of interpretation: suffice it to say that Romans had been reading Virgil for centuries without understanding him as a Christian prophet. The *Oration*'s analyses of history and literature are thus presented as correcting erroneous assumptions: Christianity was not new but foundational, restorative not subversive. Constantine's life, military achievements, and long-standing success underscore that, having truly found the divine – that is, the god who intervenes in history – he is confirmed in his discovery by the fact that he rules with God-given guidance and benefitting from divine support. 'For my part', Constantine writes at the end of the *Oration*, in an address to divine providence, 'I ascribe to Your goodwill all my good fortune and that of those who are mine. And the evidence of this (μαρτυρεῖ δὲ καὶ) is that everything has turned out according to my prayers'.[79] The audience is being instructed as to where to find proof of the validity of Constantine's claims. A striking coincidence is being explained. It is not that the victorious emperor also happens to be a sublime interpreter; instead, Constantine is victorious precisely because he is a sublime interpreter.

Interpreting Constantine's Act of Interpretation: Eusebius of Caesarea and the Celestial Cross

The transmission of Constantine's post-324 letters and his *Oration to the Assembly of Saints* within Eusebius' *Life of Constantine* is not accidental. Eusebius' final work gathers documents that produce a consistent image of Constantine as the interpreter of the divine. One of the most debated issues in Eusebian scholarship is the nature of Eusebius' relationship with

---

[79] *OC* 22 (cf. 25).

Constantine.⁸⁰ The nineteenth-century idea of Eusebius as a court historian subservient to Constantine and his ideals has been progressively replaced by an understanding of Eusebius' support of Constantine as always contingent on Constantine's support of Christianity.⁸¹ But acknowledgement of Eusebius' agenda should not lead us to conclude that he ignored Constantine's project and self-image. There were important points of misalignment between the emperor and the theologian, particularly in respect to the budding power dynamics between state and church – a point to which I return in a later chapter.⁸² At the same time, we should not underestimate Eusebius' proximity to Constantine. Especially in the final years of his life, the bishop had an opportunity to observe the emperor up close.⁸³ Eusebius' proximity presumably served the intellectualising ambitions perceptible in Constantine's delineation of his imperial profile: Eusebius enjoyed a reputation as an erudite, intellectual bishop, and Constantine acknowledged this explicitly and on multiple occasions. In his letters, the emperor praises Eusebius' treatise on Pascha, asking for more such writings (*VC* 4.35). He also entrusted the bishop with the production of fifty parchment codices of the Bible (4.36), a choice that indicates that he saw Eusebius as particularly well qualified to supervise the task. In addition, Constantine is reported to have engaged in at least one theological discussion about an address by the bishop (4.33).⁸⁴ Finally, Eusebius was entrusted with the honour of delivering an encomium of Constantine at court at a time of extraordinary symbolic significance: the celebration of Constantine's thirty years of rule, his *Tricennalia*, which were held in Constantinople in July 336.⁸⁵

It is against this background that we must read the account of Constantine's conversion during his Italian campaign of 312 offered in Eusebius' final work, the *Life of Constantine*. Eusebius' first account of the

---

⁸⁰ See, e.g., Barnes (1981) 266; Cameron and Hall (1999) 23; Drake (2000) 371; Johnson (2006) 156, (2014) 112; Corke-Webster (2019) 1–9.
⁸¹ For a reassessment of the debate, see Corke-Webster (2019) 2–9. Barnes (1981) altered perceptions of Eusebius by stressing his autonomy and distance, as a provincial bishop, from the halls of power. This led to dismissal of the idea that Eusebius was a court historian. Barnes relied *inter alia* on the consideration that only four encounters between the emperor and the bishop are documented (Barnes [1981] 26). Yet four attested meetings with the ruler of the Roman Empire cannot be described as 'few' (as Drake [2000] 370 notes). Constantine's manifestations of esteem for Eusebius (on which, see below) further help challenge the idea that he was a marginal episcopal figure. Barnes' point regarding Eusebius' autonomy, however, remains valid, as his primary allegiance was seemingly always to the Church. Eusebius, who could equate Rome with Assyria (*DE* 7.1), celebrated the empire in his later works but always saw in Christ the conquering agent of polyarchy and polytheism and the power behind Augustus' rise (Johnson (2006) 180–88).
⁸² See Chapter 5, p. 227–31.   ⁸³ Drake (1988).   ⁸⁴ Cf. Wienand (2012) 427.
⁸⁵ Cf. *VC* 4.46.

campaign, in his *Ecclesiastical History* (finished ca. 325), had already addressed the theme of Constantine's victories as a manifestation of divine will. The *Ecclesiastical History* cast Constantine's defeat of Maxentius at the battle of the Milvian Bridge, which resulted in his conquest of Rome, as a re-enactment of the biblical crossing of the Red Sea.[86] But this account differs in one important respect from that produced years later in the *Life*: it lacks the story of Constantine's vision of a cross in the sky accompanied by the motto 'By this conquer'.

Eusebius' account of the vision in the *Life* begins with the statement that, before Constantine marched against Maxentius, he realised his need for a god who would support him. The reference to this intuition is followed by an illustration of Constantine's thought processes:

> He (*scil.* Constantine) therefore considered what kind of god he should adopt to aid him, and, while he thought, a clear impression came to him (ζητοῦντι δ' αὐτῷ ἔννοιά τις ὑπεισῆλθεν), that of the many who had in the past aspired to government, those who had attached their personal hopes to many gods and had cultivated them with drink-offerings, sacrifices, and dedications, had first been deceived by favourable predictions and oracles which promised welcome things, but then met an unwelcome end .... Only his own father had taken the opposite course to theirs by condemning their error, while he himself had throughout his life honoured the God who transcends the universe and had found him a saviour and guardian of his Empire and a provider of everything good .... He marshalled these arguments in his mind (ταῦτ' οὖν πάντα συναγαγὼν τῇ διανοίᾳ) and concluded that it was folly (ματαιάζειν) to go on with the vanity of the gods who do not exist and to persist in error in the face of so much evidence (τοσοῦτον ἔλεγχον), and he decided he should venerate his father's god alone.[87]

Eusebius portrays Constantine performing inductive prognostication. The emperor stops to reflect on the past and realises that the polytheistic rulers of the Roman Empire had always come to a bad end (or so he says): he is engaging – or claiming to engage – with evidence provided by the history of Rome. His own father, 'having condemned their error' (a propagandistic theme),[88] had conversely received God's support throughout his life.

---

[86] *HE* 9.9. [87] *VC* 1.27. All translations of the *VC* are from Cameron and Hall.
[88] Cf. Constantine's reference to his father's 'gentle deeds' in his letter to the provincials in the East (*VC* 2.49). Lactantius, emphasising Constantius' different attitude to religion from the other Tetrarchs (*Mort. Pers.* 8.7), argues that he allowed the destruction of churches during the Great Persecution ('to avoid appearing to disagree') but left the Christians themselves unscathed (*Mort. Pers.* 15.7). Eusebius denies that he destroyed buildings (*HE* 8.13.12–13; *VC* 1.13). It has been argued that Constantius was a Christian or a Christian sympathizer (e.g., Barnes [1981] 19–20; and Elliott [1987] 423). But the Latin Panegyrics present him as an adherent of Greco-Roman religion. See further Smith (1997); Cameron and Hall (1999) 195; Cristofoli (2005) 85.

No evidence is provided to support this claim, perhaps because the life of Constantine, who allegedly patterned his life on the precedent set by his father, buttresses this claim retroactively. Crucially, it is only *after* having reached his conclusions, grounded on historical interpretation, that Eusebius' Constantine begins to invoke his father's god in prayer. In response, he receives a vision that reveals that he is praying to the Christian god:

> He began to invoke this god in prayer, beseeching and imploring him to show who he was and to stretch out his right hand to assist him in his plans. As he made these prayers and earnest supplications, a most remarkable divine sign appeared to the Emperor . . . . About the time of the midday sun, when the day was just turning, he said he saw with his own eyes, up in the sky and resting over the sun, a cross-shaped trophy formed from light, and a text attached to it which said 'By this conquer!' (τούτῳ νίκα).[89]

This story of the dramatic disclosure of God's identity seems to rely on the assumption that Constantine knew that his father was a monotheist but was in the dark as to the identity of the god he worshipped, perhaps a consequence of the fact that Constantine was raised apart from his father and only joined him shortly before his death. It is essential, however, that the apparition of the celestial cross reads as a response – or better, as the final step of a process begun by Constantine's interpretation. The emperor's choice of the god of his father is based on rational enquiry, and the vision stands as an act of divine endorsement sanctioning the validity of his analysis (through a sign that demands further decoding).

Eusebius' account is accompanied by the statement that the emperor himself told him this story (*VC* 1.28.1). We might be sceptical about an assertion that seeks to justify the report of a supernatural event by claiming direct acquaintance with a witness who happened to be the figure of greatest authority in the empire, the holy emperor who could not lie. Furthermore, the account likely contains Eusebian elements, for instance, the introduction of members of his own profession (priests) in the storyline in a seemingly redundant way.[90] But Eusebius' description of Constantine's thoughts fully captures the emperor's intellectual self-image as it emerges from his writings. Two options are available. Eusebius may have lied in claiming that this story of conversion came from Constantine but nevertheless produced an account resonating with Constantine's writings. Alternatively, Eusebius faithfully reported Constantine's version and, although making some additions, maintained its essential features. In this

---

[89] *VC* 1.28.   [90] *VC* 1.32. Discussion in Chapter 5, p. 228–9.

regard, we should bear in mind that Eusebius could accrue important benefits by endorsing the idea of Constantine as wise interpreter. Chapter 1 illustrated that the identification of Christianity as the greatest philosophical school of the empire was the centre of gravity of Eusebius' historical and theological production.[91] Furthermore, a ruler acknowledging that his understanding of God and providence was a matter of reasoning and method rather than innate, provided Eusebius with a springboard to negotiate the (spiritual) authority of the ecclesiastical leader vis-à-vis the power of the emperor. I return to this second point below.

Gifting Interpretation: Optatian's *Carmina*

The work of a lay author seeking Constantine's favour in the mid-320s further suggests that, at the time of the unification of the empire, the concept of the ruler as intelligent interpreter was known to imperial audiences, who could also access its theological and political significance. Publilius Optatianus Porfyrius – usually referred to as Optatian – a member of the Constantinian entourage,[92] fell into disgrace and was exiled for unknown reasons seemingly between late 322 and 323. Optatian later sought to appease the emperor by composing a collection of highly intellectualising panegyrics in verse that resurrected the Hellenistic tradition of picture poetry. Constantine received the *carmina* around the celebrations of his *vicennalia*, in July 326.[93] We learn from Jerome that Optatian was rewarded for the gift by being recalled from exile.[94] In the following years, Optatian seems to have fared well: he was entrusted with the proconsulship of Achaea and subsequently with the urban prefecture of Rome. His collection of *carmina* arguably succeeded in restoring his reputation and boosting his prestige. Constantine surely approved of a type of poetry that appeared receptive to the transformation in his public and political image.[95] Optatian's poems rubber-stamped the fundamental re-orientation of the emperor's profile after his final victory over his former co-ruler Licinius. The event was followed by a new propaganda emphasis on the theme of

---

[91] See p. 66–70.
[92] Optatian, *Carm.* 6 puts him in Constantine's court in 322 (Wienand [2017] 124).
[93] The date is debated (Barnes (1975) 184; Barbero (2016) 107–12), but Optatian asserts that his poems were meant to be given to Constantine on that occasion (*Carm.* 4.1, 5.8, 9.35, 16.35, 19.33). See Wienand (2017) 124–35; Moser (2018) 37.
[94] Jerome, *Chron.* 354 Helm. Jerome dates Optatian's release to 329. But the year is questioned and the release is tentatively dated to soon after the petition (see Polara [1974] 118–19; Barnes [1975] 175). In 329, Optatian was already serving as prefect of Rome (Wienand [2017]).
[95] Wienand (2012) 355–420. See also Van Dam (2011) 158–70.

Constantine as victor on a religious-cosmic plane. His reign was now represented as a *saeculum aureum*, the triumph of *iustitia* and *veritas*.[96]

The form of Optatian's poems also served as political commentary. If his epistolary exchange with Constantine, which survives in a number of manuscripts, is authentic – as scholars are now inclined to think[97] – this correspondence, which pre-dates the exile, is key to understanding Optatian's engagement with crucial themes. His letter to Constantine combines praise for the military excellence and scholarship of the sovereign, showing an awareness that Constantine saw value in both. Constantine's reply, suggesting that the greatness of the literary past of Rome should not prevent artists from striving towards something new, expresses a desire to act as a patron of bold new forms of art. This desire deserves contextualisation, as Constantine's praise of literary innovation arguably resonates with the new types of writing being produced around him and his court, from Lactantius' *On the Deaths of the Persecutors* to Eusebius' own remarkably innovative and ambitious oeuvre. Optatian arguably sought to carve out a space for himself in this context, responding to Constantine's invitation with poems whose Neoplatonising language and imagery sealed their author's ambition to be recognised as a unique poetic voice at court.[98]

Optatian's poems form acrostics and create pictures. Their experimental visual quality was once regarded as a sign of the decadence and abstruse character of late Latin literature.[99] Analysis of the interaction between his poetry and the imperial image, however, reveals that its forms were timely. Optatian's effort reads as an attempt to offer a poetry of reason, an intellectual act blending past literary forms from the Greek tradition (e.g., Hellenistic *technopaegnia*) with erudite echoes and allusions to the Latin poetic canon.[100] This cultural encounter acquires particular meaning since it is employed in celebration of the emperor, under whose enlightened rule such cultural efforts could be pursued. The sovereign himself, as Körfer shows, is actively involved in the process of interpreting Optatian's oeuvre: the *carmina* summon Constantine as co-producer of his own praise. The emperor is expected to detect the layers of significance, (re)constructing how their combination creates the panegyric form.[101]

---

[96] Wienand (2012) 373.
[97] Dörries (1954) 127–28; Barnes (1975), (1981) 47; Corcoran (1997) 152; Wienand (2012) 358; Van Dam (2011) 158–70. See *contra* Barbero (2016) 111–12, who tends to think that they are forgeries. Most scholars accepting their authenticity date them to ca. 312–13. Wienand (2017) 148–55 suggests a date of around 319–22.
[98] On elements of Neoplatonism in Optatian's poetry, see Habinek (2017).
[99] Surveys of older scholarship in Squire (2017b) 56; Squire and Whitton (2017) 46.
[100] On the relationship between Optatian's poems and the *cento*, see Squire (2017a) 83.
[101] Körfer (2019) 22–147.

But the *carmina* do more than massage the sovereign's ambition to be recognised as an intellectual through literature. On a more profound level, they celebrate the ruler as able to read divine meaning in literature. The dedication of picture-poems to Constantine is tantamount to offering the emperor a network of symbols. The lines are eloquently pervaded by the vocabulary of *signa* (signs).[102] I see additional meaning in the fact that this network of signs combines the classical and the Christian: the *carmina* famously alternate invocations to the Muses and Apollo with acrostics forming crosses.[103]

Seeking to force Optatian into the confessional box might not be worth the effort. Remarkable religious fluidity must have characterised elite life in the 310s and 320s, decades in which Christianity was seeking to find its identity at court.[104] It remains the case, however, that Constantine's (and Lactantius' and Eusebius')[105] interpretation of the relationship between the classics and Christianity relied on the assumption that the good elements of Greco-Roman culture were all contained in Christian doctrine. Optatian's poetry seems to provide a poetic symbolisation of this assumption. His imagery and vocabulary may be classical, but the words he puts together create Christian forms. I see this not as testimony to the author's allegiance to Christianity but as a window into what a court intellectual assumed would please the emperor who showcased his capacity to read the truth in the world.

In support of this reading, one might observe that Optatian's visual symbolisation of the classical in the Christian (or of the Christian form as containing the classical) is instrumental to his celebration of Constantine's power. This is well exemplified by *carm.* 19, dated to 329.[106] The picture poem praising Constantine's rule takes the shape of a ship, an ancient metaphor of the state used by Alcaeus (and others) and now presumably employed to refer to the naval victory of Chrysopolis of 324, in which Constantine's fleet crushed Licinius' (Figure 3.1).[107]

The mast and sails of the ship form a Christogram (or *Chrismon*), which complicates the poem's apparently classical – at least on a literary level – celebration of Constantine's rule. Just as the divine manifests itself in the world through signs the wise recognise and can decode through interpretation, so too

---

[102] Squire and Whitton (2017) 68. See, e.g., the use of terms like *vicennia signa* (4.1), *signare* (5.2, 6.34), *signatur* (7.12), *pia signa* (8.2), *insigna magna* (8.27), *caelestia signa* (19.1), *signis ... notare* (19.17), *signa ... laetissima* (19.29). On the power attached to symbols (especially crosses and the Christogram) among late antique Christians, see Lunn-Rockliffe (2017).
[103] On the Muses and Apollo, see, e.g., Optatian, *Carm.* 16.3, 7, 8. The issue is complicated by the uncertain authenticity of some of his transmitted poems (Squire [2017b] 57 n. 12).
[104] Green (2010) 66–67; Van Dam (2011) 168–70; Squire (2017a) 62; (2017b) 91; Squire and Whitton (2017) 70.
[105] See Chapter 1, p. 65–70. [106] Wienand (2012) 396; Squire and Whitton (2017) 72.
[107] Alcaeus frr. 6; 326. Cf. Wienand (2012) 396.

Figure 3.1 Optatian, *Carm.* 19. Reproduction from Squire and Wienand (2017) p. 42, following the layout of the Codex Augustaneus 9 Guelferbytanus (16th c.), folio 4r, (Herzog August Bibliothek, Wolfenbüttel)

Optatian's poetry represents Christianity as both the network of meaning permeating his literature and the form that arises visually from his classical verse. The evocative power of the Christogram is explicitly explored in poem 8 (Figure 3.2), which associates Constantine, 'golden light of the world', and Jesus, whose name is explicitly spelled in the *versus intextus*,[108] as well as in

---

[108] Optatian, *Carm.* 8.1.

Holy Hermeneutics 137

Carm. 8

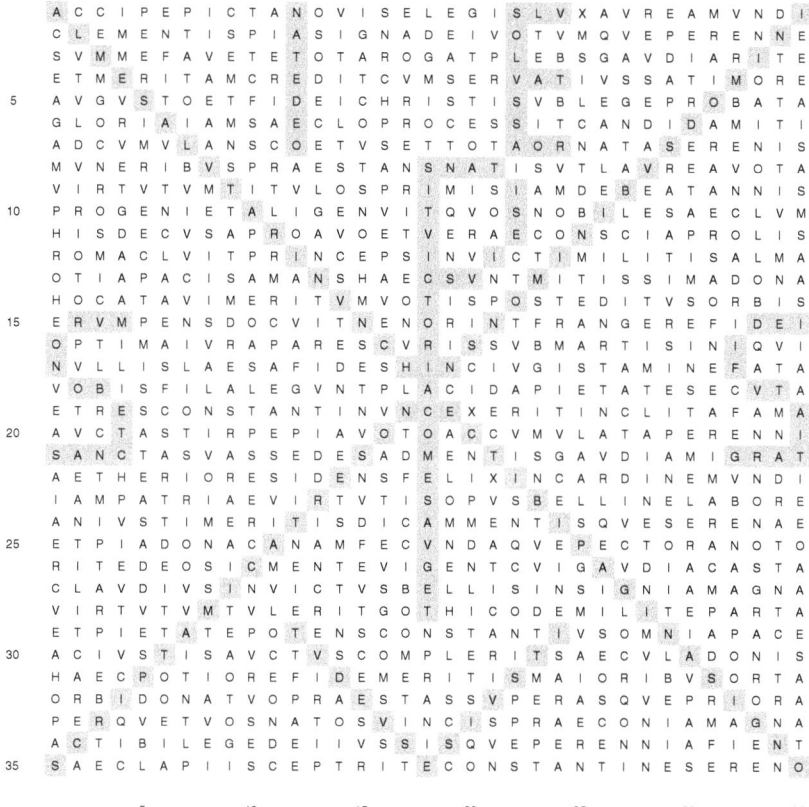

Figure 3.2 Optatian, *Carm.* 8. Reproduction from Squire and Wienand (2017) p. 8, following the layout of the poem as in P. Welser, *Publilii Optatiani Porphyrii panegyricus dictus Constantino Augusto*, Augsburg 1595, p. 33 (Munich, Bayerische Staatsbibliothek, Sign. 2 A.lat.a. 207)

poems 14 and 19 and the highly Christianising *carmen* 24.[109] In *carmen* 16, a panegyric, the convergence of a Constantinian and a Christian signification is achieved through acrostics shaped by individual letters: the left-hand acrostic dedicates the poem to the emperor, while the three mesostics celebrate his rule as a gift granted by Christ to honour Constantine's piety.

[109] The authenticity of *Carm.* 24 is debated, but the poem is compatible with a fourth-century date (see Squire and Whitton [2017]).

Staging Interpretation: Eusebius' *Praise of Constantine*

Optatian's poetry invites comparison with another macroscopic case in which Constantine is publicly addressed in his capacity of interpreter. This section will again involve Eusebius, although no longer as a biographer. Instead, I consider his *Praise of Constantine*, which he delivered at the Constantinopolitan court in July 336. The occasion was Constantine's celebration of his *Tricennalia*, the thirtieth anniversary of his ascension to the throne. Eusebius presents his delivery as a public act of 'interpreting ... the emperor's philosophical ideas'.[110]

The *Praise of Constantine* is a text whose layered complexity is the result of unprecedented ambitions. It might be defined as an act of foundation, setting the rules for interaction between the Church and emperor, whose alliance is sanctioned and regulated via a cunning exploration of the panegyric form. The *Praise* is thus a text concerned with hierarchies and expresses this concern in a self-assertive manner. I return to the demanding, controlling side of the oration later in this book, in a chapter in which I discuss how its rhetoric enabled Eusebius to negotiate ecclesiastical authority at court.[111] Here I am interested in considering what the *Praise* offers – or makes a display of offering – to Constantine.

Eusebius' encomium opens boldly. The first lines amount to a declaration of poetic independence and announce a break from panegyric literature, which Eusebius disparages as beguiling and superficial:

> I have not come before you (i.e., Constantine) with idle stories, with verbal nets spun from silken words that I might beguile your ears with Siren song .... Popularisers (δημώδεις) pursue phrases crammed with puerile conceits ... since in order to please a mundane audience they must make pleasure their criterion and limit themselves to mundane accomplishments. But those initiated in universal wisdom (οἱ δ' αὐτῆς μύσται τῆς καθόλου σοφίας) ... leave it to lesser men to celebrate the lesser of his (i.e., the emperor's) fine points.[112]

Perfunctory criticism of other rhetoricians was a recurrent oratorical device; Julian and Themistius both regularly drew on it in their panegyrics.[113] Given the easy equation between encomium and flattery, orators' attempts to distance themselves from other practitioners of rhetoric aimed to reassure the audience about the sincerity of their intentions.[114] But Eusebius distances himself not merely from other panegyrists but

---

[110] *VC* 4.45.3. [111] See Chapter 5, p. 227–8. [112] *LC proemium*, transl. Drake (modified).
[113] See Chapter 2, p. 75. [114] Goldhill (2001b) 184–93. See Chapter 1, p. 57.

also – surprisingly – from the expected subject of his encomium, declaring that he will not be praising Constantine. 'This', he states, 'is a celebration of the supreme sovereign ... and I mean by supreme sovereign the one who is truly supreme (τὸν ἀληθῶς μέγαν)'. He then moves on to praise God as the creator of the world and the Son as the teacher, Logos, and source of all wisdom.[115] The rest of the *Praise* redistributes the traditional panegyric structure to convey the message that every achievement of the emperor results from divine assistance. Despite this blunt beginning, Eusebius does bring up Constantine's successes but in a way that underscores their origin in 'the truly supreme' god, who rewarded the emperor for his devotion.[116] Following the defeat of his impious adversaries, Constantine's greatest achievements have been the defeat of polytheism, the teaching of the faith, and the construction of churches.[117] Praising the emperor means praising his Christianity. The longevity of Constantine's rule is a consequence of his faith; his intelligence and ability to reason are a gift from the Logos.

There is much within this picture that could be, and has been read, as destabilising and even threatening; the emperor's supreme authority is sidelined as he is praised.[118] We must stress, however, that Eusebius is playing with Constantine's cards. He could have come to court and delivered a standard panegyric minimally rearranged to befit his role as a high representative of the religious community now officially patronised by the emperor. If he behaved differently, this is because he envisaged the possibility of a greater gain from the subversion of encomiastic rules. This intuition was not extemporaneous but the result of observation: the *Praise* did not emerge without precedents. Other representatives of the Church had already addressed speeches to Constantine, although not in such a context as momentous as the celebration of the *Tricennalia*. We know, for instance, that a bishop (perhaps Eusebius of Nicomedia) delivered an encomium for the emperor at the Council of Nicaea in 325.[119] Eusebius of Caesarea himself had an initial opportunity to give a speech in

---

[115] The Son as a teacher: *LC* 1.3; as Logos, Law, and Wisdom: *LC* 1.6. Cf. *LC* 2.4; 3.7–8; 4.1–5.1.
[116] The pattern of the encomium is maintained (Drake [1975] 37; Wienand [2012] 428) but in a reduced capacity: Eusebius' attention constantly drifts towards the divine (Corke-Webster [2020a] 144).
[117] See especially *LC* 7 (Constantine subduing barbarians and demons), 9.14–17 (church building, with attention to Jerusalem).
[118] See especially Corke-Webster (2020a). Discussion in Chapter 5, p. 227–8.
[119] *VC* 3.11. The chapter heading identifies him with Eusebius of Nicomedia, Sozomen with Eusebius of Caesarea (*HE* I 19). Barnes (1978) 56–57 suggests Ossius of Cordoba. Discussion in Brennecke (1994) 432; Cameron and Hall (1999) 265; Wienand (2012) 421 n. 1.

Constantine's presence in Constantinople a few months before he delivered the *Praise*.[120] The eulogies for the absent emperor by the bishops gathered for the September 335 dedication of the Church of the Holy Sepulchre in Jerusalem should also be added to the list.

From these attempts to establish channels of rhetorical communication between the state and the Church, patterns emerged.[121] Constantine responded to the Nicene encomium with a counter-speech in which he deflected the praise to the 'King of All'. He reminded his audience that he had achieved his victories through God's favour and claimed that what would please him most was to see the Church reunited.[122] Eusebius' *Life of Constantine* also reports an episode in which Constantine asked his subjects to save 'adulation and honour' for God when they acclaimed his exposition of doctrine.[123] Another anecdote from the same text describes his annoyance at hearing the words of an unspecified 'minister of God' who, in an 'excess of boldness', called the emperor 'blessed' and declared that he would rule alongside Christ in the next life. Eusebius tells us that Constantine replied that the priest 'should not say such rash things, but should rather pray for him, that in both this life and the next he might be found worthy to be God's slave'.[124] Eusebius' present for Constantine's *Tricennalia*, it seems, consisted of giving the emperor what the emperor himself wanted.

In delivering his *Praise*, Eusebius lays bare the rules of the game. The *Praise* makes a display of connecting Constantine to forms of leadership the Greco-Roman tradition had sanctioned as ideal: military leadership and the construction of significant buildings (both requalified here, however, as Christian activities) and philosophical leadership. Eusebius draws on this label in a passage that eloquently presents Constantine as not only a philosopher-ruler but the only philosopher-ruler who ever lived ('truly, therefore, is only this man a philosopher-ruler [μόνος φιλόσοφος βασιλεύς] who knows himself and understands the showers of every blessing which descend on him . . . from heaven').[125] Philosophy is presented as the ruler's awareness of his subordination to the (Christian) divinity who is the source of all power and intelligence. Such an awareness was arguably for Eusebius the quintessential form of understanding.

---

[120] Wienand (2012) 422–24 suggests that he delivered a shortened version of his oration *On Christ's Sepulchre*.
[121] Wienand (2012) 424.   [122] *VC* 3.12.   [123] *VC* 4.29.2.   [124] *VC* 4.48.
[125] *LC* 5.4. Constantine has 'a mind truly fitted for the service of God' (*LC* 2.5) and leads his subjects 'to the knowledge and pious worship of God' (2.6).

The *Praise* further advises Constantine about appropriate behaviour. The document, which addresses the ruler as 'the interpreter of the All-Ruling God',[126] implicitly outlines what both emperor and bishop will gain from mutual endorsement. At its beginning, when Eusebius proclaims that he will praise the supreme sovereign above all, he takes care to stress that 'the sovereign who is present will not resent it (i.e., not being the primary subject of the praise) but will join in celebration of the divine teaching ... having fully perceived in Him the cause of his empire'.[127] Like Optatian with his *carmina*, Eusebius anticipates that Constantine will actively receive and interpret his words. If Constantine shows indignation at the *Praise*'s disruption of rhetorical conventions, he will not only deny authority to the bishop who is addressing him but will also reveal himself as someone who pretends to possess spiritual qualities but only cares about social conventions. Conversely, applause of the *Praise* will bolster not only Eusebius' reputation but also Constantine, who will be manifesting wisdom in a way that knows no (imperial) precedent. Eusebius' *Praise* thus appears as a text that massages Constantine's intellectual self-projection by offering a stage on which the ruler could perform his understanding.

The *Life* tells us that Eusebius' experiment delighted the emperor: after hearing the *Praise*, he declared his joy at dinner with the bishops.[128] Eusebius' Constantine chooses to play by the rules. He appears fully committed to the construction of his image as exegete and to the use of Christianity to highlight his interpretive abilities.

After Nicaea: Power and the Intellectual Religion

Lactantius wrote as the spokesperson of a tradition that maintained an Isocratean belief in rhetoric as education. A professional rhetorician, he proudly identified with his discipline and was wary of using the label 'philosophy'. He associated the traditional philosophical schools with what he viewed as a recipe for an epistemological disaster: an exclusive, arrogant reliance on human intelligence, which alone cannot achieve perfect knowledge. The latter was only accessible through the *sapientia* and *ratio*

---

[126] *LC* 2.4; 10.4.
[127] *LC* 1. See also his advice on pure (i.e., bloodless, made with thoughts) sacrifice at *LC* 2.5–6, and the description of God's (pleased) reaction at *LC* 3.1 (and 6.1–2, insisting on the correlation between God's satisfaction and Constantine's long rule). Eusebius' celebration of Constantine at *LC* 5.2–8 is prescriptive and conditional, because it provides the audience with an outline of the differences between a virtuous (i.e., Christian) and an impious (i.e., idolatrous) sovereign.
[128] *VC* 4.46.

originating in the Christian god.¹²⁹ Despite his explicit self-distancing from the philosophers, however, the author of the *Divine Institutes* was wrestling with the same questions, being as concerned as the philosophers were with matters such as the ultimate truth and the order of the universe.

Lactantius' understanding of Christianity as the ultimate source of knowledge is reflected in how he conceptualised its centre of gravity. Lactantius' interest in Christ lay not so much in the passion and the crucifixion but in his role as *magister* and *doctor*, teacher of true knowledge and healer of souls.¹³⁰ Constantine's *Oration to the Saints*, although it presents Christianity as a philosophy (defined as 'knowledge of what is true and good', *OC* 15) and uses Plato rather than Cicero as its crucial point of reference, also depicts Christ as a teacher.¹³¹ For Constantine, the meaning of Christ's incarnation lies in meaning itself: the Son is above all else the Logos, the principle of understanding, the 'expositor', as Constantine calls him, 'of his Father's decrees to people of intelligence ... schooling them with a life-long education'.¹³² In consequence, the theme of the Passion, which is central to his Good Friday sermon, evolves into a reflection on the interpretation of Christianity or, better put, on Christianity as interpretation. The *Oration* turns the crucifixion into the ultimate test of understanding. Wise interpreters can distinguish between the literal meaning of the event (the death of the body) and its underlying significance (eternal life).¹³³ The argument provides a clever but unmistakably defensive response to social anxieties turning on the shameful death of the founder of a religion the Romans were now being asked to associate with victory and prosperity. Constantine obliquely acknowledges this. 'Thoughtless and impious people', he writes, 'have failed to understand this properly, believing that the cause of life to those who live was himself deprived of life'.¹³⁴ His own persona is summoned to seal what I called in the Introduction the Constantinian politics of interpretation. Having fully grasped the significance of crucifixion, the ruler demonstrates through his successes the correctness of his reading of Jesus' death as a symbol of victory.

Eusebius' *Praise of Constantine* also presents Christ as the Logos. Eusebius takes this equivalence to an extreme: the name Jesus and the title Christ are absent from the oration. Instead they are replaced with

---

¹²⁹ Cf., e.g., *Div. Inst.* 1.1.21, 1.23.9. Analysis of this position in DePalma Digeser (2000) 8, 67; Garnsey (2003) 22–23; Schott (2008) 101. Lactantius argues that counting among the rhetoricians trained him to 'plead the case of truth' (*Div. Inst.* 1.1.10, transl. Bowen and Garnsey).
¹³⁰ DePalma Digeser (2000) 67–68; Garnsey (2003) 24.   ¹³¹ *OC* 15.   ¹³² *OC* 15.
¹³³ *OC* 11.   ¹³⁴ *OC* 11.

rarefied formulations such as 'the only begotten Logos of God'.[135] But rigorous terminology is key to accessing the method and finalities of the *Praise*. Since Drake demonstrated that the manuscript tradition erroneously merged Eusebius' *Praise* and his oration *On Christ's Sepulchre*,[136] the difference in terminology between the two texts has become apparent. In his *Praise*, Eusebius never quotes the Bible and avoids using Christian terms (including, as just noted, Christ's name); this is not true of the oration dedicated to the church in Jerusalem. The abstract rendition of Christianity in the *Praise* is read as an attempt to appease a pagan court by establishing a 'lingua franca' (as Drake put it)[137] that captured Christianity's affinities with the spirituality of traditional Neoplatonists, to which some give the label 'pagan monotheism'.[138]

Eusebius unquestionably wanted the *Praise* to be perceived as a text navigating the philosophical, Neoplatonic realm familiar to many of Constantine's courtiers. But this should not be interpreted as a conciliatory gesture. Current readings of the *Praise* as seeking common ground and a shared religious language disregard Eusebius' unambiguous assertion that all truth derives from a god who, although not labelled as such, is the Christian one. A bishop is speaking. As a religious leader, Eusebius attacks temples and their idols and celebrates the fact that Constantine 'stripped the gods of their outer trappings'.[139] He equates polytheism with barbarity and claims that, through Constantine's actions, Romans were redeemed from idolatry and now 'spit on the faces of the dead idols ... and ridicule the dated delusions of their forefathers'.[140]

It is often stressed that non-Christian intellectuals cultivated a philosophical ideal of supreme divinity, which tends to be referred to as the Neoplatonic One. Yet – and this is the fundamental difference between them and Eusebius – they did not consider belief in a plurality of divine entities to be impious, idolatrous, or blasphemous. To them, the traditional Greco-Roman gods were emanations or reflections of a superior divinity.[141] They conceived of the representation of gods in art and literature as a different but complementary form of worship. This was perhaps bound to a more popular type of religious sentiment, but they had

---

[135] E.g., at *LC* 2.1, 2. Drake (1975) 46–49, cf. Barnes (1981) 235. [136] Drake (1975) 30–45.
[137] Drake (1975) 54. On the *Praise* as encouraging co-existence, see Drake (1975) 46–60.
[138] See Athanassiadi and Frede (1999). The expression 'pagan monotheism' is questioned by Fowden (2005) 521–23; Cerutti (2010) 15–32; Johnson (2013) 54; Gassman (2020) 6 n. 3.
[139] *LC* 8.3.   [140] *LC* 10.2. Cf. the correlation between polytheism and war established at *LC* 9.2.
[141] Johnson (2013) 54.

no wish to eradicate it. It is difficult to imagine that the violent imagery of Eusebius' *Praise* would have won their approval.

The question therefore arises of why Eusebius avoids using Christian vocabulary in a text so evidently Christian in content, if his aim is not to establish a common ground. I suggest that Eusebius' *Praise* seeks to demonstrate that a Christian speaker can have full mastery of the cultural and ideological framework of traditional *paideia*; in other words, that he can speak the language the elites believed power should speak.[142] At court, Eusebius talks in a Neoplatonic fashion, which is tantamount to a statement of intellectual dominance. The bishop who challenged Plato (*Preparation for the Gospel*) and argued that Christian priests, being perfect intellectuals, were also perfect Roman leaders (*Ecclesiastical History*), uses his *Praise* to demonstrate that Christianity controls philosophy and its vocabulary.[143] In a sense, therefore, Eusebius is indeed addressing the expectations of Constantine's courtiers but only insofar as he is alive to their cultural concerns. He shows upper-class individuals, who might have wanted to regard Christianity as an uncultured creed, that his religion does not take second place to any other school of philosophy.

Eusebius was writing eleven years after a powerful act on the part of the state to sanction Christ as source and subject of knowledge: the Council of Nicaea of 325. The first ecumenical council in Roman history, Nicaea was summoned to address a set of controversies: the Melitian schism, the issue posed by the date of Easter, and – most important for later political and theological developments, although its prioritisation here is somewhat teleological – the Arian controversy. The council temporarily settled Arius' dispute with Alexander with a 'vague yet political' (thus Edwards) creed declaring the Son's consubstantiality with the Father.[144] Crucially, the gathering was promoted by the emperor in person and took place in a city that bore the imprint of his power. Nicaea contained in its name a twofold message of victory: both the triumph of sound doctrine and that of Constantine over Licinius, the event that made the pursuit of orthodoxy possible. Because Nicaea was only a day's journey from the residential city of Nicomedia, all the bishops were expected to travel from their sees across the empire to attend the gathering.[145] Holding the council there thus simultaneously proclaimed the symbiotic relationship between State and

---

[142] On Eusebius' use of Pythagorean elements in *LC* 6.10–17, see Wienand (2012) 430.
[143] On Eusebius' treatment of Plato and the Christian priests see Chapter 1, p. 66–70.
[144] Edwards (2006) 563.   [145] Wienand (2012) 416–17; Galvão-Sobrinho (2013) 106–7.

Church and asserted that the ruler was the guardian of Christianity's identity, whose essence is doctrine.

Constantine's engagement with theology (and Christology) thus represented an official, power-centred acknowledgement of Christianity's self-image as a philosophy. It was crucial to recognise the management of doctrinal disputes as essential to the life of the Church. To this end, Constantine encouraged a competitive relationship with Greek philosophical schools, a key indication of his points of reference. His *Letter to Alexander and Arius*, another composition transmitted by Eusebius in the *Life*, is enlightening in this regard.[146] By presenting himself as the 'peaceful arbitrator' of a controversy between the two bishops, Constantine draws on intellectualising imagery (cf. the reference to the 'hidden eye of reason' at *Life* 2.64), reminding them of their responsibilities as community leaders. The problem was not that they had quarrelled but that they did so in front of the faithful (2.69). Constantine's exhortation culminates with these words:

> You surely know how even the philosophers themselves all agree in one set of principles, and often when they disagree in some part of their statements, although they are separated by their learned skill, yet they agree together in unity when it comes to basic principles. If this is so, how is it not far more right (εἰ δὴ τοῦτό ἐστι, πῶς οὐ πολλῷ δικαιότερον) that we, who are appointed servants of the great God, should, in a religious commitment of this kind, be of one mind with each other? (*VC* 2.71.2)

The *argumentum a fortiori* gives away his intention to compete with the traditional philosophical schools. Constantine invites the bishops to improve upon the schools' practices. The fact that the emperor himself formulates the injunction is key to the picture. Constantine does not only act as a mediator but also presents himself as an authority who can dictate intellectual models. I return to the socio-political implications of this in a later chapter.[147] Here I want to underscore the importance of Constantine's vocabulary. The lack of doctrinal consensus was detrimental to the cohesion of the church. It is therefore self-evident why Constantine would need to ascertain that the doctrine presented as what gave stability to his power would not prove, conversely, a source of destabilisation.[148] But once we bring Constantine's comprehension of doctrinal debates into focus as part of the process of negotiating the place of Christianity among

---

[146] *VC* 2.64–72. [147] See Chapter 5, p. 220–43.
[148] But see Cooper (2019) for the intriguing suggestion that Constantine also saw an advantage (in the short run?) in exploiting the subdivision into factions.

the philosophical schools of Greece and Rome, his intervention acquires further, contextual meaning. Theological looseness appeared to have the potential to disqualify as arbitrary – and thus un-philosophical – the system of knowledge supporting Constantine's claim to philosophical leadership. Earlier Christian theologians had already acknowledged the problem of theological arbitrariness arising from internal divisions; as I aim to show below, this criticism resurfaced in fourth-century philosophical responses to Christianity, in particular in Julian's writings.[149]

But there is a second, fundamental consequence of Constantine's appreciation of doctrine – that is, philosophy – as a locus of state intervention. Imperial efforts to control the creed created an unprecedented scenario in which a philosophical debate relied for its resolution on a principle of authority derived by the state.[150] Nicaea is a somewhat ironic chapter in history, in that it encouraged the crystallisation of the episcopate 'into maledictory factions' (thus Edwards)[151] through episcopal appeals to the same central power that had demanded unity. Inner rivalries were fed by the creation of channels enabling the state to intervene in Christian philosophy. This eventually produced a transformation, internal to fourth-century Christianity, of the practice and regulation of philosophy – an issue to which I return in Chapter 5.[152] What remains is that Constantine's endorsement of Christianity as the highest school of philosophy, and his attempts to establish this school's reliance upon irrefutable truths, re-orientated theological confrontation around imperial power, arguably heightening it. This re-reading of Constantine's propaganda makes it evident why, as soon as his apostate nephew Julian became sole ruler, he set out to organise his reaction against Christianity starting from a refutation of its identity as a rational hermeneutic system.

Julian's Response, Part 1: Christianity and Intellectual Appropriation (*Against the Galileans*, School Ban)

We can now return to where this chapter started: Julian's impromptu elevation, his confrontation with Constantius II, and the final unification under his rule of the eastern and western halves of the empire. During the months following his entrance into Constantinople as sole Augustus,

---

[149] See, e.g., Clement of Alexandria's report that the pagans argued against Christianity due to the disagreement among its sects (*Strom.* 7.15.89.2–3). Cf. similarly Celsus *ap.* Origen, *C. Cels.* 3.12. Discussion in Boys-Stones (2001) 151–52.
[150] Humfress (2007). [151] Edwards (2018) 5–6. [152] See Chapter 5.

Holy Hermeneutics 147

Julian promulgated edicts reversing the religious policies of his predecessors. He provided for the restoration of the temples of the gods and the abrogation of the rules freeing Christian clergymen from financial obligations. In February 362, he recalled the bishops exiled by Constantius II.[153] In light of Julian's refusal to enforce religious allegiance, his act of summoning back the bishops lent itself to a twofold reading. It signalled a philosophical distance from violence, as Julian claimed to prefer debate and persuasion.[154] And it simultaneously showed by contrast the tyrannical nature of his predecessor Constantius, who had even targeted his co-religionists. Under Constantius' reign, Julian writes, many Christian leaders 'happened to be sent into exile, prosecuted, and cast into prison'.[155]

Once we acknowledge that the recalled bishops would not return to empty sees, however, we can appreciate another dimension of Julian's policy: the expectation that it would revive tensions. It should be stressed that Julian's objective was arguably as much symbolic as practical. Ammianus seems to capture the full picture when he argues that Julian had seen that 'no wild beasts are so deadly to human beings as most Christians are to each other' (*nullas infestas hominibus bestias, ut sunt sibi*

---

[153] Restoration of temples: Amm. Marc. 22.5.2; Libanius, *Or.* 18.126; Sozomen, *HE* 5.3.1; 5.5. See Caltabiano (1991) 60 n. 37; Tougher (2007) 58. Cf. Julian's relegalisation of blood sacrifice: Amm. Marc. 22.12.6; Teitler (2017) 56–63. Financial obligations: *C.Th.* 12.1.50, 13.1.4. Germino (2004) 24; Bransbourg (2009) 153–54; Teitler (2017) 68. Episcopal amnesty: Julian *ep.* 15 Wright (= 46 Bidez–Cumont); 41 Wright (= 114 Bidez–Cumont), 436a–b; Amm. Marc. 22.5.3; Sozomen, *HE* 5.5. See Germino (2004) 20; Greenwood (2021) 75.

[154] We should question, however, whether religious conflict in (late) antiquity can be discussed by drawing on a post-Enlightment ideal of 'tolerance' (cf. Garnsey [1984]; Kahlos [2009]; Van Nuffelen [2018]). The assumption that antiquity somehow cultivated appreciation for this ideal is implicit, for instance, in the claims that Julian pursued tolerance (e.g., Marcos [2009]) or that, conversely, his polemical confrontation with the Christians is incompatible with 'a politics of tolerance' (Greenwood (2021) 56–57). Julian was invested in two projects: avoiding a tyrannical reputation for violence and coercion, and philosophical self-projection (entailing the performance of intelligent communication and the development of arguments that might correct what he regarded as a theological misunderstanding). See, e.g., his order to persuade 'those who have strayed ... by reason (λόγῳ) ... not by blows or insults' in *ep.* 41 Wright (= 114 Bidez–Cumont); the definition of educational punishment as a form of philanthropy in *Ep. Fragm.* (= 89b Bidez–Cumont), 289a–b; and his letter *Against Nilus* (*ep.* 50 Wright = 82 Bidez–Cumont) declaring his preference for writing over punishing (Niccolai [2017]). On the issue posed by Julian's indulgence towards episodes of religious violence (e.g., the unpunished murder of Bishop George of Cappadocia, only criticised in *ep.* 21 Wright (= 60 Bidez–Cumont)), see Tougher (2007) 55; Nesselrath (2013) 39–42; Teitler (2017) 35–40. On Julian's religious policies, see further Mazza (1998); Bouffartigue (2004); Marcos (2009); Teitler (2017); De Vita (2022) lxxx–xc.

[155] All cults permitted: Amm. Marc. 22.5.2-3. Rejection of anti-Christian violence: Julian *ep.* 37 Wright (= 83 Bidez–Cumont) and 40 Wright (= 115 Bidez–Cumont). Cf. Libanius *or.* 18.121–25. On Julian's self-distancing from Constantius II as a persecutor of fellow Christians, see Julian *ep.* 41 Wright (= 114 Bidez–Cumont) and *ep.* 15 Wright (= 46 Bidez–Cumont).

ferales plerique Christianorum).[156] These words open up the possibility of interpreting Julian's policy as cultivating the idea that a renewed outbreak of intra-Christian conflicts would help disprove the grounding of the Church in rational agreement.[157]

Overall, a re-assessment of Constantine (and Constantius II) as navigating religious transition via intellectual self-projection illuminates the complementary but antagonistic politics of interpretation operating in Julian's mature writings. Here he sought in the first place to refute Christianity's philosophical identity by arguing that it had appropriated Greek philosophical tools that it was however unable to utilise properly. Second, Julian revisited the myths and traditions of Greek philosophy and religion with the twofold aim of showing that Christian attacks on them were the result of faulty interpretive practices and that Greek wisdom already contained everything later claimed as unique to Christian doctrine.

Julian's *Against the Galileans*, composed in winter 362/363,[158] has been effectively read as arguing for the inferiority of Christian modes of interpretation.[159] This ambition must be understood as instrumental to challenging ideas of Christianity not only as a superior philosophy but as a philosophy *tout court*. Representing the only polemical treatise ever written by a Roman emperor to address his religious adversaries, *Against the Galileans* embodies Julian's effort to project his response to Christianity as a correction of mistaken approaches to exegesis and of the theology underlying them. Even the sobriquet 'Galileans', by which Julian habitually refers to Christians, serves his project: by locating Christianity within its (narrow) region of origin, the term challenges the way Christianity interpreted itself as the universal religion.[160] The writings of Lactantius, Constantine, and Eusebius show to what extent universalising claims supported a representation of Christianity as the source of all wisdom, including the wisdom of Greece.[161] On a political level, universalism facilitated the adoption of Christianity as a system of ideological support

---

[156] Amm. Marc. 22.5.4 (on the difficulty of reading the manuscript, see Den Boeft et. al [1995] 60). This interpretation is also suggested by Sozomen, *HE* 5.5.7, Philostorgius, *HE* 7.4. See Teitler (2017) 38; Nesselrath (2013) 39.

[157] Cf. Julian's description of the 'folly' of Christian communities engaging in acts of violence in *ep*. 40 Wright (= 115 Bidez–Cumont) and 41 (= 114 Bidez–Cumont).

[158] As testified by Libanius, *Or*. 18.178.   [159] See on this especially De Vita (2022) ccxlii.

[160] The sobriquet 'Galileans' features regularly in Julian's writings (e.g., *ep*. 15, 19, 37, 39, 40, 47 Wright = 46, 79, 83, 54, 115, 111 Bidez–Cumont). Gregory of Nazianzus ascribes it directly to Julian (*Or*. 4.76). On its use, see Scicolone (1982); Robert (2008) 239–42; Teitler (2017) 25; Finkelstein (2018) 2 n. 9, 24–25.

[161] See Chapters 1, p. 65–70, and 3, p. 125–9.

for the Roman Empire, which its inhabitants perceived as a universal entity. Julian's 'Galileans' thus blurs this picture and re-opens the issue of Christianity's troubling novelty, depicting Christians as a local sect stemming from Judaism.[162]

Only fragments of *Against the Galileans* survive, for an estimated total of 20–25 per cent of the text.[163] These fragments are transmitted within a polemical work that Bishop Cyril of Alexandria composed about seventy years later to refute Julian. The third Book of *Against the Galileans*, which seemingly focused on the New Testament, did not survive Cyrillian and Christian censorship of its treatment of Jesus, and is entirely lost.[164] Despite this, it is apparent from what remains that Julian focused on challenging Christianity as the religion of the Logos and, therefore, of reason. In one fragment, he eloquently describes Christianity as making use of the part of the soul 'which loves fables (φιλομύθῳ) and is childish and foolish (ἀνοήτῳ τῆς ψυχῆς μορίῳ)'.[165]

Interpretation is the battlefield: Julian's critique of Christianity is structured as an analysis of passages from the Bible used to make the intertwined claims that the texts are fallacious and that Christians read them erroneously.[166] The argument is not innovative; Julian grafts himself onto a tradition of philosophical confrontation over exegesis that had long provided a space of interaction and conflict among Greco-Roman intellectuals. I return to this tradition in the next section, where I also consider the extent to which Julian sought to personalise it. Here suffice it to say that, with this choice of topic, Julian acknowledges interpretation as central to the negotiation of Christianity's philosophical identity. His attacks move from the contention that stories conveying divine truths cannot be incongruous or impure in their diction, a point that structures another Julianic text discussed below, the oration *Against Heraclius*, as well.[167] Aspects of incongruity and impurity in the text indicate misinterpretation – and misrepresentation – of the divine. Readers who perform

---

[162] On the novelty and transgression of Christianity, see also *ep.* 47 Wright (= 111 Bidez–Cumont) 432d.
[163] Riedweg (2020) 249.   [164] Finkelstein (2018) 47–48.   [165] *C. Gal.* fr. 1 (39b).
[166] On the hypothesis that this argument was influenced by Porphyry' *Against the Christians*, see Bouffartigue (1992) 379–97; De Vita (2011) 168; Finkelstein (2018) 52–53; Marcone (2019) 16. For a hypothesis regarding Julian's debt to Porphyry's theology, see Greenwood (2021) 81–91. Regardless of the question of direct inspiration, it can be assumed that both authors were writing with the same end in sight: to refute the claim that the Christian scriptures disclosed a superior truth. On the limits of *Quellenforschung* and on the innovative aspects of Julian's proposal, see De Vita (2022) ccxliv–cclx.
[167] Cf. *C. Her.* 218d–19a. See below, p. 159–60, and Chapter 4, 170–9.

exegesis of such texts are thus bound to falsify divine truths; it is also implicit that only a poor interpreter could assume that faulty texts convey a divine message.[168]

The deconstruction of Christian doctrine in *Against the Galileans* begins at its origins: Creation. Julian compares the account in Genesis (which he ascribes to Moses, as was customary in antiquity) with Plato's *Timaeus*.[169] This choice has been read as a response to Origen.[170] This is possible; but Julian's primary ambition appears to be a critique of how Judeo-Christian Scriptures understand the relationship between God and the world. The focus of Julian's deconstruction of the account in Genesis lies with the text's mishandling of the crucial issue of the divine as a source of knowledge. Julian lingers on the story of the Fall, arguing that God's behaviour – barring Adam and Eve from tasting knowledge – befits only a mischievous demon. The serpent who offered knowledge appears by contrast to be a benefactor.[171] It follows, Julian suggests, that this account demonstrates that Genesis provides a faulty representation of the divine. The story of the Fall of Man betrays ignorance of theology by presenting a god who is ignorant (he does not know the woman will be the root of evil), an enemy of knowledge (he refuses to let the humans taste it),[172] and jealous (he fears that Adam and Eve might achieve divine understanding). Julian's objection must be read in the light of the Neoplatonic assumption – which he endorsed – that the pursuit of divine knowledge represented the highest expression of piety and the lifelong goal of the wise.[173]

What survives of Julian's commentary on the Gospels seems to focus on showing that the search for intellectual prestige and self-differentiation from Judaism led early Christian theologians to disguise the authentic nature of their religion. Julian puts his finger in the open wound of Christology.[174] Unsurprisingly, his main polemical target is John, the gospel most committed to interpreting the life of Jesus in the light of pre-existing theological notions. John was consequently controversial not only for adherents of the Greco-Roman religion but also for Christians who opposed the principle of the co-eternity of the Son.[175] *Against the*

---

[168] Cf. his attacks on bad interpreters of Homer in *II Pan.* 74d (Chapter 2, p. 97–8).
[169] *C. Gal.* fr. 6–17 (49a–e; 52b–c; 57b–58d; 65a–66a; 69b–d; 72b; 75a–b; 80b; 85e; 89a–b; 93e–94a).
[170] De Vita (2011) 180.   [171] *C. Gal.* fr. 17 (93d–94a).   [172] *C. Gal.* fr. 16 (89a), 17 (94a).
[173] See Introduction, p. 13–15.
[174] Smith (1995) 205; and Bouffartigue (1992) 389 argue that Julian's Arian upbringing left no trace in his writings. But see Elm (2012) 317–18; Hunt (2012); De Vita (2017a) 56–57, (2022) ccliv and nn. 689–90; Greenwood (2021) 85–89.
[175] Cf. De Vita (2017a) 149–53; Boulnois (2020) 195–96, 209–12.

Galileans detects a kernel of deceptive innovation in it: the divinisation of Christ.

Julian sees two problems in John's conceptualisation of the nature of Christ. First, the proclamation that a human being born of a mortal woman might be a god carries implications of idolatry.[176] Second, and most important, Jesus' divinisation is achieved by John through an arbitrary borrowing of the philosophical category (and divine entity) of the Logos, which is identified with him.[177] Even the author of John himself, Julian writes, is 'ashamed' (αἰσχυνόμενος) to specify the ground on which such an identification is possible: he knew that his claim had neither a logical nor a theological foundation, and he disguised his lack of argumentation through an appeal to authority (John the Baptist had said this).[178] Julian is suggesting that the gospel's equation of Jesus with the Logos was driven by an urge for self-legitimisation: the author of the Gospel wanted to attach his creed to an authoritative philosophical principle. Yet by violating the tradition from which he descended (that of Moses, the Apostles, and Paul),[179] he not only ended up promoting the cult of a mortal but also transformed his monotheism of origin into a polytheistic cult postulating a second divinity.

John's awareness of the conceptual inadequacy of its religion marks for Julian the beginning of a history of duplicity in the way Christianity thought and spoke of itself and surrounding cultures. The foundation of Christology upon the theft of a Greek philosophical concept stood as the first in a series of what might be defined as acts of appropriation. The religion that claimed the partiality and fallibility of Greek wisdom in fact continued to borrow from Greek learning to support its structures. 'If the

---

[176] *C. Gal.* fr. 62 (253c–e), 64 (262c–e), 65 (276e–77a). Cf. Julian's letter to Photinus (*ep.* 55 Wright = 90 Bidez-Cumont).

[177] *C. Gal.* fr. 79 (327a–c). Celsus already rejected the claim that Jesus was the Logos (see fr. 2.30 Bader, and Porphyry, *C. Chr.* fr. 86). On Julian's targeting of John (esp. *Jo.* 1.1; 1.3; 1.4 [in fr. 50 (213a–13c), 64 (261e–62e), and 79–80 (327a–c, 333b–d)], 1.18 [in fr. 80 (333b–d)], and 3.18 [in fr. 64 (261e–62e)]), see Bouffartigue (1992) 393; Elm (2012) 316–17; De Vita (2017a) 148; Riedweg (2020) 256.

[178] *C. Gal.* fr. 79 (327a–c), 80 (333b–d). Betrayal of tradition is also evident in Christianity's rejection of blood sacrifice, which Constantinian propaganda had saluted as a victory of reason (cf. Eusebius, *LC* 2.5, *VC* 4.23). For discussions of Constantine's policy toward sacrifice and the possibility that he issued a (lost) ban, see Barnes (1984); Bradbury (1994); Cameron and Hall (1999) 243–44, 247–48; Van Dam (2007b) 31; Lee (2012) 173–74; Lenski (2016) 234. Julian contends that Christianity contradicts itself by rejecting what Abraham and Moses performed and endorsed (*C. Gal.* fr. 87 [356c–57a], 88 [358c–e]).

[179] Paul is said to have 'surpassed all magicians and charlatans' (*C. Gal.*, fr. 18 [100a]), and Matthew and Luke are self-evidently refuted by their own disagreements (*C. Gal.*, fr. 62 [253e]). Cf. Julian's challenge of the Christian interpretation of *Is.* 7.14 at fr. 64 (262d).

reading of your own Scriptures is sufficient (αὐτάρκης) for you', Julian asks, 'why do you gnaw (παρεσθίετε) at the learning of the Hellenes?'[180] He answers his own question by claiming that the Christians have knowledge of one fact: the theoretical weakness of their Scriptures. 'You yourself', he writes, 'know the very different effect on the intelligence (σύνεσις) of your scriptures as compared to ours, and that from studying yours no man could attain excellence or even ordinary goodness, whereas from studying ours every man would become better than before'.[181]

The 'knavish' (μοχθηρός) Eusebius of Caesarea, the only theologian named explicitly in the text (or at least in what we have of it),[182] is singled out as key to this process of falsification of intellectual hierarchies. Julian addresses Eusebius' argument for the priority of the Hebrews over the Greeks in several disciplines, including logic ('something whose name he learnt from the Greeks', Julian comments).[183] It has been suggested that *Against the Galileans* should be understood as a response to Eusebius' *Preparation for the Gospel*.[184] Regardless of whether this is the case (the fragmentary nature of the treatise is an obstacle to a clear-cut answer), this passage makes it clear that Julian saw the Bishop of Caesarea as a symbol of what he perceived as Christianity's intellectual rapacity.

A desire to address Christianity's reliance on the intellectual tools provided by *paideia* also explains Julian's most controversial legal enactment: the so-called School Ban that barred Christian teachers from lecturing on the classics. The School Ban is controversial not only because of the outrage it sparked among Christian theologians (beginning with Gregory of Nazianzus, to whom I shall return)[185] but also and especially because its exact nature remains uncertain due to the state of the preserved documents. It is unclear whether the only surviving edict by Julian concerning education, the *de medicis et professoribus* (issued on 17 June 362),[186] is to be identified with the Ban. The *de medicis et professoribus*, which regulates municipal procedures for the appointment of teachers and doctors, only demands that they display outstanding morality and makes no explicit reference to Christians. Various possibilities are open for consideration. The jurists compiling the *Codex Theodosianus* in the 430s may have

---

[180] *C. Gal.* fr. 55 (229c). Cf. fr. 38 (178a–b). [181] *C. Gal.* fr. 55 (229d).
[182] Cf. Chapter 1, p. 70–1. [183] *C. Gal.* fr. 53 (222a).
[184] Bouffartigue (1992) 384–89, comparing Julian's reflection with Eusebius' commentary on the *Timaeus* at *PE* 11.29, 1–4. Cf. also Elm (2012) 305–20.
[185] See Chapters 5, p. 215–17, and 6, p. 276–9.
[186] *C.Th.* 13.3.5 (also preserved, with an important variant, in *C.I.* 10.53.7). A survey of the debate in Niccolai (2023).

modified the text, removing sections that clashed with the religious policies of the now officially Christian empire.[187] This hypothesis is supported by the fact that the Theodosian jurors had permission to modify the texts they were compiling and were not expected to signal such changes in the text.[188] Alternatively, Julian's School Ban may have been an entirely different text from the edict *de medicis et professoribus*, which did not survive, likely due to a deliberate decision not to preserve it.[189]

Other, in my view less convincing, hypotheses have also been advanced. It has been suggested that the *de medicis et professoribus* did not mention Christians explicitly but targeted them allusively through its interaction with another, non-legal document, a letter in which Julian describes Christian professors as 'thinking one thing and teaching another' and therefore as immoral.[190] It has also been suggested that Julian's issue of the ban was a Christian invention aimed at casting the apostate emperor as a persecutor.[191] Post-Julianic Christianity certainly promoted the circulation of fictitious stories of Julianic martyrs, and it is also true that contemporary Christians deliberately misrepresented the nature of Julian's Ban in their writings.[192] But the hypothesis that the Ban was pure Christian invention is at odds with the indignation of Ammianus, who refers to it twice, once describing it as something that 'should be buried in eternal silence'.[193] Ammianus was simultaneously concerned with asserting his own reliability and a supporter of Julian, close enough to him to have a good sense of what was slander.[194] It seems equally bizarre that Ammianus' indignation would be triggered by a text allusively challenging Christianity via a generic requirement that professors be of outstanding morality. I am inclined to conclude that Julian's School Ban existed and targeted Christians either in

---

[187] Rosen (2006) 270; Stenger (2009) 109; Vössing (2020) 185–88. *Contra*: Germino (2004) 215–20.
[188] Kaiser (2015) 120–21.
[189] Watts (2006) 68–78; Goulet (2008); Harries (2012) 130–31; Schmidt-Hofner (2020) 161.
[190] *Ep.* 36 Wright (= 61c Bidez–Cumont), 422a–b (general law: 424a). Elm (2012) 140–41; Nesselrath (2013) 47–50; Teitler (2017) 64–67; Greenwood (2017a); Drake (2020) 169, compare the relationship between the edict *de medicis et professoribus* and *ep.* 36 Wright (= 30 Bidez–Cumont) with the relationship between Julian's funeral edict (*C.Th.* IX 17,5) and its explanatory text (*ep.* 56 Wright = 136b Bidez–Cumont). De Vita (2022) cvi–vii provisionally identifies the School Ban with the edict but acknowledges that the question remains open.
[191] Germino (2004) 163–64. See also McLynn (2014), followed by Greenwood (2021) 103, hypothesising that the edict *de medicis et professoribus* responded to a local dispute and that Julian later composed a text (*ep.* 36 Wright = 61c Bidez–Cumont) that ultimately sparked a provocative debate on the (im)morality of Christian teachers.
[192] Fictional martyr stories: Teitler (2017). Exclusion of Christian pupils from traditional education: but note that Julian's *ep.* 36 Wright (= 61c Bidez–Cumont) expresses the hope that attending classes might help them understand their error (424a). See further Vössing (2020) 197.
[193] Amm. Marc. 22.10.7; 25.4.20. [194] See Chapter 5, p. 212–14.

the form of a lost law or in a previous version of the edict. That Julian resorted to this decision despite his desire to present himself as a philosopher-ruler who shunned coercion and acts of direct hostility is not a contradiction in terms but can be explained on the basis of his understanding of Christianity as a predatory system. In this light, the Ban appears as a measure for preventing abuse. From Julian's perspective, the exclusion of Christian teachers did not amount to persecution. Instead, it was a way to restore fairness in the cultural relationship between Christians and adherents of Greco-Roman religion, allocating to each their own. The Ban, in other words, helped expose what Julian considered the original poverty of the Christian message before its encounter with Greek learning.[195] Second, Julian's intervention points to a desire to stop Christians from acquiring intellectual tools they might use at the expense of traditional culture, employing them to entice intellectually upper-class Romans. His criticism of the Christian theologian Diodorus, who – in his words 'rashly took to philosophy (*philosophans imprudenter*) and engaged in the study of literature (*musicarum . . . rationum*), and by the devices of rhetoric armed his hateful tongue (*odibilem adarmavit linguam*) against the heavenly gods', indicates this.[196] Third, as De Vita stresses, the measure also served an educational purpose: by allowing Christian pupils to attend classes, Julian was seeking to create spaces in which they might be introduced to a correct representation of the relationship between culture and the divine.[197]

A final point must be considered. Julian's decision appears to be a practical if drastic response to a state of aporia arising from the belief (shared with his adversaries) that knowledge simultaneously leads to and originates in the divine.[198] 'Was it not the gods who revealed all their learning to Homer, Hesiod, Demosthenes, Thucydides, Isocrates, and Lysias?', Julian writes, adding: 'I think it is absurd (ἄτοπον) that men who expound the works of these writers should dishonour the gods whom those writers used to honour'.[199] His focus on absurdity is essential. If

---

[195] Cf. *ep.* 36 Wright (= 61c Bidez–Cumont), 423d. De Vita (2022) xlix too suggests that Julian's project aimed to end what she labels *usurpazione culturale*.

[196] *Ep.* 55 Wright (= 90 Bidez–Cumont). The letter is transmitted, in a Latin translation, in Facondus Hermianensis, *pro defens. trium cap.* 4.2 (see Caltabiano [1991] 267 n. 1).

[197] De Vita (2022) lxxxv, cvi–cvii.

[198] Julian speaks of the canonical Greek authors as having been guided by the gods in all their learning (*ep.* 36 Wright = 61c Bidez Cumont); he identifies the Delphic God as the founder of philosophy (*I Pan.* 3c, *Cyn.* 188a) and speaks of Athena as source of wisdom, intelligence, and the creative arts (*Hel.* 150a). His belief in the identity of learning and religion is celebrated in Libanius *Or.* 18.157. See further Athanassiadi (1981) 121–23; Stenger (2009) 99–101.

[199] *Ep.* 36 Wright (= 61c Bidez–Cumont), 423a. See Niccolai (2023).

(Christian) atheism derives from ignorance and irrationality,[200] it is critical to establish why a fully educated individual would commit to endorsing such a system. Teachers, by definition, cannot justify their ignorance. Julian's answer to the conundrum – a provisional one, it should be noted, since it puts his assumption that education engenders morality between brackets – is deliberate duplicity. In what sounds like an echo of Achilles' indignation at the man 'who hides one thing in his mind and says another',[201] Julian writes that 'when a man thinks one thing and teaches another (ἕτερα μὲν φρονεῖ, διδάσκει δὲ ἕτερα) to his pupils ... he fails to educate exactly in proportion as he fails to be an honest person (χρηστός)'.[202]

Julian's Response, Part 2: From Homer to the Mother of the Gods: *Paideia* as Cult of Culture

As Julian dissected the weaknesses of Christian Scriptures, he was quite aware that Greek literature could be attacked in similar ways. Criticism of texts containing references to the divine, and of the methods for approaching such references, had a long history in Greek thinking. Already by the sixth century BCE, Greeks were debating the problematic representations of the divine found in their myths and poetry (especially in Homeric epic) and questioning the existence of belligerent, jealous, and incestuous gods.[203] Later, such content drove Plato to rule out the use of epic poetry in the education of children even when scrutinised through the device of allegory, the ancient practice of seeing an element in a text as pointing to something else (or of creating mythical and literary content pointing to a non-literal message; active allegory, however, will be the focus of a later section).[204] Hellenistic and post-Hellenistic philosophers were especially committed to developing forms of exegesis that postulated a deeper, mystical significance hidden behind the letter of the text. It is from within this context that Philo of Alexandria developed his application of Platonic exegesis to the Bible, later inspiring Origen and Clement. Exegesis,

---

[200] Cf. his statement that *paideia* 'caused every noble being that nature has produced among you (*i.e.* the Christians) to abandon impiety' at *C. Gal.* fr. 55 (229d). Those who do not worship the gods have 'strayed out of ignorance' (*ep.* 41 Wright = 114 Bidez–Cumont, 438b).
[201] *Il.* 9.312-13.   [202] *Ep.* 36 Wright (= 61 Bidez–Cumont), 422a–b.
[203] Theagenes of Rhegium seems to have explained the battle of the gods in *Iliad* 20 as an allegory of the strife of the elements (fr. 8 Diels-Kranz).
[204] See. e.g.. Pl. *Resp.* 2.378d, *Phdr.* 229c–30a (cf. Most [2010] 26). On the history of Greek allegory, see Pépin (1976); Dowson (1992); Brisson (1996); Young (2002); Boys-Stones (2003); Struck (2004); Ramelli (2006); Copeland and Struck (2010); Kahlos (2012).

allegory, and their areas of overlap thus became key fields of religious interaction in the late empire, with different groups engaging in interpretation with striking methodological similarities to competitive ends.[205]

In his *Second Panegyric to Constantius II*, Julian betrays awareness of this cultural context. He joins the Homeric detractors who disapproved of the depiction of Zeus in *Iliad* 11 and attacks those who find meanings in poetry that they themselves have imported into the text.[206] On this basis, it has been claimed that Julian rejected allegory *tout court*.[207] But a look at his mature writings, which are riddled with attempts to create and interpret myths and symbols, is enough to disprove this claim. The depiction of Julian as a literalist hides the complexity of the solution that, I suggest, he devised to challenge the Christian hermeneutics of the Bible without turning his critique into a double-edged weapon. In this, he was inspired, or rather deterred, by Porphyry, from whose methods he seems to have tried to differentiate himself.[208]

Porphyry was the first Neoplatonist to pit himself against Christianity, authoring, among other writings, a philosophical treatise that targeted the new religion. He also raised the allegorical exegesis of Homer to new heights (see especially his essay on the Cave of the Nymphs in *Odyssey* 14).[209] In the third century, when Christian allegory of the Bible was flourishing – with Origen as the undisputed leader in the field – Porphyry's exegetical efforts must have had a competitive dimension.[210] Eusebius, Porphyry's main Christian detractor, at any rate, appears especially committed in his attacks on the Neoplatonic philosopher to address the link tying Porphyry's allegory to his adherence to Greco-Roman religion. Eusebius' *Preparation for the Gospel* challenges the validity of Porphyry's claims to the divine by challenging his exegesis: Eusebius draws on what he takes to be evidence of Porphyry's poor interpretive skills to undermine his status as a philosopher and, with it, the validity of his theological system.[211]

---

[205] For a comparative analysis of such similarities, see especially Kahlos (2012).
[206] *II Pan.* 68a, 74d–75a. See Chapter 2, p. 97–98.
[207] Cf. Lamberton (1986) 134–39, defining Julian as 'the champion of a misconceived and unexamined literalism' (139). Masaracchia (1990) 38 and Riedweg (2005) also regard Julian as an anti-allegorist. On Julian's partial acceptance of Christian allegory and his engagement with the topic, see Bouffartigue (1992) 161, 384–85; De Vita (2022) ccli n. 676.
[208] Julian states at *Mat.* 161b that he does not know Porphyry's interpretation of the myth of Cybele and Attis. But as De Vita (2010) 160 suggests, this statement is open to challenge. Cf. further Greenwood (2021) 81–83, 89.
[209] Struck (2004) 74. On Plotinus' educational use of allegory, see Struck (2010) 58–59.
[210] On Origen and allegory, see, e.g., Cocchini (2006); Boyarin (2010); Turner (2010) 74–76.
[211] See especially Euseb. *PE* 4.6–10, challenging Porphyry's *Philosophy from Oracles*.

Holy Hermeneutics

Julian's layered approach to exegesis and the Greek canon suggests he aimed to redefine the terms of the debate, presumably, as De Vita suggests, in the legacy of Iamblichus' innovative approach to interpretation (which aimed at grasping the *skopos* – the overall mystical message – of a text rather than lingering on its details).[212] Above all, Julian must have understood that to persist in the *querelle* of Homeric versus scriptural allegory despite the similarity of the problems posed by both corpora, which he acknowledged,[213] bound him to operate on the level of his adversaries, the bad interpreters. Julian therefore opted for a methodological re-assessment of allegory, with the goal of disentangling Greek philosophers from problems they had refused to face. In Chapter 4, I examine how Julian's intuition shaped his engagement with creative allegory – that is, the way he wrote myth. Here I will only consider his efforts to interpret pre-existing Greek literature.

Julian's fundamental intuition lies in the acknowledgement that not everything could be salvaged: the interpretation of Homeric poetry in particular was bound to remain uncertain. This does not mean that he was not devoted to Homer.[214] But he was also aware that to advocate for the *Iliad* and the *Odyssey* as 'enigmatic' poems, that is, as poems whose divine content was accessible through interpretation, opened the door for (Christian) criticism.[215] Incidentally, this conclusion is compatible with a perception of Homer and Hesiod as inspired by the divine. Julian, who derived from Plato a belief in the divine inspiration of the poet, eloquently refers to both Homer and Hesiod as inspired by the gods 'with a frenzy for the truth, like seers'.[216] In the same text, however, he also states that, 'along with the divine', their poems 'contain a great deal that is merely human'.[217] This is the crux of the matter: in his desire to generate entertainment – a human urge, unrelated to the god – Homer, who 'embellishes (ἐπικοσμῶν) his poems with tales',[218] contaminated the divine element that had inspired his work. It is due to this tampering that Julian envisages Homeric poetry as failing to meet the criteria that

---

[212] On the possible influence of Iamblichus' exegesis on Julian, see De Vita (2022) cclxxix–xiii.
[213] Acknowledgement of affinity between Greek and biblical myths: *C. Gal.* fr. 4 (44a–b) and 15 (85b).
[214] Cf. his statement that Homer's poems were to him like an amulet in *ep.* 29 Wright (= 80 Bidez–Cumont). For the number of allusions and explicit references to Homer in Julian's writings, see Bouffartigue (1992) 52.
[215] Cf. how Eusebius eloquently draws on Plato to criticise Homer (Pl. *Resp.* 10.595b in *PE* 12.49). On the equivalence of Greek and Christian modes of interpretation, cf. Kahlos (2012).
[216] *Hel.* 136b–c; cf. 149c.   [217] *Hel.* 137c.   [218] *II Pan.* 61a.

rendered it suitable for allegory. No divine message was hidden behind Homer's depictions of quarrelling gods.

A key source for reconstructing what, for Julian, must have been a difficult conclusion to reach is the *Fragment of a Letter to a Priest*, dated to the first months of 363.[219] Here Julian provides an outline of his reform of the Greco-Roman cult. He explains what rites and forms of devotion should be practised, how priests should be selected, and how they should be trained. The stakes are high; the long fragment is ambitious and undoubtedly the product of much reflection. As has been noted, Julian lays special emphasis on the place of traditional culture: the priest must read.[220] A reading list is presented: Julian identifies the classics that should be recommended to the ministers of the cult because 'not every sort of reading is suitable for a priest'.[221] His canon, intriguingly, is structured around censorship. He takes care to explicitly recommend some topics (Plato above all) but prohibits many others, from Archilochus, Hipponax, and the Old Comedy to Sceptic philosophers and love stories. In this list, one absence stands out: Homer is left unmentioned, neither recommended nor forbidden. One could argue that Julian shaped his canon for educated individuals: if he wanted his priests to read Plato, he must have assumed that they had progressed in *paideia* up to philosophical studies. At the same time, a remark close to his reading list indicates that he did not want Homer to be read in a holy environment. Julian writes: '[We ought to] teach concerning the gods that ... they do no injury at all either to mankind or to one another, out of jealousy or envy or enmity ... the sort of things our poets (οἱ μὲν παρ'ἡμῖν ποιηταί) in the first place have brought themselves into disrepute (κατεφρονήθησαν) by writing.'[222] He names no names, but his allusion inevitably recalls the most controversial scenes in the *Iliad* and *Odyssey*.

Julian's problematisation of Homeric epic, however, comes to full fruition only in the light of his treatment – better, defence – of Greek myth. The testing-field for this assertion is the *Hymn to the Mother of the Gods* (March 362), in which Julian provides a mystical interpretation of the myth of the union between the goddess Cybele, Mother of the Gods, and her lover and son Attis. As Tougher has shown, there is a strong

---

[219] *Ep. Fragm.* = *ep.* 89b Bidez–Cumont.
[220] In this, Julian seems to be diverting from Iamblichus, whose profile of the ideal priest is unconcerned with literary education. See Borrelli (2003); De Vita (2011) 249–50.
[221] *Ep. Fragm.* (= 89b Bidez–Cumont), 301c. [222] *Ep. Fragm.* (= 89b Bidez–Cumont), 301a.

apologetic component in this text, which addresses a myth that was severely criticised by Christian contemporaries due to its incestuous theme and violent imagery (Attis' self-castration).[223] But Julian intriguingly argues that the controversial aspects of the myths are evidence of its enigmatic nature, inviting audiences 'through the paradox and the incongruity ... to search out the truth'.[224] The underlying message, he claims, is simultaneously cosmological and soteriological: the myth of the Mother must be understood as representing both the intellectual genesis of the cosmos and the process of return of the archetypical soul to the One,[225] which are the opposed elements of the eternal motion that unites all beings endowed with reason.[226] This interpretation, incidentally, seems to confirm Julian's debt to Iamblichean principles of exegesis and a desire to move away from Porphyry and his approach to the same myth.[227]

The *Hymn*'s argument that the paradoxical nature of the myth reveals its mystical kernel might seem inconsistent with Julian's treatment of the incongruity in Homer. But if we turn to the text that formulates Julian's most structured theory of allegory, his oration *Against Heraclius*, the pieces of his system come together. The highly programmatic nature of *Against Heraclius*, composed in the same Spring 362 in which Julian wrote the *Hymn to the Mother of the Gods*, is probably a consequence of the fact that this was his first public oration as Augustus.[228] The text has a complex structure organised around the theme of the didactic function of myth. In a long theoretical section, Julian defends so-called paradoxical myths (i.e., myths whose literal meaning appear obscure or puzzling) as educational by appealing to the Heraclitean concept that 'Nature loves to hide her secrets'. Such myths help communicate the secrets of Nature in a mediated form to those who are uninitiated in philosophical mysteries (and have 'childish souls').[229] The argument is not Julian's invention but a founding principle of Platonic interpretation.[230] From the way he develops this reflection,

---

[223] Tougher (2020b), considering the cases of Arnobius, *Adv. nat.* (5.8–15), and Firmicus Maternus, *Err. prof. rel.* 18; 27. Cf. Julian's apologetic remarks at *Mat.* 161b, 169d–70a, 174a–b and the definition of Cybele's love for Attis as 'passionless' (ἀπαθής) at *Mat.* 166b. See also De Vita (2010); Liebeschuetz (2012) 214–15.
[224] *Mat.* 170b. Cf. analogous statements at *Hel.* 154a; *C. Her.* 217c, 219a–c, 220a–21d.
[225] De Vita (2010) 161.
[226] On the polyvalence of Julian's interpretation, see De Vita (2011) 154.   [227] See n. 212 above.
[228] Rosen (2006) 57 defines it a programmatic manifesto. Cf. also De Vita (2022) clxix–clxx.
[229] *C. Her.* 216c (echoing Heraclitus, fr. 123 Diels-Kranz). Educational nature of myths: *C. Her.* 206d.
[230] On its fortune, see Turner (2010) 76.

however, its influence on his project of critical selection of interpretable texts becomes apparent. Julian writes:

> When we invent myths about sacred things our language must be wholly dignified .... There must be nothing base or slanderous or impious in it .... There must be no incongruous element in diction thus employed (περὶ τὰς τοιαύτας λέξεις), but all must be dignified, beautiful, splendid, divine, pure, and as far as possible in conformity with the essential nature of the gods. But as regards the thought (τὸ δὲ κατὰ τὴν διάνοιαν), the incongruous may be admitted, so that under the guidance of the gods men may be inspired to search out and study the hidden meaning.[231]

Diction versus thought, *lexis* versus *dianoia*: this distinction explains why one should not allegorise Homer's stories, whose literary agenda is set by rhetorical artifices but can interpret the naked sequence of (sacred) events in the story of Cybele and Attis. Since the myth, from Julian's perspective, does not seek to entertain but to educate, its most surprising and eccentric features should not be envisaged as formulas for enjoyment. They are enigmatic signifiers, suggesting that a kernel of superior truth is hidden in the text for those who are wise enough to see behind the paradox.

There is a degree of circularity in this reflection, which emerges fully when Julian's acknowledgement of the comparability between Greek and biblical myth is considered.[232] Julian's *petitio principii* lies in implicitly stating that the implausibility of a myth should be taken as a marker of a superior truth only if one already knows that the myth does not rely on derivative theology (i.e., Christianity) and therefore points to a superior truth. Inevitably, one can only recognise as valid myths that belong to a religious system one already knows to be valid.[233] But circularity does not undermine the internal consistency driving Julian's theory of allegory. This consistency is in fact key to understanding why he focuses primarily on Greek myth to oppose Christianity via a simultaneously apologetic and competitive reassessment. Julian's writings strive to illustrate how Greek myth provides primary evidence of a full original control over ideas Christianity later claimed as its own – beginning with the Logos. This argument is essential to rethinking the long-held assumption that Julian sought to appropriate Christian concepts in the service of Greek philosophy.[234] In fact, Julian confronted

---

[231] *C. Her.* 218c–19a.   [232] See above.
[233] This circularity, however, compares with argumentative patterns characterising the rivalries between ancient allegorists. See Kahlos (2012) 540.
[234] Cf., e.g., Greenwood (2014), (2017a).

Christianity on the topic of originality versus dependency of knowledge that, as Boys-Stones shows, shaped the interaction both among the post-Hellenistic schools of philosophy and between them and Christian intellectuals who laid claim to primacy.[235] Julian accordingly sought to (re)assert Greek thinking as original in developing concepts over which the Christian theologians of his time claimed intellectual control. The myth of Cybele and Attis exemplifies this ambition, since it is implicitly presented as capturing more effectively than Christian doctrine the process by which the divine interacts with the created world. Attis, presented as the 'substance (οὐσίαν) of the generative and creative Intellect (γονίμου καὶ δημιουργικοῦ νοῦ)' (*Mat.* 161c) and assimilated to the Logos,[236] illustrates better than Christ how the Logos can descend from the One while remaining divine. The goddess Cybele, who – like Mary – is paradoxically both a virgin and a mother, does so from a completely divine state and as the mother of a perfectly divine figure. Believers are therefore not expected to assume that her divine paradox is compatible with mortality or that a mortal woman might engender a god.[237] The myth of Attis never postulates the divinisation of a mortal but preserves the divinity of its subject as it acknowledges that Attis was drawn to matter by his superabundant creative energy but nevertheless managed to withdraw from it, setting in motion the eternal circle of generation.[238]

Questions connected with the universal divinity, the agency of a demiurgic, Logos-like deity, and the relationship between the divine and the world are also at the heart of Julian's *Oration to King Helios* (December 362), a celebration of the nature and power of the solar god inspired by Iamblichus' philosophy.[239] I will not engage in detail with the reconstruction of the *Oration*'s cosmology, which posits three superior entities: the physical sun; a second, intellectual (*noeros*) sun, which is a demiurgic entity coinciding with both Mithras and Helios; and the highest divinity,

---

[235] Boys-Stones (2001). See Introduction, p. 15.
[236] *Mat.* 161d–62a, 179c. On the Logos-like Attis in the hymn, see Wright (1913) 501; De Vita (2017) 160–61; (2022) clxxx–cxcii; Liebeschuetz (2012) 223–24; Greenwood (2018).
[237] On the possible competition between the Mother and Mary, see De Vita (2022) clxxxvi–clxxxvii.
[238] Attis' 'superabundance of generative power': *Mat.* 162a. Interruption of his descent into matter through a voluntary act (self-castration): *Mat.* 168d; 169c; 175b. See Ugenti (1992); Criscuolo (2001) 373; De Vita (2011) 161; Elm (2012) 127–31; Tougher (2020b) 79.
[239] Inspired by Iamblichus: *Hel.* 146a–b, 150d, 157c–58a. For a comparison (and problematisation) of the hymn's relationship with Iamblichus' cosmology, see Dillon (J. M.) (2012) 104–5, 109. On Julian's admiration for Iamblichus, see *C. Her.* 222b; *Cyn.* 188b; *ep.* 2 Wright (= 12 Bidez–Cumont); 58 Wright (= 98 Bidez–Cumont), 401b.

intriguingly presented as intelligible (*noetos*) rather than beyond intelligibility.[240] I want to linger, however, on how the *Oration*'s mystical elaboration of the cosmic harmony of a (tripartite) divine culminates in a special attentiveness to the notion of 'middleness' (μεσότης), Helios' divine mediation between the highest God and the sensible world.[241] Although not explicitly compared to the Logos,[242] this noeric (i.e., intellectual), demiurgic Helios has a filial relationship with the superior divinity, whose 'offspring' (ἔκγονος) it is.[243]

The meditation on the relationship between the divinity and the cosmos through a generative force that is also an intellectual principle inevitably invites comparison with Christianity's interpretation of the structured cosmos.[244] Julian seems to detect as a key element of competition the way the visible world bears witness to the metaphysical entities that structure it. He presents the visibility of solar light, through which the agency of the physical sun is manifested, as evidence: it offers proof of the validity of his philosophical examination of the cosmos. The role of Helios in delivering enlightenment is demonstrated by the light provided by his lowest hypostasis to the sub-lunar world; conversely, the supposed enlightenment provided by a Logos-like Christ leaves no visible trace on the cosmos.[245] It may be worth emphasising that a similar attempt to produce evidence in favour of his theological system underlies Julian's treatment of (and self-association with) the 'saviour' (σωτήρ) Asclepius, god of medicine.[246] Julian argues for the effectiveness of Asclepius' divine agency in a way that is comparable to his treatment of Helios' light. Asclepius' power has the epistemological advantage of being tangible, since it takes the form of an actual gift to humankind: the art of healing (that is,

---

[240] See Athanassiadi (1977); De Vita (2011) 139–53; Dillon (J. M.) (2012); Elm (2012) 293–99; Nesselrath (2020) 53.

[241] On the relationship between this tripartite divine and the Christian Trinity, see Chadwick (2001) 175; Nesselrath (2008); De Vita (2017a) 163. For a cautionary note, see Greenwood (2013). On the 'middleness' of the intellectual Helios, see *Hel.* 138c–39a. Discussion in Wright (1913) 359; De Vita (2011) 146–47; Dillon (2012) 110–11; Elm (2012) 288, 293–97.

[242] De Vita (2017a) 163.   [243] *Hel.* 133b.   [244] Cf. Greenwood (2021) 65, 80.

[245] *Hel.* 133d–34b, 151b; cf. 133a and *Mat.* 172b–73a. Discussion on Helios' agency in: Wright (1913) 349; De Vita (2011) 145–49; Dillon (J. M.) (2012) 112–15; Elm (2012) 299; Nesselrath (2020) 61.

[246] *Hel.* 144b, 153b (Helios begetting Asclepius for the salvation of the world). For the explicit juxtaposition of Asclepius with Christ, see *C. Gal.* fr. 46 (200a–b). See Athanassiadi (1981) 167–68; Bouffartigue (1992) 649; De Vita (2011) 197–98; Dillon (2012) 113; Greenwood (2017b); (2021) 75–91. Asclepius seems to have been a key figure in the debate between traditional religion and Christianity: cf. Kahlos (2007) 158–61; De Vita (2011) 197–98. On Julian's association with Asclepius in the writings of his supporters, see Athanassiadi (1981) 168; and especially Greenwood (2021) 86–89.

medicine). Conversely, Christ's healing powers are only attested within the body of literature that relies on the assumption that he had healing powers, in a circular – and fallacious – design.

My final point concerns a key consequence of Julian's systematising efforts in regard to what Greek philosophy is and how it should be understood. Julian's *To the Mother of the Gods* and *To King Helios* present Greek myth and philosophy as ideal spaces for the articulation of correct ideas about the divine and do so by programmatically merging two forms, hymn and exegetical commentary. Julian is advertising his system of belief as essentially a cult of culture. This representation, however, presents him with a further challenge: the identity of his 'cult of culture' was threatened not only by its detractors, who could be dismissed as ignorant and deceitful, but also – and more critically – by its vulgar supporters. The two orations on Cynicism that Julian composed in 362, *Against the Cynic Heraclius* (March) and *To the Uneducated Cynics* (June), are designed to address and resolve this specific issue. Both are concerned with finding a place within Julian's map of Greek philosophy for the most subversive and counter-cultural traditional philosophical school: Cynicism.[247]

The problem posed by Cynic philosophers was comparable and antithetical to that presented by Christian teachers who remained Christian despite being deeply knowledgeable about the classics. The Cynics located themselves within the Greek tradition but did so from a position of ignorance and rejection of *paideia*. Their erratic behaviour undermined Julian's claim that Greek philosophy necessarily produces reasonable, cultured individuals from the inside. Heraclius, the Cynic philosopher who serves as Julian's polemical target in the eponymous oration, is described as simultaneously blasphemous and unacquainted with key philosophical categories. He is unaware of the educational function of myth and does not understand when he should speak obliquely and when he should instead resort to direct address (i.e., *parrhesia*), as befits a philosopher addressing power.[248] Julian's solution is to disavow the ignorant Cynics as a group. *To the Uneducated Cynics* justifies this decision by arguing that their vulgarity and lack of respect for traditional culture shows that they hold beliefs they deem philosophical but that are in fact a parody of wisdom. Julian argues that Cynicism in its original form occupies a

---

[247] On Julian's perception of the Cynics as threatening his religious reforms, see Liebeschuetz (2012) 218; Marcone (2012) 240; De Vita (2022) cxcii–cxcvi. It should be noted that professional philosophers had long felt threatened by Cynics: cf. Nesselrath (1998); Goulet-Cazé (2015) 24–26.

[248] *C. Her.* 205a–b, 207d–8c.

peculiar position within the Greek philosophical system, since it is a type of universal philosophy that does not demand a commitment to learning but is suitable for anyone who desires to live according to nature.[249] For Cynicism to be valid, however, piety must be its regulating principle.[250] Julian claims that this philosophy originated as a direct response to Apollo's precept 'Know thyself!' and thus derives meaning from a lifelong engagement with the divine injunction.[251] In support of this claim, he points to Diogenes of Sinope, Cynicism's most famous representative. Julian re-interprets Diogenes as a deeply pious figure whose apparent subversiveness was an expression of his obedience to Apollo's command.[252] His unconventional lifestyle originated in his efforts to free himself from the shackles of appearance, efforts that were tantamount to a search for his true self. Conversely, contemporary Cynics who imitate Diogenes but do not share his devotion are enslaved to appearance. What drives them is 'the ambition to attract public notice' (200c). Confusing the assumption of a Cynic attitude with true philosophical practice, they 'have become rapacious and depraved, and no better than one of the brute beasts'.[253] Julian seals his argument by explicitly underscoring the resemblance between their lives and those of the (Christian) 'monks'.[254]

Conclusions

Constantine, twice subversive (as a usurper and as a Christian), consolidated his authority and legitimacy by adapting Christian theories of providence to meet elite expectations concerning the imperial self-image. Exploiting the apologetic claim that Christianity was the only wisdom inspired by the divine, Constantine pursued recognition as the only Roman emperor who ever achieved an understanding of the divine will. His advertisement of his capacity to apply his exegetical skills to both history and literature simultaneously validated his claims to a philosophical identity and invited his audiences to join in his politics of interpretation by examining the validity of his arguments. His victories were elevated into

---

[249] *Cyn*, 187d.   [250] *Cyn*, 187d–88a. Cf. Elm (2012) 137–38; Marcone (2012).
[251] *Cyn.* 188a–b.
[252] *Cyn.* 191a–d, 199b; cf. *C. Her.* 211b–d, 238b–39c. For Julian's personalisation of the doxographic material on Diogenes and his rewriting of the Cynic as a deeply pious figure, see Marcone (2012) 241; De Vita (2022) lxxx, cxcviii–cc.
[253] *Cyn.* 197b. Cf. Julian's remarks on their ignorance at *C. Her.* 225a–b; 227a–b.
[254] *Cyn.* 224b (ἀποτακτιστάς). On routine associations between Cynics and Christians, see further Marcone (2012) 239; De Vita (2022) cxcvi. Cf. Julian's accusation that Heraclius cultivated Constantius II to win patronage: *C. Her.* 223d.

evidence of the truth of his assertions. His supporters (including Optatian and Eusebius) further cultivated the image of the Christian emperor as master exegete.

Julian's commitment to competitive exegesis during the time he ruled as sole emperor must therefore be read as intrinsic to his response to Christianity. In Julian's view, the definition of Christianity as a superior hermeneutical system was the outcome of a deliberate misrepresentation of the relationship of Christian doctrine to Greek philosophy. Julian's mature writings mapped out his ambition to deny Christianity interpretive command. The new religion was presented as an irrational cult that appropriated features of Greek wisdom to compete in the socio-political arena. Julian further supported his argument with a complementary attempt to reclaim Greek *paideia* as the highest hermeneutical system. To this end, he addressed controversial matters such as the allegory of Greek myths and poetry to emphasise the inner coherence and philosophical superiority of the Greco-Roman religious system and the claim that everything Christianity called its own already existed in Greek thinking.

CHAPTER 4

A Life for a Life

In Chapter 3, I argued that Constantine's self-legitimisation as a Christian sovereign relied on an advertisement of his capacity to access the meaning of history, a capacity his ability to perform literary exegesis both foreshadowed and confirmed. Of all the proofs put forward by Constantine in support of his argument, one had special validating significance by virtue of being visible to every subject and therefore available for verification. This piece of necessary evidence – a *tekmerion*, as the ancient forensic language would term it[1] – was Constantine's own life. As was argued above, the strategy of focalising the story of the rise of Christianity through Constantine's story is a dominant mode of argumentation already in his letters from the 320s. It then arguably reaches its fullest articulation in the *Oration to the Assembly of the Saints*, underlies Optatian's poetic intertwining of Christian and Constantinian symbols, and serves as the cornerstone of Eusebius' *Life of Constantine*.

In the present chapter, I read Julian's focus on the public persona of Constantine and his complementary engagement with (auto)biography against the background of this core component of Constantinian propaganda. It is uncontroversial to state that Julian disavowed his predecessor on ideological grounds (and perhaps also out of personal resentment).[2] In his oration *Against Heraclius*, Constantine is singled out as a greedy, ignorant tyrant; in the *Caesars*, Julian's satire of the emperors who preceded him, Constantine features as a buffoon devoted to pleasure who provides the miserable foil against which Julian delineates the greatness of Marcus Aurelius. I suggest, however, that Julian – the subtle interpreter of Constantine's politics of interpretation – fully understood Constantine's use of his life as necessary evidence. To this, he opposed a complementary

---

[1] See Grimaldi (1980).
[2] See now especially Greenwood (2021) 12, arguing for retribution as the key aspect of Julian's attitude to Constantine and Constantius II.

and competitive use of his own life as the token of his truth. When seen in this light, the biographical experiments that permeate the final phase of Julian's literary production emerge as an essential component and in fact the culmination of Julian's larger project of refuting Christian hermeneutics.

From Eusebius' *Life of Constantine* to Julian's *Against Heraclius*

Eusebius' account of Constantine's vision of the cross in the first book of his *Life of Constantine* is a strikingly effective encapsulation of the principle according to which Constantine's conversion originated in his intelligent interpretation of history. The rest of the work remains faithful to this premise. The old Eusebius, who dedicated the time between Constantine's death and his own to recording the emperor's deeds, appears to have found in the biographical form an ideal space to explore Rome's first experience in Christian sovereignty. His image of Constantine, at once celebratory and prescriptive, sits at the crossroads between the two main biographical strands of antiquity: on the one hand, the lives of rulers, consolidating the collective memory of exemplary leaders, and on the other, the lives of philosophers, a genre revisited in early Christian literature in the form of saints' lives. Biographies of philosophers and holy individuals turned the most abstract of pursuits – the search for knowledge – into a living process that could be subdivided into stages, observed, admired, and reproduced.[3] Eusebius' *Life* tells us that there is one condition for these two biographical strands to merge: the Christianity of the ruler.[4]

Eusebius' *Life* introduces Constantine as 'excelling above all in literary education (παιδεύσει λόγων), natural judgment, and God-given wisdom'.[5] The organisation of Constantine's talents is programmatic: his literary education confirms that he was a man of culture; his personal qualities point to his personal inclination, as an individual, to the role of leader; his wisdom is explicitly identified as a gift from the divine. As the *Life* progresses, Constantine is presented as highly educated and eloquent: a network of allusions to his proficiency in rhetoric runs through the book.[6] He operates as a wise lawgiver and is a conqueror moved not by

---

[3] On normative biography and hagiography in late antiquity, see Momigliano (1971); Cox (1983); Hägg and Rousseau (2000); Williams (2008); Goldhill (2020) 194–235. Urbano (2013) 163–204 brings effectively into focus the competitive mobilisation of the lives of Constantine and Julian as upholding an ideal of philosophical leadership for their respective supporters.
[4] See especially Urbano (2013) 168–86; Corke-Webster (2020b). [5] *VC* 1.19.2.
[6] See, e.g., *VC* 1.19.2; 3.59.3; 4.29; 4.55.1–2.

a thirst for power but by a desire to defeat tyrants (who are, of course, his former co-rulers). He also strives to dispel ignorance and brutality by allowing (read: deporting) foreign people into the empire. In an eloquent passage, Eusebius describes the Sarmatians rejoicing at their good luck in having been defeated by such an emperor.[7]

In Eusebius' *Life*, Christianity colours all the traits of Constantine's leadership. His enlightened legislation finds its highest expression in the way it interacts with the institution of the Church, protecting and encouraging a spiritual, ascetic lifestyle.[8] His defeat of polyarchy signifies the defeat of polytheism; the crushing of external enemies seals the end of atheism. Finally, Constantine's commitment to culture is described as evolving into devotion to a Christian doctrine, explicitly called 'philosophy', whose superiority is openly acknowledged – according to the text – by non-Christian philosophers as well.[9] Book by book, Eusebius outlines the relentless process of the emperor's spiritual growth. By the time we reach Book Four, which focuses on Constantine's final years, we are presented with a ruler whose qualities have 'advanced to the peak of human perfection'[10] and who has become the teacher of divine things. The book illustrates Constantine's participation in doctrinal disputes and his study of the sacred texts. He spends the hours of the night awake, 'applying his mind to the meaning of the divinely inspired oracles'.[11] He also repeatedly composes and delivers speeches, thinking it his duty to 'rule his subjects with instructive argument' (λόγῳ παιδευτικῷ), establishing his whole imperial rule as 'rational' (λογικήν ... βασιλείαν) – arguably in the sense of both reasonable and enlightened by the (Christian) Logos.[12] Eusebius describes Constantine's instruction of his soldiers in prayers; 'countless multitudes' come 'to listen to the emperor's philosophising' (φιλοσοφοῦντος ἀκουσόμενα βασιλέως).[13] As death approaches, Constantine even indulges in the Socratic gesture of conversing on the soul's immortality.[14] All these claims converge to suggest that he alone fulfilled the ideal of philosopher-ruler that pagan antiquity had desired in

---

[7] *VC* 4.6.2. On the late third- and fourth-century representation of the forced deportation of foreign tribes in the empire as an act of benevolence, see, e.g., *Pan. Lat.* VIII (4) 1.4; 8.4–9.4 See further Barbero (2006) 81–84, 1414–2, 224–25.

[8] Constantine's legislation, for instance, is described as favouring those who chose abstinence through 'a passion for philosophy' (φιλοσοφίας ἔρωτι, *VC* 4.26.3).

[9] *VC* 4.55.2.   [10] *VC* 4.54.1.

[11] *VC* 4.17. On the study of the 'oracles' (i.e., Scriptures), see also *VC* 1.3.4; 2.12.1. Nights awake: 4.29.1.

[12] *VC* 4.29.1.   [13] Instructing in prayer: *VC* 4.19. Listening multitudes: *VC* 4.29.2, cf. 4.45.3.

[14] *VC* 4.55.2.

vain: the proof is that he alone (μόνου) worshipped God properly and was consequently rewarded as none of his predecessors had been.[15]

Eusebius' *Life of Constantine* thus offers the most explicit (and effective) exemplification of how the elevation of Constantine into a model of philosophical leadership could transform his imperial experience into a demonstration that governmental stability had to be (re)founded on Christian philosophy. After Constantine's death, Eusebius offered validation of all the claims the emperor had advanced while alive, sealing their reliability in his role of external observer and intellectual and via his episcopal authority.[16] What is more, Eusebius organised the emperor's claims within a systematic account that revisited Constantine's life and passed on his teaching to new generations. The immediate impact of Eusebius' operation is difficult to assess. The *Life* seems to disappear from all records (at least explicitly; some writings from the second half of the century have been regarded as echoing it),[17] until Socrates' *Ecclesiastical History* mentions it one hundred years later.[18] Socrates' fleeting criticism of the *Life* – he says that his own history is less rhetorical and more historically accurate – may suggest, however, that he expected his audience to be familiar with his polemical target. In any case, regardless of whether Socrates' tone suggests wide circulation, the imperial court plausibly represented a space of early fruition of Eusebius' *Life*. The opening and end of the text clearly indicate that Eusebius had an imperial readership in mind and aimed to issue what is usually regarded as a *speculum principis* for the benefit of Constantine's sons.[19] He focuses on the passage of power from Constantine to his children and celebrates the latter's harmonious rule in the legacy of their father, foreshadowing – that is, encouraging – them to pattern their rule on Constantine's. As seen in Chapter 3, his children quickly committed to presenting themselves as his sons.[20]

Julian too belonged to the world of the court. He never tells us that he read Eusebius' *Life* – although one might speculate that the biography of the first Christian ruler counted among the books 'recording the

---

[15] Eusebius, *VC* 4.75. [16] Cf. Chapter 3, p. 129–33.
[17] For instance, Libanius, *Or.* 59 (see Petit [1950]; Wiemer [1994]; Cameron and Hall [1999] 48–49) and Rufinus' *Ecclesiastical History* (Van Dam [2007b] 332). Urbano suggests that Libanius' *Epitaphius*, his funeral oration for Julian, was written in response to Eusebius' *Life* (Urbano [2013] 164).
[18] Socrates, *HE* 1.1.2. Corke-Webster (2020b) shows that the *Life* attempted to convert Constantine into a model of virtuous episcopacy, which suggests that Eusebius was writing in addition for bishops.
[19] Eusebius, *VC* 1.1, 3, 9.2; 4.72. Cameron (1997); Cameron and Hall (1999) 12.
[20] See p. 114–17.

experience of men of old' that Eusebia gave to Julian, as he tells us, before his Gallic campaign.[21] It would have been quite appropriate for the pious wife of Constantius to exhort the youngest living descendant of Constantine to mould himself after his uncle. This remains hypothesis. But the fact that Julian knew and read (and was critical of) Eusebius' writings, as already noted in this book, is not.[22]

It is unnecessary to postulate Julian's specific knowledge of Eusebius' *Life* to argue that he intended to deflate the apologetic potential embedded in the bishop's use of Constantine as evidence: Constantine's propaganda – including his iconography, to which I return later – spoke for itself. But the significance of Julian's biographical experiments emerges in full when we compare them to Eusebius' final word on the life of the Christian emperor. The *Life*'s Scripturesque refashioning of Constantine's rule, its self-presentation as a sort of interpretive handbook of the Constantinian image, and its open disavowal of Roman history prior to him are three guidelines that illuminate Julian's equally literary efforts to narrate his own life as that of a salvific agent and supreme philosopher, place the (meaning of) his image in competition with Constantine's iconography, and re-assess the significance of Rome's past as itself evidence refuting Constantine's claims.

I begin to analyse the dialogic and antagonistic quality of Julian's relationship with biography by engaging with a text that stands as a manifesto of Julian's cultural, religious, and political project. This is the oration *Against Heraclius*, a piece constructed around the question of how to write the life of an agent of providence. The oration presents itself as a response to a lecture delivered by a Cynic philosopher, Heraclius, in Julian's presence. But criticism of Heraclius' performance is a springboard for disavowing the adherents to Cynicism who, in Julian's eyes, brought Greek philosophy into disrepute. Chapter 3 considered how Julian regarded them as drawn more to the form than the substance of the intellectual life and sought to prevent them from hindering his efforts to project Greek philosophy as a cult of culture.[23] Heraclius' lecture proved, in its specifics, his ignorance of an art philosophers should master: myth-making.[24] (What we might want to define as allegorical composition, as opposed to allegory as interpretive practice.) From Julian's rebuke, we understand that the Cynic had exploited a (weak) mythical framework to

---

[21] *Eus.* 124a–b. [22] See Chapters 1, p. 70–1, and 3, p. 152. [23] P. 163–4.
[24] *C. Her.* 234c–d. Cf. Elm (2012) 111–12 and Van den Berg (2019) 426.

engage with a seemingly subversive but intellectually unsatisfying power play involving the emperor himself.[25] Julian uses his response to legitimise his intellectual authority and, much as he had done years before with the *Letter to Themistius*, seizes the opportunity to lecture a self-confessed philosopher on philosophy.[26]

I will not return at this point to the content of Julian's teaching, a clarification of the use and function of educational mythography whose finalities have already been assessed in Chapter 3.[27] But Julian's assertion that myths can serve as vehicles of divine truths, which they convey to those who are not so advanced in philosophy that they can engage directly with metaphysics and the divine mysteries, is relevant here. 'Through riddles and the dramatic setting of myths', Julian writes, 'knowledge is insinuated into the ears of the multitude'.[28] He then moves on to provide his own exemplification of this statement, and it is here that the complex machinery set up by *Against Heraclius* truly gets in motion. The material of Julian's myth is derived from the most recent events in Roman history,[29] upon which it eloquently grounds an allegory of the opposition between the rule of reason, which derives its legitimacy from the Greek gods and the rule of impiety and unreason, which connected, as we will now see, to a different and subversive type of worship.

'A certain rich man', Julian begins, 'had numerous flocks of sheep and herds of cattle . . . . He was eager to enrich himself, be it justly or unjustly, because he had no care for the gods (ἔμελε γὰρ αὐτῷ τῶν θεῶν ὀλίγον)'.[30] This man, he adds, had several sons but did not teach them how to preserve their wealth, 'for in his ignorance (ὑπὸ ἀμαθίας) he thought that their mere numbers would suffice . . . since he had not acquired his wealth reasonably (μὴ λόγῳ προσειληφώς) but rather by use and wont'.[31] The sons proved to be as irrational as their father. Indeed, all their relatives were: a general slaughter ensued, over the course of which the sons demolished temples and erected sepulchres.[32] Zeus, concerned, intervened. After inviting his son Helios to leave behind his resentment against the rich shepherd who, having forsaken the sun god, 'brought so many calamities on himself and his race',[33] Zeus drew Helios' attention to a young man, the shepherd's nephew. The boy was Helios' child – he is referred to as his 'offspring', ἔκγονος – but had been 'infected with smoke,

---

[25] See Chapter 3, p. 163. [26] See Chapter 1. [27] See p. 155–61.
[28] *C. Her.* 216c (see also 206d). See De Vita (2011) 107–19. [29] *C. Her.* 227c–34c.
[30] *C. Her.* 227c. [31] *C. Her.* 227d. [32] *C. Her.* 228c. [33] *C. Her.* 228d–29a.

filth, and darkness'.³⁴ Helios and Athena were therefore entrusted with rearing him and healing him from his malady.³⁵

The myth is transparent. The greedy and despicable rich man who breeds sons cut from the same cloth is Constantine. The principle of reason – *logos* – is here ironically denied to the emperor worshipping Logos with a capital *lambda*. The mention of the conflicts provoked by Constantine's dynasty calls to mind Ammianus' comment that Julian perceived Christianity as fostering violence (also and especially the intra-religious kind).³⁶ The themes of corpse-worshipping and replacement of temples with sepulchres (τάφοι, Julian's term for churches)³⁷ serve as evidence that, in Constantine's religion, everything is upside down – a motif Julian repeatedly explores in his efforts to bring out the implications of Christianity's fallacies.³⁸ The focus on death draws attention to the theological problem posed by the humanity of Christ: thus in the *Against the Galileans* Julian accuses John of forging Jesus' identity with the Logos.³⁹ Finally, the youth the gods rescue from the malady (of Christianity) is Julian.⁴⁰ The fact that he is described as 'reared' by Helios resonates with Julian's description of the fascination for solar light he felt in his childhood, and of how he later saw in this fascination a first stage in his conversion to the gods.⁴¹ The youth's salvation, presented as part of a divine project (Zeus summons the Fates), eloquently occurs, as the *Letter to the Athenians* had already claimed, through education.⁴²

After being raised by the gods, the youth was in torment as to how to escape from the evils that had struck his family. Hermes appeared to him as a guide and led him to the foot of a great mountain on whose summit Zeus dwelt (230d). The youth begged Helios to let him stay on the summit (231d), but he was eventually shown the misery into which the world had fallen under the depraved rule of his cousin (Constantius II, 'sunk in forgetfulness and devoted to pleasure').⁴³ Helios asked him to return to the world – much as the liberated prisoner returns to Plato's Cave – and 'cleanse away all impiety' (καθαίρειν . . . πάντα τὰ ἀσεβήματα,

---

³⁴ *C. Her.* 229c.   ³⁵ *C. Her.* 229d.   ³⁶ See Chapter 3, p. 147–8.
³⁷ Cf. *C. Gal.* fr. 81 (335c).
³⁸ On Julian's treatment of (Christian) Antioch in the *Misopogon* as a space of subversion, see Quiroga Puertas (2009).
³⁹ *C. Gal.* fr. 79 (327a–c), 80 (333b–d). See Chapter 3, p. 151–2.
⁴⁰ Bowersock (1978) 17; Athanassiadi (1981) 133–34; Smith (1995) 185; Elm (2012) 114–16; Greenwood (2021): 65–74.
⁴¹ *Hel.* 130c–31a. Eunapius of Sardis reports that 'Julian in his letters calls the Sun his own father' (fr. 28.5 Blockley (1983), transl. Blockley). Cf. Greenwood (2021) 69.
⁴² Cf. *Ath.* 272a (Julian's divine salvation by means of philosophy).   ⁴³ *C. Her.* 232b.

231d). In his desire never to leave the company of the gods, the youth protested, but Helios rebuked him. The myth closes with the youth's decision to fulfil his divinely set task (232c–d).

The myth of the *Against Heraclius* is extraordinarily complex, and I will now seek to separate its main layers in order to show how they work together to construct Julian's ideal persona from various but complementary angles. A first level of the argument relies on Julian's display of his mastery of rhetoric, the mark of *paideia*. Julian asks educated readers to recognise his oration as inspired by Dio of Prusa.[44] This (implicit) request is quite significant. Thanks to what are known as his *Orations on Kingship* – speeches that addressed Trajan on the matter of ideal kingship – Dio had become in Julian's times the paradigm of the philosopher-adviser of emperors and the architect of an enlightened synergy between Greek wisdom and Roman power.[45] I return in Chapter 5 to the importance this paradigm maintains even in a context of negotiation of the power of bishops vis-à-vis the emperor.

The first of Dio's *Orations on Kingship* is divided precisely into two parts: an exposition of theory, mostly consisting of moral advice about how to be a good emperor, and a political translation of Prodicus' myth of Heracles at the crossroads between virtue and vice, which Dio adapts for his imperial audience by setting it at the crossroads between kingship and tyranny.[46] Not only does Julian's *Against Heraclius* mirror the bipartition of Dio's oration, but the myth developed in the second half of the text clearly offers itself as Julian's adaptation of Dio's adaptation of Prodicus' story. Julian's Hermes, whose role is read by Athanassiadi as the Psychopompus leading the soul of the devotee through the degrees of initiation in the Mithraic mysteries, is in the first instance the divinity guiding Heracles in Dio's first oration.[47] Crucially, Dio's figurative opposition between kingship and tyranny is here recast as one between good leadership inspired by the gods and the irrational rule of the (Christian) tyrant. Although never confronted with the possibility of choosing between these two options, Julian is granted a vision of the latter while standing on top of Zeus' mountain. From there, he can gaze at the obscure world of Constantius, whose thick fog and darkness is reminiscent of the

---

[44] Cf. Greenwood (2021) 53.
[45] Themistius too sought association with Dio: see Jones (1978) 115; Brancacci (1985) 123; Maisano (1995) 11–12; Heather (1998) 129–30. On the case of Synesius of Cyrene's self-stylisation as a better Dio, see Chapter 5, p. 257–9.
[46] Dio Chrys. *Or.* 1.59–84.   [47] Dio Chyrs. *Or.* 1.66. See Athanassiadi (1981) 104.

fog and darkness surrounding the peak where the personification of tyranny dwells, in Dio's account of Heracles at the crossroads.⁴⁸

The refashioning of Dio's oration is part of Julian's strategy of suggesting proximity to the ideal of philosopher-ruler by flipping intellectual hierarchies and lending his own advice to self-styled philosopher-advisers. Crucially, Dio's – and Julian's – teachings focus on a specific portion of ancient political philosophy: kingship theory. A similar display of the ability to prescribe views on this matter, as shaped by Julian in his earlier *Second Panegyric to Constantius II*, had already served him as a weapon to assert his intellectual superiority over the Augustus.⁴⁹ Now that Julian is the only remaining emperor on the stage, his claims of superiority have become absolute rather than relative. Dio of Prusa could only pray to Trajan to follow his philosophical advice, but Julian does not need to pray to anyone: every exhortation is to and for himself. By the very act of advising, he is fulfilling the content of his own advice.

At the same time, the breech Julian's Dionic myth opens in the theme of the divine discloses another layer of self-stylisation at work in *Against Heraclius*: the bond Julian establishes between his cultural profile and his religious allegiance. The Sun god (who became the subject of Julian's hymn *To King Helios* a few months later, in December 362) plays a central role here. Helios is presented as the father and educator of the youth: he cures him from Christianity (229c) and sends him back to earth to replace Constantius (232c) and restore the cult of the gods (233c–d). Helios is thus irreconcilable with Christianity, despite, Julian allusively suggests, previous attempts to claim otherwise. When he addresses Helios, Zeus asks if he still resents the vicious shepherd – Constantine – for forsaking him (ὅς σε ἀπολιπὼν αὐτῷ).⁵⁰ This must be read as a comment on Constantine's conversion to Christianity. At the same time, however, the representation of Constantine's 'abandonment' of Helios as a personal betrayal seems to allude to something more specific, (the end of) the extended self-attachment of Constantine to the god, which was testified by the presence of solar imagery in Constantine's propaganda. After his early divorce from the Tetrarchs, the young Constantine sought association with

---

⁴⁸ *C. Her.* 232a, cf. Dio Chrys. *Or.* 1.68. ⁴⁹ See Chapter 2, p. 94–100.
⁵⁰ *C. Her.* 228d. This re-appropriation of the sun in Julian' propaganda is reflected by the rhetorician Himerius. His *Or.* 41, delivered in Constantinople after early December 361 (Penella (2007) 2), hails the emperor for having 'washed away ... the darkness that was preventing us from lifting our hands up to the Sun' (Him. *Or.* 41.8, transl. Penella (2007)). Himerius adds that Julian 'links his nature with the Sun both to give light and to reveal a better life' (ibid.). On Himerius' commentary on Julian's cultic revival see further Greenwood (2021) 97–8.

a divinity that set him apart from their Jupiter and Hercules. The most effective instrument for disseminating imperial messages – coinage – testifies to this ambition: between 310 and 317, all the Constantinian mints produced coins with *Sol* on the reverse.[51] After the coinage reform of 318 discontinued the bronze coinage featuring the god, *Sol* progressively disappeared from Constantine's coins in a long envoi whose final act took place only in 325, when, a few months after the defeat of Licinius, the solar god also vanished from gold coins and medallions.[52] Solar elements, it should be noted, were not completely erased from Constantinian iconography. His post-Nicene images still bear traces of what Wienand calls 'subliminal' references to the god, which create a complex interplay between solar imagery from the imperial cult and early Christian associations of Christ with light.[53] This final development, however, falls outside the scope of my analysis. Here I am primarily concerned with what I see as early evidence of Julian's ambition to ironically mobilise Constantine's iconography at Constantine's expense – an effort that, as I argue below, dominates Julian's final orations. Julian's mention of Constantine forsaking *Sol* suggests that he expected his audience to remember Constantine's past association with the god and recognise, in this association, a token of his duplicity.

But solar imagery is not the only element in Julian's myth that interacts antagonistically with the theological vocabulary supporting Constantine's

---

[51] Bergmann (1998) 282–90; Wallraff (2001); Bardill (2012) 84–104; Wienand (2012) 274–80, (2013) 177–83; Guidetti (2013) 189–91; Barbero (2016) 239–54; Lenski (2016) 49–50. The image of the god was frequently accompanied by the legend SOLI INVICTO COMITI, 'to the Unconquered Sun, the protector' (on discussion of this use of *comes*, see Bardill [2012] 86 and n. 378). Representations of Sol peaked following Maxentius' defeat in 312. Cf., in this regard, the rapid career of the solar priest Gaius Vettius Cossinius Rufinus, *praefectus urbi* of Rome in 315 and consul in 316 (Wienand [2012] 333 n. 190). On the nature of the relationship between Constantine's Christianity and his allegiance to *Sol*, see Wallraff (2001); Girardet (2007) 80; Bardill (2012); Wienand (2013). Wienand suggests that Constantine believed in the divine protector of the emperor as a *summa divinitas* that could be called by many different names while remaining the same (Wienand [2013] 181, considering the celebration of the 'supreme creator of things, whose names' are 'as many as the tongues of the nations', *Pan. Lat.* XII [9] 26.1, transl. Nixon and Rodgers [1994]). On deliberate ambiguity in iconography and the search for consensus, see Guidetti (2013) 190–91.

[52] Wienand (2012) 288z-335, (2013) 183–77; Barbero (2016) 257–61.

[53] Wienand (2012) 390–96, 448–53, (2013) 187–90. See further Tantillo (2003); Barbero (2016) 306–8; Elm (2021) 140. For the re-semanticisation of the attributes of the solar god as imperial attributes, cf. Constantine's lost statue wearing a radiate crown on the Porphyry Column in Constantinople (Bardill [2012] 28–36, 332–35) or Constantine's similarly lost statue at Termessos carrying a dedication (*SEG* 53.1612) that apparently assimilates the emperor to Helios Panepoptes (Fowden [1991] 129, Tantillo [2003]). On Optatian's association of Constantine with light, e.g., *Carm.* 7.13; 9.32; 12.15; 14.2; 15.14; 18.7; 19.2, 12. On Eusebius' use of solar imagery in connection to Constantine, see p. 189–92 below.

strategies of self-legitimisation. Another crucial element of competition is the motif of the emperor as salvific agent, which Constantine's propaganda had explored by emphasising his mimetic relationship with Christ.[54] *Against Heraclius* enhances Julian's self-projection as a soteriological figure via a literary strategy: his alter ego in the myth inhabits the role of Zeus' son Heracles in both Prodicus' version of the story and Dio's variant.[55] As Christ and Heracles were competing figures in late antiquity,[56] Julian's myth takes full advantage, as Greenwood shows, of this conflictual overlap.[57] First, the story teases the analogy between Heracles and Jesus by describing the former as walking on water and serving as a 'saviour for the world' (τῷ κόσμῳ σωτήρ).[58] Second, although the myth casts Julian in the role of Heracles, it simultaneously inserts him into a scene evoking Matthew's account of Jesus in the desert, the relevance of which for Julian is shown by his criticism of it in *Against the Galileans*.[59] It should be noted, incidentally, that Julian's implicit but competitive assimilation of Heracles with Jesus is not as much an imitation of Christian theology as an expression of his own larger project of asserting the dependence of Christian theology on Greek thinking, on which see Chapter 3.[60] Julian writes to remind his audience that the idea of a divine saviour was contained in Greek religion from its origins and was therefore original to it. His choice of the mythical Heracles implicitly contrasts the antiquity of the latter with the novelty of the historical Jesus. This claim to antiquity is also implicitly reflected in Julian's appeals to and self-association with another mythical salvific figure who epitomised with his art the care of the Greek deities for humankind: Asclepius the god of medicine.[61]

The way Julian's myth weaves together a network of references to the relationship between the ruler and the divine, pointing to culture as what provides the instruments for assessing the claims of rival rulers to both theological and intellectual priority, brings me to my final point in connection with this text. The final level of argumentation in *Against*

---

[54] On which, see especially Greenwood (2017a), (2021) 31–40.
[55] See, e.g., at *C. Her.* 220d, 231c–32a, 232c. On how the motif was reflected in his propaganda, see Conti (2009).
[56] Van Kooten (2010) 25–29.
[57] Greenwood (2014), (2021) 65–74. See further Elm (2021) 138–39; De Vita (2022) cclxxxviii–cclxxxix.
[58] Walking on water: *C. Her.* 219d (cf. Mt. 14.25–33; Mk. 6.45-52; Jo. 6.16–21). On the episode, see also *C. Gal.* fr. 50 (213b). Saviour of the world: *C. Her.* 220a.
[59] *C. Her.* 230b–33d. Greenwood (2014) 593–98, (2021) 70–74. For Julian's criticism of Mt. 4.1–11, see *C. Gal.* fr. 93 (fr. 2 Wright).
[60] P. 146–63. [61] Greenwood (2021) 75–91.

Heraclius elevates compositional experimentation into a demonstration of method. This chapter opened with the question of if and how the way a life is told can validate or challenge its ties to the divine. The form designed by Julian for his autobiography points to a personal commitment to answering this question. In the oration, he achieves self-legitimisation via the creation of a narrative that meets all the criteria for sacred myth – one might say, for Scripture. Chapter 3 considered how *Against Heraclius*' theoretical section, which focuses on the features of myths that help identify them as true vessels of divine messages, illuminates Julian's strategies for the competitive differentiation of Greek from Christian hermeneutics. Julian's reflection is also essential to understanding how he navigated the delicate passage from reception to creation of sacred stories, that is, to return to scholarly labels, from interpretive to compositional allegory. This step was necessary for an author concerned with writing himself into providential history. The autobiographical account of *Against Heraclius* thus shows that Julian's definition of the features of truly educational and divinely inspired myths prepares for his legitimisation of his providential agency in the same text through a story that derives its validation from its conformity to Julian's own criteria for assessing mythography.

The myth's handling of the divine is at the heart of this operation. In *Against Heraclius*, the gods have distinctly Homeric traits. Homeric allusions are disseminated throughout the text.[62] Epic tropes are reproduced. Zeus' resolution to intervene to save humankind, for example, is followed by his decision to summon what could be interpreted as a restricted council involving himself, Helios, and the Fates.[63] In the solitude of his journey, the Julianic youth who is a Heracles and also, in some ways, a Jesus, also acquires Odysseus-like traits: like the Homeric hero, he is destined to return to his paternal house and cleanse it.[64] But Julian also becomes an Achilles *alter*, having received divine weapons (*gorgoneion* and helmet) from the hands of his virgin 'mother' Athena.[65] One of the arms Athena entrusts to Julian, crucially, is advice. And it is here that Julian's strategy for self-legitimisation via mythical autobiography comes full circle.

According to Julian's theory of what constitutes a good myth, stories conveying divine wisdom must be characterised by diction befitting the divinity of the gods: they must serve as pure vessels of truth. *Against Heraclius* does set up a Homeric framework, but there is something striking

---

[62] See *C. Her.* 227c (quoting *Il.* 2.474; 20.221); 229d–30a (*Il.* 9.231; 11.164; 24.348); 232c (*Il.* 3.415).
[63] *C. Her.* 228d–29d.   [64] *C. Her.* 231d.   [65] Weapons: *C. Her.* 234a. Athena's virginity: 230a.

about it: all gods speak wisely at all times; their only desire is to benefit humankind. Helios and Athena give political and moral advice to the salvific agent they personally appointed, Julian.[66] Their statements are in themselves quite basic: suffice it to note that Athena's – literal – message consists of warning Julian against flattery and encouraging him to be sober and vigilant and to show respect for the gods in the first place.[67] What is essential about these words is not their content but the fact that their purity indicates the suitability of the text that reports them – Julian's myth – as a vessel of the divine truths underlining world history. When scrutinised for deeper significance, the parable of the youth reveals itself as voicing messages that go beyond the literal meaning of Athena's (or Helios') words. The myth of *Against Heraclius* makes three fundamental pronouncements: Julian's opposition to the house of Constantine is something greater than a dynastic quarrel, being rather a struggle of the rule of reason against an irrational tyranny; this struggle is sanctioned by the gods, who trained Julian (with philosophy) to accomplish his soteriological task; and the gods' theodicy rather than Christian providence controls the fate of Rome.

The function of this brief, unevenly structured pamphlet thus appears in its full significance. *Against Heraclius* is simultaneously Julian's speech on kingship – the literary enactment of his proficiency as scholar, rhetorician, philosopher – and his Scriptural *Life of Julian*, which argues that salvific leadership and true philosophy can only meet outside of Christianity rather than within it, as Eusebius would have argued. Finally – and crucially – Julian's claims of soteriological agency draw on precisely the same vantage point that Constantine exploited before him: historical success. Julian's own survival after the demise of the house of Constantine proves that Constantine's claims to insight into divine history were misplaced. At one point in the text, Julian eloquently argues that 'careful tests must be applied (ἀκριβῶς βασανιστέον) to see whether the myth is plausible (πιθανός)'.[68] The question then arises: which tests can be applied to verify the statement formulated by Julian's myth, namely that he is an agent of the divine will in history? As the next section will show, this issue is at the heart of Julian's final two orations, *Caesars* and *Misopogon*. They accordingly strive to produce evidence disproving Constantine's claims and asserting Julian's design against them.

---

[66] *C. Her.* 231c–33d.   [67] *C. Her.* 232d–33b.
[68] *C. Her.* 226d. On Julian's reflection on the validity of traditions, cf. also *Mat.* 161b (acknowledging that the story of vestal Claudia and the stone of the Mother might sound incredible, but is recorded by the Roman historians) and *Hel.* 154a (portents supporting the mythical account of the foundation of Rome).

Importantly, in both pieces confrontation over philosophical kingship is relocated from the mythical, scriptural isolation of *Against Heraclius* to an explicit use of contemporary history as Julian's weapon of choice. I examine them jointly, beginning with the one that was written last.

Handling Constantinian Evidence between *Caesars* and *Misopogon*. Part I: Features of Understanding

Antioch: Julian's final city of residence before embarking on the Persian campaign. It is February 363, the end of a long winter stay. Julian posts a piece of writing on the Tetrapylon of the Elephants, the triumphal arch facing the imperial palace. Everyone must read what the emperor has written, and what he has written is a satire of his beard. This satire, known as the *Misopogon*, is a response. We learn from Julian that the citizens of Antioch were poking fun at his outward appearance, the stand-out feature of which was his long beard where 'the lice scampered' and that could be 'used to twist ropes'.[69] At this point in his rule, Julian's facial hair had become a key element of his public image. The end of 362 witnessed the issue of a series of coins featuring Julian's last and most famous coinage type, an image of the emperor sporting a long beard (cf. Figure 4.3), a far cry from the short, trimmed military-style beard that had been a trademark of Tetrarchic coinage.[70] Julian's beard seems to have had a role in eliciting the sarcasm of the Antiochenes. The *Misopogon* accuses them explicitly of poking fun at his coins.[71]

The piece thus opens on a note of self-parody, but the self-deprecation is ironic – in the sense that it extols what it pretends to be deriding – and quickly turns into self-celebration. Julian's description of his beard provides an effective illustration of this process:

> As for eating greedily (λάβρως), or drinking with my mouth wide open, this is not in my power (οὐ συγχωροῦμαι); for I must take care, I suppose, or before I know it, I shall eat up some of my own hair. As for the business of being kissed and kissing, I suffer no inconvenience whatever. And yet for this as for other purposes, a beard is evidently troublesome (λυπηρόν), since it does not allow one to press shaven 'lips to other lips more sweetly'[72]

---

[69] *Mis.* 338c–d.
[70] For examples of Tetrarchic coinage portraits, see Figures 4.4, 4.5, and 4.6 below. Notice Maximian's short beard in Figure 4.5. Other coins of Julian Augustus too depicted him with a shorter beard that evoked the Tetrarchic precedent and military authority (cf. Figures 4.1 and 4.2, with attention to the military theme of the reverse of the *solidus* in Figure 4.2). Discussions of the evolution of Julian's bearded style, and of the Tetrarchic precedent behind his militaristic portraits, in Varner (2012); López-Sanchez (2012); Guidetti (2015); García-Ruiz (2018).
[71] *Mis.* 355d.   [72] *Mis.* 338c–d (echoing Theocr. *Id.* 12.32).

Figure 4.1 Julian Augustus, bronze, Sirmium 362–363 CE. Obverse: head of Julian, bearded, pearl-diademed, wearing cloak, with the inscription DN FL CL IVLIANVS PF AVG; reverse: standing bull with stars above, with the inscription SECVRITAS REIPVB (wreath). *RIC* VIII Sirmium 106 p. 392. London, British Museum, Department of Coins and Medals, inv. no. B.3808 (© The Trustees of the British Museum)

Figure 4.2 Julian Augustus, *solidus*, Antioch 362–363 CE. Obverse: head of Julian, bearded, pearl-diademed, wearing cuirass, with the inscription FL CL IVLIANVS P P AVG; reverse: Roman soldier (arguably Julian) holding a trophy and dragging a fettered captive, with the inscription VIRTVS EXERCITVS ROMANORVM. London, British Museum, Department of Coins and Medals, inv. no. 1921,0107.3 (© The Trustees of the British Museum)

Figure 4.3 Julian Augustus, *solidus*, Antioch 362–363 CE. Obverse: head of Julian, with long beard, pearl-diademed, with the inscription FL CL IVLIA-NVS P F AVG; reverse: Julian standing, in full figure, draped with the toga picta, bearing mappa and sceptre, with the inscription VIRTVS EXERCI-TVS ROMANORVM. London, British Museum, Department of Coins and Medals, inv. no. 1867,0101.928 (© The Trustees of the British Museum)

Julian's presents his beard as evidence of his capacity for self-restraint, his asceticism. Facial hair is quickly revealed to be the token of his virtuous countenance, as it forces him to eat and drink moderately (since he is unable to do so voraciously) and to renounce love (since he cannot exchange kisses).[73] But Julian's mobilisation of his beard as evidence is aggressive, as the continuation of the passage shows:

> But you say I ought to twist ropes (σχοινία πλέκειν) from it! Well, I am willing to provide you with ropes if only you have the strength to pull them.... And let no one suppose that I am offended by your satire (νομίση δὲ μηδεὶς δυσχεραίνειν ἐμὲ τῷ σκώμματι). For I myself furnish you with an excuse to indulge in it by cultivating a chin like the goats (ὥσπερ οἱ τράγοι).... But you, since even in your old age you emulate (ζηλοῦντες) your sons and daughters by your soft and delicate way of living (ὑπὸ ἁβρότητος βίου), or perhaps by your effeminate dispositions, take care to make your chins smooth![74]

Julian's self-explanation of his appearance is at the expense of the Antiochenes. From here on, they are described as immoral hedonists obsessed with shaving and self-care. Their appearance, Julian implies,

---

[73] Supporters of Julian celebrated his self-countenance. See, e.g., Amm. Marc. 15.8.10; 16.5.4–8; 24.4.27; 25.4.2; Mamertinus, *Pan. Lat.* III (11) 10.3; 14.3; Libanius, *Or.* 12.94–95; 13.44.

[74] *Mis.* 338b–39a.

can also serve as evidence for their lack of understanding. In his self-description, Julian is playing with an open hand. The dichotomies upon which the *Misopogon* relies – bearded vs. shaven, uncouth vs. overly refined – are rhetorical tropes. Offstage are centuries of Greco-Roman iconography of philosophers, creating a subtext of legitimisation. Especially from the time of the Principate, the beard became a visual component in the process of codification of the appearance of philosophers, being sported by Greek intellectuals among traditionally shaved Romans. A long, unkempt beard was used to signify life according to nature and nonconformity to conventional Roman aesthetic criteria.[75]

By stopping at the consideration that Julian's dichotomies resonate with rhetorical conventions, however, we fail to explain the sense of urgency his text communicates. Why did he perceive his public image as a battleground, and why was he ready to fight and shame his subjects in this matter? I aim to show that Julian's reflection on the imperial image represents a fundamental component, if not the culmination, of his response to Constantine's claims to historical interpretation. Julian understood that imperial iconography had become a fundamental tool for substantiating Constantinian propaganda. Full appreciation of Julian's use of his own image as a response to Constantine, however, requires that we put the *Misopogon* aside and go back in time two months. The *Misopogon*, in fact, was not Julian's first attempt to negotiate the emperor's value and identity by focusing on his image.

The *Caesars*, Julian's satire on his imperial predecessors, was arguably composed in December 362.[76] It presents itself at the outset as a playful piece (or better put, a semi-serious one, in that it acknowledges both serious and amusing intent)[77] written in celebration of the festival of the Saturnalia, which demands parody and laughs (306a–b). It opens – and, as we will see later on, closes – with Julian's voice. 'It is the season of the Saturnalia ... but I have no talent for being amusing or entertaining'

---

[75] Cf. Zanker (1995) 108–11, 198–200; Gleason (1995) 55–81.

[76] I follow the dating of Bidez (1930) 362, on which see also Lacombrade (1964) 27–30; Baldwin (1978) 450–52; Bowersock (1978) 15; Müller (1998) 37–38, Sardiello (2000) viii–ix; De Vita (2022) ccii n. 487. See Bouffartigue (1992) 402–3 and Greenwood (2021) 45–54 for the intriguing but indecisive (to my eyes) hypothesis that the oration should be dated to December 361 (on which, cf. also Wright [1913] 343).

[77] On the *Caesars* as *spoudaiogeloion*, see Niccolai (2017a) 615–16; De Vita (2022) ccii–cciii n. 489. Julian and Menippean satire: Marcone (1984); Bouffartigue (1992) 397–400; Relihan (1993) 119–34; Weinbrot (2005) 50–61. On the *Caesars*' engagement with Seneca's *Apocolocyntosis*, Lucian's *The Parliament of the Gods*, *Philosophies for Sale*, *Demonax*, and *Tragic Zeus*, and Plutarch's *Lives*, see König (2012) 198–99; Quiroga Puertas (2017b).

A Life For A Life 183

(306a), he complains. 'Caesar, can there be anyone so thick (παχύς) ... as to take pains over his jesting? (306a)' is the reply of a friend (perhaps the dedicatee, *Saloustios*)[78] that cuts the matter short.

What Julian has conjured up is a tale of celestial amusement but with an earthly kernel. The work features an imaginary pageant of past Roman emperors. It is set in the heavens, before an audience of Olympian divinities, and addresses a specific matter of interest to the gods, who want to know which emperor has been the best ruler of the Roman Empire. From Caesar and Augustus to Constantine, all of them (including Alexander the Great, the guest star of the contest) parade before the gods; eventually, a subset of the group is selected (317a–18a) and invited to make a short speech to advertise their merits. The shortlist features Alexander, Caesar, Augustus, Trajan, and Marcus Aurelius, the latter having been explicitly summoned by virtue of his excellence in philosophy (317c). Constantine too is invited to join, on the grounds that there should be nothing 'incomplete' (ἀτελές) among the gods (317d). It is therefore necessary to include 'a votary of pleasure' (τινα ... ἀπολαύσεως ἐραστὴν, 317d) among the contestants. Over the course of the competition, two points emerge: Marcus was certainly the best ruler and Constantine was the worst. The significance of this opposition is illuminated by its focus on Marcus as Rome's philosopher-ruler, a focus that defines his opposition to Constantine as one of rational versus irrational leadership.

Julian chooses an intriguing strategy to introduce the emperors in the *Caesars*: he focuses on their appearance. This is evident from the entrance of the first four Julio-Claudian rulers.[79] A dramatic crescendo links each of them with an impressionistic image: the tongue-in-cheek mockery of Julius Caesar's renowned baldness is followed by the chameleon-like appearance of Octavian (who 'changes colour continually [309a]', illustrating his ability to adapt but also his opportunism). Tiberius enters with a solemn countenance, but his back is revealed to be covered with 'countless scars, burns, and sores (309c)', betraying the depravity he kept hidden beneath a sober façade. The sequence ends with the entrance of an 'evil beast' (θηρίον πονηρόν, 310a) that is quickly hurled into Tartarus. This is Caligula, an emperor so disgraced that the satiric fiction denies him a name, a human figure, or any description.

---

[78] Cf. Wright (1913) 343, based on *Hel.* 157c. Σαλούστιος (in the Greek) tends to be identified with Saturninus Secundus Salutius (see Chapter 2, n. 114).
[79] *Caes.* 308d–10b.

Julian's portraits, which rely on the literary tradition of comic mockery of the human body,[80] refer to well-known features of the rulers (e.g., Caesar's baldness) but also use their image synthetically, as epitomising the significance of their rule. The description of the winner of the contest, Marcus Aurelius, is particularly indicative of this. Julian strategically delays the moment of Marcus' portrait. Whereas all the other emperors are described as they arrive at the banquet, Marcus is described only when he faces the divine jury. The special emphasis this bestows on the portrayal clearly befits his status as the hero of the story:

> He came in looking extremely dignified (σεμνὸς ἄγαν) and showing the effect of his labours in the expression of his eyes and his lined brows (ὑπὸ τῶν πόνων ἔχων τά τε ὄμματα καὶ τὸ πρόσωπον ὑπό τι συνεσταλμένον). His aspect was unutterably beautiful from the very fact that he was careless of his appearance and unadorned by art (ἄκομψον καὶ ἀκαλλώπιστον). For he wore a long beard (ἡ ... ὑπήνη βαθεῖα), his dress was plain and sober (τὰ ἱμάτια λιτὰ καὶ σώφρονα), and from lack of nourishment (ὑπὸ τῆς ἐνδείας τῶν τροφῶν) his body was shining and transparent (διαυγέστατον καὶ διαφανέστατον), like light most pure and stainless.[81]

Intriguingly, the image does not match the emperor's portraits. These show a beard – not unkempt and 'philosophical', however, but short and well groomed, like that of his predecessor Hadrian.[82] The similarities end there. What Julian offers his audience is a portrayal in which every feature alludes to virtue: Marcus' tired eyes are those of a scholar; his long beard is that of a philosopher. Marcus is careless of his appearance, leads an ascetic life, and eats little. His practices of renunciation are reflected in his spiritual body, which has become shiny and transparent, a token of his purification from bodily taints, which Neoplatonists believed philosophical souls could achieve.[83]

By suggesting how a philosopher-ruler should look, Marcus' portrait creates a bridge between literature and actuality, conflating fiction and the contemporary world. In fact, the long beard, ascetic lifestyle, and lack of care for outward appearance are all features celebrated by Julian: they

---

[80] On the role of physiognomics in imperial rhetoric and politics, see Gleason (1995). On Plutarch (Julian's model, Niccolai [2017a]) and the *eikonismos* of leaders in the *Lives*, see Tatum (1996).
[81] *Caes.* 317c–d.
[82] Zanker (1995) 218–33, suggests that Hadrian's bearded iconography expressed philhellenism and conveyed continuity with the image of the philosopher. See *contra* Vout (2006), arguing that his beard simply signalled differentiation from his predecessors and presupposed a Roman military model.
[83] On the theory of the *pneuma* (breath) and its intermedial status between soul and world, see Porph. *Abst.* 2.389. Cf. Clark (2000b) 155 n. 306, 156 n. 311.

inform the words of his supporters describing him and are the traits that, as we have seen, Julian explicitly claimed for himself shortly afterwards, in the *Misopogon*. It should be stressed that, at the time the *Caesars* was composed, the long beard – the token of Julian's philosophy – was already being introduced in his public iconography, as noted above.[84]

I return to this resonance between Marcus and Julian in the next section. Here it is essential to appreciate that the value of Marcus' portrait lies not only in the way it actualises an old, authoritative philosophical tradition but also in how it displaces its opposite. The *Caesars* dedicates attention to Constantine's appearance, and here the opposition becomes evident. Having been asked by Silenus, the arbiter of the pageant, what his ambition in life was, Julian's Constantine gives the baffling reply 'To amass great wealth and then spend it liberally'.[85] The reply contrasts strikingly with the portrayals of Constantine by his supporters; in particular, note Eusebius' claim that the Christian emperor 'laughs at his raiment, interwoven with gold' and 'abstains ... from drinking bouts and drunkenness'.[86] Constantine's words give Silenus the opening for an eloquent comment. He asks if Constantine's desire was to lead the 'life of a cook' or a 'hairdresser' (ὀψοποιοῦ καὶ κομμωτρίας βίον, 335b), thus blending criticism of haircare, another imperial rhetorical topos used to (dis)qualify sophists, with the Platonic distinction between the crafts that truly benefit body and soul and the skills that imitate them (such as the profession of the ὀψοποιός, the cook who prepares delicacies of all sorts).[87] In establishing this comparison, Silenus adds a further remark, telling the emperor that his 'hair and appearance' (ἥ τε κόμη τό τε εἶδος, 335b) already indicated his base ambitions.

Silenus' mention of Constantine's hair and appearance is a quote from Hector's description of Alexander Paris at *Iliad* 3.55. He presents Constantine, in other words, as someone who looks like a youth of outstanding – and problematic – beauty. Intertextuality enhances the

---

[84] No statues of Julian survive. Varner (2012) 187–92 defends the identification with Julian (contested in Fittschen [1992–93] and [1997], cf. Fejfer [2008] 397) of two copies of the same statuary portrait (bearded man with *pallium*) preserved at the Louvre (inv. MA 1121) and at the Musée de Cluny (inv. Cl. 18830). But see Guidetti (2015) 12 n. 2.

[85] Πολλά ... κτησάμενον πολλά χαρίσασθαι, *Caes.* 335b. Open-handedness, intriguingly, seems to have been a Constantinian trait. See, e.g., Zosimus, 2.38.1 (on Constantine oppressing some but giving to worthless people); Euseb. *SC* 11.3–4. Cf. also Eusebius' attempt to justify how Constantine's generosity had led him to trust unworthy individuals, at *VC* 4.54.3. Barnes (1981) 255; Cameron and Hall (1999) 309–11; Kelly (2012) 194–98.

[86] See respectively at *LC* 5.6 and 5.7. Cf *VC* 4.30.1 and Constantine's criticism of passions and appetites at *OC* 13.

[87] Plato, *Gorg.* 464b–65d, 521e2–4. See Moss (2007).

critical force of the passage: Hector is reproaching Paris for fleeing from Menelaus. It is intriguing that Julian seems to point to Constantine's beauty as something self-evident, which therefore testifies to his immoral nature. Silenus rounds off his attack on Constantine with a reference to a piece of evidence we are invited to take as substantiating all his accusations, the litmus test of his analysis of the Christian ruler. But why should Julian's readers accept a reference to Constantine's 'good looks' as evidence of immorality? The answer, I suggest, must be found in the efforts of the first Christian emperor to communicate the significance of his power through his public image.

As the previous section considered through the case of Constantine's association with *Sol*, the control and personalisation of the iconography of power were key Constantinian concerns. Constantine began soon to pursue a renewal of the imperial image by abandoning the military beard and hard facial features of Tetrarchic portraits (see Figures 4.4–4.6). Instead, he assumed an image of *civilitas* and *urbanitas* that recalled the emperors of the Principate (especially Augustus and Trajan), in an attempt to advertise his rule as a revival of the Roman Empire's most prosperous period.[88]

The portrait-type developed towards the end of 310 at the mint of Trier for the celebration of the fifth anniversary of Constantine's accession to the throne became in this respect a canon that would be followed for more than twenty years (although from 324 his portrait would be enriched by meaningful additions, on which see below).[89] The intriguing consequence was that Constantine never aged in his portraits. His connection with the divine also came to be signified through the celebration of his eternal beauty.[90] A few unique physiognomic features became his trademark – the shape of his nose, his chin, the fringe of curly hair elegantly arranged on his forehead and along his neck – promoting an idealised, atemporal image.

Constantine's image long remained at the centre of attention in two different but interacting ways. First, it was passed on to his descendants. When Constantine was alive, the same coinage type could signify both him and his sons, regardless of their differences in age.[91] After his death, the signification of dynastic continuity found a privileged channel in iconography, as Constantine's sons continued to adopt their

---

[88] Wright (1987); Hannestad (2001) 95–98; Elsner (2012) 260–62; Guidetti (2013) 186–89. For an early example (meaningfully produced by the mint of Trier, which, being under Constantine's direct control, operated as the epicentre of iconographic innovation) see Figure 4.7.
[89] Elsner (2012) 261; Bardill (2012) 11; Guidetti (2013) 191–94.   [90] Wienand (2012) 251.
[91] Guidetti (2013) 192, with a catalogue of relevant coins at n. 28.

Figure 4.4 Diocletian Augustus, *aureus*, Nicomedia 294–305 CE. Obverse: head of Diocletian with a laureate crown and the inscription DIOCLETIA-NVS AVGVSTVS; reverse: Jupiter wearing cloak and holding thunderbolt, with the inscription IOVI CONSE-RVATORI. *RIC* VI Rome 11 p. 554. London, British Museum, Department of Coins and Medals, inv. no. 1864,1128.165 (© The Trustees of the British Museum)

Figure 4.5 Maximian Augustus, *aureus*, Nicomedia, 294–305 CE. Obverse: head of Maximian with a laureate crown and the inscription MAXIMIA-NVS P F AVG; reverse: Hercules carrying a club and holding four apples, with the inscription HERCVLI VICTORI. *RIC* VI Nicomedia 3, p. 553. London, British Museum, Department of Coins and Medals, inv. no. 1864,1128.176 (© The Trustees of the British Museum)

Figure 4.6   Constantine, *aureus*, Rome 305–307 CE. Obverse: head of Constantine (Tetrarchic style), with a laureate crown and the inscription CONSTANT-INVS NOB C; reverse: Constantine in military dress holding standard in the right hand and a sceptre in the left, with the inscription PRINCI-PI I-VVENTVT(IS). *RIC* VI Rome 151, p. 369. London, British Museum, Department of Coins and Medals, inv. no. 1868,0331.1 (© The Trustees of the British Museum)

Figure 4.7   Constantine, *aureus*, Trier 305–307 CE. Obverse: head of Constantine (new type), with a laureate crown and the inscription CONSTAN-TINVS NOB C; reverse: Constantine in military dress, with the right hand raised and holding a sceptre in the left, between ensigns, with the inscription PRINCIPI IV-V-E-NTVTIS. *RIC* VI Trier 627, p. 204. London, British Museum, Department of Coins and Medals, inv. no. 1864,1128.187 (© The Trustees of the British Museum)

Figure 4.8 Constantius II Augustus, *siliqua*, Antioch 337–347 CE. Obverse: head of Constantius II (Constantinian dynastic style), pearl-diademed, with upward gaze; reverse: inscription VOTIS XV MVLTIS XX within a jewelled wreath. *RIC* VIII Antioch 35 (2). London, British Museum, Department of Coins and Medals, inv. no. 1950, 1006.1588
(© The Trustees of the British Museum)

father's image.[92] Julian too, as Constantine's nephew, was temporarily caught up in their visual project: following his appointment as Caesar, he adopted the shaven Constantinian appearance on coins as well as in life (Figure 4.10).[93]

Second, Constantine's supporters – in particular, Eusebius of Caesarea – sought to prescribe a univocally Christian interpretation of Constantine's images. Constantine's appeal to his Augustan precedent speaks to the complexity of his use of the visual and to how he explored this space to negotiate the support of elites of diverse sensibilities by appealing to a glorious but reassuringly traditional shared past.[94] Eusebius, as was his practice, adapted Constantine's iconography to his own agenda by erasing ambiguities and pushing for a univocal reading. In his *Praise*, Constantine's old association with *Sol* is recovered in the service of a Christian message: Eusebius shapes a complex architecture that sanctions God as the first giver of eternal light, the Logos as the mediator who brought the light (of wisdom) into the world, and Constantine as a Sun-

---

[92] Guidetti (2013) 193–94; Varner (2020). Cf. Figures 4.8–4.9.
[93] See López-Sánchez (2012) 160–71; Guidetti (2015) 16. Cf. Julian's story of how he was forced to shave at *Ath.* 274c.
[94] See especially Bardill (2012) on the Constantinian elaboration of past Hellenistic and imperial models as an anchoring strategy communicating divine favour.

Figure 4.9 Constantius II Augustus, *solidu*s, Aquileia 337–340 CE. Obverse: head of Constantius II with cloak, wearing diadem with gems, with the inscription CONSTANT-IVS P AVG; reverse: seated Victory and winged genius supporting a shield reading VOT X MVLT XX, with the inscription FELICIT-AS PERPETVA. *RIC* VIII Aquileia 5, p. 315. London, British Museum, Department of Coins and Medals, inv. no. 1974,0904.6 (© The Trustees of the British Museum)

Figure 4.10 Julian Caesar, *solidus*, Arles 355–359 CE. Obverse: head of Julian (Constantinian dynastic style), no diadem, wearing cuirass, with the inscription FL CL IVLIANVS NOB CAES; reverse: seated Victory and genius supporting a shield reading VOT V, with the inscription VICTORIA AVGVSTORVM CONST. London, British Museum, Department of Coins and Medals, inv. no. 1853,0716.64 (© The Trustees of the British Museum)

like agent of destiny in a Christian cosmos.⁹⁵ The *Life of Constantine* brings Eusebius' efforts to win Constantine's iconography for the cause of Christianity to consummation: as van Nuffelen shows, images are ubiquitous in a work that places great emphasis on the mystical significance of sight and viewing and gives constant readings of the emperor's paintings, statues, and coins.⁹⁶ Eusebius' effort to claim Constantine's aspect is evident, for instance, in his description of the emperor's entrance at the Council of Nicaea:

> Constantine finally walked along between them (i.e., the bishops) like a heavenly angel of God (οἷα θεοῦ τις οὐράνιος ἄγγελος), his bright mantle shedding lustre like beams of light, shining with the fiery radiance of a purple robe and decorated with the dazzling brilliance of gold and precious stones. Such was his physical appearance. As for his soul, he was clearly adorned with fear and reverence for God (τὴν δὲ ψυχὴν θεοῦ φόβῳ καὶ εὐλαβείᾳ δῆλος ἦν κεκαλλωπισμένος): this was shown by his eyes, were cast down (ὀφθαλμοὶ κάτω νεύοντες), the blush on his face (ἐρύθημα προσώπου), his gait, and the rest of his appearance, his height, which surpassed all those around him …⁹⁷ by his dignified maturity, by the magnificence of his physical condition (τῷ μεγαλοπρεπεῖ τῆς τοῦ σώματος εὐπρεπείας), and by the vigour of his matchless strength. All these, blended with the elegance of his manners and the gentleness of imperial condescension, demonstrated the superiority of his mind (τὸ τῆς διανοίας ὑπερφυὲς … ἀπέφαινον) surpassing all description.⁹⁸

This portrait represents a peculiar amalgam of images of physical strength, magnificence, and wealth that recalls the terminology of imperial panegyrics.⁹⁹ But these are mingled with traits of (Christian) self-countenance: the 'eyes cast down', the 'blush of modesty' characterising a 'soul adorned with fear and reverence for God'. The emperor's gaze was an attribute that panegyrists would praise, but it was also relevant to portraits of philosophers.¹⁰⁰ Eusebius uses it to open a window into the

---

⁹⁵ Wienand (2012) 436–53. Cf. *LC* 1.2, 5 (God's command over celestial light); 6.19 (God giver of light); *LC* 1.6 (Logos as mediator); *LC* 3.4 (Constantine as Sol). For Eusebius' use of light-related imagery in praising Constantine, see also *VC* 1.43.3; 2.2.3; 2.19.1; 3.10.3.
⁹⁶ Van Nuffelen (2013), with particular attention to *VC* 1.30–31; 3.2–3; 3.35–41; 4.7.2–3; 4.15; 4.69.2; 4.72–73 (and to the complementary motif of Eusebius' commentary on the fight against idols and pagan representations of gods, see, e.g., *VC* 3.26, 48, 54–58; IV 16). See also Cameron and Hall (1999) 32.
⁹⁷ Lacuna in the text.   ⁹⁸ *VC* 3.10.3–4.   ⁹⁹ Smith (1997) 194–202.
¹⁰⁰ Gaze of emperors: see, e.g., *Pan. Lat.* VII (6) 9.5 (Maximian); VI (7) 4.4 (Constantine; Themistius, *Or.* 18.219b (Theodosius); Amm. Marc. 25.4.22. Gaze of philosophers: see Eunapius of Sardis' focus on the eyes of Maximus and Chrysanthius (Eunap. *VPS* 428, 551). On the attention dedicated to face and gaze in statuary and literary portraits of late antique philosophers, see Smith (1990), Civiletti (2007) 439–40 n. 309.

'superiority of mind' (τὸ τῆς διανοίας ὑπερφυές) of the Christian philosopher-ruler, which is beyond words.[101]

Constantine's entrance at Nicaea calls to mind Marcus' arrival at the divine gathering in the *Caesars*, which has been considered above. In both cases, a ruler walks into a holy congregation and a spiritualised description of his appearance is offered to provide a commentary on the significance of the encounter. The correspondence between scenes is meaningful, however, insofar as Julian seems to be responding critically to his model. Marcus' body communicates spiritual elevation, his dignified appearance stuns those who are present, and his eyes betray the loftiness of his soul. But other attributes Eusebius ascribed to Constantine are completely absent. Bodily strength goes unmentioned, and no luxury item such as purple or jewels is included; to the contrary, Marcus' body has become immaterial, as it is now made up of spiritual light. His aspect is explicitly defined as beautiful 'from the fact of being unadorned (317c)'.

The possibilities of comparison between Constantine's image, its Eusebian interpretation, and Julian's parodic portrayal of his uncle do not end here. Another scene in the *Caesars* invites us to reach analogous conclusions. In 324, after the defeat of Licinius, Constantine's eternally youthful portrait was enriched by two new features, the diadem and the heavenward gaze. Like his other symbols (the Sun, the *labarum*), the upward gaze lent itself to multiple readings: the combination of uplifted eyes and the diadem evoked portraits of Hellenistic kings and in particular Alexander the Great, who was immortalised with a gaze directed towards the heavens by the sculptor Lysippus and who had assumed the diadem following his victory over Darius II in 330 BCE.[102] In late antique statuary, eyes looking upwards also featured in portraits of philosophers, a fact arguably instrumental in eliciting associations between Constantine and this material.[103] As one might expect, Eusebius interpreted Constantine's upward gaze as univocally signifying the emperor's faith and his special relationship with God. His *Praise of Constantine* already remarks that 'the emperor pilots affairs below with an upward gaze, to steer by the archetypical form'.[104] In the *Life*, Eusebius observes that Constantine 'had his own portrait so depicted on gold coinage that he appeared to look upwards (ἄνω βλέπειν) in the manner of one reaching out to God in prayer

---

[101] Eus. *VC* 3.10.4.
[102] Wright (1987) 505–6; Bardill (2012) 11–24; Elsner (2012) 262–63; Guidetti (2013) 191–94.
[103] Smith (1990); Zanker (1995) 307–27; Bardill (2012) 22–23. Cf. Figure 4.13.
[104] *LC* 3.5 (ἄνω βλέπων κατὰ τὴν ἀρχέτυπον ἰδέαν τοὺς κάτω διακυβερνῶν ἰθύνει).

Figure 4.11 Constantine, *solidus*, Ticinum 326 CE. Obverse: head of Constantine with plain diadem and upward gaze, with no inscription; reverse: star above intertwined wreaths, with the inscription CONSTANTINVS AVG. *RIC* VII Ticinum 192, p. 385. London, British Museum, Department of Coins and Medals, inv. no. R1874,0715.137
(© The Trustees of the British Museum)

(ἀνατεταμένου πρὸς θεὸν τρόπον εὐχομένου)', adding that 'impressions (ἐκτυπώματα) of this type were circulated throughout the entire Roman world (καθ' ὅλης τῆς Ῥωμαίων ... οἰκουμένης). In the imperial quarters of various cities, he was portrayed standing up, looking to heaven (ἄνω μὲν εἰς οὐρανὸν ἐμβλέπων)' (see Figure 4.11).[105]

The *Caesars* seems also to have something to say about Constantine's upwards gaze. The scene of Constantine's self-advertisement before the gods is marked by a special focus on Constantine's body language – in particular, on the trajectory of the emperor's gaze:

> Constantine was allowed to speak next ... He paid them (i.e., the gods) tribute, so to speak, while he gave all his attention (ἀφεώρα) to Luxury (τὴν Τρυφὴν), who stood at a distance from the gods, near the entrance to the moon. Of her indeed he was so enamoured (ἐρωτικῶς τε οὖν εἶχεν αὐτῆς) that he had no eyes for anything else (ὅλος πρὸς ἐκείνην βλέπων).[106]

Julian directs his audience's attention to Constantine's fixation on Luxury (*Truphē*): he cannot divert his eyes from her. Her position, intriguingly located apart from the gods and in proximity to the entrance of the moon, suggests that she is somewhere between the space they occupy and the

---

[105] *VC* 4.15. Cf. Lactant. *Epit.* 20.10.   [106] *Caes.* 328d–29b.

Figure 4.12 Silver tetradrachm of Lysimachus, Lampsacus 305–281 BCE. Obverse: head of Alexander the Great with gaze looking upwards, a diadem, and a ram's horn; reverse: Athena Nikephoros (seated), Nike stretching her right hand and resting her left arm on her shield, with the inscription ΒΑΣΙΛΕΩΣ ΛΥΣΙΜΑΧΟΥ (basileos lysimachou). London, British Museum, Department of Coins and Medals, inv. no. 1919, 0820.1
(© The Trustees of the British Museum)

sublunary sphere where the imperial contest takes place.[107] In order to look at her, Constantine must therefore look up to the ethereal level but also at an angle, as he speaks facing the jury of the deities. Moreover, the emperor's gaze on Luxury is what connects him to Christianity. Intriguingly, Constantine's vision of Luxury in the *Caesars* has the same outcome as his vision of the cross as described in Eusebius' *Life*: both lead him to God. When, at the end of the contest, Julian's Constantine is finally freed to reach for the object of his attention and desire, it is Luxury who brings him to meet Jesus (336a). The scene closes with a depiction of Jesus as a peddler advertising baptism and confession as a quick fix to any sin:

> She (i.e., Luxury) received him (i.e., Constantine) tenderly and embraced him, then after dressing him in raiments of many colours and otherwise making him beautiful (καλλωπίσασα), she led him away to Profligacy (τὴν Ἀσωτίαν). There he also found Jesus (ἵνα καὶ τὸν Ἰησοῦν εὑρών), who had

---

[107] This reference to the entrance of the moon might offer a further contribution to the motif of corporal degradation. On the Middle- and Neoplatonic doctrine that souls passed through the gate of the Moon to descend on earth, cf. Porph. *Antr. Nymph.* 29.11–14. See Akçai (2019) 145–52.

A Life For A Life

Figure 4.13 Shield portrait of philosopher with upward gaze from Aphrodisias (Caria), Atrium House, late fourth to early fifth century. CE Museum of Aphrodisias, inv. no. 81-112. LSA no. 207

taken up his abode with her and cried aloud to all comers: 'He that is a seducer, he that is a murderer, he that is sacrilegious and infamous, let him approach without fear! For with this water I will wash him and will straightway make him clean (ἀποφανῶ γὰρ αὐτὸν τουτῳὶ τῷ ὕδατι λούσας αὐτίκα καθαρόν)'.[108]

Having fully grasped the significance of iconography in supporting Constantine's providential(istic) argument, Julian re-opens the question of the image of the ideal philosopher-ruler. By doing so, however, he takes care to present Constantine's visual propaganda (and its Eusebian elaboration) as testifying against any association of the emperor with philosophy. Eusebius tells us that Constantine's portraits were everywhere[109] and they were highly recognisable, their main features being, as noted, the

---

[108] *Caes.* 336a–b.
[109] *VC* 4.15.2 (and cf. also *VC* 4.72, on the portraits of Constantine and his sons). On the dissemination and recognisability of imperial portraits, see Fejfer (2008) 380–90.

idealised, atemporal look that marks the beauty of those who are loved by the divine. This is the body Constantine sports in the *Caesars*, a body that exposes and condemns his vanity.[110] Julian's *Caesars* engages with the face of Constantine that he knew his subjects knew, inviting a reading of its idealised features as evidence of Constantine's hedonism and lack of intellectual authority.

Handling Constantinian Evidence between *Caesars* and *Misopogon*. Part II: Staging Interpretation

If the *Caesars* presents Constantine as deceptive evidence – a beautiful face hiding an ugly soul – we should finally consider how this claim is linked to Julian's ambition to question Constantine's capacity as an interpreter. His investment in this issue becomes evident in the section of the *Caesars* in which emperors are summoned to advertise their merits before the panel of gods. Here Constantine confronts Marcus, his reaction to the latter's words, crucially, involving misunderstanding. As Marcus is invited to illustrate his merits, Silenus, the arbiter of the pageant, loudly wonders about 'which paradoxes (παράδοξα) and wonderful doctrines (τεράστια δόγματα) this Stoic will produce' (328c), a first, although ironic acknowledgement of Marcus' philosophical expertise. Marcus, however, surprises the gods by politely refusing to deliver a speech. Aware that everything is known to them, he modestly invites them to assign him whatever they believe he deserves. Thus, as the only emperor in the competition who puts his piety before his ambition, he implicitly replies to Silenus' remark by demonstrating that his philosophy is more than scholarship. Marcus has achieved the highest goal of the wise: he knows the divine. Conversely, Constantine, who is allowed to speak next, dishonestly inflates his merits and especially his military achievements (of whose insignificance, the narrator tells us, he is fully aware). His manipulative account is confronted by Silenus, who compares Constantine's successes to the 'gardens of Adonis' (Ἀδώνιδος κήπους, 329c–d): beauties that rapidly dissolve. Remarkably, the close of Constantine's speech is a direct reply to Marcus Aurelius' words. 'As for Marcus here', he says, 'by saying nothing for himself he yields precedence (τῶν πρωτείων ἐξίσταται) to all of us,

---

[110] On the use of well-known statues as props for satire and parody, see also Lucian's *Zeus the Tragic Actor*, where the gods in assembly are described as looking like their most famous statues (*Jup. Trag.* 7-12, 33. Cf. Branham [1989] 169–72). For a hypothesis of Julianic engagement with this piece, see Bouffartigue (1992) 295–96.

329c). Constantine thus demonstrates his complete misunderstanding of Marcus' decision – which is revealing, above all else, of his ignorance of the divine.

The theme of the coincidence between Marcus' philosophy and his piety resurfaces after the gods decide to ask the imperial contestants about their governing principle in life (329d). Marcus' reply – 'to imitate the gods' (τὸ μιμεῖσθαι ... τοὺς θεούς, 333c) – is meaningful. Divine mimesis was a central Platonic tenet, and Marcus' advocacy of the principle is one of many clues suggesting the collapse – which the previous section began to address – of his persona and that of his (literary) creator, Julian. Julian's supporters testify to his ambition to seek a personal association with Marcus; this is unsurprising, if we consider that cultured fourth-century elites still looked at the Antonines as an ideal model of leadership.[111] But Marcus' Neoplatonising words show that the picture is more complex than this. Julian and his supporters might have presented Marcus as a reference point, but the character in the *Caesars*, as Hunt shows, is not a historical reconstruction of the adoptive emperor.[112] Despite Silenus' joking reference to his Stoicism and another remark about his wife and son, Julian's Marcus has almost no recognisable features. None of his utterances are modelled on Marcus' *Meditations* or the Stoic principles that shaped them. Instead, he encapsulates enlightened, wise, pious leadership, the sovereignty the gods love. He is not, however, the only symbolic figure who stands on stage in the *Caesars*. Julian's Constantine could be taken as another: mobilised as the nemesis of the philosopher-emperor, he represents profligate tyranny, since his every action is marked by a special blend of dishonesty and lack of awareness. In this too, Julian seems to be engaging with the Eusebian framing of Constantine. Eusebius' *Praise* and *Life* both illustrated Constantine's awareness of God's superior position in the hierarchies of praise.[113] Constantine's disorderly self-promotion in the *Caesars* goes in the opposite direction. But Julian's Constantine, being a braggart, also automatically qualifies himself as a bad orator with no sense of the occasion and no understanding of his audience – the very opposite of the image of Constantine as an author of religious speeches that Eusebius produced in the *Life*.[114]

---

[111] On Julian's emulation of Marcus, see Amm. Marc. 16.1.4; Eutropius 10.16. On the idealisation of Marcus in late antiquity, see Stertz (1977).
[112] Hunt (1995). See also De Vita (2022) ccix–ccxi.
[113] *VC* 4.29.2. On the handling of this theme in the *LC*, see Chapter 3, p. 138–41.
[114] See, e.g., at *VC* 4.29, 32.

Marcus and Constantine are further located within a narrative framework that constantly teases the audience's interpretive skills. I considered in the previous section how almost all the main rulers on stage, beginning with the chameleon-like Octavian, have an appearance that encapsulates the significance of their rule. Julian's gods must deduce the true nature and qualities of the emperors based on their speeches and appearance; the rulers themselves navigate the pageant by studying each other's strategies for self-promotion. What is more, Julian seems to place a further, final sign demanding interpretation at the heart of his text: the arbiter of the pageant, Silenus.

The Olympian deities who gather for the celestial banquet have appointed a non-Homeric, non-Olympian god to conduct the contest. Since the *Caesars* is a satire, Silenus evidently stands as a catalyst for subversion: he is an image of playfulness, the motor of entertainment. On closer scrutiny, however, Silenus' subversiveness appears twofold. His chatty irreverence repeatedly allows the truth to emerge. It is thanks to his questions that Marcus is recognised as the only participant in the contest who truly understands the divine. It is, again, thanks to Silenus that Constantine's false merits are exposed and condemned via a referential framework that goes back to Plato's *Gorgias*. The nothingness of Constantine's rule is thus exposed by the same semi-feral deity upon whose unflattering image the most ancient portraits of Socrates were modelled.[115] Julian was quite familiar with this iconographic overlap: he elsewhere quotes from the passage in Plato's *Symposium* where Socrates is compared with the little statues of flute-playing Sileni that, once opened, reveal images of gods inside.[116] Silenus the arbiter signals to the audience of the *Caesars* that this piece, despite presenting itself as an opportunity for pure entertainment, has a philosophical core: through the shifting symbol of the feral god, the *Caesars*' satirical tones are revealed as a vehicle for Socratic irony. The image of (a Socrates-like) Silenus interrogating the emperors suggests that Julian's subversive approach to Roman history amounts to a dramatisation of how the philosopher interprets the past.

In the end, the past and its interpretation are the true protagonist of the piece. Marcus and Constantine might be stylised figures, but their confrontation takes place within a heavily historicised context. They are

---

[115] Zanker (1995) 32–39.
[116] *Cyn.* 187a–b, quoting from Plato, *Symp.* 215a–b. On the presence and function of Socrates in Julian's speeches (cf., e.g., *II Pan.* 78d–79a; *Cons.* 243a, 249b), see De Vita (2013). On the indebtedness of the *Caeesars* to Plato's *Symposium* and the resonance of Julian's Silenus with Socrates, see also Sardiello (2000) xiii–xiv, xxii–xxiii.

immersed in the story of the empire, which is symbolised by all the rulers who preceded and followed them. This is the cornerstone of the *Caesars* and, I believe, what transforms Julian's satire into a weapon against Constantinian propaganda, especially the *Life of Constantine*. In the *Life*, Eusebius in fact made a gesture of extraordinary implications: with a sleight of hand, he subtracted Constantine from the Roman past in order to relocate him in biblical history.

Comparatio, the rhetorical practice of weighing emperors and their achievements against one another, was a standard panegyric feature in late antiquity. Panegyrists were accustomed to praise rulers by likening them to their illustrious predecessors.[117] Under Constantine, this translated visually into the Arch of Triumph, which the Roman Senate put up in 315 to celebrate the emperor's conquest of Italy. By gathering sculpted reliefs from the age of Trajan, Hadrian, and Marcus Aurelius, the Arch performed a *comparatio* through the use of spolia, implicitly locating Constantine's rule in the legacy of the Principate and presenting it as its culmination.[118] Constantine himself had a complex relationship with his imperial past. His official iconography, as noted, continued to seek association through portraiture with the models of Augustus and Trajan.[119] Yet, as Chapter 3 considered, his writings not only attacked his predecessors who had persecuted Christianity but also claimed his unique position in the imperial succession due to his piety.[120] The mature Constantine continued to speak in art the reassuring language of tradition, but his reading of Roman history as Christian implicitly entailed a problematisation of his models insofar as it subtracted value from the pagan Roman past. This tension was arguably never resolved or made fully explicit in his propaganda. But it was grasped – and brought to completion – by Eusebius in his final work.

---

[117] Cf., e.g., Themistius, *Or.* 5.63d; 13.166b; 17.215a; 19.229b; 34.7. On the *comparatio* of Constantine (and Maximian) to Augustus in the Latin Panegyrics, see Ware (2018). Cf. also the celebration of Julian through the evocation of rulers from the Principate in Amm. Marc. XVI 1.2–5. According to Eutropius, the fourth-century Senate acclaimed emperors with the cry '*felicior Augusto, melior Traiano*' (*Breviarium* 8.5, cf. Rapp [1998] 286).

[118] Many debates surround the Arch, its state of preservation, the origin of the materials employed, and the dramatic increase in the use of *spolia* in architecture and statuary under Constantine. See Elsner (2000) for the reading of the trajectory from the Arch of Triumph to Constantine's Mausoleum as one of progressive merging of the culture of *spolia* with the cult of relics.

[119] Intriguingly, however, one historical source reports that Constantine had a tendency to belittle the emperors of the Principate (*Anonymous post Dionem* (= *Dionis Continuatio*), fr. 15.2, ed. Müller). See Van Dam (2007b) 88. Whether the claim is reliable remains uncertain.

[120] See p. 121–2, 127–9.

Eusebius' *Ecclesiastical History*, his first attempt at writing Constantine in sacred history, was still shaped by the need for self-legitimisation. To this end, Eusebius pursued the connection of Christian leadership with the canonical emperors of the Principate, whom he recovered for Christianity by reconstructing their profile as that of protectors or sympathisers of the Christians.[121] By the time he set down to write the *Life of Constantine* – that is, after thirty years of Constantinian rule – the strategy pursued in the *Ecclesiastical History* had lost its appeal. In his desire to establish Christianity as the only wisdom legitimising and supporting the history of Rome, Eusebius constructs Constantine here as an emperor without precedents.[122] The first ruler able to offer to Rome a life of reason, Constantine is subtracted by the text from the linear succession of his predecessors, including those famous for their successes and wisdom. The first Book of the *Life* eloquently opens with a definition of Constantine as 'the only one of the widely renowned Emperors of all time (μόνον ... τῶν ἐξ αἰῶνος ἀκοῇ βοηθέντων αὐτοκρατόρων) whom God set up as a huge luminary (μέγιστον φωστῆρα) and loud-voiced herald of unerring devotion (τῆς ἀπλανοῦς θεοσεβείας)', and 'the only one (μόνῳ) to whom God gave convincing proofs (τὰ ἐχέγγυα) of the religion he practised'.[123] The fourth and final Book closes on a comparable note:

> He alone of all the Roman emperors (μόνου μὲν Ῥωμαίων βασιλέων) had honoured God the All-sovereign with exceeding godly piety; he alone (μόνου) has publicly proclaimed to all the word of Christ (πεπαρρησιασμένως τὸν τοῦ Χριστοῦ κηρύξαντος λόγον); he alone (μόνου) has honoured his Church as no other since time began; he alone (μόνου) has destroyed all polytheistic error and exposed every kind of idolatry; and surely he alone (μόνου) has deserved in life itself and after death such things as none could say has ever been achieved by any other among either Greeks or barbarians, or even among the ancient Romans, for his like has never been recorded from the beginning of time until our day (ὡς οὐδενὸς τοιούτου τινὸς εἰς ἡμᾶς ἐκ τοῦ παντὸς αἰῶνος μνημονευομένου).[124]

Comparatio is not entirely set aside in the work, but its function is altered in two fundamental ways. First, the Roman emperors evoked in the *Life* are summoned to their shame (as is particularly the case with Constantine's imperial adversaries, Maxentius and Licinius, both reduced

---

[121] Corke-Webster (2019) 250–68. [122] See, e.g., Barnes (1981) 271; Williams (2008) 49–55.
[123] *VC* 1.4. [124] *VC* 4.75.

A Life For A Life 201

to the grotesque type of the malicious tyrant).[125] Second, and most importantly, *comparatio* finds expression in the form of (biblical) typology, as Constantine is repeatedly presented as operating in history like a Moses *alter*: like Moses, he grew up by the hearth of a tyrant (Diocletian), from which he fled;[126] his adversary (Maxentius) drowned like Pharaoh in the Red Sea.[127] Through this use of the Mosaic paradigm, Eusebius relocates Constantine in sacred Christian history.[128] Whether this association with Moses was promoted by Constantine himself is debated.[129] But regardless of whether it is originally Constantinian, the association between Constantine and Moses bestows upon the Constantine of Eusebius' *Life* all the features his model evokes. Since Philo of Alexandria's retelling of the life of Moses with an eye to Greek and arguably non-Jewish audiences (Niehoff), Moses had acquired the status of the biblical philosopher-ruler par excellence.[130] Philo, a Platonist, refers explicitly to Moses as 'ensouled law'.[131] Constantine's connection with Moses thus not only signifies the providentiality embedded in his agency (especially in regard to his victory over the tyrannical Maxentius-Pharaoh and Licinius). It also seals Constantine's status as a philosophical, God-inspired leader and lawgiver – and, crucially, it does so without looking back even once at Greco-Roman history. Marcus Aurelius has become redundant. The 'Mosaicisation' of Constantine thus turns his life into the proof also supporting the need to sideline the whole of Rome's imperial history when looking at the empire from the perspective of Providence. The empire's pagan days are effaced. The projection of Constantine as the culmination of Rome's history must entail the

---

[125] *VC* 1.33-7 (Maxentius); 1.49–56 (Licinius). For their tyrannical characterisation, see also 1.12.2; 1.26. Licinius perishes despite – better put, on account of – his attempts to appease with sacrifices those 'he thought of as gods' (*VC* 2.4.2).

[126] *VC* 1.12, 1.20.2.

[127] *VC* 1.38.2–5, recovering the idea already exploited in *HE* 9.9.5,7. Explicit parallels between Constantine and Moses at *VC* 1.12.1, 19.1, 20.2, 38.2–5; 2.12 (and cf. also comparison of Maxentius to Pharaoh at *HE* 9.9.5–8). See Barnes (1981) 271; Hollerich (1989); Cameron (1997) 158–61; Cameron and Hall (1999) 34–35, 192–93; Rapp (2005) 129–31; Inowlocki (2007); Williams (2008) 26–31, 36–42, 54–57; Flower (2013) 72; Damgaard (2013); Urbano (2013) 175–78; Johnson (2014) 160–61; Corke-Webster (2020b) 269–70.

[128] Williams (2008) 52–55.

[129] See Damgaard (2013) for the suggestion that the Mosaic paradigm was originally Constantinian.

[130] Audience of Philo's *De Vita Mosis*: see Niehoff (2011) 169–87. On the fortune of Philo's *Life of Moses*, 'the most popular and influential of all Philo's works during the Patristic period' (so Runia [1993] 222), see Runia (1993) 132, 135–36, 185–86, 189, 221–22, 256–61, 315–16, 337. Philo in Eusebius: Inowlocki (2004), (2006) 147–222.

[131] Philo, *Vit. Mos.* 2.4 (νόμον ἔμψυχον).

paradoxical displacement of Rome's history prior to him as marking an irrelevant phase of transition.

Julian's *Caesars* problematises this displacement by presenting history itself as counter-evidence. Julian lets the past speak for itself, summoning the divinity as judge. If the *Caesars* can be interpreted, as I have argued, as the dramatisation of an act of philosophical interpretation of Rome's history, it should be further noted that the divine itself – the feasting gods – is summoned on stage to assess past Roman emperors. Constantine is put back in the imperial and historical context to which he belongs, and he is denied imperial dignity on this ground. Constantine is made to face an authentic representative of philosophical sovereignty – Marcus Aurelius – and proves by his reactions to Marcus' philosophy that he has no idea of what the divine knows and wants. Rulers whose achievements had been far greater than his (Alexander the Great, Caesar, Augustus, and Trajan) are paraded in front of him as reminders of his mediocrity. The final implication of this display of past conquerors is the debunking of Constantine's use of his own victories as a token of the providential necessity of his rule. Constantine's allegedly glorious achievements are derided, as Julian shows that they can be regarded as achievements only when Constantine, with his own words, inflates them – an oblique allusion to his propaganda?[132] And it is precisely on the theme of victory, one might argue, that Julian seals the argument of the providentiality of his own power. A final question should be raised at this point: what is it that allows Julian's argument to resonate beyond his fiction?

The *Caesars* closes abruptly but predictably on Julian's divine call. After that, Marcus is proclaimed the winner of the contest, and Constantine is thrown into Tartarus (and then rescued out of respect for his ancestor Claudius Gothicus).[133] Julian suddenly shifts back into the first person, writing: "'As for you', Hermes said to me, 'I have granted you the knowledge of your father Mithras (δέδωκα τὸν πατέρα Μίθραν ἐπιγνῶναι). Keep his commandments, and secure for yourself a cable and sure anchorage throughout your life!'".[134] Julian's sudden appearance at the very end of his own piece is a statement of his position in history, a gesture drawing attention to both his presence and his absence. Julian is present in his text as the master interpreter of history, the author of this playful but urgent re-assessment of the meaning of Rome's imperial past. His absence too, however, is crucial: he alone of all the Roman emperors in his story must remain on the threshold – the narrative framework – and

---

[132] *Caes.* 328d–29c.   [133] On this claim of lineage, see Alföldi (1968).   [134] *Caes.* 336c.

cannot join the gods' feast. Julian cannot feature as himself among the banqueting emperors because he alone is alive. Constantine had projected his life as proof of the correctness of his interpretation of providence. Now Julian projects his own life as proof that Constantine's interpretation of history was not destined to last: Julian has replaced it. In this work of a Julian who is now undisputed Augustus, it is implicit that all the threads of history lead to him. Julian in his role of narrator summons himself twice, at the opening and the close of the piece. From the outset of the text and the 'O, Caesar' put in the mouth of his interlocutor (306a), he reminds his readers that he is the authentic winner: his role as puppeteer of his predecessors signifies his control of history and its meaning.

Julian writing himself into his piece brings us back to where my analysis of Julian's mobilisation of imperial iconography started: the *Misopogon*, which commands the citizens of Antioch to read Julian's beard as evidence of his philosophy. At the beginning of my analysis, I asked why Julian is so eager to attack the Antiochenes and their misunderstanding. His ragged growth of hair is explicitly contrasted with the soft cheeks of the Antiochenes, his lifestyle with theirs. It might be argued that, by describing them as hedonists, Julian is merely replying in kind to the people who derided him, replacing topos with topos, shaming their scorn for his lack of self-care through the accusation that they care excessively for outer appearance – the token of a life led in search of pleasure. There is indeed an element of this in his reply. But Julian's strategy is, as always, complex.

Irony, the register explored and exploited in the *Misopogon* to invite the Antiochene audience to capture the true significance of things – Julian's disagreeable looks are in fact the token of his philosophical nature – is presented here, crucially, as a response to a failed act of interpretation. The inhabitants of Antioch, with their jeering remarks shaming Julian's aspect, have demonstrated their inability to understand the significance of his disregard for aesthetic conventions. But the Antiochenes are not merely vulgar and uneducated lovers of luxury.[135] They favour Christianity and are faithful to the house of Constantine, a double allegiance that they covertly profess through an obscure riddle (αἴνιγμα) that must be explained to Julian by 'interpreters' (ἐξηγητῶν).[136]

---

[135] On Julian's characterisation of Antiochenes (partly conveyed through a fictitious reported speech of some citizens who accuse Julian of being unable to adapt to their lifestyle), see, e.g., *Mis.* 342b–45b, 345d–46a, 349d–50d.

[136] *Mis.* 357a–b; 360d. On the Christianity of the Antiochenes, cf. further *Mis.* 361b–c, 63a. The percentage of Christians in fourth-century Antioch remains unclear (Elm [2012] 278). On Julian's

Julian is using his subjects' misrecognition of his image to round off his argument against Constantinian – and Christian – hermeneutics. The image of the Antiochenes is produced as the final piece of evidence substantiating his claims. Through the juxtaposition between the *Caesars* and the *Misopogon*, the first Christian emperor is revealed as upholding the same beauty standards as the Antiochenes – but also their shallowness. This points to the fact that Constantine, through Christianity, has seduced the uneducated many, creating a community in which hedonism and superficiality thrive.[137] The Antiochenes, who are loyal to Constantine and to his creed and look like him, stand for an interpretive system that does not provide understanding and is unable to control the meaning of history. Their rejection of Julian's beard seals the validity of his claims to authentic philosophical leadership: the emperor implies that it is the destiny of true philosophers – see Socrates – to be despised and misunderstood by the ignorant crowd.

Conclusions

This chapter has argued that Julian's response to Constantine's political self-legitimisation via the celebration of Christian hermeneutics had to culminate in biography because Constantine himself and his propaganda (especially Eusebius) had sealed his providential argument via an exemplary use of his life. Julian's increasing concern with translating his own life into literature must thus be seen as opposing teleological readings of Constantine's rule via his competitive experiments in autobiography, which cast Julian as the true instrument of providence. Julian's biographical and autobiographical reflection unfolds across three crucial texts. The layered *Against Heraclius* reclaims for Greco-Roman culture and religion the divine symbols Constantine had attached to his persona (the Sun god, the association with a divine agent of salvation) and validates Julian's life as providential by narrating it through a myth that meets the criteria to qualify as Scripture. The targeting of Constantine's biography – and of the strategies Eusebius' *Life* devised to encapsulate it in sacred history – continues in Julian's first satire, the *Caesars*. This piece responds to the Eusebian excision of pagan history from Constantine's imperial

---

depiction of the Antiochenes as degenerate Greeks and anti-Athenians, see Quiroga (2009) 134–35.

[137] Cf. *C. Gal.* fr. 58 (238d–e). At *C. Gal.* fr. 59 (245a–d), Julian argues that Paul's letters bear witness to the impious conduct of early Christian communities.

background, a choice dictated by the bishop's ambition to advertise Constantine as the philosopher-ruler reviving Moses. Julian confronts a fictional Constantine with the most philosophical among his imperial predecessors – Marcus Aurelius – to suggest that Constantine's triumphant self-image could only be upheld at the cost of a deceitful erasure of the past. The piece further replaces Constantine's use of his successes as evidence of divine benevolence with a reminder of Julian's victory (or survival) over his imperial predecessors. Finally, Constantine's official iconography, which the Christian emperor used to advertise across the empire the historical and theological significance of his rule, is recovered by Julian as evidence of his anti-philosophical nature and the immoral quality of the religion he endorsed. Conversely, Julian's own public image, pursued in radical differentiation from that of his predecessor, is offered in the *Misopogon* as evidence of his Socratic nature and the validity of his historical and theological claims.

PART III

After Julian: Philosophy in the World

CHAPTER 5

Those Who Know If the Emperor Knows

Soon after the composition of his final piece, the *Misopogon*, Julian embarked on the Persian campaign that in few months would result in his death. The impact of his rule on fourth-century political debate, however, did not end with his demise. Instead, this marked the beginning of a new season of Christian elaboration on the theme of divine providence, now corroborated by the parable of the emperor who had contested the Christian interpretation of history and been rewarded accordingly. In Part III, I illustrate the processes by means of which late fourth-century Christian preachers – now the de facto leaders in their urban territories – capitalised on Julian's failure while at the same time navigating the implications of the imperial endorsement of their philosophical identity.

This chapter considers how the agreement between Christian emperors and bishops in identifying Christianity as perfect knowledge affected the power dynamics of the Roman state. I show that this agreement elicited a dynamic but unstable circuit of simultaneously cooperative and competitive transactions between rulers and ecclesiastics. On the one hand, cooperation took the unprecedented form of state support for the elaboration of orthodoxy – that is, correct thinking. Imperial acknowledgement of the centrality of doctrine in Christianity both heightened intra-Christian rivalries around the issue of the knowability of the divine and created the legal conditions for their socio-political management. On the other hand, competition between State and Church arose from reflection on whether the bishops, now officially acknowledged as master interpreters, had intellectual authority over the ruler and should therefore exercise guidance of him. Julian's refutation – via his death – of his claims to divine insight unintentionally bolstered this idea, which sealed the assumption that emperors opposing episcopal advice were operating against a providential design that was also at one with perfect rationality. This reflection ultimately affected the public role of 'pagan' or non-aligned philosophers, that is, thinkers external to the interpretive system from which true and perfect knowledge was now assumed to derive.

An Exegetical Fea(s)t: Libanius, Eunapius, Ammianus, and Gregory of Nazianzus on Julian's Death

Julian had presented his life as the token of his truth. Now, after his premature death in battle in June 363,[1] his self-projection became open to an interpretation he would not have liked. The reaction of his supporters indicates a perceived need to offer post-mortem assessments of Julian's life that did not damage his cause. A case in point is Libanius, whose orations already under Julian's rule provided a resonant platform for imperial propaganda.[2] His *Funeral Oration* for Julian (*Or.* 18, composed in the late 360s)[3] argues, among other things, that Constantius was a bad, irrational ruler, who hated Julian;[4] that Julian 'ascended to the throne for the salvation of the whole world'; that the gods loved him and wanted him to be emperor; and that philosophy guided his rule and inspired his military campaigns.[5] Libanius also presents here and elsewhere philosophical practice as that which helped Julian realise that Christianity advocated 'false ideas' regarding the divine and was causing the 'ruin of the inhabited world'.[6] But Libanius' providential narrative of Julian's life left him to face

---

[1] Amm. Marc. 25.3; Libanius, *Or.* 18.268–73.
[2] See, e.g., the orations Libanius composed for Julian between 362 and 363 (*Or.* 12–16). On Julian's and Libanius' interaction – including disagreements and tense episodes – see Norman (1969) xxiii–xxxii; Sandwell (2007) 97–98 (considering Libanius' disapproval of Julian's revival of sacrifices), 163–65, 216–31; Cribiore (2013) 163–66, 233–34.
[3] On the date, see Wiemer (1995) 260–66, for 365; Van Nuffelen (2006), (2014) 293, for 368; Urbano (2013) 189–90.
[4] See, e.g., Libanius, *Or.* 18.27 (criticism of Constantius' ill temper); *Or.* 18.31 (mention of Constantius' responsibility for the murder of Julian's relatives); *Or.* 18.33, 36–37 (Constantius' dangerous alliance with the barbarians and cowardice in handling the pressure at the Gallic borders); *Or.* 18.130 (corruption and luxurious living at Constantius' court).
[5] Libanius, *Or.* 18.4 (Julian enthroned for the salvation of the world); *Or.* 18.173–74 (advice coming from the gods); *Or.* 18. 192 (the gods wanting Julian to be emperor); *Or.* 18.39, 72, 176 (philosophy guiding Julian). On Libanius' projection of Julian in the text as ideal philosopher-ruler, see Urbano (2013) 193–95. On his efforts to condition the early reception of Julian's oeuvre (vis-à-vis Gregory of Nazianzus' construction of the 'Apostate'), see Ross (2020).
[6] τὴν φθορὰν τῆς οἰκουμένης, *Or.* 18.21 (on the claim that, thanks to philosophy, 'he found it impossible to maintain false ideas [δόξαν ... παράσημον] about the divine'; see also Libanius, *Or.* 12.33). For other points of consonance of Libanius' oratory with Julian's propaganda, cf. *Or.* 18.121–25 (Julian's religious tolerance and his concern with 'handling religion with understanding' [σὺν ἐπιστήμῃ τῆς θεραπείας ἁπτόμενος, *Or.* 18.124]). Regarding the representation of Julian as interpreter of the divine, cf. *Or.* 18.40 (the sign of the garland), 103 (a response of the gods exhorts Julian to keep the throne), 176 (Julian as 'priest, writer, seer, judge,

the question of why the same gods who endorsed Julian's leadership made his rule so short.[7]

Libanius' *Funeral Oration*, an attempt to capture the meaning of Julian's life in literature that has been likened to Eusebius' *Life of Constantine* accumulates explanations.[8] Had Constantius not failed to deal with the Persians (*Or.* 18.206–7), Julian would not have needed to lead a campaign in the first place. Moreover, Constantius' inept leadership of the Roman army had corrupted the soldiery (*Or.* 18.209–12). Envious spirits snatched away Julian's hopes of success (φθονερῶν ... δαιμόνων, *Or.* 18.283). In a final twist, however, the oration recurs to prosopopoeia and summons Julian himself to have the last word on his demise. Libanius' Julian argues that he received not a punishment but a reward: the gods let him become their associate (*Or.* 18.296). This explanation seals the tragic scenario, inflated with rhetorical pathos, which Libanius delineates to conclude his commemoration (*Or.* 18.286–93): the disgraces that followed Julian's death, from poverty and despair in various parts of the empire to the persecution of traditional religion, the fall into disgrace of true philosophers, and the rise of barbarians, are all part of the divine design. Julian knew that all this was meant to come, and he deliberately chose to 'retire to make way for the onset of a degenerate age' (ὑπεχώρησε τῇ φορᾷ τῶν χειρόνων, *Or.* 18.298) – an age arguably ushered in by the (Christian) subversion of the imperial channels of communication with the divine.

The historian and philosopher Eunapius of Sardis makes similar claims. Eunapius was a critic of Christianity and a Julianic enthusiast who took pride in having been initiated into the mysteries by the same priest who initiated Julian.[9] He composed a historical work that survives only in fragments but seems to have covered the period from the reign of Claudius Gothicus to 404.[10] Julian was arguably its central figure; Photius, who could still access the work, claims that Eunapius 'worked up his history almost into an encomium (ἐγκώμιον) of that ruler (i.e., Julian)'.[11] Eunapius remembers Julian as the embodiment of the ideal of the philosopher-ruler, the model of a military commander and just judge, the son of the sun-god, and the culmination of Roman history.[12]

---

soldier, and universal saviour'), 180 (Julian's prophetic insight: seers could never mislead him, since his gaze too scrutinised omens).
[7] Libanius, *Or.* 18.281.   [8] Comparison with Euseb. *VC*: Urbano (2013) 188–203.
[9] Eunap. *VPS* 475.   [10] Discussion in Blockley (1981) 1–6.
[11] Photius, *Codex* 77 (transl. Blockley [1983] 3).
[12] See, e.g., Eunap. *Hist.* frr. 18.1 (Julian's military feats); 18.6 (on the interaction between his military leadership and political ideals); 25.1 (Julian as judge); 25.3 (Julian's demonstration of clemency and

He contends that divine providence supported Julian throughout his reign: correct worship of the true divine enabled him to access the providential design and gain the power of foreseeing the future. He knew, for instance, that Rome's control of Gaul would be temporary and limited to the period of his reign.[13] It follows that when he went to Persia, Julian was perfectly aware that he would die. The gods had announced in a prophecy – which Eunapius takes care to transcribe – that he would soon be 'taken to Olympus', freed from his body.[14] 'Elated (ἀρθέντα) by these words', Eunapius argues, Julian 'most eagerly (μάλα ἡδέως) abandoned this mortal and transitory existence'.[15]

Ammianus' *Res Gestae* is also part of this environment of negotiation of the Julianic parable. His work is marked by a blend of admiration for Julian – the centre of gravity of what survives of his text – and criticism addressing controversial aspects of his rule: Ammianus attacks Julian's School Ban, his obsessive concern with the religious allegiance of his subjects, his proclivity to superstition, and the harshness he displayed towards the Antiochenes towards the end of his stay in their city.[16] This balance of praise and blame fits Ammianus' profile as a historian and his concern with issues of authorial self-legitimisation (on which, see especially Kelly).[17] His efforts to communicate impartiality frame his assessment of Julian's rule. Writing during the reign of Theodosius, Ammianus envisaged as the turning point in the contemporary history of Rome the Battle of Adrianople in 378, which ended in the defeat of the imperial army at the hands of the Goths. A subtle critic of Christianity, but a critic nevertheless, he looked at aspects of this religion as responsible for destabilising the political and military situation of the Roman Empire.[18] He consequently

---

literary talent in responding to Heraclius); 27 (Julian's foreknowledge, originating from reasoning and/or the divine); 28.2 (Julian's acceptance of criticism); 28.5 (defence of Julian's claims to descend from Helios) Blockley. See further Breebaart (1979); Marcone (2020) 352–54.

[13] Eunap. *Hist.* fr. 27.1 Blockley. Cf. Marcone (2020) 354.   [14] Eunap. *Hist.* fr. 28.6 Blockley.

[15] Eunap. *Hist.* fr. 28.6 Blockley.

[16] Ammianus on the School Ban: 22.10.7; 25.4.20. Julian's excessive concern for religion: cf. Sandwell (2007) 19, commenting on Ammianus 22.10.2, a passage in which Julian is defined as *intempestivus* ('untimely'/'tactless') on religious matters. Superstitious more than pious: Amm. Marc. 25.4.17. Unfair treatment of the Antiochenes: Amm. Marc. 22.14.2. On Ammianus and Julian, see Rike (1987) 23, 37–51; Kelly (2008) 296–317; Ross (2016).

[17] Kelly (2008), calling attention to Ammianus' twofold strategy: on the one hand, the use of literary allusion to suggest control of Rome's literary as well as historical past, on the other, a peculiar autobiographical focus communicating Ammianus' unique position as historical witness.

[18] On Ammianus and Christianity, see, e.g., Rike (1987) 100–107, 129–33; Matthews (1989) 435–51; Davies (2004) 228–29, 242–46; Kelly (2008) 3–4, 28, 68, 157–58, 294.

found himself needing to explain why the emperor who tried to oppose Christianity had not fared better.

I am wary of converting Ammianus' engagement with religion into a univocal, clear-cut solution; his complexity as an author is reflected in the complexity of approaches he devised across the Res Gestae.[19] Nevertheless, it could be argued with Rike that Ammianus overall guides his readers to recognise in Julian a great but imperfect leader, who paid with his life for his increasing superstition and progressive loss of touch with the gods' providential design.[20]

Ammianus occasionally incorporates omens (or impressive natural phenomena with unknown causes) into his historical accounts.[21] That a late antique historian with the ambition of projecting himself as a rigorous thinker would do so is less surprising than it might seem at first sight; as this book has sought to illustrate, ambitions for rational enquiry and openness to prognostication were compatible in (late) antiquity. In Ammianus' Res Gestae, the accounts of Julian's preparation for the Persian campaign and of his expedition are punctuated by inauspicious omens, from earthquakes to deadly accidents, predictions, ominous dreams, and even the apparition of the Genius Publicus in funerary attire.[22] According to Ammianus, professional soothsayers and trustworthy advisors repeatedly asked Julian to abandon the expedition.[23] Because he listened to the wrong advisers, however, he refused to acknowledge the validity of the omens, hastening his end (which he nevertheless accepted bravely, recovering his philosophical temper *in extremis*).[24] Ammianus

---

[19] For an assessment of the contradictory elements in Ammianus' religious thinking and the difficulties of systematisation, see Ross (2016) 160–61.

[20] Rike (1987).

[21] See, e.g., Amm. Marc. 15.8.22 (prophecy of the old blind woman regarding Julian); 17.7.9–10 (unknown – and possibly divine? – causes of earthquakes); 19.12.19–20 (portents in Daphne); 20.3.1 (an eclipse of the sun); 20.5.10 (first appearance of the Genius Publicus to Julian); 20.11.26 (frequent rainbows); 21.14.1–2 (omens of Constantius' death); 22.1.1–3 (Julian receives confusing signs from augury and haruspicy; omen announcing the death of Constantius).

[22] Amm. Marc. 23.1.3 (catastrophic natural phenomena during the reconstruction of the Temple); 23.1.5–7 (deadly accidents, Constantinopolitan earthquake, advice of the Sibylline books); 23.2.6, 2.8 (deadly accidents at the beginning of the Persian expedition); 23.3.3 (Julian's ominous dreams, temple of Apollo devastated by fire); 23.3.6 (death of Julian's horse); 23.5.6 (ominous corpse); 23.5.8 (gift of the lion); 23.5.12–13 (soldier struck by lightning); 25.2.3–8 (Julian's nocturnal vision of a mournful Genius Publicus; vision of a falling star).

[23] Amm. Marc. 23.1.7; 5.10, 13; 25.2.7–8 (advice of the expert seers). Cf. also Sallustius' advice at 23.5.4–5.

[24] Amm. Marc. 23.5.5 (Julian disregards Sallustius' advice and carries on); 23.5.11, 5.14 (the 'philosophers' who surround him wrongly oppose the seers' advice); 25.2.4 (Julian's lucid acceptance of his fate). On Ammianus' judgement concerning Julian's failures in managing the cult once he was sole emperor, cf. Rike (1987) 52–68.

thus seems to imply that the emperor who had the capacity to steer Rome to safety failed to do so, since the degeneration of his piety into superstition diverted his attention from channels of communication with the gods.

Although Libanius, Eunapius, and Ammianus are writing for different audiences and to different ends, they seem to share a concern to keep interpretations of Julian's life from pointing to the need to understand Roman history as driven by Christian providence. In fact, his death was weaponised almost immediately.[25] The earliest and most effective example of this phenomenon is Gregory of Nazianzus' *Or.* 4 and 5, a diptych of anti-Julianic orations the bishop composed between 364 and 366.[26] Gregory was a key architect of the so-called Neo-Nicene Creed under Theodosius. His writings circulated among the most prominent theologians of the second half of the fourth century, including Ambrose and Augustine in the West, and he became the second most copied author in Byzantium, second only to the Bible.[27] But his work is relevant here not only by virtue of its resonance and the long-lasting influence it continued to exercise, but because Gregory always negotiated his intellectual authority with an eye to the socio-cultural expectations of the Roman elite. A professor of rhetoric,[28] he was a master in the art of literary self-fashioning.[29] Gregory committed to advocating for the idea that Christianity should be recognised as the system of knowledge presiding over Greco-Roman culture, and in laying this claim, he never lost sight of the political, as Elm shows.[30] His ambition was to see Christianity recognised as the interpretive guide for Roman governors.

When writing about Julian and assessing his legacy, Gregory relied on a unique vantage point: personal acquaintance. The emperor and the bishop studied philosophy together in Athens in the summer of 355, shortly before Julian's appointment as Caesar. That fact alone captures the extent to which upper-class religious rivals in the fourth century shared the same cultural coordinates (thus again Elm).[31] Part of the strength of Gregory's

---

[25] Christian responses to Julian in Van Nuffelen (2020).
[26] Discussion of the dating in Criscuolo (1987) 171; Kurmann (1988) 9–10; Elm (2012) 342; Van Nuffelen (2020) 363 n. 9.
[27] Goldhill and Greensmith (2020) 58–59; cf. Sterk (2004) 139; Simelidis (2009) 57–97.
[28] On Gregory's activity as a rhetorician, dated to around 358–62, see McLynn (2006) 215, 220–26; Elm (2012) 26–27.
[29] Elm (2012). See esp. 6–9 (on Gregory's self-presentation as divided between philosophical withdrawal and priestly service) and 158–65 (Gregory on *recusatio*).
[30] Elm (2012) 10–11, 166–81, 373–77, 403–32, 480–83.   [31] Elm (2012).

argument therefore lies in his reliance on a principle one could say had been operating in Greek historiographical thinking since Herodotus: autopsy, that is, direct and personal scrutiny of Julian's nature and intentions.[32] Gregory was well aware of the persuasive force of autopsy and sought to capitalise on it. This is illustrated by his (malevolent) exercise in physiognomics in regard to the young Julian:

> A sign of no good seemed to me (οὐδενὸς γὰρ ἐδόκει μοι σημεῖον εἶναι χρηστοῦ) to be his unsteady neck, his shoulders always in motion and shrugging up and down like a pair of scales, his eye rolling and glancing from side to side with an insane expression (μανικὸν βλέπων), his unsteady and stumbling feet, his nostrils breathing insolence and disdain (ὕβριν πνέων καὶ περιφρόνησιν), the ridiculous gestures of his face that expressed the same feelings, his unrestrained and gusty bursts of laughter, his nods of assent and dissent with no reason (σὺν οὐδενὶ λόγῳ), his speech stopping short (λόγος ἱστάμενος) and interrupted by his breathing, his disordered and unintelligent (ἄτακτοι καὶ ἀσύνετοι) questions, his answers no better than his questions.[33]

Gregory advances a crucial claim: thanks to his reading of Julian's appearance, he precociously understood what the world would only discover years later. 'I saw the man before his actions exactly as what I afterwards found him in his actions', he writes.[34] If the validity of autopsy was established by Herodotus, it is a story as old as Thucydides that a good interpreter of history and the world is he who reads the signs pointing to a great event, be it the Peloponnesian War or the rise of the Apostate, before anyone else can.[35] Gregory exploits his claim to an early reading of Julian's nature to assert himself as master interpreter. His anti-Julianic diptych presents itself as a grand exegetical performance, with the Apostate as the main subject of scrutiny and Gregory as the bishop who always and in all circumstances saw through the emperor.

Although the first piece of the diptych, *Or.* 4, presents itself as a critical survey of the life and rise to power of the Apostate emperor, it begins *in medias res*, as it were, with an attack on Julian's School Ban. Gregory's fundamental concern with establishing Christianity as the source and fulfilment of *paideia* explains why he bestows primacy on the Ban.

---

[32] Cf. Hdt. 2.99.1, contrasting the narration of what he scrutinised by sight (ὄψις), reasoning (γνώμη), and enquiry (ἱστορίη), to the reporting of things heard.
[33] Greg. Naz. *Or.* 5.23, transl. King. Cf. his similar characterisation of Julian in *Or.* 4.30.
[34] Τοῦτον πρὸ τῶν ἔργων ἐθεασάμην, ὃν καὶ ἐπὶ τῶν ἔργων ἐγνώρισα, Greg. Naz *Or.* 5.24.
[35] Cf. Thuc. 1.1 for his claim of precocious understanding of the magnitude of the coming war.

Moreover, Gregory arguably identifies it as the other key event that, alongside Julian's death, reveals – to intelligent interpreters – Julian's misrecognition of the relationship between human and divine. It therefore deserves first place in a critical re-assessment of the emperor's life, since it serves as an interpretive guide organising the reading of his reign as both intellectually fraught and politically abusive. 'It is a fitting judgment', Gregory writes, 'for that man to be punished by means of a word (λόγῳ κολάζεσθαι) for his transgressions against words (ὑπὲρ τῆς εἰς λόγους παρανομίας) which, although the common property of all rational beings (λογικοῖς ἅπασιν), he begrudged to the Christians . . . devising as he did a most irrational thing (ἀλογώτατα)'.[36] Derision of the man who wanted to deprive those who worship the Logos of *logoi* prepares for Gregory's argument that the divine component in culture is trivialised by ethnic and linguistic demarcations. The Logos intended people speaking all languages to be able to communicate; the use of Greek is a contingency that also befalls those who do not believe in the Greek gods.[37] In support of this argument, Gregory showcases his knowledge of Aristotelian logic, Demosthenic rhetoric, and Pindar.[38] His mastery of authors Julian claimed as non-Christian conveys the irony that they could be mobilised at the expense of Julian's cultural programme.

Gregory draws on this first, cultural, refutation to press the political point that Julian (this 'great mind', as he sarcastically calls him) was therefore also incapable of understanding the significance of Christ's incarnation for the history of Rome.[39] This was the source of his disruption of the harmony between Christianity and the empire, which was always meant to be. The claim that Julian was responsible for fostering religious violence[40] – arguably a direct response to his insistence that the Christians were the first to cultivate violence – prepares for another attempt to prove Gregory's ability to interpret Julian. Julian repeatedly stated that Christians would not be persecuted when he was on the throne.[41] Gregory contends that a juxtaposition of Julian's words with his actions disproves his claims, offering access to Julian's secret intention

---

[36] Greg. Naz. *Or.* 4.4.   [37] Greg. Naz. *Or.* 4.5, 103. See Elm (2012) 349, 387–96.
[38] Demoen (1996) 361–65.
[39] 'Great mind' (τὸν νοῦν τὸν μέγαν): *Or.* 4.1. Failure to understand that a challenge to Christianity is now a challenge to Rome: *Or.* 4.74 (cf. Elm [2012] 359–62). See also Gregory's commentary on the simultaneity of the growth of the state of Rome and of the Christians at *Or.* 4.37.
[40] Gregory's narration of violence perpetrated against the Christians under Julian: e.g., *Or.* 4.86–89, 92–96.
[41] See Chapter 3 above, n. 154.

to deprive Christians of the 'very great honour' of an open confrontation and 'introduce into his persecution the traps and snares concealed in arguments (τὰς περὶ τοὺς λογισμοὺς πλοκὰς καὶ διπλόας)'.⁴² Julian's open endorsement of paganism and the Ban demonstrated his strategy of disguising coercion 'in the mask of Minos', putting up the façade of the philosopher-ruler (τὸν φιλόσοφον βασιλέα) but de facto delegating the exercise of violence to subjects whose will becomes 'unwritten law' (ἄγραφον ... νόμον).⁴³ This reads as a dramatic reversal of the ideal of the sovereign as ensouled law.⁴⁴

Oration 5, Gregory's second invective against Julian, rounds off his character assassination by accumulating what Gregory presents as definitive evidence: the series of Julian's verifiable failures culminating in his shameful death in Persia. Eloquently, the piece opens with a meditation on the hierarchy of the signs of God's intervention in history. Diseases, plagues, unnatural deaths, and other accidents sent upon the unrighteous are defined as 'evident and public manifestations (ἐναργῆ καὶ φανερὰ γνωρίσματα) of God's anger at such doings' (*Or*. 5.2). Gregory, however, will 'willingly pass over' such things to describe the 'miracle (θαῦμα) that is in the mouth of everyone (περιβόητον πᾶσι)' and 'not disputed even by the heathens themselves (οὐδὲ τοῖς ἀθέοις αὐτοῖς ἀπιστούμενον, *Or*. 5.2)': Julian's defeat. *Or*. 4 began to introduce the motive of Julian's lack of providential insight by denying that omens announced his victory against Constantius and by going so far as to argue that Julian in fact plotted Constantius' assassination.⁴⁵ The text also produced a description of Julian's first public sacrifice as the scene of a (Christian) miracle: the entrails of the sacrificial victim, Gregory writes, displayed the figure of the Cross enclosed in a garland.⁴⁶ Readers are simultaneously invited to reflect on how, at the culmination of Julian's power, God signalled his presence and control and how Julian failed to understand the message. *Or*. 5 continues this line of argument by illustrating the outcomes of Julian's intellectual and interpretive failure. It begins by narrating the divine signs

---

⁴² Greg. Naz. *Or*. 4.61 (although claiming immediately afterwards that the 'argument of force' followed closely: see *Or*. 4.62–66).
⁴³ Julian's 'mask of Minos': *Or*. 4.79. Description of his deceitful behaviour towards the Christians: *Or*. 4.81–84. Julian's reputation as philosopher-ruler: *Or*. 4.91. Will of the people as unwritten law: *Or*. 4.61.
⁴⁴ Cf. Gregory's complementary reflection that the 'will of a prince is unwritten law' at *Or*. 4.93.
⁴⁵ Greg. Naz. *Or*. 4.47 (adding that Julian's success was consequently 'not foreknowledge [πρόγνωσις] but knowledge [γνῶσις]').
⁴⁶ Greg. Naz. *Or*. 4.54.

Julian ignored on his way to doom, in particular the earthquake that stopped the reconstruction of the Temple – an event feeding Christian supersessionism and that Gregory claims was accompanied by an apparition of yet another cross in the sky.[47] The piece then engages with Julian's failed Persian campaign and culminates in the account of the great and undisputed *thauma* announced at its opening: Julian's death, the final proof of his lack of providential insight.[48]

Elm has labelled Gregory's *Or.* 4 and 5 an 'inverted Fürstenspiegel', meaning texts that exploit the normative dimension of biography to set Julian up as a model of perverted sovereignty.[49] The assessment of a fourth-century politics of interpretation helps us see Gregory's (counter) exemplary exploitation of Julian's life as pursuing a twofold aim. First, Gregory reconfigures Julian's life as an interpretive guide to the Christianity of history. The fallacy of Julian's own hermeneutical system is shown by the fact that he 'fell a fitting victim of his own impiety'.[50] Only one event – one life – is under observation. But this life, whose trajectory is marked first by reaction against God and later by visible punishment, is universally accessible in its implications and thus demonstrates that God controls history and its course. Second, Gregory presents the parable of Julian as the instrument of a divine didactic project. Julian served as a warning and wake-up call to the Church, which had been rendered arrogant by the prosperity that followed the end of the persecutions.[51]

In light of all this, it could nevertheless be argued that Gregory's management of the memory of Julian stands as a commentary not so much on ideal leadership as on who gets to ratify it as ideal. The treatment of Constantius II in *Or.* 4 is an eloquent indication of this. The oration

---

[47] Failed reconstruction of the Temple: *Or.* 5.3–7; cross in the sky: *Or.* 5.4. The attempt is documented in Julian, *Ep. Fragm.* (= *ep.* 89b Bidez-Cumont) 295c; Amm. Marc. 23.1.2–3; Philostorgius, *HE* 7.9; Sozomen, *HE* 5.22; Socrates, *HE* 3.20.1–8. Discussion in Finkelstein (2018) 101–14; Bradbury (2020) 270–73; Greenwood (2021) 111–13. On contemporary Christian reactions to Julian's project of rebuilding, see Bradbury (2020) 282–89; Drake (2020) 191–94.

[48] Greg. Naz. *Or.* 5. 13 (with ironic commentary on how the spear pierced Julian's liver).

[49] Elm (2012) 344. [50] Greg. Naz. *Or.* 4.2.

[51] God's will behind Julian's rise and fall: *Or.* 4.28, 47, 49–50, 54. Julian's rule as a wake-up call for the Church: *Or.* 4.28, 49. On Gregory's use of this argument to admonish the clergy in *Or.* 2.87, cf. Sterk (2004) 122–23. Gregory's claim draws on a long-standing narrative of divine admonishment in times of arrogance, on which see also Eusebius, *HE* 8.1.7. Cf. John Chrysostom's rhetorical expressions of nostalgia for persecutions vis-à-vis present Christian laxity, as in *In II Cor. Hom.* 26.4 (*PG* 61.580). See Sandwell (2007) 126.

presents us with an idealised figure, described as superior in wisdom to any other emperor.[52] His only mistake – sparing Julian – was a consequence of the fact that he was too pure to suspect evil.[53] This celebration of Julian's predecessor responds to and reverses Julian's attempts to delegitimise Constantius. At the same time, Gregory was aware that by extolling Constantius, he was glossing over a well-known point (which he very briefly and obliquely acknowledges): Constantius' attempts to control intra-Christian policies had rendered him controversial among Christians.[54] Julian's self-projection as a sovereign shunning violence and coercion appealed to this shared knowledge.[55] In celebrating Constantius as a leader free of shadows, Gregory implicitly pressed the point that he, as God's minister and interpreter, had the final word over the worth of rulers. Gregory's reading of Julian's providential function illuminates the meaning of Constantius' leadership: by enthroning Julian, Constantius enabled him to serve as God's unconscious agent. But Constantius could not know this outcome. Although his rule was infused with wisdom, he evidently lacked foreknowledge. The only figure who emerges from this picture as in complete control of understanding is thus Gregory himself. He recognised Julian's nature long before the rest of the world and can now unlock the meaning of the reigns of both Constantius and Julian. His *Orations* 4 and 5, therefore, claim the bishop's place at the top of the hermeneutical ladder, highlighting his position of interpretive control in respect to all emperors, both pious and impious.

In the next section, I attempt to show that Gregory's claims of intellectual control over the emperor is not a one off, but that the negotiation of interpretive authority was in fact a crucial point of contention in the post-Constantinian interactions between Church and State. Because of the extent of the matter and the number of figures involved, however, I will proceed by case studies, with no pretence of exhaustiveness. My aims are two: to trace the coordinates of what I see as a productive framework for conceptualising fourth-century politics and to locate Julian's role within this picture.

---

[52] Greg. Naz. *Or.* 4.34.
[53] Greg. Naz. *Or.* 4.38. Gregory further argues that Constantius expected to tame Julian (*Or.* 4.40) and trusted in his power to dismiss him if he misbehaved (*Or.* 4.41). But 'true wickedness defies all calculation' (*Or.* 4.42).
[54] Constantius' interventionism (on which, see Chapter 2, p. 86–87) is obliquely and fleetingly acknowledged at *Or.* 4.37.
[55] See Chapter 3, n. 154.

Chains of Validation, Part 1: Bishops with Emperors, versus Bishops

Gregory's attempt to establish his intellectual authority over both Constantius and Julian helps identify emperors and bishops as the two main categories involved in fourth-century negotiations of interpretive control. This binary is complicated, however, by ecclesiastical fragmentation. The fourth-century 'Church' (if the singular is even appropriate) was traversed by internal rivalries. Crucially, these too relied on strategies of self-validation based on claims to control of exegesis and true knowledge – which in this context can be labelled 'orthodoxy'. Bishops expected imperial arbitration to preside over their disputes, resulting in a complex scenario in which the Church derived strength in equal measure from cooperation and competition with the State. Dynamics of alignment and tension with the central government thus coexisted. For the sake of organising my argument, however, I consider them separately, beginning with the first.

Constantine's rule as a Christian emperor constantly oscillated between bestowal of authority (for instance, in his creation of ecclesiastical privileges such as the *episcopale iudicium* and episcopal immunity from municipal duties)[56] and an ambition to exercise a degree of personal control over the Church. The interventionist side of Constantine's religious policy was perhaps the one that was most expected. *Mutatis mutandis*, it ensured that the emperor continued to meet traditional expectations. Rome had always ascribed the highest responsibility for the management of civic religion to the emperor, its *pontifex maximus*. A good relationship with the divine was regarded as a primary source of stability for the empire. Chapter 3 considered how third-century rulers sought to stabilise their power and solve socio-political tensions by strengthening their bond to the divine.[57] State-endorsed attempts to coerce sacrifice and the new phenomenon of centralised religion persecution, from Decius to the Tetrarchs, provide evidence of heightened ambitions for religious control. Even Galerius' decision to end the persecutions in 311 reads as an adjustment of current state policies aimed at preserving the channels of communication with the gods: the Edict of Serdica voices concern that persecution might cause Christians to become atheists and expresses the wish that they might at least pray to their divinity for the public welfare.[58] With a different vision but a comparable sense of connection between the state and the divine,

---

[56] Barnes (1993) 171–74; Lenski (2016) 197–206.   [57] Chapter 3, p. 122–4.
[58] Text preserved in Lactant. *Mort. Pers.* 34; cf. Euseb. *HE* 8.17.

Constantine's and Licinius' so-called Edict of Milan (313) proclaimed freedom of worship in the hope that *quidquid divinitatis in sede coelesti* might be propitious to Rome.[59]

Against this background, the summoning of the Council of Nicaea in 325 reads as Constantine's (updated) compliance with a duty he was expected to fulfil. One might add the self-evident point that the more Constantine committed to the Church, the greater the impact of the latter's instability on his rule. But I believe that an understanding of Constantine's reliance on Christianity as an instrument for intellectual self-legitimisation can enrich our reconstruction of his interventionist policies. The language he employed to address the quarrelling Alexander and Arius (see Chapter 3) betrays an awareness of debates suggesting that a lack of doctrinal agreement might qualify Christianity as a faulty system of knowledge. Constantine explicitly asks why bishops cannot agree on foundational tenets as Greek philosophers do.[60] His challenge of Christianity's divisions thus did not merely follow criticism by external detractors but resonated with a discourse that by the fourth century had become internal to Christianity. Hellenistic and post-Hellenistic concerns about primacy of access to the truth had fed both the rivalry of Christian theologians with the Greek philosophical schools and their efforts to police heresy among themselves.[61] It is an obvious point but one nevertheless worth pressing that the term 'heresy' itself is an indicator of Christianity's engagement with Greco-Roman philosophical discourse, in which *hairesis* designated the choice of a philosophical school.[62] In this light, Constantine's attempts to fix core doctrinal tenets read as an intuition that the same (theological) knowledge that provided him with intellectual authority needed to undergo a process of stabilisation initiated by the imperial authority itself, if it was to be acknowledged as authoritative.[63] But this somewhat circular design could not be finalised without episcopal acceptance that imperial power should preside over efforts to differentiate between the knowable and the unknowable in divine matters. The bishops gathered at Nicaea accepted the emperor's offer of cooperation. They did so, however, in the anticipation that an alliance between State and Church would help manage another gap – the

---

[59] Text preserved in Lactant. *Mort. Pers.* 48; cf. also Euseb. *HE* 10.5. Discussion (with scholarly review) in Kahlos (2009) 56–58.
[60] See Chapter 3, p. 145–6.   [61] Cf. Boys-Stones (2001) 179–98.
[62] Boys-Stones (2001) 154–62. Cf. the occurences of *hairesis* with a neutral meaning at Acts 5.17; 15.5; 24.5.
[63] See Chapter 3, p. 144–6.

one between disagreeing bishops – through a top-down redrawing of theological coordinates.

The resulting history of interactions between State(s) and Church(es) in antiquity and beyond falls outside the scope of this book. I will linger, however, on one example, from late fourth-century Constantinople, that is meaningful in two respects. First, it exemplifies the concern with intellectual authority driving episcopal rivalries, since its narrative relies entirely on revisiting traditional models of the philosophical quarrel of the kind implemented in the context of intellectual self-assertion explored by representatives of the so-called Second Sophistic. Second, it connects this motif with a (prescriptive) celebration of the intervention of the orthodox emperor. Gregory of Nazianzus' *Concerning his own life* (*De Vita Sua*, II 1.11) is simultaneously an apology and an act of self-celebration. It was issued by Gregory following his tormented experience as a bishop in the Eastern capital. The first part of the poem – which opens with Gregory's conception and birth – asserts two points: Gregory enjoys a privileged relationship with God (who even saved him from a shipwreck as a reward for his piety)[64] and he is devoted to the philosophical life. Gregory then discusses his study of rhetoric and philosophy in Athens, using this to re-assert the point (on which, cf. *Or.* 4) that his unbending allegiance to the Logos is a condition for his dominance of the *logoi*.[65] Gregory ascribes qualities to himself that resonate with collective expectations regarding philosophical behaviour. He is wary of office. The poem formulates repeated expressions of *recusatio* (whose philosophical implications were considered in Chapter 1) when narrating Gregory's appointment as bishop first of Sasina and later of Constantinople.[66] Second, Gregory is a master of *parrhesia*. The theme of philosophical free speech and of ambitious clergymen unworthily exploiting it is at the heart of his lengthy account of his vicissitudes in Constantinople, which occupies the entire second half of the poem. This section opens with a sustained attack on Gregory's former ally – and later enemy and rival for the episcopal see – Maximus the Cynic.[67] Gregory attempts to disqualify Maximus by presenting him as an

---

[64] Greg. Naz. *DVS* 175–204.   [65] Cf. e.g. at *DVS* 112–18, 267–76.
[66] Cf. *DVS* 277–336 (inner torment regarding the choice of the right life; admiration for biblical prophets and their ascetic life; reverence for the altar but at a distance); 337–52 (shock of the ordination, flight to Pontus); 417–25 (Gregory forced to become Bishop of Sasina); 486–91 (second flight); 529–51 (reluctance to engage in pastoral activities, flight to Seleucia); 1745–1901 (Gregory's resignation from the see of Constantinople; speeches before the bishops and the emperor).
[67] Greg. Naz. *DVS* 843–1119.

abuser of *parrhesia*. Maximus' well known adoption of Cynic practices, including wearing the Cynic tunic, are singled out in the poem as signs of what might be labelled his degenerate performativity. Maximus feigned the adoption of a philosophical lifestyle to disguise his profound ignorance. He was a 'barking dog' (κύων ὑλακτῶν, l. 813) whose verbal violence – a parody of true *parrhesia* – sought to conceal his immorality.[68]

To the negative model set up by Maximus, Gregory opposes his own person. But he does so in a section that opens and closes on the expected role of emperors in relation to episcopal debates. Gregory presents his ideal of cooperation between emperors and bishops as grounded in an agenda of differentiation of true from false practitioners of (Christian) philosophy, which the imperial authority is expected to validate. Gregory begins by celebrating his enthronement as bishop of the capital following Emperor Theodosius' expulsion of the Arian bishop Demophilus. Gregory's enthronement at the Basilica of the Apostle is led by the emperor himself:

> Then full of joy (ἄσμενος) he (i.e., Theodosius) came to me in my great joy – for he had treated me with respect at our first meeting (τετίμηκέν με τῇ πρώτῃ θέᾳ), but in the way he spoke and listened (οἷς τ' εἶπεν οἷς τ' ἤκουσεν) most kindly .... The upshot of it all was this: 'God hands the church (i.e., of the Apostles)', he said, 'through me to you and to your great efforts' ('δίδωσι", φησί, 'τὸν νεὼν θεὸς δι' ἡμῶν σοί τε καὶ τοῖς σοῖς πόνοις').[69]

The exchange between emperor and bishop is marked by ideal respect of the rules of communication – Theodosius speaks and listens 'most kindly' (εὐμενέστατα) – which translates into an equally ideal apportioning of authority. The Orthodox emperor puts his power in the service of (Neo-Nicene) orthodoxy, here embodied by Gregory himself. His understanding thus confirms that he is worthy to act as an agent of doctrinal stabilisation and as a (temporary) mediator between God and his bishop.

Gregory's retrospective celebration of his (failed) episcopal experience closes on his self-projection as a perfect speaker driven by a love of truth and a lack of ambition.[70] The stage where those qualities become manifest is the Second Ecumenical Council, held in Constantinople in 381 – the culmination and conclusion of Gregory's episcopal career. Gregory's narrative of his activity at the Council, over which he presided, is enshrined in

---

[68] Greg. Naz. *DVS* 810–14. Cf the comparison of contemporary Cynics to barking dogs at 1030–31.
[69] *DVS* 1305–12. Transl. White (1996). [70] *DVS* 1190–206.

a twofold act of *parrhesia*. First, he reports his long, bold speech addressing the assembled bishops:

> You do not all seem to me to hold the same opinion (οὔ μοι δοκεῖτε ταὐτὰ γινώσκειν), my friends, nor do I think you have any intention of resolving the issue which we have met to decide; in fact, I think you are in the highest degree failing in your duty (τοῦ δέοντος ἁμαρτάνειν).[71]

The rest of Gregory's speech accuses the bishops of being driven by what, elsewhere in the poem, he labels *philarchia*, political ambition: Gregory argues that the bishops merely need him as accomplice in their rivalries and asserts his concern with greater matters.[72] He reminds them of their responsibilities to God and invites (or orders) them to 'accept his advice, based on careful thought' (δέξασθέ μου λόγον, λόγον προμηθῆ).[73] The plausibility that such a speech was actually delivered will not be discussed here. More relevant to my argument is Gregory's commitment to constructing himself as a *parrhesiastes*: he explicitly and somewhat prescriptively draws attention to this quality of his words (τῆς ἐμῆς παρρησίας, l. 1659). The second act of *parrhesia* Gregory presents to his readers is the story of his resignation from the episcopal see, in a long scene (ll. 1797–1918) following the account of the Constantinopolitan council. Especially remarkable in this section is the blending of the theme of Gregory's *recusatio* (see above) and longing for ascetical withdrawal with the celebration of his bold speaking. After delivering a stern speech of resignation to the bishops (ll. 1827–55), Gregory goes on to address the emperor (ll. 1881–901). The striking feature of his address to Theodosius, however, is the misalignment between tone and content. This speech, like the one targeting the bishops, is punctuated with imperatives: Gregory portrays himself as issuing orders to the emperor.[74] But in terms of content, Gregory merely asks to be allowed to resign from the episcopal see after so many doctrinal quarrels. No order is actually being given; in fact, Gregory is begging for permission.[75] The imperative tone, however, allows Gregory to re-frame his retirement from what it actually was – a defeat – to a marker of his status as a fearless speaker of the truth. Equally important is appreciating that Gregory continues to prescribe communicative interactions between emperor and bishops by exemplifying the

---

[71] *DVS* 1591–679 (quoted lines: 1591–4). [72] *DVS* 1595-8. *Philarchia* as true cause: *DVS* 460.
[73] *DVS* 1620–21.
[74] E.g., 'Demand (ἀπαίτει) of these people a loving harmony!' (l. 1893), 'demand (ἀπαίτει) of these grey hairs ... that they persevere in suffering!' (ll. 1898–900).
[75] Thanks to Anna Lefteratou for drawing my attention to this aspect of the speech.

ruler's ideal reaction: Theodosius applauds.[76] His orthodoxy is confirmed via a final gesture that communicates not only approval but understanding. The emperor recognises in Gregory's desire to withdraw from ecclesiastical politics the token of a genuinely philosophical nature and allows Gregory to go and lead a life of contemplation. Somewhat ironically, the alignment in intents and ideals between emperor and bishop seals Gregory's ideal nature as bishop at the very moment he steps aside.

Gregory's story is both retrospective and self-referential. We are entitled to be sceptical about the validity of his claims. But his account provides an ideal blueprint for Church-State relations. It confirms that doctrinal disputes wrote themselves – or had the ambition of writing themselves – in the history of Greco-Roman philosophy and of its (performative) presence in society. It points to the expectation that enlightened imperial authority would be able to identify true Christian philosophers and tell them apart from those who parrot a philosophical identity for political gain. Gregory celebrates Theodosius for identifying the representatives of the former category, supporting their public commitment, and approving of their free speech and eventually their right to self-determination, even when this must result in retirement from public life.

But episcopal acceptance of the emperor's legitimising role in sanctioning orthodoxy had an inevitable impact on the dynamics regulating the strife for orthodoxy. The point I am pressing here is by no means new but is worth incorporating within a larger reflection on the fourth-century negotiation of intellectual authority. The development of mechanisms internal to Christianit(ies) for disciplining dissidents long predated Constantine's rule. As is well known, however, Constantine's injection of the principle of state authority into the management of religious disputes had an ironic consequence: imperial power became the catalyst of a process of acceleration of religious competition. Being 'in the right' now meant being close to power. The enhanced social status of bishops lent greater visibility to their doctrinal rivalries, which in turn developed into a testing field that might (or might not) prove that they were worthy of authority in the first place. Urban populations were mobilised to generate social pressure. The rise of a dynamic style of church leadership – courtesy of the Arian dispute – enabled preachers to energise their followers via antagonistic preaching and incensed tones.[77] Bishops also

---

[76] *DVS* 1902 ταῦτ᾽ ἐκρότει μὲν ἐν μέσοις αὐτοκράτωρ.
[77] Galvão-Sobrinho (2013) 66–86. This proved especially challenging in large urban contexts, since episcopal rivals could be consecrated simultaneously (cf. Van Dam [2007a] 244).

realised that power could not only provide endorsement but even serve as a 'secular arm' (thus Kahlos) via the army, with the Alexandrian revolt of 356 that set Homoian against Nicene Christians serving as a powerful test case.[78] Finally, and perhaps most important, state-endorsed Christianity gained access to the empire's legal resources.

Humfress has shown that, beginning with Constantine, the gradual integration of Christianity into the imperial judicial system created the conditions for categorising non-conforming religious beliefs as a crime under Roman law.[79] Late antique ecclesiastics trained in schools of rhetoric capitalised on this, using their legal knowledge to navigate disputes. As the law courts came to serve as an orthodoxy-defining space, the perquisites of legal management of theology became apparent. As Humfress writes, 'the dialectic of the courtroom could also offer a singular advantage over philosophical disputation, in that it produced a legally enforceable judgment as to the winner and the loser'.[80] Once we conceptualise doctrinal disputes as early Christian theologians did – as efforts to establish exact knowledge – we are also bound to note that the crystallisation of State-Church cooperation into legal language was responsible for a historically unprecedented and to some extent paradoxical injunction: to make metaphysics bite-size, so as to enable legal enforcement. Clear-cut, univocal formulations would serve as the benchmark – for fellow theologians, the state, and the faithful at large – to measure violations. We might thus entertain the idea of conceptualising the increasing demand for creeds, tenets, and dogma as the outcome of the fourth-century progressive collapse of two complementary anxieties: the search to define (and stabilise) authority-legitimising knowledge, and the elaboration of the role of power in protecting and policing what constitutes authoritative knowledge and its conditions of universal accessibility.

Cooperative dynamics between the Roman state and the bishops were thus key to establishing imperial intervention as the fundamental act of patronage regulating Church interactions. But they were also invested by what I would call Gregory's paradox. The same Gregory who wanted his audience(s) to know of his ideal synergy with Theodosius was also keen to underscore his intellectual authority over both good and bad emperors – see his treatment of Julian and Constantius II in his *Or.* 4. Both points were equally vital to him. Bishops expected the emperor to preside over their disputes, except that, at the same time, they did not.

---

[78] Kahlos (2019) 45.   [79] Humfress (2007).   [80] Humfress (2007) 234.

Chains of Validation, Part 2: Bishops with Bishops, versus Emperors

Eusebius of Caesarea, the first bishop to cast himself as the interpreter of the interpreter-ruler, already fully realised that a gesture of public validation of imperial Christianity would bestow upon the Church a form of power that, although symbolic, had concrete implications. The two works in which Eusebius illustrates his understanding of the emperor's understanding – the *Praise* and the *Life of Constantine* – consistently map out this intuition. Chapter 3 analysed the sophisticated strategy by means of which the *Praise*, delivered at court on the occasion of Constantine's *Tricennalia*, invites the emperor to partake in a joint effort to project the sovereign's piety.[81] Constantine's previous responses to panegyrics reveal Eusebius' startling request – the ruler should recognise God's primacy – as counter-intuitively seductive. Eusebius appeals to Constantine's awareness that his endorsement of the request will publicly demonstrate his identity as a philosopher-ruler. The *Praise* therefore seems – and in a sense is – an invitation to cooperation. But this cooperation simultaneously seals the bishops' right to remind the emperor that God stands above him. One of the two parties will gain more than the other from this exchange of gifts, and that is the party of Eusebius.

Corke-Webster sees in Eusebius' invitation to Constantine to join in his praise of God the subversive kernel of this text, which he reads as setting the conditions for the power struggle between State and Church. The downgrading of Constantine to the role of panegyrist in fact enables the bishop to occupy the same position of the ruler, at least on a literary level.[82]

> This is, then, a celebration of the Supreme Sovereign. And let us, the royal children, inspired by the lessons of sacred writings, rejoice in the fact that the author of our festival is the Supreme Sovereign. And I mean by 'Supreme Sovereign' the One who is truly supreme (μέγαν δ' ἐγὼ βασιλέα καλῶ τὸν ἀληθῶς μέγαν); this one, I say – nor will the sovereign who is present resent (νεμεσσήσει) it, but rather will he join in praise of the divine teaching (συνευφημήσει τῇ θεολογίᾳ) – is the One who is Above the Universe, the Highest of All, the Greatest, the Supreme Being, whose kingdom's throne is the vault of the heavens above, while the earth is footstool for His feet.[83]

---

[81] See Chapter 3, p. 138–41. [82] Corke-Webster (2020a) 161–62.
[83] Euseb. *LC* 1.1, transl. Drake. Further descriptions of Constantine as praising God at *LC* 1.3, 2.4.

The passage clearly points to the fact that, in order to symbolically enhance his power, Constantine must give it away. Eusebius' invitation amounts to an oblique request that the emperor sanction the dynamics of his relationship with God's representatives on earth – the bishops – in the way a bishop publicly formulates them. The *Praise* might help present Constantine as a sublime exegete, but it simultaneously advertises the two exegetical feats Eusebius has accomplished: interpretation of the emperor's desire to be publicly acknowledged as interpreter and interpretation of the emperor's relationship with God, which must be one of subordination.

The presentation of the priests as the ultimate interpretive authority returns in Eusebius' *Life of Constantine*. This is apparent in his account of Constantine's conversion. As was argued in Chapter 3, Eusebius' narration of Constantine's vision of the cross is a perfect encapsulation of the idea that the emperor's conversion resulted from a considered deductive process later validated by revelation.[84] We also saw, however, that the omen sanctioning Constantine's understanding – the apparition of the celestial cross – has a second function: it discloses that the true god is the Christian one to an emperor who converted as a result of a pure analysis of historical evidence, without knowing to which divinity he was turning.[85] Eusebius' Constantine, however, sees the cross and does not recognise it. At this point in the story, he finds himself in need of interpretive assistance. This comes first from Christ himself, who appears in a dream when the emperor falls asleep and urges him to make a copy of the celestial sign, for protection against his enemies.[86] It should be noted, however, that Christ's appearance in the story is not tantamount to a full disclosure of the identity of Constantine's new god. Another scene, which somewhat disrupts the flow of the narrative,[87] is later introduced to close the hermeneutical gap. According to Eusebius, Constantine, stunned by the vision, would have summoned 'those initiated in his words (i.e., the words of the god)' (τοὺς τῶν αὐτοῦ λόγων μύστας) to help him understand which divinity appeared to him, and to help him decode the divine riddle.[88] The interpreters arrive and explain to the emperor that he has received the sign of 'the only begotten Son of the one and only God', and

---

[84] Euseb. *VC* 1.27. See Chapter 3, p. 129–33.   [85] Euseb. *VC* 1.27.3.   [86] Euseb. *VC* 1.29.
[87] Cf. how Eusebius first explains Constantine's instructions for reproducing the sign on his banner (*VC* 1.30-1) and afterwards declares 'but those things happened somewhat later' (ἀλλὰ ταῦτα σμικρὸν ὕστερον, *VC* 1.32) and returns to the theme of the interpretation of Constantine's vision(s).
[88] Euseb. *VC* 1.32.1.

that 'the sign (σημεῖον) which appeared was a token of immortality (σύμβολον ... ἀθανασίας)'.[89]

> They began to teach (ἐδίδασκον) him the reasons for his (i.e. the Son's) coming, explaining (ὑποτιθέμενοι) to him in detail the story of his self-accommodation to human conditions .... Comparing the heavenly vision with the explanation (ἑρμηνείᾳ) of what was being said, he made up his mind (τὴν διάνοιαν ἐστηρίζετο), convinced (πειθόμενος) that it was as God's own teaching (θεοδίδακτον ... γνῶσιν) that the knowledge of these things had come to him. He now decided to apply himself personally to the divinely inspired writings, taking the priests of God as his advisers (παρέδρους αὐτῷ).[90]

This additional episode does not only appear redundant (compare Lactantius' version of Constantine's vision, in which no priestly intervention is mentioned).[91] It is also somewhat contradictory: it should apparently come as no surprise to Eusebius' readers that Constantine, who did not even know which god he was praying to, was fortuitously in the proximity of priests who happened to be Christian. But from an ecclesiastical perspective the addition was essential. It tempered the celebration of Constantine's intellect with an emphasis on its limits, preparing for the argument that true understanding can only be achieved through priestly advice. On the one hand, Eusebius validates Constantine's deductive process: his inductive prognostication was rewarded with the sign of the celestial cross. On the other hand, he makes it clear that Constantine's thinking needed external help to achieve full maturity. The cumbersome structure of the account speaks to Eusebius' struggle to balance praise for the first Christian sovereign with the preservation of the interests of his stakeholder group.[92]

In the course of the rest of the *Life*, Constantine's wisdom grows *pari passu* with his relationship with the priests. The emperor acknowledges their authority explicitly. The much-debated sentence Eusebius' Constantine pronounces before a gathering of bishops is emblematic in this respect: 'You are bishops of those within the Church (τῶν εἴσω τῆς ἐκκλησίας); but I am perhaps a bishop of those outside (τῶν ἐκτός),

---

[89] Euseb. *VC* 1.32.2.
[90] Euseb. *VC* I 32.2–3. Transl. Cameron and Long (1999), slightly modified.
[91] Lactant. *Mort. Pers.* 44.5. On the discrepancies between the different accounts of Constantine's vision, see – among others – Weiss (2003); Van Dam (2011); Flower (2012); Barbero (2016) 142.
[92] Van Dam (2011) 98 accepts the scene of the consultation with the priests as part of Constantine's recollections. Potter (2013) 156–57 suggests that the odd structure might indicate a conflation of materials.

appointed by God (ὑπὸ θεοῦ καθεσταμένος).'[93] Regardless of how 'those outside' are to be identified (barbarians? pagans? heretics? laymen?), this sentence conveys the emperor's acknowledgement that God himself apportioned authority (thus Johnson, who argues for 'an expression of the doctrine of the separation of Church and State'),[94] assigning the bishops the care (and leadership?) of 'those within the church'. The sentence also signals that Constantine wished to be counted among them. As Corke-Webster shows, Eusebius' portrayal of Constantine in the *Life* eventually results in his episcopalisation as the 'universal bishop appointed by God'.[95] The mature Constantine is here described in such a way that his qualities and style of leadership coincide with those ascribed to ideal bishops in Eusebius' *Ecclesiastical History* – a point that speaks to the efforts of fourth-century ecclesiastics (including Eusebius), considered below, to construct episcopacy as perfect leadership.[96]

Finally, Eusebius' addendum to the conversion story arguably addresses the crucial issue of the nature of Constantine's relationship to Christ. When we follow the main storyline of the *Life*, we find Constantine learning everything from the mouth of Christ, who visits him personally in a dream. The intervention of the priests who stand by tempers this picture of unmediated connection. Eusebius' awareness of the need to celebrate the proximity of Constantine to Christ while avoiding having the Son and the emperor come too close – let alone overlap – appears as a driving force already in the *Praise of Constantine*. Here Eusebius postulates Constantine's mimetic agency of Christ but also takes care to underscore that he was (only) a 'friend of the Logos'.[97]

In the *Life*, Eusebius' thematisation of the mimetic relationship between Constantine and Christ is infused with scriptural ambitions: Constantine's

---

[93] Euseb. *VC* 4.24.
[94] Johnson (2006) 195. For further discussion, see Cameron and Hall (1999) 320; Lenski (2016) 78; Corke-Webster (2020b) 274–76.
[95] Euseb. *VC* 1.44.1; Corke-Webster (2020b). See also Rapp (1998) 295.
[96] On Eusebius' projection of his episcopal ideals in the *Ecclesiastical History*, see Corke-Webster (2019) 89–148.
[97] Constantine's mimesis of Christ: Euseb. *LC* 2.2–5 (comparing the agency of the Logos in the cosmos and of Constantine on earth. Cf. the definition of Constantine as 'emulous of the Almighty', ὁ δὲ ζήλῳ τοῦ κρείττονος, at *LC* 2.5). See Drake (1976) 31–38; Barnes (1981) 253–55; Greenwood (2021) 33. Constantine as friend of the Logos: Euseb. *LC* 2.3, 4 (ὁ δὲ τούτῳ φίλος). On the problem a straightforward assimilation of Constantine to Christ could pose for Christians, see Bardill (2012) 338–76. But Van Dam (2011) 78–81 argues that Eusebius, as the upholder of a subordinationist position in Christology, saw an advantage in stressing the resemblance between Christ and Constantine insofar as each served as 'prefect of the Great Ruler', i.e., God (μεγάλου βασιλέως ὕπαρχος, said of Christ at *LC* 3.6 and of Constantine at *LC* 7.13).

biography looks more to the Bible than to the Roman past, with Moses serving as the emperor's typological model.[98] Drake suggests that the appeal to the Mosaic paradigm may have served to deflect another association seemingly sought by the elderly Constantine: with Paul, a source of apostolic authority.[99] If so, the delineation of the bishops' role in the *Life* as guides of the emperor reads even more as an attempt to control the clever and ambiguous attitude to ecclesiastical politics the real-life Constantine developed in his final years.

It is inevitable that Constantine's cooperation with some bishops antagonised others. He might even have operated in anticipation of this eventuality: Cooper has recently pointed to the way Constantine's attempts to stabilise doctrine simultaneously served as an opportunity to test episcopal allies.[100] His far from linear passage from endorsing the Nicene Creed in 325 to reconciling with Arian theologians and expelling the uncompromising Nicene Athanasius of Alexandria in 335 maps out a history of diffidence towards doctrinal intransigence (thus Drake).[101] Athanasius refused Constantine's request to receive Arian followers back into communion, as he himself declares in his *Apology against the Arians*.[102]

The implications of Constantine's religious interventionism are illuminated by his son Constantius, as is the case with many other policies he devised. As noted earlier, Constantius' religious policy – a key component of his self-image – was conceived in continuity with his father's legacy.[103] Yet Constantius also seems to have enhanced this legacy through his muscular presence in doctrinal debates and through the clear-cut positions he took in open letters – behaviour that elicited the resentment of various ecclesiastics.[104] Bishop Ossius of Cordoba begged Constantius – or so Athanasius tells us in the *History of the Arians* – to stop intruding into the affairs of the Church:

> Stop using force, and do not write or send *comites* . . . . Stop, I beg you, and remember that you are a moral man: fear the day of judgment and keep yourself pure for it. Do not intrude yourself into the affairs of the church, and do not give us advice about these matters, but rather receive instruction

---

[98] See Chapter 4, p. 200–2.
[99] Drake (2000) 377, 391. Cf. further Inowlocki (2007) 255. On Constantine's desire to be buried with the Apostles in the eponymous church, see Bardill (2012) 367–76; Greenwood (2021) 34.
[100] Cooper (2019).   [101] Drake (2000) 265.
[102] Athanasius, *Apol. c. Ar.* 59. See Barnes (1993) 20–21; Galvão Sobrinho (2013) 136.
[103] See Chapter 3, p. 114–7.   [104] See Baker-Brian (2020) 368–72.

on them from us. God has given you kingship but has entrusted us with what belongs to the Church.¹⁰⁵

Athanasius himself went from depending on the intercession of imperial letters in his rivalries with religious opponents to being repeatedly exiled and composing attacks on Constantius' legitimacy as emperor.¹⁰⁶ He thus fully exemplifies the fact that a thin line separated the bishops' perception that their authority depended on imperial approval from their belief that, should the emperor disappoint them, they had the power to question not only his religious piety but his political legitimacy.

In his influential *Life of Anthony*, composed between 356 and 362, Athanasius depicts his literary alter ego – Anthony the Great – as utterly indifferent to imperial authority.¹⁰⁷ The work problematises allegiance to earthly power as a source of conflict with Christian identity.¹⁰⁸ Anthony receives letters from Constantine, Constantius, and Constans, who write to him 'like a father'.¹⁰⁹ But he is unimpressed. 'Why do you marvel if the emperor writes to us: is he not a man?' he asks his monks, who eventually convince him to write back.¹¹⁰

It is against the background of this growing competition between emperors and bishops that a key but underappreciated aspect of Julian's religious policy comes to fruition. Scholars have often asked if Julian's attitude to institutionalised religion imitated Constantine's relationship with the Church.¹¹¹ His desire to rival aspects of imperial Christianity may be suggested, as Greenwood shows, by his evidently competitive articulation of the providential and soteriological role of the ruler or by his response to the Constantinian exploitation of architecture as a visual demonstration of the victory of Christianity.¹¹² I suggest, however, that Julian's relationship to the Constantinian model of interaction with priestly hierarchies was critical rather than imitative, insofar as its primary

---

¹⁰⁵ Athanasius, *Hist. Ar.* 44.6–8, transl. Barnes (1993) 174–75. The authenticity of the statement is disputed (Klein [1982] 1002–10) but, as Barnes stresses, it nevertheless expresses Athanasius' perspective (Barnes [1993] 295 n. 43).
¹⁰⁶ Athanasius and imperial correspondence: see Baker-Brian (2020) 354–67. Athanasius' reliance on imperial intercession emerges from the three letters by Constantius preserved in *Ap. c. Ar.* 51 (cf. Baker-Brian [2020] 356–57). Attacks on Constantius' legitimacy: Athanasius, *Hist. Ar.* 49–51. See Flower (2013) 89–97; Baker-Brian (2020) 356.
¹⁰⁷ Circulation of the *Life* and success of its Latin translations: Urbano (2013) 228. Dating: Brennan (1976) 52–54. For a discussion on the authenticity of the *Life*, see Barbero (2016) 465–66; Cartwright (2016) n. 1.
¹⁰⁸ Cartwright (2016). ¹⁰⁹ Athanasius, *Vit. Ant.* 81. ¹¹⁰ Athanasius, *Vit. Ant.* 81.
¹¹¹ See already Koch (1927–28) and now especially Greenwood (2017a), (2021) 100–104.
¹¹² Greenwood (2017a), (2021) 111–17.

aim was to neutralise what Julian saw as problematic features of the new dynamics between State and Church.

A bit of evidence would seem to stand in the way of my argument – and is arguably the reason why Julian's suspicion regarding Church dynamics has failed to attract scholarly attention despite the enormous attention paid to Julian's religious reforms. The text in question is Julian's famous *Letter to Arsacius* (*ep.* 22 Wright = 84 Bidez–Cumont) that addresses the high priest of Galatia and issues what reads like an invitation to imitate ecclesiastical structures and the behaviour of Christian clergymen. In this text, Julian complains that not enough people are (re)turning to 'Hellenism' (Ἑλληνισμός), that is, Greek religion. He therefore orders Arsacius and the other priests to engage in practices such as philanthropy, care of the dead, and a 'display of holiness' in behaviour, which have secured the success of 'atheism' (meaning Christianity):

> Why do we not observe that it is their benevolence to strangers (ἡ περὶ τοὺς ξένους φιλανθρωπία), their care for the graves of the dead and the pretended holiness (πεπλασμένη σεμνότης) of their lives that have done the most to increase atheism (τὴν ἀθεότητα συνηύξησεν)? I believe that we ought really and truly to practice every one of these virtues ..... In every city establish numerous hostels (ξενοδοκεῖα) in order that strangers may profit from our benevolence; I do not mean for our own people only, but also for others who are in need of money.[113]

The *Letter to Arsacius* presents Julian's relationship with Christianity as imitative and driven by an ill-concealed sense of resentful admiration. This is arguably, however, precisely what contemporary Christian intellectuals would have liked to read. The authenticity of the text, which was not part of the ancient collection of Julian's letters but was transmitted separately by the Church historian Sozomen,[114] is much debated. Although excellent Julianic scholarship defends it,[115] the issue, in my view, remains open. The points advanced by Van Nuffelen in the article that first raised the hypothesis of forgery (or of a heavily re-edited text) have not been addressed as effectively as the defenders of the text believe. For example – and crucially – it is striking that the letter's definition of Greek religion as 'Hellenism' not only is unparalleled in Julian's writings but also, as Van Nuffelen stresses, corresponds to a Christian term for Greek-speaking

---

[113] *Ep.* 22 Wright (= 84 Bidez–Cumont), 429d–30c.
[114] Sozomen, *HE* 5.16.5–15. See Van Nuffelen (2002) 136; Bouffartigue (2005) 231.
[115] See Bouffartigue (2005); Nesselrath (2013) 9 n. 28; Stöcklin-Kaldewey (2014) 73; Greenwood (2017a) 4–5, (2021) 101–2; Wiemer (2020) 227; De Vita (2022) ccxcviii, 836 n. 379.

'pagans'.[116] Bouffartigue's response to Van Nuffelen's remark relies primarily on Julian's use of the adjective 'Hellenic' (ἑλληνικός) in other texts, despite his awareness of the difference between the two words ('Hellenic' and 'Hellenism') that are cognate but not identical.[117] The close relationship between the words, however, does not diminish the fact that no pagan occurrences of 'Hellenism' are attested.[118]

Reflection on the authenticity of this text must also address the question of its function, given that, as suggested above, its claims would have likely filled late antique Christians with pride. The letter sends a clear message: philanthropy, the care of the dead, the creation of hostels/hospitals, and a holy lifestyle secured the success of Christianity, which continues to prosper despite the return of hegemonic 'Hellenism' through Julian's top-down intervention. At one point, the piece even claims:

> For it is disgraceful that, when no Jew ever has to beg, and the impious Galileans support not only their own poor but ours as well (τρέφουσι δὲ οἱ δυσσεβεῖς Γαλιλαῖοι πρὸς τοῖς ἑαυτῶν καὶ τοὺς ἡμετέρους), all men see that our people lack aid from us. Teach those of the Hellenic faith to contribute to public service of this sort.[119]

This passage compliments the Christians. Although it uses critical words to describe them (as expected: the text mimics Julian's voice), it simultaneously implies that Christians are so generous that they effectively help all the poor regardless of religious allegiance. The statement reads like a distortion of the complaint Julian raises elsewhere, namely that Christians use philanthropy to lure innocent people – a much different argument.[120] The letter thus seemingly entrusts a demonstration of Christianity's universal philanthropy to Julian's critical voice, producing overwhelming evidence, inasmuch as it comes from an active detractor.

The picture of Julian's religious reform changes remarkably once we put aside the *Letter to Arsacius*. Julian's ambition appears to be not so much to catch up with the ecclesiastical machine as to re-assert the centrality of the emperor in all religious matters, by which I mean doctrine and cultic

---

[116] Van Nuffelen (2002), *prob*. Elm (2012) 326–27; McLynn (2014) 134 n. 69.
[117] Or on the (unverifiable) argument that, given that Gregory uses the expression τὸ Ἑλληνίζειν to attack Julian's School Ban, an 'honest forger' (*honnête faussaire*, p. 235) would have used οἱ Ἑλληνίζοντες rather οἱ Ἑλληνισταί. See Bouffartigue (2005) 233–35; similarly Greenwood (2021) 153 n. 16. Other deductions in Bouffartigue (2005) that seem open to debate: *hellenismos* must have been used somewhere else in Julianic propaganda (235); although the establishment Christian *xenodocheia* targeted in *ep*. 84 was not greatly developed in Julian's times, Julian would have been alive to the phenomenon anyway (237).
[118] Van Nuffelen (2002) 138.   [119] *Ep*. 22 Wright (= 84 Bidez–Cumont), 430d.
[120] Cf. *Ep. Fragm.* (= ep. 89b Bidez–Cumont), 305b–d; *Mis*. 363a–b.

practice. Eusebius could deny Constantine absolute interpretive authority or complete identification with Christ and argue that, in order to know which god he was praying to, the ruler needed the advice of Christian priests. Julian, as noted in Chapter 3, represented himself as the alter ego of Heracles within an autobiographic myth dedicated to his providential agency (*Against Heraclius*) and sought personal association with Asclepius.[121] He claimed a status as prophet of Apollo (ἔλαχον ... τοῦ Διδυμαίου προφητεύειν) and strove to exercise direct control over his priests, whom he directed through a correspondence that still partially survives.[122] Bishops were elected by their communities; Julian personally appointed his clergymen. As his long epistolary fragment to a priest (*ep.* 89b Bidez-Cumont) shows, he aimed to determine *inter alia* where they spent their days and nights, what they wore, which forms of entertainment were suitable for them, and – as Chapter 3 noted – what they read.[123] This final point, considered in juxtaposition with Julian's theological hymns (*To the Mother of the Gods*, *To Helios King*), is particularly important. In the hymns, Julian presents himself as a conscious agent of divine providence and a sublime theologian, the master-interpreter shaping pieces that are at once mystical allegories and philosophical treatises.[124] His hymns seal his status as the leader of the cult and perfect philosopher. It is Julian who teaches his priests how to interpret the divine; he is not taught by them.

But Julian's simultaneous self-projection as hymnographer, allegorist, prophet, *pontifex maximus*, and religious leader clearly relied, in contrast with Constantine's (and Constantius') doctrinal commitment, on a vantage point of which he was arguably aware. He could rely on the unity between the Roman state and the cult that was, to draw on a term used in the study of ancient religion, 'embedded' in it.[125] Constantine's choice to seal his legitimacy by replacing the traditional interpretation of divine providence with a new one (although presented as an underlying tradition) destabilised this unity. Against the backdrop of growing tensions between the Christian emperor and his bishops, Julian seems to have tried to devise a model for imperial control over the cult that was simultaneously more centralised than

---

[121] On Julian's association with Asclepius see Chapter 3, n. 246.
[122] Prophet of Apollo: *ep.* 18 Wright (= 88 Bidez–Cumont) 451b-c. Letters testifying to Julian's ambition to personally direct his priests: *ep.* 16, 19, 20, 32, 33 Wright and *Ep. Fragm.* (= 30, 79, 89a, 86, 85, 89b Bidez–Cumont).
[123] See *Ep. Fragm.* (= *ep.* 89b Bidez–Cumont) 296d (personal qualities of the priest), 300c-2a (reading list), 302d-3b (priestly behaviour, clothing), 305a (criteria for appointment).
[124] See Chapter 3, p. 158–62.
[125] A cautionary discussion of the use of the term in Nongbri (2008).

ever and in which the ultimate interpretive authority lay unambiguously with the philosopher-ruler.[126] This might suggest that Julian perceived the new relationship between the Christian emperor and the Church as a zero-sum game he had no intention of replicating. Gregory of Nazianzus' response to Julian's project seemingly confirms this. Gregory's exploitation of the parable of Julian to re-assert the need for episcopal validation of the emperor reads like an attempt to crush not only Julian's advocacy of the old religion but also his assertion that priests must be interpretive subordinates. As noted above, Gregory responded to Julian by asserting the superiority of his interpretive control, which he eloquently proclaimed over both Julian and Constantius II – the impious and the pious.[127]

Gregory's *Or.* 4 accuses Julian's project of religious reform of being a mere imitation (μιμήματα) of the structures of Christianity.[128] We might read this accusation as Gregory's deliberate attempt to obscure Julian's effort to challenge such structures. Van Nuffelen suggests that Gregory's oration may have inspired the author of the *Letter to Arsacius*.[129] The letter seems to postulate a separation between state and religious authorities – another point that, in light of Julian's centralisation of the cult, is a non sequitur.[130] It orders priests to only meet government officials (ἡγεμόνες) within the vestibule of the temple, a space in which the official, after passing over the threshold, becomes a private citizen (ἰδιώτης). 'For you yourself', it continues, in the address of Arsacius, 'as you are aware, have authority over what is within, since this is the bidding of the divine ordinance'.[131] This sounds like the Constantine of Eusebius' *Life* praising the authority of the bishops at the banquet, this being precisely what Julian was fighting against and Gregory was fighting for.

Philosopher-Rulers or Philosopher-Advisors: The Shifting Forms of Episcopal Authority

Although this may sound obvious, it is essential to remember that episcopal claims to interpretive control developed at a time when the bishops' socio-political authority was also growing. Beginning with Constantine,

---

[126] On Julian's possible debts to the efforts of Maximinus Daia and Aurelian to re-organise priesthoods according to a hierarchical system, see Scrofani (2005) 204–9; Borrelli (2018); De Vita (2022) cviii–cvix.
[127] See p. 214–19 above.   [128] Greg. Naz. *Or.* 4.111–14.   [129] Van Nuffelen (2002) 145–47.
[130] *Pace* Bouffartigue (2005) 238.
[131] *Ep.* 22 Wright (= 84 Bidez-Cumont), 431c–d. On this passage and its clash with Julian's *Ep. Fragm.*, see Van Nuffelen (2002) 142–43.

imperial patronage transformed the episcopal urban authority and presence at court: ecclesiastical hierarchies, benefitting from new sources of revenue – they could now inherit wealth – were increasingly modelled on the imperial administration.[132] As Rapp shows, the vocabulary used by urban communities to celebrate magistrates, civic benefactors, and bishops often overlapped.[133] Ecclesiastical empowerment and the transformation of the late antique city were interlinked phenomena, with bishops steadily replacing local elites as urban patrons.[134] This process accelerated episcopal efforts to cultivate their public image through literature as part of an effort to legitimise their authority.[135] The negotiation of the public face of the episcopacy certainly predated the Constantinian turn. Like the management of orthodoxy, however, episcopal leadership was redrawn by its entrance into the public sphere and open interaction with state structures.

In this section, I seek to isolate some literary tendencies that map the rise and consolidation of a fourth-century discourse concerned with the self-projection of bishops as at once philosophers and leaders. This analysis recapitulates points made above in my examination of Gregory of Nazianzus' *Concerning his own life*, insofar as I continue to explore, albeit in a larger setting, the engagement of episcopal self-assertion with the performative rules set by the Greco-Roman tradition for the participation in society of self-confessed philosophers. What I would define as the bishops' productively ambiguous management of the repertoire of philosophical features offered by the Greco-Roman tradition is striking in this connection. In my view, the conflation of philosophical traits pertaining to different social functions indicates episcopal ambitions to inhabit different philosophical ideals simultaneously and, by so doing, to control them all.

Rapp uses the term 'mirrors of bishops' to designate (heterogenous) normative writings on episcopal leadership that idealise real-life experiences of bishops.[136] The so-called Cappadocian Fathers – Basil of Caesarea, Gregory of Nyssa, and Gregory of Nazianzus – were crucial developers of this 'genre' (a term I use here operatively and reluctantly). It is meaningful that these theologians, who were deeply invested in asserting Neo-Nicene Christianity with emperors and vis-à-vis fellow ecclesiastics,

---

[132] Transformation of episcopal urban authority: Brown (1992); Van Dam (2007a); Kahlos (2019) 40–41.
[133] Roueché (1997) 363, (1998); Rapp (2005) 168–71.   [134] See Chapter 6.
[135] Lizzi Testa (2007) 526.
[136] For the expression, see Rapp (2005) 45, 139. A survey of key treaties (such as Gregory of Nazianzus' *In Defense of His Flight*; John Chrysostom's *On the Priesthood*; Ambrose of Milan's *On the Duties of the Clergy*; Gregory the Great's *Pastoral Care*) in Rapp (2005) 41–55.

were also pioneers in establishing what a bishop was (to be). Sterk suggests that Basil's charismatic episcopal experience served as a catalyst in their reflection. After his death, Basil was elevated by the two Gregories, through speeches and treatises, to the model of perfect episcopacy.[137] This model coincided with the ideal of philosopher-leader. Basil's access to divine philosophy is presented in these writings as key to his ability to act as a shepherd of the faithful and to elevate collective life by guiding his congregation's worship.[138]

But the primary model for Gregory of Nazianzus' reflection on how to be an ideal bishop was arguably himself. As noted above, Gregory's literary production is pervaded by reflections on prescriptive episcopacy that return again and again to his own person. Among these should be mentioned his *Apology for his Flight to Pontus* (*Or.* 2), which takes its cue from his early departure from the see to meditate on pastoral duties. The text is seemingly a product of 362 or 363 and was therefore composed considerably before Basil's death, at a time when Gregory was acutely aware of Julian's presence in the East – something that might have encouraged him to think antagonistically about philosophical leadership.[139] For the rest of his life, Gregory's writings continued to alternate between self-projection as an ascetic philosopher and attacks on unworthy, power-seeking bishops.[140] Over the course of the following decades, John Chrysostom and Theodore of Mopsuestia also issued their own treatises entitled *On Priesthood* – other 'mirrors of bishops', on Rapp's formulation.[141] Around 388, the Latin West saw the publication of *On the Duties of the Clergy* by Ambrose of Milan.

All these texts engage with an idea of bishops as ideal philosopher-leaders by exploring traits that characterise philosopher-rulers in classical political theory. Eusebius is also a precursor in this respect: his *Ecclesiastical History* explored the idea of bishops as perfect philosophers and perfect leaders, and his *Life of Constantine* modelled Constantine on (Eusebius') ideal of episcopacy.[142] Fourth-century 'mirrors of bishops' draw on points the *Life* ascribes to Constantine, such as the motif of the imitation of

---

[137] Sterk (2004) 95–118, 125–26, 131–40.   [138] See Chapter 6.
[139] On the dating, see Elm (2012) 153 n. 27.
[140] Cf., e.g., *Or.* 20 and 21, both dedicated to the theme of bad bishops, and *Or.* 42. On Gregory's criticism of fellow bishops, see Sterk (2004) 122–25, 128–38; Elm (2012) 164–66, 228–39, 259–65, 403–13. On Gregory's attacks on Maximus the Cynic and on the bishops gathered at the Second Ecumenical Council (Constantinople 381) in his *Concerning his own life*, see p. 222–23 above.
[141] John wrote *On Priesthood* presumably in the late 380s (Malingrey [1980] 11; Rapp [2005] 44).
[142] Corke-Webster (2020b).

Christ and the association of the emperor with Moses.[143] Moses is treated as a model of ideal episcopacy by – among others – Gregory of Nazianzus, Gregory of Nyssa, John Chrysostom, John's biographer Palladius, and Theodoret of Cyrrhus.[144] The fact that Moses had been projected as an archetypical model of the philosopher-ruler since Philo of Alexandria's *Life of Moses* is meaningful here.[145] It is unnecessary to assume that any of these bishops used Moses because he served as a model in Eusebius' *Life*, whose early circulation, as noted in Chapter 4, remains difficult to assess.[146] But it is striking that the emperor and the bishops could be celebrated by relying on the same paradigm.

Moses, the perfect philosopher-ruler, famously begs God in Exodus to appoint someone more capable to carry out his mission. In his *Preparation for the Gospel*, Eusebius juxtaposes this passage with Plato's celebration of leaders who flee offices.[147] In other words, Eusebius celebrates *recusatio*, the practice we observed in Julian's management of his identity as philosopher-ruler and in Gregory's self-projection as ideal bishop.[148] Fourth-century prescriptions of ideal episcopacy are almost obsessed with this ideal. The writings of the Cappadocians, John Chrysostom, and Ambrose – all occupying extremely prestigious sees – are punctuated by statements of fear of office and lack of political ambition.[149] Gregory of Nazianzus is the outstanding case in point. 'I devoted the greatest part of my life to God and to purification, leaving to others the gates of the powerful', he writes at one point.[150] As a result of the effectiveness of his self-projection as a reluctant leader, his claims have only recently been re-assessed as part of a strategy to navigate public expectations.[151]

---

[143] See Chapter 4, p. 200–1.
[144] Rapp (1998), (2005) 125–36; Sterk (1998), (2004) 95–98, 102–12, 124–29, 153, 156; Williams (2008) 60–65, 80–100; Urbano (2013) 114–24. On Moses in Gregory of Nazianzus, see, e.g., *Or.* 2.92; 20.2; 28.2–3. Gregory of Nyssa explores Moses as a model of the perfect life in four works, two from the early 380s (*Funeral Oration on Basil* and the *Life of Gregory the Wonderworker*) and, a decade later, in the *Life of Moses* and *ep.* 17. John Chrysostom presents himself as Moses (cf. *Regr.* 5–6, pp. 99–100 Mayer and Allen) and is described in the same terms by his disciple Palladius in the *Dialogue on the life of John Chrysostom*. See especially *Dial.* 20 (pp. 146–47 Meyer), which establishes direct identification, but also *Dial.* 12 (pp. 80–81 Meyer), 18 (p. 122 Meyer), 19 (p. 129 Meyer). Palladius criticises Theophilus of Alexandria, a rival of Chrysostom, for calling himself 'a second Moses' (*Dial.* 7, p. 45 Meyer). Jacob Nisibis is defined as 'a new Moses' by Theodoret of Cyrrhus (*HR* 1.5).
[145] On the reception of Philo's writings in late antiquity, see Runia (1993). [146] See p. 169.
[147] Eusebius, *PE* 12.9, comparing Pl. *Resp.* 1.346e-7a with *Ex.* 4.13.
[148] See Chapter 1 and above, p. 224–5, respectively.
[149] Cf. Gaudemet (1958) 108–11; Lizzi Testa (1987) 33–50; Rapp (1998) 280–91, (2005) 143–47; Elm (2012) 6–8, 158–64; Piepenbrink (2012) 76–79.
[150] Greg. Naz., *DVS* 434–35.   [151] See especially Elm (2012) 4–14.

Gregory's autobiographical poem *Concerning his own life*, considered above, exemplifies how his claims to desire withdrawal went hand in hand with an ambition to control the ecclesiastical scene. Gregory the fleeing priest is not in contradiction with Gregory the bishop, the perpetual rival of other contemporary clergymen.[152] One point illuminates the other.

John Chrysostom too opens his *On Priesthood* by narrating an episode of *recusatio*, his decision to remove himself from the attempt by church authorities in Antioch to forcibly ordain him and his friend Basil. John claims to have fled – thus breaking a pact formerly made with his friend – because he believed he was unworthy to take up the role.[153] Reproached by Basil for his deceit, John explained to him that his decision had been taken in consideration of what would be best for the Church.[154] This retrospective reassessment inevitably ends up requalifying a surprising (and unfair) gesture as a demonstration of John's rigorous self-criticism and thus of the fact that he deserved the leadership position in the Church he held at the time he wrote.[155] Further examples could be offered, from Synesius of Cyrene's aggressive exploitation of *recusatio* when negotiating the acceptance of his bishopric (on which, see Chapter 6)[156] to the treatment of the trope in virtuoso fashion by Ambrose, possibly the most political fourth-century Western clergyman. Ambrose, the 'reluctant bishop' (thus McLynn), performatively displayed unworthiness to suggest that he should not be appointed to the see. Among other things, he fled the city and summoned prostitutes to his home in broad daylight.[157]

Unlike all the traits considered so far, however, another feature of ideal episcopacy advanced by these bishops brings into focus their identity not as powerholders but as interlocutors of power. This is the motif of *parrhesia*, freedom of speech in the presence of the powerful. In Hellenistic and post-Hellenistic political theory, *parrhesia* marked the behaviour of the philosopher who addresses the leader.[158] It summoned expectations connected to the behaviour of the philosopher in society but looked at power from a perspective not of identification but of challenge.

---

[152] Elm (2012) 147–81. See also Lizzi Testa (1987) 33–41.   [153] *Sac.* 1.3–7 (*SC* 272.72–99).
[154] Basil's criticism: *Sac.* 1.4 (*SC* 272.76–87); John's reply: *Sac.* 1.5–7 (*SC* 272.88–99).
[155] Cf. Kelly (1995) 25–28.   [156] P. 288–91.
[157] At least according to Paulinus of Milan, *V. Ambr.* 7–8. Rufinus too speaks, in very general terms, of resistance to the appointment (Rufinus, *HE* 11.11). Cf. McLynn (1994) 44–49.
[158] Momigliano (1973) 260; Bartelink (1979) 10; Van Renswoude (2019) 5. In classical Athens, *parrhesia* (or *isegoria*) denoted instead the privileged status of the free-speaking (male) citizen: see, e.g., Momigliano (1973) 259–60; Balot (2004) 233; Raaflaub (2004) 42.

Post-Hellenistic political theory prescribed endurance (even appreciation) of *parrhesia* as a quality differentiating wise sovereigns from flattery-seeking tyrants.[159] Bishops inhabiting the traditional figure of the philosopher-adviser accordingly worked to maintain the expectation that a good emperor was defined as such by his willingness to listen to them. This principle already regulates Eusebius' *Praise of Constantine*. Here the Christian sovereign reveals his worth by showing himself willing to accept the truth conveyed by the bishop's address, which coincides with a message of the ruler's subordination to the divine. Throughout the fourth century, ecclesiastical writings are consistently concerned with reflecting on the duty of the spiritual authority to admonish. I considered above the blunt speech(es) Gregory of Nazianzus puts at the heart of his revisitation of his life as one of a perfect philosopher (*Concerning His Own Life*). Basil of Caesarea, the perfect (post-mortem) exemplum of episcopal leader, was also portrayed as outstanding in *parrhesia*.[160] John Chrysostom's reputation for lambasting the rich preceded him.[161] Another bishop, Rufinus, is described (or retrospectively constructed) as having had *parrhesia* with Theodosius.[162] The latter's most famously blunt interlocutor, however, remains Ambrose of Milan.

Ambrose had already signalled his authority with Theodosius' predecessor, Valentinian II, by preventing the court from using the Basilica Nova and the Portian Basilica for Arian rites.[163] Ambrose's first confrontation with Theodosius related to the plundering and destruction of a synagogue in Callinicum. In winter 388–89, Ambrose pressured the emperor until he dropped his decision to punish the Christians who had perpetrated the act.[164] In writing to the emperor, the bishop explicitly refers to philosophical *parrhesia*. 'As it is not the part of an emperor to deny freedom of speech', he writes, 'so it is not that of a priest to refrain from saying what

---

[159] Cf. Suetonius' praise of Vespasian's tolerance of the outspoken advice of friends (*amicorum libertatem*) and philosophers (Suet. *V. Vesp.* 13) or Philostratus' celebration of Marcus Aurelius' behaviour with Herodes Atticus (Philostr. *VS* 560–61). Plutarch often addresses the issue (see, e.g., *Pomp.* 44.2; *Cat. min.* 33.1–2, and *How to Tell a Flatterer From a Friend*). Dio's *Orations on Kingship* rely on a pragmatic adaptation of this principle (see below, p. 257–59).
[160] Cf. the praise of Basil as 'addressing boldly the rulers' (βασιλεῦσι παρρησιαζόμενος) in Greg. Nyss. *In Basil. Fratr.*10 (= *PG* 46.798a) Greg. Naz. *Or.* 43.34. See Benedict (2018) 237–51.
[161] John's fame for blunt speaking: e.g., Palladius, *Dial.* 5 (p. 30 Meyer), 18 (p. 124 Meyer), 19 (p. 128 Meyer). John's powerful rhetoric and willingness to address any injustice as key to his Antiochian popularity: Sozomen, *HE* 8.2. Cf. Liebeschuetz (1990) 174–79.
[162] Theodoret, *HE* 5.17.
[163] McLynn (1994) 187–96, Liebeschuetz (2005) 125–60, with different chronologies.
[164] Ambr. *ep.* 74 (= ep. 40 Maur). McLynn (1994) 298–302; Kahlos (2019) 48.

he thinks'.[165] (It should be noted that Ambrose re-edited the text after Theodosius' revocation of the order.)[166] A later episode went down in history – via the inflated version provided by the Church historians[167] – as a symbol of imperial submission to the Church, and in this case as well Ambrose self-consciously assumed the role of philosopher-adviser.[168] Following the Massacre of Thessalonica of 390, Ambrose wrote to Theodosius to 'persuade, request, encourage, advise' him after the event (which the bishops defines as 'unprecedented in human memory').[169] In this (seemingly private)[170] missive, Ambrose explains to Theodosius that he will not celebrate the Eucharist with a blood-stained ruler, who must therefore show repentance like King David after Uriah's murder.[171] Eloquently, Ambrose also dedicated an *Apology for David* to Theodosius that focused on Psalm 50 (51), which David supposedly composed after being rebuked by the prophet Nathan.[172] Theodosius ultimately chose to make a display of penitence by humbling himself before the bishop by joining the *ordo poenitentium* in Milan – and, as McLynn argues, cleverly turned the aftermath of a massacre into a performance of piety.[173] It remains the fact, however, that this act sanctioned the emperor's reliance on episcopal approval.

All these examples point to a crucial matter: the episcopal focus on *parrhesia* might seem at first to downgrade bishops from a position of power to one of interlocutors of power. In fact, this aspect of their self-projection was the result of a skilful exploration of interpretive control.

---

[165] Ambr. *ep.* 74.2 (neque imperiale est libertatem dicendi denegare, neque sacerdotale, quod sentias, non dicere), transl. Liebeschuetz (2005).

[166] Zelzer (1982) xx–xxiii; Liebeschuetz (2005) 95–96; Van Renswoude (2019) 85–86, 103–6. The letter exists in two (modestly but meaningfully different) versions, one transmitted by Ambrose (*ep.* 74) and another by his secretary Paulinus of Milan (*ep. extra collectionem* 1a).

[167] See Sozomen, *HE* 7.25; Theodoret, *HE* 5.17–18, claiming that Ambrose opposed Theodosius in the porch of the church and forbade his entrance. A historical reconstruction of the confrontation in McLynn (1994) 315–23. Cf. Brown (1992) 110–13; Liebeschuetz (2011) 89–90; Van Renswoude (2019) 87–99.

[168] Brown (1992) 11–12; Van Renswoude (2019) 88–89, 93.

[169] Ambr. *ep. extra collectionem* 11.12 ('persuade ... advise'), 6 (unprecedented event). Transl. Liebeschuetz (2005).

[170] Cf. Ambrose's statement 'I am writing with my own hand what you alone are to read' (*ep. extra collectionem* 11.14 = *ep.* 51 Maur.). Transl. Liebeschuetz (2005).

[171] See Ambr. *ep. extra coll.* 11.13 (refusal to celebrate the Eucharist in the presence of the emperor); 7–9, 11 (invitation to repent like David).

[172] Liebeschuetz (2011) 80–82; Van Renswoude (2019) 94–95. Comparison between *ep. extr coll.* 11 and the *Apology* in Hadot (1977) 37–41. Brown (1992) 111 suggests that Ambrose appended the *Apology* to the letter. On the prophet Nathan as a model for Ambrose, see McLynn (1994) 303 (on *ep. extra coll.* 11) 306–8.

[173] McLynn (1994) 323–30.

When one considers that the episcopal exercise (or display of exercise) of *parrhesia* relied on an understanding of Christianity as perfect knowledge, it becomes clear that fourth-century bishops sought to occupy all the roles Greco-Roman society had traditionally constructed around philosophers, from philosopher-rulers to philosopher-advisers. It is on this basis that I referred to the ambiguity of the self-image of fourth-century bishops as productive. It sanctioned their ability to inhabit the two key models postulated by Greco-Roman political theory, to claim control of both, and to centre general reflection on the relationship between philosophy and power on their public selves.

Parrhesia and the Displacement of Non-Christian Philosophers: John Chrysostom on Julian

The effectiveness of episcopal claims to *parrhesia*, however, resided not only in their summoning of (interpretive) authority but also in their disqualification of philosophical rivals. A process of theological re-semanticisation of the word lay behind the possibility of employing it antagonistically. Already in the context of Hellenistic Judaism, *parrhesia* was infused with new significance as indicating a special relationship between human beings and the divine.[174] In Philo of Alexandria, the word (ἡ πρὸς θεὸν παρρησία) denotes the perfect communicative act with God of the wise – that is, those who rejoice at being servants of God and are free from all sin.[175] It is the right of God's friends (Abraham, Moses, etc.) to tell him everything.[176] This sense is also at work in early Christian writings, which identify the *parrhesiastes* par excellence as the martyr, whose self-sacrifice is rewarded in heaven by the right to speak freely to God and to intercede for the living.[177] Gregory of Nazianzus eloquently opens one of his autobiographical poems with a reference to how he would often 'reproach' Christ (πολλάκι Χριστὸν ἄνακτα ... ὠνοσάμην) for his own misfortunes.[178] Audiences acquainted with the discourse surrounding martyrdom would have recognised in Gregory's confidence with Christ the

---

[174] Momigliano (1973) 262; Scarpat (2001).
[175] Philo, *Quis rerum divinarum heres sit* 1.7 (definition of God's parrhesiastic interlocutor, 1.20–21). Analysis in Weiss (2017) 9.
[176] Philo, *Quis rerum divinarum heres sit*, 1.19–20. Weiss (2017) 9–10.
[177] Momigliano (1973) 262; Scarpat (2001) 103–17; Van Renswoude (2019) 21–40.
[178] Greg. Naz. 2.1.19 (*A complaint concerning his own calamities*), l. 1–2.

principle that legitimised any act of free speech performed by a Christian holy man. He who can freely address the Son will speak even more freely to fellow bishops and, as noted, to the emperor himself.

The productive ambiguity of fourth-century episcopal self-projections is also reflected in a complex engagement with *parrhesia*. As Gregory's writings exemplify, this category could refer both to the (traditional, political) quality of the philosopher-adviser confronting state power and to the sign of the bishop's martyr-like ability to speak freely to God and to mediate divine grace. Van Renswoude has shown that this is the case, for instance, with Hilary of Poitiers' shift from providing direct advice to Constantius II to borrowing the language of martyr acts and attacking the same ruler by appealing to his own *apostolica libertas* (*libertas* being the Latin term most closely resembling *parrhesia*). Hilary perceived both practices as complementary expressions of his control over philosophical free speech for the benefit and at the expense of the emperor, respectively.[179] Ambrose too exemplifies this complex usage. In a letter addressing Theodosius after the Thessalonica massacre, the bishop sends a message with parrhesiastic potential – his decision not to offer mass to the unrepentant emperor – but eloquently presents it as an order he has received from God as his direct interlocutor.[180]

But the figure perhaps most invested in exploiting the self-assertive (and religiously antagonistic) potential of *parrhesia* is John Chrysostom, Bishop of Constantinople from February 398 until his deposition and exile in June 404.[181] John had been a scholar of rhetoric and possibly – although this is debated – Libanius' (star) pupil.[182] Ironically, he derived from his traditional rhetorical training the cultural instruments that would make him an effective critic of the value of *paideia* to genuine – that is, Christian – philosophy.[183] In his surviving works (a massive 900 or so,

---

[179] Van Renswoude (2019) 41–62.   [180] Ambr. *ep. extra coll.* 11.13.

[181] John was appointed on 15 December 397, according to the Constantinopolitan synaxarion, but on 26 February 398, according to Socrates of Constantinople (*HE* 6.2), who is viewed as more reliable. See Kelly (1995) 104–5; Tiersch (2002) 18; Rendina (2021) 140–41 n. 8.

[182] Sozomen, *HE* 8.2 (cf. Socrates, *HE* 6.3). See Hunter (1988) 5–8, (1989); Ponzone (2018) 20–21. Against the hypothesis of John as Libanius' pupil, see Malosse (2008).

[183] The Church is defined as a 'spiritual school' (διδασκαλεῖον πνευματικόν, *In Mt. hom.* 17.7 [*PG* 57.264]). The faithful are expected to pursue 'that philosophy that is according to God' (φιλοσοφίαν ... τὴν κατὰ Θεόν, *Stat.* 18.4 [*PG* 49.186]). Paul is defined as – among other things – 'more philosopher than the philosophers' (ὁ φιλοσόφων φιλοσοφώτερος, *Laz.* 6.9 [*PG* 48.1041]). On John's depiction of Paul as a philosopher-rhetorician, see Rylaarsdam (2014) 159–66. See further Malingrey (1961) 273–74; Stenger (2016).

divided between homilies and treatises), the word *parrhesia* crops up around 1,300 times.[184] Used in a full range of meanings,[185] it primarily refers to frankness before God.[186] But this frankness must be fulfilled in the admonishment of worldly power.

The test case for this assertion is – perhaps unsurprisingly – the parable of Julian. I set aside the question of whether the *Comparison between a King and a Monk* obliquely responds to Libanius' praise of Julian and whether it is truly by John.[187] What is beyond dispute is that John sealed Julian's tyrannical image in two other pieces of uncontested authenticity, both of which are concerned with reclaiming interpretive authority at the expense of the Apostate. The first is John's homily *On Juventinus and Maximinus*. This homily narrates the alleged martyrdom of two Christian soldiers (members of Julian's bodyguard, according to Theodoret) who confronted the emperor on religious matters.[188] I will not consider it here; more important for my argument is John's second piece, his sermon *On Babylas, against Julian and the Pagans* (presumably dating to the late 370s).[189] Here John's meditation takes its cue from the fire that in October 362 partially destroyed the temple of Apollo at Daphne, a suburb of Antioch,[190] and places it at the heart of a complex demonstration of Christian providence pivoting around the figure of the third-century martyr Babylas.

A long preamble (*Bab.* 1–21) engages with two intertwined themes: the superiority of Christian revelation over Greek philosophy and the function of miracles as providing historical evidence of the agency of the Christian

---

[184] A *TLG* search showed 1,327 results.
[185] An analysis *exempli gratia* of its occurrences in one text, John's *On Priesthood*, shows that *parrhesia* is used there in the sense of general freedom of speech (*Sac.* 3.9.23 [*SC* 272.162]); license in talking, with negative connotations (3.9.42 [*SC* 272.164]); courage (5.8.47; 6.2.15; 6.4.77 [*SC* 272.302, 306, 320]); confidence in addressing God (of Moses and Elijah, 6.4.26 [*SC* 272.314]); of our soul, 6.4.63 [*SC* 272.318]); confidence in the context of the Last Judgment (6.13.98 [*SC* 272.362]).
[186] Bartelink (1997).
[187] Debated authenticity: Rapp (1998) 280; Ponzone (2018) 76. Response to Libanius: Hunter (1988) 29, 525–31; Urbano (2013) 204.
[188] Jo. Chrys. *Pan. Juv. et Max.*, PG 50. 571–78 (= *BHG* 975). See Franchi de' Cavalieri (1953); Teitler (2017) 118–22. Juventinus and Maximinus as members of Julian's bodyguard: Theodoret, *HE* 3.11.
[189] PG 50.533–72. Dating: Schatkin (1985) 15–16; Lieu (1986) 56. Discussion also in Grillet and Guinot (1990) 279–80. On the authenticity of the homily (not to be confused with Chrysostom's shorter piece *On the holy martyr Babylas*, in PG 50.527–34), see Schatkin (1970) 478–81; Lieu (1986) 55–61.
[190] Cf. Lieu (1986) 51–58; Greenwood (2021) 107–9. On the episode, see further Amm. Marc. 22.13.1–2; Julian, *Mis.* 346b, 361b–c; Sozomen, *HE* 5.20; Theodoret, *HE* 3.11.

divine.[191] This preamble is instrumental in tying together a contemporary wonder (the fire of Apollo's temple) with an illustration of how Christianity's intellectual and historical power are jointly epitomised in the figure of Babylas. His Christ-like status, acquired through martyrdom, was sealed in life by his divinely inspired *parrhesia* targeting an (unnamed) emperor; in death, it continued to manifest itself through the power of his relics over another impious emperor – Julian – and the demon Julian worshipped, Apollo. The first part of the piece narrates the events leading up to Babylas' martyrdom: he dared to expel from his church a ruler, perhaps Philip the Arab, for killing his hostage, the son of a foreign king.[192] Babylas' *parrhesia* – as John calls it – is presented as in itself a miracle, his bravery and steadfastness being only explicable as a gift from the divine.[193] His relics, it is argued in the second part of the piece, instilled fear in Apollo, whose oracle in the temple of Daphne became silent as a result of its proximity to the martyr's buried remains.[194] John narrates of how Julian would have decided on this ground to remove Babylas' relics[195] and how this triggered divine punishment: the destruction by fire of the temple, 'the miracle' – as John has it – 'which displayed not only the power but also the ineffable philanthropy of God'.[196]

On Babylas not only presents the episode of the destruction of the temple as a miraculous event targeting Julian and demonstrating the Christianity of providence but also ties this argument to a proof of the superiority of Christian interpretation over pagan claims to knowledge of the divine. (Compare Gregory of Nazianzus' use of Julian's death.)[197] The martyr Babylas is constructed as the only valid paradigm of a free-speaking philosopher. He 'taught emperors' – in the plural, his teaching extending also to Julian through the wondrous agency of his remains – 'not to carry their authority beyond the measure given to them by God'.[198] By so doing, Babylas 'showed that one appointed to the priesthood is a more responsible guardian of the earth and what transpires upon it than one who wears the purple',[199] in a striking conflation of the ideals of the bishop as

---

[191] See, e.g., *Bab.* 10 Schatkin (*PG* 50.536) (evidence of Christ's miracles; comparison with other religious figures – e.g., Zoroaster and Zalmoxis – on the ground that 'all that was said about them was fiction'); *Bab.* 11 Schatkin (*PG* 50.536) philosophers confronting Christianity 'became ridiculous and seemed no different from foolish children'). Translations from Schatkin (1985).
[192] *Bab.* 23–38 (*PG* 50.539–50). Pohlsander (1980); Shahîd (1984) 67–69; Lieu (1986) 52–53.
[193] *Bab.* 33 (*PG* 50.542). [194] *Bab.* 73–75 (*PG* 50.553). [195] *Bab.* 80–81 (*PG* 50.555).
[196] *Bab.* 87 (*PG* 50.557) (removal of the coffin); 93 (*PG* 50.559) (the fire as miracle). Cf. *Bab.* 94 (*PG* 50.559) (examination of the ruined site to argue that the symmetrical traces left by the fire prove it was divinely ordained).
[197] See p. 214–19 above. [198] *Bab.* 127 (*PG* 50.570–71). [199] *Bab.* 51 (*PG* 50.547).

philosopher-adviser and philosopher-leader. John's piece pursues simultaneously multiple aims: to disprove Julian's claims to interpretive access to divine providence, show that rulers must rely on episcopal advice (whose intellectual authority is sealed by *parrhesia*), and suggest that the highest form of leadership belongs to spiritual rather than earthly authority. There is also a fourth – fundamental – point that *On Babylas* presses by exploring *parrhesia* as a theological-political category: the disqualification of all non-Christian philosophers who claim philosophical free speech. The piece not only disavows Julian (a non-Christian philosopher) but also argues that Babylas' admonishment of the sovereign is a better instantiation of *parrhesia* than that of the Cynic Diogenes, the Greek model par excellence of the practice.[200] Babylas' example of virtue is said to 'demonstrate that the philosophers (i.e., non-Christian ones) ... are characterised by vainglory, impudence, and puerility'.[201]

John opens a window onto how a complex ideal of episcopal *parrhesia* – one that collapsed soteriological and political expectations – served as a weapon to disqualify non-Christian philosophers. If Christian *parrhesia* is grounded in a primary act of free interlocution with God, this becomes the fundamental prerequisite for laying claim to the practice. It certifies that the philosopher has genuine access to truth and can therefore offer spiritual salvation to those who agree to listen to him. Non-Christian philosophers, being deprived of this interlocution with the (Christian) divine, are cut off from the circuit of generation of free speech. In challenging political circumstances, they lack the steadfastness that proves the philosopher's connection with divine – and unshakable – knowledge.

The centrality of this claim to John Chrysostom's agenda is shown by how he seized the opportunity provided by another historical event to re-assert it. The episode was the Antiochene Riot of the Statues in 387, which brought Emperor Theodosius into collision with his subjects. John dedicated a Lenten cycle of twenty-one homilies (the *Homilies on the Statues*) to the event. The uprising, which followed extraordinary taxation, attracted the intervention of state authorities after the Antiochenes took down the imperial images.[202] John's homilies promote a narrative in which the monks' active intercession with the magistrates for the sake of the population puts to shame the cowardly behaviour of the non-Christian

---

[200] *Bab.* 48 (*PG* 50.546).
[201] *Bab.* 45 (*PG* 50.545). The attack on Greek philosophers extends from *Bab.* 37 Schatkin (*PG* 50.543) to *Bab.* 49 Schatkin (*PG* 50.546).
[202] On the event, see, e.g., Browning (1952); Liebeschuetz (1972) 278–80; van de Paverd (1991); French (1998); Quiroga (2008).

philosophers who fled the city.²⁰³ Emblematic in this respect is homily 17, delivered on 27 March 387,²⁰⁴ which pays particular attention to the monks of the city and their role in the trial. Here John writes:

> Now where are those wearing threadbare cloaks, sporting a long beard and carrying a staff in their right hands – the pagan philosophers (οἱ τῶν ἔξωθεν φιλόσοφοι), canine outcasts (τὰ κυνικὰ καθάρματα) who are more miserable than dogs under the table and do everything for the sake of their stomachs? At that time, they all left the city, they all sprinted away and hid in caves (εἰς τὰ σπήλαια κατεκρύβησαν).²⁰⁵

Conversely, the monks 'demonstrated their own kind of philosophy (τὴν οἰκείαν ἐπεδείξαντο φιλοσοφίαν)' in the face of danger and 'stated that they would not leave until either the judges spared the people of the city or sent themselves together with the accused to the emperor'.²⁰⁶ In another homily, John returns to the theme of the parrhesiastic bravery of the Christian holy man by celebrating (read: embellishing) the intervention of Bishop Flavian, who placated Theodosius by admonishing him 'by his appearance alone and his plain conversation (ἀπὸ τῆς ὄψεως μόνης ... καὶ ψιλῆς τῆς συντυχίας)'.²⁰⁷ The Cynic posture of non-Christian philosophers ('canine outcasts') is mere pretence; their *parrhesia* is empty talk, of which they fall short in difficult times.

Non-Christian Philosophers at the Imperial Court: Themistius as a Window into Christian Power

Statements such as John's could resonate in the normative and somewhat abstract space of homiletic literature, where the superiority of Christian *parrhesia* could be proclaimed apodictically. In real life, John too found himself needing to adapt his rhetoric to contextual necessity.²⁰⁸ Similarly, literary statements of the intellectual superiority of the bishops over

---

²⁰³ It compares this argument to previous apologetic treatments of Christian vs. pagan behaviour in adverse contexts. Cf. Eusebius' account of Christian charity during the plague that affected the Empire following the renewal of Maximinus' persecutions (*HE* 9.8.13–14).
²⁰⁴ Van de Paverd (1991) 352–57; Allen and Mayer (2000) 104.
²⁰⁵ Jo. Chrys. *Stat.* 17.5 (*PG* 49.173-4). Transl. Allen and Mayer (1999). On John's focus on the monks, see also *Stat.* 17.2 (*PG* 49.173–75), 19.1 (*PG* 49.189–90). Cf. Maxwell (2006) 32.
²⁰⁶ *Stat.* 17.3 (*PG* 49.173).
²⁰⁷ *Stat.* 21.16 (*PG* 49.219). On John's aggrandisement of the bishop's role, see Van de Paverd (1991) 131–49. See also Sandwell (2007) 58; Quiroga Puertas (2008) 147–48.
²⁰⁸ Testimonies to encounters between the bishop and the emperor are extremely few (Tiersch [2002] 183) and only one of John's homilies bears the title *homilia dicta presente imperatore* (*PG* 63.473–78). On the debated episode of John's confrontation with the Gothic commander Gaïnas in the presence of Arcadius on the matter of Arian services, see n. 298 below. In John's

representatives of the Greek philosophical schools must be read in the awareness that the latter continued to be present at court throughout the second half of the fourth century, as exemplified by the thirty years of political prominence of Themistius, an open adherent of the cult of the Greco-Roman gods. Yet Themistius himself provides oblique testimony to changes in the interaction between philosophy and (Christian) leadership.

Themistius' writings arguably betray some alertness to the need to thematise the validity of philosophical advice from non-Christian intellectuals.[209] In Chapter 2, I argued that his self-projection as Constantius' philosopher-adviser lent – perhaps inadvertent – assistance to Constantius' projection of Christianity as containing and fulfilling Greco-Roman culture.[210] After Julian's death, Themistius eloquently resumed his 'talismanic' role (thus Heather) by unambiguously disavowing the legacy of the Apostate.[211] In celebrating the enthronement of Julian's successor, Jovian, Themistius praises him – an imperial guardsman with no known cultural interests – for 'restoring philosophy ... to the palace once more' (φιλοσοφίαν ... ἐπανάγεις αὖθις εἰς τὰ βασίλεια).[212] Themistius extols the new ruler by criticising the faulty understanding of religion of his predecessors Julian and Constantius II, whom Themistius' piece, somewhat ironically, groups together. Contrary to them and their ambitions to exercise pervasive religious control, Jovian's attitude to religious freedom showed an awareness that 'there are some matters that ... are superior to threat and injunction ... above all, reverence for the divine'.[213] Through this piece, Themistius offers himself as the public interpreter of Jovian and his policies.[214] By so doing, he establishes a legitimising connection between Jovian and Constantine, by singling out the former, in a final

---

surviving homilies, the references to Arcadius appear in any case to be cautious (see Kelly [1995] 115–16; Tiersch [2002] 194–95) or to express what Liebeschuetz calls 'diplomatic' enthusiasm, aiming at the Christianisation of the imperial ceremonial (Liebeschuetz [2011] 220). On John's letters as testimony of his efforts to liaise with politicians (especially the powerful Anthemius), see Rendina (2021a) 139–61.

[209] Philosophers remained ideal ambassadors (Fowden (1979) 213–16). Cf., for example, the involvement of Macedonius for the city of Cyrrhus (*PLRE* s.v. Macedonius 4).
[210] P. 93–4.
[211] Jones (2010). 'Talismanic' Themistius: Heather (1998) 137–38; Heather and Moncur (2001) 23–24. Themistius remained active under Julian, although without the prominence he enjoyed under Constantius II (Elm [2012] 107; De Vita [2011] 28, Rigolio [2019] 218). According to *Suda* θ 122, he was also appointed to a prefecture (Greenwood [2021] 22).
[212] Them. *Or.* 5.63c. Transl. Heather and Moncur (2001). See also *Or.* 7.99b.
[213] Them. *Or.* 5.67c (cf. also 68b, 70a).
[214] See Vanderspoel (1995) 146–54; Heather (1998) 130; Heather and Moncur (2011) 150–56; Elm (2012) 436–38; De Vita (2014).

rhetorical flourish, as 'himself the very Constantine'[215] (arguably on account of their comparable religious policies).

In the following decades, Themistius' orations continued to celebrate the receptiveness of Roman emperors to (his type of) philosophy but with mixed results. The emperors who succeeded Jovian, the soldier Valentinian (r. 364–75) and his brother, the farmer Valens (r. 364–78), were stigmatised by their educated contemporaries due to their humble background.[216] Valens, who ruled over the *pars Orientis* until the debacle at Adrianople, did not speak Greek.[217] The imperial usurper Procopius, who rose and fell between 365 and 366, used Valens' ignorance as leverage for his propaganda; following his defeat, Themistius eloquently sought to rehabilitate Valens' image by praising him as a devotee of philosophy.[218] Lenski has shown that Valentinian and Valens were in fact more culturally aware than ancient sources acknowledge: they undertook educational reforms and sought learned tutors for their children.[219] Valens' continued patronage of Themistius could be taken to indicate such an awareness. It might also be argued, however, that these two emperors, who were external to the Constantinian dynasty, remained extraneous to its politics of interpretation. Valentinian and Valens ostensibly failed to engage with the Constantinian intuition that an emperor could derive intellectual legitimacy from his commitment to Christianity. They were unaware of, or uninterested in, the value of cultivating the image of Christian interpreter-rulers.

Themistius seems to testify to this through a change in his strategies of praise. His orations in honour of Valentinian and Valens mark a departure from the efforts to celebrate the sovereign as philosopher-ruler that characterised his speeches for Constantius II.[220] Instead, Themistius engages with (wishful) descriptions of the ideal synergy between emperor and philosopher-adviser – emphasising, however, that these figures do not overlap.[221] In a striking turn of the tables, when he addresses Valens, Themistius even criticises Plato for 'dangerously' (ἀποκεκινδυνευμένως) stating that 'evil will only end when philosophers rule'.[222] He opposes to

---

[215] Them. *Or.* 5.70d.
[216] Cf., e.g., Ammianus' description of Valens at 31.14.5. See Lenski (2014) 94–95.
[217] Cf. Them. *Or.* 6.71c–d, 11.144c–d.
[218] Them. *Or.* 7.99c–d, cf. 7.93b. On the reliance of Procopius' propaganda on Valens' reputation, see Lenski (2014) 228–29.
[219] Lenski (2014) 269–70.   [220] See Chapter 2, p. 81–6.
[221] Cf., e.g., Them. *Or.* 7.99d (also mentioning Julian, 'who lay claim to being the most philosophical of rulers', as a negative example); 8.104a–5c, 107c–d; 10.130a.
[222] Them. *Or.* 8.107c.

this an alternative model he presents as Aristotelian: the practice of philosophy is actually an obstacle (ἐμπδοδών) to rulers, who should simply listen to the advice of professional philosophers.²²³ 'Even if you don't know Plato's doctrine by heart and are unfamiliar with that of Aristotle, you none the less show in your deeds that you are their follower',²²⁴ Themistius writes to Valens in Winter 366/7, in a text composed after the emperor's (brutal) repression of Procopius' usurpation. In this piece, Themistius' difficulty in hiding or justifying Valens' vindictiveness signals the difficulties he encountered in managing the public figure of the farmer-emperor.²²⁵ I insist that a change in tone marks Themistius' addresses to the Illyrian emperor(s) because, once we bring it into focus, his recovery of the model of philosopher-ruler in his final orations appears striking. These orations are dedicated to a new leader, Theodosius (r. 379–95). In *Or.* 17, delivered after his appointment as city prefect in 384, Themistius celebrates Theodosius for 'uniting philosophy and politics within himself'²²⁶ and, apparently oblivious of his previous dismissal of this ideal, calls Theodosius 'the most philosophical emperor' (ὁ φιλοσοφώτατος αὐτοκράτωρ).²²⁷ His final panegyric (*Or.* 18, also composed in 384) praises Theodosius' commitment to philosophy.²²⁸ In this piece, incidentally, Themistius also promises to educate Theodosius' son Arcadius, whose tutor he had been appointed, through the texts of Plato and Aristotle.²²⁹

Theodosius, a soldier whose level of education remains difficult to assess,²³⁰ has not come down in history with a reputation as a philosopher-ruler. But the same could be said of Constantine. Like Constantine, Theodosius was committed to doctrine; in fact, he outdid his predecessor in this respect. What was once interpreted as Theodosius' assertion of Nicene Christianity as state religion – the 'Edict of Thessalonica' (*cunctos populos*, *CTh* XVI 1.2) – was arguably a local measure. The edict draws on universalising rhetoric ('It is our will that all the peoples who are ruled by the administration of Our Clemency')²³¹ but has been reassessed as a response to a contingent event, the struggles

---

²²³ Them. *Or.* 8.107d.   ²²⁴ Them. *Or.* 7.93b. Cf. similarly *Or.* 6.72a–b; 8.107c–d; 11.144b.
²²⁵ Vanderspoel (1995) 167; on Themistius' panegyrics to Valens as expressing disagreements and tension, see also Vanderspoel (1995) 175–76, 178–79.
²²⁶ Them. *Or.* 17.214a–b.   ²²⁷ Them. *Or.* 17.214b. cf. also 214c.
²²⁸ Them. *Or.* 18.219b–c. Cf. *Or.* 34.7, where Themistius argues that Plato's real heir is not Speusippus or Xenocrates but Theodosius himself.
²²⁹ Them. *Or.* 18.224b–25b.   ²³⁰ McLynn (2005) 100–108.   ²³¹ Transl. Pharr (1952).

between Nicene and Homoian Christians that shook the city of Constantinople in the 380s.[232] The Edict's reputation as a pivotal event in the history of late Roman religion might accordingly need to be re-evaluated. But one point stands: Theodosius espouses the rhetoric of a perfect identity of (Orthodox) Christianity with reason and understanding ('The rest ... whom we adjudge demented and insane [*dementes vesanosque*], shall sustain the infamy of heretical dogmas'). More broadly, Theodosius' government was marked by a steadfast identification of (Christian) piety as a central governmental concern: his Novel 3 states that the first task of the *imperatoria maiestas* is true religion.[233] Theodosius' complex (and debated)[234] policies for managing religious dissent between heresy and paganism thus strike one as to some extent the inevitable consequence of decades of intra-Christian debates testing the link between orthodoxy, knowledge, and salvation. His enactments consummated an argument rooted in the idea that exact knowledge must be ensured, since it has a soteriological function. If (Nicene) Christianity alone could guarantee the stability of the empire and its spiritual salvation, it follows that any other system of knowledge was either superfluous or harmful and needed to be dismissed.

Appreciation of Theodosius' general concern with Christianity as a source of knowledge also casts retrospective light on a seemingly unrelated phenomenon: the clustering of anecdotes celebrating episcopal *parrhesia* around his reign. If we return to the episodes of episcopal free speech considered above, it is striking how many have Theodosius or his sons as protagonists. This was certainly an outcome of decades of strengthening of the public authority of bishops, culminating under Theodosius' rule in the aggressively political profile of certain bishops who controlled key sees, especially Ambrose in the West and John Chrysostom in the East. At the

---

[232] Errington (1997) 36–41; Garnsey and Humfress (2001) 141–42; Kahlos (2019) 37–39. This explains the edict's exclusive focus on heretics with no reference to pagans. Moreover, the edict contains no provisions for enforcement. Only with its inclusion in the Theodosian Code (436) did *cunctos populos* serve as an Empire-wide enactment.

[233] Rendina (2021) 40–41; cf. Dermandt (1989) 164; Millar (2006) 22–45.

[234] On Theodosius' religious policies, see, e.g., Williams and Friell (1994) 30–41, 90–117; McLynn (2005) 79–88; Errington (1997), (2006) 212–59; Cameron (2011) 46–99; Kahlos (2019) 30–39, 46–48, 55. The beginning of his reign betrayed more concern for heretics than for other religious groups; Theodosius permitted pagan practices (while nevertheless banning sacrifices, magic, or divination: cf. *C.Th.* 16.10.8). His attack on pagan rites in the laws of 391–92 (*C.Th.* 16.10.10–12) tends to be read as marking the beginning of a new stage more invested in repressing traditional religion (cf. Fowden [1998] 549–54). On how Theodosius' religious legislation, however, seems to elude linear narratives, see Kahlos (2019) 35–36.

same time, we should not ignore the role Theodosius' self-image might have played in encouraging the perception that the sovereign was open to (Christian) philosophical advice. His act of repentance before Ambrose, performative though it may have been, remains a powerful symbol: it shows that, like the aging Constantine approving of Eusebius' *Praise*, Theodosius had learned that strategic submission to God's ministers could serve as a platform for projecting his piety and wisdom even after a massacre. A clear analogy between the two rulers thus emerges among the differences: both envisaged their commitment to religion as a fundamental component of their intellectual self-projection. Themistius, Constantius' experienced panegyrist, must have understood this and accordingly praised Theodosius.

From Themistius to Synesius' *On Kingship*: Philosophy Speaks up

Themistius' orations are key to my argument in three respects. First, they enable us to conclude that imperial engagement with philosophy remained a critical space of negotiation of the imperial self-image from Constantius II to Theodosius. Second, they obliquely confirm that an identification between Christianity and perfect philosophy continued to shape the coordinates of political debate for decades. Third, they introduce us to the experience and self-perception of a prominent non-Christian philosopher actively soliciting reflection on the sociopolitical utility of his public engagement. But this third point raises the question of whether Theodosius' time was also one of transformation(s) in the self-perception 'non-episcopal' philosophers had of their role as providers of intellectual resources for state power. An answer, I aim to show, may come from the writings of another self-confessed philosopher seeking prominence in Constantinople about a decade after Themistius' disappearance from public life (and presumed death): Synesius of Cyrene.

A Libyan aristocrat, *curialis*, Neoplatonic philosopher, poet, polymath, and – towards the end of his life – bishop, Synesius of Cyrene (ca. 373–414) mostly features in studies of late antiquity as a symbol of the flexibility and range of expression of early Christianity. Previously thought of as a man who converted late – if at all – in order to become a bishop, Synesius has been reassessed by recent scholarship as an eclectic Christian. Today he tends to be regarded as an intellectual who, having been born and raised in a Christian family, never perceived any tension between his religious allegiance and his commitment to *paideia*, which he cultivated by studying philosophy under Hypatia of Alexandria.[235]

There are appealing elements to this picture. The fourth century was in fact a period in which the very notion of religious identity was elaborated, and fourth-century intellectuals were scarcely all driven by normative religious ambitions.[236] At the same time, I am convinced – and have argued elsewhere – that the new image of Synesius is in some respects just as suspicious as the old, dichotomic approach that postulated his linear conversion. The making of the new Synesius has been grounded on a questionable item of archaeological evidence, the so-called house of Hesychius, and on a reading, equally open to challenge, of some of his writings (in particular his *hymn* 1) as clothing Christian ideas in classicising language.[237] We are left with the question of how to incorporate into this picture of an always-Christian Synesius his praise of traditional *manteia* the oracles of Pytho and Ammon and of the wisdom of those who practiced haruspicy – which in his time was forbidden under pain of death.[238] Some might want to qualify these statements as a gesture of cultural performance (a position that perhaps raises more questions than answers). But the defiant statement that accompanies Synesius' praise of traditional religious practices is worth stressing: his treatise *On the Dreams* argues that the 'arrogant state' (τῆς βασκάνου πολιτείας – a reference to Theodosian and post-Theodosian policies against sacrifice?) cannot prevent the form of *manteia* that occurs in the secrecy of one's own soul, through dreams.[239]

I will not seek to re-open here the question of Synesius' religion allegiance. A figure able to publicly express dissatisfaction with Christian

---

[235] This thesis finds its most structured expression in Cameron and Long (1993) 13–69. See further Lizzi Testa (1999) 710; Garzya and Roques (2000a) xlvi; Schmitt (2001); Rapp (2005) 157; Tanaseanu-Döbler (2008) 155–286, but postulating Synesius' conversion from Christianity to Neoplatonic philosophy; Criscuolo (2012); Op de Coul (2012); Pizzone (2012); Lane Fox (2015). Doubts expressed by Fowden (1985); Hagl (1997) 17–18, 30–31.
[236] An excellent introduction, through the lens of Libanius and John Chrysostom, in Sandwell (2007) 3–33.
[237] On the chronological problems posed by attempts to use the Christian inscriptions of the House of Synesius to locate Synesius' birth in a Christian family, see Niccolai (2019). Against Cameron and Long's argument that Synesius' *hymn* 1, composed a full decade before his appointment to the bishopric, described his baptism, see Niccolai (2021) 219–21, considering the theurgical function of the hymn's 'baptismal' vocabulary (on which, see also Bregman (1982) 91–92) and the impact of the codicological study in Baldi (2012) 65–110 on attempts to read *hymn* 1 as a unitary project.
[238] *Insomn.* 2.1 (haruspicy); 4.5 (sacred oracles); 11.2 (Pytho and Ammon).
[239] *Insomn.* 12.6. Schmitt (2001) 113–40 suggests that Synesius merely wants to express his dissent from a controlling state (but this leaves open the question of how to interpret religious references such as those in the note above).

dogmas even when taking up the bishopric,[240] Synesius must remain an author who challenges easy compartmentalisation. At the same time, a fuller assessment of his complex profile requires taking into account his competitive self-positioning vis-à-vis rising Christian leaders and what Goldhill labels their 'politics of culture'.[241] Even if we are wary of reducing this competition to the question of 'paganism' vs Christianity, it is essential to ask how an elusive intellectual ascribing his philosophical authority to his mastery of *paideia* would project his voice within a political discourse that increasingly prioritised Christian doctrine as a source of perfect knowledge. Here and in Chapter 6, I show that Synesius' political writings attempt to construct him as the representative of a type of philosophy threatened with displacement and in search of new strategies of self-assertion. The first such strategy is a competitive upgrade of the Themistian model of the traditional philosopher-adviser at court, which I see as the principle regulating Synesius' perhaps most controversial text, his oration *On Kingship*.

On Kingship, an address to Theodosius' son Arcadius, was composed (or presents itself as having been composed) towards the beginning of Synesius' stay at Constantinople, where he was sent, probably between 397 and 400, as a Libyan envoy tasked with obtaining tax remissions for his country.[242] His letters allow a reconstruction of this three-year sojourn as marked by a constant but eventually frustrated effort to find a political place in the capital through networking with the local aristocracy.[243] The speech seemingly interacts with Synesius' social ambitions but does so counter-intuitively. *On Kingship* presents itself as a 'crown speech' (στεφανωτικὸς λόγος), a text normally meant to accompany the delivery of tax-money to the sovereign in the form of a crown, the *aurum coronarium*.[244] It quickly transforms itself, however, into a speech of advice on kingship marked by a peculiar harshness of tone. Having announced that he is offering not one but two crowns to the emperor (the *aurum coronarium* and the crown of philosophy),[245] Synesius argues that the emperor must be brought back to the right track, since his lifestyle has been

---

[240] Synesius, *ep.* 105.   [241] Goldhill (2022) 35.
[242] I follow the dating by Barnes (1986a) and Cameron (1987) of Synesius' sojourn in Constantinople (cf. Liebeschuetz [1990] 106; Cameron and Long [1993] 91–102, 107; Rendina [2021] 71 n. 1). The alternative hypothesis, that Synesius arrived in 399 and left in 402, was first advanced by Seeck (1894) and is supported by Roques (1989) 16–17; Hagl (1997) 64–65; Lamoureux and Aujoulat (2008a) 25.
[243] Rendina (2021a) 44–51, 71–97.   [244] On this taxation, see Klauser (1944).   [245] *Reg.* 3.1.

corrupted by flatterers who surround him.²⁴⁶ The rest of the oration takes the form of an exposition on the virtues and duties of the ideal ruler, interspersed with stern remarks targeting the emperor. For example, Arcadius is unflatteringly compared to jellyfish, a peacock, and lizards.²⁴⁷ Scholarship has long debated whether Synesius could have made this speech at court and has mostly decided against the possibility. *On Kingship* tends to be read as oppositional literature, written at a time when Synesius had grown frustrated at a court unresponsive to his plea for tax remission for Cyrene (and therefore possibly later than its fictional setting). On this line of argument, Synesius composed it to seek the favour of a party that was trying to gain control of the imperial administration.²⁴⁸

There can be no doubt that the speech in its present form could never have been presented at court: it is simply too long.²⁴⁹ But assuming that Synesius' address to the emperor is mere fiction implies denying all validity to Synesius' statement, made a few years later, that he had been 'bolder (θαρραλεώτερον) than any Greek ... in addressing the emperor'.²⁵⁰ Synesius might certainly be lying, perhaps in an effort to aggrandise himself a posteriori.²⁵¹ But one wonders if he deserves such radical questioning in light of the bluntness displayed elsewhere, from his abovementioned criticism of the 'arrogant' state in *On the Dreams* to his remarkable letter of negotiation of the bishopric (on which, see Chapter 6) and his self-celebration as a shocking *parrhesiastes* in *On Providence*.²⁵² Starting from the assumption that the excessive length of *On Kingship* as it is preserved today suggests that the text was re-edited, it remains possible that there is a kernel of truth in Synesius' repeated self-congratulatory remarks for talking tough (to the ruler).

Be this as it may – the point must remain speculative – Synesius' repeated emphasis on the sincerity of his appeal serves my argument for a different reason. It reveals his clear ambition to write himself not as an oppositional author but as the latest instantiation in a long tradition of philosophical *parrhesia*. The difference between antagonism and bluntness is crucial, because parrhesiastic advice, although a vehicle of criticism,

---

[246] Cf. *Reg.* 14.2–5.   [247] Respectively at *Reg.* 14.3; 15.3, 15.7.
[248] Barnes (1986a) 108; Liebeschuetz (1990) 106; Cameron and Long (1993) 127–30; Schmitt (2001) 282–88; Hoffmann (2012) 54; Flower (2013) 53–54; Petkas (2018).
[249] A speech accompanying homage to the crown should not exceed 150/200 lines in length (Menander II 12. 423.3–5 Russell-Wilson). *On Kingship* is 1,200 lines (Cameron and Long [1993] 128).
[250] *Insomn.* 14.4.   [251] Swain (2013) 102 argues for a provincial circulation of *On Kingship*.
[252] *Prov.* 1.18. On *ep.* 105, see Chapter 6, p. 288–91.

presents itself as aiming to benefit rather than merely challenge authority. Moreover, as noted above, it obliquely validates rulers who are willing to learn from philosophy.[253]

A close reading of Synesius' self-presentation as a rough advisor shows that his concern is less with criticising Arcadius than with advertising his own speech as an exemplary philosophical exercise. The text never criticises Arcadius without qualification. When blaming him for living the life of a jellyfish, Synesius eloquently adds: 'But do not be incensed, for the fault is not yours!'[254] (it is, rather, of those who surround and corrupt the young ruler). Arcadius' errors have one trait in common: they are all caused by other people, be they his entourage of flatterers or the imperial predecessors who handed down the practice of wearing purple, gold, and jewels.[255] A parallel claim is made that Arcadius is naturally inclined to fall for true – that is, philosophical – beauty. Once the emperor understands his errors (which are the product of youth and bad company), he will 'blush' (ἐρυθριῶν) for shame', recognising that Synesius' harshness is in his service: enlightened power is expected to provide a safe space for the truth-speaking philosopher.[256] Synesius describes his words as 'pedagogues, not servants of persuasion'.[257] He explicitly presents himself as the mouthpiece of philosophy,[258] which, when truthful, is 'harsh and stern from the beginning'.[259] He professes faith in the capacity of the young sovereign to progress intellectually, becoming an ideal ruler with the help of his own advice.[260]

Synesius' repeated signalling of the philosophical meaning of his bluntness resonates with the principle, sealed in imperial literature by Dio of Prusa, of the conditionality of praise: the sovereign proves he deserves celebration if he accepts philosophical truth, even when it is harsh.[261]

---

[253] Cf. Hagl (1997) 63–102, whose reading has the merit of recognising Synesius' (literary) stance as inspired by the Hellenistic model of the philosopher-adviser of the powerful (see especially Hagl [1997] 82–91). Cf. Menchelli (2017) 93.
[254] *Reg.* 14.2 (Ἀλλὰ σύ γε μὴ δυσχεράνῃς, ὡς τοῦτό γε οὐκ ἔστι σόν). Transl. Fitzgerald (1930).
[255] *Reg.* 14.2–5.
[256] *Reg.* 3.5–6 (blushing for shame); 6.4 (youth and bad company). Cf. *Reg.* 1.4–2.1 on the ideal relationship between power and truth-speaking philosophy.
[257] *Reg.* 2.3 (μὴ εἰσὶ θεραπευταὶ πειθοῦς ... ἀλλὰ παιδαγωγοί).
[258] *Reg.* 15.1. Cf. *Reg.* 19.1–2; 29.2; 29.4.   [259] *Reg.* 3.6.
[260] *Reg.* 3.6. Synesius also puts his method as a teacher on display and advertises his knowledge of literature (*Reg.* 4.5), educational exempla (*Reg.* 7.3–4, 16), and the exact definitions of difficult or ambiguous terms (*Reg.* 4.3–4; 8.2–3; 17.2–3).
[261] See, e.g., *Reg.* 2.3; 3.5; 4.6–5.4; 6.3, 4; 9.5; 10.4; 16.1; 18.1; 25.6; 29.4. On Dio's 'conditionality', see Moles (1990) 312.

On Kingship frequently and deliberately echoes Dio's orations *On Kingship*.²⁶² Synesius' tropes are also Dio's: he speaks on behalf of philosophy and against sophists.²⁶³ Both authors recognise the noble inner nature of their addressees and explain imperial shortcomings as the product of inexperience.²⁶⁴ Dio describes himself as a wanderer, a self-taught philosopher; his alter ego Diogenes is the epitome of (philosophical) rusticity.²⁶⁵ Synesius' insistence on Cyrene's poverty is to be understood in this light as not merely instrumental to his request (be it real or performative) for a tax exemption for his hometown. Above all, it serves an image of coarse simplicity that sets Synesius in opposition to the type of the greedy sophist.²⁶⁶ 'Let not a man's prudence (φρόνησις) escape you, nor the rest of that swarm of the soul's virtues which are concealed under poor clothing (ἐσθῆτι φαύλῃ κρυπτόμενος)', the *curialis* and landowner Synesius says.²⁶⁷ The probability that the ambassador of the Libyan Pentapolis came in a tattered garment to present a crown of gold to the emperor is nil.

What complicates Synesius' interaction with the literary legacy of Dio, however, is the fact that *On Kingship* simultaneously seeks to construct itself against the legacy of the most successful fourth-century instantiation of Dio's advisory model: Themistius. 'Will you admit philosophy finally coming to reside here? And will anyone be able to recognize her appearing here after so long an interval (διὰ πλείστου φανεῖσαν)?', Synesius asks at the opening of his piece.²⁶⁸ As Schmitt has argued, this reads as a hint at the years that separated Themistius' death around 388 from Synesius' arrival in Constantinople in 397.²⁶⁹ Themistius had a habit of talking of himself in his writings as Philosophy personified.²⁷⁰

But the interaction *On Kingship* seeks between Dio and Themistius is pursued, I suggest, with the aim of sending the message that Synesius has overcome both. His bluntness displaces Dio's modulation of the criterion of the conditionality of praise. Dio tempered aspects of criticism through generalising assertions, the use of parables, and the projection of authentic acts of *parrhesia* as taking part in a distant past and involving Diogenes and

---

²⁶² See already Asmus (1900) for a list of echoes and borrowings from Dio in *On Kingship*. Synesius' *Dio* provides explicit comments on Dio's fourth oration *On Kingship* (Dio 2.4).
²⁶³ Cf. Dio Chrys. *Or*. 1.61; 3.14–25.   ²⁶⁴ Cf. Dio's description of Alexander in *Or*. 2.1–2.
²⁶⁵ See also the woman in rustic garments (ἄγροικον στολήν) who teaches Dio at *Or*. 1.53–54.
²⁶⁶ *Reg*. 3.1.   ²⁶⁷ *Reg*. 28.1.   ²⁶⁸ *Reg*. 1.2.
²⁶⁹ Schmitt (2001) 289–90; see also Tanaseanu-Döbler (2008) 261–63. For alternative – but unconvincing – interpretations, see Fitzgerald (1930) 183; and Aujoulat (2008a) 85 n. 3. The text has unmistakable Themistian echoes (Swain [2013] 104; Petkas [2018] 133–38).
²⁷⁰ Heather and Moncur (2001) 159 n. 53. Cf., e.g., at *Or*. 1.18a–b.

Alexander, alter egos of himself and Trajan.[271] Synesius, conversely, embraces the Diogenes in Dio: criticism and bluntness are pursued in his own name rather than through a historical alter ego. He depicts himself as unafraid of speaking truth to power as the Cynic archetype of *parrhesia*.

At the same time, this ideal of philosophical integrity puts Themistius in perspective as well. One might remark – without seeking to generalise – that Themistius' imperial addresses offer a twofold model. One is straightforward celebration of the ruler as a (self-sufficient) philosopher-ruler, which therefore obliquely undermines the intellectual authority of the philosopher-adviser.[272] The other, explored with the Illyrian emperors (see above), is the promotion of a synergy between philosophy and power that simultaneously deactivates the threatening elements potentially embedded in such encounters. Suffice it to recall that Themistius praised Valens' clemency after the latter's bloody repression of Procopius' supporters. Synesius' *On Kingship* reclaims philosophical authority. He projects himself as a philosopher-adviser unafraid to recover Dio's (and Diogenes') subversive side.

The overall picture that emerges is one of Synesius as an intellectual striving to signal his intellectual authority through a competitive engagement with the literary history of *parrhesia*. But what lies behind Synesius' perceptible urgency to inhabit the parrhesiastic model so assertively and to push it to its expressive limits? His main driving concern might simply have been his sense of competition with an authoritative philosophical canon. It is intriguing, however, that *On Kingship* never loses touch with an ambition to stress that Synesius' blunt, rough, subversive character is a mark of a philosophy in dialogue with the divine. He advocates for the usefulness of his advice in cultivating the piety of the emperor (which praised in abstract, metaphysical terms).[273] He professes his awareness that philosophy's chief concern is with God.[274]

---

[271] See, e.g., his cautionary revisiting of the myth of Heracles at the crossroads as advice against tyranny at *Or.* 1.58–84, or his threatening reminder of the destiny of the bad bull (i.e., Domitian) in *Or.* 2.73–74. In *Or.* 4, Alexander, Trajan's alter ego, meets the brash Diogenes and has a conversation turning on the theme of ideal kingship. Alexander is described as both delighting in Diogenes' boldness (*Or.* 4.15) and feeling threatened and challenged by some of the philosopher's statements (*Or.* 4.19, 26, 49, 61, 64).

[272] Them. *Or.* 1.9b (the philosopher as defective in his efforts to imitate God when compared to the ruler); 2.34b–c (the ruler as a true philosopher because he is a philosopher in action). In the same text, Themistius advances an idea of the ruler as 'nourishing himself and learning on his own' (αὐτοφυής ... καὶ αὐτοδίδακτος, 2.36a–b).

[273] *Reg.* 25.5–6.

[274] *Reg.* 29.2 (cf. also 29.4, on how Synesius' philosophical address was stimulated by god). Similar statements at *Reg.* 3.2; 5.3–4; 8.4–5; 9.3–4; 15.2.

At the turn of the fourth century, Synesius the envoy was living, working, and writing in the city of John Chrysostom, who saw *parrhesia* as a key weapon for challenging the political authority of philosophers coming from the traditional schools. As noted above, John claimed that distance from (Christian) truth fundamentally prevented his opponents from accessing the true instantiation of this philosophical virtue, making them weak and cowardly.[275] Synesius' self-image in *On Kingship* almost reads as a proud reply to these accusations. The question arises spontaneously: did Synesius know John?

The Philosopher and the High Priest: Allegory and Competition in Synesius' *On Providence*

No sources attest to encounters between Synesius and John, although Synesius does mention the bishop in one of his letters. The statement is sibylline: 'We cannot speak without respect now that he is no more; all enmity (δυσμένεια) ought to end with his life.'[276] We should be wary, however, of regarding this enmity as personal: the letter, written at the time of Synesius' episcopacy, is addressed to his patron Theophilus, the powerful patriarch of Alexandria. Theophilus had been one of John's most vocal and influential rivals and played a key role in securing his downfall and exile.[277] All we can extrapolate with any certainty from Synesius' letter is that John was known to him. Given the latter's fame, however, this hardly comes as a surprise. Something more might nevertheless be deduced from another Synesian text that, I suggest, bears witness both to John's political prominence and to the challenges it posed to philosophers ascribing their intellectual authority to *paideia*.

Towards the end of his sojourn in the capital, Synesius composed a piece known as *On Providence* (or *Egyptian Tale*).[278] This might be classified as a historical account, since it outlines the series of dramatic events that occurred in Constantinople in the years 399–400, from the coup led by the Gothic commander Gaïnas – the *magister militum* who allied with the chieftain Tribigild – to the exile of Synesius' patron Aurelian and the massacre of seven thousand Goths living in the capital. *On Providence* thinly disguises such events in the form of an Egyptian

---

[275] See p. 247–8.   [276] Synesius, *ep.* 67, l. 8–10.   [277] Favale (1958) 93–141.
[278] The date of the piece is debated. Book 1 was presumably composed after 12 July 400 (Cameron and Long [1993] 312–16; see also Lamoureux and Aujoulat [2008b] 4).

myth framed by the strife between two brothers and kings, the good Osiris (Aurelian's alter ego) and the mischievous Typhos.[279]

From a religious point of view, *On Providence* expresses distaste for Arianism. But it does so by pinning it to the ethnicity of its adherents, the Goths (who are referred to as 'Scythians', as was customary at the time).[280] The main villain, Typho, is said to 'have become a Scythian (ἐσκύθιζεν) even in his religious beliefs'.[281] This statement has been read as pointing to Synesius' adhesion to Nicene Christianity, although one might wonder if, in post-Theodosian Constantinople, criticism of Arianism represented a statement of personal allegiance in any way. At the same time, the piece never disguises Synesius' ambition to present himself as a special interlocutor of the divine. *On Providence* introduces the figure of a stern philosopher and poet. Left anonymous, the philosopher-poet is described as 'dignified, but nurtured by philosophy in a rather rustic manner' (ἐμβριθής ... ἀλλ'ὑπὸ φιλοσοφίας ἀγροικότερον ἐκτεθραμμένος), who composes on the lyre Doric hymns that he does not 'give to the public'.[282] Following the fall of Osiris, 'this man became even more rustic than before. It was then that he published, then that he revealed his compositions, horrifying every listener (πάντων φριττόντων τὴν ἀκοήν)'.[283] The philosopher is a thinly disguised representation of Synesius himself, devised for an audience acquainted with his poetic activity and, presumably, his efforts to cultivate a role as *parrhesiastes*.[284] Crucially, Synesius' alter ego is not just a philosopher but a prophet. *On Providence* stages his privileged access to the divine through a scene in which the philosopher, who has become the target of Typho's hostility, is visited by a god who encourages him. The god entrusts him with a prophecy on the destiny of the Egyptian kingdom, the meaning of which is revealed to the philosopher alone.[285]

---

[279] The alternative identification of Osiris with Arcadius (Hagl [1997] 145–51; cf. Lamoureux and Aujoulat [2008b] 5, 48–51) fails to convince. Arcadius was never exiled, and identifying him with Osiris would require that we recognise in his antagonist Typhos Arcadius' brother Honorius, although *On Providence* is unconcerned with Western events. Discussion of Typhos' identity in Liebeschuetz (1990) 253–72; Cameron and Long (1993) 175–82; Hagl (1997) 140–45; Lamoureux and Aujoulat (2008b) 48–51.
[280] The Arianism of the Goths was a consequence of their conversion to Christianity under Constantius II; cf. Heather and Matthews (1991) 124–32.
[281] *Prov.* 2.3. Cf. *Prov.* 1.18. Transl. Cameron and Long (1993).
[282] *Prov.* 1.18.1 οὐ μὴν ἐξέφερεν εἰς τὸ πλῆθος. On Synesius' elitist conception of philosophy, see Chapter 6, p. 285–91.
[283] *Prov.* 1.18.2.
[284] On the identification of the philosopher with Synesius, see Cameron and Long (1993) 374 n. 204.
[285] *Prov.* 1.18.5.

Another figure in *On Providence* appears to be connected – at least nominally – to the divine. This is the high priest (μέγας ἱερεύς) who features briefly in Book 2.[286] The high priest is portrayed as enjoying great social repute: the first city assembly (ἐκκλεσία in Greek) following the massacre of the Goths takes place in front of his house. Despite the acknowledgement of his prestige, however, the high priest is given little stage time. He only pronounces one line in reported speech, promising the return of Osiris and the exiles, 'if the gods grant it' (τῶν θεῶν διδόντων). Later in the text, an impersonal statement, ambiguous in its concision, adds that 'it was not right for him (i.e., the high priest) to put money before the ordinances of his father', a comment on Typhos' attempts to bribe him.[287]

Whether the high priest is to be identified with either Arcadius or John Chrysostom has long been debated, with most scholars preferring the latter.[288] Cameron and Long have tried to set aside efforts at identification by arguing that Synesius' high priest must be a 'stock character'.[289] They reject the hypothesis of the priest as John's alter ego on the ground that he promises the return of the exiles; but 'since the hostages were actually prisoners of Gaïnas, no one in Constantinople had the power to recall them'.[290] Two objections are available. The first is that the insertion of a stock character is inexplicable here: the priest serves no function in the development of the story, which his presence in fact slows down.[291] His intervention more likely derives its meaning from an allusion to a historical event. Second, we should take into consideration the political message sent by John's homily *Cum Saturninus et Aurelianus acti essent in exsilium*.[292] This text, which John Chrysostom delivered before his congregation, opens with an allusive description of John's mission to Gaïnas to request the liberation of the exiles. (If his journey had further diplomatic ends, they are not disclosed.)[293] In the homily, John seems especially concerned to assert his power. He calls himself 'the common father' of the

---

[286] *Prov.* 2.3.2.   [287] *Prov.* 2.3.4 τῷ δὲ οὐκ ἦν θέμις πρὸ τῶν πατρίων ἀργύριον τίθεσθαι.
[288] The emperor is identified with Arcadius (qua *pontifex maximus*) by Seeck (1894) 451; Fitzgerald (1930) 412; Lacombrade (1951a) 101–9. The identification with Chrysostom is preferred by Crawford (1901) 456; Nicolosi (1959) 75–76; Roques (1987); Liebeschuetz (1990) 110; Hagl (1997) 156–57; Lamoureux and Aujoulat (2008b) 51; Hoffmann (2012) 60.
[289] Cameron and Long (1993) 192.   [290] Cameron and Long (1993) 192.
[291] *Pace* their argument that 'with the old king dead and Osiris in exile, Synesius needed a force for good to oppose to Typhos' (Cameron and Long [1993] 192.).
[292] The title is arguably a label attached by a secretary (Cameron and Long [1993] 175).
[293] *PG* 52.413–20. See Kelly (1995) 153–56; Liebeschuetz (1990) 191–92.

congregation and styles himself a leader 'calming a storm ... guiding those who were sinking to a harbour and calm water'.[294]

I suggest that John's involvement in Constantinopolitan politics provides the key to unlocking the significance of the role of the high priest in *On Providence*. John's political commitment took the form in literature of a particular emphasis on the need for Christian philosophy to control the state and for an unprecedented degree of episcopal involvement in the daily life of the city (including administration and the founding of hospitals).[295] In summer 399, as the so-called Gothic crisis began to delineate itself, John seized an opportunity to press his ecclesiastical agenda by (temporarily) sheltering the once powerful *praepositus sacri cubiculi* Eutropius, condemned to death by Arcadius at the request of Gaïnas: he refused to hand Eutropius over to imperial officers and later preached to his congregation about the vanity and transience of earthly success with Eutropius clinging to his altar.[296] Not long afterwards (presumably in Spring 400),[297] he opposed – but the dynamics of the episodes are debated – the imperial concession that a Constantinopolitan church be used for the Arian services attended by Gothic soldiers.[298] According to Sozomen, this would have resulted in John confronting Gaïnas with a protest speech delivered before Arcadius. This event remains difficult to reconstruct, since it seems retrospectively aggrandizing and like a possible attempt to redeem John from accusations of ambiguous interactions with the Goths.[299] It is also the case that, in the same year, John was placed (by Arcadius?) at the head of the above-considered expedition entrusted with negotiating the liberation of Gaïnas' hostages (and arguably, as Liebeschuetz writes, with forging an agreement between the imperial and the Gothic parties).[300] He seems to have been considered the right figure

---

[294] PG 52.413. Transl. Liebeschuetz (1990) 192.
[295] On John's socio-political and cultural involvement, see, e.g., Kelly (1995) 115–80; Hartney (2004); Sandwell (2004), (2007) 185–212; Liebeschuetz (1990) 170–88, (2011) 185–204, 224–47.
[296] PG 52.391–96. On the episode, see Kelly (1995) 147–50; Liebeschuetz (1990) 104–8.
[297] Kelly (1995) 156–57.
[298] The Church historians report, with noticeable differences, an episode in which John admonished Gaïnas, possibly in the presence of Arcadius, against the cession of a Constantinopolitan church to the (Arian) Goths: Sozomen 8.4 (John admonishes Gaïnas but speaks boldly also to the emperor); Theodoret 5.32 (John gives stern advice to Arcadius and then attacks Gaïnas on behalf of the emperor). Cf. also Socrates 6.5 (mentioning only John's reproach of Gaïnas).
[299] Liebeschuetz (1990) 190, (2011) 229–30; Cameron and Long (1993) 235.
[300] Liebeschuetz (1990) 110, 192 (based on Theodoret, *HE* 5.33). On the episode, see also Kelly (1995) 153–56; John had an interest in missionary activities among the Goths living along the Danube, on which see Liebeschuetz (1990) 170, 190, (2011) 227; Kelly (1995) 142–44; Dolezal (2006).

to liaise with the Gothic general. The Gothic crisis Synesius describes in *On Providence* thus marked the culmination of John's assertion of his authority, since it put him on the front line on more than one occasion.

If the high priest of *On Providence* is identified with John Chrysostom at the peak of his influence, his implicit juxtaposition with Synesius' alter ego is ridden with significance. The high priest is the subject of an elliptical, allusive portrayal devoid of confrontational tones; it may be worth recalling that, when Synesius wrote *On Providence*, John had not yet fallen into disgrace. But compared with the rustic philosopher – a *parrhesiastes* who alone possesses true prophetic insight – the priest appears to be of modest stature. He makes unfulfilled promises. It is worth noting that the energetic tone of John's homily *Cum Saturninus et Aurelianus* seems to imply that his embassy succeeded. Historical reconstructions, however, show that the return of John to Constantinople did not coincide with the return of the hostages. When they were finally sent back, they also seemed to resent him.[301] Does Synesius' *On Providence* implicitly confront John with his failure? Furthermore, the brief, impersonal formula (οὐ θέμις) used to describe the high priest's response to Gaïnas' corrupting influence is not devoid of ambiguity, leaving it unclear whether the high priest was tempted by bribes and resisted them reluctantly. As Cameron and Long stress, some of Synesius' contemporaries seem to have perceived Chrysostom's role in the Gaïnas crisis as equivocal.[302]

Finally, the high priest never converses with the divine. The gods do not entrust him with the divine message, which is instead passed down to the rustic philosopher. The way Synesius' alter ego interacts with the gods thus displaces the relationship between the high priest and the sacred. The high priest is in the dark as to whether the gods will grant the return of the captives and can merely express his hopes. Only the rustic philosopher knows the meaning of the divine prophecy that communicates the destiny of the state: he is the exclusive interpreter of the divinely-ordained history of the kingdom of Egypt – which, outside of the fiction of *On Providence*, coincides with the history of the (Eastern) Empire.

Once the competitive nature of *On Providence* is appreciated, Synesius' concern with asserting his brand of philosophy as the primary space of interpretation of (sacred) history appears pressing. The piece does not merely put Synesius in the spotlight by describing his alter ego but strives

---

[301] Liebeschuetz (1990) 192, (2011) 227; Kelly (1995) 153–56; Tiersch (2002) 297–308. On the hostages' hostility to John, see further Cameron and Long (1993) 234–35.
[302] Cameron and Long (1993) 235.

to celebrate his intellectual identity and philosophical lineage. This celebration is achieved obliquely through the setting. Plutarch's *On Isis and Osiris* has sometimes been pointed to as the model used by Synesius to shape *On Providence*,[303] but this is both true and false. It is true insofar as Synesius himself wants his readers to know that he is familiar with Plutarch's work, which he occasionally echoes.[304] But the actual Plutarchean influence on *On Providence* is minimal. What we miss, if we look at Synesius' composition from an intertextual perspective, is his ambition to write the story of Osiris and Typhos as an Egyptian: not by birth but by (intellectual) adoption, as the disciple of Hypatia of Alexandria. 'This story is Egyptian. Egyptians are extraordinarily wise' is the opening line of *On Providence*.[305] The praise extends to Synesius: his audience would have known that everything he had learned came from Alexandria, a city he presents elsewhere as philosophy's capital, having fully replaced an Athens now living parasitically off its past.[306] Synesius is not the first Neoplatonist to use Egypt as a symbol. His gesture is made even more poignant by the fact that Porphyry's *Letter to Anebo* and Iamblichus' response, his *Reply of the Master to the Letter of Porpyhry to Anebo*, had already chosen to communicate their philosophy by ventriloquising Egyptian voices. This seems like an attempt to harvest Egypt's prestige as a land of ancient wisdom within a cultural environment obsessed with the question of cultural primacy.[307] The long speech Synesius' *On Providence* puts in the mouth of Osiris' father, a character introduced as simultaneously a 'king, priest, and philosopher',[308] is entirely Neoplatonic in content: Egyptian wisdom must culminate in Egyptian Platonism, from whose spring Synesius, the poet, prophet, and *parrhesiastes*, had drunk

Conclusions

The parable of Julian stimulated a contest of interpretation between Christians and adherents to Greco-Roman religion over the significance of his death in establishing which providence presided over the Roman Empire. Christian theologians invested in the quarrel – in particular Gregory of Nazianzus and John Chrysostom – explored readings of

---

[303] Liebeschuetz (1990) 114; Cameron and Long (1993) 256; Elm (1997) 101–2.
[304] Cf. Cameron and Long (1993) 261. Synesius echoes Plutarch's piece also in the *Praise of Baldness* (*Calv. Enc.* 7.6, cf. Plut., *Mor.* 352c–d).
[305] *Prov.* 1.1.1. [306] Synesius, *ep.* 136.
[307] On this, see Struck (2004) 206; Addey (2014) 127–70. [308] *Prov.* 1.5.1.

Julian's death as evidence that, together with his exegesis of history, disqualified his attempts to re-assert the subordination of priests to imperial authority. Julian's efforts to reform the 'pagan' clergy in fact suggest a precocious awareness of what might be labelled the paradox of Christian power: emperors choosing to seal their intellectual authority through claims to Christian knowledge had become, for the first time in Roman history, external to the hierarchies of their religion of choice.

From this initial paradox sprang a second: the emperor's exclusion from religious hierarchies coexisted with episcopal demands for intervention. These demands posited a simultaneous but irreconcilable request that the emperor help bishops control doctrinal interpretation (resulting in an unprecedented process of adaptation of theological knowledge to legislative channels) but leave all decision-making authority to the bishops. This joint demand was articulated with increasing assertiveness at a time when bishops were openly gaining socio-political prominence. The phenomenon accelerated their exploration of their public self-image, fostering the cultivation of an ideal of the bishop as a model philosopher-leader but at the same time a philosopher-adviser. The blurring of boundaries between these two figures of classical political theory enabled bishops to occupy the main roles mobilised in debates regarding the relationship between philosophy and power. Their self-positioning as philosopher-advisers, relying as it did on (expectations of) imperial endorsement, further enabled them to progressively displace philosophical advisors who lacked access to the Christian truth from politics.

In the passage from Themistius' generation to Synesius', the self-projection of philosophers grounding their intellectual authority on *paideia* seems to have responded to the episcopal challenge by becoming more competitive. This can be seen in Synesius' writings, which arguably testify to a perception of a loss of ground in the political arena. His *On Kingship* lends itself to being read as an aggressive revisitation of the traditional figure of the philosopher-adviser turning on a blunt performance of *parrhesia*, a category heavily mobilised in contemporary negotiations of intellectual authority. Synesius' *On Providence* (ca. 400) narrates contemporary history in a way that brings to centre-stage Synesius as the only authentic interpreter of the history of the Roman Empire, whose authority he derives from the Platonic tradition.

CHAPTER 6

Wisdom for the Many, and Wisdom for the Few

How did the late Roman world envisage the relationship between philosophy as a self-legitimising tool and the culture that ascribed it this legitimising force? This book has argued that Constantine's grafting of Christianity onto Roman power relied on an intuition that Christianity should be asserted as the culmination of *paideia* rather than its subversion. The Christianisation of the paradigm of philosopher-ruler proclaimed the 'religion of the simple' as capable of both inhabiting imperial structures of power and confronting the cultural capital of Greco-Roman elites.

The ideas that fed Constantine's self-image, however, developed within an environment – early Christianity – that simultaneously cultivated an ideal of universal accessibility and relied on it heavily in its efforts to mobilise consensus among the empire's populations. Bishops pressing an image of Christianity as 'wisdom for the many' did so in rivalry with the elitist demands of Platonism. As a result, they experienced various degrees of conflict with their own rhetoric insofar as most of them came out of the traditional classroom and shared its elitist values.

This final chapter explores the other side of the coin of the project of assertion of Christian religion as perfect knowledge: how did fourth-century Christianity handle the relationship of the ill-educated to theology? I argue that a history of criticism of Christianity's appeal to the many, which Julian tried to revive as his final argument against it, illuminates the socio-cultural tensions surrounding the status of the new religion in the post-Constantinian empire. Moreover, I suggest that this debate over philosophical accessibility had two outcomes. First, it ironically facilitated the unintentional self-displacement of non-Christian philosophers from the political scene. Second, it generated the final paradox shaping the history of the early Christian mobilisation of culture for self-legitimisation. The political rise of counter-cultural Christianity in fact produced forms of upper-class and hegemonic rejection of the type of cultured Christianity

Julian the Satirist: The Philosopher and the Crowd

Julian's literary output ends in a bang and a whimper. In his final piece, which responds to mocking addresses targeting his beard, the tone goes from jocular to plaintive, culminating in a lament over the Antiochenes' failure to acknowledge his governmental skills.[1] But the *Misopogon* remains explosive material. Past Roman emperors had been the target of satires, a macroscopic example being Claudius in the *Apocolocyntosis*. But they had never composed one, let alone a parody of themselves. This raises a question: why would Julian, the most powerful man in the empire, engage with a blend of oblique speech (irony regarding his beard as a vehicle for more pointed criticism targeting the Antiochenes) and open accusations, producing a literary piece that seemingly echoes forms of communication historically employed by political and cultural dissidents?

One explanation for Julian's choice of what would turn out to be his final literary register is easily available, since he himself points to it. Julian implies that he is engaging in a form of enlightened retribution. His exploration of what is properly *spoudaiogeloion* echoes Cynic models (the fictitious diatribe, the insistence on bodily functions), presumably offering Julian's personal take on that philosophical school, which he had recently sought to re-organise.[2] His engagement with *spoudaiogeloion* claims a place within his attempts to diversify his imperial profile from that of Constantius, since it continues to communicate Julian's preference for dialectic confrontation over coercion. The *Misopogon* sends the message that its author has chosen critical but educational words over violence.[3] What is more, by conveying such words – at least initially – through irony and jesting, Julian proves again the subtle interpreter of the cultural history in which he sought to write his legacy. The fourth century had behind it a long tradition of Greek and Roman reflection on the ability of laughter to define hierarchies.[4] The concern of Greek philosophers with the social

---

[1] Cf. *Mis.* 370c-1c.
[2] On Julian and *spoudaiogeloion*, see Chapter 4, n. 77. On the problem of the genre of the *Misopogon* and the relationship with Cynic diatribe, see Marcone (1984); De Vita (2022) ccxxxii. Julian as a theorist of Cynicism: see Chapter 3, p. 163–4.
[3] Comparison with Julian's treatment of the unruly senator Nilus in Niccolai (2017b).
[4] See especially Richlin (1983); Goldhill (1995) 14–20; Corbeill (1996); Agosti (2001); Halliwell (2008); Beard (2014).

anxieties laughter both feeds on and generates, translated in a post-Hellenistic environment into an expectation that the wise ruler would be able to engage in benevolent jesting. As Beard shows, Rome perceived tyranny as strongly associated with cruel entertainment at the expense of its subjects.[5] Conversely, the good sovereign was expected to know how to tolerate a wisecrack. In advising Emperor Theodosius about how to behave after the Antiochene Riot of the Statues of 387, Libanius eloquently put forward, as an *exemplum* of imperial tolerance, how Constantine once reacted to scoffing remarks by considering that 'it was proper for rulers to put up (ἀνέχεσθαι) with such skittishness (τοιούτων σκιρτημάτων)'.[6] Strikingly, in reminding Theodosius of this episode, Libanius also mentions – clearly assuming it was well known – Julian's ambition to achieve fame in the same way.[7]

Libanius' comment illuminates Julian's efforts to outdo his predecessor(s). The fact that Julian did not merely tolerate derision, however, but sent it back to the sender, inevitably sets the *Misopogon* apart from Constantine's response. Julian blends a message of superiority with an oppositional attitude that rises in tone as the text unfolds. This search for confrontation invites further reflection. As Chapter 4 argued, a joint reading of the *Misopogon* and the *Caesars* shows that these texts seek to challenge Christianity as an interpretive system. The challenge is pursued in two ways: by focusing on the emperor's hermeneutical profile as what proves – or disavows – the intellectual authority of his religion of choice and (in the *Misopogon*) by demonstrating Christianity's interpretive failure as epitomised by the inability of the Christian Antiochenes to read Julian's appearance.[8] The *Misopogon* thus presents Julian as simultaneously an emperor choosing words over violence and an individual voice confronting a challenging adversary, which we are invited to recognise in Christianity. The meaning of the piece is sealed by the image of the philosopher Julian facing the ignorant Antiochenes, whose illusion of understanding is fed by a deceptive religion.

To project his voice as antagonistic, Julian must implicitly acknowledge that what he is facing is in some form a hegemonic discourse. His self-projection as the solitary philosopher confronting the uneducated crowd does exactly that: it points to mass adhesion as explaining Christianity's new hegemony. Julian's *Misopogon*, in other words, is profoundly committed to the Platonising dichotomy of true philosophy, which speaks to a

---

[5] Beard (2004) 128–55.   [6] Libanius, *Or.* 19.19.   [7] Libanius, *Or.* 19.19.
[8] See Chapter 4, p. 179–204.

few wise auditors, versus sophistry and false knowledge, which flatter the unsubstantiated ambition of the many to control meaning. Julian qualifies Christianity as matching the latter's definition by pointing to how it derives its strength from numbers. He represents Christianity as a majority cult that feeds a collective delusion, making the many believe that their ignorance is wisdom. It comes as no surprise, therefore, that true philosophers are outnumbered. Even the emperor – who counts among them – is put in a corner, from which his reply must sound like an act of subversion.

The image of a solitary Julian facing the Christian many is more than a complaint: I see it as his last and most sophisticated strategy to challenge Christianity as an interpretive system. In fact, Julian's polemical vein re-opens the question of how the identity and validity of a philosophy are revealed by the type of practitioners it attracts. The Platonising dichotomy he activates – philosophy versus false knowledge (or sophistry) – resonated profoundly with his educated readers, for the imperial rhetoric flourishing in and since the Second Sophistic had crystallised it in its efforts to mobilise philosophy for socio-political self-assertion.[9] At the same time, the post-Hellenistic schools of philosophy – especially Platonism – cultivated within their circles the idea that knowledge is the preserve of the few. The ideal of perfection of the soul as achievable only through a life-long process of self-purification suggested that only highly cultivated individuals could access the divine message in an unmediated form. The open circulation of philosophical truths was regarded as dangerous and impious, since it exposed them to incomprehending audiences. Unmediated disclosure was an act of debasement, entailing a loss of philosophical status.[10] Porphyry eloquently writes that the philosopher must 'leave the sleepers lying in their own bed' to avoid catching their disease.[11] It is against this background that one must locate the interest of post-Hellenistic philosophers in myths, intended as the narrative form that allows one to pass on superior messages to those Julian in the *Against Heraclius* defines as 'childish souls'.[12]

Julian's investment in mythmaking claims its place in this context of elaboration of what the wise knows the unwise does not know and of how the former is supposed to educate the latter. Platonist divisions between the initiated and the profane were accompanied by a sense that the philosopher was responsible for the moral and spiritual improvement of

---

[9] See the Introduction, p. 2–3. [10] Addey (2014) 50–54.
[11] Porph. *Abst.* I 28.2, transl. Clark (2000b). [12] *C. Her.* 206d.

the collective (thus O'Meara).[13] This idea was fully compatible with the expectation that, in mediating knowledge, the philosopher would protect its divine kernel: Julian's myths are the other face of the coin of his hymnic appeals to maintain the silence that befits mysteries.[14] The same Porphyry who urged leaving 'sleepers lying in their bed', and whose writings often reveal a lack of concern with needs perceived as popular (including civic obligations), conceived of his teaching as helping pupils to progress beyond common thinking.[15] His *Philosophy from Oracles* starts from the assumption that the gods are protective of their messages, which they deliver 'through enigmas',[16] so that only those who 'arranged their plan of life with a view to the salvation of the soul' could interpret them correctly.[17] It is ironic that his concern for pedagogy and the systematising of knowledge has led past scholarship to see him as a populariser.[18]

Julian's religious reform betrays an ambition to devise strategies to guide the uninitiated without disturbing the hierarchies of knowledge or of knowers. His solutions range from the engagement with mythmaking mentioned above to supporting rites and cultic practices (e.g., blood sacrifice) and the use of icons.[19] His attempt arguably aligns with – and inspired? – the work by 'Saloustious' (who may be identical with Saturninus Secundus Salutius).[20] Saloustious' *On the Gods and Universe* articulates a project of philosophical mediation, offering a summary of theology intended 'for those who neither can be steeped in philosophy nor are incurably diseased in soul'.[21] It is repeatedly referred to as a 'pagan catechism'.[22]

The *Misopogon*'s address to the Christian Antiochenes should thus be conceptualised as among Julian's didactic efforts to target the many. By choosing to talk (tough) to the people of Antioch, Julian reinforced his identity as an educator. It is significant in this respect that he drew on a

---

[13] O'Meara (2005).
[14] See, e.g., at *Hel.* 148a; *Mat.* 159a; 169a; 172d–73a; *C. Her.* 217d–18a. On Julian's sense of the need for the philosopher to distance himself from the many, see *Cyn.* 193d; 196d; 197b–d; 198b; *Ep. Fragm.* (= 89b Bidez-Cumont) 290a–b.
[15] Johnson (2013) 102–85. [16] Porphyry, fr. 305 Smith. [17] Porphyry, fr. 304 Smith.
[18] For a scholarly overview and correction of this interpretation, see Johnson (2013) 147.
[19] Julian's reflection on the worship of images, temples, and altars is in *Ep. Fragm.* (= 89b Bidez-Cumont) 293a–95b, 296b. Commitment to acts of public devotion is reported in inscriptions celebrating him as *restitutor sacrorum* (Conti [2014]). On the pragmatics of Julian's cult, see De Vita (2017b), (2022) ccxcii–ccxcv; Marcone (2019) 60–61, 199–206.
[20] See Chapter 2, n. 114.
[21] Sallustius, *De diis* 14 (transl. Nock). See Fowden (1979) 237; Clarke (1998); Tougher (2020b) 81; De Vita (2022) ccxxcii–ccxcv.
[22] Definition by Rochefort (1956) 52.

philosophical model – Cynicism – which his oration *To the uneducated Cynics* presents as, in its noblest version, properly appealing to the simple.[23] But the *Misopogon* simultaneously conveys another message that his educated readers would not have failed to acknowledge. It communicates the impossibility of Christianity inhabiting the halls of power. If the first half of the fourth century had seen theologians and emperors claim Christianity's suitability to be in the imperial court and speak the language of the elite, Julian's *reductio* of Christianity to its mass audience denies this possibility altogether. Instead, it reinforces the reputation upper-class Christianity had long been striving to eschew, that of being an irrational cult appealing to the uneducated. Second – and most subtly – Julian spoke to the anxieties of contemporary Christian theologians. His *Misopogon* stands as a reminder of the dangers of the universalising language that bishops, for reasons I consider below, simultaneously cultivated and feared.

Early Christian Leaders between Universalism and Elitism: Gregory's Response to Julian

'Among us', Eusebius writes in the *General Elementary Introduction*, 'is a crowd (πλῆθος) of those who entirely lack a formal education (παντελῶς ἰδιωτῶν), exhibiting a virtuous, philosophic way of life (ἐμφιλόσοφον πολιτείαν) which one cannot easily find even among those trained in philology and boasting in their care for books'.[24] This is one of many examples of the praise of the simple that permeates the rhetoric of fourth-century bishops. The language is intrinsically competitive. The homilies of John Chrysostom are full of praise for the farmers and monks who understand the divine better than traditional philosophers.[25] Augustine famously remarked that Porphyry had worked hard to acquaint himself with demonology, which any old Christian woman (*quaelibet anicula Christiana*) would instantly know and detest.[26] It is fundamentally important that all these authors appealing to the wisdom of the uncultured had one trait in common: an upper-class education. As Brown saw, this is the paradox of early Christian rhetoric: the men who find evidence of Christianity's power in the miraculous spread of the preaching of humble men without *paideia* were the same ones who had enjoyed a life-long access to *paideia*.[27] An example of this is the way reflection on myth and

---

[23] Marcone (2012) 241–44.
[24] Euseb. *GEI* (= *Eclog. Prophet.*) p. 141 Gaisford (1842). Transl. Johnson (2014) 58.
[25] See p. 282–84 below.   [26] August. *Civ. D.* 10.11.   [27] Brown (1992) 75–76.

exegesis characterising the engagement of the Greco-Roman philosophers with divine mysteries found an exact counterpart in early Christian cultural debates. If both sides could be in dialogue – and rivalry – over allegory and share complementary aims and methodologies, this is because Christian theologians too cultivated the idea that their audiences possessed different degrees of intellectual understanding.[28]

In the fourth and fifth centuries, the largest recruiting ground for the episcopate was the curial class. It was an 'open secret' (thus Brown) that many Christian bishops owed much of their social prestige to the fact that they had once been rhetors.[29] This same access to rhetoric facilitated their efforts to chain doctrinal disputes to imperial legal discourse.[30] Without Eusebius' habit of incorporating all the classical texts he aimed to target in his writings, works like Porphyry's *Philosophy from Oracles* would today be lost. John Chrysostom, the lover of the poor, was in his youth a pupil of Libanius (perhaps his best one, if we are to believe Sozomen's claim that Libanius would have appointed John his successor, 'had not the Christians taken him over').[31] Augustine's celebration of the old Christian lady over Porphyry must be read against the background of his expressions of distaste, as a young scholar of rhetoric, for the poverty of the Gospels' language.[32]

These authors' appeals to the many and the simple lived off the interaction between ideology and expediency and should not be reduced to either. A belief in the Christian message as truth that could even emerge from the *sermo piscatorius* certainly structured the bishops' understanding of what they perceived as the uniqueness of their religion. At the same time, socio-political developments – the growth of the authority of the Church in the public sphere – developed jointly with the preachers' capacity to secure their status by connecting with large audiences. As bishops became aware of how much political power could be accrued from mobilising the masses (cf. the Arian dispute),[33] they also discovered that universal rhetoric gave them leverage over the traditional philosophers and members of the upper class who were their interlocutors and rivals. Peter Brown's *Power and Persuasion* illuminates the significance and impact of what could be labelled the late antique 'invention' of the poor as a

---

[28] Cf. e.g. the arguments supporting the necessity to diversify the communication of divine truths in Origen, *C. Cels.* 1.18; 1.27; 3.52. On similar statements in Justin Martyr, Irenaeus of Lyon, and Eusebius, see Harl (1982) 337, 343-50. See also Kahlos (2012) 536.
[29] Brown (1992) 75. [30] Humfress (2007). [31] Sozomen, *HE* 8.2.
[32] August. *Conf.* 3.5.9.
[33] Haas (1997) 245–77; Kelly (2007); Galvão Sobrinho (2013); Cooper (2019).

significant socio-political category.[34] Patronage of the urban crowd, now visible everywhere in the bishops' preaching and writing, was key to outflanking traditional social aristocracy.

But the in-betweenness of Christian intellectuals equally indebted to *paideia* and the urban poor left its traces. Episcopal writings are interspersed with expressions of contempt for the many, a sign of the resilience of the authors' educational background. Their criticism variously targets the ignorance of the 'most unreasoning people', the 'a-philosophical crowd', and 'the ways of the multitude' that 'reviles philosophy'.[35] Even the Mosaic paradigm, which I have treated as instrumental in shaping the bishop as philosopher-ruler, implicitly re-asserts an elitist agenda: Moses is repeatedly celebrated in episcopal writings due to his solitary penetration of the divine mysteries. He possessed exclusive access to divine law.[36]

The Cappadocians, as highly educated advocates of Neo-Nicene Christianity, effectively exemplify this tension. In a famous passage, Gregory of Nyssa mocks 'old-clothes men, money changers, food sellers ... all busy arguing. If you ask someone to give you change, he philosophizes about the Begotten and the Unbegotten'.[37] The examples he provides to ground his claim (the baker says that 'the Son is inferior', the bath attendant that 'the Son was made out of nothing') seem, incidentally, to ascribe to the simple a subordinationist position on Christological matters – something I see as another oblique layer of judgement, if we consider that this parody comes from the pen of a Nicene theologian. Gregory of Nazianzus' argument that 'discussion of theology is not for everyone ... it is not for all people, but only for those who have been tested and have found a sound footing in study',[38] contrasts with his appeals to the wisdom of simple Christians, to which I return shortly.

Even the leadership of John Chrysostom, the advocate of the urban poor, lived off this contradiction: his celebration of the simple occasionally incorporates expressions of contempt for the crowd, with which John, however, cleverly equates the masses who are ignorant of Christ, thus facilitating a divorce of spiritual ignorance from lack of (worldly) culture.[39]

---

[34] Brown (1992) 71–117; Clark (2004) 109.
[35] See, e.g., Euseb. *PE* 2.8.12; 5.33.11–12; 12.1.1. Clement of Alexandria, being convinced that Greek philosophy prepares for Christianity, implies at times that a limited education will result in a superficial understanding of catechesis (*Strom.* 6.15.119.1, cf. Eshleman [2012] 108).
[36] Sterk (1998) 232–41.
[37] Greg. Nyss. *PG* 46.557 (*On the deity of the Son and of the Holy Spirit*), transl. Ware (1963).
[38] Greg. Naz. *Or.* 27.3, transl. Williams (2002).
[39] See, e.g., Jo. Chrys. *Sac.* 3.11.29–38 (*SC* 272.190), 5.8.12–27 (*SC* 272.298–300).

But the ambiguity was never fully erased. This is captured in the way John's disciple Palladius has one of the characters of his *Dialogue on the Life of John Chrysostom* comment regarding the person who betrayed John to state authorities. 'And who else could have found fault with John's philosophy than a tanner (βυρσοδέψου)', one of the characters exclaims, 'who takes the stench of his workshop everywhere with him?'[40] This brutal line exposes, casually yet effectively, the tension between the urban poor and the upper-class clergymen who legitimised their authority by playing the part of lovers of the needy.

It is in the context of the fourth-century 'catholic' turn (as Williams puts it),[41] and its competitive and authoritative bend, that one sees a growth in both the activation of episcopal ecumenical rhetoric and its inner tensions. As Chapter 5 argued, post-Nicene Christological disputes, with their search for clear-cut formulations of divine truths, sought to provide a benchmark for orthodoxy that was available to imperial politics as well as to all the faithful. Christianity's effort to seek definitions was therefore not extraneous to a logic of universalism, since it helped provide exact theological knowledge to people from all social levels. Arius' development of his theological position, despite epitomising in many respects the intellectual legacy of Origen (thus Williams),[42] was eloquently asserted via an innovative project of interaction with ordinary people. Famously, Arius sought to turn his followers into teachers of doctrine by condensing his Christology into slogans. He used music to instruct the faithful, turning doctrinal formulations into songs that could be learned by heart and passed on even by humble people. He is reported to have composed ballads for sailors and muleteers – an anecdote that, if taken at face value, serves as a further indication of his ambition to broadcast his message.[43] Another source reports that Arius' efforts to involve the population in his preaching were criticised by fellow Christians: Constantine himself is supposed to have complained that Arius had taken divine truths to popular assemblies.[44]

This complex interplay of exploitation, distaste, and commitment that characterised the relationship of fourth-century theologians to their crowds suggests that they were likely unsettled by Julian's attempt to disqualify their religion by attacking their rhetoric of universal accessibility. Once

---

[40] Palladius, *Dial.* 19 (p. 125 Meyer). Transl. Meyer. [41] Williams (2001) 87–91.
[42] Williams (2001) 84–85.
[43] Galvão-Sobrinho (2013) 71–84. West (1982) argues that Arius' use of a metre associated with salacious entertainment, the Sotadean, also points to his efforts to appeal to a broad public.
[44] Galvão-Sobrinho (2013) 67.

more, we can turn to Gregory of Nazianzus – and his literary response(s) to Julian – to confirm this hypothesis. As Chapter 5 noted, his anti-Julianic diptych (*Or.* 4 and 5) targeting the emperor after his death betrays a deep awareness of the main strategies Julian devised to destabilise Christianity, from his challenge to its hermeneutical validity to his reading of Church-State power dynamics.[45] Julian's polemics with Christianity as the religion of the many, and the idea that this disqualified it from being identified as a philosophy, are also – unsurprisingly – addressed in Gregory's reply. The point is never acknowledged explicitly, but *Or.* 4, Gregory's response to Julian's School Ban, is a manifesto of (Christian) elitism. At the same time, it is also an attempt to outline a project of legitimisation of Christian elitism that might work in synergy with a universalising rhetoric and combine the two into an argument asserting the ideality of episcopal leadership. Julian's downfall is key to Gregory's picture. The grand argument of Julian's interpretive failure (on which, see Chapter 5) is here used to argue that the emperor's inability to understand must result in an inability to communicate – an irredeemable fault in a universal ruler.

Gregory begins his argument in a way that intriguingly testifies to his – and his colleagues' – difficulty in managing their own universalising rhetoric. His outraged commentary on the School Ban obliquely reveals his desire to reinstate his superior social position through the very act of professing distaste for aristocratic privileges:

> He (i.e., Julian) debarred us from the use of words as though we were stealing other people's goods ... fancied he should escape our notice, not in his attempt to rob us of a benefit of the first class (ἀγαθοῦ τινος τῶν πρώτων) – we who so utterly despise these mere words (οἵ γε καὶ σφόδρα τούτους περιφρονοῦμεν τοὺς λόγους) – but in his apprehension of our refutation of his impious doctrine.[46]

The comment Gregory hastens to add to his definition of *paideia* as a first-class benefit ('we who so utterly despise these mere words') is a red flag.[47] One might call the remark an *excusatio non petita* or, to draw on political vocabulary, a form of *recusatio*, since it justifies Gregory's possession of what he claims he does not desire. The good Christian leader is unquestionably the one who does not like the idea of belonging to a class that has exclusive access to specific goods.

Having indignantly rejected the notion of 'first class', *Or.* 4 moves on to posit an opposition. The first term of comparison is the history of Greek

---

[45] See Chapter 5, p. 215–17. [46] Greg. Naz. *Or.* 4.5. [47] Similarly at *Or.* 4.61.

philosophy. In Greece, only a few famous individuals such as Solon, Socrates, and Plato could become truly proficient in philosophy; they also, however, cultivated an immoral lifestyle together with their philosophy.[48] The second term of comparison is the army of 'those many in a lower station (τῶν κάτω), significant only through number (ἀριθμῷ μόνῳ γνωριζομένων)'.[49] These people, despite their simplicity, 'rebuffed' Julian's attack (i.e., on their purity) like 'some well-built wall'. They are the Christian faithful. The universalising implication is that these 'thousands and tens of thousands' (χιλιάδας καὶ μυριάδας) had access to philosophy through Christianity, regardless of their education. (Here it might also be worth asking what sense of proximity Gregory felt with those he describes as 'significant only through number'). Gregory groups together the low-born (τῶν ἀγεννῶν) and rich aristocrats, those 'once of high rank and distinguished for opulence, birth, and station',[50] who overcame the limits of traditional education to understand that true philosophy starts from the *imitatio Christi*. This principle is what renders Christian truth available to everyone, both the simple and the aristocrats, who must, ironically, achieve simplicity.

Gregory ties this argument to his refutation of Julian's understanding of philosophy via another act of interpretation of the Apostate.[51] This time the subject of scrutiny is Julian's understanding of the bond tying salvation to communication. Julian's School Ban betrayed his failure to comprehend that a classroom cannot offer the truth but only tools that can be used to express the truth. Since Julian identified salvation with culture, however, and merit with education, he looked at his universal empire from a partial perspective, his blind spot being the many who lacked access to learning. Julian had no means to communicate with them and therefore condemned everyone who was unable to follow a code of rules strictly designed for the educated to misery. Gregory substantiates this point through an anecdote. He reports an episode in which Julian supposedly tricked his army into sacrificing to the gods. On the day of the imperial distribution of gifts, he ordered them to throw some incense in a brazier. When he did so, however, he did not inform them that they were making an offering to Jupiter – the gesture that, under Diocletian, served as the test of conformity to Greco-Roman religion.[52]

---

[48] *Or.* 4.72.   [49] *Or.* 4.65.
[50] *Or.* 4.73 (τῶν λίαν ὑψηλῶν ποτε καὶ λαμπρῶν, καὶ περιουσίᾳ, καὶ γένει, καὶ δυναστείᾳ).
[51] On Gregory as Julian's interpreter, see Chapter 5, p. 214–9.
[52] *Or.* 4.82–83. Gregory's accusations might have been rooted in an Antiochene perception that Julian was bad at communicating with his subjects. Cf. Van Nuffelen and Van Hoof (2011).

I leave aside the question of the historicity of this episode. What is of interest is that, despite Gregory's claims that Julian was concerned to communicate only with the educated, his argument obliquely acknowledges – and challenges – Julian's attempt to involve his subjects through targeted forms of collective participation (in this case sacrifices). Gregory thus competes via erasure, misrepresentation, or both. To Julian's project of hierarchical but nevertheless ecumenical involvement, he opposes his own – hierarchical and ecumenical – proposal. His argument ultimately reads as a political translation of the principle of different forms of signification conveyed by different levels of allegory:

> Now if it were possible for all to be very good and attain the extreme point of virtue, this certainly would be best and most perfect.... What is the meaning of you prescribing rules that are not meant for all and then punishing those who do not keep them? It would be as if those not deserving of capital punishment were on this ground deserving of commendation; or as if those not worthy of commendation deserved, accordingly, capital punishment. On the contrary, the right thing is to demand from us correctness of conduct within the limits of our own philosophy and of human capability.[53]

An aristocrat is speaking, drawing on his cultural superiority to argue that valid leadership is generated precisely from the encounter between this superiority and Christian ideals. Gregory's proposal for a 'dual ethics' (as it tends to be labelled) was not his invention: Eusebius of Caesarea in particular had already argued that there were two lawful modes of life in the Church, one for the educated, another for the people.[54] But Gregory's celebration of what could be defined as a form of systemic flexibility re-functionalises Julian's attack on Christianity's identity-threatening compromise, presenting it as in fact a source of political strength. The universal accessibility of Christianity enables everyone to achieve the status of intelligent addressee. Every convert or believer can rely on the fundamental principle of understanding coinciding with their precise religious allegiance. Within this shared system of knowledge, however, the difference between leaders and subjects is that leaders also have a capacity to organise knowledge to the benefit of their subjects, thus helping them to achieve spiritual salvation. Gregory's fundamental point is that a genuine didactic project can take place only within a philosophical system in which leaders accept that the many have their way to access wisdom.

---

[53] *Or.* 4.99 (transl. from King, slightly modified).
[54] Euseb. *DE* 1.8. On the notion of 'dual ethics' in early Christianity, see Baynes (1955) 26; Elm (2012) 167.

Christianity's engagement with a form of dual but genuine communication is projected against what Gregory defines as Julian's duplicity. *Or.* 4 reframes Julian's interaction with his subjects as an effort that does not create the possibility of educational communication but only an illusion of interaction. This is blamed on the rigidity of the traditional cultural system: those who believe that there is only one philosophy – the one learned in school – must make ethical demands that are unattainable for most people. A leader relying on this paradigm is left to coerce or manipulate his subjects, since he has no other means of communicating with them. Gregory rounds off his argument by claiming that the obscurity and deceit in which the many are bound to live within paganism is necessarily bound to degenerate into instability. In the absence of a genuine didactic project, people are driven towards irrationality and violence. 'What has ever happened to your party from the Christians of the sort that often happened to the Christians from your party? Against whom have we stirred up furious mobs? (Τίσι δήμους ἐπανεστήσαμεν ζέοντας;)',[55] Gregory asks Julian – implicitly noting once more his understanding of his place at the top of the social pyramid. The aim of his response is not merely to re-assert Christianity as the only valid philosophy. More specifically, Gregory wants Christianity to be recognised as the only philosophy valid for rulers. His 'we' refers to a new generation of Christian leaders, whose capacity to communicate to the many is presented as the fundamental political quality establishing the superiority of the Christian educated few over the pagan educated few. It is through this simultaneous acknowledgement of an elevated position while promoting ideas of communication and education – denied to his rival – that Gregory turns Julian's final argument against Christianity into an argument against Julian. He exploits Julian's question of access to develop a challenge mirroring the one launched by the Apostate: how can a philosophy that speaks only to the few fulfil the fundamental duty of the philosopher-ruler – the spiritual elevation of the community – if it condemns most people to live as part of a mob?

Essence, and Everything Else: The rise of Counter-cultural Christian Leadership

After Julian's death, two ways opened up for Christian philosophy to challenge his re-assertion of the bond tying *paideia* to the Greco-Roman divine. One was Gregory's: to deny validity to such connections all together, using Julian's failure as proof of his misunderstanding of both

[55] *Or.* 4.98.

culture and the divine.[56] On Gregory's side of the debate were other upper-class theologians attached to the educational system within which they had been raised; consider, for instance, Basil of Caesarea's *Address to Young Men on the Right Use of Greek Literature*. These theologians remained alive to the importance of Christianity's cultural self-projection in the space of the court and among the elite – the same principle that, as I have shown, secured Christianity's claims to leadership under and after Constantine.

An alternative possibility was explored within Christian asceticism – or essentialism – and in a sense derived its strength from its agreement with Julian. Christian ascetics too believed that God should be kept separate from 'pagan' literature. If Julian could ask what type of philosophy is the philosophy that everybody can access, the counter-question raised by Christian ascetics could be summarised as follows: what type of philosophy dilutes its engagement with the ultimate truth(s) with cultural manifestations that do not generate salvation? Essentialism turned the old philosophy-sophistry dichotomy on its head by arguing that Greco-Roman culture, being mostly a distraction from the divine, catered to non-philosophers, since it led away from the pursuit of true knowledge. Genuine philosophy was therefore to be found outside the philosophical classroom and traditional education. Within this framework, *paideia* was at best redundant, at worst misleading.

It should be stressed that this approach to Greco-Roman culture always existed in some form in early Christian thinking (for example, Tertullian). But now it could rely on two new sources of support. The first was ideological: for those able to identify – with Julian – Greek culture and polytheism, the Apostate's downfall served to disprove the providential insight offered by *paideia* and the capacity of Greek philosophers to be of use in the management of the state.[57] The second was socio-political. The rise of Christian leadership in the cities noted above, the mobilisation of the urban masses through the activation of charitable projects, and universalising rhetoric progressively encouraged the cultivation of a style of episcopal leadership that derived its strength from a bond with the lower classes. This was made especially evident by the rise of charismatic asceticism, which offered the monk as a symbol of perfect purity and the highest instantiation of the (Christian) philosophical life. Sterk and Rapp have shown that the late fourth century saw many episcopal voices appropriate monastic charisma, borrowing ascetic features to communicate

[56] See Chapter 5, p. 214–9. [57] See Chapter 5.

the perfection of their spiritual life.⁵⁸ Perhaps unsurprisingly, the Cappadocians were very receptive to this development (as well). Their commitment to monasticism arose from their efforts to identify a purified, normative episcopal ideal within their projects of competitive self-assertion. Beyond any doubt, ascetic ideals permeating Greek philosophy (see Cynicism) were in the background of their thinking. The Cappadocians' projection of the ideal spiritual guide as an ideal philosopher (and leader), which I considered in Chapter 5,⁵⁹ was thus concomitant with their efforts to valorise the ascetic component structuring philosophical life.

But the cultivated Cappadocians represent figures at the intersection of two discourses: monastic idealisation, on the one hand, and attachment to traditional cultural capital, on the other. In fact, asceticism could and would be explored especially within a counter-cultural framework whose agenda was driven by an ambition to challenge traditional education and, by so doing, connect with the larger populace. The rise to fame of Anthony the Great, the desert father, exemplifies this phenomenon. Anthony lived between the third and the fourth centuries (he died ca. 356) but only became a literary phenomenon following the composition of his *Life* around 360. Its author – Athanasius of Alexandria – was another key protagonist in the joint processes of negotiation of episcopal versus imperial authority, and of Nicene vs. Arian Christianity. As Chapter 5 noted, the *Life of Anthony* is explicitly concerned with projecting a symbolic representation of the Christian holy man as above the emperors, whose letters leave Anthony indifferent.⁶⁰

Anthony, Athanasius' hero (and alter ego; Athanasius was from a humble background, and his local leadership stemmed from the support of the people of Alexandria and rural Egyptian monks) lives and speaks in the *Life* as a manifesto of counter-cultural Christianity. He uncompromisingly disavows *paideia*.⁶¹ The superiority of his knowledge, which he derives from God alone (and the Bible), is asserted through an eloquent scene in which Anthony refutes 'men who were deemed wise among the Greeks' one by one.⁶² He has a series of exchanges with pagan philosophers and exposes their fallacious assumptions in regard to the nature of God, the soul, and the mind. Eventually, the philosophers themselves are

---

⁵⁸ Sterk (2004); Rapp (2005) 137–52.   ⁵⁹ See p. 214–26, 36–43.   ⁶⁰ Athanasius, *V. Ant.* 81.
⁶¹ Cultural (and political) competition in the *Life of Anthony*: Brakke (1995) 201–65; Rubenson (2000) 115–19; Urbano (2013) 207–28; Cartwright (2016).
⁶² Learning from God alone: *Vit. Ant.* 20. Men 'deemed wise among the Greeks': *V. Ant.* 74.

described as acknowledging their defeat with astonishment.[63] By defeating the Hellenists with his essential wisdom, Athanasius' Anthony takes a position against what they represent but also within the Christian cultural debate. The *Life* does not put forward as a perfect philosopher an intellectual à la Gregory of Nazianzus, who projects himself as dominating through Christianity a traditional culture he nevertheless possesses. Instead, it extols the illiterate monk whose wisdom lies in trumping the illusion that culture has any value for knowledge. The normative – and artificial – quality of Athanasius' argument is revealed by comparison of the *Life of Anthony* with the letters ascribed to the historical desert father. As Rubenson shows, the latter present us with a man who had some culture and was not ignorant of Platonism.[64]

The other great critic of *paideia*, John Chrysostom, further illustrates how disavowal of traditional culture could help reorganise the priorities of the increasingly influential Christian leaders while simultaneously de-platforming intellectuals who came from the traditional classroom. In real life, after spending years in monastic seclusion, John Chrysostom grew progressively disillusioned with the monks, developing conflicts with urban monks (especially Isaac the Syrian).[65] In literature, however, he committed to the ideal that peasants and monks, 'who live a country life at the spade and plough' (namely, physical labour), possess a 'store of wisdom'.[66] As is customary in his thinking, John insisted on cultivating this ideal in critical juxtaposition with his assessments of non-Christian philosophers. The claims formulated in a sermon delivered in Antioch sometime between 389 and 397 indicate this clearly:

> You see this simple rustic (i.e., the monk) who knows nothing but farming and tilling the earth. Yet he takes no heed of the present life, but sends his thoughts winging to the good things that lie stored up in heaven, and he knows how to be wise about those ineffable blessings. He has exact knowledge of matters which the philosophers who take pride in their beard and staff have never even been able to imagine.[67]

---

[63] *V. Ant.* 80.
[64] Rubenson (1995) 85; Urbano (2013) 215. On the construction of the monks as illiterate despite their having a variety of cultural backgrounds, see Brown (1992) 71 and Rubenson (2012).
[65] Cf. Lizzi Testa (1987) 25; Hunter (1988) 29 n. 66; Kelly (1995) 30; Tiersch (2002) 178–81; Sterk (2004) 141–49; Rylaarsdam (2014) 203–4.
[66] Jo. Chrys. *Stat.* 19.3 (*PG* 49.189), transl. Easterling and Miles (1996) 103. See further Sterk (2004) 146; Stenger (2016) 185.
[67] *Catech.* 8.6 (*SC* 50 bis), transl. Harkins (1963).

Chapter 5 considered John's project of asserting *parrhesia* as the prerogative of Christian over pagan philosophers.[68] But this philosophical virtue is most highly fulfilled in (ideal) monasticism. The monk's honesty and straightforwardness feed on and are simultaneously testified to by his simplicity and lack of the conceit that originates in a traditional education. John's philosopher-monks show that access to the Christian divine is the exclusive prerequisite for *parrhesia*.[69]

John's early treatise *Against the Opponents of the Monastic Life* describes the desert where ascetic monastic communities are located as 'teeming with the abundant fruit of philosophy (πολλῷ ... τῷ τῆς φιλοσοφίας καρπῷ)'.[70] Monks are portrayed as pedagogues and teachers of true knowledge. The monastery is the only place appropriate for the formation of the young. To parents who object to this ('What then? Shall we all become philosophers? Shall we let everything that pertains to this life go to ruin?'), John replies that 'Not philosophy ... but the failure to philosophise destroys and corrupts everything'.[71] 'If you look at their actual substance', he writes elsewhere of the Greek philosophers, 'there is only ashes and dust and nothing healthy. Their throat is an open grave, full to the brim with defilement and blood, and their doctrines are replete with worms'.[72] 'Outside philosophy', as John refers to it,[73] is not actively conducive to the production of virtue, and exposes (the young, in particular, but everyone else as well) to vices such as pederasty, the desire for wealth, and vainglory (κενοδοξία). This point is eloquently developed in his treatise *Concerning Vainglory and the Education of Children*.[74]

The arguments voiced by Athanasius and John can serve as a thermometer of late fourth-century politics. Both authors offered in literary form, and to audiences increasingly alert to the prominence of Christian asceticism, the cultural weapons needed to challenge non-Christian intellectuals upholding culture, denying all value to advice from traditional *paideia* on this ground. What is remarkable here is not that these theologians questioned the value of Greco-Roman culture; this stance, as noted, had a long history. It is instead the fact that figures like Athanasius and John began to

---

[68] See p. 243–8.
[69] Cf. Van Renswoude (2019) 32–35 on perceptions of *parrhesia* as fitting the Christian ideal of *sermo humilis*.
[70] *PG* 47.328.   [71] *PG* 47.363.
[72] *In Jo. Hom.* 66 (*PG* 59.370). Transl. Siniossoglou (2008) 53.
[73] On John's references to the notion of 'outside philosophy' and its cognates, see, e.g., *Stat.* 17.2 (*PG* 49.173, οἱ τῶν ἔξωθεν φιλόσοφοι); *Laz.* 3.3 (*PG* 48.994); *in Jo. hom.* 66.3 (*PG* 59.369). See further Malingrey (1961) 265–69; Stenger (2016) 180.
[74] On the date and authenticity of the piece, see Malingrey (1972) 13–47; Kelly (1995) 85.

envisage the possibility that the validity of *paideia* might be denied from a position of undisputed civic prominence and socio-political leadership. Both bishops were closely involved with imperial politics and counted among the best known and most influential preachers of their times. Their disavowal of traditional education came from the highest echelons of the ecclesiastical hierarchy. Their arguments thus communicate a new confidence in the political effectiveness of the system of episcopal mobilisation of urban crowds.

All this points to what I see as a crucial paradox defining the evolution of the interaction between Christianity, philosophy, and Roman power from its Constantinian origins to the early fifth century (and beyond). The construction of Christianity as a highly cultured language was pursued, as I have argued in this book, in the awareness that only an identification of Christianity with culture could persuade Roman elites to endorse its claims to a (hegemonic) position in the empire. But Athanasius' and John's arguments show that, just a few decades after the Constantinian turn, counter-cultural arguments could be pressed by figures interacting with the court – a bastion of traditional culture – thus becoming available as a new language for the Christian(ised) elite. The challenge to the cultural capital whose creative adaptation had been necessary for Christianity's political self-assertion could now originate in and be articulated from the top of the social ladder.

I am wary of moulding the ascetic turn into a teleological story. Coexisting models of the relationship between Christianity and culture would continue to be voiced from the upper classes for centuries. A macroscopic case, and one very close chronologically to the authors I am considering, is the poet Nonnus of Panopolis. In the fifth century, Nonnus moved back and forth from an epic on Dionysiac myth to paraphrasing the *Gospel of John*, to which he applied a blend of highly philosophical language and rarefied poetic vocabulary. Nonnus thus stands as perhaps the most striking example of an extremely intellectualising version of Christianity, in which social exclusion and cultural interaction went hand in hand – a synergy that might seem jarring to contemporary sensibilities.[75] The hiatus between John and Nonnus, however, was filled by a variety of attempts to mobilise the socio-political utility of charismatic asceticism and to interrogate its limits. For Christian intellectuals who had responded to Julian's criticism by re-asserting Christianity's capacity to

---

[75] On the challenges posed by Nonnus' self-positioning in contemporary culture, see Goldhill (2020) 81–86, (2022) 223–313.

control *paideia*, Christian essentialism was quintessentially problematic. It reinforced precisely the idea of Christianity that Julian and his followers had weaponised in the service of their philosophical ideals. Most important, an image of Christianity as the religion of one book eradicated the distinction between the educated few and the uneducated many, which, as Gregory's case has shown, was still thriving in the interstices of the bishops' universalising rhetoric and was actually perceived as supporting it. Gregory's dual ethics relied on the fact that, provided everyone shared in the possibility of benefitting from revelation, cultural differences were necessary to set a class of leaders apart from their faithful subjects. Who is best equipped to rule if no *paideia* serves as a differentiating factor? As I argue in the next section, late fourth-century intellectuals – inside and outside of Christianity – were alert to this question and addressed the problematic aspects of the ascetic machine to negotiate their intellectual and socio-political standing. Some were more successful, some less so. I begin with Synesius.

Synesius Offers No Easy Solution

The way Synesius engaged with the question of the relationship between culture, Christianity, and philosophy continues to add to the puzzle of his life. Chapter 5 argued that Synesius' aggressive self-presentation in his Constantinopolitan writings (*On Kingship* and *On Providence*) betrays a competitive desire to assert his authority as a philosopher. I further suggested that his tone and argument might be explained as reacting to the philosophical expectations mobilised by and around John Chrysostom's charismatic preaching. As Synesius' epistolary works testify, he knew not only John but also Athanasius of Alexandria.[76] In this section, I aim to show that Synesius' commitment to antagonistic self-assertion as a philosophical model continued to unfold after his return from Constantinople to Libya. Here it took the form of a reflection on the superiority of that philosophy cultivated through *paideia* over other forms of philosophy, among which Christian asceticism is to be counted. I will continue to leave open the question of whether Synesius' polemics were voiced from a position external or internal to Christianity. My starting points will be two. First: Synesius' post-Constantinopolitan writings offer contradictory

---

[76] Synesius, *ep.* 66, l. 92–93, referring to Athanasius as πάμμεγας, 'truly great'. Since the letter addresses Alexandria's patriarch, Theophilus, it is unclear if the compliment truly represents Synesius' opinion.

evidence regarding his understanding of Christianity as a philosophy. This is an idea Synesius intermittently supports and challenges, depending on audience and circumstances.[77] Second: Synesius complements this twofold movement of acknowledgement and denial of Christianity's self-image with repeated reflections on the relationship between philosophy and culture, on the one hand, and the philosopher and the many, on the other.

The starting point for assessing Synesius' approach to this set of issues is the programmatic treatise he composed prior to his appointment to the bishopric, *Dio, or on Living by his Example* (dated to ca. 404, a few years after Synesius' return from the capital). The *Dio* presents itself as a celebration of Dio as a philosophical model – although arguably the utility of Synesius' celebration of his predecessor mostly lies in creating a springboard that enables him to assert his own superiority to his model.[78] Dio serves in the *Dio* as a great model from the past in the art of advising the powerful. He is a well-known example of meaningful engagement of the intellectual with politics. Synesius celebrates him for his capacity, developed after (what he narrates as) Dio's conversion from rhetoric to philosophy, to steer clear of demagogy and adopt a type of social commitment that educates 'both monarchs and citizens'.[79] Following this, the *Dio* reflects on the identity and duties of true philosophy. According to Synesius, philosophy must be understood as a widely encompassing intellectual disposition that does not disavow any manifestation of culture but enables its practitioners to move from the heights of metaphysics to the realm of human communication.[80]

This definition does not only entail criticism of the practice of sophistry, that is, communication unconcerned with wisdom, which Synesius attacks in the section of the text devoted to performing rhetoricians.[81] It also targets erroneous or limited ways of conceiving philosophy. These are identified, respectively, in the metaphysical concerns of socially withdrawn Neoplatonists, who only look at the celestial spheres and forget the world, and in Christian asceticism.[82] Of the anchorites who shun learning and prefer hard physical labour, Synesius says that they confuse the means (that is, self-control) with the purpose (wisdom and understanding). They

---

[77] On Synesius' self-projection as simultaneously a philosopher and a priest, see *ep.* 41 l. 139–45, 296–97; 62; 96. To what extent the label of 'philosopher-priest' challenges the identity between these categories by presenting Synesius' blending of them as unique?

[78] Cf. *Dio* 1.4 (Dio's conversion to philosophy was 'led more by fortune than by his own will'); 1.14 (Dio never reached the heights of metaphysics, because he found philosophy too late); 4.1 (Dio's writings are 'the boundary (μεθόριον) between preliminary instruction and true culture'.

[79] *Dio*, 1.14.   [80] See especially *Dio* 4.5–5.1.   [81] *Dio* 12–15.   [82] *Dio* 7–11.

choose extreme temperance without knowing why they ought to be temperate.[83] As a result, they never truly develop a (philosophical) method; their experience of the divine does not progress. They end up having 'scarcely travelled a path at all'.[84] Synesius is clearly not challenging the monks' practice of self-restraint but the meaning they attach to the practice. They see a school of wisdom in what is no school at all.

Synesius' *Dio* presents both targeted groups – metaphysicians and Christian ascetics – as representatives of 'the one and the other philosophy' (ἑκατέρα φιλοσοφία).[85] He remarks that his criticism (of the monks' lack of education) 'does not apply to those who follow the other way (ἐκ τῆς ἑτέρας ἀγωγῆς), but rather those who follow ours'.[86] Is this a way to differentiate between Christian and Greco-Roman philosophy, or between the philosophy cultivated within or outside of *paideia*, or both? Synesius does not say.[87] It is meaningful, however, that he unequivocally acknowledges Christian asceticism as a form of philosophy, which he sees as comparable to Neoplatonic metaphysics, insofar as both appear to him to be intellectually inadequate. In his correspondence as well, Synesius continues to represent metaphysicians and Christian ascetics as two alternatives rendered interchangeable by the fact that they are equally concerned with defining philosophy and localise it 'with divine matters only'.[88] In a letter addressing a friend described as undecided as to whether to join one of these groups, Synesius argues that, although he has a slight preference for the metaphysicians, there is no real difference between them.[89]

Synesius' choice to structure the *Dio* around Dio acquires further meaning when we bring the text into focus as striving *inter alia* to undermine the claims of counter-cultural Christianity to philosophical insight. It is essential in this respect to stress that Synesius takes time to characterise Dio as someone introduced late to philosophy. The first consequence of this, as anticipated above, is that it provides Synesius with

---

[83] *Dio* 9.7. For the hypothesis that Synesius is describing the desert communities of Nitria and Kellia, see Treu (1959); Garzya (1972), (1989) 679; Cameron and Long (1993) 64.
[84] *Dio* 8.5.   [85] *Dio* 9.6.   [86] *Dio* 11.1.
[87] Cf. however Synesius' complaint about the 'alien way of life' (ἀγωγὴ ἑτέρα) he had led, 'having been brought up outside the Church' (ἀπότροφος ἐκκλησίας), in *ep.* 66, l. 361–66. For readings of this passage as merely arguing that Synesius had not been raised to become a clergyman, see Roques (1987) 302; Cameron and Long (1993) 24–26; Schmitt (2001) 191 n. 205; Tanaseanu-Döbler (2008) 174–76; Criscuolo (2012) 164.
[88] Cf. *ep.* 154, ll. 2–8 (ca. 405). Synesius' awareness of monasticism's self-understanding as a school of philosophy also helps explain his inclusion of Anthony in a group of sages in *Dio* 10.5 (see Niccolai [2021] 219).
[89] *Ep.* 147 (ca. 408).

an easy opening to assert his own superiority. Dio, a latecomer to wisdom, never managed to become proficient in metaphysics;[90] needless to say, Synesius – Hypatia's pupil – excelled in that area. But the claim that Dio came to philosophy late is not advanced exclusively in order to support Synesius' (thinly disguised) desire to supersede his model. It also channels criticism towards ascetic monks. In the section dedicated to them, Synesius argues that monks teach without having learned because they feel shame at the prospect of becoming late learners (Ὑμεῖς δὲ ὀψιμαθίαν αἰσχύνεσθε).[91] Due to their limited understanding of the nature of education, they fail to realise what Dio, conversely, grasped: that the greatest shame is not to learn late but not to learn at all (ἡ δὲ ἀμαθία, καὶ τοῦτο μεῖζον, τοῦτο αἰσχρόν).[92]

Synesius' critical attitude towards Christian forms of self-distancing from *paideia* also appears in his *Letter* 105. His acceptance of the see was accompanied by a complex act of assertion of his intellectual profile at the expense of the Church.[93] In 410, the powerful archbishop Theophilus of Alexandria offered Synesius the bishopric of the Libyan city of Ptolemais.[94] At the time, Synesius was a layman. This should not come as too much of a surprise: it simply reminds us of the deep connection between the late antique episcopacy and issues of leadership, socio-political prestige, and wealth. The *curialis* Synesius, the leader of the embassy of the Pentapolis to Emperor Arcadius, would appeal to those expecting a bishop to act as the munificent patron of his community and a strong mediator with the imperial government.[95] Having withdrawn to Alexandria to decide whether to accept the bishopric, Synesius issued a series of letters perhaps deliberately expressing uncertainty.[96] After seven months, he decided to accept, but on his own conditions, which *Letter* 105 sets.

The letter is famous for its striking requests. Apart from a demand to be allowed not to divorce his wife, Synesius wrestles with dogma. He proclaims his unwillingness to believe that the soul is of more recent origin than the body and that the cosmos has an end (both points mirroring his Neoplatonic belief in the pre-existence of souls). He subtly challenges

---

[90] *Dio* 1.14.   [91] *Dio* 10.10.   [92] Ibid.   [93] Niccolai (2021) 227–32.
[94] I follow the dating of Lacombrade (1951b) 210–12. Barnes (1986b) prefers to date the election to 407; Roques (1987) 310 locates it in January 411 and the ordination in January 412. A summary of the discussion in Tanaseanu-Döbler (2008) 159 n. 27.
[95] On these expectations, see Brown (1992) 78–103; Hunt (1997) 240–50, 262–72; Rapp (2005) 183–207. On the famous case of Valerius Pinianus, see Augustine, *ep.* 124, 125, and 126 (*CCL* 31B: 178–94). See also Shaw (2011) 386–87. Cf. further Gregory of Nazianzus' criticism of Christians seeking pastors who are rhetors (*Or.* 42.24, cf. Sterk [1998] 243–44).
[96] See esp. *ep.* 11; 13; 41; 79; 96; 105.

resurrection.[97] The tone of the piece is also surprising. Synesius does not hide his preference for the aristocratic life over the bishopric. It could be argued that this resistance to the appointment is – as I am convinced – a performance of *recusatio*. At the same time, what sets Synesius' *recusatio* apart from other examples of bishops professing a lack of ambition is that he is somewhat offensive to his ecclesiastical addressees. He does not merely declare his unworthiness for the role and his desire to lead an ascetic, philosophical life. The *recusatio* of Gregory of Nazianzus or John Chrysostom was accompanied by expressions of unworthiness and a desire to lead the pure life of the monk. But Synesius contends that the leisure he has been enjoying till this moment seems to him a better option than sacrificing his time for Church-related commitments.[98]

Our starting point for evaluating both the strategies and the significance of this text should be its outcome. Synesius was afterwards awarded the bishopric; his requests were seemingly successful. This casts his blunt statements in a different light: if he used daring language, he arguably knew he could afford to do so. The text pretends to be private: formally, it addresses Synesius' brother Euoptius, in a performance of intimacy. But it is in fact a public, contractual document. As Synesius himself declares, he expects the letter to circulate among the clergymen, reaching Theophilus himself. The piece thus represents Synesius' opportunity to adjust his public profile as he transitions from one social status to another, claiming a superiority over his ecclesiastical interlocutors that is simultaneously social and intellectual.[99]

Synesius' direct engagement with the unspoken power dynamics regulating his relationship to his interlocutors is key to his self-assertion. The piece does not shy away from mapping out hierarchies. The community honoured Synesius by electing him, and now his reputation is at stake.[100] While expressing devotion to Theophilus and to God ('Let the beloved of God, the right reverend Theophilus ... decide on this issue concerning me!'), Synesius constructs the clergymen as his subordinates (a point to which I return below). Most important, he obliquely professes his awareness of being wanted so much as a bishop – qua a public, prominent figure – that he knows he will be allowed to control doctrine. Synesius does

---

[97] *Ep.* 105, ll. 69–78 (wife), ll. 82–90 (dogmas).
[98] Piepenbrink (2012) 76–79. On episcopal *recusatio*, see Chapter 5, p. 239–40.
[99] On *ep.* 105 as the expression of Synesius' struggle to relocate his identity on a shifting cultural map, see Goldhill (2006) 153–63.
[100] See Synesius' expression of gratitude to the inhabitants of Ptolemais for the honour of the appointment at *ep.* 105. 1–3.

not make himself acceptable by professing allegiance to orthodoxy. In fact, his assertion that the soul pre-exists the body voices a belief opposite to that of his ultimate addressee and patron, Theophilus.[101] To the contrary, Synesius asserts himself by pointing to his power to control social norms as the true stakes of the transaction. His discourse on doctrine and philosophy is at once a show of force and an open conversation about power, sending the message that at the end of the negotiations he will have obtained what he wants in either case. This is because Theophilus will either accept his conditions, or, as Synesius writes, will 'leave me by myself, to my life and philosophy' – the option that, he tells us from the start, is most appealing to him. By writing *ep.* 105, Synesius was arguably not expressing concern that he might be made bishop against his will. His aim was rather of a socio-symbolic nature: bolstering his reputation as an intellectual and leader. Synesius tells Theophilus, who wanted an authoritative figure for the see of Ptolemais, that Ptolemais could not get a bishop with more authority than him.

I am convinced, however, that Synesius' self-assertion in the letter would scarcely have worked without his anticipation that his ecclesiastical interlocutors would be alert to the tension between Christian essentialism and traditional, socially established ways to secure a philosophical reputation. He draws on this unease when he projects himself as an uncompromising intellectual. His expressions of elitist sensitivity are accompanied by repeated challenges to the lifestyle (and interpretive skills) of his interlocutors. Synesius seems to have assumed that his challenge would trigger discomfort. He obliquely criticises the clergymen's work by wondering how their 'divine flame' remains alive despite their various duties and asks how a priest 'can sustain the weight of so many cares without his intellect being submerged (τοσοῦτον ὄγκον φροντίδων καὶ μὴ κατακλύσαι τὸν νοῦν)'.[102] Synesius tempers these questions with an acknowledgement that there must be such men and adds that his personal weakness prevents him from achieving the same results (ll. 46–55). But he is still playing with fire. The key questions he raises are left unanswered: How many priests manage to preserve their full range of intellectual skills despite their duties? What is his opinion of the clergymen reading his words?

---

[101] The pre-existence of the soul would only be condemned in 553, at the fifth ecumenical council. Nevertheless, all the most prominent fourth-century theologians seem to have followed the doctrine of the simultaneous creation of body and soul (Louth (2003) 1172–73). Theophilus actively intervened against Origenists (Brown [1992] 138).
[102] *Ep.* 105, l. 41–46.

The core of the letter, Synesius' rejection of the three tenets, is eloquently presented as a refusal to believe in 'dogmas which are common talk' (θρυλλουμένοις δόγμασιν).[103] The problematisation of resurrection is in this regard especially meaningful. 'What is commonly referred to as resurrection', Synesius writes, 'I regard as a sacred mystery (ἀπόρρητον) and am far from sharing the assumptions of the many thereon'. Synesius does not say whether the view of his ecclesiastical addressees coincides with or differs from the popular understanding of resurrection, leaving them to draw their conclusions. But he is adamant that he does not divulge religious mysteries to the non-initiated. As he declares shortly afterwards, if he is allowed to hold fast to his beliefs as a preacher, he will take over the priesthood on the condition that 'I may prosecute philosophy at home, and teach outside through myth' (τὰ μὲν οἴκοι φιλοσοφῶ, τὰ δ' ἔξω φιλόμυθός εἰμι διδάσκων).[104] Synesius makes his ecclesiastical addressees confront an uncomfortable alternative: either to profess their allegiance to whatever 'the many' believe, thus exposing their proximity to the crowd, or to support his own position, betraying that they too cultivate beliefs that contradict their universalising claims. Synesius thus seems to be simultaneously condemning the cultural politics of Christian asceticism and appealing to the anxieties driving episcopal self-projections à la Gregory of Nazianzus. *Ep.* 105 cultivates the perplexities of its educated readers by making them confront the fact that their preaching must entail either a loss of (philosophical) identity or an element of compromise unmasking their rhetoric. Even Synesius' opening *recusatio*, his claim that he is not up to the task of belonging as a priest 'to all men', seems retrospectively double-edged. Could a person committed to protecting philosophy from the non-initiated see any value in becoming κοινότατος – supremely public?

How to Disappear Completely: Eunapius' *Lives of the Philosophers and Sophists*

The elitist argument explored by Julian to challenge Christianity as a vulgar philosophy – hence as no philosophy at all – created the possibility for someone like Synesius to exploit it to his (socio-political) advantage. I suggest, however, that a version of Julian's argument was also responsible for eliciting a prescriptive ideal of how non-Christian philosophers should participate in politics that eventually hampered its supporters. My case study will be the *Lives of the Philosophers and Sophists*. This series of

---

[103] *Ep.* 105, l. 84–85.   [104] *Ep.* 105, l. 99–100.

biographies was written by the pro-Julianic intellectual and historian Eunapius of Sardis between 396 and 399, only a few years before Synesius issued his *ep.* 105.[105]

Eunapius' work shares a crucial premise with the writings of the main historian of the fourth century, Ammianus: it looks back on Roman history with a perspective altered by Adrianople. Like Ammianus – although, perhaps, with lesser complexity – Eunapius both reflected on the causes of Rome's (military and general) downfall and conceived of the history of the empire as driven by political agents who could either access providence and secure prosperity or failed at doing so and damaged politics accordingly. Both Ammianus and Eunapius, finally, saw Christianity as a factor in this decline.

Eunapius' lost history celebrated the 'divine' (θειότατος) Julian as the philosopher-ruler who alone defeated the barbarians.[106] He believed that true harmony of Rome with the gods could only come from traditional piety and Neoplatonic philosophy. His *Lives* blames Rome's troubles on Christianity, although an exception is made for figures like the Christian rhetorician Prohaeresius, Eunapius' teacher, who dedicated his life to *paideia*.[107] The *Lives* presents Constantine as an anti-philosopher, a lover of flattery and the crowds. Eunapius tells us that 'he loved to be applauded in the theatres by men so drunk that they could not hold their liquor. He desired to be praised by the unstable populace (σφαλλομένων ἀνθρώπων ἀγαπήσας ἐγκώμια) and that his name should be in their mouths, although they were so stupid that they could hardly pronounce the word'.[108] The Greek philosopher Sopater temporarily brought a redeeming influence to Constantine's court. But slander – to which Constantine was receptive – brought this fortunate experience to an end, and Sopater was executed. His slanderer, Ablabius, is described as coming from 'a very obscure family' (γένος ἀδοξότατον), not even attaining to 'the humble middle class' on his father's side.[109] He is also said to have 'influenced the emperor as though the latter were an undisciplined mob' (ἀτάκτῳ δήμῳ).[110] One is inevitably reminded of the argument obliquely developed in Julian's *Misopogon*: there is no substantial difference between a Christian emperor and the mob of his coreligionists.

---

[105] On the dating of the work, see Penella (1990) 9; Civiletti (2007) 13 n. 2.
[106] Cf. Eunap. *Hist.* Fr. 1.15; 28.1 Blockley. See Civiletti (2007) 30–33; Urbano (2013) 229–30.
[107] See Civiletti (2007) 40 and 616–18 n. 699, summarising previous discussion; Urbano (2013) 239–40.
[108] *VPS* 462.   [109] *VPS* 463.   [110] *VPS* 464.

Eunapius' work reveals a special animosity towards the monks, presented as epitomising Christianity's unreason. The destruction of the Serapeum of Alexandria and Alaric's invasion of Greece (395–96) are explicitly blamed on them ('men in black robes').[111] For Eunapius, the monks are 'men in appearance but leading the lives of swine',[112] who 'fettered the human race to the worship of slaves'.[113] Non-human animals and individuals antiquity classified as sub-human are here grouped together to convey a sense of wretchedness. Eunapius also mocks the monks' mimicry of the philosophical life, pursued through an empty performance of detachment from social conventions. 'In those days', he writes, 'every man who wore a black robe and consented to behave in unseemly fashion in public possessed the power of a tyrant (τυραννικὴν εἶχεν ἐξουσίαν)'. The comment underscores Eunapius' perception of a tight connection between the acknowledgement of someone's philosophical identity and the authority deriving from it. His focus on the destructive agency of the Cynicising monks sends a political message: a state fails when government relies on the advice offered by false philosophers, vulgar figures who can only imitate the wise in appearance. His *Lives* thus perfectly captures his understanding of history as a space of interpretation struggled over by rival exegetical systems, only one of which can be exact. At the same time, Eunapius' understanding of Christianity as vulgar captures his perception that a valid interpretive system must be accessed by the educated few. The *Lives* stands as a manifesto of this belief.

Eunapius writes to celebrate the memory and legacy of the great representatives of Plotinus' lineage, starting with those he presents as the founding fathers of Neoplatonism: Plotinus, Porphyry, and Iamblichus.[114] His characters are just as towering as they are isolated. Eunapius frequently lingers on descriptions of how they cultivated their perfect wisdom in isolation, sharing their teaching only with carefully selected disciples. Of Porphyry, for instance, Eunapius writes that, after having sailed to Sicily, 'he would not endure either to see a city or to hear the voice of a man'.[115] Iamblichus, although described as having a multitude of eager disciples, is simultaneously presented as a philosopher with a tendency to seek solitude and perform his rites alone.[116] It is said of another philosopher, Aedesius, that his search for secrecy 'owed to the times' (διὰ τοὺς χρόνους, referring

---

[111] *VPS* 472 (Serapeum), 476 (Alaric). [112] *VPS* 472. [113] *VPS* 473.
[114] He also occupies himself with sophists and doctors, but both have been left out of this chapter. On Eunapius' view of sophists as guardians of *paideia* and its capacity to preserve the Greek cultural heritage, see Civiletti (2007) 36–38.
[115] *VPS* 456. [116] *VPS* 458.

to Constantine's actions against paganism) but also to the consideration that his best disciples inclined towards 'a silence appropriate to the mysteries' (μυστηριώδη τινὰ σιωπήν).[117] The great Sopater, Constantine's adviser, 'would not condescend to associate with other men'.[118] Of Sosipatra, a philosopher and prophetess initiated into Chaldean wisdom by divine beings, it is said that her father, although very proud of her, 'sometimes was ill pleased (ἐδυσχέραινεν) by her silence'.[119] Sosipatra's son Antoninus, having embraced 'the wisdom that is hidden from the crowd', lived as an ascetic at the Canobic mouth of the Nile and, while available to discuss philosophy, replied with the silence of a statue to those 'who raised questions as to things divine'.[120] Priscus is described as being 'of a secretive disposition' (κρυψίνους).[121]

This form of engagement with society – or lack thereof – is interpreted by scholarship as reflecting a social context in which Christianisation had succeeded in isolating dissenting voices. Eunapius' holy Neoplatonists are assumed to document a shrinking world in which philosophers, increasingly drawn towards elusive forms of hieraticism, were losing interest in social participation – what Fowden calls the 'drift of the pagan holy man towards the periphery of society'.[122] Non-Christian philosophers did indeed end up being pushed to the margins of the Christianised state; Eunapius seems here and there to be ascribing the secretive habits of his philosophers to a fear of religious hostility.[123] But I believe that his reasons for describing his philosophers' search for solitude lie elsewhere. The *Lives* offers a counterintuitive project of resistance addressing the (risk of) social exclusion of non-Christian philosophers.

Eunapius' idealising, normative project outlines a succession of strikingly similar philosophical portraits.[124] His characters are all aristocrats, and the aristocracy of their spirit is matched by their social positioning.[125] They are close to the divine: they practice theurgy and have prophetic skills. They are blessed by beauty.[126] Their ideal nature is further captured

---

[117] *VPS* 461. [118] *VPS* 462. [119] *VPS* 469. [120] *VPS* 472. [121] *VPS* 481.
[122] Fowden (1982) 33.
[123] Fear of hostilities is acknowledged at *VPS* 461 (Constantine targeting pagans) and, possibly, at 482 (reference to Priscus' secretive habits and mention of the destruction of temples). On religious conflicts in late antiquity and the issue of whether and to what extent literary accounts of violence should be taken at face value, cf. the nuanced assessment at Kahlos (2019) 57–81.
[124] Penella (1990); Cox Miller (2000); Goulet (2001); Civiletti (2007); Elm (2012) 93.
[125] See, e.g., *VPS* 457 (Iamblichus); 461 (Aedesius); 467 (Sosipatra); 473 (Maximus); 475 (the anonymous hierophant initiating Eunapius); 479 (Clearchus); 500 (Chrysanthios). Cf. Fowden (1982) 48–49; Civiletti (2007) 501.
[126] Cf., e.g., *VPS* 481 (Priscus), 487 (Prohaeresius), 502 (Chrysantius).

by what seems to be Eunapius' choice to downplay philosophical disagreements among them. For instance, he notoriously differentiates between Iamblichus and Porphyry based exclusively on literary style.[127] This used to be taken as a sign of Eunapius' lack of philosophical expertise, but this assessment misses the point that Eunapius did not write the *Lives* with the aim of providing accurate philosophical explanations.[128] Instead, he wished to celebrate the history of Neoplatonism as relying on the principle of harmony that the post-Hellenistic schools perceived as legitimising philosophical claims.[129]

The most prescriptive traits of the *Lives*, however, is the way Eunapius' solitary philosophers navigate the question of political engagement – in particular the ideal, which Neoplatonists cultivated, that the duty of true philosophers was to elevate society by mediating between humankind and divinity.[130] I suggest that Eunapius' *Lives* seeks to reconcile a Neoplatonic desire to contribute to politics with the question of whether a philosophy open to the public can maintain the identity necessary to legitimise its advice. Eunapius reflects on how true philosophers can serve a state in need of their interpretive insight while remaining uncontaminated by the vulgar dynamics of politics, ambition, and self-advertisement.

A crucial feature marks the desire for solitude of Eunapius' heroes: they all long for isolation but cannot find it, and when they find it, it does not last long. Iamblichus, who enjoys performing his rites alone, is eventually dragged out of isolation by his 'flocks of pupils', who ask him to share his knowledge. His obscurity in speaking and writing does not prevent those who strive towards true learning from seeking and finding him.[131] The ascetic Antoninus, having relocated as far as possible from human settlements, near the Canobic mouth of the Nile, is still sought out by all the youth who 'hungered for philosophy'.[132] This fantasy of interrupted seclusion is best captured by the story of Aedesius' prophetic dream.[133] One oracle tells him that his renown will be deathless if he chooses the cities of men, but if he becomes a shepherd, he will be the associate of the immortals. Aedesius chooses the second option and becomes a goatherd. But his decision is short-lived: Eunapius reports that 'he could not be hidden from those who longed for training in eloquence or for learning. They tracked him down and beset him like hounds baying before his doors

---

[127] *VPS* 458. Cf. Urbano (2013) 233.
[128] Praechter (1933) 117–18, see *contra* Fowden (1979) 77–82. On Eunapius' philosophical interests, see Hahn (1989) 486–90; Civiletti (2007) 23–30.
[129] Harmony and truth: see Chapter 3, p. 146.   [130] O'Meara (2005).   [131] *VPS* 458.
[132] *VPS* 471.   [133] *VPS* 464–65.

and threatened to tear him into pieces if he devoted wisdom so great and so rare to hills and rocks and trees'. Eventually, Aedesius agreed to 'return to the life and converse of ordinary men'.[134] It is not merely the case that he chose to withdraw and was prevented from finalising this decision; instead, he is recognised as worthy of becoming a public figure on account of this choice.

The pattern is clear. The paradigm that Eunapius' heroes embody and constantly re-perform is the old trope of *recusatio*. The *Lives*' normative philosophers seek withdrawal from society, but this shows that they have the modesty, lack of ambition, and distaste for public honours expected from those in positions of power.[135] His philosophers, in other words, are presented as social and spiritual leaders, but Eunapius presents this leadership as something that must be demanded from them and which is exercised reluctantly.

Eunapius engages with a political paradigm whose significance he is fully aware of. His understanding of *recusatio* is highlighted by his description of the imperial appointment of his ideal philosopher-ruler, Julian. Eunapius tells us that Julian, 'forcibly removed by Constantius (i.e., from his studies) ... obtained what he did not desire but had been thrust upon him' (ὥστε ὁ μὲν Ἰουλιανὸς ἔτυχεν ὧν οὐκ ἐβούλετο μέν, ἀλλ' ἠναγκάζετο)'.[136] I considered earlier how Eunapius' Constantine, conversely, longs for the crowd. Negative examples are also summoned to reinforce the paradigm; note in particular Eunapius' account of the parable of the philosopher Maximus of Ephesus, who is rendered arrogant by his success at court and recovers his wisdom and fortune only after losing everything.[137] But most important is Eunapius' surprising treatment – that is, erasure – of the fourth-century Greek philosopher who had been more prominent at court than anyone. Themistius is conspicuous for his absence from the *Lives*.[138] The omission is clearly not accidental but takes place within a larger discourse that Themistius' own writings help us reconstruct. During the approximately forty years of his political career, Themistius' public involvement was constantly challenged. I have already considered in Chapter 1 how Julian's *Letter to Themistius* might in a sense (also) be read as obliquely targeting Themistius' ambition and mobilisation of classical philosophical literature for socio-political self-assertion. In some

---

[134] *VPS* 465.   [135] See Chapter 1, p. 54–5; Chapter 5, p. 239–40.   [136] *VPS* 476.
[137] *VPS* 477 (arrogance at court), 478 (misfortunes and torture); 480 (return to philosophy, success, prophecy regarding Valens' death, public execution). Cf. Van Renswoude (2019) 71.
[138] Penella (1990) 134–39; Cox Miller (2000) 239.

surviving orations, Themistius personally responds to accusations that he compromised too much with public life. Already between 358 and 359, a time when he was the equivalent of a *princeps senatus* for Constantius II, Themistius wrote in response to critics who accused him of being a sophist rather than a philosopher, his reply consisting in summoning Plato's criteria for detecting sophists and claiming his distance from each of them (*Or.* 23). Elsewhere Themistius evokes Socrates' apology (*Or.* 26) as the model of his ideal of a universal philosophy that achieves the best results by targeting public assemblies, like the sun that benefits everyone without drawing distinctions.[139] Decades later, in 384, we find Themistius writing a very defensive *Speech of Thanks* (*Or.* 17) following his appointment to the urban prefecture of Constantinople. Here he draws on *recusatio* – his appointment is the will of someone else, Theodosius, whose wisdom validates the role and makes it necessary to accept it ('A philosopher who resists when a philosopher-emperor (βασιλέως ... φιλοσόφου) selects him to serve the state straightway demonstrates that the title "philosopher" does not truly belong to him', Themistius says).[140] Themistius continued to defend his prefecture in his *Orations* 31 and 34. The last of these pieces, composed after he stepped down from the prefecture, reinstates the identity of philosophy and social duty and argues that legislators and politicians were the first philosophers.[141]

In his *Oration* 28, Themistius crucially locates his harshest critics among the Neoplatonists, whom he defines as having 'a stubborn, wilful, and unyielding disposition'[142] and accuses of being 'fearful' and 'wary of public assemblies (ἀγοράς)', as they cannot even 'bear to look away from their couches and secluded corners (οὐκ ἀνέχονται παρακύπτειν ἔξω τοῦ σκίμποδος καὶ τῆς γωνίας)'.[143] These charges compare with Synesius' attacks on his unnamed critics, whom he describes as dissatisfied with his commitment to literature and politics and demanding that he return to pure philosophy.[144] Both Themistius and Synesius thus represent figures

---

[139] Them. *Or.* 26.331a. On the dating of orations 23, 26, and 29 between 358 and 359, see Dagron (1968) 24; Maisano (1995) 23. See further Heather (1998) 127; Heather and Moncour (2001) 286. Already Themistius' *Or.* 20 (funeral oration for his father, possibly dated to 355) argued for his ideal of philosophy as committed to society. *On Virtue* (transmitted in Syriac) remains of debated authenticity, but if it is Themistian (a hypothesis in favour of authenticity in Rigolio [2019]), it would provide further reflection on the social involvement of the philosopher in society.
[140] *Or.* 17.214c, transl. Penella (2000). See Heather and Moncur (2001) 289–90.
[141] *Or.* 34.3. Composed after leaving the office: Vanderspoel (1995) 214; Heather and Moncour (2001) 285–87.
[142] *Or.* 28.342b–c.
[143] *Or.* 28.341d. See Fowden (1982) 56; Penella (1990) 134–37; Quiroga (2013b) 613.
[144] Synesius, *ep.* 154.

who prided themselves on resisting compromise and objected to philosophers who followed a different agenda. As Quiroga argues, Themistius' and Synesius' responses are strategic and rhetorical: both seek to capitalise on criticism by presenting themselves as uniquely committed to politics and thus as enjoying a success that jealousy obliquely confirmed.[145] In criticising his accusers for their secluded lifestyle, Themistius argues that they are 'the silent ones (τῶν σιωπώντων)' who 'do not allow themselves to speak freely to people'.[146] He is evidently seeking to disqualify his rivals by presenting them as forsaking the parrhesiastic ideal that is the essence of civic philosophy. But once we read Themistius' – and Synesius' – critical description of the seclusive philosophers side by side with Eunapius, the suspicion arises that Themistius' response also relies on a strategy of devaluing his opponents' modality of socio-political engagement. Eunapius' exploitation of *recusatio* in constructing his heroes shows that it could be a participatory device: it signalled the right to be involved in politics by obliquely shaming those who sought blunt interactions with the public as attention-seekers. In this light, Themistius' choice to criticise his rivals' silence reads as a gesture obscuring the fact that their seclusion may have been ideological and driven not by indifference or fear but by an intention of abiding by a practice that alone would qualify them as political advisers.

As Penella observes, it is impossible that Eunapius, who knew about every intellectual associated with the imperial court in the late fourth century, was unaware of Themistius.[147] The *Lives* takes and claims its place within a complex political discourse whose competitiveness Eunapius fully embraces. His response – the cancellation of the hyper-involved Themistius from his lineage of ideal philosophers – pays Themistius back in kind. Eunapius criticises 'the professed philosophers who made a profit out of their affinity with genuine philosophy and spent most of their time running risks in the law court'. For them, he chooses *contrapasso*: 'I need not write down even the names of these men (καὶ τούτων γε τὰ ὀνόματα οὐδὲν δέομαι γράφειν)', he argues, 'for my narrative is eager to lead on to those that are not unworthy, but worthy'.[148]

Eunapius' heroes thus appear receptive to the post-Constantinian transformation of the mutually legitimising dialogue between Christian philosophy and Christian power and of the progressive erasure of traditional philosophy from the equation. His portraits construct a difference between

---

[145] Quiroga (2013b) 618. [146] *Or.* 28.342b–d.
[147] Penella (1990) 134–39. See also Cox Miller (2000) 239; and Elm (2012) 95. [148] *VPS* 471.

the modalities of communication of his heroes and those of the sophists and Christian 'philosophers' who, by seeking out the public, prove that they are not philosophers at all. Readers are profoundly involved in a normative project of this sort. By asking them to see that his ideal philosophers, although elusive prophets, can provide insightful and authoritative guidance when summoned back to society, Eunapius offers his audience coordinates that may help them recognise which philosophers should be involved in political life. The *Lives* instructs its readers not only on what constitutes the perfect philosophical life but also – and perhaps most important – on what to look for when seeking a master. Prescriptiveness, in other words, is not limited to the delineation of *exempla* of holy lives: Eunapius re-reads history to show that history itself proves a need for true philosophical advice, which cannot come from Christianity. But Christianity has deceived rulers with its availability to the political scene and by its philosophical pretensions: if the powerful want true philosophers by their side, they must seek them out, because it is a mark of true philosophers to not spontaneously pursue power. Eunapius, incidentally, expects sovereignty to be Christian by now, and – just as he approves of Prohaeresius, the Christian rhetorician who fully understands the value of *paideia* – he signals that Christian rulers in particular would benefit from the company of his true philosophers. This is shown by the *exempla* of the successes (all ephemeral, due to the intervention of jealous courtiers) of Sopater at the court of Constantine and of Eustathius under Constantius II. Eunapius says of Constantine that 'for all he was wrapped up (ἐνεχόμενος) in the books of the Christians',[149] he understood his need for help from a pagan philosopher, given the difficult situation the state was in. Subsequent events proved him right: Eustathius did wonders at court and eventually even converted the Persian king Shapur to philosophy – we are told that Shapur lay the purple aside to wear Eustathius' cloak – before falling victim to a conspiracy by the jealous Magi.[150] The *parrhesia* of another philosopher, Clearchus, is described as so forceful and sincere that it soothed the wrath of Emperor Valens and persuaded him of the validity of the philosopher's advice.[151]

A problem is apparent here. By elevating *recusatio* into a principle of self-legitimisation, Eunapius unintentionally points to the limits of a political philosophy that demands withdrawal from the political scene as the pre-condition for operating in it. It is impossible for his heroes to seek prominence and not lose their philosophical identity as a result of their

---

[149] *VPS* 465.   [150] *VPS* 466.   [151] *VPS* 479.

search. Their strategy of self-legitimisation – which, as I hope to have shown, does not coincide with indifference towards society – requires a receptive audience in order to be fulfilled. It follows that Eunapius' philosophers can only serve the state if power actively seeks for them. This was the case during the 'golden age' of Julian, who is eloquently portrayed in the *Lives* as constantly searching for philosophers, travelling to find them, and summoning them to court to become his priests and personal advisers.[152] But Julian's successors looked for wisdom elsewhere. Eunapius' oblique *recusatio* presupposes a perfectly concerted effort by two players, the withdrawing philosopher and the ruler who sees virtue in withdrawal. In the late fourth and early fifth centuries, other players – monk-bishops and charismatic preachers whose urban power was steadily increasing – were in the public eye. Their doctrinal disputes demanded attention both on account of their political potential and capacity to mobilise the population, and because they successfully constructed the question of orthodoxy as the most urgent matter on the agenda of philosophical truth. All the difficulties that arose from Christianity's negotiation of its philosophical identity between universalism and elitism could not undermine a fundamental fact: a positive feedback loop had established itself between Christian emperors and bishops. This was grounded on their mutual acknowledgement and on the validation of their joint control over the meaning of history and culture through Christianity.

Conclusions

An element of tension was intrinsic in efforts to define Christianity in competition with the post-Hellenistic schools of philosophy. On the one hand, upper-class Christian theologians shared with their non-Christian interlocutors an elite perspective on philosophy as the achievement of the highly cultured – a belief that engendered concern regarding the capacity of the ill-educated to be involved. On the other hand, their authority gained security from Christianity's rhetoric of universal accessibility, whose political utility was evident in its efforts to mobilise the urban population as a base of ecclesiastical support. This combination of universalising rhetoric with claims of Christianity's priority over Greco-Roman culture

---

[152] See, e.g., *VPS* 474 (Julian travels to Pergamon to find Aedesius; becomes a disciple of Eusebius of Myndus and Chrysanthius of Sardis), 475 (goes to Ephesus to find Maximus, and to Eleusis to meet the hierophant); 476 (summons the hierophant from Greece; sends for Maximus and Chrysanthius); 477 (summons Priscus from Greece; asks again for Chrysanthius); 478 (following Chrysanthius' refusal to join the court, Julian appoints him high priest of Lydia).

accelerated discussions regarding whether *paideia* was at best complementary to true philosophy, or at worse corrupting.

The rise to prominence of the state-sponsored Church thus appears to have been shaped by debate over two intertwined issues: what relationship, if any, was there between divine knowledge and Greco-Roman culture, and how could the un-educated be represented within projects of political (self)legitimisation that rely on claims to intellectual authority? Within this picture, Julian appears an acute reader of the complex relationship of Christian intellectuals to cultural politics and notions of cultural capital. He sought to draw on Christianity's universalising rhetoric to disqualify its intellectual authority, but his death gave his opponents another opportunity to attack him. Gregory of Nazianzus in particular used Julian's death to assert that a unique combination of universal accessibility and the intellectual authority of select leaders made Christianity not only the perfect system of knowledge but the one best suited to train (imperial) leaders. The debate, however, remained tense, as is exemplified by the way Synesius of Cyrene manipulated the problem of universal accessibility to secure his personal authority (*ep.* 105) and criticised contemporary efforts to divorce philosophy from *paideia*.

Two paradoxes, I suggest, define the late fourth-century consolidation of Christianity as the system of knowledge supporting Roman power. On the one hand, the rise to authority of counter-cultural Christian voices enabled the questioning of *paideia* by high-ranking representatives of a religion that had found space at court by successfully presenting itself as the culmination of *paideia*. Second, attempts to disqualify Christianity by attacking its universalising rhetoric eventually created the conditions for writing post-Hellenistic philosophies out of the political scene. As Eunapius' *Lives of the Philosophers* illustrates, traditional philosophers engaged in performative seclusion to signal their suitability to advise the powerful. But with the tightening of the link between Christian power and Christian philosophers, this strategy dissolved the authority of non-Christian philosophers in public life.

Conclusions

My research began in 2016 with a seemingly simple question: how did the Christianisation of the Roman Empire affect the self-representation of Roman power? As I chased down self-referential statements in the writings of emperors and bishops, I became increasingly aware that how fourth-century leaders spoke of themselves was indissolubly tied to how they spoke of their culture. Negotiating the value of traditional Greco-Roman *paideia* and its literature(s) – attacked, upheld, manipulated, and fetishised – was an obsession in all the texts I was interrogating. Students of the fourth century often contemplate the puzzling fact that the cultures and practices cultivated for centuries across the Greco-Roman Mediterranean were willingly pushed aside in the space of a few decades. This book has addressed this issue through an analysis that is both culture- and power-centred and grounded on three statements, the first two of which might seem contradictory:

(1) Greco-Roman upper classes constructed Christianity as incompatible with traditional education (*paideia*).
(2) Traditional education (*paideia*) secured Christianity's position of imperial leadership.
(3) Greco-Roman and Christian intellectuals shared above all else a philosophical identity, meaning an understanding of themselves as belonging to an intellectually rigorous and all-encompassing system of knowledge.

This philosophical identity, I contend, provided an interface for ideological confrontation, creating the conditions that enabled (1) and (2) to interact, through Constantine.

Contemporary scholarship has increasingly (and profitably) dismissed the paradigm of 'great man' histories and the narratives they have fostered. It might therefore seem reactionary to suggest that an explanation of the fourth-century revolution must start with Constantine and in particular his intuition that the potential subversiveness of his power (as Christian ruler and usurper) could be neutralised by anchoring novelty to reassuring tradition. But Constantine found himself at the receiving end of a tradition that long predated him and whose fruits he harvested. As I illustrate in the Introduction, since the Principate, Christian theologians had been advocating for an acknowledgement of Christianity as the highest expression of the category Greek and Roman thinkers were most invested in constructing, rationality. In asserting this, they deployed the language, ideas, and techniques for self-definition that were simultaneously explored by post-Hellenistic schools of philosophy. Chapter 3 contends that Constantine voiced the self-image of Christian intellectuals from the imperial platform. Leaving aside the question of the 'genuineness' of his religious allegiance, I argue that he saw the cultural and therefore political utility of endorsing Christianity's intellectual self-projection. He offered Greco-Roman elites an ideal of undisputed prestige that might entice, persuade, and intimidate them: he projected his innovative profile of Christian sovereign as fulfilling – in fact, correcting – the Greco-Roman ideal of the enlightened ruler whose agency is illuminated by understanding.

This strategy confirms recent reappraisals of Constantine as a skilful consensus-seeker able to tailor his communications to target audiences. At the same time, it invites us to re-assess aspects of the discrepancy between ancient and modern conceptions of intellectual authority that might have prevented us from looking for authoritative knowledge in Constantine's propaganda. Contemporary scholars are wary of calling him a philosopher-ruler, despite his and his supporters' attempts to demonstrate that he was one by virtue of his Christianity. Our disengagement with this aspect of his political communication results from different factors. First, it takes at face value attempts by 'pagan' philosophers to disqualify Christianity's claims to a philosophical identity. The academic separation between (ancient and modern) 'philosophy' and 'theology' is reflected in the somewhat arbitrary collocation of the post-Hellenistic schools with the former and of 'Patristics' with the latter. This has resulted in a willingness to rely on ancient oppositional constructions of Christianity as exclusively pertaining to the sphere of 'irrational belief', regardless of how early Christian theologians conceptualised themselves. Second, another reason for the dismissal of Constantine's intellectual self-image is arguably the import of modern systematisations of knowledge and how they have facilitated associations between the 'rational' and the 'secular'. This has resulted in the intellectual disqualification of ancient systems of thinking that envisaged reasoning and revelation as compatible categories. Christianity's philosophical identity thus remains the 'elephant in the room' of fourth-century political and religious debates. In this book, I have let the elephant roam free across the pages.

My reason for doing so is that reappraising the philosophical self-understanding of early Christianity not only helps us recover ancient perspectives on intellectual authority but also explains the reactions the Constantinian turn elicited among its contemporaries. Chapter 4 argues that, by representing his adhesion to Christianity as the consequence of an act of philosophical understanding, Constantine was able to devise an unprecedented strategy, transforming the Roman past into a foil against which to project his (intellectual) might. Constantine claimed insight not merely into the nature of the divine but, most important, into the divine regulations structuring the course of Roman history, which both late antique 'pagans' and Christians conceived as providential. This claim was bolstered through the construction of a circular argument, whereby Constantine's successes and longevity as a ruler served as evidence that he had found the true god, intended as the god who truly controls history. By means of this claim, Constantine infused his philosophical self-image with antagonism. He presented himself as correcting a history of (mis) understanding of the ideal of philosophical leadership. When compared to an unstable and tumultuous past, his thirty years of government demonstrated that he had finally succeeded in doing what a good philosopher-ruler should: understand which actions might meet God's favour and on that basis secure the prosperity of the state. For contemporary audiences, accepting the validity of Constantine's reasoning entailed dismissing previous, 'pagan' conceptions of philosophy. Any Greek or Roman ruler from the past who enjoyed a good reputation would never have passed the test of understanding in the way Christianity (and Constantine) set it.

The antagonistic force of Constantinian propaganda thus explains why this book on the fourth-century institutionalisation of Christianity is above all else about Julian as witness, interpreter, and catalyst. Our traditional understanding of Julian inclines towards representing him as an emperor who loved Greek philosophy, worshipped the Greek gods, disliked Christianity, and at some point decided to cultivate his role as philosopher-ruler in response to (what he perceived as) Christian ignorance. To this picture, I respond with a reading of Julian as the key to assessing how Constantinian propaganda transformed the Roman political and ideological discourse. As I show in Chapters 1 and 2, the cultural environment fostered at the court of Constantius II, the last surviving son of Constantine, inspired Julian both to cultivate a philosophical self-image and to challenge the way philosophical ideals were mobilised in the service of Christian leadership. Julian's militant self-image as a philosopher-ruler must consequently be read as a response to the claim that Christian philosophy had superseded Greco-Roman culture and philosophy, in the classroom as well as in the halls of power (see Chapter 3 and 4). Julian held that, conversely, Christianity had only been able to acquire a philosophical identity because it had taken ideas and methods from Greek philosophy. When re-assessed in this light, his entire literary production appears to be an attempt to come to terms with what we today would define as cultural appropriation. Julian's writings are designed to target what he saw as the main fallacies of Christianity's (mis)use of Greek thinking, including the abuse of concepts and principles – a phenomenon made worse, in Julian's eyes, by Christians' denial that they were using Greek intellectual tools in the first place (Chapter 3); Christianity's manipulative reading of the course of history, to which Julian responded by projecting his own successes as evidence disproving Constantinian claims (Chapter 4); and the difficult new power dynamics the institutionalisation of the Church created between emperors and ministers of the cult (Chapter 5).

We tend to read Julian in towering isolation, but he emerges from my analysis as fully embedded in the discourse of his times. He therefore serves as the key link in a sequence of cultural developments that ran across the entire century. The impact of the imperial debate I have outlined is not in fact limited to the imperial sphere: this book has experimented with reading fourth-century politics as a knock-on effect, the outcome of what might be defined a long crisis of knowledge. If the ground for Constantinian philosophical self-assertion was prepared by early Christian theologians conceptualising their identity, the clash between Constantine's and Julian's conception of philosophy ended up empowering the Church's social self-projection. Chapter 5 illustrates how the Christian exploitation of Julian's downfall immediately after his death in Persia ensured that the intellectual rivalries shaping the fourth century would be rounded off to the advantage of Christianity. Julian's end marked the demise of interpretations seeking to elevate his life into evidence for his ability to gain intellectual access to the divine meaning of history. His attempts to displace Christian hermeneutics, now refuted by what theologians read as his providential death, turned into a master argument proving the Christianity of all history at the expense of Julian's theological and political design. Bishops presented his failure as a token, visible to (and thus verifiable by) anyone, of the fact that Christian philosophy had exclusive insight into providence. From this, it followed that Christian philosophy enjoyed the exclusive right to access the halls of power.

Crucially, the episcopal response to Julian also succeeded in smothering his attempts to solve the political problem brought about by the institutionalisation of Christianity: the destabilisation of the emperor's authority through his permanent decentring from the control of divine matters. As I show in Chapters 5 and 6 through case studies of Synesius of Cyrene and Eunapius of Sardis, this process of post-Julianic consolidation of Christian philosophy at court eventually contributed to the displacement of non-Christian intellectuals, or of intellectuals who were not aligned with the dominant trends in contemporary Christian cultural discourse. These figures were now seen as having only partial access to understanding and therefore as lacking any intellectual authority that might legitimise their advisory relationship with the imperial court.

We might therefore argue that Christianity thrived at court the moment it became able to suggest, through a highly cultivated language of signification, that the ruler's Christianity meant the prosperity of the ruled. This is tantamount to saying that Christianity wove itself within an interpretive network whose two centres of gravity were (traditional) culture and (Roman) history. The promise issued by Christian theologians to the Roman Empire was that only the new religion could infuse the culture and history of Rome with meaning after centuries of ignorance, misunderstanding, and self-deceit. Once this argument is accepted, the well-studied issue of the culture of exegesis pervading late antiquity appears as one expression of what this book has identified as a 'politics of interpretation' structuring Constantinian and post-Constantinian cultural and political debate. The politics of interpretation was thus rendered effective by the ancient assumption that history is always sacred history. The political and doctrinal writings I have examined accordingly drew on an idea of divine design as demonstrable and used it to construct figures of authority as wise interpreters able to access sacred meaning anywhere, from the observation of natural phenomena to the course of history and the meaning of literature both sacred and secular. Exegesis, the foundational skill of late antique philosophers (including Christian ones), was mobilised by Roman power as the practice that legitimised the leader's capacity to intellectually dominate the course of history.

I end these conclusions with a final contention. One aim of this book has been to show that the Constantinian turn represented a fundamental moment in Western history, when power disciplined the experience of religion. This might sound obvious at first. The role Constantine's reign played in kickstarting the history of the institutionalisation of Christianity in the West is as well-known as it is undisputed. But I suggest that an institutional focus obscures how Constantine assisted Christianity's effort to identify the core of its identity in knowledge. Constantine's deployment of his religion of choice for intellectual self-legitimisation secured a conception of Christianity as perfect understanding. Appreciating this subtle but fundamental aspect of his commitment to religion bestows further meaning on the perceived necessity – outlined with and since Nicaea – that a rigorous structuring of doctrine was the primary condition for Christian interaction with structures of power. Lack of agreement on foundational theological matters in fact not merely represented a threat to the cohesion of the new religious party endorsed by the state but fundamentally undermined the idea of Christianity as the expression of rationality and exactitude, with an impact on the intellectual image imperial power was seeking to derive from doctrine. Anxieties surrounding fourth-century doctrinal rivalries pivoted around the assumption that, if something is true, this must be self-evident and everyone must agree on it. If agreement is absent, this implies that the epistemological foundations of the matter under debate are not as solid as assumed.

Constantine's engagement with doctrinal anxieties turned imperial power into the catalyst for a joint but conflicted development. On the one hand, it elicited the transformation of the pursuit of doctrinal agreement into a centralised operation driven by an authoritative injunction. Dogmatisation – the crystallisation of metaphysics into law – strove to offer clear rules enabling state authorities *inter alia* to have a safe principle to guide their efforts to police collective knowledge of the divine. On the other hand, Constantine's turn created the conditions for propagating an impossible demand. The idea (l) of Christianity as perfect knowledge engendered a detail-oriented pursuit of theological formulas that was bound to discover more problems than solutions. The demand for clear-cut definitions revealed that each formulation, once fixed in a meticulous statement, would be rendered accountable by its own finitude for its failure to grasp the fullness of the divine. But this (frustrated) search for an (impossible) agreement resulted in the upholding of categories that educated audiences would recognise as those that had regulated intellectual authority for centuries: the Christianised Roman state prioritised an agenda of understanding, interpretation, explanation, and knowledge of the divine, and an interest in searching for methods that might validate such knowledge. Constantine's rule thus provided a power-centred answer to the fundamental question that had been in the air for centuries of Greco-Roman, Jewish, and Christian thinking: what is the role of reason and wisdom (be they called Logos, Chokma, Memra, or Sophia) in the human experience of the sacred?

Bibliography

Aalders, G. J. D. 1969. 'ΝΟΜΟΣ ΕΜΨΥΧΟΣ', in P. Steinmetz (ed.), *Politeia und Res Publica: Beiträge zum Verständnis von Politik, Recht und Staat in der Antike*. Wiesbaden: Steiner, pp. 315–19.
  1975. *Political Thought in Hellenistic Times*. Amsterdam: Hakkert.
Addey, C. 2014. *Divination and Theurgy in Neoplatonism: Oracles of the Gods*. Farnham; Burlington: Ashgate.
Agamben, G. 1995. *Homo sacer. Il potere sovrano e la nuda vita*. Turin: Einaudi.
Agosti, G. 2001. 'Late Antique Iambics and Iambiké Idea', in A. Cavarzere, A. Aloni, and A. Barchiesi (eds.), *Iambic Ideas: Essays to a Poetic Tradition from Archaic Greece to the Late Roman Empire*. Lanham: Rowman & Littlefield, pp. 219–51.
Ahl, F. 1984. 'The Art of Safe Criticism in Greece and Rome', *American Journal of Philology* 105: 174–208.
Akçai, K. N. 2019. *Porphyry's* On the Cave of the Nymphs *in Its Intellectual Context*. Leiden; Boston: Brill.
Alföldi, A. 1948. *The Conversion of Constantine and Pagan Rome*. Oxford: Clarendon Press.
  1968. 'Die verlorene enmannsche Kaisergeschichte und die *Caesares* des Julianus Apostata', *Bonner Historia-Augusta Colloquium* 4: 1–8.
Alföldy, G. 1974. 'Crisis of the Third Century as Seen by Contemporaries', *Greek, Roman, and Byzantine Studies* 15: 89–111.
Allen, P., and W. Mayer. 1999. *John Chrysostom*. London: Routledge.
Alvino, M. C. 2019. *Lo specchio del principe. L'ideologia imperiale a Costantinopoli tra IV e VI secolo d.C.* Naples: Satura editrice.
Ando, C. 2012. *Imperial Rome AD 193 to 284: The Critical Century*. Edinburgh: Edinburgh University Press.
Antonova, S. E. 2018. *Barbarian or Greek? The Charge of Barbarism and Early Christian Apologetics*. Leiden; Boston: Brill.
Asad, T. 1993. *Genealogies of Religion: Discipline and Reasons of Power in Christianity and Islam*. Baltimore; London: Johns Hopkins University Press.
Asmus, R. 1900. 'Synesius und Dio Chrysostomus', *Byzantinische Zeitschrift* 9: 85–151.
  1914. 'Review of Geffcken 1914', *Wochenschrift für klassische Philologie* 31: 515–25.

Asper, M. 2016. 'Distinctive Readings: Callimachus and Roman Knights', *Philologia Antiqua* 9: 21–32.
Atack, C. 2015. 'Aristotle's Pambasileia and the Metaphysics of Monarchy', *Polis* 32: 297–320.
Athanassiadi, P. 1977. 'A Contribution to Mithraic Theology: The Emperor Julian's *Hymn to King Helios*', *Journal of Theological Studies* 28: 360–71.
  1981. *Julian and Hellenism: An Intellectual Biography*. Oxford: Clarendon Press.
Athanassiadi, P., and M. Frede (eds.) 1999. *Pagan Monotheism in Late Antiquity*. Oxford: Clarendon Press.
Badham, C. 1855. *Platonis Philebus*. London: J.W. Parker.
Baker-Brian, N. 2020. '"I have taken pains to get copies of them" (Athanasius, De Synodis 55): Epistolary Relations between the Sons of Constantine and the Christian Church', in Baker-Brian and Tougher (eds.), pp. 347–87.
Baker-Brian, N., and S. Tougher (eds.) 2012. *Emperor and Author: The Writings of Julian the Apostate*. Swansea: Classical Press of Wales.
  2020. *The Sons of Constantine, A.D. 337–361: In the Shadows of Constantine and Julian*. Cham: Palgrave Macmillan.
Baldi, I. 2012. *Gli Inni di Sinesio di Cirene: vicende testuali di un corpus tardoantico*. Berlin: De Gruyter.
Baldwin, B. 1978. 'The *Caesares* of Julian', *Klio* 40: 449–66.
Balleriaux, O. 1994. 'Themistius et le néoplatonisme. Le Nous pathêtikos et l'immortalité de l'âme', *Revue de Philosophie Ancienne* 12: 171–200.
Balot, R. K. 2004. 'Free Speech, Courage and Democratic Deliberation' in I. Sluiter and R. M. Rosen (eds.), *Free Speech in Classical Antiquity*. Leiden; Boston: Brill, pp. 232–59.
Barbagli, N. 2019. 'Il perdono degli Alessandrini. Fortuna di un episodio di clemenza imperiale', in G. A. Cecconi, R. Lizzi Testa, and A. Marcone (eds.), *The Past as Present: Essays on Roman History in Honour of Guido Clemente*. Turnhout: Brepols, pp. 43–91.
  2020. 'The Emperors in the Province: A Study of the Tetrarchic Images from the Imperial Cult Chamber in Luxor', in F. Guidetti and K. Meinecke (eds.), *A Globalized Visual Culture? Towards a Geography of Late Antique Art*. Oxford; Havertown: Oxbow Books, pp. 91–131.
Barbero, A. 2006. *Barbari. Immigrati, profughi, deportati nell'impero romano*. Rome: Laterza.
  2016. *Costantino il vincitore*. Rome: Salerno editrice.
Barceló, P. A. 2004. *Constantius II. und seine Zeit: die Anfänge des Staatskirchentums*. Stuttgart: Klett-Cotta.
Bardill, J. 2012. *Constantine, Divine Emperor of the Christian Golden Age*. Cambridge: Cambridge University Press.
Bardy, J. 1949. 'Philosophie et philosophe dans le vocabulaire chrétien des premiers siècles', *Révue d'Ascétique et de Mystique* 25: 97–108.
Barker, A. 2015. *Porphyry's Commentary on Ptolemy's Harmonics: A Greek Text and Annotated translation*. Cambridge: Cambridge University Press.

Barnes, T. D. 1975. 'Publilius Optatianus Porfyrius', *American Journal of Philology* 96: 173–86.
  1976. 'The Emperor Constantine's Good Friday Sermon', *Journal of Theological Studies* 27: 414–23.
  1978. 'Emperor and Bishops, A.D. 324–44: Some Problems', *American Journal of Ancient History* 3: 53–75.
  1981. *Constantine and Eusebius*. Cambridge, MA; London: Harvard University Press.
  1984. 'Constantine's Prohibition of Pagan Sacrifice', *American Journal of Philology* 105: 69–72.
  1986a. 'Synesius in Constantinople', *Greek, Roman, and Byzantine Studies* 27: 93–112.
  1986b. 'When Did Synesius Become Bishop of Ptolemais?', *Greek, Roman, and Byzantine Studies* 27: 325–29.
  1993. *Athanasius and Constantius*. Cambridge, MA: Harvard University Press.
  1998. *Ammianus and the Representation of Historical Reality*. Ithaca; London: Cornell University Press.
  2001. 'Constantine's Speech to the Assembly of the Saints: Place and Date of Delivery', *Journal of Theological Studies* 52: 26–36.
  2008. 'Aspects of the Severan Empire, Part I: Severus as a New Augustus', *New England Classical Journal* 35: 251–67.
  2011. *Constantine: Dynasty, Religion, and Power in the Later Roman Empire*. Chichester: Wiley–Blackwell.
Barnes, T. D., and J. Vanderspoel. 1981. 'Julian and Themistius', *Greek, Roman, and Byzantine Studies* 22: 187–89.
Bartelink, G. M. 1970. *Quelques observations sur παρρησία dans la littérature paléo-chrétienne*. Nijmegen: Dekker & van de Vegt.
  1997. 'Die Parrhesia des Menschen vor Gott bei Johannes Chrysostomus', *Vigiliae Christianae* 51: 261–72
Bassett, S. 2004. *The Urban Image of Late Antique Constantinople*. Cambridge: Cambridge University Press.
Bausi, A., B. Reudenback, and H. Wimmer (eds.) 2020. *Canones: The Art of Harmony: The Canon Tables of the Four Gospels*. Berlin; Boston: De Gruyter.
Baynes, N. H. 1929. *Constantine the Great and the Christian Church*. London: Humphrey Milford.
  1955. 'The Thought-World of East Rome', in *Byzantine Studies and Other Essays*. London: Historical Association, pp. 24–46.
Beard, M. 1986. 'Cicero and Divination: The Formation of a Latin Discourse', *Journal of Roman Studies* 76: 33–46.
  2014. *Laughter in Ancient Rome: On Joking, Tickling, and Cracking Up*. Berkeley: University of California Press.
Beckwith, C. L. 2005. 'The Condemnation and Exile of Hilary of Poitiers at the Synod of Béziers (356 C.E.)', *Journal of Early Christian Studies* 13: 21–38.
Benedict, J. L. 2018. 'Truth to Power: The Politics of Theological Free Speech in the Cappadocian Fathers and Augustine of Hippo'. Diss. Duke University.

Béranger, J. 1948. 'Le réfus du pouvoir', *Museum Helveticum* 5: 178–96.
Bergmann, M. 1998. *Die Strahlen der Heerscher. Theomorphes Herrscherbild und politische Symbolik im Hellenismus und in der römischen Kaiserzeit*. Mainz am Rhein: von Zabern.
Bidez, J. 1930. *La vie de l'Empereur Julien*. Paris: Les Belles Lettres.
  1932. *L'empereur Julien. Œuvres complètes*, I.1 *Discours de Julien César*. Paris: Les Belles Lettres.
Bidez, J., and F. Cumont. 1922. *Iuliani imperatoris Epistulae Leges Poematia Fragmenta varia*. Paris; Oxford: Les Belles Lettres.
Bleckmann, B. 1994. 'Constantina, Vetranio, und Gallus Caesar', *Chiron* 24: 29–68.
  1997. 'Ein Kaiser als Prediger: zur Datierung der konstantinischen Rede an die Versammlung der Heligen', *Hermes* 125: 183–202.
  1999. 'Die Schlacht von Mursa und die zeitgenössische Deutung eines spätantiken Bürgerkrieges', in H. Brandt (ed.), *Gedeutete Realität. Krisen, Wirklichkeiten, Interpretationen (3.–6. Jh. N. Chr.)*. Stuttgart: Steiner, pp. 47–102.
  2012. 'Sources for the History of Constantine', in Lenski (ed.), pp. 14–32.
  2020. 'From Caesar to Augustus: Julian against Constantius', in Rebenich and Wiemer (eds.), pp. 97–123.
Blockley, R. C. 1981. *The Fragmentary Classicising Historians of the Later Roman Empire: Eunapius, Olympiodorus, Priscus and Malchus*. Liverpool: Cairns.
  1983. *The Fragmentary Classicising Historians of the Later Roman Empire: Eunapius, Olympiodorus, Priscus and Malchus. Vol. 2: Text, Translation and Historiographical Notes*. Liverpool: Cairns.
Borrelli, D. 2003. 'Il sacerdos del *De Mysteriis* e il sacerdos di Giuliano', in U. Criscuolo (ed.), *Da Costantino a Teodosio il Grande. Cultura, Società, Diritto*. Naples: D'Auria, pp. 105–17.
  2018. 'Identità e funzioni dello *hiereus* nel 'religious revival' di Massimino Daia e Giuliano imperatore', in D. Dainese and V. Gheller (eds.), *Beyond Intolerance: The Milan Meeting in AD 313 and the Evolution of the Imperial Religious Policy from the Age of the Tetrarchs to Julian the Apostate*. Turnhout: Brepols, pp. 67–104.
Bosworth, B. 1999. 'Augustus, the *Res Gestae*, and Hellenistic Theories of Apotheosis', *Journal of Roman Studies* 89: 1–18.
Bouffartigue, J. 1992. *L'Empereur Julien et la culture de son temps*. Paris: Institut d'Études Augustiniennes.
  2004. 'Philosophie et antichristianisme chez l'empereur Julian', in M. Narcy and É. Rebillard (eds.), *Hellénisme et Christianisme*. Lille: Presses Universitaires du Septentrion, pp. 111–31.
  2005. 'La lettre de Julien à Themistius: Histoire d'une fausse manœuvre et d'un désaccord essentiel', in Á. González Gálvez and P.-L. Malosse (eds.), *Mélanges A.F. Norman*. Lyon: Maison de l'Orient méditerranéen, pp. 113–38.
Boulnois, M.-O. 2020. 'Le prologue de l'évangile de Jean au cœur de la polémique entre l'empereur Julien et Cyrille d'Alexandrie', in G. Huber-

Rebenich and S. Rebenich (eds.), *Interreligiöse Konflikte im 4. Und 5. Jahrhundert. Julian* Contra Gailaeos-*Kyrill* Contra Iulianum. Berlin; Boston: De Gruyter, pp. 195–227.

Bourdieu, P. 1986. 'The Forms of Capital', in J. G. Richardson (ed.), *Handbook of Theory and Research for the Sociology of Education*. New York: Greenwood Press, pp. 241–58.

Boyarin, D. 2004. *Border Lines: The Partition of Judaeo-Christianity*. Philadelphia: University of Pennsylvania Press.

2010. 'Origen as Theorist of Allegory: Alexandrian Contexts', in Copeland and Struck (eds.), pp. 39–54.

Boys-Stones, G. R. 2001. *Post-Hellenistic Philosophy: A Study of Its Development from The Stoics to Origen*. Oxford: Oxford University Press.

(ed.) 2003. *Metaphor, Allegory, and the Classical Tradition: Ancient Thought and Modern Revisions*. Oxford: Oxford University Press.

2016. 'Providence and Religion in Middle Platonism', in E. Eidinow, J. Kindt and R. Osborne (eds.), *Theologies of ancient Greek religion*. Cambridge: Cambridge University Press, pp. 317–38.

Bowen, A., and P. Garnsey. 2003. *Lactantius: Divine Institutes*. Liverpool: Liverpool University Press.

Bowersock, G. W. 1978. *Julian the Apostate*. London: Duckworth.

1982. 'The Emperor Julian on His Predecessor', *Yale Classical Studies* 27: 159–72.

Bowman, A. 2005. 'Diocletian and the first Tetrarchy, A.D. 284–305', *Cambridge Ancient History* XII: 67–88.

Bradbury, S. 1987. 'The Date of Julian's *Letter to Themistius*', *Greek, Roman, and Byzantine Studies* 28: 235–52.

1994. 'Constantine and the Problem of Anti-Pagan Legislation in the Fourth Century', *Classical Philology* 89: 120–39.

2020. 'Julian and the Jews', in Rebenich and Wiemer (eds.), pp. 267–92.

Brakke, D. 1995. *Athanasius and the Politics of Asceticism*. Oxford: Clarendon Press.

Brancacci, A. 1985. *Rhetorike philosophousa. Dione Crisostomo nella cultura antica e bizantina*. Naples: Bibliopolis.

Branham, R. B. 1989. *Unruly Eloquence: Lucian and the comedy of traditions*. Cambridge, MA; London: Harvard University Press.

Bransbourg, G. 2009. 'Julien, l'*immunitas Christi*, les dieux et les cités', *Antiquité Tardive* 17: 151–58.

Breebaart, A. B. 1979. 'Eunapius of Sardes and the Writing of History', *Mnemosyne* 32: 360–75.

Bregman, J. 1982. *Synesius of Cyrene, Philosopher–Bishop*. Berkeley; London: University of California Press.

Brennan, B. 1976. 'Dating Athanasius' *Vita Antonii*', *Vigiliae Christianae* 39: 209–27.

Brennecke, H. C. 1994. 'Nicäa', *Theologische Realenziklopädie* 24: 429–41.

Briquel, D. 1995. 'L'empereur Claude comme auteur des 'Tyrrhenika', in D. Briquel and C. Guittard (eds.), *Les écrivains et l'Etrusca disciplina de Claude à Trajan*. Tours: Université de Tours, pp. 88–93.
Brisson, L. 1990. 'L'Oracle d'Apollon dans la vie de Plotin', *Kernos* 3: 77–88.
  1996. *Introduction à la philosophie du mythe. Tome 1: Sauver les myths*. Paris: Vrin.
Brown, P. 1988. *The Body and Society: Men, Women and Sexual Renunciation in Early Christianity*. New York: Columbia University Press.
  1992. *Power and Persuasion in Late Antiquity: Towards a Christian Empire*. Madison: University of Wisconsin Press.
Browning, R. 1952. 'The Riot of A.D. 387 in Antioch: The Role of Theatrical Claques in the Later Roman Empire', *Journal of Roman Studies* 42: 13–20.
  1975. *The Emperor Julian*. London: Weidenfield & Nicolson.
Bruch, J., and K. Hermann. 2012. 'The Reception of the Philosopher-King in Antiquity and the Medieval Age', in M. van Ackeren (ed.), *A Companion to Marcus Aurelius*. Chichester; Malden, MA: Wiley–Blackwell, pp. 483–96.
Brunt, P. A. 1977. 'Lex de imperio Vespasiani', *Journal of Roman Studies* 67: 95–116.
Bryan, J. 2012. *Likeness and Likelihood in the Presocratics and Plato*. Cambridge: Cambridge University Press
Burckhardt, J. 1853. *Die Zeit Constantins des Großen*. Basel: Schweighauser'sche Verlagsbuchhandlung.
Burgersdijk, D. W. P. 2020. 'Neoplatonic Philosophy in Tetrarchic and Constantinian Panegyric', in Ross and Omissi (eds.), pp. 167–89.
Burgersdijk, D. W. P., and A. J. Ross (eds.) 2018. *Imagining Emperors in the Later Roman Empire*. Leiden; Boston: Brill.
Burgess, R. 2008. 'The Summer of Blood: the 'Great Massacre' of 337 and the Promotion of the Sons of Constantine', *Dumbarton Oaks Papers* 62: 5–51.
Burnyeat, M., and M. Frede. 2015. *The Pseudo-Platonic Seventh Letter*. Oxford: Oxford University Press.
Caltabiano, M. 1991. *L'epistolario di Giuliano Imperatore. Saggio storico, traduzione, note e testo in appendice*. Naples: D'Auria.
Cameron, Al. 1987. 'Earthquake 400', *Chiron* 17: 343–60.
  2011. *The Last Pagans of Rome*. New York; Oxford: Oxford University Press.
Cameron, Al., and J. Long. 1993. *Barbarians and Politics at the Court of Arcadius*. Berkeley: University of California Press.
Cameron, Av. 1965. 'Procopius and the Church of St. Sophia', *Harvard Theological Review* 58: 161–63.
  1991. *Christianity and the Rhetoric of Empire: The Development of Christian Discourse*. Berkeley: University of California Press.
  1997. 'Eusebius' *Vita Constantini* and the Construction of Constantine', in M. J. Edwards and S. Swain (eds.), *Portraits: Biographical Representation in the Greek and Latin Literature of the Roman Empire*. Oxford: Oxford University Press, pp. 145–74.

1998. 'The Perception of Crisis', *Settimane di studio del centro italiano sull'alto medioevo* 45: 9–31.
2005. 'The Reign of Constantine, A.D. 306–337', *Cambridge Ancient History* XII: 90–109.
Cameron, Av., and S. G. Hall. 1999. *Life of Constantine. Eusebius. Introduction, Translation, and Commentary.* Oxford: Clarendon Press.
Carlà-Uhink, F. 2019. *Diocleziano.* Milan: Il Mulino.
Cartwright, S. 2016. 'Athanasius' *Vita Antonii* as Political Theology: The Call of Heavenly Citizenship', *Journal of Ecclesiastical History* 67: 241–64.
Célérier, P. 2013. *L'ombre de l'empereur Julian: le destine des écrits de Julien chez les auteurs païens et chrétiens du IVe au Vie siècle.* Paris: Presses universitaires de Paris Ouest.
Centrone, B. 2000. 'Platonism and Pythagoreanism in the Early Empire', in Rowe and Schofield (eds.), pp. 559–83.
Cerutti, M. V. 2010. "Pagan Monotheism'? Towards a Historical Typology', in S. Mitchell and P. Van Nuffelen (eds.), *Monotheism between Pagans and Christians in Late Antiquity.* Leuven; Walpole, MA: Peeters, pp. 15–32.
Chadwick, H. 2001. *The Church in Ancient Society: From Galilee to Gregory the Great.* Oxford: Oxford University Press.
Chantraine, H. 1993–94. 'Die Kreuzesvision von 351 – Fakten und Probleme', *Byzantinische Zeitschrift* 86–87: 430–41.
Chiaradonna, R. 2015. 'La Lettera a Temistio di Giuliano imperatore e il dibattito filosofico nel IV secolo', in Marcone (ed.), pp. 149–71.
Chin, C. M. 2008. *Grammar and Christianity in the Late Roman World.* Philadelphia: University of Pennsylvania Press.
Civiletti, M. 2007. *Eunapio. Vite di Filosofi e Sofisti.* Milan: Bompiani.
Clark, G. 1989. *Iamblichus, On the Pythagorean Life.* Translated with notes and introduction. Liverpool: Liverpool University Press.
2000a. 'Philosophic Lives and the Philosophic Life. Porphyry and Iamblichus', in T. Hagg and P. Rousseau (eds.), *Greek Biography and Panegyric in Late Antiquity.* Berkeley: University of California Press, pp. 29–51.
2000b. *Porphyry. On Abstinence from Killing Animals.* London: Duckworth.
2004. *Christianity and Roman Society.* Cambridge: Cambridge University Press.
Clarke, E. C. 1998. 'Communication, Human and Divine. Saloustious Reconsidered', *Phronesis* 43: 326–50.
2004. *Iamblichus, De mysteriis.* Translated with an introduction and notes by E. C. Clarke, J. M. Dillon, and J. P. Hershbell. Leiden: Brill.
Cocchini, F. 2006. *Origene. Teologo esegeta per un'identità cristiana.* Bologna: EDB.
Conti, S. 2009. 'Da eroe a dio: la concezione teocratica del potere in Giuliano', *Antiquité Tardive* 17: 119–26.
Conybeare, C., and S. Goldhill (eds.) 2021a. *Classical Philology and Theology: Entanglement, Disavowal, and the Godlike Scholar.* Cambridge: Cambridge University Press.
2021b. 'Philology's Shadow', in Conybeare and Goldhill (eds.), pp. 1–11.

Coogan, J. 2021. 'Transforming Textuality: Porphyry, Eusebius, and Late Ancient Tables of Contents', *Studies in Late Antiquity* 5: 6–27.
Cooley, A. 2007. 'Septimius Severus: the Augustan Emperor', in S. Swain, S. J. Harrison, and J. Elsner (eds.), *Severan Culture*. Cambridge: Cambridge University Press, pp. 381–93.
 2009. *Res Gestae Divi Augusti. Text, Translation, and Commentary*. Cambridge: Cambridge University Press.
Cooper, K. 1992. 'Insinuation of Womanly Influence: An Aspect of the Christianisation of the Roman Aristocracy', *Journal of Roman Studies* 82: 150–64.
 1996. *The Virgin and the Bride: Idealized Womanhood in Late Antiquity*. Cambridge, MA; London: Harvard University Press.
 2019. 'Constantine the Populist', *Journal of Early Christian Studies* 27: 241–70.
Copeland, R., and P. T. Struck (eds.) 2010. *The Cambridge Companion to Allegory*. Cambridge: Cambridge University Press.
Corbeill, A. 1996. *Controlling Laughter: Political Humor in the Late Roman Republic*. Princeton: Princeton University Press.
Corcoran, D. 1997. *The Empire of the Tetrarchs: Imperial Pronouncements and Government, AD 284–324*. Oxford: Clarendon Press.
 2013. 'The Gregorianus and Hermogenianus Assembled and Shattered', *Mélanges de l'Ecole française de Rome* 125: 285–304.
Corke-Webster, J. 2019. *Eusebius and Empire: Constructing Church and Rome in the Ecclesiastical History*. Cambridge: Cambridge University Press.
 2020a. 'How to Praise a Christian Emperor: The Panegyrical Experiments of Eusebius of Caesarea', in Omissi and Ross (eds.), pp. 143–65.
 2020b. 'A Bishop's Biography: Eusebius of Caesarea's *Life of Constantine*', in K. de Temmerman (ed.), *Oxford Handbook of Ancient Biography*. Oxford: Oxford University Press, pp. 297–312.
Cox, P. 1983. *Biography in Late Antiquity: A Quest for the Holy Man*. Berkeley: University of California Press.
Cox Miller, P. 'Strategies of Reprentation in Collective Biography: Constructing the Subject as Holy', in Hägg and Rousseau (eds.), pp. 209–54.
Crawford, M. R. 2019. *The Eusebian Canon Tables: Ordering Textual Knowledge in Late Antiquity*. Oxford: Oxford University Press.
Crawford, W. S. 1901. *Synesius the Hellene*. London: Rivingtons.
Cribiore, R. 2013. *Libanius the Sophist: Rhetoric, Reality, and Religion in the Fourth Century*. Ithaca: Cornell University Press.
Criscuolo, U. 1983. 'Sull'epistola di Giuliano Imperatore al filosofo Temistio', *Koinonia* 7: 89–111.
 2001. 'La religione diGiuliano', *Mediterraneo Antico* 4: 365–88.
 2012. 'Sinesio di Cirene tra neoplatonismo e teologia patristica', in Seng and Hoffmann (eds.), pp. 164–82.
Cristofoli, R. 2005. *Costantino e l'Oratio ad sanctorum coetum*. Naples: M. D'Auria.

Curta, F. 1995. 'Atticism, Homer, Neoplatonism, and *Fürstenspiegel*: Julian's Second Panegyric on Constantius', *Greek, Roman, and Byzantine Studies* 36: 177–211.

Dagron, G. 1968. *L'Empire romain d'Orient au IVe siècle et les traditions politiques de l'hellénisme. Le témoignage de Thémistios*. Paris: de Broccard.

Damgaard, F. 2013. 'Propaganda against Propaganda. Revisiting Eusebius' Use of the Figure of Moses in the Life of Contantine', in Johnson and Schott (eds.), pp. 115–49.

Davies, J. P. (2004) *Rome's Religious History: Livy, Tacitus, and Ammianus on their Gods*. Cambridge: Cambridge University Press.

Dawson, D. 1992. *Allegorical Readers and Cultural Revision in Acient Alexandria*. Berkeley: University of California Press.

Dearn, A. 2003. 'The Coinage of Vetranio: Imperial Representation and the Memory of Constantine the Great', *Numismatic Chronicle* 163: 169–91.

De Blois, L. 1976. *The Policy of Emperor Gallienus*. Leiden: Brill.

2002. 'The Crisis of the Third Century A.D. in the Roman Empire: A Modern Myth?', in L. De Blois and J. Rich (eds.), *The Transformation of Economic Life under the Roman Empire: Proceedings of the Second Workshop of the International Network Impact of Empire*. Amsterdam: Gieben, pp. 204–17.

Demoen, K. 1996. *Pagan and Biblical Exempla in Gregory Nazianzen: A Study in Rhetoric and Hermeneutic*. Turnhout: Brepols.

Den Boeft, J., J. W. Drijvers, D. den Hengst, and H. C. Teitler (1995) *Philological and Historical Commentary on Ammianus Marcellinus XXII*. Leiden; Boston: Brill.

DePalma Digeser, E. 2000. *The Making of a Christian Empire: Lactantius and Rome*. Ithaca; London: Cornell University Press.

Desideri, P. 1978. *Dione di Prusa. Un intellettuale greco nell'impero romano*. Messina; Florence: G. d'Anna.

2012. 'Introduzione', in Vagnone (ed.), pp 7–21.

De Vita, M. C. 2006. 'Socrate filosofo politico e maschera letteraria nelle orazioni di Temistio: strategie di appropriazione di un mito', in G. De Gregorio and S. M. Medaglia (eds.), *Tradizione, ecdotica, esegesi. Miscellanea di studi*. Naples: Arte Tipografica, pp. 7–41.

2010. 'Cibele Neoplatonica: alcune osservazioni sull'inno giulianeo Alla Madre degli dèi (or. 8 Rochefort)', in C. Talamo (ed.), *Saggi di commento a testi greci e latini*. Pisa: ETS, pp. 154–77.

2011. *Giuliano imperatore filosofo neoplatonico*. Milan: Vita e Pensiero.

2013. 'Alcune variazioni sul mito di Socrate nella tarda antichità', χώρα 11: 37–58.

2014. 'Una nobile gara di pietà: il dibattito interreligioso nel panegirico di Temistio a Gioviano', in M. Coppola, G. Fernicola and L. Pappalardo (eds.), *Dialogus. Il dialogo fra le religioni nel pensiero tardo-antico, medievale e umanistico*. Rome: Città Nuova, pp. 119–34.

2017a. 'Giuliano l'Apostata e il Vangelo di Giovanni', *Koinonia* 41: 147–67.

2017b. 'Giuliano Imperatore e il culto delle immagini sacre: un esempio di *philosophia telestike*?', in L. Canetti (ed.), *Statue. Rituali, Scienze e Magia dalla Tarda Antichità al Rinascimento*. Florence: Sismel, pp. 67–85.

2022. *Giuliano imperatore: Lettere e discorsi*. Milan: Bompiani.

DeVore, D. J. 2013. 'Greek Historiography, Roman Society, Christian Empire: The Ecclesiastical History of Eusebius of Caesarea'. Diss. University of California.

Dillon, J. M. 1986. 'Plutarch and Second Century Platonism', in A. H. Armstrong (ed.), *Classical Mediterranean Spirituality: Egyptian, Greek, Roman*. London: Routledge and Kegan Paul, pp. 214–29.

2001. 'The Neoplatonic Reception of Plato's Laws', in Lisi (ed.), pp. 241–54,

2006. 'Pedantry and Pedestrianism? Some Reflections on the Middle Platonic Commentary Tradition', in H. Tarrant and D. Baltzly (eds.), *Reading Plato in Antiquity*. London: Duckworth, pp. 19–31.

2012. 'The Theology of Julian's Hymn to King Helios', in J. Dillon (ed.), *The Platonic Heritage*. Farnham: Ashgate Variorum, pp. 103–15.

Dillon, J. M., and L. P. Gerson. 2004. *Neoplatonic Philosophy: Introductory Readings*. Indianapolis: Hackett.

Dillon, J. N. 2012. *The Justice of Constantine: Law, Communication, and Control*. Ann Arbor: University of Michigan Press.

Dolezal, S. 2006. 'Johannes Chrysostomos and the Goths', *Acta Universitatis Carolinae* 2: 165–85.

Dörrie, H. 1981. 'Die Andere Theologie: Wie stellten die frühchristlichen Theologien des 2.–4. Jahrhunderts ihren Lesern die ‚Griechische Weisheit' (= den Platonismus) dar?', *Theologie und Philosophie* 56: 1–46.

Dörries, H. 1954. *Das Selbstzeugnis Kaiser Konstantins*. Göttingen: Vandenhoeck & Ruprecht.

Dossey, L. 2010. *Peasants and Empire in Christian North Africa*. Berkeley: University of California Press.

Downey, G. 1959. 'The Name of the Church of St. Sophia in Constantinople', *Harvard Theological Review* 52: 37–41.

Drake, H. A. 1976. *In Praise of Constantine: A Historical Study and New Translation of Eusebius' Tricennial Orations*. Berkeley: University of California Press.

1988. 'What Eusebius Knew: The Genesis of the Vita Constantini', *Classical Philology* 83: 20–38.

2000. *Constantine and the Bishops: The Politics of Intolerance*. Baltimore; London: Johns Hopkins University Press.

2012a. 'The Impact of Constantine on Christianity', in Lenski (ed.), pp. 111–36.

2012b. 'But I Digress . . . Rhetoric and Propaganda in Julian's Second Oration to Constantius', in Baker-Brian and Tougher (eds.), pp. 35–46.

2020. *A Century of Miracles: Christians, Pagans, Jews, and the Supernatural, 312–410*. New York: Oxford University Press.

Drinkwater, J. F. 1983. 'The 'Pagan Underground', Constantius II's 'Secret Service' and the Usurpation and Survival of Julian the Apostate', in C. Deroux (ed.), *Studies in Latin Literature and Roman History III*. Brussels: Latomus, pp. 348–87.
  2005. 'Maximinus to Diocletian and the "crisis"', *Cambridge Ancient History* XII: 28–66.
Drijvers, J. W. 2004. *Cyril of Jerusalem: Bishop and City*. Leiden; Boston: Brill.
Drozdek, A. 2007. *Greek Philosophers as Theologians: The Divine Arche*. London: Routledge.
Duncan-Jones, R. 2004. 'Economic Change and the Transition to Late Antiquity', in S. Swain and M. Edwards (eds.), *Approaching Late Antiquity: The Transformation from Early to Late Empire*. Oxford: Oxford University Press, pp. 20–52.
Dvornik, F. 1955. 'The Emperor Julian's "Reactionary" Ideas on Kingship', in K. Weitzmann et al. (eds.), *Late Classical and Medieval Studies in Honor of Albert Mathias Rend*. Princeton: Princeton University Press, pp. 71–81.
  1966. *Early Christian and Byzantine Political Philosophy: Origins and Background*. Washington, DC: Dumbarton Oaks Center for Byzantine Studies.
Easterling, P., and R. Miles. 1996. 'Dramatic Identities: Tragedy in late Antiquity', in R. Miles (ed.), *Constructing Identities in late Antiquity*. London; New York: Routledge, pp. 95–111.
Edwards, M. 1995. 'The Arian Controversy and the *Oration to the Saints*', *Vigiliae Christianae* 49: 379–87.
  2003. *Constantine and Christendom: The Oration to the Saints; the Greek and Latin Accounts of the Discovery of the Cross; the Edict of Constantine to Pope Silvester*. Liverpool: Liverpool University Press.
  2006. 'The First Council of Nicaea', *The Cambridge History of Christianity. Origins to Constantine*. Cambridge: Cambridge University Press, pp. 552–67.
  2018. *Catholicity and Heresy in the Early Church*. London: Routledge.
Elliott, T. G. 1987. 'Constantine's Conversion: Do We Really Need It?', *Phoenix* 41: 420–38.
Elm, S. 1997. 'Isis' Loss – Gender, Dependence and Ethnicity in Synesius' *de providentia* or *Egyptian Tale*', *Zeitschrift für antikes Christentum* 1: 86–115.
  2012. *Sons of Hellenism, Fathers of the Church: Julian the Emperor, Gregory of Nazianzus and the Vision of Rome*. Berkeley: University of California Press.
  2013. 'Priest and Prophet: Gregory of Nazianzus' concept of Christian leadership as Theosis', in G. Stroumsa, R. Parker and B. Dignas (eds.), *Priests and Prophets in the Roman World*. Leuven: Peeters, pp. 162–84.
  2021. 'Julian the Emperor on Statues (of Himself)', in Conybeare and Goldhill (eds.), pp. 128–48.
Elsner, J. 1995. *Art and the Roman Viewer: The Transformation of Art from the Pagan World to Christianity*. Cambridge: Cambridge University Press.

1996. 'Inventing Imperium: Texts and the Propaganda of Monuments', in J. Elsner (ed.), *Art and Text in Roman Culture*. Cambridge: Cambridge University Press, pp. 32–53.

2000. 'From the Culture of Spolia to the Cult of Relics: The Arch of Constantine and the Genesis of Late Antique Forms', *Papers of the British School at Rome* 68: 149–84.

2012. 'Perspectives in Art', in Lenski (ed.), pp. 255–77.

2020. 'Introduction', in J. Elsner (ed.), *Empires of Faith in Late Antiquity: Histories of Art and Religion from India to Ireland*. Cambridge; New York: Cambridge University Press, pp. 1–24.

Elsner, J., and J. Hernández Lobato (eds.) 2017. *The Poetics of Late Latin Literature*. New York; Oxford: Oxford University Press.

Errington, M. 1997. 'Church and State in the First Years of Theodosius I', *Chiron* 27: 36–41.

2000. 'Themistius and His Emperors', *Chiron* 30: 861–904.

2006. *Roman Imperial Policy from Julian to Theodosius*. Chapel Hill: University of North Carolina Press.

Eshleman, K. 2012. *The Social World of Intellectuals in the Roman Empire: Sophists, Philosophers, and Christians*. Cambridge: Cambridge University Press.

Esmonde Cleary, A. S. 2013. *The Roman West, AD 200–500: An Archaeological Study*. Cambridge: Cambridge University Press.

Falls, T. B. 2003. *St. Justin Martyr. Dialogue with Trypho*. Washington, DC: Catholic University of America Press.

Favale, A. 1958. *Teofilo di Alessandria. Scritti, vita e dottrina*. Turin: Società editrice internazionale.

Feeney, D. 1988. *Literature and Religion at Rome: Cultures, Contexts and Beliefs*. Cambridge: Cambridge University Press.

Fejfer, J. 2008. *Roman Portraits in Context*. Berlin; New York: De Gruyter.

Feissel, D. 2009. 'Les acts de l'Etat impérial dans l'épigraphie tardive (324–610). Prolégomènes à un inventaire', in Haensch, R. (ed.), *Selbstdarstellung und Kommunikation. Die Veröffentlichung staatlicher Urkunden auf Stein und Bronze in der Römischen Welt*. Munich: Beck, pp. 97–128.

Ferguson, J. 1991. *Clement of Alexandria, Stromateis. Books One to Three*. Washington, DC: Catholic University of America Press.

Ferrar, W. J. 1920. *The Proof of the Gospel Being the Demonstratio Evangelica of Eusebius of Caesarea*. London: Society for Promoting Christian Knowledge.

Ferrari, G. 1990. 'Plato and Poetry', in G. Kenney (ed.), *The Cambridge History of Literary Criticism*. Cambridge: Cambridge University Press, pp. 92–148.

Finkelstein, A. 2018. *The Specter of the Jews: Emperor Julian and the Rhetoric of Ethnicity in Syrian Antioch*. Berkeley: University of California Press.

Fittschen, K. 1992–93. 'Ritratti maschili privati di epoca adrianea. Problemi della loro varietà', *Scienze dell'antichità. Storia, archeologia, antropologia* 6/7: 445–85.

1997. 'Privatporträts hadrianischer Zeit', in J. Bouzek and I. Ondrejová (eds.), *Roman Portraits: Artistic and literary*. Mainz: von Zabern, pp. 32–36.

Fitzgerald, A. 1930. *The Essays and Hymns of Synesius of Cyrene*. Oxford: Oxford University Press.

Flaig, E. 1999. 'Über die Grenzen der Akkulturation: Wider die Verdinglichung des Kulturbegriffs', in G. Vogt-Spira, B. Rommel, and I. Musäus (eds.), *Rezeption und Identität: die kulturelle Auseinandersetzung Roms mit Griechenland als europäisches Paradigma*. Stuttgart: Steiner, pp. 81–112.

Flower, R. 2012. 'Visions of Constantine', *Journal of Roman Studies* 102: 287–305.

2013. *Emperors and Bishops in Late Roman Invective*. Cambridge: Cambridge University Press.

Flower, R., and M. Ludlow. 2020. *Rhetoric and Religious Identity in Late Antiquity*. Oxford; New York: Oxford University Press.

Fontaine, J. 1987. 'Introduzione', in Fontaine, Prato, and Marcone (eds.), pp. ix–lxxvii.

Fontaine, J., C. Prato, and A. Marcone. 1987. *Giuliano Imperatore. Alla madre degli dèi e altri discorsi*. Milan: Arnaldo Mondadori Editore.

Ford, A. 2002. *The Origins of Criticism: Literary Culture and Poetic Theory in Classical Greece*. Princeton: Princeton University Press.

Fowden, G. 1978. 'Bishops and Temples in the Eastern Roman Empire A.D. 320–435', *Journal of Theological Studies* 29: 53–78.

1979. 'Pagan Philosophers in Late Antique Society with Special Reference to Iamblichus and His Followers'. Diss. Oxford University.

1982. 'The Pagan Holy Man in Late Antique Society', *Journal of Hellenic Studies* 102: 33–59.

1985. Review of Bregman (1985) in *Classical Philology* 80: 281–85.

1991. 'Constantine's Porphyry Column: The Earliest Literary Allusion', *Journal of Roman Studies* 81: 119–31.

1998. 'Polytheist Religion and Philosophy', *Cambridge Ancient History* XIII: 538–60.

2005. 'Late Polytheism: The World-View', *Cambridge Ancient History* XII: 521–37.

Fowler, R. (ed.) 2014. *Plato in the Third Sophistic*. Berlin; Boston: De Gruyter.

Fowler, R., and A. Quiroga Puertas. 2014. 'A Prolegomena to the Third Sophistic', in Fowler (ed.), pp. 1–30.

Franchi de' Cavalieri, P. 1953. 'I SS. Gioventino e Massimino', in *Note agiografiche* 9: 167–200.

Frede, M. 2000. 'The Philosopher', in J. Brunschwig and G. E. R. Lloyd (eds.), *Greek Thought: A Guide to Classical Knowledge*. Cambridge, MA; London: Harvard University Press.

Freisenbruch, A. 2007. 'Back to Fronto: Doctor and Patient in his Correspondence with an Emperor', in R. Morello and A. D. Morrison (eds.), *Ancient Letters: Classical and Late Antique Epistolography*. Oxford: Oxford University Press, pp. 235–56.

French, D. R. 1998. 'Rhetoric and the Rebellion of A.D. 387 in Antioch', *Historia* 47: 468–84.
Freudenburg, K. 2014. '"Recusatio" as Political Theatre: Horace's Letter to Augustus', *Journal of Roman Studies* 104: 105–32.
Gaisford, T. 1842. *Eusebii Pamphili episcopi Caesariensis, Eclogae Propheticae, e codice manuscripto bibliothecae Caesareae Vindobonensis*. Oxford: Oxford University Press.
Galvão-Sobrinho, C. R. 2013. *Doctrine and Power: Theological Controversy and Christian Leadership in the later Roman Empire*. Berkeley: University of California Press.
Gangloff, A. 2018. *Pouvoir impérial et vertus philosophiques: l'évolution de la figure du bon prince sous le Haut-Empire*. Leiden: Brill.
García-Ruiz, M. P. 2015. 'Una Lectura Conjuncta del Primer Encomio A Constancio y el Encomio A Eusebia de Juliano', *Exemplaria Classica* 19: 155–73.
  2018. 'Julian's Self-Representation in Coins and Texts', in Burgersdijk and Ross (eds.), pp. 204–33.
Garnsey, P. 1984. 'Religious Toleration in Classical Antiquity', *Studies in Church History* 21: 1–27.
  2000. 'Introduction: The Hellenistic and Roman Periods', in Rowe and Schofield (eds.), pp. 397–414.
  2003. 'Introduction', in Bowen and Garnsey, pp. 1–54.
Garnsey, P., and C. Humfress. 2001. *The Evolution of the Late Antique World*. Cambridge: Cambridge University Press.
Garnsey, P., and R. Winton. 1981. 'Political Theory', in M. I. Finley (ed.), *The Legacy of Greece*. Oxford: Oxford University Press.
Garzya, A. 1972. 'Il 'Dione' di Sinesio nel quadro del dibattito culturale del IV secolo d.C.', *Rivista di Filologia e Istruzione Classica* 100: 32–45.
  1989. *Opere di Sinesio di Cirene*. Turin: UTET.
Garzya, A., and D. Roques. 2000a. *Synésios de Cyrène, tome I: Correspondance (lettres I–LXIII)*. Paris: Les Belles Lettres.
  2000b. *Synésios de Cyrène, tome II : Correspondance (lettres LXIV–CLVI)*. Paris: Les Belles Lettres.
Gassman, M. 2016. 'Eschatology and Politics in Cyril of Jerusalm's *Epistle to Constantius*', *Vigiliae Christianae* 70: 119–33.
  2020. *Worshippers of the Gods: Debating Paganism in the Fourth Century Roman West*. New York; Oxford: Oxford University Press.
Gaudemet, J. 1958. *L'Église dans l'Empire Romain: IVe–Ve siècles*. Paris: Sirey.
Geffcken, J. 1914. *Kaiser Iulianus*. Leipzig: Dieterich.
Germino, E. 2004. *Scuola e cultura nella legislazione di Giuliano l'Apostata*. Naples: Eugenio Jovene.
Gifford, E. H. 1903. *Eusebii Pamphili Evangelicae praeparationis libri XV. Ad codices manuscriptos denuo collatos recensuit, anglice nunc primum reddidit, notis et indicibus instruxit*. Oxford: Oxford University Press.

Girardet, K. M. 2007. *Die Konstantinische Wende: Voraussetzungen und Geistige Grundlagen der Religionspolitik Konstantins des Grossen*. Darmstadt: Wissenschaftliche Buchgesellschaft.
  2013. *Konstantin. Rede an die Versammlung der Heiligen*. Freiburg: Herder.
Gleason, M. 1995. *Making Men: Sophists and Self-Presentation in Ancient Rome*. Princeton: Princeton University Press.
Goldhill, S. 1995. *Foucault's Virginity: Ancient Erotic Fiction and the History of Sexuality*. Cambridge: Cambridge University Press.
  2001a. *Being Greek under Rome. Cultural Identity, the Second Sophistic and the Development of the Empire*. Cambridge: Cambridge University Press.
  2001b. 'The Erotic Eye: Visual Stimulation and Cultural Conflict', in Goldhill (2001a), pp. 154–94.
  2002. *Who Needs Greek? Contests in the Cultural History of Hellenism*. Cambridge: Cambridge University Press.
  2006. 'Rethinking Religious Revolution', in Goldhill and Osborne (eds.), pp. 141–63.
  2009. 'Constructing Identity in the Love Letters of Philostratus', in E. Bowie and J. Elsner (eds.), *Philostratus*. Cambridge: Cambridge University Press, pp. 287–308.
  2020. *Preposterous Poetics: The Politics and Aesthetics of Form in Late Antiquity*. Cambridge: Cambridge University Press.
  2021. 'The Union and Divorce of Classical Philology and Theology', in Conybeare and Goldhill (eds.), pp. 33–62.
  2022. *The Christian Invention of Time: Temporality and the Literature of Late Antiquity*. Cambridge: Cambridge University Press.
Goldhill, S., and E. Greensmith. 2020. 'Gregory of Nazianzus in the *Palatine Anthology*: The Poetics of Christian Death', *The Cambridge Classical Journal* 66: 29–69.
Goldhill, S., and R. Osborne (eds.) 2006. *Rethinking Revolutions through Ancient Greece*. Cambridge: Cambridge University Press.
Goulet, R. 2008. 'Réflexions sur la loi scolaire de l'empereur Julien', in J. Hugonnard-Roche (ed.), *L'enseignement supérieur dans les mondes antiques et médiévaux*. Paris: Vrin, pp. 175–200.
Grafton, A. 2008. *Christianity and the Transformation of the Book: Origen, Eusebius, and the Library of Caesarea*. Cambridge, MA: Belknap Press of Harvard University Press.
Green, R. P. H. 2010. 'Constantine as Patron of Christian Latin Poetry', *Studia Patristica* 46: 65–76.
Greenlee, C. 2020. 'The Ideology of Imperial Unity in Themistius (Or. 1) and Libanius (Or. 59)', in Baker-Brian and Tougher (eds.), pp. 133–56.
Greenwood, D. N. 2013. 'A Cautionary Note on Julian's Pagan Trinity', *Ancient Philosophy* 33: 391–402.
  2014. 'Crafting Divine Personae in Julian's *Or. 7*', *Classical Philology* 109: 140–49.
  2017a. 'Constantinian Influence upon Julian's Pagan Church', *Journal of Ecclesiastical History* 68: 1–21.

2017b. 'Julian's Use of Asclepius against the Christians', *Harvard Studies in Classical Philology* 109: 491–509.
2019. 'Homer and the Wrath of Julian', *Classical Quarterly* 69: 887–95.
2021. *Julian and Christianity*. Ithaca: Cornell University Press.
Gregg, R. C. 1980. *The Life of Antony; and the Letter to Marcellinus*. Athanasius. London: SPCK.
Grethlein, J. 2013. *Experience and Teleology in Ancient Historiography: 'Future Past' from Herodotus to Augustine*. Cambridge: Cambridge University Press.
Grillet, B., and J. -N. Guinot. 1990. *Homélie sur Babylas. Introduction, texte critique, traduction et notes*. Paris: Éditions du Cerf.
Grimaldi, W. M. A. 1980. '*Semeion, Tekmerion, Eikos* in Aristotle's *Rhetoric*', *American Journal of Philology* 101: 383–98.
Gruen, E. S. 1984. *The Hellenistic World and the Coming of Rome*. Berkeley: University of California Press.
1992. *Culture and National Identity in Republican Rome*. London: Duckworth.
Guidetti, F. 2013. 'Iconografia di Costantino. L'invenzione di una nuova immagine imperiale', in A. Melloni (ed.) *Costantino I. Enciclopedia costantiniana sulla figura e l'immagine dell'imperatore del cosiddetto editto di Milano, 313–2013*, Rome: Treccani, II 185–200, 961–79
2015. 'I ritratti dell'imperatore Giuliano', in Marcone (ed.), pp. 12–49.
Haas, C. 1997. *Alexandria in Late Antiquity: Topography and Social Conflict*. Baltimore: Johns Hopkins University Press.
Habinek, T. 2017. 'Optatian and His Oeuvre: Explorations in Ontology', in Squire and Wienand (eds.), pp. 391–425.
Hadijttofi, F., and A. Lefteratou (eds.) 2020. *The Genres of Late Antique Christian Poetry: Between Modulations and Transpositions*. Berlin; Boston: De Gruyter.
Hadot, P. 1977. *Ambroise de Milan, Apologie de David. Introd., texte latin, notes et index*. Paris: Éditions du Cerf.
1981. *Exercices spirituels et philosophie antique*. Paris: Etudes augustiniennes.
Hafner, M. 2017. *Lukians Schrift 'Das traurige Los der Gelehrten': Einführung und Kommentar zu* De Mercede Conductis Potentium Familiaribus. Stuttgart: Steiner.
Hägg, T., and P. Rousseau (eds.) 2000. *Greek Biography and Panegyric in Late Antiquity*. Berkeley: University of California Press.
Hagl, W. 1997. *Arcadius Apis Imperator: Synesius von Kyrene und sein Beitrag zum Herrscherideal der Spätantike*. Stuttgart: Steiner.
Hahn, J. 1989. *Der Philosoph und die Gesellschaft: Selbstverständnis, öffentliches Auftreten und populäre Erwartungen in der hohen Kaiserzeit*. Stuttgart: Steiner.
Haines, C. R. 1962. *The Correspondence of Marcus Cornelius Fronto*. Cambridge, MA; London: Heinemann.
Hall, S. G. 1998. 'Some Constantinian Documents in the *Vita Constantini*', in S. N. C. Lieu and D. Monstserrat (eds.), *Constantine: History, Historiography and Legend*. London; New York: Routledge, pp. 86–103.
Halliwell, S. 2008. *Greek Laughter: A Study of Cultural Psychology from Homer to Early Christianity*. Cambridge: Cambridge University Press.

Hannestad, N. 2007. 'Die Porträtskulptur zur Zeit Konstantins des Grossen', in A. Demandt and J. Engemann (eds.), *Konstantin der Grosse*. Trier: Rheinisches Landesmuseum, pp. 96–116.

Harkins, P. W. 1963. *St John Chrysostom: Baptismal Instructions*. Translated and annotated. New York: Newman Press.

Harl, M. 1982. 'Origène et les interpretations patristiques greques de l'obscurité biblique', *Vigiliae Christianae* 36: 334–71.

Harries, J. 2012. 'Julian the Lawgiver', in Baker-Brian and Tougher (eds.), pp. 121–36.

Hartmann, U. 2008. 'Claudius Gothicus und Aurelianus', in K.-P. Johne (ed.), *Die Zeit der Soldatenkaiser. Krise und Transformation des Römischen Reiches im 3. Jahrhundert n. Chr. (235–284)*. Berlin: De Gruyter.

Hartney, A. M. 2004. *John Chrysostom and the Transformation of the City*. London: Duckworth.

Heather, P. J. 1998. 'Themistius: A Political Philosopher', in Whitby (ed.), pp. 125–50.

  2020. 'The Gallic Wars of Julian Caesar', in Rebenich and Wiemer (eds.), pp. 64–96.

Heather, P. J., and J. Matthews. 1991. *The Goths in the Fourth Century*. Liverpool: Liverpool University Press.

Heather, P. J., and D. Moncur. 2001. *Politics, Philosophy, and Empire in the Fourth Century: Select Orations of Themistius*. Liverpool: Liverpool University Press.

Heck, E. 2009. 'Constantin und Lactanz in Trier – Chronologisches', *Historia* 58: 118–30.

Heim, F. 1992. *La Théologie de la victoire de Constantine à Theodose*. Paris: Beauchesne.

Helm, R. 1956. *Die Chronik des Hieronymus*. Berlin: Akademie Verlag.

Henck, N. 2001. 'Constantius' *paideia*, Intellectual Milieu and Promotion of the Liberal Arts', *Proceedings of the Cambridge Philological Society* 47: 172–82.

  2002. 'Constantius ὁ Φιλοκτίστης?', *Dumbarton Oaks Papers* 55: 279–304.

Henderson, J. 2002. *Pliny's Statue: The Letters, Self-Portraiture and Classical Art*. Exeter: University of Exeter Press.

Henrichs, A. 1995. 'Graecia Capta: Roman Views of Greek Culture', *Harvard Studies in Classical Philology* 97: 243–61.

Hidber, T. 2006. *Herodians Darstellung der Kaisergeschichte nach Marc Aurel*. Basel: Schwabe.

Hoffmann, L. M. 2012. 'Die Lebenswelt des Synesius von Kyrene – ein historischer Überblick', in Seng and Hoffmann (eds.), pp. 35–65.

Hoffmann, P. (2009) 'What Was Commentary in Late Antiquity? The Example of the Neoplatonic Commentators', in M. L. Gill and P. Pellegrine (eds.), *Companion to Ancient Philosophy*. Oxford: Wiley-Blackwell, pp. 597–622.

Hollerich, M. J. 1989. 'The Comparison of Moses and Constantine in Eusebius of Caesarea's *Life of Constantine*', *Studia Patristica* 19: 80–95.

Hopkins, K. 1998. 'Christian Number and Its Implications', *Journal of Early Christian Studies* 6: 185–226.
Horst, C. 2013. *Marc Aurel: Philosophie und politische Macht zur Zeit der Zweiten Sophistik*. Stuttgart: Steiner.
Humfress, C. 2007. *Orthodoxy and the Courts in Late Antiquity*. Oxford: Oxford University Press.
Humphries, M. 1997. 'In Nomine Patris: Constantine the Great and Constantius II in Christological Polemic', *Historia* 46: 448–64.
  1998. 'Savage Humour: Christian Anti-panegyric in Hilary of Poitiers' Against Constantius', in Whitby (ed.), pp. 201–23.
  2012. 'The Tyrant's Mask? Images of Good and Bad Rule in Julian's Letter to the Athenians', in Baker-Brian and Tougher (eds.), pp. 75–90.
Hunt, D. 1995. 'Julian and Marcus Aurelius', in D. Innes, H. Hine, and C. Pelling (eds.), *Ethics and Rhetoric: Classical Essays for D. Russell on his Seventy-Fifth Birthday*. Oxford: Oxford University Press, pp. 287–98.
  1997. 'The Church as a Public Institution', *Cambridge Ancient History* XIII: 238–76.
  2012. 'The Christian Context of Julian's against the Galileans', in Baker-Brian and Tougher (eds.), pp. 251–61.
Hunter, D. G. 1988. *A Comparison between a King and a Monk; Against the Opponents of the Monastic Life: Two Treatises by John Chrysostom*. Lewiston: Edwin Mellen Press.
  1989. 'Libanius and John Chrysostom: New Thoughts on an Old Problem', *Studia Patristica* 22: 129–35.
Huttner, U. 2004. *Recusatio imperii: ein politisches Ritual zwischen Ethik und Taktik*. Hildesheim: Olms.
Hutchinson, G. 1998. *Cicero's Correspondence: A Literary Study*. Oxford: Oxford University Press.
Inowlocki, S. 2004. 'Eusebius of Caesarea's 'interpretatio Christiana' of Philo's *De vita contemplativa*', *Harvard Theological Review* 97: 305–28.
  2006. *Eusebius and the Jewish Authors: His Citation Technique in an Apologetic Context*. Leiden; Boston: Brill.
  2007. 'Eusebius' Appropriation of Moses in an Apologetic Context', in A. Graupner and M. Wolter (eds.), *Moses in Biblical and Extra-Biblical Traditions*. Berlin; New York: De Gruyter, pp. 241–55.
Ip, P. H. 2022. 'Thinking with Origen Today: Hermeneutical Challenges and Future Directions', *Modern Theology* 38: 191–203.
Isele, B. 2010. *Kampf um Kirchen: religiöse Gewalt, heiliger Raum und christiche Topographie in Alexandria und Konstantinopel (4. Jh.)*. Münster: Aschendorff.
James, L. 2012. 'Is There an Empress in the Text? Julian's Speech of Thanks to Eusebia', in Baker-Brian and Tougher (eds.), pp. 47–60.
Johnson, A. 2006. *Ethnicity and Argument in Eusebius'* Praeparatio Evangelica. Oxford: Oxford University Press.
  2013. *Religion and Identity in Porphyry of Tyre: the Limits of Hellenism in Late Antiquity*. Cambridge: Cambridge University Press.

2014. *Eusebius*. London: I. B. Tauris.
2020. 'The Rhetoric of Pagan Religious Identities: Porphyry and his First Readers', in R. Flower and M. Ludlow (eds.), *Rhetoric and Religious Identity in Late Antiquity*. Oxford: Oxford University Press, pp. 28–47.
Johnson, A., and J. Schott (eds.) 2013. *Eusebius of Caesarea: Tradition and Innovations*, Washington, DC: Center for Hellenic Studies.
Jones, A. H. M. 1949. *Constantine and the Conversion of Europe*. London: Hodder and Stoughton.
1964. *The Later Roman Empire, 284–602: A Social, Economical and Administrative Survey*. Oxford: Oxford University Press.
Jones, A. H. M., and T. Skeat. 1954. 'Note on the Genuineness of the Constantinian Documents in Eusebius' *Life of Constantine* and Appendix', *Journal of Ecclesiastical History* 5: 196–200.
Jones, C. P. 1978. *The Roman World of Dio Chrysostom*. Cambridge, MA; London: Harvard University Press.
2010. 'Themistius after the Death of Julian', *Historia* 59: 501–6.
Kahlos, M. 2007. *Debate and Dialogue: Christian and Pagan Cultures c. 360–430*, Aldershot; Burlington, VT: Ashgate.
2009. *Forbearance and Compulsion: The Rhetoric of Religious Tolerance and Intolerance in Late Antiquity*. London: Duckworth.
2012. 'Pagan-Christian Debates over the Interpretation of Texts in Late Antiquity', *Classical World* 105: 525–45.
2019. *Religious Dissent in Late Antiquity, 350–450*. New York; Oxford: Oxford University Press.
Kaiser, W. 2015. 'Justinian and the *Corpus Iuris Civilis*', *The Cambridge Companion to Roman Law*. Cambridge: Cambridge University Press, pp. 119–48.
Karla, G. 2020. 'Libanius' Imperial Speech to Constantius II and Constans (Or. 59): Context, Tradition and, Innovation', in Omissi and Ross (eds.), pp. 67–90.
Kaster, B. 1983. 'The Salaries of Libanius', *Chiron* 13: 37–59.
Kelly, C. 2007. 'Riot Control and Imperial Ideology in the Roman Empire', *Phoenix* 61: 150–76.
2012. 'Bureaucracy and Government', in Lenski (ed.), pp. 183–204.
Kelly, G. 2008. *Ammianus Marcellinus: The Allusive Historian*. Cambridge: Cambridge University Press.
Kelly, J. N. D. 1995. *Golden Mouth: The Story of John Chrysostom, Ascetic, Preacher, Bishop*. London: Duckworth.
Kennedy, G. A. 1983. *Greek Rhetoric under Christian Emperors*. Princeton: Princeton University Press.
Key Fowden, E., and G. Fowden. 2008. *Contextualising Late Greek philosophy*, Athens; Paris: National Hellenic Research Foundation.
King, C. W. 1888. *Julian the Emperor: Containing Gregory Nazianzen's Two Invectives and Libanius' Monody with Julian's Extant Theosophical Works*. London: Bell.

Klauser, T. 1944. 'Aurum Coronarium', *Römische Mitteilungen* 59: 129–53.
Klein, R. 1977. *Constantius II. und die Christliche Kirche*. Darmstadt: Wissenschaftliche Buchgesellschaft.
(1982) 'Zur Glaubwürdigkeit historischer Aussagen des Bischofs Athnasius von Alexandria über die Religionspolitik des Kaisers Constantius II', *Studia Patristica* 17: 996–1017.
Koch, W. 1927–28. 'Comment l'empereur Julian tâcha de fonder une église païenne', *Revue Belge de Philologie et d'Historie* 6: 123–46; 7: 42–82, 511–50, 1363–85.
Kofsky, A. 2000. *Eusebius of Caesarea against Paganism*. Leiden; Boston: Brill.
Kolb, F. 2004. '*Praesens Deus*: Kaiser und Gott unter der Tetrarchie', in A. Demandt, A. Goltz, and H. Schlange-Schöningen (eds.), *Diokletian und die Tetrarchie: Aspekte einer Zeitwende*. Berlin; New York: de Gruyter, pp. 27–37.
König, J. 2012. *Saints and Symposiasts: The Literature of Food and the Symposium in Greco-Roman and Early Christian Culture*. Cambridge: Cambridge University Press.
König, J., and T. Whitmarsh (eds.) 2007. *Ordering Knowledge in the Roman Empire*. Cambridge: Cambridge University Press.
Körfer, A. L. 2019. *Kaiser Konstantin als Leser: Panegyrik, performance und Poetologie in den carmina Optatians*. Berlin; Boston: De Gruyter.
Kurfess, A. 1918. 'Das Akrostichon Ἰησοῦς Χρειστὸς Θεοῦ Υἱὸς Σωτὴρ Σταυρός', *Sokrates* 6: 99–105.
Kurmann, A. 1988. *Gregor von Nazianz, Oratio 4 gegen Julian: ein Kommentar*. Basel: Reinhardt.
Labriola, I. 1972. *Messaggio agli Ateniesi. Saggio e traduzione*. Florence: La Nuova Italia Editrice.
Lacombrade, C. 1951a. *Synésios de Cyrène Hellène et chrétien*. Paris: Les Belles Lettres.
1951b. *Le Discours sur la Royauté de Synésios de Cyrène à l'empereur Arcadios*. Paris: Les Belles Lettres.
1964. *L'Empereur Julien, oeuvres complètes*, t. II, 2e p.: *Discours de Julien Empereur*. Paris: Les Belles Lettres.
1978. *Synésios de Cyrene, tome I: Hymnes*. Paris: Les Belles Lettres.
Lacoste, J.-Y. 2014. 'Theōria, vita philosophica, and Christian Experience', in *From Theology to Theological Thinking*, translated by W. C. Hackett. Charlottesville: University of Virginia Press, pp. 1–30.
Lamberton, R. 1986. *Homer the Theologian: Neoplatonist Allegorical Reading and the Growth of the Epic Tradition*. Berkeley: University of California Press.
Lamoureux, J., and N. Aujoulat. 2004. *Synésios de Cyrène, tome IV: Opuscules I*. Paris: Les Belles Lettres.
2008a. *Synésios de Cyrène, tome V: Opuscules II*. Paris: Les Belles Lettres.
2008b. *Synésios de Cyrène, tome VI: Opuscules III*. Paris: Les Belles Lettres.
Lane Fox, R. 1986. *Pagans and Christians*. London: Viking.
2015. *Augustine: Conversions and Confessions*. London: Penguin.

Lauwers, J. 2013. 'Systems of Sophistry and Philosophy: The Case of the Second Sophistic', *Harvard Studies in Classical Philology* 107: 331–63.

Lavan, M. 2018. 'Pliny *Epistles* 10 and Imperial Correspondence: The Empire of Letters', in A. König and C. Whitton (eds.), *Roman Literature under Nerva, Trajan, and Hadrian. Literary Interactions, D 96–138*. Cambridge: Cambridge University Press, pp. 280–301.

Lee, A. D. 1993. *Information and Frontiers: Roman Foreign Relations in Late Antiquity*. Cambridge: Cambridge University Press.

  2012. 'Traditional Religions', in Lenski (ed.), pp. 159–80.

Lenski, N. (ed.) 2012a. *The Cambridge Companion to the Age of Constantine*. Cambridge: Cambridge University Press.

  2012b. 'The Reign of Constantine', in Lenski (ed.), pp. 59–90.

  2014. *Failure of Empire: Valens and the Roman state in the fourth century A.D.* Berkeley: University of California Press.

  2016. *Constantine and the Cities: Imperial Authority and Civic Politics*. Philadelphia: University of Pennsylvania Press.

Lettieri, G. 2013. 'Lattanzio ideologo della svolta costantiniana', in *Enciclopedia Costantiniana*. Milan: I 45–57.

Levick, B. 2010. *Augustus: Image and Substance*. Abingdon: Routledge.

Lianeri, A. 2016. *Knowing Future Time in and through Greek Historiography*. Berlin; Boston: De Gruyter.

Liebeschuetz, J. H. W. G. 1990. *Barbarians and Bishops: Army, Church, and State in the Age of Arcadius and Chrysostom*. Oxford: Oxford University Press.

  2005. *Ambrose of Milan: Political Letters and Speeches*. Liverpool: Liverpool University Press.

  2007. 'Was There a Crisis of the third Century?', in O. Hekster, G. de Kleijn and D. Slootjes (eds.), *Crises and the Roman Empire: Proceedings of the Seventh Workshop of the International Network Impact of Empire*. Leiden: Brill, pp. 11–20.

  2011. *Ambrose and John Chrysostom: Clerics between Desert and Empire*. Oxford: Oxford University Press.

  2012. 'Julian's Hymn to the Mother of the Gods', in Baker-Brian and Tougher (eds.), pp. 213–27.

Lieu, S. C. 1986. *The Emperor Julian: Panegyric and Polemic. Claudius Mamertinus, John Chrysostom, Ephrem the Syrian*. Liverpool: Liverpool University Press.

  2004. *Christian Identity in the Jewish and Graeco-Roman World*. Oxford: Oxford University Press.

Lisi, F. L. 2001. *Plato's Laws and Its Historical Significance: Selected Papers of the International Congress on Ancient Thought*. Sankt Augustin: Academia Verlag.

Lizzi Testa, R. 1987. *Il potere episcopale nell'Oriente romano. Rappresentazione ideologica e realtà politica (IV–V sec. d.C.)*. Rome: Edizioni dell'Ateneo.

  1999. 'Synesius', in G. W. Bowersock, P. Brown, and O. Grabar (eds.), *Late Antiquity, a Guide to the Postclassical World*. Cambridge, MA; London: Belknap Press of Harvard University Press, p. 710.

2007. 'The Late Antique Bishop: Image and Reality', in Ph. Rousseau (ed.), *A Companion to Late Antiquity*. Chichester: Wiley–Blackwell, pp. 525–38.

Long, J. 1996. *Claudian's in Eutropium: Or, How, When, and Why to Slander a Eunuch*. Chapel Hill: University of North Carolina Press.

2012. 'Afterword: Studying Julian the Author', in Baker-Brian and Tougher (eds.), pp. 323–38.

López-Sánchez, F. 2012. 'Julian and His Coinage, a Very Constantinian Prince', in Baker-Brian and Tougher (eds.), pp. 159–81.

Lössl, J. 2012. 'Julian's Consolation to Himself on the Departure of the Excellent Salutius: Rhetoric and Philosophy in the Fourth Century', in Baker-Brian and Tougher (eds.), pp. 61–74.

Louth, A. 2003. 'The *Collectio Sabbaitica* and Sixth Century Origenism', in L. Perrone (ed.) *Origeniana Octava. Origen and the Alexandrian Tradition*. Leuven: Leuven University Press, pp. 1167–76.

Lowrie, M. 2009. *Writing, Performance, and Authority in Augustan Rome*. Oxford: Oxford University Press.

Lucrezi, F. 1995. *Aspetti giuridici del principato di Vespasiano*. Naples: Eugenio Jovene.

Lunn-Rockliffe, S. 2017. 'The Power of the Jewelled Style: Christian Signs and Names in Optatian's versus intexti and on Gems', in Squire and Wienand (eds.), pp. 427–60.

Lutz, C. E. 2020. *Musonius Rufus. That One Should Disdain Hardships: The Teachings of a Roman Stoic*. New Haven: Yale University Press.

MacCormack, S. 1981. *Art and Ceremony in Late Antiquity*. Berkeley: University of California Press.

MacMullen, R. 1969. *Constantine*. New York: Dial Press.

1976. *Roman Government's Response to Crisis, A.D. 235–337*. New Haven: Yale University Press.

Maisano, R. 1994. 'La funzione dei richiami platonici nei discorsi di Temistio', in C. Curti and C. Crimi (eds.), *Scritti classici e cristiani offerti a Francesco Corsaro*. Catania: Università degli studi di Catania, pp. 415–29.

1995. *Temistio. Discorsi*. Turin: UTET.

2006. 'Patrimonio culturale "di prima mano" e "di seconda mano" nei discorsi di Temistio', in E. Amato (ed.), *Approches de la Troisième Sophistique. Hommages à Jacques Schamp*. Brussels: Éditions Latomus.

Malingrey, A.-M. 1961. *Philosophia. étude d'un group des mots dans la littérature grecque, des présocratiques au IVe siècle après J.-C*. Paris: C. Klincksieck.

1972. *Jean Chrysostome. Sur la Vaine Gloire et l'Éducation des Enfants. Introduction, texte critique, traduction et notes*. Paris: Éditions du Cerf.

1980. *Jean Chrysostome. Sur le Sacerdoce (dialogue et homélie); introduction, texte critique, traduction et notes*. Paris: Éditions du Cerf.

Malosse, P.-L. 2008. 'Jean Chrysostome a-t-il été l'éleve de Libanios ?', *Phoenix* 62: 273–80.

Maltagliati, G. 2020. 'Persuasion through Proximity (and Distance) in the Attic Orators' Historical Examples', *Greek Roman and Byzantine Studies* 60: 68–97.

Mantovani, D. 2009. 'Lex 'regia' de imperio Vespasiani. Il *vagum imperium* e la legge costante', in L. Capogrossi Colognesi and E. Tassi Scandone (eds.), *La Lex de Imperio Vespasiani e la Roma dei Flavi. Atti del Convegno, 20–22 novembre 2008*. Rome: l'Erma di Bretschneider, pp. 125–55.

Maraval, P. 2013. *Les fils de Constantin: Constantin II (337–340), Constance II (337–361), Constant (337–350)*. Paris: CRNS Editions.

Marcone, A. 1984. 'Un panegirico rovesciato. Pluralità di modelli e contaminazione letteraria nel *Misopogon* giulianeo', *Revue d'Études Augustiniennes* 30: 226–39.

2012. 'The Forging of a Hellenic Orthodoxy: Julian's Speeches against the Cynics', in Baker-Brian and Tougher (eds.), pp. 239–50.

2015. *L'imperatore Giuliano. Realtà storica e rappresentazione*. Milan; Florence: Le Monnier Università.

2019. *Giuliano*. Rome: Salerno editrice.

Marcos, M. 2009. '"He Forced with Gentleness". Emperor Julian's Attitude to Religious Coercion', *Antiquité Tardive* 19: 191–204.

Markus, R. A. 1990. *The End of Ancient Christianity*. Cambridge: Cambridge University Press.

Marlowe, E. (2016) 'The Multivalence of Memory: The Tetrarchs, the Senate, and the Vicennalia Monument in the Roman Forum', in K. Galinsky and K. Lapatin (eds.), *Cultural Memories in the Roman Empire*. Los Angeles: Getty: 240–62.

Marchesi, I. 2008. *The Art of Pliny's Letters: A Poetics of Allusion in the Private Correspondence*. Cambridge: Cambridge University Press.

Martens, J. 1994. 'Nomos Empsychos in Philo and Clement of Alexandria', in W. E. Helleman (ed.), *Hellenization revisited*. Lanham; London: University Press of America, pp. 323–38.

Masaracchia, E. 1990. *Contra Galilaeos. Giuliano Imperatore; introduzione, testo critico e traduzione*. Rome: Edizioni dell'Ateneo.

Mathew, G. 1943. 'The Character of the Gallienic Renaissance', *Journal of Roman Studies* 33: 65–70.

Matthews, J. 1989. *The Roman Empire of Ammianus*. London: Duckworth.

Maxwell, J. L. 2006. *Christianisation and Communication in Late Antiquity: John Chrysostom and His Congregation in Antioch*. Cambridge: Cambridge University Press.

Mazza, M. 1986. 'Filosofia religiosa ed *Imperium* in Giuliano', in M. Mazza (ed.), *Le maschere del potere. Cultura e politica nella tarda antichità*. Naples: Eugenio Jovene, pp. 95–148.

McCormick, M. 1986. *Eternal Victory: Triumphal Rulership in Late Antiquity, Byzantium, and the Early Medieval West*. Cambridge: Cambridge University Press.

McLynn, N. B. 1994. *Ambrose of Milan: Church and Court in a Christian Capital*. Berkeley: University of California Press.

2005. '"Genere hispanus": Theodosius, Spain, and Nicene Orthodoxy', in K. D. Bowes and M. Kulikowski (eds.), *Hispania in Late Antiquity: Current Perspectives*. Boston; Leiden: Brill 77–120.

2006. 'Among the Hellenists: Gregory and the Sophists', in N. McLynn (ed.), *Christian Politics and Religious Culture in Late Antiquity*. Farnham: Ashgate Variorum, pp. 213–38.

2014. 'Julian and the Christian Professors', in G. Harrison, C. Humfress, and I. Sandwell (eds.) *Being Christian in Late Antiquity: A Festschrift for Gillian Clark*. Oxford University Press, pp. 120–38.

Metzger, E. 1998. *A Companion to Justinian's Institutes*. London: Duckworth.

Meyer, R. T. 1985. *Palladius. Dialogue on the Life of John Chrysostom*. New York: Newman Press.

Moles, J. L. 1990. 'The *Kingship Orations* of Dio Chrysostom', *Papers of the Leeds Latin Seminar* 6: 297–365.

Momigliano, A. 1963. 'Pagan and Christian Historiography in the Fourth Century A.D.', in *The Conflict between Paganism and Christianity in the Fourth Century: Essays*. Oxford: Oxford University Press, pp. 79–99.

1971. *The Development of Greek Biography: Four Lectures*. Cambridge, MA: Harvard University Press.

1973. 'Freedom of Speech in Antiquity', in P. P. Wiener (ed.), *Dictionary of the History of Ideas: Studies of Selected Pivotal Ideas*. New York: Scribners, II pp. 252–63.

1987. 'Ancient Biography and the Study of Religion in the Roman Empire', in *On Pagans, Jews, and Christians*, Hanover, NH: Wesleyan University Press, pp. 159–77.

Morgan, T. 2015. *Roman Faith and Christian Faith:* pistis *and* fides *in the Early Roman Empire and Early Churches*. Oxford: Oxford University Press.

Moser, M. 2018. *Emperors and Senators in the Reign of Constantius II: Maintaining Imperial Rule between Rome and Constantinople in the Fourth Century AD*. Cambridge: Cambridge University Press.

Moss, J. 2007. 'The Doctor and the Pastry Chef: Pleasure and Persuasion in Plato's *Gorgias*', *Ancient Philosophy* 27: 229–49.

Most, G. W. 2010. 'Hellenistic Allegory and Early Imperial Rhetoric', in Copeland and Struck (eds.), pp. 26–38.

Müller, F. L. 1998. *Die beiden Satiren des Kaisers Julianus Apostata*. Stuttgart: Franz Steiner.

Naber, S. A. (1867) *M. Cornelii Frontonis et M. Aurelii Imperatoris Epistulae: L. veri et T. Antonini Pii et Appiani Epistularum Reliquiae*. Leipzig: Teubner.

Nasrallah, L. S. 2010. *Christian Responses to Roman Art and Architecture: The Second-Century Church amid the Spaces of Empire*. Cambridge: Cambridge University Press.

Nesselrath, H.-G. 2008. 'Mit "Waffen" Platonis gegen ein christliches Imperium: der Mythos in Julians Schrift Gegen den Kyniker Herakleios', in Schäfer (ed.), pp. 207–19.

2020. 'Julian's Philosophical Writings', in Rebenich and Wiemer (eds.), pp. 38–63.

Nesselrath, T. 2013. *Kaiser Julian und die Repaganisierung des Reiches. Konzept und Vorbilder*. Münster: Aschendorff.

Niccolai, L. 2017a. 'Julian, Plutarch, and the Dangers of Self-Praise', *Greek, Roman, and Byzantine Studies* 57: 1058–84.
　2017b. '"Avrei potuto punirti, ma ho preferito scriverti": regole della politica e regole della satira tra *Contro Nilo* e *Misopogon*', *Athenaeum* 105: 601–20.
　2019. 'The "House of Hesychius" and the Religious Allegiance of Synesius' Family', *Historia* 68: 368–85.
　2021. 'Synesius of Cyrene, Sophist-Bishop: Rhetoric and Religion in the Greek East at the Turn of the Fifth Century CE', *Rhetorica* 39: 209–33.
　2023. 'Julian the Emperor and the Reaction against Christianity: A Case Study of Resistance from the Top', in J. Elsner and D. Jolowicz (eds.), *Articulating Resistance under the Roman Empire*. Cambridge: Cambridge University Press, pp. 219–238.
Nicolosi, S. 1959. *Il* De providentia *di Sinesio: studio critico e tradizione*. Padua: CEDAM.
Niehoff, M. 2011. *Jewish Exegesis and Homeric Scholarship in Alexandria*. Cambridge: Cambridge University Press.
Nixon, C. E. W. 1983. 'Latin Panegyrics of the Tetrarchic and Constantinian Periods', in B. Croke and E. M. Emmett (eds.), *History and Historians in Late Antiquity*. Sydney; Oxford: Pergamon Press, pp. 88–99.
Nixon, C. E. V., B. S. Rodgers, and R. A. B. Mynors. 1994. *In Praise of Later Roman Emperors: The Panegyrici Latini. Introduction, Translation and Historical Commentary*. Berkeley: University of California Press.
Nock, A.B. 1926. *Sallustius: Concerning the Gods and Universe*. Edited with prolegomena and translation. Cambridge: Cambridge University Press.
Nongbri, B. 2008. 'Dislodging "Embedded" Religion: A Brief Note on a Scholarly Trope', *Numen* 55: 440–60.
　2013. *Before Religion: A History of a Modern Concept*. New Haven: Yale University Press.
Noreña, C. 2001. 'The Communication of the Emperor's Virtues', *Journal of Roman Studies* 91: 146–58.
Norman, A. F. 1969. *Libanius. Selected Orations*, vol. 1. London; Cambridge, MA: Harvard University Press.
　1977. *Libanius. Selected orations*, vol. 2. London; Cambridge, MA: Harvard University Press
　1992. *Autobiography and Selected Letters*. London; Cambridge, MA: Harvard University Press.
Odahl, C. M. 2010. *Constantine and the Christian Empire*. London: Routledge.
O'Meara, D. J. 2005. Platonopolis: Platonic Political Philosophy in Late Antiquity. Oxford: Oxford University Press.
　2014. 'Political Theory', in P. Remes and S. Slaveva-Griffin (eds.), *The Routledge Handbook of Neoplatonism*. London; New York: Routledge, pp. 471–81.
　2017. 'Plato's Political Dialogues in the Writings of Julian the Emperor', in H. Tarrant et al. (eds.), *The Brill Companion for the Reception of Plato in Antiquity*. Leiden; Boston: Brill, pp. 400–11.

Omissi, A. 2018. *Emperors and Usurpers in the Later Roman Empire: Civil War, Panegyric, and the Construction of Legitimacy*. Oxford: Oxford University Press.

2020. 'Civil War and the Late Roman Panegyrical Corpus', in Omissi and Ross (eds.), pp. 211–31.

Omissi, A., and A. J. Ross (eds.) 2020. *Imperial Panegyric from Diocletian to Honorius*. Liverpool: Liverpool University Press.

Op de Coul, M. 2012. 'Aspects of Paideia in Synesius' Dion', in Seng and Hoffman (eds.), pp. 110–24.

Pack, R. 1953. 'Julian, Libanius, and Others. A Reply', *Classical Philology* 48: 173–74.

Pagliara, A. 2012. *Retorica, filosofia e politica in Giuliano Cesare*. Alessandria: Edizioni dell'Orso.

2015. 'Giuliano Cesare panegirista di Costanzo II', in Marcone (ed.), pp. 87–118.

Pellegrin, P. 2012. 'Aristotle's *Politics*', in Shield, C. (ed.), *The Oxford Handbook of Aristotle*. Oxford: Oxford University Press, pp. 558–85.

Pelttari, A. 2014. *The Space That Remains: Reading Latin Poetry in Late Antiquity*. Ithaca: Cornell University Press.

Penella, R. J. 1990. *Greek Philosophers and Sophists in the Fourth Century A.D. Studies in Eunapius of Sardis*. Leeds: Frances Cairns.

2000. *The Private Orations of Themistius, Translated, Annotated, and Introduced*. Berkeley: University of California Press.

2007. *Man and the Word. The Orations of Himerius, Translated, Annotated, and Introduced*. Berkeley: University of California Press.

Pépin, J. 1976. *Mythe et allégorie: les origines grecques et les contestations judéo-chrétiennes*. Paris: Aubier-Montaigne.

Perl, G. 1996. 'Die Rede des Kaisers Claudius für die Aufnahme römischer Bürger aus Gallia Comata', *Philologus* 140: 114–38.

Pernot, L. 1993. *La rhétorique de l'éloge dans le monde gréco-romain*. Paris: Institut d'études augustiniennes.

2000. *La rhétorique dans l'antiquité*. Paris: Libraire générale française.

2015. 'Greek Figured Speech on Imperial Rome', *Advances in the History of Rhetoric* 18: 131–46.

2021. 'The Concept of a Third Sophistic: Definitional and Methodological Issues', *Rhetorica* 39: 177–87.

Petit, P. 1950. 'Libanius et la *Vita Constantini*', *Historia* 1: 562–82.

Petkas, A. 2018. 'The King in Words: Performance and Fiction in Synesius' *de regno*', *American Journal of Philology* 139: 123–51.

Pharr, C. 1952. *The Theodosian Code and Novels and the Sirmondian Constitutions: A Translation with a Commentary, Glossary, and Bibliography*. Princeton: Princeton University Press.

Piepenbrink, K. 2012. 'Selbsdarstellung des Synesius als Bischof', in Seng and Hoffman (eds.), pp. 73–94.

Pietri, C. 1989. 'La politique de Constance II. Un premier 'césaropapisme' ou l'Imitatio Constantini?', in A. Dihle (ed.), *L'église et l'empire au Ive siècle*. Vandoeuvres-Genève: Fondation Hardt, pp. 113–72.

Piganiol, A. 1932. *L'empereur Constantin*. Paris: Rieder.
Pizzone, A. M. V. 2012. 'Christliche und heidnische Träume: versteckte Polemik in Synesios, De insomniis', in Seng and Hoffman (eds.), pp. 232–47.
Poggi, V. 2003. 'Costantino e la chiesa di Persia', in G. Bonamente and A. Carile (eds.), *Costantino il Grande nell'età bizantina*. Spoleto: Fondazione centro di studi sull'alto Medioevo, pp. 61–97.
Pohlsander, H. 1980. 'Philip the Arab and Christianity', *Historia* 29: 466–67.
Polara, G. 1973. *Publii Optatiani Porfyrii Carmina*. Turin: UTET.
　1974. 'Cinquant'anni di studi su Optaziano', *Vichiana* 3: 110–24, 282–301.
Ponzone, V. 2018. 'Giovanni Crisostomo: retorica e politica cristiane'. Diss. University of Pisa.
Potter, D. S. 1994. *Prophets and Emperors: Human and Divine Authority from Augustus to Theodosius*. Cambridge, MA: Harvard University Press.
　2013. *Constantine the Emperor*. Oxford: Oxford University Press.
Pownall, F. (2020) 'Sophists and Flatterers: Greek intellectuals at Alexander's Court', in M. D'Agostni, E. M. Anson, and F. Pownall (eds.), *Affective Relations and Personal Bonds in Hellenistic Antiquity: Studies in Honor of Elizabeth D. Carney*. Oxford: Oxbow Books, pp. 243–65.
Praechter, K. 1933. *Richtungen und Schulen im Neuplatonismus*. Berlin: Wiedemann.
Prato, C., and A. Fornaro. 1984. *Giuliano Imperatore. Epistola a Temistio*. Lecce: Milella.
Puech, B. 2002. *Orateurs et sophistes grecs dans les inscriptions d'époque impériale*. Paris: Vrin.
Quiroga Puertas, A. 2007. 'From *Sophistopolis* to *Episcopolis*. The Case for a Third Sophistic', *Journal for Late Antique Religion and Culture* 1: 31–42.
　2008. 'Deflecting Attention and Shaping Reality with Rhetoric (the Case of the Riot of the Statues of A.D. 387 in Antioch', *Nova Tellus* 26: 135–53.
　2009. 'Julian's *Misopogon* and the Subversion of Rhetoric', *Antiquité Tardive* 17: 127–35.
　2013a. *The Purpose of Rhetoric in Late Antiquity: From Performance to Exegesis*. Tübingen: Mohr Siebeck.
　2013b. 'Themistius *or*. 28. Between Singing and Philosophy', *Athenaeum* 101: 605–19.
　(ed.) 2017a. *Rhetorical Strategies in Late Antique Literature: Images, Metatexts and Interpretation*. Leiden; Boston: Brill.
　2017b. 'In Heaven Unlike on Earth: Rhetorical Strategies in Julian's Caesars', in Quiroga Puertas (ed.), pp. 90–103.
　2018. *The Dynamics of Rhetorical Performances in Late Antiquity*. London; New York: Routledge.
Raaflaub, K. A. 2004. 'Aristocracy and Freedom of Speech in the Greco-Roman World', in I. Sluiter and R. M. Rosen (eds.), *Free Speech in Classical Antiquity*. Leiden; Boston: Brill, pp. 41–61.
Ramelli, I. 2006. *Il basileus come nomos empsychos tra diritto naturale e diritto divino: spunti platonici del concetto e sviluppi di età imperiale e tardoantica*. Naples: Bibliopolis.

Rapp, C. 1998. 'Comparison, Paradigm, and the Case of Moses in Panegyric and Hagiography', in Whitby (ed.), pp. 277–98.
  2005. *Holy Bishops in Late Antiquity: The Nature of Christian Leadership in an Age of Transition*. Berkeley: University of California Press.
Rawson, E. 1989. 'Roman Rulers and the Philosophical Adviser', in M. T. Griffin and J. Barnes (eds.), *Philosophia togata I: Essays on Philosophy and Roman Society*. Oxford: Oxford University Press, pp. 233–58.
Rebenich, S., and H.-U. Wiemer. 2020. *A Companion to Julian the Apostate*. Leiden; Boston: Brill.
Rebillard, E. 2012. *Christians and Their Many Identities in Late Antiquity, North Africa, 200–450 CE*. Ithaca: Cornell University Press.
Rees, R. 2002. *Layers of Loyalty in Latin Panegyric, AD 289–307*. Oxford: Oxford University Press.
  2004. *Diocletian and the Tetrarchy*. Edinburgh: Edinburgh University Press.
Relihan, J. C. 1993. *Ancient Menippean Satire*. Baltimore: Johns Hopkins University Press.
Remes, P., and S. Slaveva-Griffin. 2014. 'Introduction', in S. Slaveva-Griffin and P. Remes (eds.), *The Routledge Handbook of Neoplatonism*. London; New York: Routledge.
Rendina, S. 2021. *La prefettura di Antemio e l'oriente romano*. Pisa: ETS edizioni.
Richlin, A. 1983. *The Garden of Priapus: Sexuality and Aggression in Roman Humor*. New Haven: Yale University Press.
Riedweg, C. 2008. 'Julians Exegese der Rede des Demiurgen an die versammelten Götter in Platons *Timaios* 41a–d: Anmerkungen zu *Contra Galilaeos* fr. 10 Mas.', in D. Auger and É. Wolff (eds.), *Culture classique et christianisme. Mélanges offerts à Jean Bouffartigue*. Paris: Picard, pp. 83–95.
  2020. 'Anti-Christian Polemics and Pagan Onto-Theology: Julian's Against the Gailaeans', in Rebenich and Wiemer (eds.), pp. 245–66.
Rike, R. L. 1987. *Apex omnium. Religion in the* Res Gestae *of Ammianus*. Berkeley: University of California Press.
Riggsby, A. M. 2019. *Mosaics of Knowledge: Representing Information in the Roman World*. New York; Oxford: Oxford University Press.
Rigolio, A. 2019. 'Themistius: On Virtue', in J. Wildberg, J. Trompeter, and A. Rigolio (eds.), *Michael of Ephesus: On Aristotle's Nicomachean Ethics 10. Themistius: On Virtue*. London: Bloomsbury Academic, pp. 207–73.
Robert, F. 2008. 'La rhétorique au service de la critique du christianisme dans le *Contre les Galiléens* de l'empereur Julien', *Revue d'études augustiniennes et patristiques* 54: 221–56.
Roberto, U. 2015. 'Giuliano e la memoria politica della tetrarchia', in Marcone (ed.), pp. 50–62.
Rochefort, G. 1956. 'Le περὶ θεῶν καὶ κόσμου de Saloustios et l'influence de l'Empereur Julien', *Revue des études grecques* 69: 50–66.
  1963. *L'Empereur Julien. Oeuvres complètes,* tome II, 1e part: *Discours de Julien Empereur*. Paris: Les Belles Lettres.

Rohrbacher, D. 2005. 'Why Didn't Constantius II Eat Fruit?', *Classical Quarterly* 55: 323–26.
Rolfe, J. C. 1935–40. *Ammianus Marcellinus: With an English translation*, London; Cambridge, MA: Harvard University Press.
Roller, M. B. 2001. *Constructing Autocracy: Aristocrats and Emperors in Julio-Claudian Rome*. Princeton: Princeton University Press.
Roques, D. 1987. *Synésios de Cyrène et la Cyrénaïque du Bas-Empire*. Paris: Editions du CRNS.
  1989. *Études sur la Correspondance de Synésios de Cyrène*. Brussels: Latomus.
Rosen, K. 2006. *Julian. Kaiser, Gott und Christenhasser*. Stuttgart: Klett-Cotta.
Ross, A. J. 2016. *Ammianus' Julian*. Oxford: Oxford University Press.
  2018. 'The Constantinians' Returns to the West: Julian's Depiction of Constantius in Oration 1', in Burgersdijk and Ross (eds.), pp. 183–203.
  2020. 'Text and Paratext: Reading the Emperor Julian via Libanius' *Epitaphios*', *American Journal of Philology* 141: 241–81.
Ross, A. J., and A. Omissi (eds.) 2020. *Imperial Panegyric from Diocletian to Honorius*. Liverpool: Liverpool University Press.
Rostagni, A. 1920. *Giuliano l'apostata: saggio critico con le operette politiche e satiriche tradotte e commentate*. Turin: Bocca.
Rothrauff, C. M. 1965. 'The *Philanthropia* of the Emperor Julian'. Diss. University of Cincinnati.
Roueché, C. 1997. 'Benefactors in the Late Roman Period: The Eastern Empire', in M. Christol and O. Masson (eds.), *Actes du Xe Congrès International d'Épigraphie Grecque et Latine, Nimes 4–9 Octobre 1992*. Paris: Éditions de la Sorbonne, pp. 353–68.
  1998. 'The Functions of the Governor in Late Antiquity: Some Observations', *Antiquité Tardive* 6: 31–36.
Rowe, C., and M. Schofield (eds.) 2000. *The Cambridge History of Greek and Roman Political Thought*. Cambridge: Cambridge University Press.
Rubenson, S. 1995. *The Letters of St. Antony: Monasticism and the Making of a Saint*. Minneapolis: Fortress Press.
  2000. 'Philosophy and Simplicity: The Problem of Classical Education in Early Christian Biography', in Hägg and Rousseau (eds.), pp. 110–39.
  2012. 'Monasticism and the Philosophical Heritage', in S. F. Johnson (ed.), *The Oxford Handbook of Late Antiquity*. Oxford: Oxford University Press, pp. 487–512.
Runia, D. 1993. *Philo in Early Christian Literature: A Survey*. Assen; Minneapolis: Fortress Press.
Russell, D., and N. G. Wilson. 1981. *Menander Rhetor*. Oxford: Oxford University Press.
Sabbah, G. 1984. 'De la rhétorique à la communication politique: les panégiriques latins', *Bulletin de l'Association Guillaume Budé* 43: 363–88.
Salzman, M. R. 2008. 'Pagans and Christians', in S. Ashbrook Harvey and D. G. Hunter (eds.), *The Oxford Handbook of Early Christian Studies*. Oxford: Oxford University Press, pp. 186–202.

Sandwell, I. 2004. 'Christian Self-Definition in the Fourth Century AD: John Chrysostom on Christianity, Imperial Rule and the City', in I. Sandwell and J. Juskinson (eds.), *Culture and Society in Later Roman Antioch*. Oxford: Oxford University Press, pp. 35–58.
  2007. *Religious Identity in Late Antiquity: Greeks, Jews, and Christians in Antioch*. Cambridge: Cambridge University Press.
Sardiello, R. 2001. *Giuliano Imperatore. Simposio I Cesari*. Lecce: Milella.
Scarpat, G. 2001. *Parrhesia greca, parrhesia cristiana*. Brescia: Paideia.
Schäfer, C. (ed.) 2008. *Kaiser Julian 'Apostata' und die philosophische Reaktion gegen das Christentum*. Berlin: De Gruyter.
Schatkin, M. 1970. 'The Authenticity of St. John Chrysostom's *Contra Julianum et Gentiles (de Sancto Babyla)*', in *Kyriakon: Festschrift Johannes Quasten*. Münster: Aschendorff, pp. 474–89.
  1985. *Discourse on blessed Babylas and against the Greeks*. Washington, DC: Catholic University of America Press.
Schlange-Schöningen, H. 1995. *Kaisertum und Bildungswesen im spätantiken Konstantinopel*. Stuttgart: Steiner.
Schmidt, P. L. 1994. 'Claudius als Schriftsteller', in V. M. Strocka (ed.), *Die Regierungszeit des Kaisers Claudius (41–54 n.Chr.). Umbruch oder Episode?* Mainz: von Zabern, pp. 119–32.
Schidmt-Hofner, S. 2020. 'Reform, Routine, and Propaganda: Julian the Lawgiver', in Rebenich and Wiemer (eds.), pp. 124–71.
Schmitt, T. 2001. *Die Bekehrung des Synesius von Kyrene: Politik und Philosophie*. Munich: Saur.
  1997. *Bildung und Macht: zur sozialen und politischen Funktion der zweiten Sophistik in der griechischen Welt der Kaiserzeit*. Munich: Beck.
Schofield, M. 1999. *Saving the City: Philosopher-Kings and Other Classical Paradigms*. London: Routledge.
  2000. 'Epilogue', in Rowe and Schofield (eds.), pp. 661–71.
Schott, J. 2003. 'Founding Platonopolis: The Platonic Politeia in Eusebius, Porphyry, and Iamblichus', *Journal of Early Christian Studies* 11: 501–31.
  2008. *Christianity, Empire, and the Making of Religion in Late Antiquity*. Philadelphia: University of Pennsylvania Press.
Schramm, M. 2014. 'Platonic Ethics and Politics in Themistius and Julian', in Fowler (ed.), pp. 131–43.
Schrenk, S. 1995. *Typos und Antitypos in der Früchristliche Kunst*. Münster: Aschendorff.
Scicolone, S. 1982. 'Le accezioni dell'appellativo "Galilei" in Giuliano', *Aevum* 56: 71–80.
Scott, A. G. 2015. 'Cassius Dio, Caracalla and the Senate', *Klio* 97: 157–75.
Sedley, D. 1989. 'Philosophical Allegiance in the Graeco-Roman World', in M. T. Griffin and J. Barnes (eds.), *Philosophia Togata: Essays on Philosophy and Roman Society*. Oxford: Oxford University Press, pp. 269–96.
Seeck, O. 1894. 'Studien zu Synesius', *Philologus* 52: 442–83.
  1906. *Die Briefe des Libanius*. Leipzig: Hinrichs.

1920. *Geschichte des Untergangs der antiken Welt. Band I*. Stuttgart: J. B. Metzler.
Seiler, E.-M. 1998. *Konstantios II. bei Libanios. Eine kritische Untersuchung der überlieferten Herrschenbildes*. Frankfurt: Peter Lang.
Seng, H., and L. M. Hoffmann (eds.) 2012. *Synesius von Kyrene: Politik, Literatur, Philosophie*. Turnhout: Brepols.
Shahîd, I. 1984. *Rome and the Arabs: A Prolegomenon to the Study of Byzantium and the Arabs*. Washington, DC: Dumbarton Oaks Research Library and Collection.
Shaw, B. D. 2011. *Sacred Violence. African Christians and Sectarian Hatred in the Age of Augustine*. Cambridge: Cambridge University Press.
Sheppard, A. 2007. 'Porphyry's Views on Phantasia', *Bulletin of the Institute of Classical Studies* 89: 71–76.
Sidebottom, H. 2009. 'Philostratus and the Symbolic Roles of the Sophist and the Philosopher', in E. Bowie and J. Elsner (eds.), *Philostratus*. Cambridge: Cambridge University Press, pp. 69–99.
Siecienski, A. E. (ed.) 2017. *Constantine: Religious Faith and Imperial Policy*. London; New York: Routledge.
Silli, P. 1987. *Testi costantiniani nelle fonti letterarie*. Milan: Giuffrè.
Simelidis, C. 2009. *Selected Poems of Gregory of Nazianzus*. Göttingen: Vandenhoeck & Ruprecht.
Simmons, M. B. 2015. *Universal Salvation in Late Antiquity: Porphyry of Tyre and the Pagan-Christian Debate*. New York; Oxford: Oxford University Press.
Siniossoglou, N. 2008. *Plato and Theodoret: The Christian Appropriation of Platonic Philosophy and the Hellenic Intellectual Resistance*. Cambridge: Cambridge University Press.
Sissa, G. 2009. 'Gendered Politics, or the Self-Praise of *Andres Agathoi*', in R. K. Balot (ed.), *A Companion to Greek and Roman Political Thought*. Malden, MA; Chichester: Wiley–Blackwell.
Sluiter, I. 2017. 'Anchoring Innovation: A Classical Research Agenda', *European Review* 25: 20–38.
Smith, C., and L. M. Yarrow (eds.) 2012. *Imperialism, Cultural Politics, and Polybius*. Oxford: Oxford University Press.
Smith, M. 1997. 'The Religion of Constantius I', *Greek, Roman, and Byzantine Studies* 38: 187–208.
Smith, R. B. E. 1995. *Julian's Gods: Religion and Philosophy in the Thought and Action of Julian the Apostate*. London; New York: Routledge.
Smith, R. R. R. 1990. 'Late Roman Philosopher Portraits from Aphrodisias', *Journal of Roman Studies* 80: 127–55.
  1997. 'The Public Image of Licinius I: Portrait Sculpture and Imperial Ideology in the Early Fourth Century', *Journal of Roman Studies* 87: 170–202.
Sordi, M. 1993. 'Il *De Vita Sua* di Claudio e le caratteristiche di Claudio come storico di se stesso e di Roma', *Rendiconti* 127: 213–19.

Squire, M. 2017a. 'POP art: the Optical Poetics of Publilius Optatianus Porfyrius', in Elsner and Hernández Lobato (eds.), pp. 25–99.
  2017b. 'Optatian and His Lettered Art: A Kaleidoscopic Lens on Late Antiquity', in Squire and Wienand (eds.), pp. 55–120.
Squire, M., and C. Whitton. 2017. 'Machina sacra: Optatian and the Lettered Art of the Christogram', in I. Garizpanov (ed.) *Graphic Signs of Identity, Faith, and Power in Late Antiquity and the Early Middle Ages*. Turnhout: Brepols, pp. 45–108.
Squire, M., and J. Wienand (eds.) 2017. *Morphogrammata: The Lettered Art of Optatian Figuring Cultural Transformations in the Age of Constantine*. Padeborn: Wilhelm Fink.
Stanton, G. R. 1973. 'Sophists and Philosophers: Problems of Classification', *American Journal of Philology* 94: 350–64.
Stenger, J. 2009. *Hellenische Identität in der Spätantike: pagane Autoren und ihr Unbehagen an der eigenen Zeit*. Berlin; New York: De Gruyter.
  2016. 'Where to Find Christian Philosophy? Spatiality in John Chrysostom's Counter to Greek Paideia', *Journal of Early Christian Studies* 24: 173–98.
Sterk, A. 1998. 'On Basil, Moses, and the Model Bishop: The Cappadocian Legacy of Leadership', *Church History* 67: 227–53.
  2004. *Renouncing the World Yet Leading the Church: The Monk-Bishop in Late Antiquity*. Cambridge: Cambridge University Press.
Stertz, S. A. 1977. 'Marcus Aurelius as Ideal Emperor in Late Antique Greek Thought', *Classical World* 70: 433–39.
Stöcklin-Kaldewey, S. 2014. *Julians Gottesverehrung im Kontext der Spätantike*. Tübingen: Mohr Siebeck.
Strobel, K. 1993. *Das Imperium Romanum im 3. Jahrhundert: Modell einer historischen Krise? Zur Frage mentaler Strukturen breiterer Bevölkerungsschichten in der Zeit von Marc Aurel bis zum Ausgang des 3. Jh. N. Chr.* Stuttgart: Steiner.
Struck, P. T. 2004. *Birth of the Symbol: Ancient Readers at the Limits of Their Texts*. Princeton; Oxford: Princeton University Press.
  2010. 'Allegory and Ascent in Neoplatonism', in Copeland and Struck (eds.), pp. 57–70.
Swain, S. 1989. 'Plutarch: Chance, Providence, and History', *American Journal of Philology* 110: 272–302.
  1996. *Hellenism and Empire: Language, Classicism, and Power in the Greek World, AD 50–250*. Oxford: Oxford University Press.
  2013. *Themistius, Julian, and Greek Political Theory under Rome: Texts, Translations and Studies of Four Key Works*. Cambridge; New York: Cambridge University Press.
Szidat, J. 1981. *Historischer Kommentar zu Ammianus Marcellinus Buch XX–XXI*. Wiesbaden: F. Steiner.
Tanaseanu-Döbler, I. 2008. *Konversion zur Philosophie in der Spätantike. Kaiser Julian und Synesios von Kyrene*. Stuttgart: F. Steiner.
  2013. *Theurgy in Late Antiquity*. Göttingen: Vandenhoeck & Ruprecht.

Tantillo, I. 1997. *La prima orazione di Giuliano a Costanzo*. Rome: L'Erma di Bretschneider.
  2003. 'Costantino e Helios Paneptotes': la statua equestre di Termessos', *Epigraphica* 65: 159–84.
Taoka, Y. 2013. 'The Correspondence of Fronto and Marcus Aurelius', *Classical Antiquity* 32: 406–38.
Tarrant, H. 2014. 'Platonist Curricula and Their Influence', in P. Remes and S. Slaveva-Griffin (eds.) *The Routledge Handbook of Neoplatonism*. London; New York: Routledge, pp. 15–29.
Tatum, J. 1996. 'The Regal Image in Plutarch's *Lives*', *Journal of Hellenic Studies* 116: 135–51.
Teitler, H. C. 2017. *The Last Pagan Emperor: Julian the Apostate and the War against Christianity*. Oxford: Oxford University Press.
Thesleff, H. 1965. *The Pythagorean Texts of the Hellenistic Period*. Åbo: Åbo Academi.
Tiersch, C. 2002. *Johannes Chrysostomus in Konstantinopel (398–404): Weltsicht und Wirken eines Bischofs in der Hauptstadt des Oströmischen Reiches.* Tübingen: Mohr Siebeck.
Tor, S. 2017. *Mortal and Divine in Early Greek Epistemology: A Study of Hesiod, Xenophanes and Parmenides*. Cambridge: Cambridge University Press.
Tougher, S. 1998a. 'In Praise of an Empress: Julian's Speech of Thanks to Eusebia', in Whitby (ed.), pp. 105–23.
  1998b. 'Advocacy of an Empress. Julian and Eusebia', *Classical Quarterly* 48: 595–99.
  2007. *Julian the Apostate*. Edinburgh: Edinburgh University Press.
  2012. 'Reading between the Lines: Julian's First Panegyric on Constantius II', in Baker-Brian and Tougher (eds.), pp. 22–30.
  2020a. 'Julian and Claudius Mamertinus: Panegyric and Polemic in East and West', in Omissi and Ross (eds.), pp. 117–40.
  2020b. 'Julian the Apologist: Christians and Pagans on the Mother of the Gods', in Flower and Ludlow (eds.), pp. 67–82.
Trapp, M. 2007. *Philosophy in the Roman Empire: Ethics, Politics, and Society*. London: Routledge.
Treu, K. 1959. *Synesios von Kyrene. Dion Chrysostomos oder vom Leben nach seinem Vorbild*. Berlin: Akademie-Verlag.
Tuori, K. 2016. *The Emperor of Law: The Emergence of Roman Imperial Adjudication*. Oxford: Oxford University Press.
Turner, D. 2010. 'Allegory in Christian Late Antiquity', in Copeland and Struck (eds.), pp. 71–82.
Tversky, A., and D. Kahneman. 1974. 'Judgment under Uncertainty: Heuristics and Biases', *Science* 185: 1124–31.
Ugenti, V. 1992. *Alla madre degli dèi: edizione critica, traduzione e commento*. Lecce: Congedo.
  2014. *Giuliano imperatore. A Salustio. Autoconsolazione per la partenza dell'ottimo Salustio*. Pisa; Rome: Fabrizio Serra.

Ullmann, W. 1975. *Law and Politics in the Middle Ages*. Cambridge: Cambridge University Press.
Urbano, A. P. 2013. *The Philosophical Life: Biography and the Crafting of Intellectual Identity in Late Antiquity*, Washington, DC: Catholic University of America Press.
Vagnone, G. 2012. *Dione di Prusa: orazioni I–II–III–IV (Sulla regalità), orazione LXII (Sulla regalità e sulla tirannide)*. Rome: Edizioni dell'Ateneo.
Van Dam, R. 2007a. 'Bishops and Society', in A. Casiday and F. Norris (eds.), *The Cambridge History of Christianity*. Cambridge: Cambridge University Press, pp. 343–66.
  2007b. *The Roman Revolution of Constantine*. Cambridge: Cambridge University Press.
  2011. *Remembering Constantine at the Milvian Bridge*. Cambridge: Cambridge University Press.
Van den Berg, R. M. 2019. 'The Emperor Julian, *Against the Cynic Heraclius* (Oration 7): A Polemic about Myths', in G. van Kooten and J. van Ruiten (eds.), *Intolerance, Polemics, and Debate in Antiquity: Politico-Cultural, Philosophical, and Religious Forms of Critical Conversation*. Leiden; Boston: Brill, pp. 423–39.
Van de Paverd, F. 1991. *St. John Chrysostom, the Homilies on the Statues: An Introduction*. Rome: Pontificium Institutum Orientalium Studiorum.
Vanderspoel, J. 1995. *Themistius and the Imperial Court. Oratory, Civic Duty, and Paideia from Constantius to Theodosius*. Ann Arbor: University of Michigan Press.
Van Hoof, L. 2010a. *Plutarch's Practical Ethics: The Social Dynamics of Philosophy*. Oxford University Press.
  2010b. 'Greek Rhetoric and the Later Roman Empire: The Bubble of the Third Sophistic', *Antiquité Tardive* 18: 211–24.
  2013. 'Performing Paideia. Greek Culture as an Instrument for Social Promotion in the Fourth Century A.D.', *Classical Quarterly* 63: 387–406.
Van Hoof, L., and P. Van Nuffelen. 2011. 'Monarchy and Mass Communication: Antioch AD 362/3 Revisited', *Journal of Roman Studies* 101: 166–84.
  2015. *Literature and Society in the Fourth Century AD: Performing Paideia, Constructing the Present, Presenting the Self*. Leiden: Brill.
Van Kooten, G. H. 2010. 'Christianity in the Graeco-Roman World: Sociopolitical, Philosophical, and Religious Interactions up to the Edict of Milan (313 AD)', in D. J. Bingham (ed.), *The Routledge Companion to Early Christian Thought*. London; New York: Routledge, pp. 3–37.
  2021. 'The Johannine Christ, the "Only-Begotten" Athena, and the Platonic Difference between "Begotten" and "Made"', in J. Frey, F. Kunath, and J. Schröter (eds.), *Perspektiven zur Präexistenz im Früjudentum und frühen Christentum*. Tübingen: Mohr Siebeck, pp. 209–45.
Van Nijf, O. 2008. 'Athletics and Paideia', in B. Borg (ed.), *Paideia: The World of the Second Sophistic*. Berlin; Boston: De Gruyter, pp. 203–28.

Van Nuffelen, P. 2002. 'Deux fausses lettres de Julien l'apostat (la Lettre aux Juifs, ep. 51 [Wright], et la Lettre à Arsacius, ep. 84 [Bidez]', *Vigiliae Christianae* 56: 131–50.
  2006. 'Earthquakes in A.D. 363–68 and the Date of Libanius, Oratio 18', *Classical Quarterly* 56: 657–61.
  2011. *Rethinking the Gods: Philosophical Readings of Religion in the Post-Hellenistic Period*. Cambridge: Cambridge University Press.
  2013. 'The Life of Constantine: The Image of an Image', in Johnson and Schott (eds.), pp. 133–49.
  2014. 'Not the Last Pagan: Libanius between Elite Rhetoric and Religion', in L. Van Hoof (ed.), *Libanius. A Critical Introduction*. Cambridge: Cambridge University Press, pp. 293–314.
  2018. *Penser la tolérance durant l'Antiquité tardive*. Paris: Publications de l'École Pratique des Hautes Études.
  2020. 'The Christian Reception of Julian', in Rebenich and Wiemer (eds.), pp. 360–97.
Van Renswoude, I. 2019. *The Rhetoric of Free Speech in Late Antiquity and the Early Middle Ages*. Cambridge: Cambridge University Press.
Varner, E. R. 2012. 'Roman Authority, Imperial Authoriality, and Julian's Artistic Program', in Baker-Brian and Tougher (eds.), pp. 183–212.
  2020. 'Innovation and Orthodoxy in the Portraiture of Constantine and His Sons', in Baker-Briand and Tougher (eds.), pp. 97–132.
Veyne, P. 2010. *When Our World Became Christian, 312–394*, trans. J. Lloyd. Cambridge: Cambridge University Press.
Vössing, K. 2020. 'The Value of a Good Education: The School Law in Context', in Rebenich and Wiemer (eds.), pp. 172–206.
Vout, C. 2006. 'What's in a Beard? Rethinking Hadrian's Hellenism', in Goldhill and Osborne (eds.), pp. 96–123.
Yarnold, E. 2000. *Cyril of Jerusalem*. London; New York: Routledge.
Young, F. 2002. *Biblical Exegesis and the Formation of Christian Culture*. Cambridge: Cambridge University Press.
Walker, J. 2000. *Rhetoric and Poetics in Antiquity*. New York; Oxford: Oxford University Press.
Wallace-Hadrill, A. 2008. *Rome's Cultural Revolution*. Cambridge: Cambridge University Press.
Wallraff, M. 2001. 'Constantine's Devotion to the Sun after 324', *Studia Patristica* 34: 256–69.
Ware, C. 2018. 'Constantine, the Tetrarchy, and the Emperor Augustus', in Burgersdijk and Ross (eds.), pp. 113–36.
Ware, T. 1963. *The Orthodox Church: An Introduction to Eastern Christianity*, London: Penguin Books.
Washington, B. 2020. 'Playing with Conventions in Julian's Encomium to Eusebia: Does Gender Make a Difference?', in Omissi and Ross (eds.), pp. 93–116.
Watson, A. 1999. *Aurelian and the Third Century*. London: Routledge.

Watts, E. J. 2006. *City and School in Late Antique Athens and Alexandria*. Berkeley; Los Angeles: University of California Press.

Weinbrot, H. D. 2005. *Menippean Satire Reconsidered: From Antiquity to the Eighteenth Century*. Baltimore: Johns Hopkins University Press.

Weis, B. K. 1973. *Julian. Briefe*. Munich: Heimeran.

Weiss, D. 2017. *Pious Irreverence: Confronting God in Rabbinic Judaism*. Philadelphia: University of Pennsylvania Press.

Weiss, P. 2003. 'The Vision of Constantine', *Journal of Roman Archaeology* 16: 237–59.

Weisweiler, J. 2015. 'Domesticating the Senatorial Elite: Universal Monarchy and Transregional Aristocracy in the Fourth Century AD', in Wienand (ed.), pp. 17–41.

2016. 'From Empire to World-State: Ecumenical Language and Cosmopolitan Consciousness in the Later Roman Aristocracy', in M. Lavan, R. E. Payne, and J. Weisweiler (eds.), *Cosmopolitanism and Empire: Universal Rulers, Local Elites, and Cultural Integration in the Ancient Near East and Mediterranean*. New York; Oxford: Oxford University Press, pp. 187–208.

West, M. L. 1982. 'The Metre of Arius' *Thalia*', *Journal of Theological Studies* 33: 98–105.

Westerink, L.G. 2011. *Anonymous Prolegomena to Platonic Philosophy*. Edited with translation. 2nd ed. Dilton Marsh: Prometheust Trust (1st ed. Amsterdam: North-Holland Pub. Co, 1962).

Whitby, M. L. (ed.) 1998. *The Propaganda of Power: The Role of Panegyric in Late Antiquity*. Boston; Leiden: Brill.

1999. 'Images of Constantius', in J. W. Drijvers and D. Hunt (eds.), *The Late Roman World and Its Historian: Interpreting Ammianus Marcellinus*. London; New York: Routledge, pp. 77–88.

White, C. 1996. *Gregory of Nazianzus, Autobiographical Poems: Translated and edited*. Cambridge: Cambridge University Press.

1998. *Early Christian lives. Translated, Edited and with Introductions*. London: Penguin.

Whitmarsh, T. 2001. *Greek Literature and the Roman Empire: The Politics of Imitation*. Oxford: Oxford University Press.

2018. 'How to Write Anti-Roman History', in D. Allen, P. Christesen, and P. Millet (eds.) *How to Do Things with History: New Approaches to Ancient Greece*. Oxford: Oxford University Press, pp. 365–90.

Whitton, C. 2015. 'Grand Designs: Unrolling *Epistles* 2', in I. Marchesi (ed.), *Pliny the Book-Maker: Betting on Posterity in the Epistles*. Oxford: Oxford University Press, pp. 109–45.

Wiemer, H.-U. 1994. 'Libanius on Constantine', *Classical Quarterly* 44: 511–24.

1995. *Libanios und Julian: Studien zum Verhältnis von Rhetorik und Politik im vierten Jahrhundert n. Chr*. Munich: Beck.

Wienand, J. 2012. *Der Kaiser als Sieger. Metamorphosen triumphaler Herrschaft unter Constantin I*. Berlin: Akademie Verlag.

2013. 'Costantino e il Sol Invictus', in *Costantino I. Enciclopedia costantiniana sulla figura e l'immagine dell'imperatore del cosiddetto Editto di Milano 313–2013*. Roma: Treccani, pp. 177–95.

2014. Review of Girardet (2013), *Sehepunkte* 14 , www.sehepunkte.de/2014/12/24081.html.

2017. 'Publilius Optatianus Porfyrius: The Man and His Book', in Squire and Wienand (eds.), pp. 121–63.

Williams, F., and L. Wickham. 2002. *St. Gregory of Nazianzus: On God and Christ: the five theological orations and two letters to Cledonius*. Crestwood, NY: St Vladimir's Seminary Press.

Williams, M. S. 2008. *Authorised Lives in Early Christian Biography*. Cambridge: Cambridge University Press.

Williams, R. D. 2001. *Arius: heresy and tradition*. London: SCM.

Williams, S., and J. G. P. Friell,. 1994. *Theodosius: The Empire at Bay*. London: Batsford.

Wilson, N.G. 1994. *Photius. The Bibliotheca. A Selection Translated with Notes*. London: Duckworth.

Witschel, C. 1999. *Krise-Rezession-Stagnation? Der Westen des römischen Reiches im 3. Jahrhundert n. Chr.* Frankfurt: Marthe Clauss.

2004. 'The Roman West in the Third Century A.D.', *Journal of Roman Archaeology* 17: 251–81.

Wintjes, J. 2005. *Das Leben des Libanius*. Rahden: Leidorf.

Wright, W. C. 1913–23. *The Works of the Emperor Julian*. London; Cambridge, MA: Harvard University Press.

1921. *Lives of the Philosophers and Sophists*. London; Cambridge, MA: Harvard University Press.

Wright, D. H. 1987. 'The True Face of Constantine the Great', *Dumbarton Oaks Papers* 41: 493–507.

Zanker, P. 1995. *Die Maske des Sokrates: das Bild des Intellektuellen in der antiken Kunst*. Munich: Beck.

Zeiner-Carmichael, N. K. 2013. *Roman Letters: An Anthology*. Chichester: Wiley–Blackwell.

Zelzer, M. 1982. *Ambrosius: Epistulae et Acta. Tom. Iii: Epistularum Liber X, Epistulae Extra Collectionem, Gesta Concili Aquileiensis*, Vienna: Verlag der Österreichischen Akademie der Wissenschaften.

Zucker, A. 2016. 'Themistius', in A. Falcon (ed.), *The Brill's Companion to the Reception of Aristotle in Antiquity*. Leiden; Boston: Brill, pp. 358–73.

Subject index

Achilles, 95–96, 103, 105
Adrianople, battle of, 212, 250, 292
Aedesius, 293, 295
Agamemnon, 95–96, 103–4
Alexander the Great, 43, 79, 183, 192, 202, 259
allegory. *See* Interpretation
Ambrose
  Apology for David, 242
  on the Callinicum synagogue, 241–42
  fashioning the episcopal self-image, 34, 239–42
  negotiating Church-State interactions, 241–42
  On the Duties of the Clergy, 238
  and *parrhesia*, 241–42, 244
  on *recusatio*, 240
  and Theodosius, 241–42, 253
  on the *Thessalonica* massacre, 242
  and Valentinian II, 241
Ammianus
  as critic of Constantius II, 86, 90, 117
  as interpreter of Julian's life, 212–14
  on omens, 213–14
  views on religion of, 89–90, 212, 292
  witness of Julian's policies, 48–49, 54, 95, 101, 147–48, 153
anchoring, model of, 4, 25, 35, 119, 268, 303
Anthony the Great
  as countercultural model, 281–82
  indifferent to worldly power, 232
Antiochenes (citizens of Antioch), 179–82, 203–4, 212, 247, 268–69, 271
Antonines (emperors), 2–3, 7, 16, 39–40, 45, 47, 80, 166, 173–74, 183–86, 196–99, 201–2, 259
Apollo, 45, 76, 118, 122, 127, 135, 164, 235, 245–46
Apollo, oracle of. *See* oracles:of Apollo
Arcadius (emperor), 248, 251, 255–57, 262–63, 288
Argentoratum, battle of, 95
Arian controversy. *See* heresy:Arianism

Aristotle, 13, 23, 41, 57–58, 82, 85, 216, 251
  Politics, 43, 49–53, 61
  as teacher of Alexander, 79
Arius of Alexandria
  and mass preaching, 275
  dispute with Alexander, 122, 144, 221
asceticism, Christian. *See* Christianity: countercultural
Asclepius, 162, 176, 235
Athanasius of Alexandria
  and Constantine, 120, 231–32
  as critic of Constantius II, 86, 88, 90–91
  as critic of *paideia*, 281–84
  fashioning the episcopal self-image, 34
  frictions with the government, 91, 231–32
  Life of Anthony, 232, 281–82
  negotiating Church-State interactions, 86, 88, 92, 231–32, 281–82
Athena, 102, 154, 172, 177–78, 194
Athenagoras of Athens, 16
Attis, 158–61
  as Logos, 161
Augustine, 4, 120, 126–27, 214, 272–73, 288
Augustus, 1–3, 40, 45, 118, 183, 186, 199, 202
Aurelian (emperor), 118, 236
Aurelian (patron of Synesius), 260, 262, 264

Basil of Caesarea
  and *paideia*, 280
  fashioning the episcopal self-image, 237–38
  as model of perfect episcopacy, 237–38, 241
  and *parrhesia*, 240–41
biography
  of philosophers, 29, 63–65, 291–300
  of rulers, 29, 166–204, 218
bishops
  between universalism and elitism, 267, 273–75, 290–91
  as community leaders, 18–23, 34, 236–37, 264, 267–68, 273–74, 288

345

bishops (cont.)
  competing among themselves, 5, 147, 220–26, 238, 240
  competing with the emperor, 219, 227–32, 237–40
  defining Christian identity, 19, 34
  fashioning the episcopal self-image, 34, 222–25, 236–43, 280–81
  as ideal philosophers, 222–25, 236–43, 280–81
  as imperial advisers, 5, 227–31, 240–43, 263
  mirrors of, 237–38
  mobilising masses, 272–75, 79
  as philosopher-rulers, 237–40
  and *recusatio*, 224–25, 239–40, 289
  seeking imperial support, 220–26
  upper-class background of, 273–75, 290–91

Caesar, Julius, 183, 202
Caligula, 3, 47, 84, 183
Caracalla, 47, 118
Christ
  and Constantine. *See* Constantine:mimesis of Christ
  deceptive preaching of, 194–95
  as interlocutor of the *parrhesiastes*, 243
  as Logos, 12, 16, 25, 139, 142, 151, 161, 168, 172, 189, 222, 230
  passion of, 126, 142
  as teacher, 142
Christianity
  and charity, 233–34
  as condition for a philosophical leadership, 11, 17, 31–34, 67–68, 72, 84, 113–14, 129, 140, 144, 167–70, 191–92, 209, 214, 229–30, 238, 251–53, 276–80, 304–5
  as condition for the exercise of *parrhesia*, 240–43, 248, 260, 283
  countercultural, 279–87
  as damaging the Roman *oikoumene*, 210–12, 292–93
  'dual ethics' of, 278, 285
  and essentialism. *See* Christianity: countercultural
  and intellectual appropriation, 146–55
  as irrational, 146–55, 203–4, 269–70, 272, 292–93
  as philosophy, 10–18, 22–23, 34–35, 65–70, 89–94, 124, 144–46, 276–88, 302–7
  and the support of the ill-educated, 269–70, 291
  and universal accessibility, 22, 34–35, 267–85
  as upgrading *paideia*, 10, 15–17, 65–70, 92–94, 135, 167–70, 214, 267–85, 303
Cicero, 27, 66, 68–69, 102, 118, 128

Claudius (Julio-Claudian), 40, 268
Claudius Gothicus, 202, 211
Clement of Alexandria, 12, 15, 146, 155, 274
coercion, religious, 147, 216, 294
consolation (genre). *See* Julian:*Consolation to Himself*
Constans (son of Constantine), 48, 88, 115
Constantine
  Arch of Triumph, 123, 199
  as consensus-seeker, 8–11, 19, 40, 119, 220–21, 269, 303
  controlling doctrine. *See* orthodoxy:as governmental responsibility
  conversion of, 4–5, 10–11, 113, 119, 129–33, 228–29
  Edict of Milan. *See* Milan, Edict of
  emulating bishops, 229–30, 236
  as father of Constantius, 75, 114–17
  forgeries of, 120
  on his predecessors, 121, 127–28, 200
  iconography of, 119, 186–96
  as interpreter, 5, 10–11, 17, 26–27, 33, 113–14, 120–41, 228–30, 304
  as irrational emperor, 8, 171–72, 183, 196–97, 202
  Letter to Alexander and Arius, 122, 145–46, 221
  Letter to Shapur II, 122
  Letter to the Provincials of Palestine, 120–21
  life of, as evidence, 26–27, 33–34, 129, 142, 166–70
  mimesis of Christ, 176, 230
  as model to his sons, 114–17, 169, 186–89, 304
  and Moses. *See* Moses:and Constantine
  Oration to the Assembly of the Saints, 8–11, 16, 26–27, 125–29, 142, 166
  as philosopher-ruler, 8–11, 17, 33, 123–29, 140, 167–70, 192, 303–4
  position in history of, 200–3
  religious allegiance of, 8–11, 117–19, 220–21, 303
  and *Sol*, 174–75, 189–91
  Tricennalia (celebration of), 138, 227–28
Constantine II, 76, 115
Constantius I, 132
Constantius II
  Address to the Senate, 82–83, 88
  addressed with *parrhesia*, 244
  concern with self-projection, 17, 25, 31–33, 48, 73–81, 87–89, 92–93, 115
  and Constantinople, 84–85, 87, 115
  controlling doctrine, 91–93, 231–32
  early benevolence towards Julian, 77–78
  as enemy of culture, 86–87, 89–90

as heir to Constantine's cultural policy, 17,
    31–33, 94, 114–17, 186–89
as heir to Constantine's religious policy, 91,
    94, 231
iconography of, 186–89
as interpreter, 79, 91–92, 116
as Julian's addressee, 28, 32–33, 48, 73–81,
    94–107
as Julian's nemesis, 74, 97–107, 112, 147,
    172–74, 210, 218–19, 268
and learning, 75, 77–78, 85, 87–90
as lover of philosophy and wisdom, 32–33, 78,
    81–94
patron of Themistius. *See* Themistius:as
    panegyrist of Constantius II
as philosopher-ruler, 17, 81–85
and Rome, 84–85
Cybele. *See* Mother of the Gods
Cynicism (school), 163–64, 170–71, 223,
    247–48, 259, 268, 272, 281, 293
Cyril of Alexandria, 149
Cyril of Jerusalem: *Letter to Constantius*, 91–92, 116

Daniel, Book of, 10, 126
Decius, 10, 118, 127, 220
dependency theme, 15, 65–68, 113–14, 148,
    161, 221, 281
Dio Chrysostom, 2, 46, 83, 173–74, 241,
    257–59, 286–88
Dio of Prusa. *See* Dio Chrysostom
Diocletian, 10, 45, 122, 127, 187, 201, 277
Diogenes of Sinope, 164, 247, 258–59
divination. *See* prophecy
doctrine, State control of. *See* orthodoxy:as
    governmental responsibility
Domitian, 2–3, 47, 84, 122, 259

epic poetry. *See* Interpretation:of Homer
epideictic rhetoric. *See* panegyric
epistolography
    and Church-State interaction, 91–92, 115,
        232
    Constantinian, 120–22
    and self-projection, 30, 39–59, 120–22, 134,
        288–91
Erythraean Sibyl. *See* Oracles:Sibylline
Eunapius of Sardis
    on Constantine, 292–94
    as critic of Christianity, 291–93, 298–99
    as interpreter of Julian's life, 211–12, 291–92,
        296, 300
    Lives of the Philosophers and Sophists, 23, 29,
        35, 291–300
    and political competition. *See* Eunapius of
        Sardis:prescriptiveness of

prescriptiveness of, 294–300
on *recusatio*, 295–300
and Themistius, 296, 298
Universal History, 172, 211–12
Eusebia (empress), 53, 73–74, 78–81, 170
Eusebius of Caesarea
    challenging Porphyrian exegesis, 14, 156
    on Christianity's universal accessibility, 272,
        278
    and codex technology, 24–25
    competing with *paideia*, 16, 32, 66–70, 72,
        93, 135, 143–44, 148, 152
    on Constantine's iconography, 189–92
    on Constantine's position in history,
        199–202
    Ecclesiastical History, 17, 69, 130–32, 144,
        200, 238
    interpreting Constantine's policies, 17, 31,
        117, 129–33, 138–41, 167–70, 189–92
    as Julian's polemical target, 70–71, 113, 152
    Life of Constantine, 113, 115, 120, 130–33,
        166–70, 189–92, 197, 199–202, 211,
        228–31, 238–39
    negotiating Church-State interactions, 17, 20,
        29, 31, 70, 72, 138–44, 167–70, 197,
        227–28, 238–39
    Oration in Praise of Constantine, 17, 20, 29,
        31, 130, 138–44, 189–91, 197, 227–28,
        241, 253
    Oration on Christ's Sepulchre, 140, 143
    Preparation for the Gospel, 16–17, 32, 67–69,
        144, 152, 156, 239
    preserving Constantine's writings, 120, 125
    proximity with Constantine, 129–30
exegesis. *See* interpretation

Fausta (empress), 76
Flavian (Bishop), 248
Florentius (praetorian prefect), 101, 107
Fronto, 39–41

Gaïnas, 248, 260, 262–63
Galerius, 220
Gallienus, 124
Gallus (Julian's brother), 73–74, 76, 79–80, 89
Genesis, 150
Goths: Arianism of. *See* heresy:and the Goths
Greco-Roman political theory
    active vs. contemplative life, 42–43, 59, 82, 84
    comparatio, 199
    conditionality of praise, 19, 141, 240–43,
        257–58
    divine protection, 118–19, 123
    flattery, problem of, 57, 83, 97, 138, 178,
        240–43, 256–57

Greco-Roman political theory (cont.)
  Golden Age, 42, 50–51, 61, 127, 134
  laughter and power, 268–69
  law and the principle of authority, 49–53, 62–64
  parrhesia, 20, 163, 222–25, 240–43, 248, 256–60, 264, 298–99
  philanthropy, 82, 84, 93, 233–34
  philosopher-adviser, ideal of, 19–20, 173, 240–43, 251–53, 255–60, 286
  philosopher-ruler, ideal of, 7, 9, 19–21, 42, 49–65, 81–85, 94–107, 117–41, 148–64, 168, 174, 177–79, 183–85, 192, 196–97, 202–3, 238–40, 251–53, 269–70, 303
  philosophers vs. the irrational crowd, 269–72, 286, 290–91, 293–98
  piety (*eusebeia*), 93, 98–99, 105–6, 178, 259
  recusatio, 54–55, 222–25, 239–40, 276, 289
  ruler as *civilis princeps*, 45–49
  ruler as living law, ideal of, 32, 44–49, 58, 62–63, 123, 201, 217
  sophistry vs. philosophy (trope), 57, 76, 97, 138, 185, 269–70, 280, 286
Gregory of Nazianzus
  Apology for his Flight to Pontus, 238
  asserting Christianity as ideal philosophy, 218–19, 222–25, 274–79
  asserting his interpretive authority, 25, 214–19, 277–78
  between universalism and elitism, 35, 274–79
  competing with fellow bishops, 222–25, 238
  competing with imperial power, 35, 214–19, 236, 274–79
  Concerning His Own Life, 222–25, 237, 240
  on Constantius II, 87, 218–19
  controlling *logoi* through the Logos, 215–16, 222–24
  and cultural competition, 214–16, 226, 276–79
  defining Christian leadership, 214, 218–19, 222–25, 238, 276–79
  on divine admonishment, 218–19
  as interpreter of Julian, 22, 214–19, 236, 276–79
  on Julian's School Ban, 152, 215–16, 276–79
  on Moses, 239
  negotiating Church-State interactions, 214, '222–26, 236, 276–79
  Oration 4, 215–17, 236, 276–79
  Oration 5, 214, 217–18
  and *parrhesia*, 222–25, 240–43
  on *recusatio*, 222–25, 240, 276, 289
  self-projection as ideal bishop, 222–25, 237–40
Gregory of Nyssa, 237, 239, 274

Hadrian, 184, 199
hagiography, 29, 167–69, 232, 281–82
Helios. *See* Solar deity
Heracles, 42, 57, 173–74, 176–77, 187, 235
Heraclius (Cynic), See Julian:*Against the Cynic Heraclius*
Hercules. *See* Heracles
heresy
  Arianism, 86, 122, 144–45, 221, 223, 225, 231, 241, 261, 263, 273–74, 281
  competition over the definition of. *See* orthodoxy:and episcopal rivalry
  etymology of, 221
  and the Goths, 261, 263
  inspired by Greek philosophy, 15
  and the uneducated, 274
Hermes, 172–73, 202
Hesiod, 154, 157
Hesychius, house of, 254
Hilary of Poitiers, 86, 90, 116, 244
Himerius, 87, 174
Homer. *See* Interpretation:of Homer
Hypatia of Alexandria, 254, 265, 288

Iamblichus
  according to Eunapius, 293, 295
  and exegesis. *See* Interpretation:Iamblichean
  idea of cosmos, 28, 161
  Letter to Agrippa, 63
  Life of Pythagoras, 63–65
  political theory of, 63–65
  Reply of the Master, 265
  syllabus of, 52
inductive prognostication. *See* Interpretation:of history
inspiration, poetic. *See* prophecy:and poetry
Interpretation
  biblical, 91–92, 126, 149–52, 156–58
  Christianity's control of, 14–16, 23–28, 65–70, 125–33, 141–46, 209–48
  Constantine's control of. *See* Constantine:as interpreter
  of the crucifixion, 142
  of divine providence, 5, 10, 22, 26–28, 118–19, 121–22, 209–48, 276, 304
  of the emperor's image, 179–96, 215, 269
  of the emperor's life, 33–34, 166–204, 209–19, 279–80, 305
  episcopal control over, 5, 20, 22, 138–41, 214–48
  of history, 5, 10, 121, 124, 126, 129, 131–32, 166–204, 209–19, 228, 260–65, 293, 304
  of Homer, 97–98, 154–58, 177–78
  Iamblichean, 157
  Julian's control of. *See* Julian:as interpreter

of literature, 10, 12, 16, 23–31, 49–53,
    59–62, 65–70, 97–98, 126–27, 133–37,
    155–58
of miracles. *See* miracles
of myth, 14, 27, 158–61, 170–79, 260–65,
    270–71
of nature, 9, 27–28, 114–15, 121–22, 124,
    128, 159–63
of omens. *See* miracles
of oracles. *See* oracles
politics of, 6–7, 22–31, 33–34, 111–205,
    209–48, 260–65, 304–6
rhetoric of, 28–31
Stoic, 14, 24, 27–28

Jerome, 89, 133
Jesus. *See* Christ
John Chrysostom
    between universalism and elitism, 273–75
    Comparison between a King and a Monk, 245
    competing with Greek philosophers, 245–48,
        260
    competing with state authorities, 245–48,
        263–64
    as critic of *paideia*, 23, 244–48, 272, 282–84
    fashioning the episcopal self-image, 34, 238,
        240
    as high priest in Synesius' *On Providence*,
        262–64
    on Julian, 244–47
    on the monks, 247–48, 272, 282–84
    on Moses, 239
    On Babylas, 245–47
    On Priesthood, 238, 240
    and *parrhesia*, 241, 243–48, 260, 283
    political prominence of, 23, 252, 262–64,
        274–75
    praising the simple. *See* John Chrysostom:as
        critic of *paideia*
    on *recusatio*, 239–40, 289
    on the Riot of the Statues, 247–48
John, Gospel of, 12, 150–51, 172
Jovian (emperor), 54, 93, 249–50
Judaism, Hellenistic, 12, 24, 46, 155, 201, 239,
    243
Julian
    acclamation in Paris, 111–13
    Against the Cynic Heraclius, 159, 163–64, 166,
        170–79, 270
    Against the Galileans, 33, 70–71, 148–52, 172
    as agent of providence, 112–47, 170–79,
        202–3, 232–36
    and Asclepius. *See* Asclepius
    beard of. *See* Julian:iconography
    Caesars, 166, 182–204, 269

challenging Christian supersessionism of
    Greek philosophy and religion, 94, 98–100,
    146–55, 160–63, 305
challenging Christology, 150–51, 172
on Christianity's use of Greek philosophical
    concepts, 32–33, 148–53, 160–63, 305
on coercion, 146–47, 154, 268–70
competing with Themistius, 53–59
Consolation to Himself, 33, 73, 100–7
as critic of Church-State interactions, 33–34,
    232–36, 306
on Cynicism, 163–64, 170–71, 268, 272
death of, 22, 209–19, 280, 305
as deceitful leader, 216–17, 279
de medicis et professoribus, edict, 152–55
as episcopal target, 34, 214–19, 236, 245–47,
    275–79
as exegete. *See* Julian:as interpreter
First Panegyric to Constantius II, 32, 44–45,
    73–78
Fragment of a Letter to a Priest, 158, 235
in Gaul, 32, 73, 94–95, 100–8, 111–13
iconography, 28, 179–96, 203–4, 268–70
on the ideal of philosopher-ruler, 7–8, 11,
    49–59, 78, 96, 98–99, 100–7, 170–79
interacting with Constantius' propaganda, 18,
    31–32, 73–81, 94–108
as interpreter, 25, 28, 32–33, 41, 49–53,
    79–80, 96–100, 113, 150, 155–63,
    170–79, 196–204, 270–71, 275–79,
    304–5
Letter to Arsacius, 233–34, 236
Letter to the Athenians, 53–55, 74, 101–7,
    111–13
Letter to Themistius, 28, 30–31, 41–59, 61–65,
    70–72, 81, 99, 107, 171
life of, as evidence, 22, 28, 33–34, 166,
    170–205, 210–19, 305
Misopogon, 59, 179–82, 185, 203–4, 268–72
and myth, 155–63, 170–79, 270–71
as panegyrist, 73–81, 94–100
and Platonic elitism, 34, 269–72
as prophet of Apollo, 45, 235
and *recusatio*, 53–55
refuting the Christian hermeneutics of
    history, 28, 33–34, 167, 170–79, 182–203,
    269–70
rejecting Christianity's philosophical identity,
    7–8, 32–34, 148–63, 167, 268–72
as religious leader, 45, 146–48, 158, 232–36,
    271–72
responding to constructions of Constantine as
    philosopher-ruler, 7–8, 32, 170–205, 305
rethinking Greek philosophy and religion,
    7–8, 148–52, 155–63, 232–36, 271–72

Julian (cont.)
  reversing Constantius' policies, 146–48
  on the ruler as ensouled law, 31, 44–46, 48–49, 51
  on sacrifice, 147, 213–17, 271, 277–78
  as satirist, 179–205, 268–70
  School Ban, 152–53, 212, 215–17, 276–79
  Second Panegyric to Constantius II, 32, 94–100, 156
  as son of Helios, 171–72, 212
  Speech in Praise of Eusebia, 53, 78–81
  as theologian, 7–8, 98–99, 158–63, 170–79
  To King Helios, 161–63, 174, 235
  To the Mother of the Gods, 28, 158–61, 235
  as tool of Christian providence, 22, 214–19
  To the Uneducated Cynics, 163–64, 272
Justin Martyr, 12, 16

Lactantius
  Divine Institutes, 16, 32, 65–66, 68–69, 124–25, 141–42
  On the Deaths of the Persecutors, 16, 127, 134, 229
Libanius
  as (alleged) teacher of John Chrysostom, 244, 273
  as critic of Constantius II, 86–89, 92, 108, 210–11
  Funeral Oration for Julian, 210–11
  as interpreter of Julian's policies, 77, 101, 210–11, 214, 269
  as John Chrysostom's target, 245
  as Julian's addressee, 39, 41, 77
  as panegyrist of Constantius II, 88, 116
Licinius, 16, 69, 120, 133, 135, 144, 175, 192, 200–1, 221
Lucian of Samosata, 20, 182, 196
Lucifer of Cagliari, 86, 90

Magnentius (usurper), 48, 78, 90
Mamertinus, Claudius, 54, 86–87, 90, 92, 108, 112, 114–15, 117
Marcus Aurelius, 39–40, 166, 183–85, 192, 196–99, 201–2, 205, 241
Matthew, Gospel of, 91, 126
Maxentius, 113, 123, 131, 175, 200–1
Maximian, 117, 123, 187
Maximinus Daia, 236
Maximus of Ephesus, 294, 296, 300
Maximus the Cynic, 222–23, 238
Milan, Edict of, 16, 69, 125, 221
Milvian Bridge, battle of, 96, 113, 131
miracles
  apparition of Christ, 228–29
  fire of Apollo's temple, 245
  as interpretive guide, 25–26, 91–92, 116, 122, 127, 131–32, 213–14, 217–18, 245–47
  in panegyrics, 76, 96
  power of relics, 256
  rejection of, 106
  vision of Apollo, 117–18
  vision of crosses, 91, 113, 116, 131–32, 167, 217–18, 228–29
  vision of Luxury (*Caesars*), 193–94
  Zeus, sign of, 112–13
Mithras, 161, 173, 202
monasticism, ideal of, 232, 245, 247–48, 272, 280–83, 286–89
Moses
  and Constantine, 201, 231
  as holding privileged access to the truth, 67, 274
  as imperfect theologian, 150
  model of episcopacy, 239, 274
  model of philosopher-ruler, 46, 231, 239
  as *parrhesiastes*, 243
Mother of the Gods, 158–61
Musonius Rufus, 3, 46, 102
mythography (allegorical), 170–79, 260–65

Nazarius, 96
Nero, 47
Nicaea, Council of, 8, 17, 21, 139, 141, 144–46, 191, 191–92, 221, 307
nomos empsychos. See Greco-Roman political theory:ruler as living law, ideal of
Nonnus of Panopolis, 284

oblique speech, 30–31, 55–59, 74–81, 94–107, 138–41, 234, 258, 268–72
Octavian. *See* Augustus
Odysseus, 102–3, 105, 177
Oenomaus of Gadara, 14
omens. *See* miracles
On the Gods and Universe, 271
Optatian
  as interpreter of Constantine's policies, 17, 133–37, 166
  letter to Constantine, 134
Optatus of Milevi, 120
oracles
  of Apollo, 13–14, 98, 122, 246
  criticism of, 14
  in Neoplatonism, 13–14, 64, 271, 295
  as Scripture, 168
  Sibylline, 10, 117, 126–27
Oribasius, 101
Origen of Alexandria, 12, 21, 150, 155–56, 275
orthodoxy
  and episcopal rivalry, 21, 34, 146, 220–26
  as exact knowledge, 21, 220–26

as governmental responsibility, 21, 90–91,
    115, 144–46, 209, 220–22, 225–26, 275,
    307
  and imperial control. *See* orthodoxy:as
    governmental responsibility
  and law, 21, 146, 225–26
  Nicene. *See* Nicaea, Council of
  and universal accessibility, 275
Ossius of Cordoba, 139, 231

pagan monotheism, theory of, 143–44
paideia
  and philosophy. *See* philosophy: as (un)related
    to paideia
  competition over the role and significance of,
    11–16, 22, 35, 267–301
  as deceptive, 275–79
  display of, 142–46, 173–74, 272
  as partial knowledge, 22, 65–70, 279–85
  as polemical target, 65–70, 244–48, 272–74,
    279–85
Palladius, 239, 275
panegyric
  of Claudius Mamertinus, to Julian. *See*
    Mamertinus, Claudius
  of Eusebius, to Constantine. *See* Eusebius of
    Caesarea: *Oration in Praise of Constantine*
  and flattery. *See* Greco-Roman political
    theory:flattery, problem of
  of Julian, to Constantius II. *See* Julian:as
    panegyrist
  and oblique criticism. *See* oblique speech
  and Platonism, 30, 119, 122–23
  of Pliny to Trajan, 47
  of Themistius. *See* Themistius
  Tetrarchic, 122–24
Paris, Alexander, 185–86
patronage, 2, 32, 41, 55, 79–81, 88–89, 92–93,
    99, 108, 133–37, 226, 237, 250–51, 274,
    288
Paul of Tarsus, 12, 151, 204, 231
Pericles, 103–5
persecutions, religious, 10, 16, 18, 69, 91, 122,
    127, 129, 153–54, 199, 220
phantasia, faculty of, 104–5
Philo of Alexandria, 12, 46, 155, 201, 239,
    243
philosophy
  as mystery. *See* philosophy:as preserve of the
    educated few
  as preserve of the educated few, 267–74,
    285–301
  and prophecy, 13–14, 64, 270, 295–96
  as (un)related to *paideia*, 267–74
physiognomics. *See* Interpretation

Plato, 9–11, 13–15, 32, 75, 103, 116–17, 126,
    142, 144, 155, 157–58, 172, 277
  Gorgias, 198
  Laws, 42–44, 50–53, 56, 59–61, 67–68, 97
  Menexenus, 97, 99
  as polemical target, 67–68, 83
  Republic, 2, 54, 67–68
  Symposium, 198
  as theorist of philosophical leadership, 82
  Timaeus, 150
Pliny the Younger, 40, 47, 118
Plotinus, 13–14, 69, 124, 293
Plutarch, 3, 29, 46, 82, 102, 118, 184, 241, 265
poetry
  as deceptive, 76, 157–58
  Homeric. *See* Interpretation:of Homer
  oracular. *See* oracles
  and prophecy. *See* prophecy:and poetry
  and rhetoric, 76
Porphyry
  and biography, 13–14, 63–65
  and Christianity, 66, 156–57
  according to Eunapius, 293, 295
  as Eusebius' polemical target, 156, 273
  as interpreter of divine utterances, 270–71
  as interpreter of Homer, 156–57
  as interpreter of myth, 159
  Letter to Anebo, 265
  Life of Plotinus, 13
  Life of Pythagoras, 63–65
  Philosophy from Oracles, 13, 270–71, 273
  and Platonic elitism, 270–71
portents. *See* miracles
Procopius (usurper), 250–51
Prohaeresius, 292, 299
prophecy
  and philosophy. *See* philosophy:and prophecy
  and poetry, 10, 97–98, 127, 154–58
  and political legitimisation, 26–28, 91–92,
    114–19, 210–14
Pythagoras, 9, 14, 63–65, 103, 126, 144

reason
  as Christ-derived. *See* Christ:as Logos
  as divine, 9–10, 13–14, 16, 25, 27, 43, 46,
    62–64, 97, 105, 123–24, 128, 139, 159
  as perfect law, 43, 46, 49–53, 82–83

Sallustius, Flavius, 101
Salutius, Saturninus Secundus, 100–6, 183
satire. *See* Julian:as satirist
Saturnalia, festival of, 182
Scepticism (school), 158
Seneca the Younger, 102, 182, 268
Serdica, Edict of, 90, 220

Severans (emperors), 3, 47
Silenus (*Caesars*), 185–86, 196–98
Sirmium, creed of, 90
Socrates, 9, 13, 43, 98, 105, 126, 168, 198, 277
Sol Invictus, See Solar deity
Solar deity, 118, 161–63, 171–72, 174–75, 177–78, 186, 189–92
Sopater, 292, 294, 299
sophistry. *See* Greco-Roman political theory: sophistry vs. philosophy (trope)
Sosipatra, 294
spoudaiogeloion. *See* Julian:as satirist
sympathy (Stoic), 27–28
Synesius of Cyrene
  and Dio Chrysostom, 257–59, 286–88
  baptism of, 254
  competitive self-assertion of, 35, 259–60, 264–66, 285–91
  and dogma, 288–89, 291
  envoy in Constantinople, 255–66
  Ep. 105 30, 288–91
  and episcopacy, 254–55, 288–91
  as interpreter of providence, 261, 264–65
  and John Chrysostom, 260–65, 285
  On Dio, or Living by His Example, 285
  On Kingship, 255–59, 286–88
  On Providence, 256, 260–66, 285
  On the Dreams, 107, 254
  on *manteia*, 254
  on monasticism, 286–88
  on *parrhesia*, 256–61, 264
  and *recusatio*, 240, 288–91
  religious allegiance of, 231, 253–55, 285–91
  and Themistius, 258–59
  upholding *paideia*, 23, 35, 255–59, 285–91

Temple of Jerusalem, reconstruction of, 218
Tertullian, 280
Tetrarchy
  downfall of, 127–29
  image and ceremonial, 30, 40, 45, 117–19, 122–24, 174–75, 179, 186–88
  and persecutions, 10, 91, 122, 127–29, 131, 199, 220, 248, 277
Themistius
  career under Constantius II, 41, 55–56, 85–86, 88, 91–94, 297
  on Constantine, 116, 240–50
  as Constantius' panegyrist, 47, 55–56, 81, 87, 93, 116–17, 249
  criticised for political involvement, 296–98
  criticising Julian, 249–50
  criticising Plato, 250–51
  criticising seclusive philosophers, 297–98
  and Dio Chrysostom, 83, 173, 258–59

  handling philosophical sources, 43, 52, 55–58, 60–61, 70, 82, 250–51, 297
  as interpreter of power, 43, 47, 55–56, 65, 81–86, 114–16, 248–53, 258–59
  on Jovian, 249–50
  as Julian's addressee. *See* Julian, *Letter to Themistius*
  Or. 1, 44, 47, 83–84
  Or. 2, 48, 55–56, 81–83
  Or. 3, 48, 60, 84–85
  Or. 4, 48, 55, 60, 85, 92, 115–16
  Or. 5, 44, 54, 250
  Or. 6, 250
  Or. 7, 249–51
  Or. 8, 60, 250–51
  Or. 9, 44
  Or. 16, 44
  Or. 17, 60, 251, 297
  Or. 18, 251
  Or. 19, 44
  Or. 20, 297
  Or. 23, 297
  Or. 26, 4, 297
  Or. 28, 297–98
  Or. 31, 56, 297
  Or. 34, 44, 60, 297
  on *recusatio*, 54–55
  on religious freedom, 249–50
  in Synesius of Cyrene. *See* Synesius of Cyrene: and Themistius
  as 'talismanic' figure, 93–94, 249–51, 253
  on Theodosius, 251, 253, 297
  as theorist of the ruler as living law. *See* Greco-Roman political theory:ruler as living law, ideal of
  on Valentinian and Valens, 250–51
  as witness of the circulation of the *Letter to Themistius*, 56
Theodosius
  and Ambrose. *See* Ambrose:and Theodosius
  as episcopal interlocutor, 224–25, 241–42, 244, 252–53
  and intellectual self-projection *via* Christianity, 251–53
  and Libanius: 269
  and *parrhesia*. *See* Theodosius:as episcopal interlcutor
  in Themistius' writings, 44, 251–53
Theophilus of Alexandria, 239, 260, 285, 288–90
Thessalonica, Edict of, 251–52
Thessalonica, Massacre of, 242, 244
theurgy, 14, 28, 61, 254, 294
Third-Century Crisis, 5, 18, 40, 45, 118–19
Tiberius, 183

tolerance, religious. *See* coercion, religious
traditional philosophers, marginalisation of, 5–6, 22–23, 211, 243–48, 259–60, 294–96, 298–301, 306
Trajan, 2, 40, 47, 80, 118, 173–74, 183, 186, 199, 202, 259
typology (Biblical), 201–2, 230–31

upward gaze. *See* Constantine:iconography of

Valentinian and Valens (emperors), 250–51, 259
Valerian, 10, 127
Vespasian, 46, 241
Vetranio, 78, 83, 85, 113
violence, religious. *See* coercion, religious
Virgil, 4, 10–11, 127–29

Zeus, 53, 98, 105, 111–13, 156, 171–74, 176–77

Index Locorum

Ambrose of Milan
  Ep. 74.2: 242
  Ep. extra collectionem 11.12-13: 242
Ammianus
  Res Gestae
    15.8.17: 54
    16.5.12: 48–49
    21.6.2-3: 117
    21.16.4: 86, 90
    21.16.5-7: 89–90
    21.16.18: 90
    22.5.4: 147–48
    23.1.3, 5-7: 213
    23.1.7: 213
    23.5.5, 11, 14: 213
    22.10.7: 153, 212
    25.2.3-8: 213
    25.4.17: 212
    25.4.20: 153, 212
Aristotle
  Pol.
    3.16.1287a: 43, 49–50
Athanasius
  Apol. c. Ar.
    59: 231
  Hist. Ar.
    44.6-8: 231–32
  Vit. Ant.
    74: 281
    80: 281–82
    81: 232, 281
Augustine
  Civ. D.
    10.11: 272
Cicero
  Div.
    1.18 (34): 27–28
Constantine
  OC
    3-4: 9
    7: 9
    8-10: 128
    9: 9–10, 126
    11-12: 128, 142
    15: 126, 142
    17: 126
    18: 127
    19-20: 127
    24-25: 10, 127–28
  To Alexander and Arius: 65, 69, 71 See Eusebius, VC 2.64,
  To Shapur: see Eusebius, VC 4.9
  To the provincials of the East: 54 See Eusebius, VC 2.48-49,
  To the provincials of Palestine: See Eusebius, VC 2.24-27
Constantius II
  Dem.
    20a-23d: 82
    23c: 88
  C.Th.
    6.4.12: 85–86
    13.3.5: 152–53
    14.1.1: 87–88
    16.1.2 (*cunctos populos*): 251–52
Cyril of Jerusalem
  Ep. Const.
    2: 92
    3: 116
    5: 92
    6: 92
Dio Chrysostom
  Or. 1
    59-84: 173
    66: 173
  Or. 3
    10: 47
Eunapius of Sardis
  Hist
    Fr. 1.15: 292
    Fr. 18.1: 211
    Fr. 18.6: 211

Index Locorum

355

Fr. 27: 211–12
Fr. 28.1: 292
Fr. 28.6: 212
Fr. 38: 211–12
VPS
  456: 293
  458: 293, 295
  461: 294–95
  462: 292, 294
  463: 292
  464: 292
  464-65: 295–96
  465: 299
  466: 299
  469: 294
  471: 295, 298
  472: 293, 294
  473: 293
  474: 300
  475: 211, 300
  476: 296, 300
  477: 296, 300
  479: 299
  481: 294
Eusebius
  DE
    6.20.16: 69
  GEI
    p. 141 Gaisford: 272
  LC
    Proemium: 138
    1.1: 227
    1.3: 139, 141
    1.6: 191
    2.1: 143
    3.4: 191
    3.5: 192
    5.4: 17, 140
    5.6-7: 185
    8.3: 143
    10.2: 143
    10.4: 141
  PE
    4.6-10: 156
    12.1: 67
    12.9: 239
  VC
    1.4: 200
    1.12: 201
    1.19.2: 167
    1.27: 131–32, 228
    1.29: 228
    1.32-3: 228–29
    1.38: 201
    2.24-27: 120–21

    2.46: 122
    2.48-49: 121–22
    2.54: 122
    2.64: 145
    2.65: 121–22
    2.69: 145
    2.71: 145
    3.10.3-4: 191–92
    3.11: 139
    3.12: 140
    3.29.2: 117
    3.30.3: 122
    4.6.2: 168
    4.9: 122
    4.15: 192–93, 195
    4.17: 168
    4.24: 229–30
    4.29.1: 168
    4.29.2: 140, 168
    4.33: 130
    4.35: 130
    4.36: 130
    4.54.1: 168
    4.45.3: 138
    4.46: 141
    4.48: 140
    4.75: 169, 200
Gregory of Nazianzus
  Carm. 2.1.11 (*De Vita Sua*)
    175-204: 222
    434-35: 239
    460: 224
    810-14: 223
    843-1119: 222–23
    1305-12: 223
    1591-4: 224
    1595-8: 224
    1620-21: 224
    1659: 224
    1797-1918: 224
    1881-901: 224
    1902: 22
  Carm. 2.1.19
    1-2: 243
  Or. 4
    4: 216
    5: 216, 276
    34: 219
    38: 219
    47: 217
    61: 217
    65: 277
    72: 277
    73: 277
    79: 217

Gregory of Nazianzus (cont.)
  82-83: 277
  98: 279
  99: 278
  103: 216
  111-14: 236
  Or. 5
    2: 217
    3-7: 218
    23: 215
    54: 217
  Or. 27
    3: 274
  Or. 43
    14.1: 87
Gregory of Nyssa
  PG 46.557: 274
Heraclitus
  Fr. 123 Diels-Kranz: 159
Himerius
  Or. 62
    7: 87
Homer
  Iliad
    3.55: 185–86
    9.312-13: 155
    11.202-4: 98
    11.401: 102
    11.437-55: 102
Iamblichus
  Ep. Fr. 2 (*Letter to Agrippa*): 63
  Pyth.
    93: 64
    23: 65
John Chrysostom
  Bab.
    1-21: 245–56
    23-38: 246
    33: 246
    73-75: 246
    80-81: 246
    87: 246
    127: 246
    51: 246
    48: 247
    45: 247
  Catech.
    8.6: 282
  In Jo. Hom. 66 (*PG* 59)
    370: 283
  Opp. (*PG* 47)
    328: 283
    363: 283
  Sac.
    1.3-7: 240

Stat.
  17.3: 248
  17.5: 248
  19.3: 282
  21.16: 248
Julian
  I Pan.
    1d: 78
    3c: 76
    10b: 76
    11d-12b: 75
    12c-14a: 75
    23b: 76
    32d-3d: 78
    42b: 48
    45d: 44–45, 47–48
    47d: 78
  II Pan.
    49c-d: 95
    60d-61b: 98
    61a: 157
    68a: 156
    68c-9a: 97
    69c: 97
    70d: 98
    74d-5a: 97, 156
    79a-92d: 96
    80c: 98
    82b-d: 98
    86a: 98
    92b: 99
    89a: 98
  Ath.
    270c-71a: 74
    272a: 112, 172
    284b-c: 112–13
  Caes.
    306a-b: 182–83, 203
    309c-10a: 183
    317a-18a: 183
    317c: 192
    317c-d: 183–84
    328c: 196
    328d-9b: 193
    329c-d: 196–97
    333c: 197
    335b: 185
    336a-b: 194–95
    336c: 202
  C.Gal.
    Fr. 1 (39b): 149
    Fr. 16 (89a): 94a
    Fr. 17 (93d-94a): 150
    Fr. 53 (222a): 70–71, 152
    Fr. 55 (229c-d): 151–52

Index Locorum

Fr. 62 (253c-e): 151
Fr. 79 (327a-c): 151, 172
Fr. 80 (333b-d): 151
C.Her.
  205a-b: 163
  206d: 270
  207d-8c: 163
  206d: 159
  216c: 159, 171
  218c-9a: 160
  219d: 176
  226d: 178
  227c-9a: 171
  228d: 174
  228d-92d: 172
  229c-d: 172, 174
  230b-33d: 176
  230d-1d: 172–73
  231c-33d: 178
  232a: 174
  232c-d: 173–74
  233c-d: 174
  234a: 177
Cons.
  240a: 101
  241a-c: 103
  241c-d: 104
  241d-42a: 102
  243d-54a: 106
  246a-8b: 103–5
  249a: 107
  249b-c: 105
  252b: 106
  252b-c: 105
  152c: 107
Cyn.
  187a-b: 198
  187d: 164
  188a-b: 164
  191a-d: 164
  197b: 164
  199b: 164
  200c: 164
  224b: 164
De medicis et professoribus: See *C.Th.*
  13.3.5
Ep.
  18 W. (= 88 B.-C.): 235
  22 W. (= 84 B.-C.): 233–34, 236
  36 W. (= 61c B.-C.): 153
  53 W. (= 97 B.-C): 39–40
  55 W. (= 90 B.-C.): 154, 154–55
Ep. Fragm. (= 89b B.-C.)
  300c-2a: 235
  301a-c: 158

Eus.
  107b: 79
  111a-b: 80
  118b: 80
  121a-c: 80
  124a-b: 170
Hel.
  130c-31a: 172
  133b: 162
  136b-c: 157
  137c: 157
  138c-9a: 162
  144b: 162
Mat.
  161c: 161
  161d-2a: 161
  162a: 161
  168d: 161
  170b: 159
  179c: 161
Mis.
  338c-d: 179
  338b-9a: 181
  355d: 179
  357a-b: 203
  360d: 203
  370c-1c: 268
Them.
  253a-4a: 42
  254b-c: 57
  255d-6c: 42
  257d: 56
  257d-8a: 43
  258a-9a: 50
  258d: 44
  261a-c: 49–50
  261d-2a: 50
  262a-c: 44, 51
  263c-66a: 43
  263c-d: 57–58
Lactantius
  Div. inst.
    1.1.13: 125
    1.1.21: 142
    1.23.9: 142
    5.4.4: 66
    3.15.1: 66
  Mort. Pers.
    1.5-7: 127
    44.5: 229
Libanius
  Ep. 369 Foerster: 72
  Or. 18
    4: 210
    21: 210

Libanius (cont.)
    27: 210
    192: 210
    206-7: 211
    209-12: 211
    283: 211
    286-93: 211
    296: 211
    298: 211
  Or. 19
    19: 269
  Or. 62
    10: 86, 89
Marcus Aurelius
  Ep. 2.3.1: 39–40
Optatian
  Carmina
    8: 136–37
    19: 135–36
  Ep. Const.: 134
Palladius
  Dial.
    19: 275
Pan. Lat.
  III (11) (Mamertinus)
    14.6: 114
    19.3-20.4: 86
    23.4: 114
    23.5: 114–15
    27.2: 114
  IV (10) (Nazarius)
    14: 96
  V (8)
    10.2: 123
  VI (7)
    21.4-5: 117–18
  VII (6)
    7.1: 123
  XII (9)
    4.2: 123
    2.5: 123
    11.4: 123
Philo of Alexandria
  Abr.
    5: 46
  Mos.
    1.162: 46
  Quis heres
    1.7: 243
Plato
  Leg.
    257d-9a: 42–43
    709e: 60
    715c-d: 50

Pliny the Younger
  Pan.
    65.1-2: 47
Porphyry
  Abst.
    1.28.1: 270
  Phil. Or.
    Fr. 34 Smith: 271
    Fr. 305 Smith: 271
  Plot.
    10-11: 13
    22: 14
  Pyth.
    20: 64
    42: 64
Socrates of Constantinople
  Ecclesiastical History
    1.1.2: 169
Synesius
  Dio
    1.4: 286
    1.14: 286, 288
    4.5-5.1: 286
    7-11: 286–87
    8.5: 287
    9.6: 287
    9.7: 287
    10.10: 288
    11.1: 287
  Ep.
    66: 285
    67: 260
    105: 288–91
    154: 287
  Insomn.
    2.1: 254
    4.5: 254
    11.2: 254
    14.4: 256
    12.6: 107, 254
  Prov.
    1.1.1: 265
    1.5.1: 265
    1.18.1-2: 256, 261
    1.18.5: 261
    2.3: 261
    2.3.2: 262
    2.3.4: 262
  Reg.
    1.2: 258
    2.3: 257
    3.1: 255
    3.5-6: 257
    6.4: 257

14.2-5: 256–57
25.5-6: 259
28.1: 258
29.2: 259
Themistius
  Or. 1
    1a-2b: 83
    8d-9b: 84
  Or. 2
    29c-30a: 82
    31a-32d: 82
    34b-c: 82
    37d-8a: 83
    38b-c: 83
    40a: 55, 81, 83
  Or. 3
    45b: 85
    46a: 117
    46b: 85
  Or. 4
    51c-2a: 85
    54b-c: 85
    56b: 85
    59c-60a: 85
    62d: 85
  Or. 5
    63c: 249
    67c: 249
    70d: 250
  Or. 7
    93b: 251
  Or. 8
    107c-d: 250–51
  Or. 17
    214a-b: 251
    214c: 297
  Or. 18
    219b-c: 251
    224b-25b: 251
  Or. 26
    331a: 297
  Or. 28
    341d: 297
    342b-d: 297–98
  Or. 31
    354d: 56
  Or. 34
    3: 297

For EU product safety concerns, contact us at Calle de José Abascal, 56–1°,
28003 Madrid, Spain or eugpsr@cambridge.org.

www.ingramcontent.com/pod-product-compliance
Ingram Content Group UK Ltd.
Pitfield, Milton Keynes, MK11 3LW, UK
UKHW021354290425
457986UK00014B/566